Winner of the Jules and Frances Landry Award for 1991

THE KINGFISH AND HIS REALM

THE

KINGFISH

AND HIS REALM

THE LIFE AND TIMES OF
HUEY P. LONG

WILLIAM IVY HAIR

LOUISIANA STATE UNIVERSITY PRESS
BATON ROUGE AND LONDON

Designer: Amanda McDonald Key
Typeface: Aster
Typesetter: Graphic Composition, Inc.
Printer and binder: Thomson-Shore, Inc.

Library of Congress Cataloging-in-Publication Data

Hair, William Ivy.
    The kingfish and his realm : the life and times of Huey P. Long /
William Ivy Hair.

        p.   cm.
    Includes bibliographical references (p.   ) and index.
    ISBN 0-8071-1700-5
    1. Long, Huey Pierce, 1893–1935.   2. Legislators—United States—
Biography.   3. United States. Congress. Senate—Biography.
4. Governors—Louisiana—Biography.   5. Louisiana—Politics and
government—1865–1950.   6. United States—Politics and
government—1933–1945.   I. Title.
E748.L86H25 1991
976.3'06'092—dc20
[B]   91-18546
                                                                              CIP

The author is grateful to the Louisiana and Lower Mississippi Valley Collections, Louisiana State University, Baton Rouge, for permission to quote from
the Huey Long Papers, and to the Southern Historical Collection, Library
of the University of North Carolina at Chapel Hill, for permission to quote from
the John M. Parker Papers.

For Frank B. Vinson
and Ralph W. Hemphill

I was born into politics, a wedded man,
with a storm for my bride.

—*Huey Long*

CONTENTS

ILLUSTRATIONS

ACKNOWLEDGMENTS

Many good people, too numerous to mention all, helped me make this book on Huey P. Long. But I owe special debts to certain individuals and to one institution—Georgia College. I am dedicating the book to Ralph W. Hemphill, vice-president and dean of faculties at Georgia College, and to Frank B. Vinson, chairman of the Department of History and Geography. They, along with my dear friends and colleagues in the department— Emily Abdi-Wheeler, Rosemary Begemann, Victoria Chandler, Martha Turner, Robert J. Wilson III, and Mary DeVries (the over-qualified secretary who keeps the department running)—deserve special recognition because of their unfailing kindness and encouragement, and most of all for the bolstering effect of their confidence in me.

A faculty research grant from Georgia College helped defray expenses during one of the several summers of my research. This book has been many years in the making, and over time I have become indebted to numerous librarians at various institutions, most of all to these: Mary Jones (a marvelous interlibrary loan specialist) and R. Neil Scott, coordinator of communication services, both of the Georgia College Library; Faye Phillips, director, and M. Stone Miller, head of acquisitions, of the Louisiana and Lower Mississippi Valley Collections, Hill Memorial Library, Louisiana State University; Harriet Callahan and Shelby Jung of the Louisiana Department, Louisiana State Library, Baton Rouge; Wilbur "Bill" Meneray of the Special Collections Division at Tulane University; and Sarah L. Lockmiller, libraries photographer at the University of Georgia.

ACKNOWLEDGMENTS

I owe a considerable debt to Edward F. Haas, formerly president of the Louisiana Historical Association and currently chairman of the history department at Wright State University in Dayton, Ohio. Professor Haas carefully read the final manuscript and offered numerous helpful suggestions. I also relied upon advice from a former student, Glen Jeansonne, who is now a professor of history at the University of Wisconsin, Milwaukee. Both Haas and Jeansonne are working on their own books about Long, so by coming to my aid they showed not only a dedication to scholarship, but also their unselfish natures.

Louisiana State University Press was my obvious first choice for a publisher, and the courtesy that its director, Leslie E. Phillabaum has extended to me over the years made my preference for the Press and its capable staff all the stronger. Margaret Fisher Dalrymple, editor in chief, deserves more thanks for her encouragement and advice than these few words can convey. John Easterly, production editor, went about his task with exemplary professionalism. Readers of this book should know that Gerry Anders, a superb copy editor, deserves credit for improving my prose and correcting my occasional lapses of grammar. It was my good fortune to have his help.

As always, my wife Karolyn has been my mainstay. Without her love and support this book might never have been finished.

THE KINGFISH AND HIS REALM

Louisiana Parishes

SCALE OF MILES

10 5 0   10   20   30

Louisiana's Parishes and Parish Seats
Courtesy Forum Press, Inc.

· 1 ·

LOUISIANA, 1893

Huey Pierce Long was born during a hard time. "A season of disaster, that year of 1893," reflected the New Orleans *Picayune* one day after what seemed twelve months of manifold woes for the United States, and especially for Louisiana, ended. "May we never see another like it."[1]

Economic and climatic troubles combined in 1893 to intensify life's usual hazards. A nation-wide depression, worst of the nineteenth century, began in May with the so-called panic of '93 on Wall Street. By year's end most Americans' standard of living had deteriorated. Louisiana, where the majority of whites and blacks were already poor, additionally suffered from severe and unstable weather conditions. Flood waters inundated portions of northeastern Louisiana during May and June, ruining the newly planted cotton and leaving 40,000 farmers, mostly black, destitute and homeless. Later, a long summer drought scorched crops in the northwestern parishes.[2] Southern Louisiana's sugar and rice belt fared better overall, but on October 1 the deadliest hurricane in the state's history killed an estimated 2,500 people in the marshes and coastal islands south of New Orleans. "Louisiana," declared a Texas paper following the great storm, "is accursed of God."[3]

Reverend Benjamin M. Palmer of New Orleans' prestigious First Presbyterian Church never imagined that he or his beloved adoptive state was cursed by the Almighty, but during 1893 his favorite sermon topic, "Christian Fortitude," seemed particularly appropriate. Palmer—"the first citizen of Louisiana" as many called him—at seventy-five was painfully ill with an en-

1

larged prostate. For the remainder of his life he would urinate through an inserted catheter, which was "a constant source of grief and annoyance to him." Yet Palmer's voice remained as thunderous as it had been in November of 1860, when his Thanksgiving sermon, subsequently widely published in newspapers and pamphlets, was credited with swinging the voters of New Orleans toward secession.[4]

The big, solemn, Gothic-style First Presbyterian at Lafayette Square, usually referred to as "Dr. Palmer's Church" from the time he became its pastor in 1859 until his death in 1902, attracted many of New Orleans' elite. One who had been a youthful member, the writer Grace King, said in 1932 that "the remembrance of his awe-inspiring presence has lasted through the years. Others might be forgotten, but not Dr. Palmer." Someone else who grew up as a member of Palmer's congregation and thought of him often was John M. Parker, Louisiana's businessman-progressive governor from 1920 to 1924. Parker, who in his lifetime battled such diverse enemies as the Mafia, the Ku Klux Klan, and Huey Long, credited "my lamented friend, the Rev. Doctor Palmer," with instilling in him the values of "True Christianity."[5]

Palmer carried into the twentieth century both the virtues and faults of the antebellum South's patrician class. His attitudes congealed early and never changed. A sense of duty impelled him in 1878, and again in 1897, to terminate summer vacations in Virginia's cool mountains and return to a New Orleans stricken by yellow fever. Born in Charleston, South Carolina, he came from a family that had produced Puritan preachers since the early days of Massachusetts Bay Colony.[6] Palmer was short in stature, and as a child had been kicked in the face by a horse, so that his nose and lips were somewhat misshapen, but in the pulpit his powerful melodious voice made him seem tall and handsome.

As a young South Carolinian during the 1830s, Palmer became a believer in Senator John C. Calhoun's philosophy of slavery and society: that building a high civilization, such as that of ancient Athens, requires a controlled class of slaves or serfs to do the hard and dirty work, thus providing the ruling gentry with leisure time for intellectual and cultural pursuits. The American South, Calhoun and Palmer maintained, was blessed in having procured its primary labor force from equatorial Africa. These

2

ebony toilers, strong of body but weak of mind, were a people evidently designed by God to perform the role of society's mud-sill.[7] "This system of servitude," Palmer explained in one of his most quoted New Orleans sermons, "underlies and supports our material interests . . . our wealth consists in our lands and the serfs who till them," and such labor "must be controlled," especially because in Louisiana's climate "any other but a tropical race must faint and wither beneath a tropical sun."[8]

Knowing that "[my] argument will be scoffed abroad as the hypocritical cover," Palmer tried to mask the odor of selfishness with idealism. He insisted that white slave-owners (and after the Civil War, landlords and employers) were bound by obligations that went with their God-given right to rule: obligations to Christianize and care for the lesser race, just as a dutiful father should look after his small children. After all, what is a brief life of labor, compared with eternal salvation? Blacks owe us service, he explained to his congregation, but we owe them a righteous guardianship, and those few whites who abuse blacks will suffer hell's torments. Palmer had viewed the Confederate states' struggle for independence as a holy war against both atheistic abolitionism and Yankee materialism. Like Jacobins in the French Revolution, northern meddlers were striking at the South's divine principle of subordination actually to strike at God.[9]

Why did God allow the holy war to be lost? The Almighty's will must not be questioned, yet Confederate defeat—when Palmer had been so sure of victory—puzzled him for years. Finally he solved the riddle. "Can a cause be lost which has passed through such a baptism as ours?" he asked.[10] The answer was that righteous "principles never die, and if they seem to perish it is only to experience a resurrection in the future." By the 1890s, old and ill, Palmer was convinced that the ideals of the Confederacy would ultimately triumph; he welcomed signs that northerners were accepting the racial views of the white South. Indeed, as the twentieth century approached, he decided that the United States was now ready to march with the Nordic nations of Europe in the task of subordinating and Christianizing inferior peoples all over the earth.[11]

Henry J. Hearsey, the hard-drinking editor of the New Orleans *States*, had more impact than his old friend Palmer in conveying to a new generation the burning need "to prevent Louisiana from being Africanized and to sustain white supremacy."[12] Despite their friendship, Hearsey and Palmer spent little time together, since Hearsey seldom attended church and Palmer did not hang around barrooms.

Everyone called him "Major Hearsey," and unlike many who sported such titles, he really had been a major in the Confederate Army. In 1893 he was fifty-three. He had edited the *States* since the day he founded it in 1880. For most years of the late nineteenth and early twentieth centuries, his newspaper was named the official journal of the city of New Orleans. The *States* rolled off the press at 4 P.M. six days a week, with a morning *Sunday States* on the seventh. The weekday *States* was Louisiana's leading afternoon newspaper, and the major's sizzling editorials helped make it so. Its circulation was notably large along the Red River parishes—Louisiana's backbone. Bundled copies, placed on the Texas and Pacific's Cannonball just before the express train left New Orleans, were tossed out during the night at whistle stops along the 324 miles to Shreveport, where the Cannonball arrived each morning. Since the Shreveport and Alexandria dailies did not reach rural areas until later in the day, the *States* brought to the backbone parishes their freshest outside news and opinion. (Major Hearsey's rhetoric was always colorful, although not necessarily logical: in March of 1893, he referred to another editor as "a malignant ass and miscellaneous fraud.") Reading the major's editorials early in the morning, commented an envious Shreveport editor, was "an invigorating tonic," a "bracer" to start the day.[13]

More racist and less paternalistic than Palmer, the major became increasingly hostile toward blacks during the 1890s. Like Palmer, Hearsey was heavily involved in promoting the mystique of the Lost Cause. Yet the major was reluctant to share Palmer's optimism about the North's coming around to Confederate principles. Hearsey would not forgive the Yankees and could not forget. Civil War emotions remained with him on his deathbed. He always wore a little rebel battle flag in his lapel. "The major," someone who knew him recalled in 1940, "never became reconciled to General Lee's defeat."[14]

Of medium height and lacking good looks or robust health, Hearsey was saved from a mediocre appearance only by his luminous eyes. Like his friend Palmer, he had a gentler side. When not fulminating against blacks, Yankees, or anyone who disagreed with him, he could be sympathetic and generous. An easy touch, known to empty his pockets for the down-and-outs on the streets of New Orleans, the major was also a comforting friend to the mistreated animals of the city. Money matters bored him, and he scorned suggestions he run for public office. The young man he appointed circulation manager of the *States* in 1893, Robert Ewing, became business manager five years later and after Hearsey's death in 1900 purchased a controlling interest in the *States*. Ewing later added the Shreveport *Times*, the Monroe *Morning World*, and the Monroe *News-Star* to his list of properties, became an ally and then a foe of Huey Long, and tried to surpass the influence Hearsey once had held in Louisiana affairs.[15]

Usually, Major Hearsey endorsed the widespread practice of lynching because he assumed it deterred black crime against whites. Of the fourteen or more Louisiana lynchings in 1893, the major frowned on only three. These happened at dawn on Sunday, September 17, in the suburbs of New Orleans, when a mob led by some of the most prominent whites in Jefferson Parish hanged three black men. What angered all the metropolitan dailies was that the victims were not even accused of a crime: they merely had the misfortune to be brothers of Roselius Julian, who two days before had shot and killed a local magistrate, Judge Victor Estopinal. The judge's killer escaped. Frustrated at not laying their hands on him—they were planning to burn him at the stake—the mob's members turned their fury on Julian's relatives. They killed his brothers by slow strangulation; they also severely beat his old mother, his two sisters, and two male cousins.[16] Roselius Julian was never found.

It surprised some that "the leading negro hater of the state," as a letter to the editor depicted Hearsey, would condemn the mob violence in Jefferson Parish. But the major always believed that blacks should not be murdered unless suspected of a serious crime—or unless they posed a political threat to white domination. Neither was the case here: the dead or flogged victims were not involved in the shooting of Estopinal or accused of hiding his killer, and Jefferson was a white majority parish where every official was a white Democrat. Moreover, the major's sense of gallantry extended, if but feebly, to black women; he was upset upon learning that three females were flogged.[17]

Major Hearsey's best young reporter in 1893 was Thomas O.

Harris. "He possesses my full confidence," wrote Hearsey after he sent the twenty-three-year-old Harris to interview whites and blacks in Jefferson about the mob violence. Blacks were afraid to talk, and not all whites approved of what had happened, but most whites, Harris found, believed that occasional lynchings were needed to keep blacks in line. Harris' frankest source was the parish assessor, Henry Long, who said the recent violence was "perfectly justifiable" because "now the negroes were afraid to call their souls their own"; he added that "the most prominent men in Jefferson Parish were among those who strung the negroes up." Asked specifically who, Long mentioned, among others, State Senator L. H. Marrero.[18]

Pressured by the city newspapers, Governor Murphy J. Foster reluctantly sent an investigator to Jefferson Parish. Harris testified at the hearing in October of 1893, as did Long, the assessor. On the stand, Long cursed Harris, denied giving him names, and claimed that "Mr. Harris was drunk" when their meeting took place. The district attorney who conducted the hearing did not reprimand Long for his profanity. After testimony concluded, Harris was arrested and taken to jail on a charge of carrying a concealed weapon. The charge was true. As his boss observed, "Mr. Harris would have been a young idiot to have gone there unarmed." But Major Hearsey, who could speak authoritatively on liquor's effects, added that he knew Harris to be a temperate man—and also a truthful one.[19] Probably Long's accusation was inspired by the fact that Harris worked for Hearsey, and the major was a notoriously heavy drinker.

Forty-two years later, on the night of September 7, 1935, the same Thomas O. Harris, working as the Louisiana publicity director for a federal agency, was cursed by another man named Long. Huey Long, the forty-two-year-old United States senator and political "Kingfish" of the state, had called another session of his subservient legislature in Baton Rouge. Harris was there as a hostile observer. Long, seeing Harris at the press table in the House of Representatives, hurried over to curse him. "I replied in kind," Harris later said, "and he asked me to repeat it." Harris did so, whereupon Long called his bodyguards. One of Huey's guards slapped the elderly man and took him to jail. This time Harris was found to be unarmed, but was booked for being drunk and disorderly. "I was neither," Harris insisted.[20] The swearing match with old Harris would be Long's last confrontation with an enemy until the next evening, when in a corridor adjoining the House of Representatives he met a foe who was armed, Dr. Carl Austin Weiss.

Overshadowed but not forgotten during the passage of 1893 was the nineteenth anniversary of an episode then considered by most Louisiana whites to be the grandest military achievement in the state's history—the White League uprising of September 14, 1874. Only the 1815 victory over British forces in the Battle of New Orleans was comparable. Because of economic conditions, and since the twentieth anniversary came next, September 14 was not celebrated with as much pomp as usual in 1893. Still, ceremonies were held, flags displayed from buildings and residences, and flowers placed on the graves of those White Leaguers who fell in the uprising against Reconstruction Republican rule.[21] Louisiana whites considered September 14 to be their emancipation day.

The Battle of Liberty Place was the name later bestowed upon the brief clash between Republicans and Democrats near the foot of Canal Street on the sultry afternoon of September 14, 1874. Twelve years earlier, during the Civil War, the South's largest city had fallen to Union forces without a fight, but as a modern guidebook aptly puts it, "The shooting did not start in New Orleans until after the Civil War was over."[22]

Louisiana during Reconstruction was in effect a conquered province. Yet the conquest was welcomed as liberation by a majority of the state's population, for blacks slightly outnumbered whites after the Civil War, 364,000 to 362,000. This black majority was politically enhanced by the temporary disfranchisement of leading ex-Confederates and by the fact that thousands of ordinary whites who could have registered to vote under federal guidelines did not do so. Politics during Reconstruction became racially polarized in all the former Confederate states, and nowhere more than in Louisiana. But the Pelican State was never under black rule: most Republican officeholders were white, and most "black" politicians were of mixed blood, and educated, having come from Louisiana's sizable antebellum free Negro population. Even so, the white Republican governors—carpetbaggers Henry Clay Warmoth (1868–1872) and William Pitt Kellogg (1873–1877)—owed their elections to the votes of the newly freed and as yet mostly illiterate black majority.[23] Increasingly, whites viewed the Republicans who occupied the State House (then in New Orleans) as alien, oppressive, and without legitimacy.

Even though the Confederacy was lost as a separate nation and blacks were no longer property to be bought and sold, the struggle for what the Confederacy had been about was not necessarily over. "Reconstruction," Grace King pointed out with shattering insight, "was also the war."[24]

White Louisiana was more unified during Reconstruction than ever before or probably since. Secession in 1861 had been closely contested, and the Confederacy during its four years of life never possessed the overwhelming support that the White League enjoyed in 1874. This unity developed because whites came to view the reconstruction experiment in Louisiana as an attempt to turn the state into another Haiti.[25] Reconstruction was not that, at least not in the minds of most state or national Republican officeholders. But fear of black retaliation against whites for slavery's past, and dread of black domination through sheer numbers and the machinations of northern politicians—such anxieties engendered a unifying obsession within the state's white minority.[26]

Race was the most powerful magnet in drawing whites together against the Republican state government, but there were other reasons. Although Louisianians have usually shown high tolerance for official corruption, Governor Warmoth was a corrupt outsider, and Governor Kellogg, albeit more honest, appeared surly and incompetent. The Republican party in Louisiana further weakened itself with internecine power struggles. Finally, whatever hope the Republicans had of being accepted by a significant minority of whites vanished in the face of burdensome taxes that hurt small property-owners proportionally more than the big cotton and sugar planters. Here the Republicans faced one of their worst dilemmas. To provide the propertyless black masses with education and modest social services, higher property taxes were necessary. But rank-and-file white families, most of them owners of small farms, were having to pay far more in taxation, and usually receiving less in benefits, than before the war.[27] When a nation-wide economic depression hit in 1873—similar to, although not as bad as, the one to come in 1893—falling prices for market crops made taxes even more onerous, especially for marginal producers. Whites living on the edge were concerned with their own survival, not with helping blacks.

By September of 1874, White League partisans controlled most of the rural parishes and towns. They had been conducting a low-intensity guerrilla war, of the type often proved effective in other parts of the world. The hated alien regime, propped up by outside support, had lost the countryside and was isolated in the capital, New Orleans. There, Governor Kellogg had at his disposal about 4,000 local troops: the mostly white Metropolitan Police, commanded by the former Union general Algernon S. Badger, and the mostly black state militia, under former Confederate general James Longstreet, who had turned Republican after the war. By September 14, the White League, which was in effect the military arm of Louisiana's Democratic party, decided the time had come for armed confrontation in the city.[28]

The White League troops were commanded by Frederick N. Ogden, formerly a Confederate colonel in Nathan Bedford Forrest's cavalry. Ogden's force of 8,400 included whites of all economic strata, their names indicating a variety of ethnic and religious backgrounds: Anglo-Protestant, German, Latin Catholic, and Jewish. Most of Ogden's men were armed with cheap old muzzle-loading rifles imported from Belgium. The Republicans had better arms—Winchester repeating rifles, artillery, and two Gatling guns—but they were outnumbered over two to one. On Canal Street, about 4 P.M. on September 14, the two armies faced each other. Longstreet's and Badger's troops lined up in front of the United States Custom House, along the street entrances to the Vieux Carré, and at the leveed riverfront.[29]

Thousands of spectators in and around nearby buildings watched the ensuing brief battle. The White Leaguers charged, the Metropolitan defensive line caved in, and the militia fled down the Vieux Carré toward Jackson Square. Governor Kellogg and General Longstreet found sanctuary inside the granite Custom House; General Badger, hit four times by rifle fire, was carried to Charity Hospital by "my White League friends," as he good-naturedly called them. He recovered. No federal soldiers were involved in the battle. The only United States Army company stationed in the city gazed upon the fighting from windows in the Custom House, which the White League had no intention of attacking.[30]

Casualties on both sides were light: eleven dead, sixty

wounded for the Republicans; sixteen dead and forty-five wounded for the attacking Democrats. During the Civil War, the Battle of Liberty Place would hardly have been considered a skirmish. But as Major Hearsey observed in noting the firefight's 1893 anniversary, "The importance of battles are [sic] not to be estimated by the number of men engaged"; rather, "the results achieved determine their importance."[31]

The results of September 14, 1874, gradually became apparent. For three days the White Leaguers controlled New Orleans (except for the Custom House) and everything else in the state. Ecumenical services were held, as the New York *Times* reported, "at Dr. Palmer's church . . . for thanksgiving at the White League victory." Then President Ulysses S. Grant made a show of force. Federal troops poured into Louisiana, and a squadron of six warships anchored at the New Orleans docks—whereupon the White Leaguers, determined to avoid a fight with the federal military, handed over all the state property and offices they had recently won. Grace King, whose father was a sergeant in a White League company, best summed up what had happened: "The citizens . . . had proven their point, the carpet-bag government could be placed and kept in power by the United States soldiery, and in no other way whatever."[32] Louisiana's whites were betting that the North, the federal government, was losing the will to continue military intervention in the South, and they were correct. The Battle of Liberty Place was the beginning of the end of Reconstruction. Louisiana was Reconstruction's crucible, and in less than three years it and every other southern state would be under white Democratic control.

Well into the twentieth century, a man who had fought at Liberty Place could claim special status in Louisiana. Even the children of White Leaguers shone in the reflected light. John M. Parker took pride in his father's role as a leader in the uprising, and he himself, as a frail, asthmatic child of eleven in 1874, had watched as the dead body of a White League warrior, Samuel Newman, was carried home. Of all White League soldiers, the one who eventually achieved highest national prominence was a private who fired one of Company D's hard-kicking Belgian muskets at the Republicans: Edward Douglass White, who a month later began his political career with election to the state senate. By 1893, White was a United States senator, and the next year he was appointed by President Grover Cleveland to the

United States Supreme Court. From 1910 until his death in 1921, he was chief justice. Had he lived three more years, Chief Justice White probably would have been asked to be orator of the day at the elaborate fiftieth anniversary of the White League uprising. On September 14, 1924, that role was filled by John M. Parker.[33]

In 1893, at thirty, John M. Parker was already a leader of Louisiana's business elite, and a political activist. From his father (John M. Parker, Sr.), who died that year, he inherited substantial mercantile and agricultural properties, augmenting the wealth he had achieved on his own as a shrewd but honest young New Orleans cotton broker. Parker's immediate ancestors were plantation gentry from Mississippi, Kentucky, and Virginia; one of his great-grandfathers, Robert Parker, was also a grandfather of Abraham Lincoln's wife, Mary Todd. In 1888, John M. Parker married Cecile Airey, a member of an upper-class New Orleans Catholic family. Probably in part because of his bride's status and activities, he soon joined Louisiana's two most exclusive men's clubs, the Boston and the Pickwick.[34]

Despite his urban residence, his social life, and his business duties, Parker was always happiest in the countryside. He loved to grip the handles of a plow or to hunt with a pack of dogs, and he had an obsession with physical exercise. By such activities he was able to put muscles on his thin body and partly overcome his respiratory problems. Once, he admitted that he went into business not out of enjoyment, but only because "there was more money to be made."[35]

Parker became politically active in the 1880s, as soon as he could vote. Not until 1916 would he run for office, but like his father and like his minister, Dr. Palmer, he believed that right-minded, successful people have a duty to organize resistance— including violence, if needed—against any person or movement, political or otherwise, that prevents or threatens the maintenance of an orderly, upright, and hierarchical society. To do less would be to violate a commitment to civilization.

Louisiana's only metropolis, where Parker grew up and lived, was run by a political machine that in the late nineteenth century woefully failed to measure up to Parker's or the Reverend Dr. Palmer's standards, although Major Hearsey of the *States*, needing the public printing contract, could usually find some good in it. "The Ring," as New Orleans' machine was called, was nominally Democratic, but hardly patrician. Few, if any, of its members were greeted at the Boston or Pickwick clubs; typically, they were of working-class background and stressed that fact to the voters. The Ring's primary objectives were keeping its leaders in office and providing jobs for key supporters. Of far lesser priority were such matters as public safety, sanitation, and fiscal responsibility.[36] Yet even at its worst, the Ring was backed by large numbers of working-class whites, including most of the newly arrived immigrants. This was understandable, for the machine at least pretended to identify and sympathize with the disadvantaged. It also found jobs for as many friendly voters as circumstances permitted, and was more tolerant of their vices, such as gambling, than were the upper-class reformers. Blacks, who could still cast ballots in New Orleans until the late 1890s, made up a swing vote that might go either with the Ring or with reform tickets.[37]

John M. Parker was no strict puritan. He drank beer and an occasional tumbler of whiskey, chewed tobacco, and sometimes placed bets on elections and cockfights. But the New Orleans Ring, which happened to be at its most corrupt and inefficient the very year (1884) that young Parker became a voter, offended his strong sense of decency and public order. The vile Ring stood in the way of the clean, prosperous, businesslike way of life he envisioned for Louisiana in the approaching twentieth century. Consequently, in 1888 he helped organize the Young Men's Democratic Association, which backed a winning reform candidate, Joseph Shakspeare, for mayor.[38] The Ring, however, would be back in power four years later.

In March of 1891, Parker undertook what he considered to be another civic duty. He was one of the organizers of a lynch mob that slaughtered eleven Sicilian immigrants accused of being members of the first Mafia organization in the United States, reputedly established in New Orleans in the 1880s. By the early 1890s as many as fifteen thousand Italians, mostly from Sicily, were living in the Crescent City. Most were hard-working, frugal, and peaceable folk, but centuries of oppression in Sicily had made them secretive and suspicious of all authority.[39] And scattered among them were thugs who claimed to be *mafiosi*, members of the notorious criminal brotherhood.

Homicide was a common event in the city, and as long as one

ethnic or racial group killed its own members, no one outside the tribal boundary much cared. But one October night in 1890, the New Orleans chief of police, David Hennessy, who had inserted himself into a rivalry between two Sicilian families, was gunned down by blasts from sawed-off shotguns. Before he died, when asked who did it, Hennessy muttered: "Dagoes."[40] Nineteen men who were either members of or associated with the Matranga family were indicted (Hennessy had sided with the Provenzano family in accusing the Matrangas of being *mafiosi*). Eleven of these men were charged with murdering the chief, eight with being accomplices. Nine of the alleged killers went on trial first. When the jury, on March 13, 1891, refused to convict because of inconclusive evidence, public outrage rocked the city. Especially wrathful were business and professional groups, who considered the murder of Chief Hennessy to be part of a plot by alien criminals to take control of the city. Mayor Shakspeare and the new chief of police, Dexter Gaster, believed that next on the Mafia's agenda was the assassination of Shakspeare and Gaster. They were convinced the Mafia planned to rule New Orleans.[41]

Morning newspapers the next day announced a mass meeting for 10 A.M. at Henry Clay's statue on Canal Street. Ominously, it had been a similar call to gather at the Clay statue, signed by Parker's father and others in 1874, that led to the Battle of Liberty Place.

John M. Parker, Jr., was likely the youngest of the sixty-one signers, all of them leading citizens, of the 1891 call:

MASS MEETING

All good citizens are invited to attend a mass meeting on Saturday, March 14, at 10 o'clock A.M. at Clay Statue, to take steps to remedy the failure of justice in the Hennessy case. Come prepared for action.[42]

After listening to fiery speeches about liberty and justice, and carrying a death list of those believed most involved in Chief Hennessy's death, the enormous mob—"a jury of twenty thousand" as one leader described it—rushed the nearby Orleans Parish Prison and shot or hanged eleven of the supposed *mafiosi*. (Also on the mob's death list was one non-Italian, an Irish-born private detective named Dominick C. O'Malley, who was said to have been hired by the Matrangas to distribute bribe money to the jury. But O'Malley saved himself that bloody day by finding sanctuary in the office of the editor of the *Times-Democrat*.) Whether all or any of the mob's victims were guilty of murder or of being part of a conspiracy is still unclear. As the New Orleans historian John Smith Kendall wrote in 1939, "We never did get to know exactly who killed Hennessy."[43]

Among the thousands who rushed the parish prison to kill the Sicilians was John M. Parker. Apparently he did not personally shoot or string up any of the eleven victims, but he helped lead the massacre, he was there, and he never expressed regret. He believed it was another battle for civilization, like that of Liberty Place in 1874. Most state newspapers, city and rural, agreed—the *St. Mary Banner*, published in the town of Franklin, was simply more enthusiastic than most in hailing "the killing of the dagoes" as "the greatest event of the year. The 14th of March will last as long in the history of Louisiana as any other struggle for liberty and safety." Parker's minister—Palmer— added his blessing to the murders. "The instinct of self- preservation," Palmer said in a public address, made necessary "extra-legal measures . . . to stamp out the existence of the Mafia in our midst."[44]

Fallout from the lynching of the Sicilians was still being felt two years later, in 1893. By that time, a grand jury had refused to indict any of the mob's members. (The jury did hand down a true bill against O'Malley for attempting to bribe a juror in the Hennessy murder trial; the charge was later dismissed.) Indeed, the action of John M. Parker and other leaders of the lynch mob was taken by most upper- and middle-class Louisianians as additional proof of their public spirit. "It was a movement conceived by gentlemen and carried out by gentlemen," explained an approving article in the *American Law Review*. During 1893, Parker became the youngest-ever president of the New Orleans Board of Trade and was named by the city council to the board of police commissioners.[45]

Vengeance of a sort was exacted by New Orleans' Italian community in the municipal election of 1892, when Mayor Shakspeare was narrowly defeated by the Ring candidate, John Fitzpatrick. For obvious reasons, the Sicilian vote went heavily for Fitzpatrick, and probably gave him his victory margin. Sicilian voters continued to be one of the machine's strongest ethnic voting blocs, and during John M. Parker's political career he got few votes among the Italian-speaking. As governor in 1924, Parker refused to grant reprieves to six men of Sicilian background who were sentenced to hang for murdering a Tangipahoa Parish store-owner. On his way to the gallows, one of them was heard to remark: "Governor Parker has now made it seventeen Italians. Eleven lynched and six hanged."[46]

Even Dominick O'Malley enjoyed a measure of long-term vengeance against the New Orleans patricians who had wanted to lynch him. O'Malley's fee as a private investigator for the alleged Mafia defendants had been five thousand dollars, a nice sum in the 1890s. When tempers cooled, he came out of hiding and by 1893 was again operating his detective agency on Gravier Street.[47] His reputation as a jury fixer probably helped business, and at various times he would be accused of other crimes, such as blackmail, arson, rigging horse races, running a numbers racket, criminal libel, and soliciting for contract murder. In 1893 his arrest record already was one of the longest in the city's history. It would grow longer. Through it all, O'Malley seemed determined to be a center of attention, and as a self-educated immigrant he delighted in tormenting the uptown establishment. What better way to realize both goals than by owning a newspaper? In 1894 he purchased a struggling New Orleans daily, the *Item*, for only half the amount of his fee in the Hennessy case. Under O'Malley's ownership, the afternoon *Item* emphasized sensation and scandal, and it quickly became a force in Louisiana, rivaling the more sedate *Picayune*, the *Times-Democrat*, and the *States*. His style of journalism brought O'Malley additional familiarity with the effects of gunshot wounds and with the interior of Orleans Parish Prison. By the time he died—of natural causes—in 1920, he boasted of fourteen bullet wounds to his body.[48]

For Louisiana's ruling class, 1893 was a time of increasing concern. Their right to govern was being seriously contested for the first time since Reconstruction. What the Baton Rouge *Advocate*, the official journal of the state government, referred to as "wild-eyed demagogues" were busy among white farmers, organizing support for the new People's (Populist) party. In the past, these same white farmers had overwhelmingly backed the conservative Democratic party's call for political and racial unity, but as early as 1890 signs of Populist revolt—carried in by traveling agrarian crusaders from Kansas and Texas—had been visible in north central Louisiana's Winn Parish, and by 1893, largely as a consequence of the economic depression, Populist ideas were spreading across the South's poorer white agricultural areas, including the clay uplands of Louisiana.[49]

Populism was an effort to break the bonds of the past. Its leaders dreamed of organizing southern and northern farmers and other working people, black as well as white, into a new political force that would bury the old sectional and racial hostilities of the Civil War and Reconstruction years. From this unity would be born a more equitable society, free of hierarchical domination or corporate manipulation. Populism hoped to lessen the unfairness of life. Some planks in the new party's platform were socialistic, such as those supporting government ownership of railroad, telegraph, and telephone lines; other proposals were a generation ahead of their time—for example, woman suffrage. But fundamentally, Populism was a movement of small landowners in the South and the Plains States who wanted to redirect governmental priorities in such a way as to provide a measure of security and dignity in the lives of ordinary people.

Huey Long's birthplace, the hardscrabble parish of Winn, became Populism's bastion in Louisiana. Indeed, no county in any other southern state gave the new third party such overwhelming support. In 1892 the People's party gubernatorial candidate, Robert L. Tannehill, running against Democratic and Republican opponents, received 76.7 percent of Winn's vote. The parish's leading newspaper during the 1890s, the Winnfield *Comrade*, was the first People's party newspaper in the South.[50]

The People's party in Louisiana, as in other southern states, alarmed conservatives by openly appealing for black support. White Populists were hardly racial liberals by modern standards, but in the context of their time and place they took an advanced position. "We declare emphatically," read the state Populist platform, "that the interests of the white and colored races of the South are identical. . . . Equal justice and fairness must be accorded to each." In Winn Parish, where 14 percent of the population was black, Populists on at least two occasions held interracial picnics; although separate tables were provided, a Democratic observer from an adjacent parish nevertheless registered disgust. The Winnfield *Comrade* also violated southern white racial etiquette by referring to local black schoolteachers as "Mr." and "Miss."[51]

As late as the 1890s, Louisiana still narrowly had a black majority, both in population and in voter registration (even though most blacks no longer cast a free ballot), and the state's Democratic party used this fact to discourage the spread of Populism. Democratic leaders had been profoundly impressed by how well the White League worked in 1874, both in uniting all classes of whites and in overthrowing Republican rule, and they continued to play the racial card long after Reconstruction was over. It was, to quote an old Louisiana expression, "the black ace from the bottom of the deck."[52] Usually it provided a winning hand.

If racist appeals failed to keep rank-and-file whites in line, there was always fraud. The mystery about the Populist party in Louisiana is how it expected to gain power peacefully in a state where the ballot box was scarcely more sacrosanct than in, say, Honduras. Louisiana's politicoeconomic oligarchy of cotton and sugar planters, timber owners, merchants, and professional men made up less than a quarter of the registered voters.[53] But as the self-styled "better element" or "real people," and thus the standard-bearers of civilization, they were determined to do whatever was necessary to prevent Louisiana from falling into the hands of blacks, white dissidents, or any combination thereof—such as the coalition that the state's official journal said in 1893 was being hatched by the "Jacobins of Winn Parish." In other southern states, Democrats also used fraud and violence to subdue the People's party, but Louisiana was a special case. "Its Populism," as a classic study of regional politics points out, "was repressed with a violence unparalleled in the South."[54]

The governor of Louisiana in 1893 was Murphy J. Foster. According to the "official" returns, he was elected the state's chief executive in 1892, and by massive vote fraud he would be reelected over a Populist-Republican coalition in 1896. Personally honest and soft-spoken, Foster was described by a Tennessee admirer as a well-dressed gentleman whose "deportment and distinguished bearing are entirely in accord with what might be expected of a State famous for its dignity and polite manners."[55] He was also probably the most authoritarian and reactionary governor ever endured by an American state during the nineteenth century.

17

Concentrating power in the office of governor has been standard practice in Louisiana since colonial times. Under French and Spanish rule, royally appointed governors and courts exercised all authority. When Louisiana became an American state, its constitution granted more power to the chief executive than that enjoyed by virtually any other governor. During Reconstruction, the Republican governor Henry Clay Warmoth augmented his constitutional powers by intimidating legislators into granting him control over local officials and election procedures (sixty years later, Huey Long would say privately that he had learned something by Warmoth's example).[56] When conservative Democrats gained control of Louisiana after Reconstruction, the Constitution of 1879 granted authority unprecedented for a governor of any American state: this constitution, in effect when Foster became governor, gave his office not only the power of line-item veto, but also the right to appoint all parish assessors (who also acted as voter registrars), all police jury members (the equivalent of county commissioners in other states), and the state school board (which in turn appointed parish school boards).[57] With only slight overstatement, a book about Louisiana published in the 1890s declared: "The people have abdicated the right of local self-government."[58]

Governor Foster inherited such power mainly because of white Louisiana's obsessive fear of black political activity. This worry had always been intense in the alluvial parishes where blacks outnumbered whites by as much as ten to one; allowing one man in Baton Rouge the authority to name local officials gave plantation owners a measure of security. To have summarily disfranchised blacks by law—for example, by statutes directly or indirectly limiting the right to vote to white people—was not considered a feasible solution during the years just after Reconstruction. The memory of federal military occupation was still too fresh. But since white Louisiana had got away with overthrowing Reconstruction by violence and vote fraud, it seemed safe to continue these extralegal devices during the 1880s and into the 1890s. Blacks could still register—indeed many lingered on the registration rolls years after they died— but particularly in the plantation parishes, there was seldom a free or honest election. As a Populist critic acidly observed, "A dead darkey makes a good Democrat and never ceases to vote."[59] The role of the governor was crucial. Former governor Samuel

D. McEnery frankly remarked during the 1890s that Louisiana's election system "was intended to make it the duty of the governor to treat the law as a formality and count in the Democrats."[60]

Foster's official organ, the Baton Rouge *Advocate,* referred to the governor as "Commander-in-Chief Foster," as if he were the president of an independent nation of dubious stability.[61] He virtually was that. Already having more power than other governors, Foster came to office at a time when the federal government was more reluctant than previously to become involved in state affairs. Moreover, the governor of Louisiana was also *ex officio* head of the state Democratic party, which comprised the ruling elite of Louisiana.

The governor actually was commander in chief of a military force, the state militia. Louisiana's militia had dwindled during the 1880s, but because of what Foster perceived as stormy days ahead, in 1893 he set about promoting enlistments and more public funding for the militia; he also sought and received donations from those he called "prominent men of the state."[62] To publicize his martial buildup, the governor arranged for a sham battle, fought on the campus of Louisiana State University in May of 1893 between rival militia units (a baseball game between LSU and Tulane helped draw a big crowd). In August of the same year, despite a depressed economy, Foster selected 350 militiamen for a well-publicized trip to the Chicago World's Fair, where "Louisiana Day" at the fair was celebrated with a military review. A large crowd, reported the Chicago *Tribune,* watched the parade and its fancy uniforms. Governor Foster was given a twenty-one-gun salute when he appeared on the reviewing stand. Three years later, during his disputed reelection in 1896, the governor would call out his militia to put down disturbances by white and black Populists and Republicans.[63]

Huey Long, destined to become the best-known Louisianian of the twentieth century, began life in remote Winn Parish the same year that the state's most famed Civil War leader died in New Orleans. Pierre Gustave Toutant Beauregard, "Napoleon in Gray," last survivor of the original (1861) full generals of the Confederacy, suffered a fatal heart seizure on the night of February 20, 1893, at his home on Esplanade Avenue. He was seventy-four. Active until the end, he two nights earlier had visited La Variété

Club and attended the play *Cleopatra* at the Grand Opera House.[64]

Beauregard's prestige had suffered after the war because he sold his services to the Louisiana Lottery Company, a gambling syndicate notorious for bribing legislators into giving it a legal monopoly on numbers betting within the state. (Samuel McEnery, as governor from 1881 to 1888, was so visibly tied to the company he was called "McLottery.") The lottery company's annual income vastly exceeded that of the state and all parish governments combined, and part of its overhead from 1877 to 1893 consisted of paying Beauregard, along with another former Confederate general, Jubal Early, handsome salaries to supervise the public drawings, so as to lend Lost Cause respectability to a gambling company of carpetbagger origins.[65] But the lottery was an anathema to "good government" reformers of both right and left; its three leading religious foes in New Orleans made up a formidable ecumenical front: Dr. Palmer of First Presbyterian; the Catholic archbishop, Francis Janssens; and Rabbi Max Heller. In 1892 the Anti-Lottery League's efforts inside the Democratic party led to McEnery's defeat and the election of Murphy J. Foster as governor. Simultaneously, the Louisiana State Lottery was compelled by the federal government to discontinue using the United States mail—a heavy blow, for most of its ticket sales were out of state. The same year that Beauregard died, 1893, was also the last year the lottery legally operated in Louisiana. In 1894 it moved to Honduras.[66]

The funeral of General Beauregard was a time for forgetting his lottery association and remembering the heart-pounding battle glories of First Manassas and Shiloh, and his defense of Charleston and Petersburg against the Yankee hordes. He was Louisiana's most visible link to the Lost Cause. Prior to the funeral, his body, still handsome in old age and death, lay on display in City Hall, and all night long thousands walked by his bier. When the doors closed next morning for the religious ceremonies, thousands more were waiting outside, disappointed at not seeing the gallant Creole's face one more time.[67]

Beauregard had wanted a private funeral with little ceremony, and had asked to be cremated: his will revealed he was horrified by the thought of his body rotting away in this "low, warm and damp country." These wishes were all ignored. His funeral procession was the largest New Orleans had seen since that of Jefferson Davis four years earlier. Among Beauregard's pallbearers were Governor Foster, ex-governor McEnery, United States Senator Edward D. White, and Captain Thomas P. Leathers of the steamboat *Natchez* (still considered the best boatman on the river even though he had lost a famous race with the *Robert E. Lee*). A line of carriages several miles long followed the horse-drawn hearse to Metairie Cemetery, where Beauregard was placed in the great tomb of the Army of Tennessee, alongside the remains of another general whose statue stood above the tomb, Albert Sidney Johnston, killed at Shiloh.[68]

Riding in Beauregard's cortege was E. Kirby Smith, now the Lost Cause's last living full general. General Smith happened to be in New Orleans because he chaired the historical committee of the United Confederate Veterans, and this group was meeting in the city "for the purpose of agreeing upon a history of the late war for use in the public schools of the South." Smith fell ill shortly after Beauregard's funeral but returned to his teaching post at the University of the South in Tennessee. There he died in late March, a month after Beauregard. In accordance with his wishes, Kirby Smith was buried in Metairie Cemetery, in the same tomb with Generals Beauregard and A. S. Johnston and John Bell Hood.[69]

Since Metairie is the showplace of New Orleans' "cities of the dead," bodies interred there are seldom moved elsewhere, but in May of 1893, a few weeks after Beauregard and Kirby Smith were laid to rest in Metairie, an even more famous resident was removed. Jefferson Davis' remains were taken from the tomb of the Army of Northern Virginia in Metairie and, with elaborate ceremony, put on a flag-draped train for Hollywood Cemetery in Richmond, Virginia. Davis had died at eighty-one while in New Orleans in 1889. His pallbearers had included the Reverend Dr. Palmer, Major Hearsey, and Captain Leathers. Noticeably absent from Davis' funeral had been P. G. T. Beauregard. Beauregard had been invited to ride at the head of the Confederate president's funeral procession but had refused. He blamed Davis for losing the war, and hated him personally. Privately, Beauregard told his family that since "we have always been enemies," he was not sorry Davis was dead.[70]

The timing of the removal of Davis' body from Metairie, shortly after Beauregard's was taken there, probably was not coincidental. Davis' widow, Varina Howell Davis, had decided two years earlier that the Confederate capital of Richmond should be her husband's final place of interment, but the date for the removal apparently was not set until after Beauregard died. Mrs. Davis knew that her husband and Beauregard could not stand being near each other while alive, and it surely occurred to her that they would not want to be near in death. (Beauregard had wanted his own ashes placed "in our family tomb," although to no avail.)[71]

Few situations better illustrate the late nineteenth century's morbid fixation with death than Mrs. Davis' decision to move her husband's bones. It was more than Victorian sentimentality, more than a desire to see him buried beneath his own monument in the city where he had been the only president of a now-vanished nation. It also represented a profound longing of the human spirit, more palpable than in most other times and places, to attain a permanence in stone that was impossible in this fragile and melancholy earthly life.

Where and when Mrs. Davis would decide to transfer the Confederate president's remains had been a standard topic of conversation throughout the South since 1889. Louisiana, Mississippi, Georgia, and Virginia were considered the leading candidates for his permanent interment. Her final choice narrowed down to Beauvoir (their home in Mississippi) and Richmond. Mrs. Davis decided against Mississippi because Beauvoir was along the Gulf coast at Biloxi and she was afraid "my husband's mortal body" might be washed out to sea.[72]

In 1893, on the September 14 anniversary of the White League uprising, four months after President Davis' bones were removed from Metairie, there took place in that cemetery a ceremonial placing of flowers on the grave of Frederick N. Ogden, commander of the paramilitary force that had hastened the end of Reconstruction. Ogden died in 1886, but unlike most laid to rest in Metairie, he was placed inside a mound of earth instead of a mausoleum. The Fourteenth of September Memorial Committee authorized Ogden's widow to select an appropriate monument, much to its regret. She saw something in the Tennessee mountains that would do: a forty-thousand-pound granite boulder. Faithful to its word, the memorial committee hauled the huge rock from a wilderness gorge and transported it by railroad flatcar to New Orleans. "Here a difficulty presented itself," noted the *Picayune* in 1893. Teamster wagons could not handle the boulder; planks had to be laid down the middle of the streets so that the monstrosity could be tumbled by hand seven miles from the railyards to Metairie Cemetery. It took a week. But the granite mass was finally situated, properly inscribed, at the head of the White League commander's grave mound. "Unto all ages," an admirer wrote, it would stand "as a symbol of the memories of this day, and of the hero who led his people to victory." [73]

Huey Long, on a day near the end of his hectic life, invited the New York *Times* reporter Raymond Daniell and two other out-of-state newsmen to ride with him from Baton Rouge to New Orleans. As they passed Metairie Cemetery, recalled Daniell, "Huey remarked that of all forms of human vanity, the building of monuments over graves seemed to him the silliest." One of the reporters, who had been nursing a whiskey bottle all the way from Baton Rouge, looked at the Kingfish and predicted that "one day Huey would have a finer one than any in that cemetery." [74] For once, Huey Long seemed unable to think of a reply.

· 2 ·

THE BOY WHO WOULD BE KINGFISH

A big log house on a 320-acre farm was the birthplace of Huey Pierce Long, on August 30, 1893. He was the seventh of nine surviving children of Huey P. Long, Sr. (known as Hugh), and Caledonia Tison Long. Hugh and Caledonia must have made a strong genetic match: seeing nine out of ten offspring grow to maturity was exceptional for that time and place. Hugh, six feet tall, enjoyed physical strength and a roaring voice. Caledonia, a slender woman, passed to their children her retentive intelligence and firm will. She could hear a song or poem once and repeat it verbatim. All the Long siblings—five girls, four boys—were bright, and all except Huey and Earl graduated from high school and attended at least two years of college. But Huey, as his envious younger brother, Earl, conceded, was "a genius."[1]

Oxen pulling a wagon took Huey's paternal grandparents, John and Mary Long, to the forested hills of north central Louisiana's Winn Parish in 1859. The Longs had traveled three hundred hard miles from a poorer place, Sullivan's Hollow in Smith County, Mississippi. Texas was their intended destination, but relatives had already homesteaded in Winn, so John and Mary Long, with their wagonload of supplies and children (Hugh was one of fourteen), decided to remain. The presence of available land and abundant water, including saline springs from which salt could be made by boiling, was probably more of an attraction than having kin nearby. Salt, a scarce commodity in the 1850s, was needed by livestock as well as by humans, and John Long preferred stock raising and corn farming over cultivating cotton. Decades later his grandson Julius, who collected family history, declared this resource to be the Longs' primary reason for settling there. "My folks were looking for salt and found it in Winn Parish."[2]

Winn Parish first earned its reputation for dissent during the Civil War. Its delegate to Louisiana's 1861 secession convention was one of only seven who refused to sign the ordinance dissolving the bonds of union. The parish's loyalty to the Confederacy became increasingly doubtful as the war wore on; along with neighboring Jackson Parish it was the state's most notorious center for desertion and draft avoidance. General Kirby Smith had to detach five companies sorely needed to fight Yankees in a vain effort to "clear out Jackson and Winn Parishes."[3] Up to half of Winn's able-bodied young white men may have hid in the forests rather than be conscripted in the southern army; they saw no reason to fight for "rich men's niggers." Some managed to get through Confederate lines and join the Union army. John Long, Huey's grandfather, did not serve in either army, nor did he "take refuge in the arms of General Green," as hiding in the woods was called. It is likely he avoided conscription because of a hernia. His son Hugh (Huey Sr.) told an interviewer in 1935 that his father "was with the North during the war, but he stayed here and kept his mouth shut."[4]

The Longs were not "poor white trash," but neither were they gentry. It was a point of family pride that they always owned the land they worked. Yet their Winn Parish land was thin upland soil, and like most of the white families who settled there, they possessed no slaves. Winn at the time of the Civil War did include a minority of slave-owners: about one white family in three owned slaves, usually six or fewer. The Tisons—Huey Long's maternal grandparents—were small slave-owners in antebellum Winn Parish, so they could be considered marginally part of Louisiana's gentry or patrician class. But with Emancipation, followed by Reconstruction taxes, the Tisons lost their slaves, land, and status. In 1875, Caledonia Tison, orphaned and penniless at age fifteen, married Huey P. Long (Sr.), who had dreamed of going to college and becoming a physician but, because of his father John's illness, had stayed at home and taken over management of the family farm.[5]

Eldest of the four sons of the Long-Tison marriage was Julius Tison Long, born in 1879. Julius grew up to become a lawyer, and he took a special interest in the brightest of his siblings, his younger brother Huey. Family status was of utmost importance to Julius. The Longs were beginning to rise above their ordinary yeoman-farmer past, and Julius believed that with proper guidance his unruly but gifted little brother would surely move the family further along the road to gentility.[6]

Huey was *different*. Virtually all who knew him as a child or as a teenager used that word when trying to sum him up. Other descriptions of young Huey Long by relatives and classmates have depicted him as being bright, boundlessly energetic, nervous, bossy, "always butting in," a braggart, "ornery," belligerent, and as his brother Earl added, "curious about everything." Today a child psychologist might say he was precocious. Little Huey learned to walk at nine months; even earlier, his older sister Olive recalled, if not restrained he would crawl to the front gate of the yard, somehow unlatch it, and sit by the side of the road to stare at those who passed by.[7]

Huey Long truthfully wrote in his autobiography that he was born in a "comfortable, well-built split log house," although in recalling it he managed to reduce its six rooms to four. Sometimes in emotional speeches he summoned up the image of a little log cabin, uncannily resembling Abraham Lincoln's birthplace (after Huey's assassination, one of the orators at a memorial ceremony shrank the cabin to near-invisibility).[8] In 1894, the year after Huey's birth, his family moved into "a better house," as his autobiography says. But he never mentioned that when he was thirteen, in 1907, the saltbox-style "better house" was relocated and on its site the Longs built one of Winnfield's finest residences. Ten big high-ceilinged rooms and curving verandas on both stories made it, by hill-country standards, a mansion.[9]

The Long family's rising affluence was due mostly to the fortunate location of their 320-acre farm. When Huey was born, the Long's land was on the outskirts of town, but in 1901 Winnfield got its first railroad—the Arkansas Southern—and the previously isolated, unincorporated parish seat of 1,400 began a period of growth and relative prosperity. Hugh, then forty-seven, began selling off parcels of the farm as residential lots for Winnfield's expanding population (2,925 by 1910, and incorporated). This income allowed Hugh to invest in rural land and stock, as well as to build a fine home. In 1910 the Winnfield *Comrade* declared, "Few, if any, have greater proprietary interests at stake in our town than Mr. Long."[10]

A myth persisted during Huey's lifetime—and he encouraged it—that the Longs were impoverished farmers, eking out a hard-scrabble living on barren ground, with young Huey sweating in the fields alongside his kinfolk. Huey's autobiography makes some concession to the truth, such as admitting that "I hated farm work"—although that loathing was based upon slight acquaintance. The myth was largely dispelled by T. Harry Williams' detailed biography *Huey Long*. What is still not understood, however, is the status of the Long family in the politico-economic structure of Winn Parish during the time of Huey's childhood—and that family's perception of themselves as being, in the words of a neighbor, "of the upper crust."[11]

Being "of the upper crust" in Winn Parish did not signify much to the great landlords along the Mississippi and Red rivers, or to the top businessmen in New Orleans and Shreveport. Yet it mattered terribly to the Long family, especially to brother Julius and to four of the sisters: Lottie, Olive, Clara, and Lucille. During his senatorial career, Huey was referred to by a conservative journal in Vienna, Austria (*Neues Wiener Tagblatt*), as "this peasant's son." The Austrian paper added that "his achievements are strongly reminiscent of Adolf Hitler's." Had they read this, most of Huey's immediate family probably would have resented most the words "peasant's son."[12]

In fact, Huey's paternal forebears were, by the standards of continental Europe, small landowning peasants (the nicer British-American expression was *yeoman farmer*). John and Mary Long, and their children, were people who had little schooling, and upon entering Louisiana in 1859 they had come to a land where, more than in any other southern state except possibly South Carolina, a man who tilled the soil with his own hands, particularly if his wife or daughters labored beside him, was—according to the gentry—doing "niggers' work" and was therefore a white person of low status. Work itself was acceptable to the patrician class as long as it did not involve manual labor, especially not in the earth. Supervising laborers was a suitable gentleman's role, even if it included demonstrating to your sharecroppers how best to plow, as John M. Parker enjoyed doing. Keeping account books in a family business was also approved activity, as was practicing law or medicine or holding an elective or appointive public office. Probably more than in any other American state, holding public office in Louisiana signified special achievement. It meant rising above the herd. Even a justice of the peace was called "judge," and in rural areas ward constables sometimes put "honorable" in front of their names.

The maternal Tison line of Huey's ancestry, being small slaveowners, well understood the importance of gentility and status, and if Hugh Long did not perceive this before he married Caledonia (Callie) Tison, he did afterward. Of their children, only Julius, the oldest son, knew what it was like to regularly plow and plant and weed and gather the family's crops of cotton and corn. By the time Huey would have been expected to do such labor, his father had divided the family farm into town lots and most of his other acreage was being used to raise hogs and cattle. When Huey described how "we" arose before sunup, "toiled until dark, after which we did nothing except eat supper, listen to the whippoorwills, and go to bed," he must have been thinking of the Longs' less fortunate neighbors, or what Julius had told him. Huey's siblings did not recall him working in the fields at any time. If such a thing ever occurred, the veteran reporter Thomas O. Harris suggested, it was like snow in June—a rare happening that lasted briefly.[13]

Huey's mother and sisters probably never worked in the fields. Upland north Louisiana's social stratification was, by necessity, more elastic than that of the plantation parishes or the cities, but having sunbonneted womenfolks toiling among the cotton and corn rows was something not done in families with any pretensions to gentility. Even before prosperity came to the Long family in 1901, women's work would have been restricted to the home and possibly the vegetable garden. At the turn of the century, Huey's mother Callie somehow found time, amidst nine children, to make extra money with her skill at hat making: the federal census taker who visited the Long home in June of 1900 listed Hugh's occupation as "farmer" and by Callie's name wrote "milliner."[14]

Mrs. Long of course relied upon her older children to help take care of the younger ones. But Huey, who turned seven in 1900, was already making trouble for anyone who tried to tell him what to do. Predictably, he hated school. Neighbors could recall, decades later, the sight of his mother herding the protesting little boy to school with the aid of a peachtree switch.[15]

After Huey Long became governor, United States senator, and finally dictator of Louisiana, the thing his sisters and brother Julius most resented was his misrepresentation of the family's social and economic status. Huey's strongest support came from voters of humble background, and he wanted them to identify with him. But probably another impulse was also at work. A supreme egoist such as Huey could make his struggle against the odds seem all the more heroic by depicting his origins as pathetic and obscure. By downgrading his family, he made his rise appear all the higher.

"He made us all so mad," Huey's eldest sister, Lottie, recalled when in her eighties; Huey "warped things for political reasons." What made her the maddest was his portraying the Longs as ragged rednecks. His family cringed when, as governor, he declared that "this state's full of sapsucker, hillbilly and Cajun relatives of mine, and there ain't enough dignity in the bunch to keep a chigger still long enough to brush his hair." On the floor of the United States Senate in March of 1935, he claimed that "my brothers and sisters, my uncles and aunts, my relatives and friends, are starving to death."[16] But Julius was angriest over something Huey said in a 1931 radio address over KWKH, Shreveport, when he emotionally described a fictitious childhood scene: "I have seen my mother cry," exclaimed Huey, "because I did not have shoes to wear." Julius revealed emotions of his own in a published rebuttal. "Nothing could better portray [Huey's] true character, his lack of love," wrote Julius, than to "tell such a falsehood about his dead mother."[17]

At least Huey never claimed his family was Populist. Winn Parish, storm center of the 1890s Louisiana People's party, had no Long among its leaders; nor did Huey's father or any of his several uncles ever support the agrarian movement. The Longs were part of the better-off Democratic minority in the parish. When Hugh made his first unsuccessful political race—as an Independent Democrat in 1900, hoping to become state senator for the district comprising Winn, Grant, and Caldwell parishes—he stressed that he was "a Democrat" and had "always cast his lot with that party." The Colfax *Chronicle* in Grant Parish described Hugh as a "stock raiser, frugal and industrious, who is opposed to corporate control . . . of the government [and is] a firm believer in a better school system." [18] Hugh's platform, what there was of it, did have a Populist ring and touched upon points that his son would adopt a generation later. But the victor in that race was J. T. Wallace of Winnfield, a regular Democrat, whose eleven-year-old son, George, grew up to become not only one of the state's best lawyers, but also chief legal aide to Governor Huey Long. [19] J. T. Wallace's win over both a Populist and Hugh Long (who came in last) marked the first Democratic victory in that senatorial district since 1888; Populists had held it during the 1890s.

Like his father, but many times magnified, Huey Long would borrow rhetoric from the People's party heritage. Huey's anti-corporation stance, his denunciations of the "plutocrats" whose fortunes he promised to cut down to "frying size," and most of all, his verbal assaults upon Louisiana's haughty patrician rulers—all this was an updated, more explosive rendition of the Populist oratory that once had saturated Winn Parish. Huey was still a small child when the People's party faded out at the turn of the century, but he grew up "surrounded by men," as Alan Brinkley writes, "whose political views had been shaped by the struggles of the 1890s." Huey never mentioned his debt to Populism. But he had to be aware of it. [20] Perhaps he did not want his name linked to a movement that had failed. More likely, he knew that Populism had suffered from the taint of racial liberalism. As an astute politician, Huey saw no advantage in being associated with something that would remind whites of a troubled time when blacks still played a role in state politics and thousands of ordinary white people were momentarily allied with them.

What was it like being around him when he was a child? Mildred Adams speculated on that subject when she interviewed Senator Long in 1933. "One guesses," she wrote, "that he was a red-headed insurgent in a crowded farmhouse, that he fought with his brothers and sisters." Except for the Long residence not being so crowded, her surmise was correct. Huey was hyperactive from infancy. He had to hold center stage at all times, and whether the attention he got was positive or negative did not seem to be of much importance. He submitted to the authority of parents or older siblings only with great reluctance, and only temporarily. The regimentation of the classroom galled

30

him even more. As early as grade school, he considered himself a superior being to whom the rules did not apply. A classmate recalled that he wrote in his frayed books, "Hon. Huey P. Long."[21]

Quiet was almost as unendurable as discipline or lack of attention. Sometimes Huey sneaked over to the Baptist church and rang the bell, which was supposed to be sounded only for services or fires. When a circus came to Winnfield and held a parade, twelve-year-old Huey could not stand seeing the elephants get all that attention. He ran out in the street and threw a rock at the beasts.[22]

Inevitably, this assertiveness led to schoolyard fights. Early on, Huey became adept at insulting others. He seemed unable to hide his contempt for mentally slower classmates (and probably they were all slower, by comparison). But bodily rough-and-tumble was something the boy preferred to avoid. A verbal bully, he lacked the muscles and animal courage necessary to reinforce his words with action. Yet it is unfair to label Huey Long, as many have done, a physical coward. Sometimes he may have resembled one, but a real coward would not habitually say things that led to violent confrontations. Huey knew from experience what was coming when he belittled other boys, yet he kept it up. Nor would he apologize. If it came to fisticuffs, he preferred to leave that to his younger but stronger brother Earl. "Fighting," Huey explained in later years, "is not my occupation."[23]

The boy's restless nature made it difficult for him to sit still long enough to read books. Nor were there many books in Winnfield. In those years the town did not have a library. Neither did the school. Most homes would have had a Bible, perhaps some religious tracts, copies of one of the town's two weeklies (the *Comrade*, which had become politically independent after Populism died, or the *Southern Sentinel*, always Democratic), a Sears, Roebuck catalog—and little else in the way of reading material. But because of Callie's desire to see her children improve themselves, the Long home contained more books and periodicals than most in Winnfield. The family's favorite magazine was the weekly *Saturday Evening Post*, a pillar of middle-class respectability. When the eldest son, Julius, enrolled at Louisiana Tech in Ruston, he would come home on weekends with an armful of books from the college library, and encourage his brothers and sisters—most of all, Huey—to read them. The boy would flip through the volumes, scanning pages here and there. But once he grasped the main points of a book, he usually put it down. Reading out of intellectual curiosity or for enjoyment's sake was contrary to his nature. Huey's older sister Lottie said, "I never saw him study."[24]

Around the house, little Huey sometimes read, or pretended to, as a ploy to avoid work. "Mama never disturbed a child as long as he was reading, or pretending to read," Lottie recalled. Huey was often able to intuit the advent of a chore, and would bury his head in a book. His mother, coming into the room, would look over her brood and call on "one that wasn't reading to do the job at hand."[25] Yet a few books keenly interested Huey, and he read these more than once. His favorite novel was *The Count of Monte Cristo*, Alexandre Dumas' story of a hero who early in life was denied his rightful place of power by corrupt men, but who ultimately triumphed over his enemies and exacted stern revenge on all. It made a lifelong impression on him.

"That man in that book knew how to hate," Senator Huey Long mused in 1933, "and until you learn how to hate you'll never get anywhere in this world." But he also enjoyed, and in rare gentle moods recommended, Victor Hugo's *Les Miserables*, a melodramatic novel about the sufferings of society's outcasts. Huey's favorite poem, William Ernest Henley's "Invictus," would also be quoted by brother Earl in his political campaigns of the 1940s and 1950s. The New York journalist A. J. Liebling dubbed the poem "the family battle ode." The Long brothers particularly favored the following two stanzas:

> In the fell clutch of circumstance
>   I have not winced nor cried aloud.
> Under the bludgeonings of chance
>   My head is bloody, but unbowed.
>
> It matters not how strait the gate,
>   How charged with punishments the scroll,
> I am the master of my fate;
>   I am the captain of my soul.[26]

Huey's readings in history were limited partly by lack of access, but mainly by his narrow interests. Recitals of the doings of great men excited him—Napoleon most of all. Frederick the Great ranked second. Of the nonfiction works he looked into, James Clark Ridpath's *History of the World* made the strongest

impression. Designed for popular readership, Ridpath's pano-
rama of great men and events filled several volumes and was a
basic part of the Long family's modest library. It is hardly surprising that a bright boy of ten or twelve would be taken with
such an overview of the past, yet Huey never progressed to Thu-
cydides or Macaulay; during his last year of life, at age forty-one,
he still admired Ridpath as his favorite historian. Senator Long
would point to a set of *History of the World* shelved near his office
desk in Washington when he wanted to direct an interviewer's
attention to the wisdom of the past. It had faded bindings and
was likely the same set that Huey had perused as a child in
Winnfield.[27]

Whether Huey's career would have differed significantly had
he been raised in a more enlightened community is impossible
to say. Probably under any circumstances he would have tried to
become a leader. Huey grew up in one of Winnfield's better
households, but the best the town offered was none too good.
Louisiana's public schools, except for those open to privileged
white children in the cities and plantation parishes, were among
the worst in the South—"sloughs of contented ignorance," a
state school journal called them in 1904.[28] Winnfield's poorly
paid, ill-equipped teachers tried to cope with overflowing students in dilapidated classrooms; they could not be expected to
handle properly a gifted but troublesome child such as Huey
Long. The town itself had nothing resembling urban culture.
Chili con carne was the nearest thing to exotic cuisine on the
menus of local restaurants. Winnfield boasted a place called the
Opera House, but Mozart and Verdi were not on the bill. Instead,
for five cents (ten cents for front seats) the audience could watch
"Toten the Magician," silent film comedies and melodramas, and
Negro minstrel shows such as "Shufflin' Sam from Alabam'" or
"Jolly Joe, the Sooty Comedian."[29]

Briefly during his boyhood, Huey talked of entering the ministry—of becoming a Baptist preacher. Religion held a central
place in the Long household, chiefly because of mother Callie's
insistence. Every evening she would read a Bible chapter to the
family. The First Baptist Church saw all the Longs, unless one
was ill, at every service, including Sunday school, Wednesday
night prayer meeting, and revivals. Huey candidly admitted
that until he left home at sixteen, "I was, under compulsion, a
regular attendant at all religious ceremonies." He resented being

made to go but was less obstreperous about it than he was concerning school attendance. Some church activities he enjoyed, particularly group singing, because music appealed to him and he possessed a fair singing voice. Once, his closest companion, Harley Bozeman, recalled, Huey took a temporary job as a delivery boy for a bakery and gave his entire week's wages, $3.50, to the church. Much to his mother's satisfaction, Huey made his "decision for Christ" and underwent immersion in Crawford's fishpond, thereby becoming a member of the First Baptist Church of Winnfield.[30]

Whether he was serious when he told his mother that he wanted to become a minister cannot be known. Perhaps at the moment he was, for he had observed that preachers could be centers of attention and hold power over their congregations. Or he may have simply been trying to please and flatter his mother, who had spoken of her wish to see him become a cleric. (That someone of her intelligence would think a child of his disposition was pulpit material says something about the self-deluding tendency of parental love.) Huey's alleged interest in the ministry soon faded. After leaving home he almost never went to church. Yet as a politician he delivered his booming speeches with overtones of evangelical fervor, his opponents cast in the role of Satan.[31]

Huey had listened to his mother read the entire Bible during those hundreds of evenings in his childhood home. Upon becoming a politician he increasingly quoted from the Bible, beginning with his first foray into state-wide politics in 1920 when, too young to run for governor himself, he campaigned on behalf of the patrician reformer, John M. Parker. In the 1930s he would claim that his Share Our Wealth plan was based upon holy writ. "Huey," a New Orleans newspaperman once said, "is the only man who ever rose to political power in this country solely on the Pentateuch and brass-bound gall."[32] He could quote many passages from memory, and generally kept one or more Bibles near him, since (in his words) "two Bibles is never too many." Yet his method of reading and retaining Scripture offers a glimpse of Huey Long's strange inner conflicts. Sometimes while a senator, he would lie in bed at night and, with careful penmanship, copy verses from the Bible. "Suddenly," according to henchmen who shared his apartment, "in a burst of profanity [he would] decide to visit Washington's fashionable nightclubs."[33]

Whatever Huey's use of the Bible might indicate about his religiosity, it raises a question concerning his reputed photographic memory. That from early childhood he possessed remarkable powers of retention is indisputable. But his ability for recall seems to have been limited in much the same way as was his intellectual curiosity. He would focus his superb mind upon something only if there was a specific, tangible benefit for him— a prime example being the ability he developed, first as a salesman and then as a politician, to remember thousands of ordinary people's faces and names. Also, the deeds of those who crossed him were never forgotten. Yet passages from the Bible, useful as they were in his speeches, apparently took considerable effort to commit to memory. There is no denying, however, the swiftness and resourcefulness of his mentality, especially when he had a big audience. From childhood on he could speak effortlessly whether he knew what he was talking about or not. "As a boy, were you ever shy?" a biographer asked him in 1935. Without a hint of humor, Senator Long replied: "I can't remember back to a time when my mouth wasn't open whenever there was a chance to make a speech."[34]

Huey may have been the laziest youngster in Winn Parish when it came to farm work or house chores, but he was never slothful if the work involved using words. Early in life he became impressed with the impact of both spoken and written words on people. He never seems to have considered any career outside of ones where communication skills were paramount. The ministry was one such profession. But so was journalism. So also was the life of a salesman, and of a lawyer, and of a politician.

In 1906, at thirteen, Huey learned to set type and worked after school for the *Baptist Monthly Guardian*, published in Winnfield as a newsletter for the district convention of the denomination. When his skill at typesetting improved, he was employed part-time, during 1906 and 1907, by the *Southern Sentinel*. Journalism interested Huey all his life, and eventually he would establish a newspaper for his political machine. There is no evidence that Huey ever seriously thought of writing as a career, although the editor of the New Orleans *Item* claimed that in 1911, when Huey was eighteen, he applied for a job as a political reporter for that paper.[35]

Politics inevitably drew him. His combination of skills, mania for attention, and urge to dominate others meant there could be only one gratifying profession for Huey Long. A letter to his older brother George, written when he was twenty-five, indicates that when Huey was only ten years old, he began to fret over the fact he was too young to run for governor of Louisiana. As to his ultimate goal, he startled grownups by solemnly assuring them that someday he would be president of the United States. In 1935 a Winn Parish physician who had known all the Longs since the turn of the century told a writer for *Forum* magazine that, in his opinion, Huey was "a twisted psychological type, with a power fixation dating from boyhood." As an adult, Huey admitted he had always been driven. "I was born into politics," he once explained, "a wedded man, with a storm for my bride." [36]

Senator Long also said that his first involvement in politics came during a gubernatorial race in March of 1908, when Jared Y. Sanders opposed Theodore Wilkinson for the Democratic nomination. (Louisiana by then had adopted the party primary system, and because of Democratic dominance, virtually all officeholders were chosen in those primaries, not general elections.) "At the age of 14," one of Huey's publicists insisted, "in Winn Parish he worked at a precinct for Theodore Wilkinson against J. Y. Sanders." Allegedly, Huey was sent there by brother Julius, a local Wilkinson leader. Years later, however, Julius denied that Huey had played any role in that election. Other Longs were active in Sanders' campaign, including Huey's uncle George, who was president of the Bank of Winnfield. [37] It may be that the Long organization's claim in the 1930s concerning what Huey did in 1908 is accurate, but at the time Huey was making the point that he had "always" fought the New Orleans machine. Also, the elderly ex-governor Sanders had become one of his bitterest enemies.

More certain is that in the autumn of 1908, Huey and his slightly older friend Harley Bozeman were sent by local Democrats (Huey probably importuned for the chance) to a place called Mineral Springs, in the woods of upper Winn Parish, to represent the Democratic side in a debate with a traveling lecturer for the Socialist party. Socialism was beginning to spread into Winn and the other hill parishes where the Populists had recently thrived. Its followers primarily came from the more radical ex-Populist farmers and timber workers who remained alienated from the traditional parties. Sending two high school boys instead of the state senator and representative the Socialists had requested was almost certainly a studied insult by Winn's Democratic leadership, but the Socialists at Mineral Springs allowed the debate to go on. "Huey lost the debate," according to the biased recollection decades later of a Socialist who was present.[38] At that time, the Socialists were gaining strength in Winn Parish; for the next few years they would be the Democrats' only serious opposition. One of the few Socialist newspapers in the South, the *Toiler*, was published a few miles from Winnfield at the village of Dodson, and in elections from 1912 through 1914, the quasi-Marxist party won up to 40 percent of the Winn Parish vote, its highest percentage in the state; the Socialists elected an entire slate of municipal officials in the town of Winnfield. But Socialism never overwhelmed Winn the way Populism once had done, and except for a few of his numerous cousins, Huey had no relatives in the movement.[39]

Debate was the one extracurricular Winnfield High activity that Huey enjoyed and at which he excelled. Twice, in the springs of 1909 and 1910, he among others represented the school in the annual state "rally" for high school debaters, elocutionists, and athletes held on the Louisiana State University campus in Baton Rouge. These trips marked the first times he had been more than fifty miles from home—he had run away twice, but got no farther than Alexandria. Of his first rally appearance, Long wrote that "I fared badly." But in the second, in April of 1910, he won third place in debate. Placing third meant that Huey, then sixteen and a high school senior, was offered a modest scholarship to LSU.[40]

While in Baton Rouge the second time, Huey and other members of the Winnfield High team competing in various events were house guests of T. H. Harris, who in 1910 was state superintendent of education. He would continue to be for three decades. In his memoirs, Harris vividly recalled the first time he met Huey Long: "The boy was a perfect portrait of the man to follow. He came swaggering into the house, leaving the baggage for the others to bring in, and introduced himself to Mrs. Harris. He was all over the place in a few minutes and met all members of the family, including Lily, the cook. He was always late for meals, left his clothes all over the bathroom floor, and had everybody in the house awake by five or six o'clock in the morning."[41]

Huey was furious at not winning first prize. "When he returned from the contest," Harris wrote, the boy cried out: "The committee [of LSU professors] was ignorant, or bought, and gave me *third* place." But Huey had calmed down by the time he prepared to board the train back to Winnfield; he thanked Mrs. Harris for her hospitality by saying: "Mrs. Harris, you have been mighty good to me, and when I get to be Governor, United States Senator, and President of the United States, I am going to do something for you. I am on my way and will not be stopped by a committee of ignorant professors."[42]

Eighteen years later, in 1928, Mr. and Mrs. Harris stood in a reception line at the Louisiana governor's mansion to shake hands with the state's newly inaugurated chief executive, Huey Long. As they were about to pass on, the young governor said to Mrs. Harris: "Do you recall what I told you? Well, I am on my way, and I'll make the rest of the journey." He then inquired about their four children, whom he had last met in 1910, calling each by name. As an afterthought he asked, "And Lily, the cook?"[43]

· 3 ·

SELLING ANYBODY ANYTHING

Huey did not, could not, accept the scholarship at LSU. His autobiography implied finances as the reason, since the award would have paid only tuition and the economy of Winnfield had taken a downturn by 1910.[1] What Huey said about the scholarship's limitation and Winnfield's recession was true, and his father's resources may have been strained by building such a massive house three years earlier. But Huey's implication was false. He was unable to attend LSU because he did not graduate from high school.

He either was expelled or quit because he was about to be expelled during May of his senior year, shortly after returning from the debate rally in Baton Rouge. There are several versions of events leading up to his departure without a diploma from Winnfield High, but Huey later admitted to a respected New Orleans journalist that he had "formed a secret society" among those classmates who accepted his leadership, aiming "to run things" as far as student activities were concerned, irrespective of faculty rules. Huey had been openly contemptuous of the faculty, most of all the principal, who proposed to add a twelfth year to the curriculum as a requirement for receiving a diploma (only eleven years were required at the time). The teachers now considered Huey a menace to the stability of the school, whereas in earlier years they had viewed him merely as an impudent nuisance. The event that seems to have triggered his departure minus a diploma was his distribution around town of a circular. Probably printed at the shop of the weekly *Comrade*, whose editor admired Huey, the circular criticized Winnfield High's fac-

39

ulty and principal. Moreover, Huey subsequently asked citizens to sign a petition demanding that the principal be removed.[2]

By the time he abruptly left high school, Huey had learned to partially camouflage his contempt for others. No longer did he randomly insult his slower classmates. He had come to realize that to be a leader one must have followers. Setting up his "secret society" at Winnfield High required persuading its members that it was to their advantage to accept his leadership, and in attacking the principal's well-intentioned plan for adding another year to the curriculum, he was pandering to a natural human desire to achieve goals as quickly and cheaply as possible.

Yet Huey's obstreperousness toward authority figures intensified. The idea of anyone, of whatever age or relationship, passing judgment upon him or attempting to govern him had become intolerable. At home there were certain minimal rules he had to obey; otherwise, by the time he was a teenager, he would not have been allowed to stay there. He did not curse or smoke around his family, and he continued to attend church with them. But Huey's parents came to understand that they did not really control him. Even in his preteen years, whippings had done little or no good. His mother once said that she would "have to whip him to death" to stop him from doing anything he really wanted to do. Callie had the reputation of being a strong-willed woman, and it was a wonder to some elderly residents of the community that she tolerated as much as she did from him. One neighbor declared, "He ain't never been nothing but a pesterance to her."[3]

What control there was over young Huey came from his mother. His father, Hugh, although physically powerful with a voice to match, was in fact a gentle, tolerant man who, as Huey's childhood friend Harley Bozeman recalled, "never interfered with home and family affairs"; Callie was "the boss." When in his eighties, after his famous son was killed, old Hugh remembered that he had administered bodily punishment to the boy only once, when Huey was about ten or twelve, for staying out all night with the "wild Wallace boys" (George and the other sons of J. T. Wallace): "I got a little switch. He didn't say a thing."[4]

A usually astute commentator on Long's meteoric career, Raymond Gram Swing, wrote in 1935 that the "implacable resentment" boiling within Huey must stem from "a humiliating and harsh childhood." He also supposed that Huey's notorious habit of profanity was a reaction to enforced churchgoing when he was young. The surmise about cursing was probably correct, but Long's childhood was not humiliating or harsh; in fact, it was a soft upbringing by the standards of that time and place. And Swing guessed wrong in thinking that a domineering father caused all that resentment.[5] The most likely target of Huey's life-long anger toward authority would have been his mother. She had tried, with limited success, to govern him.

Huey's feelings toward individual family members may be inferred from surviving letters to and about them written during the years 1915 to 1921, when Huey was in his twenties. Overall, these letters are unpleasant; some are brutal. Yet what he felt about his mother he kept to himself. Callie Tison Long died in 1913, of typhoid fever, at age fifty-two. Huey's subsequent extant letters never mention her. His autobiography refers to her once, as "my mother, Caledonia." That is all.[6] About Hugh his sentiments, expressed in letters and by lack of attention, seem clearer. Huey neither loved nor hated the man. But he wanted as little to do with him as possible, especially after old Hugh began a slow descent into lethargy and near-poverty after his wife's death. Something that happened early in 1910, two months before Huey went to the high school rally in Baton Rouge, almost certainly caused a lessening of any respect he might have had for his father: Hugh failed in his second attempt to win public office. He ran for alderman in Winnfield, making much of the fact that he was one of the largest property-owners in the town. His chances seemed good. Five positions were to be filled, and there were only six candidates in the Democratic primary. But Hugh came in sixth.[7]

When a census taker stopped by the Long household in May of 1910, eight people resided there. "Hugh P.," fifty-seven, designated "stock raiser" as his work. Callie no longer listed an occupation. Julius, thirty-one, was now a lawyer; Clara, twenty-one, a schoolteacher. Three siblings had departed: George S. (known as Shan) was a dentist in Oklahoma; Charlotte (Lottie) and Olive were married and living elsewhere in Louisiana. Daughter Callie (named for her mother), nineteen, was still at home, as was Earl, fourteen, and the youngest child, Lucille, age twelve. Also there, for the last weeks he would live with his parents, was "Huey P. Long, Jr.," sixteen.[8] This listing was probably given to the census taker at parental direction, because the Long child

41

who was named for his father almost never used "Jr." after his name, even though Hugh outlived him. The future Kingfish could never stand being junior to anyone—and especially not to a loser who embarrassed him by running last in elections.

Huey took his first away-from-home job in July of 1910, one month short of his seventeenth birthday. His former classmate Harley Bozeman had become a salesman in northeastern Louisiana for a company that marketed by door-to-door sales a cooking oil named Cottolene, made from processed cottonseed. Bozeman told his district supervisor that he had a friend who would make a hotshot salesman, and the man agreed to let this someone, named Huey Long, join the sales team in Monroe. Huey arrived by train the next day and, for a starting salary of nineteen dollars a week, began knocking on doors.

He already knew something about salesmanship. Two summers earlier he and Bozeman had accepted a consignment of used books from a dealer passing through Winnfield, and the two boys had hitched up a rented buggy and begun peddling these books, everything from rubbish to classics, in the villages of Winn and neighboring parishes. Because of Huey's persuasiveness, they were able to get something for almost every volume. It was a remarkable achievement in a region where reading was not a widespread habit. If he could sell books in north central Louisiana, Huey decided—as he later bragged—"I can sell anybody anything."[9]

Cottolene thus acquired probably the best junior salesman it ever had. Most Louisiana housewives never thought of using anything but pig lard or cow butter in frying or baking, but during the summer and fall of 1910, many who met young Huey at their front door decided to give Cottolene to try. He made it seem a crime to turn such a bright-eyed, earnest lad away without giving his product a chance—and a sin to continue using pork fat, since those housewives who did not immediately slam the door in his face were likely to hear that the Holy Bible forbade eating "anything from the swine," which Huey interpreted as meaning that although it was permissible to eat pork flesh, God frowned upon using lard rendered from it. Huey left the impression that he was not just selling a product. He was also doing the Lord's work.[10]

The company required its salesmen to hold baking contests, and at one of these, at Shreveport in September of 1910, Huey met his future wife, Rose McConnell. She was a year older than he and worked as a secretary. Both Rose and her mother prided themselves on their baking talents, and a Cottolene advertisement had led them to enter a contest held in Shreveport's West End neighborhood. The judge was Huey Long. What he really thought about the cakes he tasted will never be known, but obviously he was smitten by the attractive, petite brunette who said she had baked one of them (Huey's sisters always believed her mother had prepared it). Showing acumen that would do credit to a seasoned politician, Huey awarded Rose a prize, then gave one to a cake her mother had entered.[11]

Huey told Harley Bozeman he had "found the girl he was going to marry." Their courtship, however, would have its bumpy moments and last more than two years; Huey and Rose were not wed until April of 1913. When they met he was only seventeen, working at a low wage for a company with a mania for cost cutting, and he had no high school diploma. In overall appearance, Huey at that age bore slight resemblance to the heavyset, floridfaced politician he would become by forty. Although five feet ten in height, he looked small for his age because of a spindly frame and undersized hands and feet. Rose noticed his clothes seemed too big for him. His red-brown hair, darker than in childhood, was frizzly, and his nose was too large for his face. Three distinguishing features would always be with him: a wide mouth, strong cleft chin, and expressive brown eyes that could instantly change from dancing merriment to a chilling stare.[12]

Early in November, 1910, both Long and Bozeman were unpleasantly surprised by dismissal notices from the marketers of Cottolene. They were good salesmen, but the company had decided to terminate door-to-door sales in north Louisiana, and the two were not offered territory elsewhere. The boys went back to Winnfield and began mailing letters of application to other sales concerns. Huey managed to turn his dismissal into the appearance of a triumphal return home. The *Comrade* told the good news: "Our young friend Huey Long, who left the home nest . . . to try his fortune in the wide, wide world as a commercial traveler, and who has made good, as we predicted, came home Wednesday to visit his family and friends. He looks fine and received a royal welcome from a host of well wishers, one of whom we are proud to be."[13]

Julius Long, now a successful Winnfield lawyer, had more influence over his bright younger brother than anyone else in the family. He kept insisting that Huey get a high school diploma so he could enroll, as Julius had done, in the Tulane law school; Julius planned for the two to eventually form a Long and Long partnership. By January of 1911, without offers of employment as a traveling salesman, Huey agreed to enter the senior class at Shreveport High, since his past trouble at the Winnfield school made reenrollment there unlikely. An aunt in Shreveport let him stay with her, and Julius probably paid the incidental expenses. Huey remained in the city from January until March, attending classes only in the morning (which would have made graduation impossible) while working as a clerk-typist for a plumbing company in the afternoons and seeing Rose McConnell in the evenings.[14]

Rose did not know whether to be impressed or disturbed by what seemed a peculiar hobby of her teenage boyfriend. "He was always writing letters to United States senators on any excuse," she recalled a half-century later. It made no sense to her, so she asked him why. "I want to let them know I'm here," was his explanation. Then he added, "I'm going to be there someday myself." Later, by the time they were married, Huey confided that he had already mapped out his entire political career: he first would run for and win some relatively minor office; then in turn would come the governorship of Louisiana, a United States Senate seat, and finally the presidency of the United States. "It almost gave you the cold chills to hear him tell about it," Rose related in 1960. "He was measuring it all."[15]

By early spring of 1911, Huey had departed Shreveport, still without a diploma, and was in Austin, Texas, working for a food wholesaler. He now solicited orders from retail stores instead of knocking on housewives' doors. (Once again he owed his job to the recommendation of Harley Bozeman, who had joined the company in February.) It was Huey's first time outside Louisiana. His new employer, the Houston Packing Company, quickly realized Huey's capabilities and, despite his not yet being eighteen, sent him to Little Rock as the sales manager for all of Arkansas. Huey remained there until midsummer, and since he knew politics would be his future career, he listened admiringly to several speeches by the most colorful politician Arkansas ever produced: United States Senator Jeff Davis. Opponents called Davis the "Karl Marx of the Hill Billies," a nickname that later would be one of many applied to Huey Long. Davis' neo-Populist, arm-waving emotional appeals endeared him to poor white voters; he never lost an election. Yet his radical rhetoric was not backed up by a program that significantly changed the economic structure of Arkansas.[16] Young Huey was highly impressed with Davis' style.

The Houston Packing Company, satisfied with Huey's work in Arkansas, sent him to Memphis in July, 1911, to open up a new sales territory covering western Tennessee and northern Mississippi. This was too tough an assignment even for Huey—a crop-killing drought that summer made retailers unwilling to give business to a youthful drummer from an unfamiliar company. Huey received his letter of dismissal toward the end of August. For the next month he stayed in Memphis looking for employment but found nothing except dirty, low-paying jobs as a common laborer. He was kicked out of a boarding house for nonpayment (they kept his clean clothes), and for several nights he stayed at a Salvation Army mission. Huey disliked having to importune his family for help, and doubtless they did not relish being asked, especially after he had disappointed them in Shreveport. But he was in desperate straits, and an appeal via Winnfield resulted in his older brother George (Shan), who practiced dentistry in Shawnee, Oklahoma, wiring him train fare to Shawnee.[17] Late in September, wearing the only clothes he owned, Huey arrived in Oklahoma penniless, frowzy, and probably ill-smelling.

Now it was Shan's turn to help Huey straighten out. Mother Callie still nourished her forlorn hope of making a Baptist preacher out of Huey, and the agreement by which he was sent train fare was that he would enroll as a theology student at Oklahoma Baptist University, a struggling institution in Shawnee ready to overlook the fact that he had not graduated from high school. Dr. Long provided tuition expenses and gave him a place to stay, but the records at OBU do not indicate that Huey actually enrolled; apparently he hung around campus off and on, but spent the tuition money as he pleased. During the Christmas holidays of 1911, he soberly informed Shan that he "had decided he was not cut out to be a preacher." Then he asked for, and received, a hundred dollars to enter the University of Oklahoma Law School at nearby Norman.[18]

Close by Shawnee and Norman, but unlike those smaller

communities, Oklahoma City had a bustling night life, including gambling dens. Instead of going straight to Norman, Huey decided to enjoy the city first; he promptly lost his hundred dollars at a roulette wheel. With fifty-five cents in his pockets, and without any explanation Shan might accept, he wandered the frigid streets of Oklahoma City (it was New Year's Day, 1912) until he happened to see the doors of a wholesale produce company. An idea dawned. Walking into owner K. W. Dawson's office, he eloquently described both his experience as a produce salesman and his desire to attend the law school in Norman. Dawson, mentioned in Huey's autobiography as "a very serious but kindly faced gentleman," after listening to a mixture of boasting and pleading, told Huey to come back the next day for an answer. The answer was yes, the young man could be his drummer on a part-time basis in the Norman area, which would give him time to attend law classes at OU.[19] Dawson had acquired an energetic salesman, and Huey never forgot a sympathetic stranger who gave him work at a desperate moment in his life. On what would be his last trip from Washington to Baton Rouge, in 1935, Senator Long swung by Oklahoma City to make a Labor Day speech, and while there took time to visit the home of a retired businessman, K. W. Dawson.[20]

In Norman, Huey could not enroll in law school—or even eat—until he obtained some money. Immediately he set about getting orders for Dawson Produce from retail grocers, but his first commission payments would not arrive for a week or more; until then, the problem was one of survival. He did not have a cent left, or an overcoat to ward off the snowy cold (he had pawned his coat to pay his hotel bill in Oklahoma City). With typical bravado, Huey stepped into a Norman bank to negotiate a loan, insisting on seeing its president. Their conversation was brief. "The banker wasn't crazy," Huey recalled. Then, in Huey's words, "I strolled over to the [train] depot." There he took on a forlorn and hungry appearance that indeed reflected his condition. He caught the eye of a local businessman named Ralph O. Jackson, who listened to the youth's tale of woe and was so impressed that he loaned him enough money to tide him over. Jackson also arranged Huey's credit at a store that sold law books. Gratitude was not one of Long's consistent traits, but this was a critical time in his life, and Jackson's help, like Dawson's, would be remembered. During the Great Depression of the 1930s, the

Kingfish, hearing that Ralph Jackson was in economic distress, gave him a decent job in Louisiana.[21]

Huey enrolled as a regular student at the University of Oklahoma Law School for the second (spring) semester of the 1911–1912 academic year. How he managed this without even a high school diploma is a question his biographers have never answered, or even asked. As far as is known, he took no special qualifying examination. That he was an out-of-state student in an era more relaxed and trusting about paper work than today probably holds the answer. Huey was not above telling fibs about his background. Probably he informed the registrar that he had graduated, and his fertile imagination then summoned up plausible reasons why proof of that event could not be produced.[22]

The new student promptly telephoned Shan for an additional seventy-five dollars, and got it. Huey's autobiography neglects to mention that Dr. Long helped him at all, perhaps because none of the money given him for tuition actually went for that purpose. In 1920, when Huey was a prospering lawyer and a Louisiana railroad commissioner, Shan asked for a five-hundred-dollar loan. Huey agreed, "on account of the fact that you let me have money once [*sic*] when I needed it and otherwise showed a very brotherly attitude toward me." But Huey reminded Shan that the total amount he had been given was (according to his reckoning) no more than two hundred dollars, and he insisted Shan repay the entire five hundred in ninety days. Huey soon wrote Julius—with whom he was temporarily on good terms— that "I permitted Shan to draft on me for $500. No doubt he will calculate some time when he performed some service for me . . . which entitles him not to pay it back if he should not want to."[23]

From January until May of 1912, Huey more or less attended law classes at the university, while also working part-time for the Dawson Produce Company and spending most weekends gambling in Oklahoma City. His luck, or whatever it was that caused him to win more than he lost, had greatly improved since the previous New Year's disaster. Now he shunned the roulette wheel and became adept at dice and poker. His course work consequently suffered: he missed many classes and was late to others. At the end of the term in May his grades were three C's and an E (incomplete or conditional). As Huey admitted to Mildred Adams twenty years later, "I didn't learn much law there. Too

much excitement, all those gambling houses and everything."
His dexterity at poker and dice became so impressive that the
bosses in one Oklahoma City den, realizing their interests would
be better served by having him on the house side, employed
Huey Long as a dealer and dice thrower.[24]

The year 1912 brought a national election, and among his
other activities while a student at OU, Huey somehow found
time to organize—and become president of—a campus club
supporting the Missouri congressman Champ Clark for the
Democratic presidential nomination. Clark and Woodrow Wilson were the major candidates, and on the university campus
the Greeks (fraternity men) were whooping it up for Wilson.
Huey, miffed because he was not asked to play a role in the campus Wilson for President club, persuaded the Barbarians (non-
fraternity men) to form a Clark for President club; they did, and
made Huey Long its head. He then wrote and had printed a circular similar to the one he had composed at Winnfield High, this
time assailing Wilson, who was the governor of New Jersey and
a former president of Princeton University, as being a mere
"schoolteacher." After Wilson won the Democratic nomination,
however, Huey became a supporter and helped form a Young
Democratic League in Oklahoma to boost the party's ticket in
November.[25]

By late summer of 1912, Huey had grown weary of Oklahoma
and once again became a traveling salesman, this time with the
Faultless Starch Company. For the third time, it was Harley
Bozeman's recommendation that got him the job; Bozeman had
been with Faultless several months and persuaded his boss to
interview Huey. After meeting him and taking him on a trial
road trip for a week, the supervisor was so impressed that, despite the fact that Huey had just turned nineteen, he sent him to
Memphis as head of a new sales team covering four states. "He's
the damndest character I ever met," the supervisor told Bozeman. "I don't know if he is crazy or a genius." Huey returned to
Memphis and the near-swank Gayoso Hotel, which ranked next
to the Peabody as the city's best. His salary was $125 per month
plus expenses—excellent for someone his age at that time. Huey
began to think of Rose McConnell and his need for the stability
she might provide, and during the Christmas holidays he went
to Shreveport, intent on asking her to marry him.[26]

Part of him desired tranquility, but something stronger inside

Huey Long drew trouble as a magnet pulls iron. In November of 1912 he was arrested in a Memphis election-eve street brawl. Why or how he was involved remains unclear, but he was taken into custody. At the police station Huey insisted he had fought for the side of "Boss" Edward Crump, mayor of Memphis, so he was soon released.[27] An even more bizarre brush with the law awaited him in Shreveport when he went there to see Rose.

In his autobiography, Huey claimed that while in Shreveport over the holidays, he was arrested and put in jail, "charged with having shot at some one." It was, he indicated, a case of mistaken identity: "at the time [of the shooting] I had been at the Grand Opera House." He wrote that he was released because Rose and others could attest he was with her, attending a performance of *Lohengrin*. He claimed that she produced the ticket stubs to prove it. His autobiography took pains to set the record straight.[28]

His story, however, does not square with the police report. Every day, the Shreveport *Times* recorded all arrests on the police blotter. Huey was in fact arrested for creating a disturbance in the city's whorehouse district, located in a black section known as St. Paul's Bottom. "CUTTING UP IN THE BOTTOM," read the little headline on an inside page, and the story below it described how "A. P. Long [*sic*], a white man," was taken to jail for "raising a rough house around one of the resorts in the restricted district," and charged "with carrying concealed weapons." He "was released later in the evening when one of his friends put up a cash bond of $150." (That friend was Harley Bozeman. Huey's brother Julius, who was then district attorney for the Winnfield area, apparently was able to get the charge dropped.) The episode happened on the night of December 20. Rose could not have gotten Huey out on the alibi he related in his autobiography, because *Lohengrin* was presented on December 16, for one night only. And despite the initials' being reported as "A. P." instead of "H. P.," the person involved was Huey, for no other Long appears on the Shreveport arrest record that entire month.[29]

Questions about the embarrassing affair remain. In his recollections, Bozeman wrote that when he visited Huey in jail, he was given to understand that the trouble supposedly occurred in St. Paul's Bottom, but Huey told him "this is nothing but a damn outrage and frame up."[30] Whatever else happened, Huey probably was carrying one concealed weapon at the time of his arrest. Later in life he frequently put a small pistol in one of his pockets, and the custom likely started during his salesman days, although he was never known to use a pistol, or any weapon, on anyone. No doubt Rose and her parents heard about Huey's arrest and read the brief Shreveport *Times* story; the event may well have delayed Huey and Rose's marriage. In later years Huey's enemies—of whom many lived in Shreveport—never rehashed the story of his arrest in the whorehouse district; at the time it happened he was a teenage nobody, and when he brought it up in his 1933 autobiography, his foes did not bother to look up the actual charge.

Rose's uncertainty about marrying Huey was increased by her visit to his family in Winnfield. They thought he was too young and unsettled to take on the responsibility of a wife, and without directly telling her so, probably got the message across. Huey wanted her to marry him immediately, and return with him to Memphis. For once his powers of salesmanship were inadequate: she refused. Understandably, she had concerns about what life with him would be like, and the circumstances of his arrest a few days earlier can only have added to her doubts. Huey angrily left for Memphis, and for several weeks it seemed their romance was over. In March, however, Rose began receiving a barrage of pleading, lovesick letters and telephone calls from Huey, and in April she boarded a train for Memphis.[31]

The day Rose arrived, April 11, 1913, she and Huey went to the Shelby County clerk's office and signed a marriage license. The next day they were wed in what was described as "a very simple ceremony" in the Gayoso Hotel. Huey had phoned the pastor of Memphis' First Baptist Church, whom he did not know, and asked him to come over to the hotel to perform the ceremony. The Reverend Arthur Boone did so, and years later he could vividly recall the appearance of the "fine looking young couple." He also remembered the groom as having a "stirring personality." (They would have left an even stronger impression had the preacher known he was marrying two future United States senators.) Typically, Huey had spent all his previous month's salary. One of his Memphis friends, C. O. Scott, had loaned him the money for Rose's wedding ring and the marriage license, and after the ceremony Rose had to search in her purse for something to pay the preacher.[32]

Until October, the couple lived in a Memphis apartment.

Then the Faultless Starch Company entered a time of financial trouble, and its Memphis office closed. Huey was transferred, at a reduced income, to Louisiana. Instead of managing salesmen as he had done in Tennessee, Huey once again went on the road, drumming up orders from retail stores across the state. He was seldom at home, and indeed now had no home of his own. Rose sometimes stayed with the Long family in Winnfield, at other times with her parents in Shreveport. In the spring of 1914, Huey was laid off. The founder-owner of Faultless Starch had died, and until his estate was litigated, all sales operations ceased. By now, however, Huey knew which companies might need experienced salesmen, and within a matter of days he signed on as the sales representative in north Louisiana for the Chattanooga Medicine Company.[33]

Of all his sales experiences, this was the one that Governor and Senator Huey Long's enemies would most delight in bringing up. The Chattanooga Medicine Company produced and sold patent nostrums. Its best-seller was particularly attacked by the American Medical Association for using misleading advertising and for being of dubious benefit. The product in question was "Wine of Cardui," an elixir for menstrual pain and other gynecological problems. It was considerably stronger than wine: forty-proof alcohol was its active, potent ingredient.[34] Huey peddled the stuff for several months, and doubtless many pious, abstemious housewives in the hill parishes temporarily felt better as a result of his sales. Coincidentally, articles in two 1914 issues of the *Journal of the American Medical Association* pounced on Wine of Cardui as "a vicious fraud," most of all because of its claim to uplift fallen wombs.[35]

Huey sold plenty of patent medicine during the summer of 1914, but in September he was fired. The Chattanooga Medicine Company, like many businesses, suffered from the American economy's temporary downturn owing to the outbreak of World War I in Europe, and as usual in personnel reductions, the newest employees were laid off first. Being let go as a salesman was getting monotonous for Huey; it had happened, through no fault of his own, four times in four years. Huey later claimed he decided at this point that "I'd accept no other job from any other living man. I'd be in no position again where I had to say 'yes, sir' and 'no, sir.' [Now] I accept no job except at the hands of the people."[36] (Later, as a lawyer, he started as a junior partner, and subsequently he worked part-time as a sales agent for kerosene containers, but the Chattanooga Medicine Company was indeed the last employer to order him around. Brother Julius, his senior law partner, would try to, but to no avail.)

Losing his job as a patent medicine salesman, coming on top of previous setbacks, caused cracks to appear in Huey's monumental self-image. It was one of the low points in his life, and he turned to Julius for advice and financial help. Both Julius and Rose urged him to attend law school and—unlike his effort in Oklahoma—to concentrate on his studies. Julius still hoped Huey would conquer his wild streak and live up to his potential. Besides, Julius had promised their mother, Callie, on her death-bed, in October of 1913, that he would help Huey get an education. And Huey, out of work in a time of recession, pressured by his wife and successful older brother, for once agreed to let others help him make decisions. He would enroll at Tulane University's law school, where Julius had attended. He would have to be a noncredit special student: since Tulane was an in-state institution, Huey did not try to bluff his way in as a high school graduate, as he probably had done at the University of Oklahoma. But becoming a lawyer in Louisiana did not necessarily require a law degree: if a candidate could pass a bar examination administered by a committee of senior lawyers from the judicial district where he intended to practice, then he was licensed for the profession of law.[37]

Julius had graduated from Tulane (LL.B., 1907), but he proposed that Huey follow the shortcut path that a majority of Louisiana lawyers of that time had used: take selected law courses for a year or two, and cram for the bar exam. Huey agreed to join Julius as a junior partner in his Winnfield law office once he was admitted to the bar. In 1912, Julius had been elected district attorney for Winn and Jackson parishes, and he needed a partner more than ever. With $400 provided by Julius and $250 more borrowed from State Senator S. J. Harper ($650 was the equivalent of about $7,200 in 1991 money), Huey and Rose moved to New Orleans late in September of 1914, renting what he described as "a dingy two room apartment" on Carrollton Avenue. Huey then enrolled as a noncredit student at the Tulane law school.[38]

For the first and only time in his life, Huey Long forsook other activities and applied himself to classrooms and books. He always considered himself a superior being, and had engaged in some big talk about climbing the political staircase until he became president of the United States, but at this point it seems to have dawned on him that a concentration of mind on achieving specific objectives was necessary if his journey to the top were ever to be more than a daydream. Traveling salesmen were not likely to become successful politicians; neither were card dealers in gambling dens, typesetters, or journalists. But lawyers often did.

"I studied law as much as from sixteen to twenty hours each day," Huey wrote, and he probably was not stretching the truth. (As a political leader he often followed an even longer work schedule, leaving only two or three hours for sleep.) At Tulane he avidly absorbed lecture and text material, then waylaid professors outside of class with questions and requests for more reading suggestions. Toward evening, he would take the St. Charles Avenue trolley to the tiny apartment on Carrollton, where he studied until past midnight. He hardly touched the food Rose prepared; always slim before, he now became emaciated, his weight dropping to 112 pounds. By May of 1915, he had been at Tulane seven months, and the borrowed money was almost gone. Huey approached a young lawyer, Charles J. Rivet, who recently had passed the bar exam. He importuned Rivet into coaching him on what questions individual members of the examining committee were prone to ask, and in what law books the correct responses were to be found.[39]

The next bar exam for the New Orleans district was set for late June, but Huey decided he wanted his now. Massive ego and gall impelled his next move. Huey walked into the office of the elderly chief justice of the Louisiana Supreme Court, Frank A. Monroe, and poignantly described his impoverished condition and his need to take the examination immediately. Chief Justice Monroe was surprised, but also sympathetic. Huey recalled feeling "perfectly at ease." He asked the old jurist "how to go about getting the bar committee." Monroe replied, "Why, just go to them like you came to me." By the same brash method, Huey then persuaded the committee of senior New Orleans lawyers to meet the next day just for him, and he easily passed their oral exam.[40] Either they assumed he intended to practice in that district, or if they did inquire about the matter, he must have lied. For it was a strict requirement that all prospective lawyers for the Winnfield vicinity take their bar examination in Shreveport. Once again, effrontery and deception had paid off.

At age twenty-one, Huey Long on May 15, 1915, was—in his words—"sworn in and declared a full-fledged lawyer in the State of Louisiana." And although three years would pass before he first stood before the voters as a candidate, he was not exaggerating when he said, "I came out of that courtroom running for office."[41]

Running for office, but also running against time. For he was in the grip of impatient and boundless ambition; clocks and calendars represented the enemy. His obsession with time had begun and would grow worse. Huey Long could not have known—although he acted as if he did—that on the day he became Louisiana's youngest lawyer he already had lived more than half his life.

· 4 ·

RULING THE ROOST

In Louisiana, proclaimed Bastrop's *Clarion-Appeal* in 1896, white people "own thirteen-fourteenths of the property and about ninety-nine one hundredths of the virtue and intelligence, and by the gods, they propose to rule the roost."[1] That statistic on property was approximately correct. Any estimate on innate superiority had to be fanciful, but the expressed determination about ruling the roost was absolutely real.

Race tension permeated Louisiana like August heat. The Populist-Republican fusion effort of the mid-1890s had revived the specter of Reconstruction, when the state's black majority enjoyed a measure of civil rights and even officeholding. When Populism collapsed—defeated by massive fraud in the 1896 gubernatorial election—any real hope for a working-class white-black political coalition disappeared. With new registration and election laws, restrictive suffrage provisions in the Constitution of 1898, and a palpable atmosphere of hostility toward voting by even literate or propertied blacks, white Louisiana by 1900 seemed to have no cause to fear the possibility of black domination—of being brutishly transformed, as the old rallying cry warned, into another "Hayti or San Domingo."[2]

The federal census figures for 1900 gave added comfort. For the first time since before the Civil War, Louisiana reported a white majority (729,612 to 650,804). "The change," announced the New Orleans *Times-Democrat*, "will be welcome news from every point of view." Yet there were suspicions that much of the white gain was due to thousands of the lightest-skinned among the state's 91,000 "mulattoes, quadroons, and octoroons" listed in the previous census having decided, because of worsening race discrimination, to pass as Caucasians.[3]

Louisiana has been called the "strange sister in the family of American states" because so much about it is untypical.[4] But in race relations during the late nineteenth and early twentieth centuries, the Pelican State tended to follow the South's pattern. This was the time, as Joel Williamson points out, when racial extremism grabbed hold of the region. Not all whites fell prey to the new strain of Negrophobia virus, but in the Deep South, including Louisiana, radical racism achieved hegemony over the white community as disfranchisement and segregation, reinforced by both legal and extralegal violence, sought to provide what Major Hearsey called "the final solution" to "the negro problem."[5] (Although Hearsey and others like him did not rule out annihilation, the "solution" in mind was to make permanent a narrower role for blacks in society. "The nigger's all right in his place," a New Orleans city official explained in 1902, but "when he tries to get out of it, hit him on the head, and next time he'll come in with his hat off.")[6]

This "final solution" represented a synthesis of the earlier dominative racism of upper-class whites and the avoidance racism of those too poor to regularly employ black labor. Blacks were to remain nearby as an agricultural and menial work force, but must stay out of politics and, except as needed for labor, keep away from white people. As a St. Francisville paper, in an orotund restatement of the Reverend Benjamin Palmer's famous 1860 sermon, explained things in 1901: "Conditions of climate and temperament make it necessary for the Caucasian, in this section, to have the African's assistance in all manual and outdoor activities."[7] Whites who governed Louisiana and other Deep South states, no longer greatly worried about federal interference, were by 1900 busily experimenting to see how close to actual slavery blacks could be pushed. Their goal, their hoped-for final solution for both races, was an organic society in which whites of all classes would stand united in *Herrenvolk* identity with the patrician Democratic party leadership, and blacks would cheerfully accept the subordinate role assigned them by Providence. The ideal black person, as one planter described him, was one who "will do the dirty work and not fuss about it."[8]

Not all blacks or whites took the roles assigned to them, but by the opening years of the twentieth century, it was clear that a more rigid caste system had been put in place. Although the system was never as binding as antebellum slavery—the postwar amendments to the United States Constitution could not be entirely ignored—neither was it softened by slavery's paternalism. The "providential trust" preached by the Reverend Dr. Palmer had little place in a world where labor was looked upon as a mere commodity, to be bought as cheaply as possible. From the standpoint of all except the poorest whites, this system was in many ways better than the old slavery: here was an impoverished caste, nearby but not in the way, to whom no obligations were due except—so they would be able to show up for work—a bare survival wage or share of the crop, which by necessity would be spent on usually exorbitantly priced goods at local stores. These mercantile establishments were scattered across Louisiana's plantation regions; many, particularly the ones owned by landlords, were known as "pluck me stores."[9]

"What a mistake we made," an aging planter of St. Landry Parish told his fellow landowners, to have gone to war attempting to preserve "an institution we are now better off without." Under slavery, W. T. Brashear explained, "we had to pay from $1,500 to $2,000 for a good hand," but now "you can hire [one] for $12.50 per month." And there is "no risk, no doctor's bills, no clothing, and if he don't suit you send him away." Brashear carefully added that ordinary whites also benefited from the contemporary system of cheap black labor: "Every one who has a dollar can get a negro to work for him now, when in slavery it took thousands."[10] This rosy view, however, could not appeal to whites at the lower end of the economic scale, who had to compete with blacks in what were called the "H" jobs—hot, hard, and heavy. Particularly in New Orleans and the other cities, common work in a free market economy went to whoever would accept the least pay.

White unity was never absolute. A tiny minority of Louisiana racial moderates during the first decades of the twentieth century echoed (although softly) the objections to a caste system made by George W. Cable in the 1880s. The Reverend Quincy Ewing, an Episcopal priest in Napoleonville, frequently sermonized against the grosser aspects of racism, but since more than ninety percent of Napoleonville was Catholic, few people heard him. The well-to-do among Ewing's small congregation either were related to him or tolerated his deviation from racial orthodoxy. In 1909, Ewing published an article in *Atlantic Monthly* that was gently critical of segregation, and the town courteously ignored it. An LSU sociology professor, William O. Scruggs, spoke out in 1916 against the rankest forms of racial injustice, such as the inequitable distribution of school funds, but he hastened to add that no criticism of social segregation was implied.[11] Andrew A. Gunby, a Monroe attorney and newspaper publisher (of the weekly *Bulletin*), had been one of the few Louisianians of patrician background to join the People's party of the 1890s. Into the new century Gunby tried to keep alive the Populist belief in political and educational equality for black people. "All they want is fair treatment," he pleaded. But even Gunby shrank from opposing segregation in public accommodations.[12] And this—Ewing, Scruggs, Gunby—was the entire list of prominent resident white Louisianians who in the early 1900s dared even mildly criticize injustices toward blacks.

An echo of Populist biracialism faintly reverberated, as late as World War I, among white and black timberworkers in the hills of north central and west Louisiana, and in New Orleans, dockworkers of both races continued their strained efforts to act in unison, because experience had taught that employers always used race as a wedge whenever strikes were attempted. The Brotherhood of Timber Workers, founded at a Beauregard Parish lumber camp in 1910, held its first official convention in Alexandria two years later. In defiance of state law, black and white BTW delegates met in the same hall; together they voted to affiliate with the radical, Chicago-based Industrial Workers of the World. Because of the highhanded tactics of timber companies who at that time were clear-cutting Louisiana's forests, the BTW-IWW found numerous sympathizers among the white hill farmers in several parishes. The "Red," or more radical, faction of the Socialist party, allied with the BTW, won minor election victories in the hill parishes in 1912, including all municipal officers in Winnfield and the mayorship of DeRidder, the seat of Beauregard Parish.[13]

Yet because virtually no blacks still voted and poorer whites often did not pay the poll tax, the Socialists could not possibly attain the political strength that the Populists briefly had enjoyed in those parishes. Moreover, the little Socialist party of Louisiana was itself divided into "Moderate" and "Red" factions, with the Moderates (mostly trade unionists in New Orleans) being less confrontational and more willing to endorse racial segregation. Even the "Red" Louisiana timberworkers' newspaper freely used the epithet "nigger" when denouncing blacks who hired on as strikebreakers.[14]

A 1907 New Orleans dockworkers' strike marked the last of several attempts, going back to the 1880s, to present a black-white united front in demanding better wages from the city's commercial interests. The strike was initially so successful that a committee of state legislators, anxious to end a situation beginning to paralyze the city's economy, reluctantly agreed to meet with a biracial delegation of strike leaders.[15] When State Senator Charles C. Cordill of Tensas Parish seemed about to have a stroke at the prospect of meeting with "watah rats and niggas," Dan Scully, leader of the white longshoremen, is reported to have replied: "Oh, we're water rats, are we? But you can't run your goddam port without us. I guess before long you'll call us nigger lovers too. . . . You talk about us conspiring with niggers . . . there was a time I wouldn't even work beside a nigger [but] you made me work with niggers, eat with niggers, sleep with niggers, drink out of the same water bucket with niggers, and finally [you] got me to the place where if one of them comes to me and blubbers something about more pay, I say 'come on nigger, let's go after the white bastards.'"[16]

Scully's vehemence notwithstanding, 1907 was a year of widespread unemployment, and the New Orleans dock strike collapsed when shipping companies brought in trainloads of black and white strikebreakers. Biracial labor unity usually accomplished little when employers were colorblind about importing nonunion workers. Oscar Ameringer, a German-born Socialist, came to New Orleans in 1907 to act as a liaison between white and black dockworkers. Ameringer admitted the strike was a failure, but from his point of view the effort seemed worthwhile just to hear Dan Scully tell off Senator Cordill.[17]

The last tragic effort, prior to the 1930s, to achieve solidarity between white and black laborers in Louisiana occurred at Bogalusa, sixty miles north of New Orleans, in 1919. The "Magic City" or the "New South's Young City of Destiny," as Bogalusa's boosters liked to say, had not existed until 1905, when the Goodyear family of Pennsylvania decided to build the world's largest sawmill on a site along the Pearl River, in one of the last great tracts of virgin timber in the United States. By 1919, Bogalusa was a busy milltown of 8,000, where the Great Southern Lumber Company's enormous saws screamed all night and day, turning out a million board feet every twenty-four hours and gradually transforming a splendid subtropical forest into a desolate horizon of rotting stumps that stretched from Lake Pontchartrain northward 130 miles into central Mississippi.[18] A big pulpwood paper mill meanwhile was added to the company's Bogalusa properties. At both mills, whites were given preference in hiring, with blacks used for the most menial tasks.

"There were no labor troubles" at the Bogalusa mills, declared Charles W. Goodyear's history of the town and its industry, until "outside agitators" showed up, beginning in 1917, to organize white employees. The recruiters were from the American Federation of Labor, not the Marxist IWW, and at first showed no interest in black workers. But in 1919 the company laid off 2,500 white union members and hired nonunion blacks in their place. By necessity, the AFL decided biracial organization was the only answer, and agreed to help the head of the local Colored Timberworkers' Union, Sol Dacus. Alarmed, the company and town leadership (Great Southern's general manager was also mayor of Bogalusa) announced that radicals were trying to "stir up" black violence. Local deputy sheriffs, assisted by members of a paramilitary "Loyalty League" attempted to run Dacus out of town and riddled his home with bullets, but the black organizer was protected by several armed white union leaders. In the ensuing gunfire, four of Dacus' white defenders were killed.[19] Dacus managed to get away; he was last seen fleeing into the Pearl River swamp, and what became of him is still a mystery. The biracial strike at Great Southern was over. A grand jury investigated the killings but did not indict anyone. And the company, as its historian noted with satisfaction, "remained on friendly terms with all Louisiana administrations, including Huey Long's."[20]

Louisiana, with its close numerical division of black and white, was always one of the most intensely race-conscious of southern states. Even without the explosive, racially focused gubernatorial campaign of 1896, the state almost certainly would have drifted into the increasingly repressive racial atmosphere that enveloped the rest of the South, and to some extent the entire nation, by the early twentieth century. (As Jack Temple

Kirby points out, "Nearly all pre–World War I white Americans were racists.")[21] But in the Pelican State during this time, two special circumstances added fuel to the racial fire: the determination among upper- and middle-class ("better element") whites that a political threat like the one posed by the biracial Populist-Republican fusionists in 1896 must not be allowed to emerge again; and tensions engendered by the South's highest proportion of racial admixture. Particularly in south Louisiana, various old families, including some of the more prominent, were rumored to have what was called "a touch of the tarbrush."[22]

Again, the critical year was 1896. Prior to that time, even the most race-minded Louisiana newspapers, including Major Hearsey's New Orleans *States* and Victor Grosjean's Shreveport *Caucasian*, customarily referred to black people by supposedly benign terms such as *colored* or *negro* or *darkey*, although unflattering adjectives such as *ignorant* or *shiftless* or *brute* were frequently attached. But with the frenzied gubernatorial campaign of 1896, vile racial epithets suddenly became commonplace in the leading Democratic papers: *nigger* alternated with *coon* and *burr head*, and all of these were accompanied by adjectives such as *loud-smelling* and *bestial*. Populist and Republican whites were "nigger lovers" committing "treason to their race" and thus, said the relatively sedate *Picayune*, "must expect to be classified with their allies . . . the black cattle."[23] Extravagant language, especially when used by persons fearful of losing control of a situation, tends to be believed by those who express it. Louisiana's threatened oligarchy probably convinced itself that its racial propaganda was true. Pandora's box lay open; the hateful words kept flying out long after the crisis of 1896 was over.

The *Plessy* v. *Ferguson* decision, in an unhappy coincidence for Louisiana blacks, was decided by the United States Supreme Court in 1896. By eight to one, the nation's highest tribunal ruled favorably on a Louisiana statute of 1890 requiring "separate but equal" accommodations for "white and colored" railroad passengers within the state. It was the legislature's first segregation law. *Plessy* v. *Ferguson* is referred to as a "landmark decision" because by saying the separate but equal device was constitutional, the Supreme Court signaled to all states that racial segregation by law was permissible. The decision engendered a flood of similar legislation not only for transportation, but also for every other sort of facility or accommodation serv-

ing the public.[24] Two years later the *Williams* v. *Mississippi* decision in effect declared that neither the literacy, property, and
poll-tax requirements for voting nor the ways in which these restrictions were actually applied by local officials violated the
Constitution so long as the wording of the laws did not specifically mention race. The *Williams* decision emboldened Louisiana's constitution makers of 1898 to limit black participation in
politics almost to the vanishing point.

Political disfranchisement and social segregation by local
custom had been widely yet haphazardly practiced in all ex-
Confederate states since the fade-out of Reconstruction. But
with the *Plessy* and *Williams* decisions, caste discrimination increasingly took on the force and respectability of law. The few
southern whites who previously had opposed, for whatever reasons, a further eroding of black civil rights on the claim that it
would violate the American Constitution, no longer had that argument. Now the question seemed to be, How far can we go and
still have blacks around as a cheap labor force? The Abbeville
Meridional, endorsing in 1902 the concept of keeping the two
races "as far apart as possible," opined that "we cannot have too
much of a good thing."[25]

Racial contempt fed upon itself and became self-perpet-
uating, since whites could suppress guilt feelings by thinking of
blacks as vile creatures who deserved bad treatment. The system was best rationalized if it was total. In 1911 an Opelousas
paper was outraged to learn that black schoolchildren in New
Orleans still had a few white teachers. "The very idea," cried the
St. Landry Clarion, "of a pure, Anglo-Saxon waxen-faced girl,
teaching a lot of foul-smelling, monkey-faced negroes is too re-
pulsive to contemplate."[26]

It was imperative that at least some blacks become partners
in the degradation, so as to help prove to whites that their image
of the supposed inferior and clownish race was true—just as the
"Sambo" image of childlike slaves on antebellum plantations
once was used to rationalize slavery. But by 1900 a new form of
ridicule helped bolster the caste system: popular entertainment
in Louisiana now included "coon" performances, in which
blacks cavorted in grotesque dances and sang demeaning lyrics
for the amusement of whites. Saloons along the Orleans-
Jefferson parish line specialized in such shows, but they were
commonplace across the South. "The Chinee and the Coon," "Dat

Graveyard Rabbit," and "All Coons Look Alike to Me" were three favorite tunes.[27] As late as the 1920s, attractions at parish or county fairs sometimes included a black man whose head appeared through a hole in a canvas; he would attempt to dodge baseballs thrown at him by white fairgoers. The sign read: "Hit the coon and get a cigar."[28]

By 1900, black political disfranchisement was largely achieved in Louisiana, with only mopping-up operations left. "Colored" registration had been 45.5 percent of the total as late as 1896; it was down to 4 percent four years later when William W. Heard, outgoing governor Murphy J. Foster's hand-picked Democratic successor, was elected over Don Caffery, Jr., the last Populist-Republican coalition candidate for the state's highest office. Heard won 60,206 to 14,215 and later persuaded the legislature to make Foster a United States senator.[29] As to the recent *de jure* disfranchisement, Governor Heard in part justified it by saying, "The negroes are happier now." A St. Mary Parish newspaper picked up the governor's point and elucidated on it: "The negroes of Louisiana are now living in . . . the happiest and most contented period they have ever enjoyed since the abolition of slavery."[30]

During the first decade of the twentieth century, many American states shifted from the convention method of choosing party nominees to the direct primary. Under this system, registered voters had to indicate a party affiliation and, in "primary" contests, decide which candidates would represent their party in the general elections. Primaries were part of the Progressive era's laudable desire to bring government closer to the people, but in the South that era meant—in the apt words of C. Vann Woodward—"progressivism for white men only, and after the poll tax took its toll not all the white men were included." The Louisiana primary law of 1906, like that of other southern states, had a racial joker in it: under the law, political parties were considered private organizations, distinct from government itself, and thus could admit or reject applicants to party membership for any reasons they might see fit—including explicit racial reasons. Throughout the South, the Democratic party allowed only whites to register as Democrats. Not until 1944 was the "white primary" held unconstitutional by the Supreme Court.[31]

Louisiana's white primary was mostly symbolic. By 1906,

only 1,342 blacks in the state were registered to vote (1.4 percent of the total, although blacks made up 47 percent of the general population). From 1906 until the 1970s, Democratic primaries in Louisiana would determine all state-wide and virtually all local struggles for office. General elections were almost always formalities that ratified the selection of Democratic nominees. A few blacks, prior to the white primary's overturn in 1944, were allowed to register as Republicans, Independents, or under some other designation, but they could cast ballots only in the usually meaningless general elections, since no party except the Democratic bothered to hold primary contests in Louisiana. The year Huey Long was elected governor (1928), eight years after women had been granted the right of suffrage, Louisiana's voter registration afforded the following figures:[32]

REGISTRATION	PARTY AFFILIATION	
White 367,286	Democratic	365,321
Colored.... 1,960	Republican	4,181
	Other..........	539

"It is certainly no crime to be colored, but it is fearfully inconvenient," a black Louisiana newspaper grimly remarked in 1880. A generation later it was actually a crime to be "colored" if someone of that legal definition attempted to enter a public facility or accommodation that served whites. The *Plessy* decision meant that racial segregation might, in a legal sense, be limited only by the human imagination. Whether racial antagonism represents a summoning up of ancient tribal instincts is debatable, but Louisiana's political leadership believed that it did, and their chief concern after the political scare of 1896 was to solidify white *Herrenvolk* identity by the further isolation and degradation of blacks. Legal segregation of the races, State Representative Harry D. Wilson of Tangipahoa Parish asserted in 1900, was good because it convenienced whites, but "the demonstration of the superiority of the white man over the negro is the greater thing."[33]

Following railroad coaches in 1890 (and depot waiting rooms in 1894), streetcars in 1902 became the next public accommodation segregated by Louisiana law. Only three communities in the state at that time had trolleys—New Orleans, Shreveport, and Baton Rouge. A bill introduced two years earlier by Wilson of Tangipahoa to compel segregation on streetcars had failed mainly because of opposition from the New Orleans trolley companies, whose directors dreaded the prospect of their conductors' having to make decisions about racial identity. "The greatest ethnologist the world ever saw," moaned one company president, "would be at a loss to classify street car passengers in this city." But in 1902 the General Assembly passed such a law, allowing trolley companies the option of dividing their cars with screens (which they did) or running separate cars. As in numerous cities across the South where such laws or ordinances were passed, blacks in New Orleans and Shreveport boycotted the segregated trolleys for several months. But the boycotts finally failed—nowhere were concessions made or laws repealed. Most blacks were too poor to regularly ride the trolleys anyway.[34]

What New Orleans' turn-of-the-century *Harlequin* magazine sadly called "the wall between humanity in this part of the globe" grew higher as the twentieth century progressed. A few urban saloons served both white and black until 1908, when a state law forbade it. Hotels, restaurants, theaters, and whorehouses were segregated by municipal ordinances; only in New Orleans had such places ever been in the habit of serving the races together, and that had virtually stopped by 1890 because of white customers' complaints.[35] In 1912 a state law provided for residential segregation by authorizing municipalities to forbid persons of one race from building or purchasing homes in a neighborhood "inhabited principally" by persons of the other race, "except on consent of the majority of the inhabitants." This prohibition was applied to renters in 1921, whether neighbors consented or not. By that time internal segregation was mandatory, both by race and sex, in jails, prisons, and other public institutions. Perhaps the oddest of the state's Jim Crow laws was one of 1914 specifying that all "shows" and "circuses" must have "separate ticket offices and entrances for the accommodation of the different races."[36] After 1920—in fact up to the 1950s—Louisiana's legislature continued to pass segregation statutes. But usually these merely supplemented previous laws.

A telling illustration of segregation's new grip on the white South's emotions came in October of 1901, when President Theodore Roosevelt invited the nation's most prominent black educator, Booker T. Washington, to dinner at the White House.

From Virginia to Texas, politicians and editorial writers boiled over in outrage, and Louisiana's rhetoricians were among the hottest. That a black person, however distinguished, would be served dinner in the nation's presidential residence was, exclaimed the New Orleans *States*, a "studied insult" to the South and a deliberate assault upon segregation. The president was dumbfounded by such reaction; he had never dreamed he would be accused of turning the White House into a "nigger restaurant."[37] Booker T. Washington, because of his accommodating approach to racial issues, was as respected as a black could be in Louisiana: the Baton Rouge *Advocate* called him "a useful negro." But that was the key point. As the St. Francisville *True Democrat* explained, "Washington . . . though the foremost of his race, is still but a negro." Professor William B. Smith of Tulane University, considered the state's leading academic champion of white supremacy, explained that Washington's "personal qualities" were irrelevant; putting individual merit above the fact of race was, to Professor Smith, "the profound and disastrous significance" of that White House dinner. One group of Louisiana whites decided the event called for action; they tried to have Booker T. Washington assassinated.[38]

Lynching, as a noted scholar of race relations points out, represented the ultimate method of race control. Between 1882 (when records of it first were kept) and 1952, a reported 391 persons were lynched in Louisiana. But that figure is based only on instances mentioned in the New Orleans press. The actual number was probably close to 500. Most lynch mob victims were black, but 56 of the 391 reported were white, including the "Mafia" Sicilians killed in 1891. At least a dozen blacks murdered by Louisiana mobs were female. As elsewhere in the South, most victims died by hanging or were shot in firing-squad style—or were finished off by bullets while strangling on a rope. The least fortunate, usually black males accused of raping a white woman, were burned at the stake. As one journalist vividly depicted such a horror, "He passes, like Elijah, in a chariot of fire, and is wafted to his reward on wings of kerosene."[39]

Louisiana ranked behind only Mississippi in lynchings per capita. A 1923 article in the reliable *Survey* magazine pointed out that on the basis of state subdivisions, Louisiana had the top three lynching counties (parishes) in America for the years since 1889: Ouachita led with nineteen, Caddo was second with eighteen, and Bossier came in third with fifteen. Morehouse Parish tied with Marion County, Florida, for fourth in the nation with thirteen. The worst years were 1896 to 1903, during which time Louisiana reported ninety-two lynchings (again, the real number most probably was higher). Several of these killings, according to white sources, were caused by Negroes' becoming more assertive in the aftermath of the bloody deeds of a black nationalist, Robert Charles, who shot twenty-seven whites in New Orleans before he was gunned down in July of 1900. Even Booker T. Washington's 1901 White House dinner supposedly led to several Louisiana lynchings because it encouraged black pride.[40]

A few Louisiana officials and newspapers mildly deplored lynching, but usually excused it in cases of rape. Others treated the subject in jocular fashion: ANOTHER NEGRO BARBECUE, read a small headline in Rayville's weekly paper in 1901. The New Orleans *States* in 1898 described a St. Helena Parish hanging as "artistic," while on the same day thinking it humorous that an accused black rapist burned to a crisp in Bossier Parish was named Will Steak. The only Louisiana governor ever to officially denounce lynching in the state was Newton C. Blanchard (1904–1908); he also posted rewards for those responsible. But Governor Blanchard conceded that "it is well-nigh impossible to secure indictments." The law's impotence was symbolized by the 1912 lynching of a black man, Nom Cadore, on a telephone pole in Port Allen, across the river from Baton Rouge. His body dangled within sight of the state capitol building.[41]

Sexual contact was the most emotional of all racial subjects. Cohabitation between white and black was an old and sensitive fact of life in the South, most of all in Louisiana, where libido had scored a multitude of victories over racial prejudice. That interbreeding (called "miscegenation" in race-minded societies) had taken place early and often was not denied even by so defensive a writer as Major Hearsey, who accepted Louisiana's responsibility for the better-looking people of mixed blood, but insisted that the ugly and "depraved" ones were the fault of Yankee invaders.[42]

Louisiana's high degree of racial admixture did not, as might be thought, lessen societal tension between white and black. Instead, it seemed to make the problem worse. Whites who believed themselves to be of pure Caucasian blood were all the more anxious that their children marry into equally unpolluted families. Conversely, there is evidence that the lighter-skinned among Louisiana's "mulattoes" crossed over, or at least preferred to associate with whites if that were allowed. Those who decided not to pass as white, or who could not do so because their features and complexions looked insufficiently European, were considered full members of the despised caste.[43] The Shreveport *Caucasian* (official journal of Caddo Parish) in 1909 summed up the general white attitude: "A negro is a negro, whether he is black or yellow or nearly white."[44]

Not all who believed in strict segregation and disfranchisement were actually fearful that Louisiana would otherwise be in danger of black domination, of becoming another Haiti. After all, by 1900 whites were in a majority, and the possibility of federal intervention on behalf of blacks was increasingly remote. Politically, the hue and cry for further subordination of blacks seemed designed primarily to solidify whites behind the ruling Democratic party. But occasionally there came hints of a more genuine fear from those who, like Major Hearsey, desired by repression to achieve a "final solution" to the race problem. Louisianians were certainly aware that race mixing already had gone far in their state, and those who knew something about the world and its history understood that whenever different races inhabited the same area in large numbers, the ultimate result was generalized amalgamation. It was not Haiti that educated whites feared as the model for Louisiana's future—it was Central America or India.

This was "the latent wisdom" of racism. As the New Orleans *Southwestern Presbyterian* explained, "Prejudice stands as an alert sentinel on duty." Only by keeping blacks firmly controlled and stigmatized as a pariah caste might the catastrophe be averted. To allow them political and social equality "would lead to intermarriage, miscegenation, and the production of a hybrid race, inferior to the whites, mentally, and to the blacks, physically." Professor Smith of Tulane agreed, yet went further. He admitted that some blacks were superior to some whites—but so also were a few dogs. The "inescapable result" of permitting the caste system to become less rigid, he insisted, "would be the mongrelization of the South and her reduction below the level of Mexico and Central America." Smith, however, was an optimist of sorts: he believed that "the Afro-American race stands even now at the entrance of the Valley of the Shadow of Death," and unless do-gooders intervened in nature's process of survival of the fittest, blacks in America would become extinct after a few generations.[45] Others were not so sure. Joe Leveque, editor of New Orleans' *Harlequin*, feared the "remedy" of more repression "will wear out in a generation," and disliked thinking about the future. The author Oliver La Farge, who lived in Louisiana during the 1920s, got the impression that thoughtful whites realized they had created "only a postponement, a makeshift."[46]

Both marriage and concubinage between whites and blacks had been illegal in Louisiana during Spanish (but not French) colonial rule. When Louisiana became an American territory and state, the ban against interracial marriage continued, but the law said nothing about cohabitation or concubinage. Antebellum New Orleans was famous (or notorious) for its quadroon balls, where wealthy white men courted prospective mistresses who were light-skinned, free Creoles of color. The children born of such marriages customarily were provided for by their fathers, and often educated overseas or in the North. During Reconstruction, interracial marriage was specifically approved by Louisiana law, while less formal sexual liaisons between the races continued as before. For years after white Democratic rule was restored, public outrage against interracial coupling, whether in marriage or otherwise, typically was expressed only if the female partner was white. The census of 1880 listed 205 mixed marriages in New Orleans, of which 29 involved white women wed to black men, but the fiercest scorn was directed toward the more numerous white females who had "colored" boyfriends. "A HANDSOME WHITE WOMAN INFATUATED WITH A COON," headlined the *Mascot* in 1894, describing a breach of racial decorum within the city. "Every week," the New Orleans tabloid complained, "instances are reported of white women ignoring white men for the sake of coons." The year before, this scandal sheet had been outraged upon learning that "a young lady, a member of one of our first families, was married to a nigger . . . lawyer." The bridegroom appeared Caucasian, but allegedly "the blood of Ham runs through his veins."[47]

The Louisiana legislature in 1894 finally revived the old antebellum law against marriages "between white persons and persons of color." Yet most interracial sex took place outside of marriage, and by 1908 Louisiana was the only Deep South state *not* outlawing white-black cohabitation—a fact the *Times-Democrat* attributed to "white degenerates" in the legislature: those politicians "who denounce social equality yet practice it." A. A. Gunby, Monroe's white liberal, estimated in 1903 that in his little city of ten thousand, "five hundred negresses are supported in idleness by white paramours."[48] But a popular history of Louisiana published in 1905 put primary blame for the state's past and present interracial sex upon the white men's partners, especially "the comely quadroon woman," whose "hereditary temperament was of necessity lascivious and unmoral, as she was the product of the lust and weakness of two races."[49]

Reacting to voter pressure, the General Assembly in 1908 made concubinage between the races a felony, and defined the practice as "cohabitation of persons of the Caucasian and of the negro races [sic] whether open or secret." Yet the law failed to answer a critical question: how is *Negro* defined in Louisiana? Other states specified what degree or percentage of black African blood made one a Negro, but not Louisiana. The original bill at the 1908 session had stipulated that "a person who is as much as one thirty-second part negro [is] of the negro race," but that provision had been removed.[50]

Showing a way out of this legal swamp was the case of *State v. Treadaway* (1910), in which the Louisiana Supreme Court accepted a defense argument that since Octave Treadaway was an "octoroon" (seven-eighths white) and not a "negro"—which by the court's definition meant all or mostly black—the 1908 law against interracial cohabitation did not apply in this case. The legislature and governor got the message. One month after *Treadaway*, the General Assembly's 1910 session passed an act that duplicated the previous one except that, at Governor Sanders' urging, the word *colored* was used instead of *negro*. Again, the racial term was not defined.[51] By using the word *colored*, however, the legislature aimed to avoid the delicate task of defining proportions. The Louisiana Supreme Court already had done so. Although the cohabiting couple in *Treadaway* was found innocent because the law under which they were tried said "negro," the court made it plain that if that law had read "colored," then no specificity by statute would be required. Included in the *Treadaway* decision was this vital passage: "The word 'colored' when used to designate the race of a person, is unmistakable. . . . It means a person of negro blood pure or mixed; and the term applies no matter what may be the proportions of the admixture, so long as the negro blood is *traceable*."[52]

Traceable. A chilling word for quite a few Louisianians, because it cast a wider and longer net than the explicit fractions used in some other states: one-fourth African ancestry made one a Negro in Virginia, one-eighth in Mississippi. Seven southern states said, in effect, that any ascertainable amount of Negro blood classified one as either "negro" or "colored." But only Louisiana, relying upon the *Treadaway* decision instead of statute definition, used "traceable." Unfortunately, the word encouraged hostile-minded research in musty public and church records of marriages, births, baptisms, and wills. Some of these records went back to Louisiana's early colonial years.[53]

"There is no telling where it might hit," *Independent* magazine predicted in 1911, referring to the recent Louisiana law and its court application. Some individuals brought suits for slander when the press described them as "colored," and in at least two of these cases, the defendants offered documentary proof that the plaintiffs *were* "colored." In the same vein, one Louisiana sheriff reportedly amused himself by looking through old courthouse records until he came upon something pertaining to his own ancestors that visibly upset him. The offending document was soon destroyed by fire.[54]

The court's 1910 interpretation of *colored* put in jeopardy others besides cohabiting men and women of questionable ancestry. Because the 1894 felony law against interracial marriage had used the phrase "persons of color," numerous married couples in Louisiana were now at risk. With the exception of Orleans Parish, there were virtually no reports of married partners being prosecuted. In New Orleans, however, several couples were arrested and their unions declared null and void. At least one suicide resulted. Among those whose marriages were broken up was a white man, John Lawrence, who cried out in Orleans Parish Criminal Court: "But she's my wife. We have lived together thirty-eight years."[55]

In a rural, marshy section of eastern Orleans Parish, what was described as a "hard situation" came to light. The *Picayune* late in 1912 reported that "a number" of white fishermen and farmers from the Lee Station vicinity were arrested because the women they had married, and raised large families with, had traceable Negro ancestry. Yet none of these arrests led to convictions. All the white men, in acts of love and courage, took the stand and swore they too were "colored."[56]

More widespread than arrests were rumors about particular families, some of them politically important. In 1931, Governor Huey Long was alerted to a whispering campaign that his registrar of the state land office, Lucille May Grace, "was tainted with a touch of Negro blood." Before he would endorse her for reelection, the Kingfish insisted she prove to his satisfaction that the story was groundless. Miss Grace was able to do so, with birth and baptismal records going back to the eighteenth century.[57] In 1935 a similar rumor was circulated, or was threatened to be circulated, about the aristocratic Pavy family, leaders of the anti-Long faction in St. Landry Parish. Apparently the resulting anger by an in-law of the Pavys, Dr. Carl Austin Weiss, led to the death of Huey Long.

· 5 ·

LAWYER LONG

Lawyer Huey Long, age twenty-one, returned to Winnfield immediately after being admitted to the Louisiana bar in May of 1915, and became a junior partner in brother Julius' law firm. It was a doomed arrangement from the beginning. Huey could never be junior to anybody, least of all to another Long; Julius could never stifle the urge to dominate his younger brother, often reminding him, "You are 14 years younger than I am." Julius was also district attorney, and Huey wanted to defend clients his brother was prosecuting. By September, their partnership had rancorously dissolved.[1]

The brothers had quite different recollections of their brief Long and Long association. "You took me in as a partner," Huey complained to Julius, "kept me three months and then turned me out, after I had made the sum of $2.00." But Julius recalled: "When you came out of [Tulane] I paid your grocery bill for a number of months and threw civil business to you till you were on your feet." Whatever the actual circumstances, it is clear their temperaments made partnership impossible, and during September, Huey set up his own practice in a tiny room on the second floor of the Bank of Winnfield's building. His elderly uncle, George Long, was president of the institution; its vice-president was B. W. Bailey, the former Winn Parish People's party leader and *Comrade* editor, who by 1915 had become a banker.[2]

Winnfield was a litigious community, but it had an oversupply of lawyers. For several months, Huey's clients were few and quite poor; Uncle George's bank almost evicted the young attorney when the four-dollars-per-month rent became overdue. He also fell into arrears for his law books, typewriter, and scruffy office furniture.[3] A temporary solution was to go on the road again as a salesman.

That he was a lawyer with sales experience impressed Never Fail, makers of home kerosene cans with built-in pumps, and during the winter of 1915–1916 he was their drummer for north Louisiana. Business was good; electricity had not yet reached most farms and villages, and kerosene lamps still provided evening light. The company was so delighted with Huey's sales record that they advanced him money to buy his first car, a second-hand Model T Ford. His brother-in-law David McConnell taught him how to drive—a difficult task, as Huey was not mechanically minded and grew frustrated when he discovered that automobiles were not as easily manipulated as people. By the spring of 1916, Huey was financially solvent and able to spend most of his time building up the law practice in Winnfield. For extra income and for personal publicity, he became the Winn Parish correspondent for Shreveport's three dailies—the *Times*, the *Journal*, and the *Caucasian*. Several of the local news items he sent happened to be about the brilliant courtroom victories of a young lawyer named Huey Long.[4]

Amidst these activities, Huey found little time for reading. But he still flipped through the weekly magazine familiar to his childhood home, the *Saturday Evening Post*. An article in its September 23, 1916, issue, "Are We Rich or Poor?" caught his attention and made a lifelong impression. Based on figures from the United States Industrial Relations Commission, it claimed that only 2 percent of America's people owned 60 percent of the national wealth. This vivid statistic further stimulated Huey's journalistic and political ambitions. In the year he first ran for public office, 1918, he quoted the article in a letter he sent to the New Orleans *Item* and other papers. Three years later, he wanted to submit an article for the *Saturday Evening Post* proposing a solution to the problem of "swollen fortunes," but the *Post* editors turned him down. As a United States senator in 1935, in a radio address over NBC boosting his Share Our Wealth movement, Huey referred to the *Post* article of 1916, saying: "It helped push me along in this fight."[5]

Although 1916 was an election year for the presidency as well as state and local offices, as usual in Louisiana, internal politics mattered more than the question of who would occupy the

White House. Huey at twenty-two was now eligible to run for parish office or for the state House of Representatives. After weighing his chances he decided to wait two years before making his debut as a candidate. A rumor circulated around Winnfield in 1916 that he might announce for district attorney against Julius, the incumbent; Huey did toy with the idea, but his friend Harley Bozeman helped persuade him this would be unwise. Bozeman pointed out that a seat on the Railroad Commission was open for contest in 1918, and it held greater promise for the beginning of a political career.[6]

All the while, Huey kept at his penchant for writing letters to prominent politicians in both state and nation. He knew that the most effective way of catching a Louisiana politico's attention was to urge him to run for governor, for higher flattery could scarcely be imagined in a state where, as *Time* once observed, most people "would rather be governor than President." In the summer of 1915, as candidates began announcing for the next gubernatorial contest, Huey wrote one of his letters to a patrician Alexandria lawyer, John H. Overton. As things turned out, Overton never ran for governor, but became one of Huey's most prominent backers when Long won that office in 1928.[7]

Some of the usual excitement was missing in Louisiana's Democratic gubernatorial primary of 1916. Ruffin G. Pleasant, the state attorney general who in 1893 had quarterbacked and captained LSU's first football team, easily defeated Lieutenant Governor Thomas C. Barrett, who urged state-wide liquor prohibition and ran as the "anti-Ring" candidate—Pleasant was endorsed by the New Orleans machine (the Choctaw Club). Huey lukewarmly supported Barrett; indeed, he seems to have been uncharacteristically detached from politics that year, once he decided not to make a race.[8] Instead, his attention was focused on achieving prominence as a lawyer and on making plans for the 1918 railroad commissioner's race.

A curious thing happened in Louisiana politics in 1916. For the first time since 1896, the Democratic party faced more than token opposition. The millionaire businessman-planter John M. Parker, the state's best-known patrician reformer, announced for governor as the Progressive party nominee. As Major Hearsey pointed out in 1893, "Mr. Parker is not a politician." But Parker was persuaded, partly through his friendship with Theodore Roosevelt, to run for governor as a Progressive. The new Progres-

sive party had been created nationally in 1912 as a personal ve-
hicle for Roosevelt, who as president from 1901 to 1909 had been
a liberal Republican but was denied the GOP's nomination
when he tried to return to the White House in 1912. As a Progressive, Roosevelt ran second to the Democratic nominee, Woodrow Wilson; the badly divided Republican party's candidate, incumbent President William Howard Taft, came in third. The
Progressive party, however, had no national future. In every
state but one, after 1912, most of its adherents began drifting
back into Republican ranks.[9] The exception was Louisiana.
There, for a special reason, the Progressive party grew stronger.

As had happened the last time (1894) a Democratic president
and Congress approved a lower tariff, Louisiana's sugar growers,
hurt in their pocketbooks by the Wilson administration's Underwood Tariff of 1913, reacted by breaking with the state Democratic leadership. This time the Progressive party offered white
people a rallying place more comfortable than Republicanism
because the new party was not so easily identified with Reconstruction and blacks. In 1914, Louisiana's Third Congressional
District, where sugar growing was concentrated, elected Whitmel Pugh Martin as the first and only Progressive member of
Congress from the South.[10] Martin was also the state's first non-
Democrat sent to Congress since 1888.

John M. Parker reluctantly accepted the Louisiana Progressive party's 1916 gubernatorial nomination. He correctly believed that victory against the Democrat's nominee, Pleasant,
was virtually impossible. Even so, Parker was one of the state's
most admired men; his reputation for honesty, independence,
and sincerity of purpose stood in shining contrast to most of
Louisiana's politicoeconomic leadership. Democrats, Populists,
and Republicans all had courted him. Yet Parker lacked char-
isma; he gave short, unemotional speeches in an age and place
where bombastic, long-winded oratory was an anticipated form
of public entertainment. The fact that he had taken a leading
role in the 1891 lynching of eleven suspected Mafia members in
New Orleans was no political handicap except within the Italian
community. His racial views were vintage paternalism—he believed blacks should be treated kindly but were innately inferior
and must not participate in politics. He also wrote that "demagogues" who pandered "to the passions of the 'poor whites'" by
stirring up race hatred were contemptible.[11]

Parker's friendship with Theodore Roosevelt dated back to a meeting in New Orleans in 1898, during the Spanish-American War, when Teddy and his volunteer Rough Riders were on their way to Cuba and the charge up San Juan Hill that made Roosevelt a national hero. (Parker tried to enlist in the Rough Riders, but was turned down for chronic asthma.) During his presidency, Roosevelt spent several vacations as Parker's guest; both men were avid hunters, and on their 1907 expedition into Tensas Swamp, the president enjoyed meeting the legendary Louisiana hunter and guide Ben Lilly, who sometimes slept in trees.

On an earlier (1902) hunting trip with Parker in Mississippi, reporters for the national press were told that Roosevelt had spared a bear cub because it was too small; the Washington *Post* ran a cute cartoon of the alleged event, and a German toy-maker sent the White House the first of the soon-to-be-popular stuffed "Teddy bears." Actually, as Parker recalled the hunt, the bear was a 335-pounder, and the president neglected to shoot the cornered animal only because he lacked a good angle of fire. Instead, Parker stabbed the bear to death with a hunting knife.[12]

Although the odds against Parker in the 1916 gubernatorial race were heavy, the Democratic establishment reacted in much the same way it had done twenty years earlier when facing the Populist-Republicans: with racist tirades. This time, however, the propaganda was not quite as venomous nor were emotions as high; after all, there were only 1,979 registered black voters in the entire state (1 percent of the total), and Parker made it clear he wanted the Progressive party to be, as the expression went, "lily white." The image of Parker as a "nigger lover" was preposterous, but Democratic speakers and editorial writers tried anyway, on the grounds that anyone who opposed the Louisiana Democratic party was either willingly or unwillingly a tool of evil forces desiring to reimpose, as Congressman James B. Aswell cried out, "the dark shadow of Republicanism and negroism . . . upon our beloved State." Aswell also implied that the chastity of white womanhood depended upon beating Parker. In a press release, John Overton referred to Parker's Progressive organization as the "pickaninny Republican party." According to the Kinder (La.) *Gazette*, Parker was a "nigger loving republican mongrel, half southern half northern simian." A strained example of guilt by association was a Democratic advertisement (written by the state central committee chairman, Lee E.

Thomas) pointing out that Parker went on hunting trips with Teddy Roosevelt, who had dinner with Booker T. Washington.[13]

In the general election of April, 1916, Pleasant easily beat Parker, 80,801 to 48,068. Still, it was a respectable performance for a non-Democratic gubernatorial candidate. Parker carried sixteen parishes, mostly in the sugar belt. His Progressive party elected twelve representatives and four senators to the General Assembly—the first legislators of any affiliation except Democratic to be elected since 1896. In the hill parishes where the Populists and Socialists had once been strong, Parker did poorly; the Democrats, who in towns and plantation parishes depicted him as a "nigger-loving Republican," told the upland farmers that Parker was a rich cotton-broker and big landowner (which he was). Yet in some parishes, notably Grant, Parker reportedly got the old, hard-core Populist and Socialist vote simply because he was running against the Democratic oligarchy. In June of 1916, the remnants of the national Progressive party nominated Parker for vice-president, but since the leader of the party—Teddy Roosevelt—refused to accept the top position and announced his return to the Republicans, Progressivism as a separate party collapsed. Parker, for his part, went back to the Democratic party and campaigned for President Wilson's reelection.[14] Four years later, in a remarkable turnabout, Parker—as a Democrat, and with help from Huey Long—would be elected governor of Louisiana.

If Huey voted in the Louisiana general election of 1916, it was probably for Pleasant. As far as is known, he never cast anything but a Democratic ballot in his life. At the time of the Pleasant-Parker election, Huey was involved in his biggest court case to date. A Mrs. Martha DeLoach was suing George Long's Bank of Winnfield. The case was complicated and the amount of money involved was less than a thousand dollars, but Huey gladly became the advocate of this "poor widow woman," as he called her, because it gave him an opportunity to pose as a champion of the oppressed, fighting a heartless financial institution. Also, he was angry at the bank for pressuring him about his office rent and for bouncing a small check on his overdrawn account. He sent word to "Uncle George and Mr. Bailey that they should feel complimented," because "Huey Long don't take out after topwaters, but only after the big fish." When the case went to trial, Huey made sure Mrs. DeLoach's numerous children, clad in pathetic rags, were in court every day, sitting in front of the jury box. Mrs.

DeLoach won her damages, and Huey's local reputation as a lawyer was assured. "I cleaned hell out of them in that suit," he boasted, "and after that I had all the law business I could handle."[15]

Winnfield's older, established lawyers were stunned at the procession of clients flocking to young Mr. Long's office. As one of these attorneys, Harry Gamble, recalled in a 1957 interview, they had underestimated the brash fledgling, which was "a great mistake." Gamble never ceased to wonder how "anybody born in this semi-tropical climate could have so much energy." Summer's heat or winter's chill made no difference. Nor did day or night: Huey once told Gamble that "three o'clock in the morning is just the same as three in the day to me," and his schedule for the remainder of his life bore out that statement.[16]

Huey visited Baton Rouge in May of 1916 and took his first look at the Louisiana legislature. "To my mind," he later wrote, the scene was "disgusting." He was there to attend a meeting of the senate committee on capital and labor, where Senator S. J. Harper (who had loaned Huey money for Tulane and had otherwise befriended him) introduced amendments to the Employers' Liability Act of 1914. The act, Huey and Senator Harper believed, did not provide sufficient compensation for injured workers; since much of Huey's practice involved the claims of lumber-mill laborers, he had a personal interest in seeing benefits liberalized—Harper's amendments were in fact drawn up by Huey. When the senate committee met, Long showed up to speak for the amendments as a concerned citizen, but was denied permission. Except for Harper, the senators were in no mood to listen to a babyfaced, twenty-two-year-old country lawyer.[17]

Suddenly Huey began speaking without permission. What he said got the senators' attention—most of all his accusation that "for twenty years has the Louisiana legislature been dominated by the henchmen and attorneys for the interests." The stunned committeemen angrily voted down most of the Harper amendments, as they probably would have done anyway, but several amendments were adopted a few days later by a full vote of the senate. (When Huey first announced for governor, in 1923, he claimed to have personally "carried the fight to the floor of the Senate," but this must be translated as meaning he encouraged Harper to resist the committee's unfavorable recommendations.) Huey was now as proud of himself as he was scornful of the General Assembly, and on returning to Winnfield, he wrote an acquaintance in Oklahoma that he was "making certain plans for a political future among the people of this state, and knowing more personally than the ordinary man [here]," it would be unwise to move his practice to Oklahoma, as the friend had suggested. Years later, as governor, Huey put this thought more succinctly: "Listen, there may be smarter men than I am, but they ain't in Louisiana."[18]

During the winter of 1916–1917, Huey learned that an assistant's position was open in the United States district attorney's office in Shreveport. He had already decided Winnfield was too small for him and targeted Shreveport as his next place of residence. President Wilson's Justice Department would make the appointment, and as some influential north Louisiana politicians had promised him their support, Huey led himself to believe "the position was practically mine for the asking." But he had not reckoned on the opposition of Eighth District Congressman Aswell who, probably influenced by lumber companies or other regional interests that perceived Huey as a nuisance, managed to block the appointment. From that point onward, "Chicken Jim" Aswell, "this scoundrel . . . liar . . . notorious demagogue," as Huey described him, became Long's first sworn political enemy. As Huey observed in his autobiography, "Once disappointed over a political undertaking, I could never cast it from my mind."[19]

America's entry into World War I, in April of 1917, affected Louisiana more than most states. The warm climate attracted military bases for year-round training; Camp Beauregard, near Alexandria, was one of the army's largest during the war. New Orleans, as a major port and gateway to the Mississippi River Valley, grew busier than ever. Louisiana's oil and gas industry witnessed its first big boom in this, the first war to rely heavily upon internal combustion engines. Tens of thousands of Louisiana's young men, white and black, volunteered for military service, and even more were drafted as the United States had its first conscription since the Civil War. The state's Creoles and Cajuns supported the war effort with special exuberance, for the fight against Imperial Germany centered in the land of most of their ancestors. Paris, as Grace King wrote, was "the mother of New Orleans," and when trains full of departing soldiers pulled out of the stations in Louisiana's metropolis, bands played the *Marseillaise*.[20]

World War I brought the first taste of prosperity that many

Louisianians had ever known. Cotton, sugar, and timber prices, after faltering when the war began in Europe, climbed steadily higher once America entered the conflict. With a labor shortage caused by the draft, employers and landowners found they had to offer better terms to retain their workers. Cotton, still Louisiana's top commercial product, reached its highest value since 1866; the New Orleans cotton exchange quoted an average price of thirty cents per pound for middling grades during the war years of 1917–1918.[21] On the other hand, cotton production was down because of the voracious boll weevil, the "little black bug" that came out of Mexico and in 1904 began eating and multiplying its way across Louisiana's fields. By 1907 the insect had crossed the Mississippi River, dashing the hopes of cotton growers in the "Florida" parishes and in the state of Mississippi that the great stream would provide a barrier (only later was it learned that adult boll weevils can fly). The weevil's ravages occurred in hit-or-miss fashion: some fields were relatively unharmed; others, particularly in the lush bottomlands along the Mississippi, were devastated.[22] Relentlessly, the weevil continued its eastward spread across the cotton South, reaching North Carolina by 1920.

In spite of disfranchisement, Jim Crow laws, and lynchings, few blacks left Louisiana or other Deep South states prior to 1916. Until then there were no economic opportunities elsewhere, no real hope for a better life. But beginning in 1916, northern industries, cut off from their customary European sources of cheap labor because of the war, looked south. Labor agents were sent into Dixie to recruit any able-bodied people willing to relocate in Chicago, Detroit, Newark, or other smokestack cities. The recruiters had their best luck among impoverished blacks in places where the boll weevil was creating havoc: the cotton-plantation areas of Louisiana, Mississippi, and Alabama. By the end of the war, in 1918, approximately 500,000 blacks from those and other ex-Confederate states had gone north. The Pelican State furnished about one tenth of the total.[23] For the first and only time in Louisiana history, the number of black people—not just the percentage, but the actual number—declined:[24]

	WHITE	BLACK
1910	941,086	713,874
1920	1,096,611	700,257

Across America, World War I promoted a greater sense of national unity, but it also produced hysteria as passions unleashed by the war proved hard to control. Louisiana was no exception. Efforts were made to eradicate German influences: Berlin Street in New Orleans was renamed General Pershing Street; the General Assembly made "the teaching of the German language" an offense punishable by fine or imprisonment; a state-wide, paramilitary Loyalty League was formed to supervise enforcement of a wartime act of the legislature requiring "all able-bodied male persons between the ages of 18 and 50 years, inclusive, to be . . . continuously employed in some lawful useful and recognized business, profession, occupation, or employment," an act commonly known as Louisiana's "Work or Fight" law. The Loyalty League engaged in more talk than action, but it allegedly was involved in the destruction of several houses belonging to the pacifist Jehovah's Witnesses sect.[25] After the war the league's Bogalusa branch, as described earlier, killed four AFL organizers in the Great Southern Lumber Company strike.

Black Louisianians were sometimes praised by whites for their willingness to enter the armed services and otherwise contribute to the war effort, but concerns were expressed that black soldiers who were sent to racially more tolerant France might return with dangerous notions. In New Orleans, a group of departing black soldiers listened to words of warning from a white speaker: "You niggers are wondering how you are going to be treated after the war. Well, I'll tell you, you are going to be treated exactly like you were before the war; this is a white man's country and we expect to rule it."[26]

"Slackers"—men who tried to avoid military service in World War I—became special targets of contempt. Actual draft dodgers were, of course, subject to arrest. There was no legal difficulty for able-bodied young men who managed to get deferments, but in the public mind they, too, were likely to be considered "slackers." In a place such as Louisiana, where warrior virtues were glorified, a man who appeared to have strained a point to avoid putting on a uniform would have a problem if he ever entered politics, and Huey Long's questionable deferment in World War I became something of a problem for him.

To his credit, Huey never pretended that he had wanted to fight in the First World War. "I did not go because I was not mad at anybody over there," he explained. "Of course," he added in a

1932 speech in Arkansas, "if they had come around and got me, I'd have grabbed a flag and yelled . . . let's go!" But it never came to that; Huey was able to importune the Winn Parish draft board into forestalling such an event. The board placed him in Class IV, a deferment granted to men with dependents (Huey and Rose had their first child in April of 1917, a daughter they named Rose. Russell, the second child, was born just before the Armistice, in November of 1918). Years later, when Huey's lack of a war record became politically embarrassing, he persuaded the draft board's former chairman, W. T. Heflin, to issue a statement on his behalf. Its unfortunate opening was not entirely helpful: "I, W. T. Heflin, Sheriff of Winn Parish . . . hereby certify that I was chairman of the Draft Board of Winn Parish during the world war, and that Huey P. Long was exempt from military service because of the fact that he had a wife and child, lived in two or three rented rooms, was buying his household furniture on time, and owed money I loaned him."[27]

What Huey really wanted, and pleaded for in vain, was a Class V exemption as a "state official," which would have virtually guaranteed him against being called up. He tried to claim it on the tenuous basis of being a notary public, but not even Heflin (despite his vested interest in keeping Huey away from the battlefields) could accept that. During Long's first gubernatorial campaign, in 1923, former governor Ruffin G. Pleasant accused him of being a slacker who flirted with treason. Huey always preferring offense over defense, struck back by denouncing Pleasant, who had served as a volunteer lieutenant colonel in the Spanish-American War, for being an "evader of military duty who had no dependents" during World War I.[28] Huey neglected to add that Pleasant was governor at the time, married, and not draft-eligible because he was forty-seven years old.

When Huey had needed money to attend the Tulane law school in 1914, State Senator S. J. Harper had loaned him $250. At the time, Harper's daughter voiced doubt that the loan would ever be repaid, but the senator replied that he might need a good lawyer some day, and if he did, Huey Long would help him. In February of 1918, amid America's involvement in World War I, Harper found himself sorely in need of legal talent: he was indicted by a federal grand jury for violating the Espionage Act, and faced, if convicted, up to twenty years in prison.[29]

Harper was a radical in the Winn Parish tradition. Although

a store-owner, a Democratic member of the legislature, and a director of the Bank of Winnfield, he was in ideology a left-wing Populist if not a Socialist. He had vehemently opposed America's entry into the war. Shortly before his indictment, Harper announced he planned to run against Congressman Aswell in the autumn (1918) Democratic primary. He also published a pamphlet titled *The Issues of the Day: Financial Slavery, Free Speech.* The pamphlet claimed that international bankers, especially those on Wall Street, were responsible for dragging the United States into the war, and further proposed that the war should be paid for by confiscating the profits of bankers, munitions makers, and others who sought to gain from the deaths of America's young men.

Only by a stretch of the imagination, even during wartime, might such statements be viewed as treasonable. But Harper was indicted. A particularly explosive count in his indictment said that in June of 1917 he "obstructed the recruiting and enlistment" of American servicemen by making public statements such as, "This is a poor man's fight and a rich man's war. President Wilson and Congress ought to be assassinated. My boy and I will take to the woods and die here before we would go to the war."[30] Harper probably did say things of that nature prior to America's joining the war, but there was no reliable evidence he uttered them afterward. His trial took place during March, 1918, in an Alexandria courtroom. Defending him were Winnfield's two best lawyers, Julius and Huey Long.

Huey would always be proud of standing by Harper's side in that courtroom, and rightly so. Ordinarily he did not place gratitude and friendship above political considerations, but here was an exception. By defending Senator Harper under such circumstances, during wartime and in a year when Huey himself was planning to run for office, with his own draft deferment already making him vulnerable to questions about patriotism, Huey Long performed the most courageous and unselfish act of his life. He did it because, in Huey's words, Harper was "my one great friend in Winnfield."[31]

The government's case against Harper was weak, but people had gone to federal prison under the Espionage Act on flimsier evidence. The best thing Harper had going for him was the younger member of his defense team, who craftily manipulated the process of jury selection in such a way as to determine the outcome before the trial began. Huey, after the jury pool was named, decided that several potential jurors, considering their appearance and background, would probably be hostile to Senator Harper. He could have kept them off the jury with challenges during the selection procedure, but he had something better in mind. Huey knew that all the potential jurors were being watched by the United States attorneys, as well as by other men who looked like government agents. In his best smarmy manner, Huey approached those persons he did not want on the jury, bought them drinks or dinner, and made sure he was seen talking and laughing with them as if they were partners in some shady endeavor. It was a trap, and the prosecution fell into it. On the day jury selection began, the people who had been Huey's guests were questioned and truthfully answered that he had not discussed the case with them (he was probably telling the latest dirty jokes), but the prosecutors suspected otherwise—and used their own challenges to prevent the seating of exactly those individuals Huey did not want on the jury.[32]

The presiding judge, George W. Jack, suspected Huey of mischief and was upset by his abrasive statement defending Harper, published in the New Orleans *Times-Picayune* before the trial began. Several times during the proceedings Jack reprimanded the young lawyer, at one point threatening him with jail for contempt of court. Julius and Huey worked well together on the Harper case, even though their office partnership had dissolved in acrimony three years previously. The judge, Huey claimed shortly after the trial, was "so hostile to me" that the brothers agreed Julius should make the closing argument. On March 19, 1918, the case went to the jury. They deliberated only seven minutes. Harper was acquitted on all counts. Judge Jack, visibly angry at the verdict, ordered Harper to turn all remaining copies of his "disloyal and seditious" pamphlet over to a United States marshal "to be burned."[33]

Soon Harper was pressured into resigning from the legislature. He did so reluctantly, still denying any act of disloyalty, and added: "I have devoted the greater part of my life trying to do something to better the condition of the common man."[34] Harper's career in politics was finished. But that of his resourceful twenty-four-year-old lawyer, Huey Long, was about to begin.

· 6 ·

COMMISSIONER LONG

Huey announced for north Louisiana's seat on the three-member Railroad Commission several weeks before his twenty-fifth birthday on August 30, 1918. He had said that one of the lesser state offices would be his first step toward the governor's chair, and ultimately the White House. Now the journey commenced.

The Railroad Commission (later the Public Service Commission), created by the Constitution of 1898, supposedly set rates and otherwise regulated all forms of public transportation in the state, as well as telephone and telegraph lines. Yet it was not an active body. Prior to 1918, the commissioners were all traditional Louisiana politicians who drew their salaries, posed as defenders of the public interest, but tended to be keenly sympathetic to the corporations they regulated. In the Third District, comprising north Louisiana's twenty-eight parishes, the incumbent was Burk A. Bridges of Claiborne Parish, a patrician conservative in his fifties, well connected with the courthouse rings in his district. Bridges undoubtedly thought he would have no trouble winning a second six-year term.[1] He was in for a rude surprise.

Perhaps by oversight, the state's constitution did not specify a minimum age for railroad commissioners. Any voter was eligible. Huey apparently had been planning this campaign for two years, and he enjoyed active backing from his brothers Julius and Earl; in all likelihood, Julius' endorsement and financial aid were based on an understanding reached in 1916: that Huey would not run against Julius for district attorney if Julius promised to help him in the commissioner's race against Bridges. Five candidates, including Bridges and Long, ran in the September Democratic primary. Huey was the youngest and least experienced of the lot, and he carried heavy political baggage—America was still at war with Germany, and outside Winn Parish Huey was chiefly known as the lawyer for the accused "traitor" S. J. Harper; his deferment also left him vulnerable to questions about his patriotism.[2] With such handicaps, and in light of Bridges' ties to local politicians, Huey would have to wage an unorthodox campaign.

"I can beat that old man," Huey boasted in 1918. Bridges was actually middle-aged, but to a challenger thirty years his junior he seemed ancient. For the remainder of his life, all of Huey's election opponents would be middle-aged or elderly men, and it became his habit to invidiously comment on their years or grayish appearance. In fact, Huey would do this to any prominent person who criticized him, if he or she were up in years. "Fossil"; "Old Buzzard Back"; "Hilda, the Antique Queen"; "Old Sack of Bones"—these were sample epithets.[3] This mode of attack became so characteristic that it signified something deeper than youthful arrogance. Probably, Huey instinctively disliked older people because they often tried to tell him what to do, and he retained a lifelong resentment against authority figures. Perhaps he also was jealous of them for having enjoyed a long life. Huey suspected that he himself would not.[4]

Against advice, Huey decided to make his first campaign in a shiny, albeit secondhand, Overland 90 automobile. Cars were still suspect in the hinterlands as "devil wagons"; the Winnfield *Comrade* had recently noted "very serious preachments" against these noisy machines. "Hell," Huey exclaimed, "they told me I'd have to drive around in an old buggy with a horse, and wear slouchy clothes and chew tobacco. But not me . . . I wanted them to think I was something, and they did." His favorite campaign apparel, brushed every day, was a $37.50 white linen suit from The Biggest Little Store of Shreveport, paid for by a grateful ex-senator Harper.[5]

Huey's days as a traveling salesman through north Louisiana now paid political dividends. He seemed to remember every farmhouse and country store he visited as a teenager selling Cottolene or Wine of Cardui, or as a young lawyer promoting Never Fail kerosene cans. His former customers usually remembered him and were flattered that he could still call them by name and seemed truly concerned with their individual problems. Louisiana politicians customarily spoke only in courthouse towns and depended on parish organizations to bring out the rural vote. But here was a candidate who took time to visit lonely little dwellings and who could make country folk believe that if he were elected they would have, for the first time, a personal friend in a notable office. Campaigning far into the night, Huey discovered that most farmers did not object to being roused from their beds to talk politics and religion with him.[6] It made them feel important.

Huey's basic message in the railroad commissioner race of 1918 would be repeated until the end of his days: he was a young warrior of and for the plain people, battling the evil giants of Wall Street and their corporations; too much of America's wealth was concentrated in too few hands, and this unfairness was perpetuated by an educational system so stacked against the poor that (according to his statistics) only fourteen out of every thousand children obtained a college education.[7] The way to begin rectifying these wrongs was to turn out of office the corrupt local flunkies of big business—in this case, Burk Bridges—and elect instead true men of the people, such as Huey Long.

During the late summer and early fall, Huey's message was carried to all twenty-eight parishes in the district. Abbreviated versions were printed on circulars mailed out by Huey's wife; some were tacked to telephone and telegraph poles by the candidate himself. The Overland's tires wore thin, and Huey almost ran out of gas money before making it back to Winnfield to borrow more campaign funds. His law practice came to a standstill; nothing mattered except the election. Several persons countersigned loans for him, including the local draft board chairman, W. T. Heflin, who now had a big stake in keeping Huey out of the trenches in France.[8]

Oscar K. Allen—known as O. K.—assessor of Winn Parish, bore the brunt of Huey's plaintive appeal: "Oscar, I haven't a penny in the world that I can get my hands on to continue the race. I don't see that I can go any further." Without hesitation, O. K. walked over to the bank, borrowed five hundred dollars, and in Huey's words, "brought me back the money in cash." Allen, eleven years older than Huey and turning prematurely gray, was a plodding, mild-mannered individual from the poorest neighborhood of the parish—a dismal thicket east of Dugde-mona Bayou. Winnfield residents looked down upon people from there, referring to them as "the yan-side element." Allen was almost the only yan-sider to have achieved status in Winn Parish. Befriending Huey would ultimately make Allen a wealthy man and—in title at least—governor of Louisiana.[9]

Huey ran a good second, behind Burk Bridges, in the September Democratic primary. Because the three other candidates rolled up respectable totals in their home parishes, Bridges did not have a majority and was forced into a run-off with Long. Too late, the incumbent awoke to his danger and began a more active campaign, but he was no match for the hyperenergetic Long, who again took to the bumpy dirt roads in his Overland. Despite the handicap of youth and attacks on his patriotism— attacks he tried to deflect by participating in war bond rallies— Long beat Bridges by 635 votes, 7,286 to 6,651. Huey lost most of the courthouse towns and did quite badly in the three urban centers of the district—Shreveport, Monroe, and Alexandria— but the rural precincts put him in. Among the congratulations was a letter from State Senator Delos Johnson of Franklinton, in southeastern Louisiana, who recognized Huey as a comer and admired him for defending their mutual friend S. J. Harper. Johnson forecast what kind of commissioner Huey would be: "I predict that you will have them sit up and take notice."[10]

The same month Commissioner Long took office, December of 1918, he moved both his residence and his law practice from Winnfield to Shreveport. Huey now dreamed of wealth as well as political power. Shreveport had become an oil and gas boom town; Caddo and nearby parishes seemed to be floating on a sea of petroleum. Like many other lawyers in the area, Huey did legal work for various independent ("wildcat") oil companies and often accepted stock as his fee. Although anti–big business in rhetoric, he was never anticapitalist when it came to small enterprises. By early 1918, he owned or would presently own stock in the Banks Oil Company, the Bayou Oil Company, and the Claiborne Oil Company. These three companies were among the independents that, beginning in 1917, brought in the Pine Island wells, fifteen miles north of Shreveport.[11]

Pine Island crude was of low-gravity grade, meaning that it made good diesel fuel but had limited potential as gasoline or kerosene. Demand was high during World War I, but after November of 1918, the United States government canceled its orders for diesel fuel, whereupon the three major oil companies—Standard, Texas, and Gulf—announced they would no longer purchase Pine Island oil "at any price," or even carry it in their pipelines. The independents were furious at what they called a "freeze-out" by Standard and the other majors.[12] Railroad Commissioner Long had both economic and political reasons to champion the independents' cause—and to pillory John D. Rockefeller's Standard Oil. The political reason was uppermost.

A veteran newsman, Thomas O. Harris, was at that time secretary of the Independent Oil and Gas Producers Association of North Louisiana. Harris had first met Huey in 1917, when the young lawyer from Winnfield was a local correspondent for the Shreveport newspapers, and had mistrusted him ever since. Writing later about Huey and the IOGPA, Harris asserted that the independents would have preferred that the new railroad commissioner not become their champion, since they suspected his motives; "but that made little difference to Huey, who . . . recognized at once the political value of a successful fight against the Standard. Suppressing him was like trying to empty the Mississippi River with a dipper."[13]

The Railroad Commission possessed what little regulatory power existed over oil and gas pipelines in Louisiana. But the law was so vague that the companies could not be told how much, or whose, oil to transport or to buy. Standard by far was the biggest purchaser, carrier, and refiner in Louisiana; its sprawling Baton Rouge refinery was one of the world's largest, and by 1919 had become the capital city's chief employer.[14] Huey always preferred big targets. At the March, 1919, meeting of the Railroad Commission, he coaxed the other two members into approving a manifesto urging Governor Pleasant to call a special session of the legislature for the purpose of declaring the pipeline companies public utilities, which would have placed them specifically under the commission's control. Pleasant hesitated, so Huey took out an ad in the Shreveport *Times* calling upon "the people of Louisiana" to prod the governor into action. Late in June, Governor Pleasant announced his decision: the problem did not merit a special session.[15]

Huey pretended to be furious. Actually he was delighted, for now the two largest targets in the state loomed in his sights:

Standard Oil and Governor Pleasant. Up to this time not many people outside of north Louisiana's twenty-eight parishes knew Huey Long's name. He craved wider attention, and soon he was going to get it.

Following the governor's refusal to call a special session, Huey insinuated to a *Times-Picayune* reporter that Pleasant took his marching orders from Standard Oil. Reading this, the governor concluded he should not dignify such juvenile clatter with a direct reply; he assigned an underling, State Fire Marshal William Campbell, the task of handling Long. Campbell issued a statement claiming that Huey was motivated by greed in that he owned stock in Pine Island companies. This, said the fire marshal, was "the first time anyone had the brass to get an extra session of the state legislature to pull off a stock-jobbing deal." Campbell then challenged Long to respond at a state-wide political rally already scheduled for a place called Hot Wells on July 4.[16] If Huey had written the scenario, he could not have given himself a better role.

The July 4, 1919, Democratic party rally at Hot Wells, a health spa in Rapides Parish, was supposed to kick off the gubernatorial campaign and election of 1920. Pleasant would not be there, as Louisiana governors at that time could not succeed themselves. But various hopefuls were expected to attend. Huey himself was five years too young to be a candidate for governor, for which office the state constitution specified a minimum age of thirty. Yet because of his clash with the Pleasant administration and Fire Marshal Campbell's challenge, Huey arranged a spot for himself at the end of the program, after the gubernatorial aspirants were done.[17]

Hot Wells, with a water temperature of 116 degrees, seems less than ideal for a July gathering in Louisiana. Predictably, outdoor heat would be close to the century mark, with humidity not far behind. But the resort, fifteen miles from Alexandria, was near the geographic center of the state. A large crowd showed up. Besides political speeches, the rally featured swimming, dancing, and "good music all day," along with a greasy-pole contest and long distance running from Boyce to Hot Wells.[18] Reporters from the New Orleans dailies came up by train to jot down what the candidates for governor might say. They knew that the young railroad commissioner Huey Long was scheduled to speak last, in reply to the Pleasant administration, but they probably did not imagine he would figure prominently in their stories.

Yet he did. As soon as the last candidate uttered his final platitude, Huey strode over to a clutch of city reporters. Some of what he was going to say, he warned the newsmen, "would not be printable." Now he had their attention. Huey then bounded up the speaker's stand and launched a verbal assault upon Standard Oil and Governor Pleasant, after dismissing Campbell as a "barfly." True to his word, Huey made some remarks that the New Orleans *States* called "unprintable." But the gist of his speech was reported, and it overshadowed the candidates' orations. Standard Oil was both an "octopus" and a "highway bandit," exclaimed Huey, and its stooge, Pleasant, was "the criminal who disgraces the gubernatorial chair." [19]

Attack was always preferable to defense, Long reasoned, and the attack should be all-out, aimed at the jugular. This he believed at Hot Wells in 1919 and at Washington in 1935. He was also convinced of the need to speak from a position of authority, even if only that of railroad commissioner, so that his accusations would have an official imprimatur. From the time he blasted Governor Pleasant until he took on President Franklin D. Roosevelt, Huey would never speak without an official title: Railroad Commissioner Long; Public Service Commissioner Long (after the designation was changed in 1921); Governor Long; Senator Long. Reading or hearing his scathing accusations, unsophisticated people would ask how someone in his position could say such things unless they were true.

Often Huey's charges had a legitimate basis, although he invariably exaggerated for effect. And by habit, beginning with the Hot Wells tirade, he embedded somewhere in his onslaughts a brief denial of self-interest. "Mr. Long," the *States* reporter noted at Hot Wells, "took the audience into his confidence. 'I haven't got a dime,' he said, 'but I'm not afraid for my political future and I don't care whether I've got any or not.'" [20] This colossal falsehood would, with variations, be repeated on many occasions.

As Huey anticipated, Hot Wells gave him his first state-wide attention. The fact that much of it was negative bothered him not at all. "Vicious," was the Alexandria *Town Talk*'s description of his speech. "An outrage," State Representative J. Martian

Hamley called it, although he conceded that "Huey seems to have taken all the political excitement from that meeting." Long was euphoric. In a July 30 letter to his brother Shan (Dr. George S. Long) in Oklahoma, Huey wrote that he was "over the first shock of being vilified, complimented, cartooned and ridiculed," and that "all of the New Orleans newspapers have been running stories for a number of days that I was looked upon as an aggressive candidate for governor [but] as you know, I am but twenty-five. . . . I cannot run on account of my age."[21] Huey was grossly overstating the impact of Hot Wells. He had not turned the state upside down, as the letter to Shan implied. Stories about him ran a day or so and that was it. But it was his first taste of real publicity, and he loved it.

The gubernatorial campaign of 1920 was in full swing by September of 1919, as soon as John M. Parker announced he would seek the Democratic nomination. His candidacy has no parallel in Louisiana's political history. Defeated in 1916 as the Progressive party's gubernatorial aspirant and never a politician in the usual sense, Parker became the favorite to succeed Ruffin G. Pleasant through unique circumstances. Parker's path to the state's highest office was traveled by him alone.

He was in many ways the antithesis of Huey Long. Parker was dignified, honor-bound, and taciturn; Huey was indecorous, devious, and loquacious. Parker thought first of principles, Huey of results. Parker actually was indifferent about his political future; Huey pretended not to care, but in fact nothing was more important. Parker thought leadership meant pointing the right way and setting a good example; Huey believed a leader should compel. Parker lacked imagination but had integrity; Long possessed imagination without integrity. Unavoidably, the two were fated eventually to become the worst of enemies.

In the 1919–1920 campaign, however, Huey joined an improbable coalition of Governor Pleasant, former governor J. Y. Sanders, Shreveport politico Lee E. Thomas, and John Patrick Sullivan of New Orleans (leader of a dissident city machine faction) in supporting the patrician reformer J. Parker for governor. Parker, who had only lately returned to the Democratic party, had to be cajoled—as in 1916 when he ran as a Progressive—into announcing for the Democratic gubernatorial nomination.[22] At fifty-six, he was one of Louisiana's wealthiest and most respected men. The Democratic politicians who pushed him into the race in 1920 did so because, for various reasons, they disliked or had broken with the New Orleans machine, and because they hoped some of Parker's prestige would rub off on them.

World War I had enhanced Parker's reputation in several ways. During 1917 and 1918, he served the national government as the head of the Food Administration for Louisiana, and did so with such efficiency that his program became a model for the wartime agency in other states. He was also on good terms with President Wilson—in itself remarkable, since Parker was a longtime friend of Teddy Roosevelt, and Wilson and Roosevelt despised each other. In 1918, Governor Pleasant offered Parker an appointment as United States senator, following the death of Louisiana's senior incumbent, Robert "Coozan Bob" Broussard. But Parker turned it down because he believed his work as food administrator for the nation's major sugar-producing state was important to the war effort. He had tried to serve in a more direct way: Parker and Roosevelt, after America entered the war, implored President Wilson to authorize, and send to the battlefields of France, a volunteer "Rough Rider Division" commanded by Roosevelt, in which Parker would be the colonel of a Louisiana regiment. Those who pledged to serve under Parker were mostly middle-aged or older; some had helped him lynch the Mafia suspects in 1891, others were veterans of the White League uprising of 1874, and one ancient volunteer had fought in the Civil War. Understandably, Wilson denied Roosevelt and Parker's request.[23]

Almost everybody who knew him trusted Parker's motives, whether they agreed with him or not. Career politicians such as J. Y. Sanders hoped by endorsing Parker to have his blessing in future campaigns; also, they probably assumed that after a term as governor he was unlikely to run for office again and so would not pose a direct threat to their ambitions. Moreover, John M. Parker had attained something that, for anyone involved in state politics, was almost as rare as gold ore in Louisiana—national respectability.

Parker's Democratic platform for the 1920 governor's race resembled his Progressive party utterances of earlier years. He was in favor of a new state constitution, increased funding for education and roads, woman suffrage, tariff protection for sugar, conservation of natural gas reserves, and help for the independent oil producers in their struggle with Standard Oil. He was stridently against the thing he had hated since coming of voting age in the 1880s—New Orleans' political machine. He promised, if elected governor, the Ring's "destruction." On alcohol prohibition, which was about to go into effect nationally (January 26, 1920) under the Eighteenth Amendment and the Volstead Act, Parker took no public stand. Privately, however, he always thought Prohibition was unworkable, particularly in Catholic south Louisiana.[24]

Colonel Frank P. Stubbs of Monroe, recently commander of the First Louisiana Infantry Regiment in France, was Parker's opponent in the January, 1920, Democratic gubernatorial primary. (The winner would face a nominal Republican foe in April.) Stubbs's platform included most of the reforms proposed by Parker, but the colonel's endorsement by Mayor Martin Behrman and the New Orleans machine made his promises for change sound hollow. World War I apparently left a majority of Louisiana voters in an untypical moralistic, reformist mood, and Parker would owe his margin of victory to that spirit. As Mayor Behrman later noted ruefully, "the people were wild for change."[25]

Commissioner Long campaigned across north Louisiana for Parker, fervidly attacking "X-Col. Stubbs," as he called him, and harping upon Stubbs's ties to the New Orleans Ring. Huey possessed a perfect instinct for guilt by association. It was an old ploy in Louisiana politics, but with him it became a fine art. Stubbs was endorsed by the Ring, and the Ring included State Representative Tom Anderson of New Orleans' Fourth Ward— the red-light district known as Storyville. Anderson was indeed a notorious character, whose career included dealing in cocaine and opium as well as female flesh; he had the unofficial title "Mayor of Storyville," and the district was sometimes referred to as "Anderson County."[26] His biography in *Who's Who in Louisiana Politics in 1916* roguishly congratulated Anderson for "always standing for the better class of politics." As a legislator, Anderson was a member of the House Ways and Means Committee, and made a splendid target for Huey Long to pin on Colonel Stubbs. How awful, Huey roared, that Stubbs's "New Orleans Ring has sent to the legislature this Tom Anderson, the King of the red light district . . . to make laws for the young boys and girls of Louisiana!"[27]

By the time Huey was fulminating about it, Storyville no

longer legally existed. In October of 1917, New Orleans had been forced to shut down the district on orders of the United States War and Navy departments. Mayor Behrman did his best to keep Storyville open, even going to Washington to protest—with justification—that closing the district would worsen the prostitution problem by scattering it throughout the city. But his warning was ignored. Shortly before the gubernatorial election in 1920, the *Times-Picayune*, supporting Parker and deciding to use Huey's methods, ran a series called "New Orleans Nights," in which Mayor Behrman, Representative Anderson, and other members of this "crawling, fetid, contaminating monster of . . . RING RULE" were held responsible for the proliferation of vice throughout the city. One procurer who specialized in arranging sex with children told an investigator posing as a customer: "She is just a little kid, and you'll like her fine, I'm sure." The price was ten dollars, plus four for a room with "police protection."[28]

Stubbs's backers predictably responded by attacking Parker's inconstancy as a Democrat. The charges used against him four years earlier when he ran as a Progressive were exhumed: his election would jeopardize Caucasian rule; he associated with "nigger-loving" Republicans; he was a rich man who cared nothing about ordinary people. Eighth District Congressman James Aswell, whose orations about the Lost Cause could make elderly Confederate veterans weep, campaigned for Stubbs in the same mode he had adopted for Pleasant in 1916, describing Parker as weak on white supremacy and as "a boll weevil eating at the heart of Louisiana Democracy."[29] Huey Long voiced outrage at "such unfair tactics" as trying "to place John M. Parker in the light as a negro lover," although in a campaign advertisement Huey brought up the irrelevancy that back in the 1880s, "the New Orleans Ring voted every negro within the city limits." Thus race remained an issue in Louisiana politics, despite the fact that by the time of the Parker-Stubbs campaign a mere 725 blacks were registered state-wide—.05 percent of the total electorate—and they could vote only in the meaningless general elections.[30]

Economically, the picture was a little brighter for Louisiana blacks. They, too, benefited from the wartime prosperity that lasted into 1920. Migration northward continued, although at a lower pace during the year following the Armistice. Blacks were still on the bottom rung, but the majority were no longer as desperately poor as before. In order to retain laborers, many planters began offering sharecroppers preharvest advances in cash. Agriculture remained Louisiana's economic base, but most field work was still done by hand. As of 1920 there were only 2,815 tractors in the state, and mechanical cotton pickers suitable for Louisiana's moist fields would not arrive until after World War II.[31] With middling cotton reaching forty cents a pound by late 1919, plantation owners were paying laborers better and making efforts to discourage migration in other ways. Out-of-state labor agents met open hostility from local officials and were required to post a five-thousand-dollar bond. The sheriff of Caddo Parish wanted the Chicago *Defender*, a black paper promoting migration north, barred from the mails. The state secretary of agriculture, Harry D. Wilson, journeyed to Chicago seeking former field hands and offered free transportation for those willing to return to Louisiana.[32]

Regardless of such inducements, life was still degrading for blacks in Louisiana, and it became unusually hazardous during the year following World War I. Thousands of black soldiers from the state had served in France; for the first time, they had glimpsed a society where race was not of overriding importance. Upon their return, many whites looked for signs of trouble. "Frenchwomen ruined niggers," was one blunt summation of that concern.[33] The result was an upsurge in the number of lynchings (eighty-two was the national total reported in 1919).[34] Significantly, neither John M. Parker nor Colonel Stubbs uttered a word of criticism about Louisiana's contribution to that sum, even though two of these public murders during the year they ran for governor were among the most egregious in the state's history. The victims were black men named Sampson Smith and George Bolden.

Sampson Smith was on trial in Columbia, seat of Caldwell Parish, charged with killing a white man. Early in 1919, an all-white jury surprised and outraged spectators by finding the defendant guilty, but without capital punishment. Immediately, the rule of law vanished from the courthouse. The spectators became a mob, and Smith was dragged outside and hanged. North Louisiana's leading afternoon paper, the Shreveport *Journal*, criticized such disrespect for judicial procedure but added that the verdict "was almost as bad" as the lynching.[35]

George Bolden's lynching, later that year, became known as the "Monroe Horror." Ordinarily, Louisiana's press either excused lynching or was only mildly critical of the practice, but the circumstances of this one were so revolting that most of the state's leading newspapers denounced it. Politicians, however, were not quoted as commenting upon it at all.

Bolden was a black artisan of Monroe, Ouachita Parish, who specialized in carpentry repairs. White competitors resented his underbidding them on jobs; apparently, one of them wrote what was described as "an insulting note to a white woman" and signed Bolden's name. Bolden could not have written it; several of his white employers later testified that he had to endorse checks with an X. But as word spread that this "nigger" had suggested sex to a white woman, a lynch mob gathered. Bolden was caught, shot several times, and left for dead. Later, after friends came and saw he was still alive, he was taken to the "colored ward" of Monroe's St. Francis Sanitarium, where he underwent surgery that included the amputation of a shattered leg. Presently the mob, hearing Bolden was alive at St. Francis, burst into the hospital. Seizing a black patient they mistook for Bolden (this man, too, had just come out of surgery), the mob dragged him out of bed, but after discovering their mistake, dropped him. He died of shock the next day. Bolden, meanwhile, had been hidden by white nurses, but knowing he could not be protected there, they told Bolden's wife to get him out of town on the next train. He was placed in the baggage car of a Shreveport-bound train, but eight miles west of Monroe, the mob, having learned his whereabouts and determined to finish the job, stopped the train, pulled the luckless man out, and shot him repeatedly to make sure he was dead. George Bolden may be the only person ever lynched twice. Monroe added to its shame by taking no serious legal action against the perpetrators. A grand jury placed two alleged mob members under bonds of a hundred dollars each; that was the only consequence. A letter from "The Nurses" to the Monroe *News-Star* expressed outrage not at Bolden's death, but at the mob's disrespect for the hospital. "We think it a disgrace to Monroe," read the letter, "for a mob to come to the sanitarium to carry out their vengeance, and to scare the nurses and patients, when they easily could have waited until the patient was carried home."[36]

The many surviving letters Huey Long composed in 1919

make no mention of Bolden's lynching, although he did write Harley Bozeman, "I have always said there was one of the lowest-down bunch of . . . scoundrels around Monroe that ever was." But Huey was referring to another, lesser "Monroe Horror" of 1919: a football game between visiting Winnfield and Monroe High School, in which his cousin Otho Long, Winnfield's star running back, was stopped from making a touchdown by a mob of spectators who ran onto the field, tripped him up, and kicked his face. The referee tried to forfeit the game to Winnfield, but when surrounded by a threatening crowd, reversed his decision.[37] Huey also disliked Monroe because he had done poorly there in the recent railroad commissioner's election.

Huey never endorsed lynching, but he considered an occasional one just part of life in Louisiana. (When quizzed about a Washington Parish lynching in 1935, he replied, "Anyway, that nigger was guilty.") Overall, his attitude toward blacks mirrored that of paternalistic patricians such as John M. Parker. "The poor negroes have got to live too," he would say, hastily adding that although he would feed a hungry black, he would never call him "mister."[38] From the beginning until the end of his stormy career, Huey's seemingly reckless disregard of consequences never extended to suggesting that blacks should be provided with the legal protection or voting rights that, as citizens, the United States Constitution granted them. Black rights was one issue Huey Long was afraid to touch. He knew what had happened to the Populists.

As a young lawyer, Huey sometimes handled cases for blacks who were injured, or whose relatives had been killed, in sawmill accidents. These suits involved small monetary settlements. Once, however, in 1920, he was asked to take on a civil rights case, involving blacks being whipped and otherwise abused at the Caddo-Winn Lumber Company's mill in the town of St. Maurice, near Winnfield. Huey refused and candidly explained why: "It is a matter which I cannot handle, although I don't doubt everything you say being true. . . . It would merely injure me and we would never get anything out of a suit." He added that mistreated blacks should console themselves with the knowledge that for white bullies, "there is such a thing as hell."[39]

Whether Huey actually believed in hell is open to question, but he knew there was a limbo for any Louisiana politician who allowed himself to be stuck with the tag of "nigger lover." In the

1919–1920 campaign, that was the only charge against John M. Parker causing concern, but with Huey's help the accusation was blunted. Huey was also able to forecast, with remarkable accuracy, the results of the Parker-Stubbs contest. He predicted that "Parker will be elected governor by a majority of ten thousand." Final returns from the January, 1920, Democratic primary were: Parker, 77,868; Stubbs, 65,685.[40] Parker went on to overwhelm a Republican opponent in the general election and was inaugurated governor in May. But Parker's most vocal supporter, Huey Long, would quickly become his nemesis.

· 7 ·

DISGUSTED

"We have played too much politics and too little common sense," John M. Parker lectured the crowd attending his swearing-in as governor on a bright May day in 1920. Parker's inaugural address of 295 words was and still is the briefest in the state's history. He spoke of ideals and called for higher standards of civic behavior, so that the world might see "a new Louisiana." Twice during the ceremony, a spectators' stand built for the occasion swayed and threatened to collapse.[1]

Parker sincerely wanted regulation and taxation of the oil and gas industry, but he held an even stronger belief in cooperation between business and government. He also admitted ignorance about the industry's problems, and prior to his inauguration he hosted a conference, arranged by Thomas O. Harris of the Independent Oil and Gas Producers Association, to discuss regulation and tax proposals. Spokesmen for small and large producers and pipeline carriers—including the big one, Standard Oil—were present. So was Huey Long, whom Parker naively asked to lay aside his bitterness and "adopt a conciliatory attitude." The governor-elect asked the group to advise him on specific legislation. But Standard and the independents could not agree, and Huey disagreed with them both, for he wanted a bill to divorce pipelines entirely from the producing and refining companies. When the General Assembly met and appeared headed toward deadlock on the issue, Governor Parker continued to hope for something mutually acceptable, and called another conference. This meeting included the legal counsel for Standard Oil; it resulted in a compromise concerning pipeline regulation, which the legislature quickly passed and the governor signed.[2] But the measure was not what Huey desired, and his alienation from Parker began.

Commissioner Long believed he had even greater reason to be dissatisfied with Governor Parker because of what he considered to be a sellout on the issue of taxation. Prior to 1920 no extractive industry—not oil, gas, timber, sulphur, or salt—paid any meaningful amount of severance taxes on the removal of Louisiana's natural resources. (Beginning in 1910, the legislature had placed minuscule taxes on these concerns, but through litigation Standard Oil and other companies had blocked all but a few thousand dollars in collections.) Parker, a few days prior to his inauguration, made a controversial "gentlemen's agreement" with the oil giant. In brief, Standard agreed not to oppose passage of, or later litigate against collection of, a 2 percent severance tax on the value of natural resources (for example, petroleum) taken in Louisiana, and Parker pledged that during his term of office, 1920 to 1924, he would not approve of any increase in the tax rate.[3]

The smaller oil and gas producers, along with other extractive enterprises such as timber companies, likewise opposed all severance taxes. But they had anticipated Standard's battery of expensive lawyers' doing all the fighting. Standard's "gentlemen's agreement" with Parker took them by surprise; after brief outcries, however, they endorsed the understanding. The governor's 2 percent tax easily passed the legislature. Parker had wanted a higher rate, but was anxious to see increased revenue for state institutions—his favorite project being a new and better Louisiana State University—and he feared, with sound reason, that litigation would stall for years the collection of a larger severance tax. Parker had a lifelong abhorrence of legal delays and obfuscations, and he generally disliked lawyers.[4] One young lawyer in particular was beginning to arouse his ire.

Huey Long's first public attack on Parker came while the General Assembly debated oil and gas pipeline legislation; the commissioner said the governor was "going soft" on his campaign pledges. He also criticized the "gentlemen's agreement" on severance taxes as being too low (by this time, Huey had sold most of his stock in Pine Island oil). The break with Parker had become irrevocable by November, when Huey wrote one of Parker's closest friends that "the Standard Oil Company has practically taken charge of affairs" and that the governor was an egotistical weakling "who must be daily and weekly told of his wonderful greatness and . . . beautiful characteristics." Huey closed the letter by declaring: "I am not worrying about my own political future. I am disgusted with public life."[5]

Huey's alleged disgust with politics seemed less genuine than his expressions of disdain, during this same period, for various members of his family. By 1920, his Shreveport law practice and railroad commissioner's salary had made him moderately prosperous, and he was called upon to financially aid two siblings—Callie and Earl—and to help his father. He resented it. Callie, named for her deceased mother, was two years older than Huey and suffered from tuberculosis. At the time, a dry climate and rest were considered the best treatment for the disease, so Callie traveled to New Mexico and later to Arizona. Huey reluctantly agreed to contribute thirty dollars per month for her board. But he became increasingly suspicious of two things: that Callie was not following the regimen she was supposed to, and that nobody else in the family was doing much toward her support.[6]

His suspicion had some foundation. Callie moved about from one desert town to the next, writing "Huey dearest" that she was in debt and needed more money. When he heard she had gone to a party, he did not chide her, but wrote Julius: "This thing has now gone on for three years and it has gotten down to the point of being ridiculous. She is attending social functions and playing the society game while I am here starving to death." In another letter to Julius he demanded to know, "just who is sending her money besides me, and how much and how often?" It was a reasonable question, but Huey followed with the brutal remark that sister Callie reminded him "of a blind ox traveling over the country expecting to be sheltered at whatever place it might stop."[7]

Toward his younger brother, Earl, Huey was often critical and suspicious. "Earl," he wrote Julius in 1920, "shows less hope of being any thing than anybody that I know of." He asserted that Earl "never appreciated any single thing that I ever did for him," although there is little evidence Huey at any time helped Earl, besides giving him a lucrative state job when Huey became governor—in return for which Earl took care of their aged father. Yet it was Earl who paid Huey's $125 qualifying fee for railroad commissioner in 1918 and who campaigned across the district for him. A year later, Huey refused to contribute toward sending Earl to law school. (Huey did try, unsuccessfully, to persuade New Orleans attorney Charles J. Rivet, who had coached him for his own bar exam, into providing Earl with cheap board.) "I have only one objection to sending Earl to law school," Huey explained to Callie. "And that is I know he does not want to study law." Besides, he told Julius, "I am not going to raise up a man with no more principle than he [Earl] has, to do me harm." [8]

Julius and Huey continued to have the rockiest relationship of any of the Long siblings. "Julius always felt that Huey would look to him like an older brother," sister Callie once observed, then added, in a model of understatement: "But Huey had a mind of his own." [9] Prior to becoming a lawyer, Huey occasionally took Julius' advice; afterward, he would not. By 1920, Huey was trying to tell Julius what to do, as if he were Julius' uncle instead of a younger brother. Huey advised Julius not to make a planned race for district judge; rather, Julius should work hard to become a better lawyer. This was good advice, but it must have burned like fire. Later, after Julius' defeat in the judicial contest, Huey suggested they once again form a law partnership. Julius unwisely agreed; in December of 1920, at age forty-one and newly married, he joined his twenty-seven-year-old brother in Shreveport as, in effect, a junior partner. For the second time, the firm of Long and Long would have a brief life. [10]

In asking Julius to join him in Shreveport, Huey probably acted out of convoluted motives. He wanted to help the elder brother who had often aided him yet also had tried to boss him; now Huey had an opportunity to play the same game. He would show Julius, and the entire family, who was the top Long. Inevitably, the partnership was as doomed as the one five years earlier. Within seven months, by August of 1921, Huey had ordered Julius to vacate the premises. Julius then set up independent practice in Shreveport. An acrimonious correspondence followed, focusing on who had helped whom in the past. Julius also referred to "your disposition to boss and show off," whereas Huey summed up his own view in these words: "After you were defeated for judge, I found you in Winnfield, a broken-down and past-handed politician. . . . I picked you up and brought you here to Shreveport." Yet toward year's end, in a rare admission of any blame, Huey mailed a sad note to Julius. "It is . . . unfortunate," he wrote, "that our mutual faults and temperaments [made it impossible to work in harmony]. I am only too sorry."[11]

For Huey, close personal relationships were difficult to establish and harder to maintain. Toward people in the mass—particularly the poor and suffering—he commiserated, but with few exceptions he distrusted and scorned individuals. True, Huey never liked being alone. Yet his need for companionship revealed an even stronger urge: he must always be the central figure. So powerful was his self-absorption that little affection could be felt for anyone else, and his cynicism about the motives of others bordered on the absolute.

Huey almost never spoke about his deceased mother, but what he thought of his father, who would outlive him, may be gleaned from comments to other family members and from his deliberate lack of contact with the old man. His feelings were an amalgam of indifference and disdain. Of all Hugh's sons, the one he named after himself most resembled him physically, and both men possessed what was described as "a roaring voice." But in a family of assertive personalities, Hugh was relatively timid. He permitted others to take charge of his life—first his father, John, then his wife Caledonia. Huey knew this and apparently concluded that his father was a weakling. Old Hugh loved to talk, and twice he ran for local office; he was badly whipped both times.[12] After his wife's death he became increasingly dependent on his children. This dependence most annoyed the son who bore his name.

When, in 1920, Hugh asked his sons for a loan to buy land on which to raise hogs, Huey wrote brother Shan in Oklahoma: "If the old man can't make out on what he has got we will just have to let [him] go. It may be the best thing any way not to put out any more money. Let him piddle around on what he already has." A year later, Hugh remarried and moved near the village of Montgomery, twenty-five miles south of Winnfield, in Grant Parish. Scornfully, Huey wrote Shan that their father was now "in a new community, where he can find several hundred people who will be glad to listen to him talk at all hours of the day or night time, and possibly will be immeasurably contented."[13]

Huey resented members of his family when they looked to him for assistance. In his opinion, their aid to him when he was younger had been insufficient. Nor had they recognized his superiority. Moreover, he began saying, the Longs were trying to thwart his ambitions—to hold him back. Only with his sister Charlotte, known as Lottie, was he able to remain on relatively cordial terms. Oldest of the Long children, Lottie was seventeen years Huey's senior and had departed Winnfield when he was quite young. Their general lack of hostility probably reflected their minimal contact. Apparently, Lottie never made demands on Huey. In a remarkable 1920 letter to her, referring to their kin, he wailed:

> It seems that every member of my family thinks that if I get 15¢, I should send it to some member of it; they all want to borrow, want gifts, in fact want everything I make, and they offer on top of this to write me any kind of ridiculous and insulting letter that may come into their heads.
>
> Every cent I've got I made. I was never sent to school by any body; I came back and had to fight the whole family to accumulate any reputation. I am very much disgusted with their present and their past attitude and snarl of their teeth.[14]

Huey also denigrated his wife Rose's two brothers, David and Lee McConnell. "They borrowed incessantly," he wrote their sister Aline, "and never repaid; they used every piece of property that I owned and used it as their own."[15] Aline McConnell, however, was one in-law he did not belittle. Judging by his letters to her, he esteemed Aline more than any of his blood sisters, including Lottie. Aline was also nearly unique in being someone Huey helped from his own pockets without expecting repayment.

Aline, like Huey's sister Callie, sought recovery from tuberculosis in the arid Southwest. But there the similarity ended. Aline followed orders; she checked into the Long Sanitarium (run by Dr. Arthur Long, a cousin of Huey's) in El Paso, Texas, and remained there through 1921. Huey regularly paid her expenses of $125 per month with no hint of complaint. He also mailed Aline spending money—for which she never asked—and told her, "When you need more let me know and I will send it." Aline's letters to Huey indicate the reason for his uncharacteristic generosity. "Peaches" (as she signed her letters to him) obviously adored him, although their relationship seems to have been platonic. He was her hero, and she—a sweet, helpless, undemanding young female—summoned forth his latent sense of chivalry.

Huey was delighted when he learned she was reading one of his favorite novels, *Les Miserables*. Predictably, he advised her to read Ridpath's *History of the World*.[16]

A month after Julius' forced departure from the Shreveport Long and Long law firm, Huey composed another of his many letters to Aline. It is one of the most revealing he ever wrote anyone. "My offices are pretty now," Huey began. "I have large nice rugs on all three floors. . . . Only the name 'Huey P. Long' adorns these offices. I am governor, mayor, king and clerk. No . . . other authority has a right even to be heard." Less happily, he told Aline that "Julius seems to regard me as a dangerous power." He closed, "Sincerely, your brother, Huey P. Long."[17]

For all his attention to family matters and his legal practice, Huey always subordinated them to the pursuit of politics. To someday be governor had been one of his goals since childhood. By 1920, he apparently had decided that the next gubernatorial election, in 1924, was his target date, for at this time he ceased flattering other politicians by suggesting them as candidates. More to the point, in August of 1923 he would reach his thirtieth birthday, and the state constitution specified "the age of thirty years" as the legal minimum for a governor. Huey often had complained about his youth being a handicap, and he resented not being able to run in 1920.[18] He was caught in the grip of restless ambition of a strength few individuals have ever known; his urge to hold a powerful office was of primal force.

To Governor John M. Parker, 1920 was the most gratifying year of his life, despite the loud barking of his recent supporter Commissioner Huey Long. Being governor was never in itself one of Parker's goals, but his sometimes self-righteous sense of duty impelled him toward specific objectives he believed to be in the public interest, and by year's end three of these had been accomplished: First, the "gentlemen's agreement" with Standard Oil, and its approval by the legislature, guaranteed the state a modest severance tax revenue for upgrading LSU and other institutions. Second, Parker's proposal for a constitutional convention, to be held early in 1921, was approved by the voters in November. Third—and best of all from Parker's viewpoint—New Orleans' municipal election in September had dealt the hated Ring machine its first defeat in over twenty years.[19]

The Ring—also known after 1896 as the Choctaw Club and as the Regular Democratic Organization—had become the nearest thing in the South to New York's Tammany Hall. That is to say, it was a big-city combine of ward politicians, often corrupt but supported by most working-class voters, that existed chiefly to perpetuate its leaders in office. The organization depended upon patronage for survival. Patronage meant not only dispensing municipally selected positions and jobs, but also controlling state employment within the city. In highly politicized (and poor) Louisiana, lacking effective civil service laws, public workers voted for those who could give, or take away, jobs. Since families customarily voted as a bloc, one state or parish or municipal paycheck usually meant four or five votes. Voting strength based on patronage was augmented by fraudulent ballots. Successful fraud depended upon manipulating the selection of the precinct commissioners, who policed election-day activity at the voting booths and who signed the tally sheets as "correct." More common than outright fraud was the payment of poor supporters' poll taxes; the machine then made sure its people went to the polls on election day. Even at its worst, however, the Ring never perpetrated—because it dared not—the stupendous vote trickery evident in upstate cotton-plantation parishes during the 1890s. Active opposition by much of New Orleans' business elite kept that sort of thing from happening. City elections were hotly contested. The Ring was not invincible.

Martin Behrman's portly torso filled the New Orleans mayor's chair from 1904 until his 1920 defeat. He was also the Ring's leader in the Fifteenth Ward (Algiers, across the river from downtown). Although Mayor Behrman was the organization's central figure, he shared power with sixteen other ward bosses; they regularly caucused as the "Council of Seventeen." Every four years a crucial decision had to be made—which of the various Democratic aspirants for Louisiana's governorship should the Ring endorse? Ring support did not always mean victory in the state-wide election, but it usually did. With a high machine-organized voter turnout, New Orleans accounted for about 30 percent of the total vote in Louisiana elections, although by 1920 the city held only 21.5 percent of the state's population. New Orleans' delegation in the General Assembly, 20 percent of both senators and representatives, ordinarily formed a bloc to protect the city's interests. Thus, the city machine was a force both in Louisiana elections and in legislation. But in both cases the Ring's basic objectives were defensive: to prevent state interference in New Orleans affairs, and to confer with a friendly governor about state patronage in the metropolis.[20]

Behrman was born to a poor Jewish couple in New York City shortly before the end of the Civil War. This family of three moved to New Orleans while Martin was still an infant. Soon after their arrival the father died, and Martin's first memories were of his mother and a little dry goods stall she set up in the French Market. At age nine he witnessed the September 14, 1874, White League uprising that hastened the end of Reconstruction. The boy found and kept a souvenir of the event—a rifle tossed away by a fleeing member of the Republican Metropolitan Police. Three years later, when Martin was twelve, his mother died. If he had relatives, he did not know where they were.

Martin was now a street waif, relying on his wits to survive. Because he was energetic and eager to please, the boy found employment in various New Orleans stores; he spent part of his meager pay to study mathematics and English in a night school. At twenty-two he became a partner in an Algiers grocery store. Converting to Catholicism, he married into a gentile family and began working his way up the Ring's Fifteenth Ward organization. Behrman explained his success in politics by saying, "I made a great many friends simply by being polite and cordial to people."[21]

But growing up alone, without opportunity for a decent education, left lifelong scars on Martin Behrman. As mayor, he resented the "silk stockings"—those patrician reformers, including John M. Parker, who fought him politically and, he suspected, made fun of his manners and diction from the elegant confines of their Boston and Pickwick clubs. Yet opponents conceded him innate ability. Behrman had many political but few personal enemies; conciliatory by nature, he generally followed his slogan: "Let's get togedder." The mayor lived frugally and was never seriously accused of private dishonesty, although some of the Ring's leaders were transparently corrupt. Reformers frequently admitted that "Martin Behrman is better than his crowd."[22]

For all its shortcomings, the machine during Behrman's years seems to have provided New Orleans with a government that satisfied a majority of voters most of the time. Certainly it was an improvement over the Ring of the 1880s, which almost took the city to anarchy. During its reorganization following defeat in the mayoralty race of 1896, when the Ring reemerged as the Choctaw Club (Regular Democratic Organization), its circle was widened to take in part of the city's economic and social elite, even including several members of the Boston and Pickwick clubs. By 1920, Mayor Behrman could point to marked improvements in public services and health that had taken place during his sixteen-year regime: the first public sewage and waterworks systems in the city's history; the first effective storm drainage system; the eradication of yellow fever; the paving of most streets (at least in white neighborhoods); and considerably more. New Orleans, after all, was then the only major American city at a subtropical latitude, and its flat, sea-level topography always created special difficulties for health and services. That Behrman tolerated some graft and much vice is hardly praiseworthy, but those practices began concurrently with the city in 1718, and were as bad or worse both before and after he was mayor. During the Prohibition years 1920 to 1933, New Orleans was considered "the worst wet spot in the country" by the Washington chief of prohibition agents. And prostitution, as Behrman had warned, moved from Storyville to the streets after the district was closed by federal pressure in 1917. Behrman thought it foolish to try to change the habits and morals of such a cosmopolitan port city. He probably would have agreed with H. L. Mencken's 1930 summation of New Orleans as being a place "with a touch of Paris, and another of Port Said."[23]

Although Behrman and his reformer opponents were about equally guilty of placing special business interests above the common good, Behrman was the less culpable, for he insisted upon a municipally owned waterworks, and in 1915 arranged a reduction in electricity rates. But both the Ring and John M. Parker's reformers kept on friendly terms with the New Orleans Railway and Light Company, which employed a monopoly on trolley, electricity, and gas service to the city. The monopoly's rates were among the nation's highest, and years after Louisiana became an abundant producer of cheap natural gas, the company still insisted on supplying New Orleans with only high-priced artificial gas. Public ownership of these utilities was never seriously considered, and regulation was ineffectual at best. Other major business interests in the city received equally respectful consideration. The Ring expressed more sympathy

for labor—at least, voting laborers—than did the patrician reformers, and it tried to provide jobs and charity for its poor supporters, but businessmen who contributed generously to the
Ring's Choctaw Club found sympathetic ears in City Hall. Did
the Ring sell itself? An astute observer said no, the machine was
not for sale—it was for rent.[24]

Crushing the Ring was John M. Parker's obsession. He had
hated it all his adult life, and now, as governor, he successfully
used patronage to defeat Behrman and all but one Ring council-
man in the September, 1920, municipal elections. The mayor, as
was his nature, had been willing to make a deal with Parker, just
as he had done with the one previous governor (Luther Hall,
1912–1916) who came to office as a foe of the Ring. For his part,
Parker claimed he held no personal animosity toward Behrman.
But "Let's get togedder" proved impossible with a governor bent
on destroying the system Behrman represented. Ironically, the
narrow mayoralty victory of Parker's businessman candidate,
Andrew McShane, was accomplished by a new, rival city machine built up with patronage dispensed by Governor Parker.
This was the Orleans Democratic Association.[25]

Huey Long applauded Parker's ODA victory over the Ring,
but having broken with the governor over pipeline regulation
and the tax agreement with Standard Oil, Huey fought Parker's
call for a constitutional convention in 1921. He claimed that
"henchmen . . . of the Standard Oil Company and other monop-
olies" would be in charge. Huey was able to persuade Winn and
most old Populist parishes to vote against having a convention,
but the proposition won easily state-wide.[26] Since most of the
convention delegates were chosen in a general election and not
by an all-white Democratic primary, the state's few hundred registered blacks were entitled to vote as well as to announce for
delegate posts. None did run—the racial climate by this time
was so harsh that becoming a corpse would have been more
likely than being elected. Yet the fact that it was even possible
for black candidates to enter delegate races so alarmed ex-
governor Pleasant that he suggested a new way of exclusion—
without mentioning race. Only those Louisiana citizens should
be eligible, Pleasant advised, "whose ancestry immediately previous to the discovery of America by Christopher Columbus in
the year 1492, anno Domini, inhabited any part of the earth
north of the 20° north latitude, as shown by historical and an-

thropolitical [*sic*] evidence."[27] This proposal was not acted upon by the legislature, it being unnecessary: the 118 elected and 12 appointed delegates were all presumably Caucasians.

The Constitution of 1921 emerged as a watered-down version of Governor Parker's original proposals, but it satisfied him. Most of the convention's time was taken up with severance tax arguments. Article X authorized the legislature to raise the tax above 2 percent, a proposal Parker at first opposed because it violated his "gentlemen's agreement." Later, after talking with spokesmen from Standard Oil and other extractive interests, he and they agreed: on condition that the constitution specify that no other taxes, state or local, could be levied upon the removal of, or assessments raised upon the land bearing, these natural resources, the industries would accept a modest increase in the severance tax. As part of the deal, Parker and his followers in the legislature informally agreed that during his administration the tax would not be raised above 2.5 percent.[28] (In 1922 the legislature increased the rate on oil and gas to 3 percent, with Parker's approval, after he and the industries made another adjustment in their agreement.) This understanding would bring additional revenue for upgrading Louisiana's public institutions, but like the original "gentlemen's agreement," it could be interpreted as a capitulation, or even a sellout, to Standard Oil. To Huey Long, it was just more ammunition.

On matters less controversial at the time, the Constitution of 1921 was hesitantly progressive. Previously, road construction and maintenance had been the task—often ignored—of local government. Now the state shouldered this responsibility. In the early 1920s, Louisiana's "highways" were arguably the worst in America, partly because of public indifference, but also because of the semiaquatic terrain of much of the state. Expensive raised roadbeds and pavement were necessary in the alluvial parishes if automobiles were to go from one town to the next without bogging down, while in the hilly districts, the red clay roadbeds changed with the weather from rock-hard to a gluelike substance. Louisiana also contained more rivers than any state of comparable size—a transportation advantage in the age of steamboats, but not in the twentieth century. Bridges were needed to replace slow ferries, but bridges spanning the numerous wide rivers meant great additional expenses. Governor Parker, recognizing the need for better public transportation but

being innately cautious, accepted the advice of former governor
J. Y. Sanders and persuaded the constitutional convention to
adopt a "pay-as-you-go" plan for road construction, instead of
floating bond issues.[29] Parker also suggested, and the new constitution included, a provision for the state's first tax on incomes.
It was not progressive. "My personal viewpoint," Parker wrote,
"is a flat income tax is preferable." Indeed it was flat: the Constitution of 1921 set the maximum rate at 3 percent, and subsequent legislatures failed to enact even this. Not until 1934,
during Huey Long's regime, was an income tax (with rates graduated up to 6 percent by constitutional amendment) voted by
the legislature.[30]

John M. Parker seldom went back on his word, but he did so
on the issue of civil service in New Orleans. At the time of the
1921 convention, Parker's prestige was—temporarily—stronger
than that most Louisiana governors have enjoyed, and at his
urging the new constitution authorized the legislature to "provide for civil service in municipalities having a population of
100,000 or more [i.e., New Orleans], and for the recognition and
adoption of the merit system in the employment or appointment
of all applicants." In his campaign, Parker had pledged "true
civil service" for the city, in order to destroy the patronage
power of the Ring. But he seemed satisfied merely to have this
high-sounding declaration written into the constitution; he
never asked the legislature to pass an enabling act.

Apparently Governor Parker's failure to pursue civil service
was due to pressure from the new mayor, and also from the real
power behind the "reform" ODA organization, John P. Sullivan.
A former Ring ward leader, Sullivan had fallen out with Mayor
Behrman, had backed Parker for governor and McShane for
mayor, and hoped to be the next boss of New Orleans. Parker
hated the old Ring so much that he was willing to cooperate
with a new machine trying to take its place.[31]

On political rights, the Constitution of 1921 accepted women
as voters because it had to, female suffrage having come the previous year through the Nineteenth Amendment to the United
States Constitution; Louisiana was one of the few states that
had refused to ratify the amendment. Most Louisiana politicians, and even the sisters Kate and Jean Gordon, leaders of the
largest woman-suffrage organization in the state, opposed the
federal amendment because they feared its wording would open

the door to black women as voters. (A false rumor circulated in Louisiana that the federal amendment "had been written by a negro.") Black women, according to John M. Parker's campaign manager, were "far more fearless" than black men. Jean Gordon warned that "a federal amendment" would place "negro women . . . on the same basis with white women, and while white men [are] willing to club black men away from the polls they would not use the club upon black women." [32] The accuracy of this prediction was not tested; few Louisiana black women bothered to register, since the state Democratic party still excluded blacks from membership and thus from participation in the only elections that usually meant anything.

The new constitution's provisions for voter registration demonstrated Louisiana's continuing fixation upon race. Although the Democratic party managed to keep itself specifically all-white until 1944, a state constitution had to avoid treading directly on the Fourteenth and Fifteenth amendments, so subterfuges were still required to discourage blacks, now including women, from voting in general elections. An old device in the 1898 constitution, the "grandfather clause," was no longer usable because in 1915 the Supreme Court had declared it unconstitutional.[33] In its place, the 1921 state constitution substituted an "understanding" and "good character and reputation" clause, as other southern states had already done, authorizing registrars to accept illiterate applicants who, in the registrars' opinion, could understand the state or federal constitution when read to them *and* were persons "of good character and reputation." (Translation: uneducated whites would be allowed to vote, but not blacks.) The clause also required that literate persons, in addition to filling out the proper forms, must be able to read "and give a reasonable interpretation" of a passage selected by the registrar from either the federal or state constitution. A handful of blacks were still permitted to register as Republicans or independents in New Orleans, but in most parishes after 1921, all voters for all elections were listed as white.[34]

In some ways, the Constitution of 1921 reflected the impact of progressivism in Louisiana. Among the reforms already effected in several other southern states, the new document created a Public Service Commission to replace the feeble Railroad Commission, and it authorized juvenile courts of justice. It also empowered the legislature to levy gasoline taxes and automobile license-tag fees (to be used for building a pay-as-you-go highway system), and to regulate the hours, working conditions, and wages of females. This last reform was intended only for white women or children, as witness a telltale "except" that crept into the provision: "except those employed in agricultural pursuits or in domestic service."[35]

Aside from its racial purposes, the Constitution of 1921—which, with multitudinous amendments, would serve Louisiana until 1974—was guilty of excessive detail. Most constitutions are blueprints for legislative action, but from its inception this one was a three-dimensional edifice, and the General Assembly (which, incidentally, the new document would rename as the "Legislature") kept adding to its baroque superstructure by piling on amendments, most of which the voters, in low turnouts, approved. Governor Parker had not intended this agglomeration of minutiae, but his ignorance of law and his deficiencies as a leader allowed it to happen. He told the convention delegates what he thought they ought to do, then stepped aside with these words: "Put in whatever else your independent and wise judgment dictates."[36] The result was the longest written constitution in the history of the United States, if not of the world. By 1964, it had ballooned to 277,000 words. "Specialists in state government," an authority on Louisiana history has written, "came to regard the [Constitution of 1921] as a perfect example of what a . . . constitution should *not* be."[37]

When the constitutional convention renamed and strengthened the Railroad (Public Service) Commission, the delegates who were closest to Parker tried, and failed, to have the incumbent commissioners thereby removed from office. Obviously, their target was Huey Long. Huey had already been alienated from the Parker administration; now he was disgusted—or pretended to be. As happened so often, Huey's foes were playing into his hands. He could cite the attempt to end his term as proof that Standard Oil's Louisiana flunkies were trying to silence the people's one true champion. His launched his severest attack in a mimeographed circular of September 27, issued while the legislature was meeting in special session to pass enabling acts pursuant to the new constitution. Every legislator had a copy placed on his desk. The circular was Huey's roughest yet. It claimed that Standard and allied corporations were brazenly running Louisiana's government and that the Parker administration was acting "in a manner unbecoming an ancient ruler of a Turkish domain." For an example, he cited Parker's appointing the son of Standard Oil's chief Louisiana legal counsel as superintendent of Charity Hospital in New Orleans. By the time of his assault on the governor, Huey also had taken on his two fellow members of the Public Service Commission, implying to reporters that both had sold out to a Louisiana subsidiary of Bell Telephone. Most legislators were shocked at these charges. Representative John Dymond said it was time "to appoint a lunacy commission to inquire into the sanity of Huey P. Long."[38]

Promptly, Governor Parker filed affidavits against Huey for criminal libel. John M. Parker had been called many things before—a "nigger lover" (which he decidedly was not), a consorter with Republicans, and a murderer. But the commissioner's accusations were, in Parker's opinion, worse; Huey Long, the governor exclaimed, was "the only man who had ever attacked [my] character." Parker added that if Long's charges were true, he was unfit to be governor—but if they were false, Long should be removed from office and put in jail. The sheriff of Caddo Parish phoned Huey at his Shreveport home and told him warrants had been issued for his arrest. Immediately, Long drove to Baton Rouge and posted bond. His trial was set for November (1921). Meanwhile, during October, the legislature investigated his charges against the other commissioners and passed a resolution, never acted upon, recommending impeachment proceedings against all three members of the Public Service Commission.[39]

Criminal libel trials were rare in Louisiana. In earlier times, those among the leadership class, such as politicians and newspaper editors, were apt to use the *code duello* if their honor or character were questioned; ordinary men often resorted to unannounced affrays with pistols, knives, or fists. Bloody street encounters still took place fairly frequently in Louisiana during the 1920s and 1930s, but the state's last formal duel had occurred near Shreveport in 1893—the year of Huey Long's birth—when the editors of the Baton Rouge *Advocate* and the Shreveport *Progress* exchanged shots with dueling pistols; neither was hurt, which disappointed a throng of spectators.[40] Parker in 1921 believed he must respond to Huey Long's insults in some decisive fashion, and since the dignity of his office as well as changing times seemed to rule out personal violence, the gov-

ernor decided to employ the legal weapon of a criminal libel
suit. It had been successfully used only once before by a prominent Louisiana politician, in 1905, when Mayor Behrman was
able to have the New Orleans *Item*'s publisher, Dominick O'Malley, sent to parish prison.[41]

Governor Parker did not fare as well in his suit as Behrman
had against O'Malley. For once, Huey placed caution above ego,
and used a team of reputable lawyers instead of acting as his
own counsel. Heading his defense was James Palmer of Shreveport, who nourished gubernatorial ambitions and, according to
Julius Long, took the case without a fee in return for Huey's
worthless promise of support in the 1924 state election. Working
with Palmer was Robert E. Reid of Tangipahoa Parish. Huey rewarded both men by naming his newborn son Palmer Reid
Long. Julius also joined his brother's team, despite the recent
blowup of their partnership in Shreveport. The trial began November 3 and lasted six days. It was highlighted by lengthy testimony from the two antagonists, Governor Parker and Commissioner Long. The governor bristled under defense questioning
about his "gentlemen's agreement" with Standard Oil, which he
admitted entering because he saw nothing wrong with it. Long,
he kept saying, was "a liar" in ascribing evil motives to the arrangement. Huey's testimony was the more restrained and effective; he made telling use of Parker's own words. Judge Harney F.
Brunot's decision allowed both sides to claim victory. The commissioner was found guilty on two counts of criminal libel, but
received only a thirty-day suspended sentence on one count and
a one-dollar fine on the other. When Huey refused to pay the fine,
his lawyer Palmer paid it instead.[42]

Thomas O. Harris, once a reporter for Hearsey's *States*, then
an editor for O'Malley's *Item* and for Ewing's Shreveport *Times*,
and more recently employed by the Independent Oil and Gas
Producers Association, by 1921 had taken on a new job—personal secretary to Governor Parker. Probably no one knew both
Parker and Long better than Harris, who admired the former
and detested the latter. In his biography *The Kingfish*, published
three years after Long's death, Harris insisted that "since vindication was all that Governor Parker had sought," the verdict satisfied him. More likely, Parker would have relished seeing Huey
in jail. Huey, for his part, adroitly used the trial to help make
himself chairman of the Public Service Commission. In this he

also had a piece of morbid luck: the death, late in November of 1921, of Commissioner John T. Michel of New Orleans. Michel, a Ring personage, always voted for rate increases; in a special election, his seat was won by Francis Williams, an anti-Ring city politician allied with John P. Sullivan. As soon as Williams took his seat, in April of 1922, he moved that Huey P. Long be made chairman of the three-man commission. The motion passed two to one.[43]

Huey and his ally Williams were masters of the Public Service Commission. The third member was the former chairman, Shelby Taylor of Baton Rouge, whom Long had castigated as a "tool" of the corporations who ought to be removed in a recall election. (Taylor presently saw the light and went over to Huey's side).[44] A whopping rate increase that the telephone company had been granted in 1921 over Huey's objections was now suspended, and after litigation going all the way up to the United States Supreme Court, the Bell System in 1923 compromised by accepting a more modest rise in rates and refunding $440,000 to its 80,000 Louisiana customers. Huey knew how to exploit victories, and although most of his potential supporters in the pending gubernatorial race did not have telephones, poor people across Louisiana were beginning to believe that somebody important named Huey Long was fighting on the side of working folk. "You would be surprised," the New Orleans *States* was told by "a prominent man" from rural southeastern Louisiana, "how overwhelming this Long sentiment is with the rank and file of our people. They don't know Huey Long. They never saw him. . . . But they know him in name and you can't make them believe he is not their defender."[45]

During 1922 and 1923, Huey's fight against Standard Oil continued, but without a decision. Using the courts, Standard was able to prevent both its pipelines and its huge Baton Rouge refinery from being classified as public utilities, which would have meant regulation by the Long-controlled PSC. Huey probably did not desire a real victory over Standard at this time, even if one could have been achieved. A dragon should not be slain by a mere public service commissioner. St. George ought to have at least the title of governor.

· 8 ·

LONG OUR NEXT GOVERNOR

Huey announced for governor the day he turned thirty, August 30, 1923. The Democratic primary was five months away, but already several hopefuls either had announced or were sending up trial balloons. Holding that powerful office was the ultimate dream of most local politicians. As a future chief executive, Edwin Edwards, correctly observed, "The governor of Louisiana is the keystone of political life in our state."[1]

One candidate who declared but soon withdrew because he saw no chance for victory was James Palmer of Shreveport. Huey apparently had offered to support him in exchange for Palmer's unpaid work in the 1921 libel trial; according to some reports, Palmer even paid Huey's five-thousand-dollar bond. But soon after the wealthy jurist announced, Huey issued a press release attacking him for having once represented Sinclair Oil, a subsidiary of John D. Rockefeller's Standard. "Four years ago," Huey added, "we put one millionaire Governor in office. We have paid a sad and heavy price for our super-folly, and we do not want another one." As for Palmer's aid to Huey, the commissioner dismissed that by pointing out, "He was in only one [of my battles] and no more."[2]

Months prior to his formal announcement, Huey tantalized those urging him to run by first indicating he would, then saying he would not, be a candidate in the January, 1924, gubernatorial primary, victory in which would be the same as election to the office, as the Republicans did not bother to put up a token candidate that year. Huey's personal files for 1923 include many penciled letters on cheap composition paper from admirers across rural north Louisiana who were encouraging him to run. Typical was the note sent by a former Socialist of Winn Parish, Rich P. Parker, who had moved to Franklin Parish and now offered "to lend every available assistance possible" if Huey decided to become a candidate. An echo from the Populist-Republican coalition of the past was also heard: Don Caffery, Jr., the last fusionist gubernatorial candidate (1900) to oppose the state's Democratic oligarchs, wrote the youthful commissioner several prodding letters during 1923, having sensed in Huey an opportunity at last for vindication and revenge against those Caffery called, in old Populist terminology, "the plutocrats."[3]

Huey's monumental ego sometimes tugged against reality's anchor, but never broke loose. He regularly deceived others, but seldom if ever himself. His chances of winning the governorship in 1924 were slim at best, and he understood that. He did not have a working organization in most parishes, virtually all the state's power brokers disliked him and scoffed at his candidacy, and as expected, his conservative opponents gathered in more campaign money. Nevertheless, there was a possibility his energy and ingenuity might overcome all obstacles. He was already a master at grabbing headlines, and his platform spoke to needs that had not been met by Louisiana's previous leadership.

Good roads and schools were Huey Long's positive themes during the gubernatorial campaign of 1923–1924. Compared with most other states, Louisiana was still in the mud, and illiterate. There were reasons beyond official indifference for this backwardness: roads were difficult to build or maintain in such a watery environment, and public education had special problems in a society that was not only poor and biracial, as in other southern states, but was also divided by language and religion. Even so, the unconcern of Louisiana's politicoeconomic elite was the root problem—an indifference owing to both short-sightedness and an aversion to taxation.

"When you mention 'good roads' to some people," the St. Francisville *True Democrat* complained, "they act as though a death had occurred in the family, and begin to conjure up visions of excessive taxation, bankruptcy, graft, and such kindred bug bears." That attitude on the part of the elite was beginning to change, but only slightly, by the time Huey Long first ran for governor. The first Louisiana chief executive to realize the need for improved roadways was J. Y. Sanders, under whose administration (1908–1912) the Highway Department was created; yet that department had little more than a paper existence, since construction was still the responsibility of parish governments. Beyond trying to stir public interest, there was little that Governor Sanders could do. He concisely described most Louisiana roads as "trails that could be traveled sometimes in good weather."[4]

The Pelican State had seen its first automobile in 1899, when a little Montgomery Ward electric braved the streets of New Orleans. Excited boys ran after it for blocks. But not until the end of World War I were autos a common sight outside the cities; postwar prosperity allowed many ordinary whites, and some blacks, to buy at least a Model T Ford. Only then did the good-roads movement stir to life in Louisiana, as thousands of first-time car owners began to complain of wretched streets and roadways. Even the tall and rugged Model T had difficulty coping with Louisiana mud, but its popularity was such that in 1922 a "Ford Day" festival was held at Opelousas, in which Auguste Jeansonne, at age 111 the state's oldest white person, was chauffeured across town, accompanied by his 92-year-old daughter.[5]

The need for better roads was dramatized by mishaps occurring on a 1919 trip by Governor Pleasant, Mayor Behrman, and other Louisiana dignitaries along the so-called Jefferson Highway, a muddy, gravel-scattered route that ran diagonally across the state from New Orleans to Shreveport, then northward to Winnipeg, Canada. Nine automobiles left New Orleans on July 1, but "only six of the cars got through to Baton Rouge," and it took those all day. Once out of Louisiana, the survivors' journey to Canada was relatively swift and easy.[6]

The Constitution of 1921 recognized the need for a state highway system, but by adopting former governor Sanders' "pay-as-you-go" plan, meaning no bond issues for construction, Louisiana remained behind even Mississippi in paved mileage. Governor Parker responded to appeals from "the country people"—who, as one spokesman said, "have been kept in the mud long enough"—by primly agreeing that Louisiana needed better roadways, but stating that it was not his responsibility to propose how they might be built.[7] Nor did leadership on the matter come from Parker's successor, the winner of the 1924 governor's race, Henry L. Fuqua. The issue of good roads simply became more urgent as years passed, and would serve Huey Long admirably in the election of 1928.

Louisiana in the early 1920s was still the most illiterate part of America. Progress had been made since the dreadful time thirty years earlier, when 45.8 percent of all persons aged ten and above could not read and write in any language, but Louisiana remained at the bottom, below even Mississippi and South Carolina, the only states still with majority black populations. In 1920 Louisiana's illiteracy stood at 22 percent, more than three times the national average. Predictably, blacks were the worst off: 38.5 percent were unable to read and write in 1920, compared with 11.4 percent of whites.[8] Illiteracy among older blacks and whites was even higher because of neglect in the past (as late as 1906, over half the white adult males of Vermilion and Lafourche parishes could not read or write). "I admit," the state superintendent of education said in 1925, "it is . . . a little uncomfortable to occupy the top rung of the ladder in the matter of adult illiteracy."[9]

Private education had always been a refuge for well-to-do whites and Creoles of color. Public instruction in Louisiana also heavily favored whites, especially if they lived in localities where most inhabitants were blacks. The state dispensed its modest educational funds on the basis of total childhood population; each parish (and the subdivisions, called "wards") could distribute state money, plus local school taxes, as the all-white school board saw fit. Consequently, white children in mostly black districts enjoyed better schools than whites in the predominantly white parishes. As one patrician spokesman candidly admitted: "We get the benefit of [Negro] labor and help him use his school money. Don't you see?"[10]

Although white schools in most of the plantation parishes and adjacent urban areas (such as Shreveport and Monroe) were relatively good, education in areas where poorer whites were in the majority (such as Winnfield) lagged far behind. And throughout Louisiana public schools for blacks ranged from miserable to nonexistent. "The average negro school is little better than a farce," State Superintendent of Education T. H. Harris declared in 1909. He suggested that public education for blacks be either upgraded or abolished. Several legislators did propose virtual abolition, but by 1923 modest improvement had taken place even in black schools, largely because of outside charitable donations by the Rosenwald, Jeans, and Slater funds. Even so, in 1923 Louisiana had 280 high schools for whites and only 3 for blacks. During the 1920s Superintendent Harris noted that public transportation (buses and wagons) accommodated 32,495 rural white children but not a single black child because, in Harris' words, "public sentiment in Louisiana would not endorse the proposition of providing transportation for negro children at public expense." After 1916, state law required school attendance for children age seven to fourteen, yet the statute contained an ingenious catch that, without mentioning race, rendered it inoperative for blacks: "*exempted* . . . children living more than 2½ miles from a school of suitable grade where no free transportation is available; and children for whom adequate school facilities have not been provided."[11]

Huey's platform for his first gubernatorial campaign included the mendacious promise uttered by countless American politicians before and since: that he would increase public services, yet lower taxes, "by eliminating extravagance." But in advocating good roads and schools Huey was more emphatic than his two opponents, who uttered vague, cautious words of assent on those two needs. "We continue to wade in the mud where we had expected asphalt," Huey exclaimed, indicating that when he became governor he would propose a constitutional amendment to allow bond issues for construction. As to Louisiana's backward school system, Huey insisted the state should assume a much greater share of the burden, and provide free textbooks for school children. To conservatives, this was a radical proposal.[12]

As always, Huey was in his prime element when attacking. He understood the need for making constructive proposals, but hurling insults and ridicule was more fun. Besides, his core clientele enjoyed hearing him say those things: the poor and lower-middle-class rural whites, who had been deceived and bypassed so often, were listening to a man who seemed an instrument of their retribution. As W. J. Cash pointed out, whatever Huey might fail to do for his followers in the future, he did give them a delightful "vision of themselves, made one flesh with him, swarming over the battlements of Wall Street . . . and driving out of power its minions, the haughty gentlemen of New Orleans and Baton Rouge."[13]

Those among Louisiana's poorer whites who did not know, or

were only dimly aware, that they had been lied to and side-tracked in the past by what Huey called "the old political gang" were now told so in earthy language. His speaking style would improve in future years, as would his taste in clothes (although his still slim and youthful figure soon began to take on a hint of paunch and jowls). But the man's essential mannerisms were in place by 1923. He did more than just "speak" to a crowd or even a small group—he roared until his voice was hoarse. By contrast, in private with someone he wished to charm, he sometimes took on what a female reporter described as "magnetic gentleness." Usually he did not simply look at people during conversations, he leaned forward and stared, giving his dark brown eyes a protruding appearance. In front of an audience, "some part of him was always in motion"; he also had a propensity for scratching his left buttock—this habit was later modified to an occasional tug at his left trousers leg. On the rare occasions when he was listening to another public speaker, Huey's movements reminded a New York observer of the jerky, flickering figures in early silent films.[14]

After others withdrew their names, Huey faced two well-organized opponents in the 1923–1924 campaign for governor. Lieutenant Governor Hewitt Bouanchaud of Pointe Coupee Parish, who had faithfully served Governor Parker's administration, gained Parker's blessing. As the only Catholic in the race during a time of religious tension, Bouanchaud had a strong following among French Catholic voters. He also was endorsed in New Orleans by John P. Sullivan's "New Regulars," a revamped version of the anti-Ring Orleans Democratic Association that in 1920 had helped elect Parker governor and drive Behrman from the mayor's office. Henry L. Fuqua, Long's other rival, was an affable Baton Rouge hardware merchant who since 1916 had been general manager of Angola, the state penitentiary. "Marse Henry," as black convicts in Angola reportedly called Fuqua, was a Protestant of French Huguenot background, and his most important endorsement came from the rebuilding New Orleans Ring—the Choctaw Club, commonly referred to in the press as the "Old Regulars" to distinguish them from Sullivan's organization. Behrman and the Ring—the Old Regulars—were bouncing back from their defeats of 1920, and they proved strong enough to give Fuqua a lead in New Orleans. Soon Martin Behrman would again be mayor.[15]

Huey was attempting something that had never been done in Louisiana politics: to win the governorship without endorsements in New Orleans from either the machine or its "good government" opponents. Such a campaign had been seriously tried only once before, in 1912 by James B. Aswell, whose Populist-style rhetoric drew heavy support in rural north Louisiana. But Aswell made little headway in the French parishes and got virtually nothing in the metropolis. He came in a respectable third in the state (20 percent), but a miserable third in New Orleans (4.6 percent) even though he had backing from New Orleans *States* publisher Robert Ewing, who was also the Ring's maverick "Boss of the Tenth Ward." [16] But Huey, in his first race for the governorship, did not have a single Louisiana daily behind him, nor was he endorsed by more than three of the over one hundred weeklies in the state.

Seeing that he had virtually no press support, that his ballot potential among the poor was limited by the poll tax, and that there were few men of local power behind him, some observers marveled that Huey or anyone else could imagine he had a chance. A Thibodaux editor dismissed his prospects by pointing out that not one local banker, physician, or lawyer was supporting Long.[17] Yet Huey did have a few affluent contributors. Probably the wealthiest was William K. Henderson, a Shreveport iron manufacturer, realtor, and owner of the pioneer radio station KWKH. A Shreveport banker, Ernest Bernstein, whom Huey was representing in litigation against the Commercial National Bank, contributed $4,600 to his lawyer's campaign. One of Huey's numerous relatives, Swords Lee of Alexandria, a lumberman and road contractor, gave generously; he liked cousin Huey's highway-building proposals. As the race heated up, former governor Pleasant charged Huey with accepting $10,000 in cash from a public utility, Southwestern Gas Company, in return for a rate concession—Huey still chaired the Public Service Commission while he campaigned for governor. Later, Julius Long swore under oath that Pleasant's accusation was true.[18]

Ironically, New Orleans was the only place where Huey enjoyed something resembling an organization in the campaign of 1923–1924. A small team was patched together there by Francis Williams, Huey's ally on the Public Service Commission. Francis and his brother Augustus—"Gus"—were rising stars in Sullivan's New Regulars, but as soon as it became evident that the

125

New Regulars would stay loyal to Parker and support Bouanchaud, and that the Old Regulars were ready to endorse Fuqua,
the Williams brothers—who like Sullivan hoped to someday
control the city—decided to place their political bets on Huey's
future, and formed the Independent Regulars in his behalf.
"Give me a handful of city votes—no more than 15,000, and I'm
good as elected," Huey told the Williamses. "Just wait and see
what I do in the country."[19] Yet it was a large handful he asked
for, and the IR "organization" was merely a skeleton entity.

Although Huey lacked structured support, he had sufficient
money for a state-wide campaign, and he possessed more energy
than Fuqua and Bouanchaud combined. Crisscrossing Louisiana in a sturdy Hupmobile, he was up before daybreak, travers-
ing the muddy flatland or bumpy hill roads toward his next
scheduled speech. Most evenings he politicked until after midnight. Sometimes he would see that one of his posters had been
ripped from a tree or building, and he would tell his driver to
stop while he got out, stood on the hood of the Hupmobile, and
tacked a replacement higher up. A favorite poster had an image
of Huey and a simple slogan:

> Long
> Our
> Next
> Governor[20]

Rose accompanied Huey when he spoke in or near Shreveport, but usually she remained at home and mailed out campaign circulars. The two older children, Rose (six) and Russell
(five) helped her stuff envelopes.[21] By this time, however, Huey's
campaign team included a pert eighteen-year-old named Alice
Lee Grosjean, who many of Long's associates believed was his
mistress for most of the rest of his life.

Alice's physical attributes were obvious. Her face, excepting a
hard-lined mouth, was delicate; her hazel eyes were bright, her
dark hair stylishly done. She possessed a slim yet bosomy figure.
But some of Alice's less obvious qualities also recommended
her to a public man such as Huey. She was intelligent and dis-
creet; when interviewed, she demonstrated a talent for talking
without saying anything controversial. Moreover, although one
writer described her as coming from a "poverty-stricken" family,

she in fact boasted a patrician lineage: her paternal grandfather was Major Victor Grosjean, who from 1891 until 1926 was editor-publisher of the Shreveport *Caucasian*.[22]

When she was fifteen, Alice had dropped out of high school to elope with an Arkansan named James Terrell. By the time she met Huey three years later, she was working as a secretary in her hometown of Shreveport; she and Terrell seldom saw each other, although not until 1928 did they legally separate and divorce. Huey, for his part, was not a compulsive womanizer. His urge for public attention and power was far stronger than his sex drive. Some members of his entourage later claimed that he occasionally indulged in casual sex with other women, but that Alice Lee Grosjean was his only mistress—his only serious extramarital affair.[23] Apparently he cared about her and trusted her as much as his nature allowed for anyone.

"You tell 'em, Huey! Pour it on!" That and considerably less decorous shouts often punctuated the youthful candidate's orations to rural audiences in the Anglo-Protestant parishes. In December the school auditorium at Ringgold, in Bienville Parish, was for the first time "crowded to capacity" to hear him; a few days later the village of Pollock, in Grant Parish, witnessed "the largest crowd ever assembled" when Huey Long arrived. In the Acadian ("Cajun") parishes, crowds also turned out to hear the young candidate, but more out of curiosity than enthusiasm—for this was Catholic, Bouanchaud territory, and Huey was an upstate Baptist with rumored Ku Klux Klan connections. He tried to allay the Cajuns' suspicions, but with limited success. Occasionally, he endeavored to speak their *patois*, while claiming that his ancestry was partly French and Catholic. (Julius Long once grumbled that if Huey were running where blacks voted he would say "there is part nigger in us in order to get the nigger vote.")[24]

Wherever he spoke, Huey's fundamental message was the same. Louisiana's people were poor, oppressed, and kept in mud and ignorance by a corrupt gang of so-called gentlemen who ran the state in the interests of Wall Street, so that they might gobble up the scraps tossed them from Rockefeller's and J. P. Morgan's tables. According to Huey's rhetoric, New York's millionaires possessed their most fawning lap dog in Governor Parker. Huey treated his two actual opponents, Fuqua and Bouanchaud, with relative restraint, for he hoped to get into a second primary—a run-off election—with one or the other, and if that happened, he would seek the support of whoever ran third. But he did accuse both of being Governor Parker's candidates: Bouanchaud was an "egg" laid in Sullivan's nest and Fuqua was an "egg" laid in Behrman's nest. When hatched, Huey said, both would have the same old Parker "cackle, cluck and strut." Referring to the incumbent governor, Huey attacked his "rotten administration" for squandering money on a new campus for LSU and for appointing fifty new game wardens (he called them "coon chasers and possum watchers") to harass poor folks trying to obtain food. Higher education and conservation were patrician fancies. "Our kind don't need college," Huey declared. Instead, "our kind" needed free schoolbooks, along with free hunting, trapping, and fishing unmolested by Parker's nosy game wardens.[25]

Huey staked his hope for victory on class resentments. Most of the poorer voters in Protestant north Louisiana stood with him, but that was not enough to slip into a second primary, much less win it—unless he managed to come in a strong second in the rural Catholic parishes of south Louisiana. In New Orleans he would surely come in third. The issue that snatched away Huey's chance for winning in 1924 was the Ku Klux Klan, because it separated the Catholic voters he needed from the Protestant voters he already had.

The Klan of the 1920s adopted the name of a white counterrevolutionary movement of Reconstruction times, but it was different. "Foreign" and "immoral" elements, rather than blacks, were the reborn Klan's major targets. The new KKK stood for enforcing "100% Americanism," meaning white, native-born, fundamentalist Protestant values, including Prohibition and sexual probity. Postwar fears of change—of alien influences and of nonconformity in general—spread Klan membership beyond the South. Oregon and Indiana became two of the organization's strongest states. Nationally, the Klan enrolled three million or more members by 1923. The KKK of the 1920s was more a bigoted fraternity than a paramilitary force, although a few local units—the one in Morehouse Parish, Louisiana, being the most notorious—decided to shed blood.[26]

Louisiana was not one of the Klan's strongholds. Nor could it be. Since anti-Catholicism was the national Klan's primary theme (popery being "un-American"), more than half the state was enemy territory for the hooded order. Probably no more than 25,000 Louisianians were members of it at any given time; only in the Protestant northern parishes and in the Florida parishes east of the Mississippi River was it, temporarily, a potent force. Louisiana in the 1920s was the only southern or western state where a majority (almost 60 percent) of church members were Catholic. As in Ireland, religious affiliation showed a geographic split: of Louisiana's sixty-four parishes, all but ten "were either more than two-thirds Catholic or more than two-thirds Protestant."[27]

The post–World War I KKK first penetrated Louisiana in, of all places, Catholic New Orleans. Late in 1920 the imperial wizard arrived from national headquarters in Atlanta to begin organizing the Pelican State. By July of 1921, "Old Hickory Klan Number One" had signed about five hundred members in New Orleans. Ironically, the exalted cyclops of Louisiana's first Klan chapter was of Italian ancestry—Thomas DePaoli, a member of the state legislature and a militant Protestant. But the Klan had limited appeal in the Crescent City. Shreveport was another matter. Overwhelmingly Protestant and fiercely conservative, distant from New Orleans both geographically and temperamentally, Shreveport soon became the seedbed of Klan activity in Louisiana. The KKK dared not hold parades in New Orleans, but in the state's second largest city its public gatherings were "greeted with enthusiasm."[28] Much of the local business elite joined, as did ordinary citizens; endorsement came from the pastor of Shreveport's largest church (M. E. Dodd of First Baptist), who said the Klan stood "for nationality, race and religion . . . the deepest, highest and mightiest motives of man." The exalted cyclops of the city's three thousand members was the Reverend E. L. Thompson of Central Christian Church. In 1922 the Klan's candidate for mayor, Lee E. Thomas, won against the combined opposition of Catholics, Jews, tolerant Protestants, Huey Long, and Governor Parker.[29]

With Shreveport as their state headquarters, KKK organizers fanned out across north Louisiana during 1921 and 1922. Monroe quickly became a secondary Klan center. In scattered parts of south Louisiana where Protestantism was strong—the Florida parishes, Lake Charles, the piney woods near Texas—the KKK also recruited heavily. Violence was not a widespread Klan tactic in the 1920s. Boycotts and threats were more typical.

THE KINGFISH AND HIS REALM

Catholic and Jewish businessmen were shunned but seldom harassed; blacks, except those suspected of bootlegging or other
illegal activities, were usually left alone. The individuals most
likely to see hooded visitors were whites who led "irregular
lives"; they would be warned, on the first visit, to either mend
their ways or leave the area—or to expect big trouble. Klansmen
assembled mostly to socialize and reinforce their dogmas, enjoy
fiery oratory, experience the thrill of frightening others, and ca-
vort in a perpetual Halloween.[30]

Yet the Klan's ability to intimidate depended on the organization's violent potential. In certain localities, threats turned
into action. Texas evidently witnessed more Klan-related violence than any other state, but Louisiana's troubles received the
widest publicity. The episodes that brought this notoriety began
when Jack Morgan of Shreveport, white, a reputed wife-beater
and layabout, was tarred, feathered, and escorted out of town.
Another tarring and feathering—of a white Methodist minister
who had deserted his wife—occurred at the Beauregard Parish
town of DeRidder in February of 1922. A month later four members of a white family, including two girls aged thirteen and
fourteen, were dragged from their Vernon Parish home and severely flogged; their alleged offense was not reported.[31] These
were isolated events. But in Morehouse Parish, along the Arkansas border, terror became systemic.

Vigilante action was a tradition in Morehouse. From the
1880s on, Morehouse and neighboring Richland Parish had led
Louisiana in lynchings per capita.[32] One of America's most bizarre mob actions took place in Morehouse Parish in 1881, when
a black cattle rustler was trussed up alive inside a dead cow,
"leaving only his head sticking out" so carrion birds could pick
out his eyes. "The tortures that the buzzards gave the thief," the
Morehouse Clarion punned, constituted "COW-PITAL . . . punishment."[33] That Morehouse's reputation would suffer new wounds
was practically guaranteed by the KKK's selection, in 1921, of
J. K. Skipwith as the local exalted cyclops. "Old Skip," as friends
called him, was within a year or so of eighty. A Confederate army
veteran, he had been active in the original Klan of Reconstruction times. The past and present tended to jumble in his mind.[34]

Old Skip's objective was to rid the parish of "disorderly persons" who led "irregular lives." That category included moon-
shiners and bootleggers, immoral women, and white men who,

in Skipwith's words, "associated with niggers." There seemed no point in harassing Morehouse's intimidated black majority; they were said to be "scared stiff" of the Klan, and propertied whites wanted them to remain in the parish for the purpose of menial labor. Klan membership was largest in the parish seat of Bastrop, a town beginning to attract industry because of nearby natural gas wells. As elsewhere in north Louisiana, the hooded order's Morehouse membership crossed class lines. Leadership, however, came from the so-called "better element," including courthouse politicians and the pastor of Bastrop's First Baptist Church, while the rank and file, according to a federal investigator, were poor and "uneducated" men.[35]

"Sometimes bad diseases require heroic treatment," explained the parish's official journal as justification for vigilantism. Morehouse took its doses of Skipwith's prescription during July and August of 1922. Several white men were severely flogged, "undesirable women" put on trains to Arkansas, and the school board compelled to fire its only Catholic teacher. The Bastrop Ice Company's manager, a Catholic who had made "scurrilous remarks" about the Klan, was escorted to the train station and warned never to return.[36] Those happenings attracted little outside notice, but on August 24 the Morehouse Klan went too far. Late that afternoon, on a road outside Bastrop, about fifty masked and armed men stopped all automobiles headed toward Mer Rouge, the parish's second-largest town. The Klansmen were looking for specific individuals, and found them. Five men were forced out of their cars and taken into the woods, where one was released unharmed. The others were interrogated and "severely beaten." Afterward, two of the beating victims—including J. L. Daniel, one of the region's largest planters—were allowed back to their Mer Rouge homes. But the remaining two, as the *Morehouse Enterprise* crisply noted, "were retained by their captors." Four months later the decomposing bodies of Watt Daniel (J. L.'s son) and Watt's friend Thomas F. Richards rose to the surface in nearby Lake Lafourche.[37]

After the two had disappeared, a threat of mini–civil war developed between Bastrop and Mer Rouge, Daniel and Richards' hometown. Citizens of both communities barricaded their streets, fearing attacks from the other. Exalted Cyclops Skipwith told a reporter that Klansmen had "cleaned up" Morehouse Parish, "except for Mer Rouge."[38] In fundamentalist Bastrop, Mer Rouge was viewed as a place where the sins of moonshining and cohabiting with black women were tolerated. Watt Daniel was accused of both transgressions, but as the son of a leading planter, a World War veteran, and a graduate of LSU, he held patrician status in Mer Rouge. Also, because of the roadblock where he and others were abducted and many automobiles searched, Mer Rouge developed a siege mentality. It became the most anti-Klan community in north Louisiana.

Why did Skipwith's men murder Daniel and Richards? After they were flogged, Daniel had torn the mask off one of his assailants and recognized him. Moreover, he and his friend Richards—the two had served together in a tank battalion during the war—were suspected of having made an earlier attempt on the life of a prominent Klansman, Dr. B. M. McCoin. That suspicion was probably unfounded; more likely, Dr. McCoin had been shot at by someone seeking revenge for his killing of another physician, Dr. K. P. Thom, in a gunfight at the village of Galion six years earlier.[39]

Mer Rouge appealed to Governor Parker for help. The beleaguered community was outnumbered by Bastrop's Ku Kluxers, and Skipwith had sent a warning to the people of Mer Rouge to "behave themselves and stop discussing Daniel and Richards" or he would "come over some night and get a few more." The governor at first responded by trying to prod Morehouse's law enforcement into action, but soon learned that both the district attorney and Sheriff Fred Carpenter were Klansmen. Then Parker came to suspect the Klan of tapping his telephone and intercepting letters to him.[40] At last he was roused to action. Passive most of the time ("I plod along as best I can"), he seldom proposed legislation and, except in New Orleans, avoided interference in local elections. Yet Parker's latent combative instincts could be triggered by anything he perceived as taking part in a conspiracy against the structured, decorous society that was his ideal.[41] The New Orleans Ring was one such foe; the presumed *mafiosi* he had helped lynch in 1891 had represented another. During 1922 and 1923, Parker's head devil was the Ku Klux Klan.

The governor decided to petition Washington for assistance. He wrote President Warren G. Harding on November 3, 1922, asking for federal help against the Klan because *"These condi-*

132

tions are beyond the control of the Governor of this State." Parker cited the United States Constitution's Article IV, Section 4, which provides a federal "guarantee to every State in this Union a Republican [representative] Form of Government, and shall protect each of them . . . against domestic Violence." Two weeks later, Parker and his attorney general, A. V. Coco, took a train to Washington for a meeting with the president and Attorney General Harry M. Daugherty. They apparently asked for the dispatch of United States marshals, and troops if necessary, into Morehouse Parish—and possibly to other Klan-infested areas of the state. Although not politically adept, Parker understood that requesting such federal help might remind Louisianians of Reconstruction, so he merged his plea to the president with appeals that would be more palatable back home: monetary aid for building the new LSU campus, and withdrawal of the appointment of a black man, Walter Cohen, as comptroller of customs for the port of New Orleans.[42]

Parker was turned down on all requests, although Washington agreed to send agents of the newly created Federal Bureau of Investigation into Morehouse Parish. Meanwhile, Skipwith's Klansmen dragged three more "disorderly persons" from their homes and flogged them, and boasted that they would "give the [FBI] agents the same treatment Richards and Daniel got." Pro-Klan newspapers pointed out that as Governor Parker's wife was Catholic, he must be a tool of Rome, and that in trying to protect the "degenerates" of Mer Rouge, he was "lined up with the most depraved nigger lovers the South has ever known." State attorney general Coco, a Catholic of Latin ancestry, became known in Klan circles as "Dago Coca Cola."[43]

Ultimately, the Klan sustained heavy damage, locally and nationally, because of its savagery in Morehouse Parish. Pathologists' examinations of Daniel's and Richards' bodies, partly preserved by the mud of Lake Lafourche, revealed that both had been tortured—bones broken, hands, feet, and testicles cut or mashed off before death. The story became a national sensation. Ku Kluxers were suspected of murders elsewhere, but these two could be laid unquestionably at the Klan's door. The state suffered its worst publicity in years. "In Darkest Louisiana" was the title of one magazine article, and major American dailies used similar phraseology. Both in state and nation, the "Murders of Mer Rouge" became a rallying cry for anti-Klan elements. After the bodies were discovered, Parker had sent national guardsmen into Morehouse. Attorney General Coco tried to obtain murder indictments against Skipwith and others, but twice grand juries in Bastrop returned no true bills. Skipwith of course denied the charges, and Klan publications claimed the bodies in Lake Lafourche were "stiffs" shipped in by Governor Parker from some morgue or medical college. Yet in the long run, the fact that Old Skip and his vigilantes literally got away with murder served to intensify hostility toward the KKK.[44] (It also may be assumed that had the Morehouse Klan flogged and murdered black sharecroppers instead of prominent white men, there would have been far less outcry.)

The Mer Rouge murders created an especially strong backlash in the Catholic, Cajun parishes. Several south Louisiana KKK chapters decided, for safety's sake, to disband. In New Iberia, the names of suspected Klansmen were posted in the courthouse, along with the advice that they should move to Morehouse Parish. In Lafayette, a similar posting led the Catholic bishop, Jules Jeanmard, to urge restraint toward Klansmen and others of the Protestant minority, since "they are entirely at our mercy."[45] North Louisiana was still a Klan bastion, but even there its popularity began to ebb. The congregations of some Protestant churches that had hitherto accepted contributions from Klan delegations now divided on whether to continue welcoming hooded visitors to their services. At the Tullos Baptist Church in LaSalle Parish, this question "resulted in the outbreak of fist fights among members of the congregation."[46]

Much to Huey Long's dismay, the Klan issue occupied center stage throughout the 1923–1924 gubernatorial campaign. Never had religion been so divisive in state politics. Of the three contestants—Fuqua, Bouanchaud, Long—none desired or received the Klan's official blessing, but only Lieutenant Governor Bouanchaud was openly anti-Klan. Both Bouanchaud's and Fuqua's platforms pledged to forbid the Klan or similar groups from wearing masks or facial hoods in public and to require the filing of complete membership lists from such organizations, but only Bouanchaud, a Catholic backed by Governor Parker, straightforwardly blasted the Klan and promised to put it "out of business"; he also criticized Prohibition and opposed efforts to close New Orleans' race track.[47]

Fuqua avoided specificity about anything, yet he pleased

Protestants simply by being one and by endorsing Prohibition, and he mollified Ku Kluxers by not attacking the order. There were suspicions, probably correct, that he was supported by the Klan's upper echelon as being less objectionable than Bouanchaud or (for class reasons) Long. One Bouanchaud campaigner referred to Fuqua as "Klandidate Kenry Kuqua." Even so, Fuqua was endorsed by the largely Catholic Old Regular machine in New Orleans, mainly because he seemed the best of bad choices.[48] To Martin Behrman and the ward bosses, supporting either Parker's candidate or a redneck radical was unthinkable.

Huey tried to straddle the Klan issue, but his home base consisted of parishes where the KKK was potent, and although well-to-do Klansmen leaned toward Fuqua, lesser members tended to identify with Long. Even Huey's fertile brain could not solve the problem of how to hold on to his Klansmen while building enough strength in Catholic areas to outpoll either Bouanchaud or Fuqua, and thus win a place in the run-off. Huey early realized the Klan's danger to his state-wide ambitions; back in December of 1921, he had written his brother Shan—who, as he knew, was a Klan organizer in Oklahoma—that "I am not a member, and while I have never taken a line either way, I requested some of my good friends whom I know to be members, that I not be asked to join."[49]

But rumors persisted that Huey was a member, even a genii (secondary local leader), of the Klan. He was not, but tenuous links to the KKK were visible. His cousin and wealthy contributor, Swords Lee, was the exalted cyclops of the large Alexandria Klan, and presented Huey with an unwanted certificate making him an "honorary member." Also, the largest Klan newspaper in Louisiana, *Sgt. Dalton's Weekly,* was published in Huey's hometown of Winnfield.[50]

Once Huey realized the Klan issue would not go away, he tried to play a double game. In north Louisiana he claimed to oppose laws against masking or secrecy, and said of his adversaries: "Bouanchaud wants to hang all the Klansmen before the election and Mr. Fuqua wants to wait till after the election in hopes some of them will vote for him, and then hang them." But a few days later, speaking in the Cajun town of Abbeville on the topic of the Klan, Huey said he was "opposed to that organization" and "made it clear he was in favor of laws against the mask." He was not yet accustomed to being followed around by city report-

135

ers, and having his contradictions spread over the state by the *Times-Picayune*, the *Item*, and the *States* made him furious. He was not able to convince a sufficient number of poor Catholic voters either that class interests overrode the Klan question or that he was genuinely anti-Klan.[51]

The Parker administration's tenacious efforts to prosecute Skipwith's vigilantes helped keep the KKK in the news. In November, 1923, as the gubernatorial campaign began to peak, Attorney General Coco finally succeeded in bringing to trial Exalted Cyclops Skipwith, Dr. McCoin, and eighteen other Morehouse Parish Klansmen. The charges, however, were relatively minor—assault with a dangerous weapon, carrying firearms on someone else's property, and related offenses. Skipwith and two of his codefendants were found guilty on the firearms-carrying charge and fined ten dollars each. All other charges were eventually dismissed. But to be convicted of anything, when he felt so justified in everything, dumbfounded Old Skip. He muttered, "What is this world coming to?"[52]

All three candidates for governor wound up their campaigns with weekend appearances in New Orleans. Huey's Saturday night rally at the Athenaeum drew entertainment seekers along with believers. His crowd filled the auditorium and overflowed into the street, as he described Fuqua and Bouanchaud as "the Gold Dust twins of Mr. Parker." Huey's Athenaeum address was carried over one of New Orleans' pioneer radio stations, WCAG. It marked the first time he or any Louisiana politician made a campaign speech over radio. WCAG's owner estimated that more than eight thousand homes in the state had "receiving stations," as early radio sets were called.[53] At that time, radios were still considered expensive toys, and it is doubtful Huey had many fans among the well-to-do who might have listened in that night. In the future, however, he would use the airwaves to great advantage, even becoming, not long before his death, a national radio personality with an audience rivaling that of a different kind of countrified entertainer, Will Rogers.

Cold, wind-whipped rain fell across Louisiana on election day, January 15, 1924. Huey later attributed his defeat to the bad weather's reducing his supporters' turnout. Had the day been sunny, he might have come closer to gaining a second primary spot, but the other candidates' totals must also have suffered; the rain alone did not keep Huey in third place. In his autobiography, written a decade later, Huey claimed he knew he had lost "when the first box was reported," from a place called Clay, where he had 60 votes out of 61 cast. "I'm beat," Huey recalled himself as saying. "There should have been 100 for me and 1 against me. Forty per cent of my country vote is lost." Actually, the Clay voters went 60 for Long, 6 for Fuqua, and 0 for Bouanchaud. And the first precinct to come in was not Clay, but the Baker box, in a rural part of East Baton Rouge Parish, where Huey had been considered strong. Baker gave him only 4 out of 51 votes. Seeing Baker's total in the late afternoon election-day edition of the New Orleans *States*, Huey understood it was a sign he was not going to make it this time.[54]

Considering his disadvantages, Huey ran remarkably well. State-wide totals in the first primary gave Bouanchaud 84,162, Fuqua 81,382, and Long 73,985. Although coming in third, Huey won an absolute majority in twenty-one rural parishes and had a plurality in seven others. Outside of New Orleans, he actually enjoyed a slight plurality over his nearest competitor, Bouanchaud (61,798 to 60,862). But Fuqua's lead in the metropolis put him into the run-off with Bouanchaud, who ran a good second in the city. Huey finished a weak third in New Orleans, with 12,187 votes, only 17.7 percent of the city total. Francis and Gus Williams' Independent Regulars were of little help; they could not even deliver their home Third Ward.[55] The vote Huey did receive in New Orleans was, as he knew, owing to personal appeal.

Fuqua was bound to win a second primary and become the next governor. With or without Huey's endorsement, he was virtually certain to pick up Long's north Louisiana Protestant vote. Because of the New Orleans Old Regulars' backing of Fuqua, and the candidate's benign slogan of "Peace" on questions about the Klan and religion, the Catholic vote was divided. The Protestant vote was not. Fuqua beat Bouanchaud in the run-off by (in round figures) 126,000 to 92,000. The only Protestant community in the state Bouanchaud carried was Mer Rouge.[56]

With his political future intensely in mind, Huey declined to endorse either man in the run-off, even though Bouanchaud, desperately bidding for the Long vote, came out in favor of free school textbooks. "I shall make no choice," Huey announced, "nor shall I enter the polls on the day of election." He added that "Standard Oil . . . has won a victory and . . . probably will maintain the control of this state under either Mr. Fuqua or Mr.

Bouanchaud for four more years."[57] Analyzing the returns, and already planning for the next gubernatorial contest in 1928, Huey understood he must somehow improve his standing with the Catholic voters of south Louisiana. He set about that task immediately.

Much of Louisiana's old ruling class still did not comprehend the threat posed by Huey Long. They had beaten the Populist-Republican coalition a generation earlier; now they thought they had beaten this new challenge to their hegemony. After all, "Huey Promise Long," as some called him, had run third. They wanted to believe he was finished, so they believed it. One plantation-parish leader rejoiced that he would "not have the pleasure of again casting a vote against him." But a wiser conservative, writing in the *Times-Picayune*, had a different prediction about the brash young redhead from Winn Parish: "He went into districts that have been hibernating and laying [sic] dormant for over 30 years. He aroused them and opened their eyes. We may just as well try and charge hades with a bucket of water as to try and stop Huey P. Long."[58]

· 9 ·

RISING AND SHINING

Defeat served as a stimulant for Huey Long. His energy level, always high, climbed to almost inhuman elevations as he immediately and simultaneously began preparing for a second try at the governorship in 1928, working to enhance his reputation as the people's champion on the Public Service Commission, and spending more time in his Shreveport law office on litigation that might bring in big fees. "I was seriously in need of money," he acknowledged. Considering both political and financial requirements, Huey wrote: "It was a case of rise and shine." [1]

Having failed to become governor in 1924, Huey later that same year sought reelection to the Public Service Commission. This pursuit took little of his time. He had swept most of the twenty-eight-parish north Louisiana district during the January gubernatorial primary; his September reelection as commissioner seemed a certainty. Nevertheless, Governor Fuqua promoted the candidacy of Huey's only opponent, State Senator Walter L. Bagwell of West Carroll Parish. Huey hardly bothered to campaign for himself, instead speaking mostly of the need to reelect United States Senator Joseph E. Ransdell; when Ransdell toured north Louisiana, Huey accompanied him. Naive persons thought this a strange thing for Huey to do. Senator Ransdell was an elderly (sixty-five) conservative patrician from Lake Providence, in the plantation parish of East Carroll. He and Huey agreed on virtually nothing. But Huey was looking ahead. Ransdell, although a north Louisianian, was devoutly Catholic and was actually more popular in the southern parishes. Huey did not expect Ransdell to reciprocate by endorsing him for governor in 1928; rather, he believed that campaigning for a Catholic would boost his own standing where he needed it most. As a budding politico from Abbeville, Dudley LeBlanc, telegraphed Huey: "YOU HAVE MADE MANY FRIENDS IN SOUTH LOUISIANA BY SUPPORTING RANSDELL." Besides, the senator's opponent was, as Huey wrote, "my very bitter, personal enemy, Mayor Lee E. Thomas of Shreveport."[2]

Huey and others pinned the nickname "Wet Jug" on Mayor Thomas: the man's bald head and protruding ears resembled a jug with handles, while "wet" described his wide, moist mouth and his tendency to perspire. But Thomas was not "wet" in a 1920s meaning of the word; he stood firmly for Prohibition. In that respect, former governor J. Y. Sanders observed, "Wet Jug" was "as dry as a bone." Mayor Thomas was superintendent of Sunday schools in Shreveport's First Baptist Church and a director of Continental Bank and Trust. Everyone knew the Ku Klux Klan had helped elect him mayor in 1922.[3] Yet Thomas shied away from the Klan in his senatorial bid, and for good reason.

By September of 1924, Louisiana's KKK was disintegrating even in Shreveport and the rural northern parishes. The Daniel-Richards murders and Parker's relentless crusade against the "Invisible Empire" had given the Klan undesirable visibility. Upper-class members, especially, were bailing out. Before he left office in May, Governor Parker had the pleasure of removing from office Sheriff Carpenter of Morehouse Parish after a shortage of $18,953.54 was discovered in Carpenter's accounts; the governor appointed Samuel A. Leopold, a Jew, as Morehouse's new sheriff. The Louisiana Klan was also in trouble with the national KKK leadership for several reasons, chiefly because Klansmen who were members of the legislature had supinely voted for Governor Fuqua's antimasking and antisecrecy laws at the 1924 session.[4]

Those acts, agreed to by the state's Klansmen out of fear that harsher measures might be the alternatives, forbade the wearing of "any facial disguise"—except during Mardi Gras, children's Halloween activities, and blackface minstrel shows. The Klan or any similar organization was required to file "a full, complete and true list" of the names and addresses of all members (many patrician Klansmen had feared a possible requirement that *previous* enrollment be disclosed; Fuqua's measure gave them time to get out or to conceal their membership by transferring it out of state). The national Klan headquarters in Atlanta also criticized the Louisiana branch for being insufficiently anti-Semitic: The Monroe KKK twice defied orders from Atlanta by refusing to oppose the reelection of Monroe's popular Jewish mayor, Arnold Bernstein.[5]

Huey coasted to reelection to the Public Service Commission, trouncing Bagwell in all twenty-eight parishes and winning 83.9 percent of the total vote. But the Ransdell-Thomas race, also decided in the Democratic primary of September, 1924, was fairly close: state-wide, the old senator defeated "Wet Jug" 104,312 to 85,547. Huey later claimed credit for Ransdell's victory, even saying that Ransdell "told me after his election that if it hadn't been for me he would never have gone back to the Senate."[6] Whatever Ransdell might have told him, Huey's boast of providing the senator's margin of victory was untrue; Ransdell ran far behind in twenty-six of north Louisiana's parishes, winning only Tensas and his home parish of East Carroll. Huey's coattail effect was minimal at best. As a salient example, Huey carried Winn Parish 1,770 to 221 in the PSC race, but Ransdell lost it 1,338 to 578. What took Ransdell back to the Senate was endorsement by the Old Regulars of New Orleans, who helped him carry the city by a two-to-one margin, plus his winning the rural Catholic parishes as heavily as he lost the Protestant ones. The chief beneficiary of the ephemeral Long-Ransdell alliance was Long, who made sure south Louisiana's Catholics knew he had campaigned for Ransdell.[7]

From this time on, Huey inserted himself into every important political fight in the state. The New Orleans mayoralty contest of 1925 gave him an opportunity to build support precisely where he had fared worst in the previous governor's race. Huey sided with John P. Sullivan's (New Regulars) candidate Paul Maloney, against the Old Regulars' Martin Behrman. Mayor McShane, an inept reformer who had beaten Behrman in 1920 with help from Sullivan and Governor Parker, was also in the race, but McShane had no effective backing and would run third. Behrman, using the slogan "Papa's Coming Home," edged out Maloney and returned to the City Hall office he had occupied from 1904 to 1920. Limited in vision though he was, Behrman had always tried to be a good mayor, and now—despite warnings from his physician—worked harder than ever. One year after his election victory, in January of 1926, Martin Behrman

THE KINGFISH AND HIS REALM

collapsed and died. His doctor said he died of "a degeneration of the heart muscles due to overwork." Governor Fuqua wrote, "He died in harness, as he would have liked to die."[8]

More important to Huey's future than either the winning effort with Ransdell or the losing Maloney venture was his 1926 campaign for the reelection of United States Senator Edwin S. Broussard. Not only was Broussard Catholic, but he was also a Cajun from coastal Iberia Parish. "Coozan Ed," as he was often hailed, had served one term in the Senate seat earlier occupied by his more personable brother Robert ("Coozan Bob"), who had died in 1918. The Broussard name was political magic in the French parishes. It was also ubiquitous; there were thousands of Broussards in south Louisiana. A generation earlier, Sheriff Ike Broussard had estimated that his Lafayette Parish alone contained four hundred, not counting blacks (he added that he knew "every one of them").[9] And with each generation the number of Broussards multiplied.

But "Coozan Ed" faced tough opposition in 1926. J. Y. Sanders, a former governor and perennial office seeker, backed by the Fuqua administration, was making his third try for a Senate seat. Twice, in 1912 and 1920, he had lost tight senatorial contests—first to Bob Broussard, then to Ed. Yet as Hewitt Bouanchaud remarked, "J. Y. always has the catlike habit of coming back."[10] Sanders, as a Protestant and foe of liquor and gambling, drew most of his support from the northern parishes; yet because he lived in south Louisiana and always upheld sugar planter interests, he also had strength there. While governor from 1908 to 1912, Sanders had enjoyed ties to Mayor Behrman and the New Orleans machine, but he never forgave the Ring for what he considered betrayal in his 1912 Senate race. A portly, old-fashioned orator full of clichés about the Lost Cause, J. Y. could always draw a crowd. He considered himself a progressive in that he advocated better schools (for white children) and good roads, yet as a fiscal conservative he believed improvements must be paid for out of current revenue, and "good roads" to him meant gravel roads. Whenever the subject of race came up, Sanders had few peers in extolling white supremacy. The *Tensas Gazette* adoringly described J. Y. as a "virile . . . clean, brainy, fearless white man's man."[11]

Broussard needed Huey's help in 1926, and Huey needed to help Broussard so as to ingratiate himself with Cajun voters.

Neither man relished the other's company, but for mutual advantage they traveled together across Louisiana. Broussard spoke in French when addressing Cajun audiences, and Huey was introduced as Huey Polycarp Long—Polycarp being the name of a Christian martyr revered among the French. Wherever they appeared, Senator Broussard uttered benign platitudes, and Huey attacked Sanders, "that long-legged sapsucker," in vituperative and colorful language. Huey accused J. Y. of everything from cutting funds for handicapped children at "the poor deaf and dumb asylum" to riding around in a big Packard. Sanders scarcely knew whether to run against Broussard or to defend himself against Long.[12]

Just as Huey had tried to duck the Ku Klux question during his recent try for the governorship, he now found Prohibition to be another Protestant-versus-Catholic issue to avoid. The national ban on alcoholic beverages had never been popular in the southern parishes and was notoriously ignored in New Orleans, whereas in Protestant north Louisiana, despite much moonshining and bootlegging, "dry" sentiment still prevailed at the ballot box. Sanders was a dry, but Broussard—"as wet as Lake Pontchartrain," as one writer described him—urged repeal of Prohibition.[13] In the September, 1926, primary, Senator Broussard won a second term by edging out Sanders, 84,041 to 80,562. Huey, of course, took credit for Broussard's victory, and unlike the case in Ransdell's reelection, his support probably was decisive. The Cajun Senator ran better than had Ransdell in most Protestant areas and even carried four parishes in Huey's upland stronghold. Huey also benefited greatly; within a year he was again running for governor, and Cajuns would remember his joint appearances with Coozan Ed. As Thomas O. Harris observed, "Support of Edwin S. Broussard was the best political investment Huey P. Long ever made."[14]

Not everything went Huey's way. Recently he and his previous ally on the Public Service Commission, Francis Williams, had fallen out after Williams complained that Huey was hogging all credit for PSC actions. Then, on the same day Senator Broussard was reelected, Shelby Taylor—who had become Huey's new friend on the PSC—lost his Second District seat. Dudley LeBlanc of coastal Vermilion Parish replaced Taylor on the three-man commission, and LeBlanc promptly (December 3, 1926) voted to oust Long as chairman. Aware of what would occur,

143

Long avoided the meeting, in which Francis Williams was elected by 2 to 0 to chair the PSC.[15] One usually astute observer of Louisiana politics believed this setback might injure Huey's prospects of becoming governor, since he "lost a lot of pull he had on big business. They were afraid of him then; they may not be afraid of him now."[16] Actually, Huey's career was on track. He had milked the Public Service Commission for about all the publicity it could provide. The governorship was next.

Huey's financial situation improved in 1926 when he received approximately $40,000, his largest fee to date, for representing a Shreveport businessman, Ernest Bernstein, in protracted, successful litigation against the Commercial National Bank. It was a huge fee for the time, roughly equivalent to $250,000 today. Huey always charged as much as the law allowed. "Why not?" he once explained. "I admit I'm the best lawyer in Louisiana." The Bernstein case provided Huey enough money to move his family into a large, Mediterranean-style white brick home. He built it, he wrote, "in the best residential section of the City of Shreveport at a cost of $40,000." The house featured wrought-iron grillwork, which had a mocking design: "I took this architect downtown," Huey recalled to journalist Hermann Deutsch, "and showed him the windows in the Commercial National Bank [featuring a fancy grille monogram] and said for him to fix up my house with windows just like that, to remind 'em of how I had cleaned 'em on those lawsuits, only he was to use my initials in place of the bank's initials."[17]

The Bernstein case also provided an ominous glimpse of the future. Huey's abrasive tactics, whether in lawsuits or politics, could arouse violent emotions. Randall Moore, president of the Commercial National Bank, grew so enraged at Huey's accusations against CNB that he could not restrain himself when, one day, he saw him in downtown Shreveport. Moore shoved Huey against the side of a building, then pulled a knife and said, "I ought to cut your goddamned throat." Huey stood still and said nothing. Moore left him unharmed.[18]

On two other occasions, Huey was assaulted by rival Shreveport attorneys who took offense at his remarks: J. U. Gallaway gave him a black eye, and elderly John D. Wilkinson pounded him with an umbrella. It was soon evident in Shreveport, as it had been in Winnfield during his school days, that Huey's com-

bativeness was almost entirely verbal. Often he cursed enemies
to their face, but rarely did he strike the first blow. The first public encounter in which Huey was the physical aggressor happened outside the Shreveport *Journal* building, when Long assaulted the paper's diminutive editor, Adolph Franz, who had
accused him of drunkenness. "I am tired of your lies," Huey exclaimed as he struck the small man. They grappled, rolling into
the gutter. Alarmed spectators quickly separated the two, and
Franz was led away with a bleeding mouth.[19]

To spread his reputation for cowardice, Huey's enemies set a
trap for him during the Broussard-Sanders campaign of 1926.
The bait was a one-legged man named Robert Prophit. A legislator from Monroe, Prophit also held a position with the state
Department of Conservation—one of the "possum watchers"—
and because of that, received unflattering mention by Huey.
Friends of Sanders and Governor Fuqua put Prophit up to a
physical confrontation with Huey. They reasoned that when Prophit hit him, Huey would either run or return the blow. To do
either in an altercation with a crippled man—who was undersized as well—would look bad indeed. Huey surpassed the plot-
ters' hopes by doing both. The fight occurred at a Broussard
rally in the town of Columbia, south of Monroe. As Huey approached the courthouse steps to speak, Prophit swung at him,
missed, then broke his cane against a gate as he hobbled toward
the fleeing Huey. Associates of Long quickly formed a circle
around Prophit and restrained the little man. Seeing this, Huey
returned to the scene and took a wild swing at Prophit. Incredi-
bly, later the same day, Long proudly displayed a trophy of the
fight: half of Prophit's shattered cane.[20]

"Who wants a rank coward for governor?" asked the Shreveport *Caucasian*.[21] In years to come, Huey's foes continued to assume that this frailty of his, which was repeatedly demonstrated
and broadcast, must necessarily destroy him politically. Louisiana's white males, after all, enjoyed a deserved reputation for
bravery in war and affairs of honor; the state's shortcomings
were notorious, but at least its men had usually been recognized
as fighters. Yet to those ordinary Louisianians who believed in
Huey—and their number kept growing—stories about his encounter with Prophit and other shameful affrays were dismissed
as being either irrelevant or newspaper lies. Certainly it is a trib-

145

ute to Huey Long's personal magnetism that so many voters clung to him despite his failure to comply with traditional standards of manly honor.

A hypnotic presence was always Huey's greatest political asset. But much of his rise to power during the late 1920s can be attributed to worsening economic conditions for average people. The flush times of World War I and the immediate postwar period soon faded. Southern farmers and workers witnessed a decline in living standards several years before the Great Depression hit the entire nation in 1929.[22] Their expectations had been raised by temporarily good income, but now the supposedly bright future began to glimmer. Huey Long told these unhappy people that their troubles were not their fault, that he was one of them, and that with their help he could punish their oppressors and make things right. Any politician could have said such things. The words alone were not enough. What carried Long into the governor's office was his mysterious gift for making everything he said sound believable.

In the spring of 1927 a natural disaster temporarily sidetracked the state's preoccupation with politics. Even Huey Long's doings could not compete with the mighty Flood of '27. Overflows often befell Louisiana; the state is the spout of an enormous funnel draining half the United States into the Gulf of Mexico. But the high water of 1927, in the United States Weather Bureau's words, "exceeded any flood since the settlement of this section more than 200 years ago."[23]

Abnormally cold and wet weather had prevailed across most of the Mississippi-Missouri-Ohio river valleys since the preceding October. In April, 1927, snowmelt and rainstorms in the upper states emptied vast amounts of water into the already high Mississippi. Rain and chill seemed to follow the rising torrent southward. Within a twenty-four-hour period beginning Good Friday morning, fourteen inches of rain fell in New Orleans, overwhelming several pumping stations and submerging those neighborhoods that lay below sea level. A week later, on April 22, killing frost struck as far south as central Louisiana—the latest freezing date known there. The Colfax *Chronicle* surmised that between the frost and approaching high water, "a great deal of cotton will have to be planted again."[24]

But a worse fate than replanting cotton was in store. A levee system that had begun as a small dike built by French colonists at New Orleans in 1718 now paralleled the Mississippi with high, thick earthen walls all the way to Illinois. The response to previous floods had been to build the levees still longer and higher, although as early as the 1880s Major Hearsey's New Orleans *States* had argued that outlets (spillways) along the lower Mississippi, as well as levees, were needed to control the periodic flooding. But upriver cotton planters and the Mississippi River Commission always insisted that taller levees would suffice. The unprecedented high water of 1927 proved how fallacious it was to rely on levees only. This time the confined Mississippi could accept no more water; its tributaries backed up and overflowed their banks, while the high levees along the great river became saturated and unstable. Late in April, eighty miles above the Louisiana border, the Arkansas River's levees crumbled, spilling a vast sheet of water, upon which rode a growing accumulation of debris and dead animals, southward toward the Pelican State. During the first week in May, Arkansas water crossed the state line. Simultaneously, levees along the Mississippi in Madison and Tensas parishes broke beneath their strain. Soon most of northeast Louisiana lay beneath what *National Geographic* called "a foul and swirling sea."[25]

Engineers saved New Orleans by dynamiting the levee at Caernarvon, twelve miles downstream from the city, thus sacrificing St. Bernard and Plaquemines parishes to spare the metropolis. Residents of the doomed area had been evacuated, and later were compensated by the city and state for most of their losses. But trouble was coming for the Cajun country of south central Louisiana, for in mid-May the Bayou des Glaises levees of Avoyelles Parish collapsed, sending waters from both the Red and Mississippi rivers cascading southward toward the Gulf of Mexico. Then the adjacent Atchafalaya River's levees broke. With that, a great stretch of Louisiana lowland, from the Arkansas line to the Gulf, 70 miles wide and 240 miles long, was inundated. In all, about one fourth of the state (along with smaller portions of Mississippi, Arkansas, Missouri, and Kentucky) was submerged.[26]

President Calvin Coolidge sent his secretary of commerce, Herbert Hoover, an engineer experienced in humanitarian work, to coordinate rescue and relief operations in the disaster area. Hoover in turn chose former governor Parker as his Louisiana director. "M'sieu Jean," as Cajuns had come to call Parker, worked efficiently and tirelessly to move Louisianians out of the flood's path to higher ground and to provide tents and food for the two hundred thousand and more white and black Louisiana refugees who crowded into what Hoover innocently described, in these pre-Nazi days, as "concentration camps." Some residents in the afflicted parishes climbed to safety in two-story houses or buildings and waited for the waters to subside; Helen Murphy of Tallulah, looking out from her large home's upper windows and thinking more of refugee neighbors than herself, wondered "if we must always be a poor, shabby, struggling people, battling against a foe too great for us."[27]

It was cold for May. The chill accompanying 1927's water-logged spring added to the misery. But the state was lucky in loss of life. Tens of thousands might have died if Louisiana had not been alerted by the April flooding farther north. As it was, of the flood's 237 total dead, no more than 16 were in the Pelican State. (By contrast, the hurricane of 1893 had killed 2,500 Louisianians.) Fortunately, too, old racial hostility was lessened by the threatened catastrophe to all. Blacks and whites each heroically saved those of the other race from drowning, and labored together in sometimes futile efforts to pile more earth upon threatened levees. "White and colored alike have worked like Trojans," observed the *Tensas Gazette;* the races had "stood shoulder to shoulder on the breastwork." Along the Red River levees, one newspaperman wrote (revealing his descending scale of respectability), "businessmen, doctors, prisoners, lawyers and negroes worked side by side."[28]

Occasionally, the flood revealed humanity's primal bond with all living creatures. People came first, as rescuers in crowded boats had to tell families they must leave even their dogs and cats behind; but at times the flood illuminated the unity of life. Will Irwin, a sensitive reporter, observed several farm animals stranded on the fast-crumbling remains of a Bayou des Glaises levee near Bordelonville: "There were three cows, one trailed by a calf not more than two days old, a great sow, and a white mare with her spindly colt. She, most highly organized of these beasts, was all atremble; and she was nuzzling her infant ahead of her. As we landed, they crowded round our boat, staring at us with mute appealing eyes. They were asking to be rescued! Fortunately, an empty cattle boat [soon arrived]. I looked back to see these perturbed beasts moving aboard with the sober regularity of Noah's animals in an old-fashioned print."[29]

During June the waters receded, leaving battered muddy dwellings, rotting animal carcasses, and stagnant pools as filthy mementos of the Flood of '27. But the disaster had one beneficial result: it proved beyond doubt that spillways as well as levees were needed to protect Louisiana from the Mississippi, especially at New Orleans, where it actually had been necessary to destroy the levee at Caernarvon in order to provide a makeshift outlet to the Gulf and save the city. Congress presently approved a flood control plan that would build spillways along with better levees, and—to the delight of Louisiana taxpayers—the federal government agreed to pay all the construction costs.[30] Since then, the levee-spillway system has worked.

The flood also provided upper-class Louisianians their best available candidate to match against Huey Long in the upcoming gubernatorial election. Riley J. "Riley Joe" Wilson, fifty-six, had been northeastern Louisiana's congressman since 1914 and was chairman of the House of Representatives committee on flood control. In that role, Congressman Wilson kept insisting the federal government should pay for levees, spillways, or whatever was needed to control flooding in the Mississippi valley; thus, Wilson could be displayed to Louisiana voters as their champion. Like Huey Long, he was born in Winn Parish and—as a sarcastic commentator added—"went barefoot as a boy."[31]

A third aspirant entered the race: Oramel H. Simpson, fifty-seven. A man of hitherto modest ambitions and a poor public speaker, Simpson would not have been a serious candidate except for the fact that Governor Fuqua had dropped dead one October evening in 1926, and as the elected lieutenant governor, Simpson was serving out the last year and a half of Fuqua's term and relying on the patronage power of the governorship to create a state-wide organization. In his bid for a full term, Governor Simpson anticipated a big vote in New Orleans, for he had given the saving order to dynamite the Caernarvon levee.[32]

As the Shreveport *Caucasian* pointed out, however, most of Louisiana's upper class, awakened at last to the menace of Huey Long, believed that Governor Simpson "does not possess the punch and wallop [needed] to stop the untamed youth from Winn." Simpson had various liabilities, including a reputation for heavy drinking. "You are a booze hound," Sheriff L. A. Meraux of St. Bernard told Simpson, and both Long's and Wilson's organizations echoed the charge. Although Simpson had some prominent supporters, including Mayor Thomas of Shreveport, a growing conviction among the old elite that the governor could not possibly beat Huey Long had prompted a frantic search for a better candidate.[33] The white-haired congressman from the Eighth District, James B. Aswell, renowned as a Populistic-cum-racist orator, was courted and told he was "the only man who can beat Long." But Aswell, who had locked horns with Huey in the past, wrote his supplicants that he had no desire to "face a sewer-line-filthy campaign which no worthwhile man craves." Besides, he thought it "very doubtful" Long could be stopped.[34] Aswell's flat refusal impelled some politicians to approach John M. Parker. But the former governor kept his vow to never again run for public office.[35]

"The highbrows," as Robert Ewing of the States termed them, "who imagine dreadful things . . . if Long is elected governor," met in Alexandria's Bolton High School auditorium on July 8, 1927, to proclaim Riley Joe Wilson as their candidate. Congressman Wilson lacked Aswell's presence or Parker's credentials, but at least he was willing to make the race. Some two thousand politicians and other personages came to the Alexandria conclave, including Adolph Franz of the Shreveport Journal, numerous bankers, and the Old Regular ward bosses of New Orleans. The Old Regulars wore lapel badges with the slogan "It Won't Be Long Now!" Huey and some of his friends tried to enter the meeting and make a scene, but according to Huey, "they had the place guarded."[36]

Wilson soon proved as uninspiring a campaigner as Governor Simpson. In dull speeches, the congressman presented himself as a "safe and sane" alternative to radicalism, while emphasizing his role in urging federally financed flood control. That he was a gentleman with no known bad habits seemed sufficient for his core supporters. But even the Homer Guardian-Journal, one of Wilson's most ardent backers, soon concluded that "Riley has been entirely too serious; he orta loosen up." A young patrician who volunteered as Wilson's chauffeur presently discovered another flaw in the candidate. "I drove that old man all over the state and paid the expenses," Roland B. Howell recalled. "He was really a tightwad."[37]

Huey decided that if the Wilson people could kick off their activities with a gathering in Alexandria, so could he—and with a bigger one at that. Three thousand people filled the seats and aisles of Bolton High's cavernous auditorium on the evening of August 3 to hear Long, age thirty-three, open his second campaign for the governorship. An estimated five thousand more stood in the schoolyard outside, listening to his speech through loudspeakers. Banners above the stage where Huey spoke proclaimed his new slogan: "Every Man a King, but No One Wears a Crown." [38]

Radio station KWKH in Shreveport, owned by Long's wealthy backer William K. Henderson, aired the event by remote control. Reporters from city dailies and small-town weeklies attended; Louisiana's journalists had found out that their readers, whether admirers of Huey or not, were interested in what he did and said. The Donaldsonville *Chief*, a formerly Republican newspaper that for decades had fulminated against the state's Democratic oligarchy, hailed Huey's Alexandria event as "the spontaneous outburst of a political boss-ridden people." [39]

Long's platform for the gubernatorial campaign of 1927–1928 mostly repeated positions he had taken four years earlier. He promised to build highways and better schools, provide free textbooks for schoolchildren, and upgrade institutions for the handicapped and mentally ill. He also would end corruption and extravagance in government by getting rid not only of "possum watchers" in the Department of Conservation, but also of all the assorted "trough feeders and pie-eaters" who held state jobs under the old regime. Again he attacked big business "plutocrats" and their political stooges who oppressed working men and women. Yet now that he smelled victory, Huey became circumspect on two matters. Charges that he was a "Radical Bolshevik" apparently bothered him. Huey insisted that fighting for the rights of laborers and farmers "in no manner means that I am now or have ever been unjust or unfair to any of our legitimate business or commercial interests." Of still more concern to him was the predictable complaint that his free schoolbook plan would benefit black as well as white children at the taxpayers' expense. Huey answered by insisting his chief concern was to see that "every *white* child in Louisiana shall receive the benefits of an education." [40]

Previously, a candidate who ran for governor in Louisiana's

151

Democratic primaries usually allied himself with a politician from another part of the state who was seeking the lieutenant governorship. But except in New Orleans and adjacent St. Bernard Parish, where the Ring (Old Regulars) and their opponents announced full slates of candidates, there had been no specific "tickets" in Democratic primaries until Huey Long announced his in 1927. Long's candidate for lieutenant governor was Dr. Paul N. Cyr, a dentist from the coastal town of Jeanerette. A Catholic of French descent—"I was ten years old before I could speak a word of English"—Cyr provided the ethnic balance Huey's ticket needed. The Long slate also listed candidates for three of the seven lesser state-wide positions: attorney general, state treasurer, and superintendent of education. Numerous candidates for legislative or parish offices also identified with Long, none more than Oscar K. Allen, running for state senator in the district that included Winn Parish.[41]

Of Huey's two opponents, only Governor Simpson dared show up at joint appearances, and Simpson soon realized this was a mistake. At a rally and barbecue one November day at the town of Colfax, Huey—in the local paper's words—"dramatically proclaimed it to be the proudest moment of his life that he had Gov. Simpson where he could tell it to him good and proper." Huey mentioned Simpson's shortcomings as governor, then lingered over his opponent's alleged personal weaknesses, including his fondness for liquor and race tracks. The governor tried to demur but was drowned out by Huey's foghorn blasts.[42] On other occasions, Long accused Simpson of having divorced his first wife, of shirking military duty in the Spanish-American War (although there was no draft then), and of manufacturing "gambling devices." The only basis for the latter charge was that Simpson owned stock in the Adonis Candy Company, and Adonis displayed punchboards that allowed a purchaser of its sweets to try for a free piece of candy.[43]

Huey yearned in vain for a face-to-face confrontation with his other adversary, Riley Joe Wilson. Lacking such a meeting, Long at some point in every speech turned his talent for sarcasm upon the absent congressman. Wilson's chief selling point was his work in Congress on flood control. Remarking on that, Huey sneered: "He has been in Congress for fourteen years and this year the water went fourteen feet higher than ever before, giving him a flood record of one foot of high water to the year, if that's what he's claiming credit for." He also referred to Wilson as "Prince Riley of Ruston," accused him of riding around in Cadillacs, Lincolns, and even Rolls Royces, and belittled the congressman's career by saying, "Wilson's autobiography reads like the obituary notice of a village alderman."[44]

Four years earlier, in his first try for the governorship, Huey had learned that contradicting himself—for example, by taking one position before a Catholic audience and another when speaking to Protestants—was apt to be reported in the city press and spread over the state. That experience had taught him something. He wanted newspapermen to publicize him and report most of what he said; the problem was how to keep them from hearing his worst contradictions. Huey devised a solution. As George Healy, a young *Times-Picayune* reporter assigned to cover him during the 1927–1928 campaign recalled: "Huey made five or six speeches a day in communities anywhere from fifty to two hundred miles apart. . . . Better than any other politician I've known, Huey knew what his different audiences wanted to hear. . . . When he changed stories, it generally was at the beginning of his speech, before reporters assigned to cover him had caught up with him after an earlier rally."[45]

"Louisiana elections are won and lost in the newspapers," *Time* magazine noted, with only slight exaggeration, when summarizing the Long-Wilson-Simpson race. This time, at least, Huey had impressive support from publishers. In 1924 no dailies and only two or three weeklies had backed Huey; now he was endorsed by the state's biggest press magnate, "Colonel" Robert Ewing, owner of the New Orleans *States* and Shreveport *Times*. More than twenty weeklies also supported Long's second try for the governorship. John Ewing, the colonel's son and editor of the *Times*, must have privately gagged at his father's endorsement of Huey, for—as Thomas O. Harris wrote John M. Parker, the younger Ewing "appears to hate [Long] with a deadly and unholy hatred."[46] But the old colonel always had yearned to be a power behind the throne in Louisiana politics, and Huey led him to believe he would be just that in a Long administration.

Despite his impressive gain in press support, more newspapers still fought against Huey than backed him. Wilson boasted endorsements from the New Orleans *Item* and its morning edition, the *Tribune*, along with two of Shreveport's three dailies (the *Journal* and the *Caucasian*) and more country weeklies than either Long or Simpson. Governor Simpson's chief journalistic backer was Louisiana's leading morning paper, the New Orleans *Times-Picayune*.[47] The fact that in this race Huey enjoyed, for his first and only time, significant newspaper support did not mean he stopped using his personal journalistic device of circulars; indeed, he issued more than ever. His belief in the attention-getting value of these one-page bombshells had commenced with the Winnfield High circular that led to his departure from school without a diploma at age sixteen. Broadside circulars remained his favorite method of disseminating printed propaganda until, as governor, he began his own newspaper, the *Louisiana Progress*.[48]

Huey was also coming to believe in radio. Broadcasting in Louisiana dated from April of 1922, when WAAB, owned by the *Times-Picayune*, began transmitting music, news, and demeaning "negro stories" rendered in dialect by a "Mr. Kennedy," who was white.[49] Another early New Orleans station, WCAU, had carried Huey's maiden radio address in January of 1924, his only use of the airwaves during his first run for the governorship. By the 1927–1928 campaign, however, radio was becoming commonplace in Louisiana; even poor households were likely to have cheap battery sets, purchased secondhand or on credit. Huey realized radio's potential and took increasing advantage of it. Radio seemed made for him. His strong, confident voice could override all but the heaviest static, and he enjoyed free time over the state's most powerful station, Henderson's KWKH in Shreveport. At night KWKH's signal blanketed all of Louisiana and Arkansas and most of Texas, and could be heard as far away as Canada.[50]

In this, his second race for governor, Huey had far more money, organization, and local politicos behind him than in his first campaign, although Congressman Wilson seemed to possess more of all three. Simpson, as the incumbent, enjoyed a built-in organization of state employees but, judging by his smaller advertisements and fewer endorsements, had less money and fewer men of vote-pulling influence than either Wilson or Long. The state's two United States senators, Ransdell and Broussard, took no public part in the governor's race, even though Huey recently had campaigned for both their reelections. Huey did not ask them for public support. He did not want either senator to be able to claim credit for his victory. Ransdell and Broussard did, however, help Huey by sending word to their key people to support him.[51]

Money along with endorsements drifted toward Huey because, increasingly, he looked like a winner. W. K. Henderson and Swords Lee again sent generous contributions, and this time funds also arrived from numerous contractors hoping to build roads or other projects in a Long administration. Huey's brother Earl, now a prosperous shoe-polish drummer, handed over ten thousand dollars. Two of Shreveport's wealthiest businessmen, Leon Kahn and Ernest Bernstein (the latter being Huey's client in the winning suit against Commercial National Bank), sent large amounts. But the most bounteous contributor to the Long campaign of 1927–1928 was a rich New Orleanian of Sicilian descent, Robert S. Maestri.[52]

Maestri was born into a family of immigrant entrepreneurs who had a furniture store on the edge of Storyville, the old red-light district. The Maestris also owned a row of cut-rate whorehouses inside Storyville, on Conti Street, space in which they rented out by the day to overaged or uncomely prostitutes. Business acumen rather than formal education personified the Maestri family; young Robert quit school after the third grade to become a clerk in his father's store, and eventually assumed management of the family properties. Through shrewd investments and carefully cultivated friendships with police captains and others in places of power, Robert Maestri by 1928 was one of the wealthiest men in New Orleans.[53] Income from vice probably was not his chief source of income—allegations that he controlled gambling dens in neighboring St. Bernard Parish were always denied—but some of his properties evidently were associated with illegal activities. Short and swarthy, ill at ease with people of gentility (it was he who asked President Franklin D. Roosevelt, during an oyster dinner at Antoine's, the legendary question, "How ya like dem ersters?"), Maestri became virtually inarticulate at public or ceremonial events.[54] He understood that his only chance of achieving real status and respect in Louisiana was to attach himself and his money to a charismatic leader such as Huey Long.

In Huey's previous race for governor, his New Orleans organization, such as it was, had been provided by the Williams brothers; this time he enjoyed backing by the supposedly more potent New Regulars of John P. Sullivan and Colonel Ewing. The New

Regular leadership must have decided Huey was headed for victory, and swallowed their misgivings about him in order to have a friendly governor. The Old Regulars, headed by Mayor Arthur J. O'Keefe, who had succeeded to the office when Behrman died, came out for Congressman Wilson; Governor Simpson's organization in the city was managed by Paul Maloney, a dissident Old Regular ward boss who in 1925 had run as the New Regulars' candidate against Behrman.[55]

As the campaign wore on, Huey shifted the brunt of his attacks from Wilson and Simpson to the "evil forces" behind them. Wilson's Shreveport organizer, Andrew Querbes, and that city's leading Simpson backer, Mayor "Wet Jug" Thomas, were favorite targets. Huey claimed that Querbes, a bank president, once operated a low "nigger" saloon and dive. Thomas caught even worse. Speaking in Shreveport, Huey accused the mayor of: (1) friendship with the Negro Republican leader Walter Cohen, (2) being so odorous that a skunk could not stay in the same room with him, and (3) being a "trough feeder" and "a low down, dirty thief and liar."[56] Querbes and Thomas were disliked or envied by many of their fellow townsmen, and the crowd in City Hall Auditorium howled its approval: this was excitement, this was retribution, this was entertainment. Triple-horned loudspeakers blared Huey's tirade into the streets below. One listener, Arthur M. Shaw, stood for a few minutes at the back of the upstairs auditorium and "watched and heard the jubilant orator, who was obviously having a good time." Shaw then walked down to the street. "Here as I heard the greatly amplified voice, the strident tones of which seemed to shake that part of town," he recalled, "I tingled with an excitement that was not altogether pleasant."[57]

Mayor Thomas was more agitated than that. He sued Huey for slander; the case eventually was dismissed on a technicality. The Shreveport *Caucasian* thought it was "unmanly" of Thomas to sue Huey; instead, the two should be "fighting it out in the good old-fashioned way." Another writer, also attuned to Louisiana's violent past, suggested that "Huey P. Long . . . would not have been allowed to live a week if the *code duello* had still been in force."[58]

No duel, but a public brawl, erupted between soon-to-be Governor Long and one target of his abuse. Ex-governor J. Y. Sanders, still smarting from his previous year's loss to Long-backed

Senator Broussard, again found himself pounded by Huey's verbal guns. Sanders was supporting Riley Joe Wilson, but Huey insisted—much as he had done with Governor Parker four years earlier—that Sanders actually controlled both of Huey's opponents. The charge was untrue. "J. Y.," as other politicians always called him, seemingly had dominated the administration of deceased Governor Fuqua, and he hoped to control Wilson, but he had no influence with Simpson. Nevertheless, Sanders was vulnerable because he symbolized the shortsightedness of the old regime and was chief legal counsel to two business interests that Huey correctly opposed as being contrary to the public good: a planned private toll bridge across the narrows of Lake Pontchartrain, and the carbon-black industry, which was wasting north Louisiana's natural gas and polluting its streams.[59]

On the afternoon of November 15, 1927, Long and Sanders fought in the lobby of New Orleans' Roosevelt Hotel. They did not plan the encounter—the block-long chandeliered lobby of the Roosevelt was simply a likely place for prominent Louisianians to meet—but when Sanders saw Long he called him a liar and other uncomplimentary things. Huey responded with a glancing blow to the former governor's jaw. Then, according to most witnesses, Huey turned and ran down the lobby toward an elevator, with Sanders in close pursuit. Huey was thirty-four and weighed about 170; J. Y. was fifty-nine and corpulent, weighing well above 200. Their running fight—Sanders moved quickly for his age and heft—would be diagrammed in a map of the lobby for readers of next day's New Orleans *Morning Tribune*. The combat concluded in the elevator. Huey later emerged with one of J. Y.'s cuff links, exhibiting it as a trophy. Sanders also claimed victory, telling reporters that Long crouched "in the elevator like a terror-stricken kitten."[60] Actually, neither man suffered more than slight bruises. The lobby portion of the fight was observed by Orange Crush delegates attending a national bottlers' convention, giving those visitors something to talk about when they returned home to more sedate parts of America.

Widespread publicity of Huey's hit-and-run brawl with J. Y. gave conservatives additional ammunition and new hope that their enemy might be defeated. It seemed inconceivable to many that Louisiana, with its virile heritage, would elect someone so evidently lacking in manly honor. "A state is frequently judged through the character of its governor," warned New Iberia's *Enterprise*, and several other papers began referring to Long as "Hot Foot Huey." Questions about his manhood became more explicit. "It is not so bad that he has the fights," opined a Rayville editor. "It is the running which makes it so shameful and disgraceful." The Shreveport *Caucasian* began spelling his name in lower case, "huey p. long." In New Orleans, "red-blooded" union men were said to be disavowing earlier support for a "running yellow candidate" who struck old men, dwarfs, and cripples. The *Federationist*, a city labor paper, decided Huey was insane as well as a coward: "There is only one place in the state that befits Huey and that is Jackson [the state asylum]. They could let him imagine he is the Governor and he would not annoy the public."[61]

Probably no Louisiana politician before him could have survived this kind of notoriety. But he was Huey Long, a unique being; J. Y. Sanders was the first to call him "sui generis," a term Huey liked and appropriated when asked to categorize himself. Ordinary people flocked to hear him and to cheer, not merely because he put on a good show while excoriating the rich and powerful, but also because he addressed real problems and pledged to bring Louisiana out of its dirt and darkness. "Long," Alan Brinkley pointed out, "tapped not only the anger and resentment, but also the hopes that lay just beneath them."[62]

Huey made sure all the state's voters got his message. Ewing's newspaper support and the circulars helped, as did radio, but personal appearance was the thing Long did best and enjoyed the most. If his campaign pace four years earlier had been hectic, that of 1927–1928 was frenetic. His schedule, the reporter Harnett Kane claimed, "would have killed a man with anything short of a mule's constitution." As election day approached, Huey estimated that he had made six hundred speeches and traveled fifteen thousand miles. His crowds grew ever bigger and more enthusiastic. "They came from every bottom in the country, by car, wagon, horseback, on foot," Oscar Guidry, a Long backer in Acadia Parish recalled. After listening in rapt attention, many would head for Huey's next scheduled stop to hear him again; some who had automobiles followed him all day. On a rainy night in Ruston, after the auditorium in which he spoke became so packed that no one else could enter, people stood out-

side in the downpour. Most ominous to his foes, Huey was drawing such crowds in the Cajun as well as the Anglo parishes.[63]

The most-quoted example of Huey at his melodramatic best
is his speech beneath the Evangeline Oak, in the Cajun town of
St. Martinville, toward the end of this campaign. When Huey
wrote his autobiography, *Every Man a King*, he proudly included
a florid but effective portion of his St. Martinville speech:

> And it is here, under this oak where Evangeline waited in vain for
> her lover, Gabriel, who never came. This oak is an immortal spot,
> made so by Longfellow's poem, but Evangeline is not the only one
> who has waited here in disappointment.
>
> Where are the schools that you have waited for your children to
> have, that have never come? Where are the roads and the highways
> that you sent your money to build, that are no nearer now than ever
> before? Where are the institutions to care for the sick and disabled?
> Evangeline wept bitter tears in her disappointment, but it lasted
> through only one lifetime. Your tears in this country, around this oak,
> have lasted for generations. Give me the chance to dry the eyes of
> those who still weep here![64]

Election day, January 17, 1928, dawned over Louisiana cool
and sunny. The anti-Long *Tensas Gazette* had vainly hoped "it
will rain like the devil in the hill-billy parishes," as had happened in 1924, so as to keep this "clown" out of the governor's
mansion. The good weather must have gratified Huey, but the
New Orleans returns, coming in first on election night, proved
disappointing for him: once again he ran a poor third in the metropolis, despite Sullivan's and Ewing's backing. Huey had
known he would not carry New Orleans. Still, he had anticipated doing better than that. More grim news came over the radio: he also was losing the second and third largest cities in the
state, Shreveport and Baton Rouge, by substantial margins.
Then, after midnight, the country returns began pouring in.
Louisiana in the 1920s was still predominantly rural: fully 65
percent of the state's population, including 60 percent of the voting whites, lived in the countryside and villages. Huey was
sweeping both the Anglo uplands and the Cajun parishes, losing
only the cotton plantation areas, where voters were relatively
few. When all precincts were in, the "windjammer from Winn,"
as the Shreveport *Journal* called him, had 43.9 percent of the

vote to Wilson's 28.3 and Simpson's 27.8. In absolute numbers, the state-wide returns showed Long with 126,842 votes, Wilson with 81,747, and Simpson with 80,326. Huey had run first in forty-seven of the sixty-four parishes, carrying thirty-eight by outright majorities.[65]

Die-hard conservatives urged Wilson to fight a second primary with Long, since to be certified as the Democratic nominee Huey would have to win a state-wide majority or be conceded victory by the withdrawal of the second-place candidate. The New Orleans *Item-Tribune* advanced the dubious proposition that "99 out of 100 of [Simpson's voters] would turn cheerfully to ... Mr. Wilson." Governor Simpson himself remained secluded for several days following the vote count, raising suspicions he had "gone on a prolonged drunk."[66] But within a week the governor's New Orleans organization endorsed Huey. Presently Simpson did too; he would be rewarded with a lucrative job in the Long administration. The influential *Times-Picayune*, meanwhile, told Wilson he should withdraw from a hopeless battle that would further divide the city from rural Louisiana and also "disturb" the upcoming Mardi Gras celebrations. Wilson's Old Regular backers agreed. The congressman then conceded the governorship to Huey Long.[67]

Long went on to easy victory over a Republican nonentity in the April general election, 92,941 to 3,733. But Huey had known he would be Louisiana's next governor from the moment, late at night following the January Democratic primary, when returns from Cajun parishes started rolling in. That night Hamilton Basso, a journalist who concealed from his bosses an admiration for Huey, walked into Long's littered headquarters at the Roosevelt Hotel and heard him exclaim to his lieutenants: "You fellers stick with me. We're just getting started. This is only the beginning. . . . From now on I'm the Kingfish. I'm gonna be President some day."[68]

Reverend Benjamin M. Palmer of New Orleans' prestigious First Presbyterian Church. From the Civil War to the early twentieth century, Palmer was the most influential Protestant preacher in the state, and a mentor to many Louisiana leaders, including Governor John M. Parker.

From Thomas Cary Johnson, *The Life and Letters of Benjamin Morgan Palmer* (Richmond, 1906)

John M. Parker. A progressive reformer who in some ways embodied the best of Louisiana's Establishment, Parker served as governor from 1920 to 1924. Long, after supporting Parker in the 1920 election, soon turned against him. The two became bitter enemies.

A statue dedicated to "the good darkies of Louisiana," erected in Natchitoches in 1927. It now stands at the LSU Rural Life Museum in Baton Rouge.

Photo by Edwin L. Wisherd © 1930 National Geographic Society

A lynching near Labadieville, Louisiana, in 1933. The victim, Freddie Moore, was accused of murdering a white girl. The girl's stepfather later confessed to the crime.

Courtesy Louisiana and Lower Mississippi Valley Collections, Louisiana State University

Huey Long's boyhood home in Winnfield, *ca.* 1913.
Courtesy the Bettmann Archive

Huey Long as a young traveling salesman, age sixteen or seventeen.
Courtesy Louisiana State Library

Huey and Rose McConnell Long early in their marriage.

A flyer from Huey's first political campaign, his 1918 run for the post of railroad commissioner. He won.

Courtesy Louisiana and Lower Mississippi Valley Collections, Louisiana State University

They Couldn't Live on Potlikker, Could They, Huey?

A typically unflattering New Orleans *Times-Picayune* cartoon of Huey, showing him with a glowing nose and a pot belly, running the state to ruin.
From New Orleans *Times-Picayune*, July 5, 1934

Alice Lee Grosjean, Huey's confidential secretary, in 1930, the
year Huey had her appointed,
at age twenty-four, as Louisiana's secretary of state.
Courtesy Louisiana State Library

Hilda Phelps Hammond. An
implacable enemy of Huey's,
Mrs. Hammond organized the
Women's Committee of Louisiana to promote anti-Long
activity. To her, the Kingfish
"represented pure evil."
Courtesy the Bettmann Archive

Seymour Weiss (no kin to Dr. Carl Austin Weiss), the financial manager of Huey Long's organization, confers with his boss during the Overton hearings. The anti-Long newspaperman Hodding Carter referred to Weiss as "an oily former shoe clerk."

A Philadelphia *Inquirer* cartoon depicting Franklin D. Roosevelt as smiling at Huey Long's political threats.

Courtesy Philadelphia *Inquirer*

TIME

The Weekly Newsmagazine

International

Volume XXV

CANDIDATE LONG
Give him honor or give him death:
(See NATIONAL AFFAIRS)

Number 13

Time magazine's cover for April 1, 1935. This was the second cover story *Time* had done on Long.

Dr. Carl Austin Weiss, Huey Long's presumed assassin.
Courtesy Louisiana State Library

Huey makes his celebrated windmill gesture.
Courtesy AP/Wide World Photos

· 10 ·

"I'M THE KINGFISH"

"LOUISIANA TO HAVE COLORFUL GOVERNOR," prophesied a New York *Times* headline following Huey's victory in the Democratic primary. America's foremost newspaper had begun paying attention to what it called this "amazing personality" from the South's hinterland at the time of his seriocomic fight with J. Y. Sanders in the Roosevelt Hotel; now, with his upcoming inauguration, the *Times* advised its readers to learn how to pronounce the name of a place called Baton Rouge.[1]

The thirty-four-year-old governor's inauguration on May 21, 1928, illustrated his penchant for mixing tradition with change in Louisiana's public affairs. All the usual ceremonies took place: a parade in the morning through downtown Baton Rouge; the swearing-in ritual at noon beside the old Gothic-style capitol building that Mark Twain had derided as a "little sham castle . . . with turrets and things"; the inaugural address; afternoon concerts; and an evening reception at the governor's mansion followed by an inaugural ball. Yet there were unaccustomed Winn Parish touches: a country music band, water buckets with tin dippers, and unstylishly dressed rural folk taking part in the festivities. Governor Long's formal remarks were mostly standard for the occasion and approached John M. Parker's for brevity. Twice during his address, however, Huey characteristically declared that he had no further political ambitions.[2]

The legislature had begun meeting a week prior to the inauguration. Only 18 of the 100 representatives and 9 of the 39 senators were elected as Long supporters; legislators firmly opposed to him numbered about the same. Most members in both houses, mindful of the extraordinary patronage power vested in Louisiana's governor, were uncommitted but flexible. To help organize the majority behind his agenda, Huey depended upon two old acquaintances from Winn Parish who had been elected on his ticket: Senator O. K. Allen and Representative Harley Bozeman. Allen and Bozeman did their work well. Long's choices for president *pro tempore* of the senate (Philip H. Gilbert) and Speaker of the House (John B. Fournet) were seated by sizable margins. Huey then told Gilbert and Fournet whom to appoint to all committees—something no governor had ever done.[3] The outvoted opposition was stunned; they were still only dimly aware of what they were facing.

Controlling the 1928 legislature, Huey was able to ram through much of his progressive program. The free schoolbook bill passed; to win Catholic support, it included parochial as well as public schools. In reply to objections that providing books to religious private schools unconstitutionally mixed church and state, Huey said the books were for individual children, who after all were citizens; the schools would merely distribute the books. The $30-million bond issue for highway and bridge construction needed a two-thirds majority because it had to be submitted to the voters as a constitutional amendment (a provision of the Constitution of 1921, still in effect, required roads and bridges to be financed out of current revenues only). Louisiana in 1928 had just 331 miles of hard-surfaced (concrete or asphalt) highways, excluding paved streets in the cities. There were only three bridges over major rivers: two across the Red (one at Shreveport, another at Alexandria), and one across the Ouachita at Monroe. The state had no bridges over the Mississippi or Atchafalaya rivers; slow ferries had to suffice. In 1928 it took at least six hours to drive from Opelousas to Baton Rouge, fifty miles away. Yet J. Y. Sanders, symbol of the old regime, boasted of "the splendid highway system we now have and enjoy in Louisiana."[4]

Understandably, since the free textbooks and bond issues for highways and bridges necessitated tax increases, Huey could not seriously try to carry out all his promises at once. Appropriations for colleges and other public institutions were modestly increased, but by a smaller percentage than during Governor Parker's administration.[5] And the methods Huey used to pass his bills (particularly the bond-issue bill, requiring a two-thirds majority) demonstrated his scorn for the principle of separation of powers, as well as his determination to accomplish objectives regardless of means.

At least sixteen legislators—probably more than twenty—were given what amounted to deadhead jobs in state agencies; others who already had relatives on the payroll were told to "get right," or their kinsmen would be removed. One legislator believed that some of his colleagues sided with Long because they were blackmailed by threats to reveal things in their past, or situations concerning their relatives. "Huey studied and catalogued skeletons in the families of old aristocrats," a lieutenant later remarked. He was the first governor since Reconstruction's Henry Clay Warmoth to walk uninvited into senate or House sessions or committee hearings and tell legislators what they should do. When one opposition member thrust a copy of the state constitution at him and asked if he knew what it was, Huey replied: "I'm the constitution around here now."[6]

Huey led by compulsion instead of statesmanship because he was internally driven by a force he seemed unable to control. His brilliant and retentive mind took no time for reflection or intellectuality; he denied himself both restraint and breadth of vision. Instead, Huey focused his genius on specific situations that could be aimed toward the only goal that truly mattered—the domination of everybody around him. Domination was of the utmost importance because only by making others recognize the centrality of Huey Long's existence could he validate, confirm, that Olympian self-image without which life would be meaningless.

Anti-Long sentiment in the 1928 legislature grew strongest in the lower house, where twenty-seven opponents called themselves the "Dynamite Squad." Although heavily outnumbered, the Dynamiters were astute parliamentarians; they would have succeeded in blocking most of Long's legislation had not their foe been so resourceful. Cecil Morgan of Caddo Parish, Norman Bauer of St. Mary, Mason Spencer of Madison, and J. Y. Sanders, Jr., of East Baton Rouge were the ablest among them. Every evening during the session, leaders of the Dynamite Squad plotted strategy at J. Y. Jr.'s downtown Baton Rouge law office in the Reymond Building. It was a prestigious address. One of Louisiana's most respected physicians, Dr. Carl Adam Weiss, had his office there; he was a friend both of former governor Sanders and Sanders' son, and of ex-governor Parker, who was one of his patients. Four years later, in 1932, Dr. Weiss's brilliant son, Dr. Carl Austin Weiss, joined his father's practice in the Reymond Building.[7]

Years later, reflecting on their failure to stop Long or his legislation, some members of the Dynamite Squad agreed that much of what Huey advocated was good, and that they had been wrong in so intransigently opposing everything in his program. Bauer said he fought any Long bill mainly because of "his overbearing ways. . . . We resented being told we had to be with him." Cecil Morgan admitted that "the stodginess of the old-line politicians who had been running the state and who had not done anything to meet the needs of the people" unlocked the door to power for Huey Long. After Long was killed, Mason Spencer's hometown *Madison Journal* conceded that Huey had accomplished much for Louisiana, but the paper still objected to "the methods employed." Hodding Carter, editor of a bitterly anti-Long newspaper and friend of J. Y. Sanders, Jr., criticized Huey's opponents most succinctly: "Looking back," Carter wrote from the perspective of 1949, "I know now that part of our failure arose from an unwillingness to approve any Long-sponsored proposal for change, regardless of its merits."[8]

To pay for free textbooks, highways, and bridges, Huey persuaded the legislature to raise severance taxes on oil, gas, lumber, and other natural products by shifting the levy from percentages of gross market value (3 percent on oil and gas, 2 percent on the others), to rates set by the quantity and quality extracted. (Notably, four to eleven cents per barrel of oil, depending on grade.) The actual increase was modest, but litigation by one of the oil companies delayed collections until 1930. Meanwhile, Huey's constitutional amendment for a bond issue to build roads and bridges received voter approval by a three-to-one margin; only Caddo and DeSoto parishes voted against it. Temporary funding for state purchase of schoolbooks was arranged with New Orleans banks through the governor's "negotiations"—the bankers agreed to advance the money as soon as Huey threatened to withhold payments on previous state debts.[9]

Huey Long in 1928 signed two bills into law that could not be considered progressive. One was in the tradition of using the "separate but equal" subterfuge to maintain racial discrimination: motor buses were beginning to compete with trains, so Act

204 of 1928 applied Louisiana's railroad segregation law of 1890 (which had resulted in the *Plessy* v. *Ferguson* decision) to bus passengers, with a fine or thirty-day jail sentence for anyone "insisting upon going to a seat or compartment to which by race he or she does not belong." In Huey's defense, he could not have vetoed that bill and expected any political future in Louisiana; as he later told Roy Wilkins of the NAACP, "there are some things even Huey Long can't get away with."[10] Another bill, this one Huey's own brainchild, hinted of the police state to come: Act 99 created a Bureau of Criminal Identification, with the governor appointing its board of managers and serving as chairman. The BCI was independent of all police, sheriffs, or constables, and was "empowered to make arrests anywhere in the State of Louisiana, without warrants, for all violations of the law." Act 99 passed partly because Huey dangled bait for the Caddo Parish representatives: the bill designated Shreveport as BCI headquarters. This ominous act was strengthened in 1934, when the Bureau of Criminal Identification was totally subordinated "to the orders of the Governor," its location moved to the capitol building in Baton Rouge, and the restriction that its personnel be "of good moral character" removed.[11]

Increasingly fearful for his safety, Governor Long surrounded himself with bodyguards who drew salaries ostensibly as members of either the BCI or the state police. His first full-time bodyguard was Harry "Battling" Bozeman (no relation to Harley Bozeman). Bozeman was an ex-prizefighter of limited intelligence. When Huey began to doubt his loyalty, he fired him. Joe Messina took Battling's place. Messina, a World War I veteran who allegedly had suffered shell shock, was working as a menial at Baton Rouge's Heidelberg Hotel when Huey met him; Messina seemed even stupider than Bozeman, but his devotion to the governor was described as "doglike." Messina would also act as Huey's valet. Other, more alert bodyguards were soon added to Huey's retinue: Murphy Roden, Louie Jones, George McQuiston (who carried a sawed-off shotgun in a paper sack, with a hole for his trigger finger), Paul Voitier, Elliott Coleman, and James Brocato (who used the alias "Jimmy Moran").[12]

Brocato (Moran) was part of the New Orleans underworld in the 1920s and 1930s. Born of immigrant parents, he once had been a barber and a little-known prizefighter, but with Prohibition he turned to gambling and bootlegging. Physically, he resembled Robert Maestri, with whom he was often seen. Brocato was an excellent cook and often prepared Italian dishes for Huey. His duties as a bodyguard were minimal. Usually, he stayed with the governor only on weekends and special occasions, because he had business interests in New Orleans that required attention—in 1930, he was sent to federal prison for a year "as a second offender for violation of the Prohibition law." When released on parole, Brocato was welcomed back into the Long retinue.[13] Huey did not entirely trust anyone, but since being alone was unendurable, and because he needed protection more than any American politician of his day, he was compelled to draw around him armed men such as Messina, Brocato, and Roden who, whatever their shortcomings, not only appeared to share Huey's opinion of himself, but also reacted instantly to potential danger.

Patronage—the dispensing of government jobs—had been essential to the power of Louisiana's chief executives since colonial times. Huey Long's knowledge of state history was superficial at best (for instance, he thought the British in the War of 1812 had "whipped the whole United States except Louisiana," which then saved America from "surrender").[14] Yet by observation or instinct he understood that his domination of the state would hinge upon absolute control of patronage. More than highways, schools, or anything else, obtaining allegiance through patronage occupied Huey's time during his first months as governor. Vengeance also played a role. Huey confessedly enjoyed firing people who were not on his side (hiring their replacements was less pleasurable). "No music ever sounded one-half so refreshing," he noted, "as the whines and moans" of "pie-eaters when shoved away from the pie."[15]

During 1928 Huey succeeded—by patronage and threats—in pressuring the legislature to pass laws giving him control of all major state agencies, including the Board of Health, the Department of Conservation, Charity Hospital in New Orleans, and the New Orleans Levee Board. The Highway Commission, with more jobs than any other agency, fell to him immediately because an earlier law empowered the governor to name all commissioners, who in turn selected all workers from engineers to night watchmen. To chair the Highway Commission, Long chose O. K. Allen. Maestri headed the Department of Conservation. Dr. Arthur Vidrine, a surgeon from Ville Platte, was appointed superintendent of Charity Hospital, the largest medical facility for indigent patients in the South. (Vidrine, ironically, would be called upon to operate on the dying Huey in 1935.) Huey required most appointees to managerial positions to sign undated letters of resignation.[16]

New Orleans remained a problem. The metropolis had disappointed Huey in both his gubernatorial races: neither the Williamses' backing in 1924 nor that of Sullivan and Ewing in 1928 had given Long anything better than a distant third-place finish. The Old Regular machine still controlled City Hall, and its legislators made up most of the anti-Long bloc in Baton Rouge. During Huey's winning campaign for governor, he had pledged to bring cheap natural gas from north Louisiana to the city, instead of seeing the resource "wasted in the manufacture of carbon black." By the time he became governor, New Orleans' franchised monopoly on gas, electricity, and streetcar service had been reorganized as NOPSI (New Orleans Public Service, Inc.); it was still privately owned, mostly by northern stockholders, although the city retained an option to purchase the company. Like its predecessor, New Orleans Railway and Light, NOPSI refused to pipe in natural gas, claiming that because of the city's warm climate, high-priced artificial gas ($1.35 per thousand cubic feet) was all the company could profitably provide. Huey promised to make NOPSI bring in natural gas and sell it at $.70 per thousand cubic feet.[17]

Eventually, Long and NOPSI agreed to a rate of $1.15 per thousand cubic feet (including a monthly meter charge) on piped-in natural gas. The savings to consumers was actually greater than the figure indicates, since artificial gas is only half as efficient as natural. While Huey was negotiating with company spokesmen, the city council at last proposed municipal ownership, and a New Orleans legislator introduced bills to provide for the necessary bond issue. Naturally, NOPSI preferred the governor's compromise rates to municipal ownership. So did Huey, and the bond-issue bills died in committee, as he decided they should. Soon New Orleans businesses and homes received natural gas, Huey claimed the credit, and NOPSI decided the governor was a reasonable man after all.[18] Rudolph Hecht, chairman of NOPSI's board of directors, soon became known as "a close friend of Long." For decades the New Orleans Ring had made behind-the-scenes deals favorable to business while posing as the people's champion. Now, as Harnett Kane observed, Huey "had beaten the Ring at its own game."[19]

As Huey plunged deeper into taking charge of Louisiana, he spent less and less time at the old governor's mansion. It stood several blocks from the capitol building, whereas the Heidelberg Hotel, Baton Rouge's best, loomed across the street from the capitol. Besides, ever since his traveling salesman days, Huey had liked staying at hotels. Finally, he disliked anything that seemed antique, and the columned mansion, built before the Civil War, was an example of plantation architecture. It was full of "damn rats," Huey complained, and "there were too many clocks in the place"—their unsynchronized striking kept him awake during the brief time he allowed himself for sleep. The roof leaked. Also, according to one employee, "he asserted he found it galling to live in a house that John Parker and Ruffin Pleasant had occupied." Worst of all, Huey felt unsafe in a place with so many high windows, facing a boulevard. One evening, a visiting politician wondered aloud why the governor was pulling down all the shades. Huey replied, "I'm a cinch to get shot."[20]

Rose did not like the mansion either, although for another reason. When Huey, Rose, and their three children moved into the place in May, Huey, with consummate brazenness, furnished his personal secretary, Alice Lee Grosjean, with living quarters there. This was too much, even for gentle Rose. She took the children, returned to their Shreveport home, and according to several members of Huey's entourage, threatened a divorce suit. Alice then moved out of the mansion and into room 720 in the Heidelberg Hotel. Soon Rose, daughter Rose, and sons Russell and Palmer came back to the mansion, but when Huey began spending most nights in his hotel suite (room 738, the Heidelberg), his family again left for Shreveport. Thereafter, while Huey was governor, Rose appeared in Baton Rouge only on special occasions.[21]

Huey also took a twelfth-floor suite in New Orleans' finest hotel, the Roosevelt. It had been his state headquarters during the last campaign for governor. During that time, Huey had come to know and like the hotel's assistant manager, Seymour Weiss (no relation to the Weiss physicians of Baton Rouge), who quickly became an important figure in Long's retinue. Weiss also climbed rapidly at the Roosevelt: soon he was general manager, and within a few years, principal owner. Born to a poor Jewish family in the town of Bunkie, Avoyelles Parish, Weiss had only a third-grade education. As a teenager he worked at various lowly jobs in nearby Alexandria. In 1925, at twenty-eight, he moved to New Orleans—having left Alexandria "at the urgent request of a committee of citizens," according to one source. Weiss first found employment in New Orleans at a footwear store (years later, Hodding Carter disdainfully referred to him as "an oily former shoe clerk"); he initially came to the Roosevelt as manager of its barber shop. His rapid advancement at the hotel was at least partly the result of his friendship with the new governor, who was in a position to adjust tax rates. Within a year after meeting Huey, Weiss became financial manager of Long's political organization. Most of the money received—a large portion being kickbacks from contractors doing business with the state—went to Weiss for safekeeping at the Roosevelt Hotel.[22]

Whenever Huey visited New Orleans, which was often, Weiss also served as his major-domo, admitting visitors to the governor's suite and making sure Huey's food, drinks, and garments were to satisfaction. Seymour Weiss had worked hard to improve himself culturally as well as financially. A biographical sketch described him as "immaculate in dress, and unusually suave in speech and manner. . . . He is almost entirely self-educated, yet . . . possesses the vocabulary of a college professor." Weiss also deserved credit for some improvement in Huey's sartorial style. Huey had always liked flashy clothes and jewelry, and he continued to wear bright colors, but Weiss taught him that certain combinations, such as brown shoes with a blue suit, did not work. On one formal occasion when Huey's flaming red tie clashed with his swallowtail coat and striped trousers, Weiss exclaimed: "Jesus Christ! You can't go down there like that."[23]

The old mansion was doomed from the moment Huey learned, in October of 1928, that it had termites. This was the excuse he needed to tear it down. He applied to the Board of Liquidation for a $150,000 loan to build a new mansion. The request was granted contingent upon the results of a mail poll of members of the legislature. Huey apparently contacted only those legislators he thought would approve, and early in 1929, in what was surely a studied gesture of contempt for the old Louisiana that the mansion symbolized, he summoned a gang of convicts from state prison to tear the building down. Joe Messina supervised its demolition. What became of most of the mansion's antique furniture, fine china, and silverware remains one of Louisiana's mysteries.[24]

In the November general election of 1928, when voters approved Governor Long's bond issue for roads and bridges, Louisiana also overwhelmingly endorsed his choice in the presidential race, Al Smith (D), over Herbert Hoover (R). This was the first national election since Reconstruction in which the Deep South's electoral votes were in doubt, for the Democratic nominee that year was a Catholic, a "wet" who urged repeal of the Prohibition amendment, and a New Yorker whose accent came over the radio as a harsh, alien sound. These perceived defects caused Smith to lose five former Confederate states. Louisiana, the only southern state with a Catholic voting majority, was considered safe for Smith, but disaffection toward the Democratic nominee was widespread in Protestant parishes. There, as in most of the rest of the South, the choice between Hoover and Smith was a hard one, since Republicans were still identified as the party of Yankees and blacks. Bible-belt voters, the acerbic Baltimore *Sun* columnist H. L. Mencken wrote, were having to select between "the Catholic bugaboo and the nigger bugaboo."[25]

That choice posed no problem for Huey. On the stump his Bible quoting sometimes made him sound like a rural Baptist evangelist, yet never did he show bigotry toward Catholics, Jews, or any other group that voted. He had no religious prejudice, one Long legislator recalled, "but he didn't have much religion either."[26] Huey's racial attitudes, on the other hand, seemed to fluctuate between traditional paternalism and plain indifference. By comparison with many contemporary southern politicians, especially Theodore Bilbo of Mississippi and Eugene Talmadge of Georgia, he was not a racist demagogue; he came to power by appealing to class antagonism, not hatred of blacks. Yet Huey was always mindful of racial reality in Louisiana: blacks could not vote, but whites did, and the vast majority of voters believed that keeping blacks economically dependent and legally helpless was part of the natural order of things. Being called a coward, a liar, a crook, and a dictator did not particularly worry Huey, but "nigger lover" was one tag he evidently feared, and he made special efforts to prevent it from sticking to him.

Speaking in support of Al Smith, Governor Long denounced

religious bigotry while appealing to racial bigotry. "I have no patience with two-bit ministers who are injecting religion into this campaign," Huey shouted, and in the next breath warned that if the South strayed from the Democratic party, "negro domination or social equality" would be the result. He added, "We believe this is a white man's country and are not willing to turn it over to the negroes."[27]

Ironically, Huey's blend of religious toleration and racial prejudice echoed the Louisiana patrician tradition. The Reverend Benjamin M. Palmer and Major Hearsey of the *States*, had they been alive in 1928, undoubtedly would have despised Huey Long personally, but could not have faulted what he said during the Hoover-Smith campaign. Louisiana's old ruling elite of well-to-do Protestants, Catholics, and Jews had smoothed over their religious and ethnic differences for the sake of achieving hegemony of their class over the state. Huey realized the value of that approach and believed, correctly, that he could similarly unite the poorer whites of both the Latin and Anglo parishes. Like his aristocratic predecessors, he understood the depth of racial feelings among the mass of whites; playing to that prejudice was not his favorite tune, but it was part of his repertoire.

Hoover's victory over Smith in the national returns was no surprise, and Huey probably did not much care which man occupied the White House. He may have secretly preferred to see conservative Republicans hold on to the presidency until he was ready to make his bid. What Huey campaigned for in the autumn of 1928, besides his road-and-bridge bond amendment, was to keep the Republican vote in Louisiana as low as possible. Most of all, he wanted to discourage a split of the electorate along religious lines, since that had been a problem to him in the past. Smith's big vote in Louisiana gratified Huey Long; the Democratic nominee carried all sixty-four parishes, although Hoover ran better than Republicans usually did in north Louisiana. Smith's overwhelming support in Catholic parishes, including New Orleans, gave the Democratic national ticket 76.3 percent of Louisiana's vote, third highest among the eight states Smith carried.[28]

When Huey's free schoolbooks were ready for distribution in the autumn of 1928, two parish school boards, in Caddo and Bossier, refused to accept them. Bossier's board soon changed its mind; Caddo's was more adamant. "This is a rich section of the

THE KINGFISH AND HIS REALM

state," exclaimed Mayor Thomas of Shreveport, the seat of
Caddo Parish. "We are not going to be humiliated by . . . our
children [being] given the books free."[29] Unfortunately, Shreveport presently needed a favor from Governor Long. The federal
government announced the city's vicinity as its first choice for a
new Army Air Corps base, but eighty acres would have to be do-
nated before construction began. A location across the Red
River from Shreveport had been selected, but because of legal
technicalities, a special act of the state legislature was needed to
transfer the land to the army. Huey, it so happened, was preparing to call the lawmakers into special session on December 10,
to pass enabling legislation for his recently approved bond-issue
amendment. Because it was a special session, the governor controlled the agenda; his approval was required for any other matter to be voted upon. Since an air base would benefit the economy of northwestern Louisiana, and since Huey owned a home
and other properties in Shreveport, the city fathers assumed the
governor would support the land transfer.[30] They were in error.

"You have decided here that your children can't have free textbooks," Huey reminded Louisiana's second-largest city. "People
so well off don't need an airport." William K. Henderson of
KWKH, one of Huey's biggest contributors, pleaded with him in
vain, and their telephone conversation ended in reciprocal cursing, with Henderson telling Long he was "a damned fool." Huey's
anger at Shreveport stemmed from more than the schoolbook
issue: he had run a poor second there in the recent gubernatorial
contest, he hated Mayor "Wet Jug" Thomas and other leading
citizens who had opposed him in the past, and he believed he
had been snubbed by not being invited to several banquets the
city's chamber of commerce had recently given for visiting War
Department and military personnel. Elderly Robert Ewing of
the New Orleans *States* and his son John D. Ewing of the Shreveport *Times*—Huey's most important newspaper backers in
1928—held what was described as "a very stormy" meeting with
the governor over the air base matter. The younger Ewing later
told legislators that Huey "demanded that the people of Shreveport recognize him in the future as Governor, and said something about bowing and scraping when he came along the
street."[31]

Specifically, Huey told the Ewings that certain terms had to
be met before he would include the needed air base bill on the

upcoming legislative session's agenda. His conditions included a published letter of apology from the Shreveport Chamber of Commerce for having slighted him in the banquet invitations, a promise of more front-page favorable publicity in the Shreveport *Times*, the support of Caddo Parish's legislative delegation for all bills he might introduce in the December special session, and immediate distribution of the free schoolbooks. These demands were indignantly refused; and indeed, this time Huey was mainly bluffing—or had second thoughts. On the second day of the special session, Huey put the air base bill in a supplemental agenda, and by agreement, the Caddo school board distributed the free books. The base, to be named Barksdale Field, could now be built. When the Kingfish was later questioned about "coercing" Shreveport and the school board, he answered: "I didn't coerce them. I *stomped* them into distributing the books."[32]

Precisely when Huey began referring to himself as "Kingfish" is uncertain. Two of Louisiana's best journalists of that period, Hamilton Basso and Hermann Deutsch, give a different time and place. Basso reported him saying "I'm the Kingfish" late on election night of 1928. Deutsch, whose coverage of Huey dated back to the rally at Hot Wells a year after World War I, first heard the epithet at a Long organization meeting in 1930, when Huey silenced his arguing lieutenants by roaring: "Shut up, you sons of bitches, shut up! This is the Kingfish talking!" There is no doubt, however, that the nickname derived from radio's most popular comedy serial of the 1920s and 1930s, "Amos 'n' Andy." One of the characters in this airwaves adaptation of blackface minstrel shows was known as Kingfish, chief of a fictitious Negro lodge, the Mystic Knights of the Sea. Huey came to prefer the nickname for self-identification, especially on the telephone. When a Louisianian's phone rang at two or three o'clock in the morning (Huey's favorite time for calling) and a commanding voice announced, "This is the Kingfish," the listener had no doubt who was on the other end of the line.[33]

Huey's self-image had been colossal since childhood, and his election as governor, followed by legislative triumphs and popular approval of his road-and-bridge bond amendment, so fed his ego that for a time he seemed in danger of drifting from reality. According to Thomas O. Harris, a Baton Rouge physician decided the Kingfish was a reincarnation of Napoleon Bonaparte, and half-convinced Huey of it; intrigued by the notion, Huey began looking at books about the French emperor.[34] One resemblance to Napoleon's life drew uncomfortably close: Huey in 1929 nearly suffered a Waterloo.

His impatience and sense of destiny, enhanced by recent successes, prodded Huey into deeds rash even by his standards. Tearing down the old mansion (with the mysterious disappearance of its contents) was only one of several exploits early in 1929 that caused him to lose majority control of the legislature, which in turn resulted in his impeachment by the House and trial before the senate. Anti-Long journals started cartooning Huey as a comic-opera Napoleon. The New Orleans *Item* editor Z. Marshall Ballard, who had become one of Huey's severest critics, now congratulated himself for having "known [from the beginning] that he could not endure . . . because of his utter lack of character, of mental balance."[35]

The brash young governor's capacity to endure was in doubt because he had overextended himself. In February of 1929, Huey forced a split with his three most prominent supporters: John P. Sullivan, Robert Ewing, and Lieutenant Governor Paul Cyr. Apparently he believed Sullivan and Ewing were expendable because their backing in the previous year's gubernatorial election had done little for him where it was supposed to help, in New Orleans; also, both Sullivan and Ewing were strong-willed personalities who insisted on giving him unwanted advice. His reasons for parting company with Dr. Cyr were more complex.

Sullivan and Ewing permanently broke with the governor after he ordered the National Guard to raid the largest gambling casinos in suburban New Orleans (St. Bernard and Jefferson parishes). Two earlier raids, in August and November of 1928, had been carried out by the guard, at Huey's command, on smaller gambling dens in those parishes, but the raid of February, 1929, hit big establishments thought to be under Sullivan's protection. (Gambling houses were illegal under state law, but New Orleans and its environs had always had them, and until Huey Long's governorship, potential problems with the law were customarily avoided by paying off local officials and police.) Unlike Sullivan, Ewing was not directly connected to casinos, but Sullivan was his friend and political ally. Moreover, Ewing was still fuming over Huey's actions in the Shreveport air base matter. On top of everything else, the *States* publisher had learned that Huey privately called him "Colonel Bow Wow" (Ewing's speech resembled barking), and contemptuously referred to his son John, of the Shreveport *Times*, as "Squirt."[36]

Lieutenant Governor Cyr's break with Huey at this same time was probably caused mostly by Long's reluctance to promise Cyr his support in the next (1932) gubernatorial election—Louisiana governors were limited to one full term. The public reason for the rift, however, was Huey's refusal to commute the death sentences of Dr. Thomas Dreher and his paramour, Ada LeBoeuf, who were hanged on February 1, 1929, for having had Ada's husband murdered. Dr. Dreher, a physician from Morgan City, happened to be a personal friend of the dentist from nearby Jeanerette, Dr. Cyr, who as lieutenant governor was an *ex officio* member of the Board of Pardons.[37] A majority of the board listened to Cyr's entreaties and recommended to Governor Long that the sentences be commuted to life in prison. Huey said no; Dr. Dreher and Mrs. LeBoeuf had been found guilty of premeditated murder and must die. The Pelican State had executed many persons and had witnessed even more lynchings, but this was "the first time," as the Mansfield *Enterprise* noted, "that a white woman had been hanged in Louisiana . . . and the first time that a wealthy and influential citizen [Dreher] has suffered the extreme penalty." Ewing's *States* accused Huey of lacking old-fashioned chivalry for permitting a Caucasian female to hang. (Mrs. LeBoeuf agreed. "Isn't it a terrible thing?" she said on the way to the gallows.) That Long meanwhile commuted the death sentence of a New Orleans pimp and rumrunner named Pleasant Harris, who had killed a prostitute, made the governor's obstinacy in the Dreher-LeBoeuf case seem all the more egregious to tradition-minded persons.[38]

Governor Long showed courage by ordering the gambling raids and ignoring the clamor to commute Mrs. LeBoeuf's and Dr. Dreher's death sentences, but it was an uneven and inequitable courage. The equally illegal gambling and bootleg dives in New Orleans proper—where Huey's underworld associates held sway—were not hit in the National Guard raids, and the reprieved murderer Harris evidently had supplicants closer to the governor than were Dr. Dreher's friends. Also, Huey's behavior while his third (February) raid was in progress showed a degree of effrontery that under the circumstances seemed pathological: he was drinking bootleg liquor in New Orleans' French Quarter, at a party where women in skimpy costumes danced the hula. One of the performers, Helen Clifford, clad in what was described as "a short crop of alfalfa," later testified the governor had pulled her in his lap. She added, "He got very frisky." [39]

Prohibition was never popular or locally enforced in New Orleans. Federal agent Isadore Einstein of the famed "Izzy and Moe" team, in his evidence-gathering trips during the 1920s, compared how long it took him to find available booze in various American cities. New Orleans came in first, timed at thirty-seven seconds after Izzy stepped off the train. In Protestant parishes where Huey had his strongest support, on the other hand, Prohibition retained the allegiance of most voters, and accounts of the governor's drinking either disturbed or were disbelieved by his throngs of followers. His propensity for liquor, and for cavorting in public while under its influence, had increased since his inauguration. The owner of the Frolics, a night club in New Orleans, testified that the governor twice "got drunk" in that establishment, then mounted the orchestra's platform and, to the delight of patrons, sang various numbers. Such antics gave the *States* an excuse, after Huey split with Ewing and Sullivan, to describe Long as "a tyrant suffering from delusions of grandeur, and the singing fool of New Orleans cabarets." [40]

Huey meanwhile handed his enemies more ammunition by purchasing a new Buick coupe for $1,300 (plus a trade-in) out of $6,000 in state funds specifically appropriated for hosting a national governors' conference in New Orleans. Louisiana did not provide its chief executive with an official automobile, and Huey had tried in vain to persuade the legislature to take care of this need. But he expected too much: a $10,000 appropriation. In the late 1920s that much money would purchase a Rolls Royce—which was what Huey had in mind. When even his loyalists in the legislature balked at his request, the governor retorted: "You damned suckers would not give me $10,000 for a car, but I will get the car just the same." The red '29 Buick was no Rolls Royce, but Alice Lee Grosjean liked it. [41]

In February of 1929, two months before his impeachment, the governor met with a group of dignitaries from Caddo Parish. They had come to Baton Rouge because the Highway Department had abruptly cut off state funds for the maintenance of roads around Shreveport. Knowing Huey's hostility toward their city, the group had selected as its spokesman Ernest Bernstein, the Kingfish's former client and wealthy contributor. It did no good. Spewing profanity, Long told the delegation what he thought of their locale, starting with "Caddo Parish can go to hell." Then he referred to some of its leading citizens: "that god-damned nigger loving Andrew Querbes . . . that god-damned son of a bitch [Randall] Moore . . . and that god-damned shit ass Ewing."[42] He recalled how Shreveporters had slandered him in the past, and he warned: "If people throw snowballs at me I throw brickbats at them. . . . I can be just as dirty as anybody." Huey also elaborated on his earlier comments to the Ewings about Shreveport needing to "bow and scrape" in his presence. "You haven't treated me with the respect that is due a Governor," Huey informed the stunned gathering, "and I will teach you to get off the sidewalk, take off your hat, and bow down damn low when Governor Long comes to town." Then, witnesses testified, "he got up and bowed low to illustrate the correct manner."[43]

Huey, unaware of his peril, in March of 1929 called two special sessions of the legislature for the purpose of enacting a manufacturer's tax of five cents on every barrel of petroleum refined in Louisiana. This was something new—a levy on the refineries' products (gasoline, diesel oil, kerosene), not another severance tax on crude oil at the wellhead. By far the largest refinery in the South was Standard Oil's facility in Baton Rouge. Huey's motives in calling for a refinery tax included revenge against his old enemy Standard Oil, but probably his primary intent was to pressure Standard and other oil companies to call off their litigation against his still-uncollected severance tax. The only certainty about his latest proposal was that Louisiana needed additional revenue, and quickly, to pay for the free schoolbooks and improve state institutions.[44]

No doubt Standard and the other refiners would have fought Huey's proposed new tax even in the best of times—and these were not good times. A glut in the oil market was developing in early 1929, with new discoveries in Oklahoma and more to come in east Texas. Within two years the price would drop to an all-time low of 21.5 cents per barrel. Standard threatened to close its Louisiana refinery if Huey's tax passed, a move that would devastate the Baton Rouge economy, since half the city's population depended upon Standard, either directly or indirectly, for livelihood. Huey charged in a radio address that legislators who said they would not vote for the refinery tax had been "bought."[45]

Some probably were, either by Standard or by Baton Rouge businessmen fearful of losing the big refinery. But Huey's insinuation that anyone who voted against the tax must be a bribetaker caused more than a few legislators to decide that the governor ought to be removed from office. Elderly and deaf Representative Gilbert Dupre of St. Landry Parish, after reading Huey's radio accusations, defended his colleagues in blunt language: "This House is not a den of thieves. There may be a lot of damned fools and there may be some damned rascals, but the majority of [us] are intent upon doing their duty."[46]

The second special session of 1929, called for March 20, was scheduled to last eighteen days. The evening it began, Huey, irked by editorials against the refinery tax in Baton Rouge's two dailies, the *Morning Advocate* and the *State-Times*, sent word to publisher Charles Manship that if his newspapers "don't lay off me I am going to have to publish a list of the names of people who have relatives in the insane asylum." Huey was referring, as Charles understood, to his brother Douglas Manship, a mental patient at East Louisiana State Hospital. The next day's *State-Times* revealed this attempted blackmail on its front page, in an open letter to legislators under the headline "THIS, GENTLEMEN, IS THE WAY YOUR GOVERNOR FIGHTS."[47]

Huey's tactic was cruel and rightly backfired, but his threat was not—as has been assumed—intended merely to embarrass the Manships by revealing Douglas' illness; he was also telling the publisher that a wealthy family that placed one of its members in a public hospital so crowded that not all persons needing treatment could be admitted, and then opposed taxation to upgrade the institution, was vulnerable to criticism on several counts. Huey spelled out this point in a subsequent radio broadcast when he spoke of Douglas Manship's "occupying a place in the insane asylum that could be used by people less fortunate." He added reproachfully, "Charlie Manship is down here fighting me and I am taking care of his brother in the insane asylum."[48] Huey saw no distinction between himself and the state.

The Dynamite Squad resumed its nightly meetings in J. Y. Sanders, Jr.'s law office. Now they talked of impeaching their enemy. These members of the House of Representatives, who in vain had opposed the governor's program at the previous year's regular session, now began to count heads—and realized that

Long had lost control of both houses, mostly because of outrageous words and deeds. A few months earlier, Huey had boasted that the legislature was "a deck of cards" he could shuffle at will. Now, as had happened to Alice in Lewis Carroll's *Alice in Wonderland*, the deck of cards was about to put him on trial.[49]

Huey soon understood that his refinery tax could not pass, but it took him several days, after the crucial second special session began, to grasp the fact that his office was in jeopardy. No Louisiana governor had been forced out by the impeachment process since Henry Clay Warmoth, the Republican carpetbagger, in 1872. Warmoth was still living in 1929, an alert octogenarian, and he resented comparisons between himself and Huey Long. After listening to Huey on the radio, Warmoth wrote in his diary that Long's speeches were "disgusting."[50]

Not since Warmoth's stormy Reconstruction days had there been a scene in Louisiana's legislature to rival the Monday evening meeting of March 25, 1929. It would become known as "Bloody Monday." Over the weekend, Huey had realized for the first time that he was in real danger of impeachment, and his loyalists in the legislature had agreed that the safest course was to adjourn the House sine die immediately after Monsignor Leon Gassler gave the invocation. No more session, no impeachment. But before Speaker of the House John Fournet could recognize another Longite member for the purpose of adjournment, Dynamite Squad leader Cecil Morgan arose, waved a piece of paper, and shouted he had an affidavit from Long's former bodyguard, Battling Bozeman, stating that the governor had offered Bozeman money to assassinate a member of the House—J. Y. Sanders, Jr. Representative Morgan demanded the House stay in session until this charge was investigated.[51]

Speaker Fournet ordered Morgan to sit down. When the Caddo Parish representative refused, Fournet instructed the sergeant-at-arms to "put Mr. Morgan in his seat." More than twenty members of the Dynamite Squad—including two members weighing above 250 pounds, George K. Perrault and Mason Spencer—formed a defensive circle around Morgan, who continued to shout above the banging of Fournet's gavel. The Speaker then called for a vote of adjournment, and solons dashed to their seats to push buttons—an electric voting machine, one of the first of its kind in the nation, loomed above the

Speaker's rostrum. The lights flashed: sixty-eight green (yes, for adjournment); thirteen red (no). Fournet declared the House adjourned sine die.[52]

"You goddamn crook!" someone screamed from the floor. Dozens of other anti-Longites, momentarily stunned at seeing the big board show green instead of red beside their names, gulped for air, and began to yell: "The machine is fixed! The machine is fixed! Oh, God, don't let 'em get away with this!" Several Dynamiters made for the rostrum, intent on taking the gavel from Fournet and calling for a new vote. One of them, Clinton Sayes of Avoyelles Parish, leaped from desk to desk on his way up front, until a Longite felled him with a blow to the forehead. So blood, although slight, had been shed. In the words of Thomas O. Harris, who was at the press table, "pandemonium broke loose." Fistfights erupted around desks and in the aisles; inkstands and other objects flew. Spectators in the gallery, excited beyond expectations, added to the noise with what was described as "one maniacal screech."[53] The more decorous senate, meeting across the hall, wondered what all the racket was about.

Mason Spencer, the loudest and, next to Perrault, the largest member of the House, hoisted his bulk atop the press table and after overriding everybody else's noise with a piercing "hog call," managed to restore a semblance of order. He then polled the House by name. The result was seventy-nine votes against adjournment, nine in favor, with eleven absent or not voting. Calm now followed the storm, and the legislature voted to adjourn—not sine die, but until eleven the next morning. Several representatives, earlier pro-Long, talked to the press on the way out of the chamber, anxious to have their changed affiliation reported in Tuesday's papers.[54]

When the House reconvened, Speaker Fournet apologized for his role in the previous evening's disgraceful episode, but he denied having "fixed" the voting machine, and there is no evidence he did; electrical contrivances of that sort were still primitive, and apparently the machine simply repeated the roll call vote of a few minutes earlier. Whether the Speaker realized this when he declared adjournment instead of calling for a new vote is another question. Fournet continued to preside during the impeachment proceedings that followed.[55]

On Tuesday, March 26, the Dynamite Squad, having stayed up

all night preparing the case against Huey, submitted nineteen impeachment charges. From then until April 26, the House would listen to testimony, debate, and finally vote on the various accusations. Some of the charges were frivolous, and the most serious—that the governor tried to hire Battling Bozeman to kill J. Y. Sanders, Jr.—was almost certainly untrue. The ex-prizefighter had been fired by Long prior to filing his affidavit with the Dynamite Squad, and his testimony at the impeachment proceedings sounded more like attempted vengeance than a truthful account (years later, Mason Spencer admitted he did not believe a word of Battling's charges).[56] Huey Long had grievous flaws, but he was no murderer. Dominating and humiliating people were the satisfactions he enjoyed. Dead enemies would provide no pleasure. Why, Huey playfully asked, should he want to kill "Little J. Y."? He elaborated: "If J. Y. Sanders, Sr., had died twenty years ago I wouldn't be governor. If J. Y. Sanders, Jr., lives twenty more years I may be President of the United States. A Sanders is what I need for my political future."[57]

Eventually the attempted murder charge was dropped, as were several others—"habitually carrying concealed weapons," engagement in "immoral and illegal activities in night clubs," and the uttering of "blasphemous and sacrilegious expressions by comparing himself to the Savior." One charge, that he had "tyrannically used the state militia [National Guard]" in gambling raids, was defeated, fifty-five to forty-three. Yet by separate votes the House did approve eight articles of impeachment, including bribery and attempted bribery of legislators, seeking to intimidate the press in the Manship affair, and various misappropriations of state funds (including the Buick purchase). Article VIII, approved fifty-nine to thirty-nine, was a blanket charge of "incompetency, corruption . . . and gross misconduct." This catchall article included Long's having required undated letters of resignation from appointees and his habitual use of "vile, obscene and scurrilous language."[58]

Tickets to the House gallery were at a premium during the impeachment proceedings. Some of the testimony about Huey's cursing could not be printed verbatim in the newspapers, although it was published uncut in the *Official Journal* of the House of Representatives, leaving Secretary of State James Bailey to wonder if this hitherto staid document could be sent through the mail without violating a federal law about obscene material.[59] Huey never testified, nor was he required to. But fascinating witnesses did appear.

Seymour Weiss, although evasive when questioned on how state funds were used in hosting the recent national governors' conference in New Orleans, left an impression that the entertainment had included bootleg liquor and loose women. Old Representative Dupre, cupping his ears to hear Weiss testify, called him "an insect" and complained that Huey Long had spent "state money in a whore house."[60] Joe Messina, Huey's faithful bodyguard-valet, who drew a salary as "license checker" with the state police, became confused when quizzed about delinquent license plates, since he did not know the meaning of the word "delinquent." Messina admitted he never worked at his highway job, but assured the House that if called upon, "I could tell a 1928 from a 1929 plate." Helen Clifford, the sexy hula dancer who sat on Huey's lap at that French Quarter party, seemed to hold the legislators' attention more than any other witness. At the end of her testimony, as the *Official Journal* recorded, several representatives insisted she give them her telephone number.[61]

Happenings outside the House chamber while the impeachment hearings continued—some reported in the press and others recalled by participants—rivaled the central event in tragicomedy. Earl Long gave the rowdiest performance. Unlike Huey, Earl relished physical combat. When Earl saw Robert Maestri discussing something in a capitol corridor with Harney Bogan, a Dynamiter from Caddo Parish, he strode up and asked Maestri, "What are you talking to that son of a bitch for?" Whereupon Earl and Bogan fought, and Earl drew blood by using his teeth on the representative's face and neck. Bogan later took an injection to ward off tetanus. When Huey learned of the fight, he exclaimed: "I bet Earl bit him, didn't he? Earl always bites."[62]

Huey's self-confidence was temporarily shaken by the charges of impeachment. He had not known many setbacks in his life. This one hit him far harder than not winning first place in the high school debate at LSU; it was worse than being hungry in Memphis after losing a salesman's job. The process of removing a governor of Louisiana by impeachment and trial was the same as for a president under the United States Constitution: the House could impeach (indict) by simple majority vote, but the governor would remain in office pending trial by the senate. It took a two-thirds vote of the senate to convict. If Huey Long were convicted on any one of the eight impeachment charges, it would mean political death: not only would he be removed as governor, but never again could he hold any public office in Louisiana.[63]

When the House first began debating impeachment, Huey seemed paralyzed by anxiety and depression. Julius Long visited Huey's Heidelberg suite to offer legal advice, and later said he had found his brother sobbing in bed; Julius had feared he was thinking of suicide. Within a few days, however, the governor recovered his nerve and struck back with a series of circulars accusing Standard Oil of being the evil force bent on his ruin because he was trying to "educate our children and care for the destitute, sick and afflicted."[64]

In the evenings, after Huey had composed the next circular's wording, the text would be rushed to Franklin Printing Company in New Orleans. Minutes after receiving it, Franklin set the type, and copies began rolling off the press. Huey no longer used the mail for distribution. As governor, he had a faster system. Unmarked highway patrol cars and other state vehicles picked up the printed, bundled circulars and transported them through the night to the homes of Huey's parish leaders. These individuals, from the Arkansas line to the Gulf, had been phoned and told when the next circular was coming; it was their responsibility to get it into the hands of local voters. One observer who studied Huey's propaganda techniques estimated that during the impeachment crisis, his several circulars totaled 900,000 copies. Huey also counterattacked with emotional radio broadcasts, principally by remote control over KWKH (Henderson was still his friend despite their recent cursing match), and he made occasional public appearances to arouse the rural constituents of wavering legislators.[65]

That some anti-Long representatives and senators took money from either Standard Oil or other Louisiana businesses is hardly debatable. The president of Standard's Louisiana division, Daniel R. Weller, reserved a suite at the Heidelberg Hotel for the length of the session—first for the purpose of stopping the refinery tax, and then to impeach Huey. But had the Louisiana legislature been as corrupt as it was sometimes depicted, Standard, with its vast financial resources, could have engineered Huey's removal from office in 1929. Standard and its allies may have paid for the votes of fifteen or twenty legislators, mostly in the House; the company either did not or could not buy enough senators to convict. Huey's bankroll could not compete with Standard's—Maestri's $40,000 (or perhaps $50,000) was Long's largest contribution, and it mostly went to pay Franklin Printing Company. But Huey could and did use, to great advantage, patronage and promises of other political rewards. He also knew how to wave the stick as well as the carrot: legislators who had already been given state jobs for themselves or for relatives were warned of the consequences if they did not "vote right."[66]

Huey was quick to accuse Standard and specific anti-Long legislators. He even publicly sneered at one, W. H. Cutrer, for allegedly selling his vote to Standard at a bargain price: "They . . . bought Representative Cutrer so cheap they felt like they had stolen him." But Huey's boasting of having purchased Representative William H. Bennett's support with a Highway Department position—"I bought and paid for him like you would a load of potatoes"—so angered Bennett when he learned of the remark that he resigned from the department and voted for impeachment.[67] The damage was done, however, and Bennett would carry through life the nickname "Sack of Potatoes." Neither side came away from the impeachment fight with clean hands. Even so, the majority of legislators, both those for and against impeaching and removing Huey Long, seem to have voted their convictions, or at least voted according to the presumed view of their constituents.

Several occurrences during the impeachment fight bordered on the grotesque, but the April 6 address of Representative George Delesdernier ("of the last," in French) from distant, roadless Pilot Town in Plaquemines Parish, was in a class by itself. A tall, cadaverous man, who seldom made speeches, Delesdernier this day decided to let everyone know how much he loved Huey Long. "Bear with me in patience while I say what I have to say," he began in a trembling voice. "The title of my speech will be 'The Cross of Wood and with Shackles of Paper.'" Delesdernier began by portraying Jesus' trial and crucifixion, then shifted gears to describe the similar suffering of the Kingfish, who like the "Divine Creature" of Biblical times, was "relieving the sick and the blind, aiding the lame and the halt, and trying to drive

illiteracy from the state." With incredulity, the opposition realized that Delesdernier was comparing Huey Long to Jesus
Christ. Cries of "Blasphemy!" and "Sacrilege!" interrupted the
oration. But Delesdernier managed to add that this "Divine
Creature . . . I mean this creature of today, is being shackled
with paper to a cross." The *Official Journal* dryly noted that "at
this juncture Mr. Delesdernier fainted, and was carried from the
floor of the House."[68] And no wonder: as Webster Smith wrote,
Delesdernier "had become immortal. He will long be known as
the man who made the most absurd address ever heard in the
Louisiana legislature. Which is quite a feat."[69]

On April 27, 1929, Governor Long was summoned to appear
before the senate for trial on the eight charges of impeachment,
which the day before had been approved by majority vote in the
House. Chief Justice Charles O'Niell of the Louisiana Supreme
Court, who recently, while intoxicated, had referred to Huey as
a "thieving son of a bitch," would preside. Lieutenant Governor
Cyr, who in a March speech had asked God to forgive him for
running on Huey's ticket in 1928, would be the next governor if
the required two-thirds majority found Long guilty.[70] Most senators were known to favor conviction. But if only fourteen of the
thirty-nine voted in Huey's favor, he would keep the governorship.

Huey's senate trial was short-circuited only two days after it
began. Its opening had been delayed to May 14 because lawyers
on both sides said they needed time to prepare their cases. "I am
ready, if your honor please," Governor Long said with a smile to
Chief Justice O'Niell as the senate assembled on that date. Huey
knew something that O'Niell and most senators were soon to
learn: he already had won the fight, and would continue as governor. Huey's legal staff, which included John H. Overton and
Leander Perez, had prepared a defense claiming that all but one
of the eight charges could not even be considered, as the House
had voted on them after April 6, the last date the legislature was
scheduled to meet in the special session for which it had been
called. The only article of impeachment the House had approved by that date was the Manship charge, the least substantial of all.[71]

On May 15 the senate rejected the Manship article of impeachment. Next day, when the senators reassembled, Longite
leader Philip Gilbert filed a motion to halt proceedings. Fifteen

senators, one more than needed for Long's acquittal, had earlier signed a document, now presented by Senator Gilbert, "officially" announcing that they would not vote to convict on any of the seven remaining charges, on the ground that these had been approved by the House after April 6. When questioned by Chief Justice O'Niell, seven of the fifteen admitted they would vote against conviction "regardless of the evidence." Gilbert's motion pointed out that since the signees made up more than one third of the senate, continuing Long's trial would be a waste of time. Minutes later, the senate adjourned sine die.[72]

A "Round Robin," the document was called, although not signed in the circular fashion by which similar motions or petitions had earned that name. Who thought of this device to terminate Huey's trial is not clear, although it probably was Leander Perez. Promises as well as threats were used to induce the fifteen senators to sign, and all would be rewarded with patronage. Possibly, had the trial continued, anti-Long money might have produced a two-thirds majority; more likely, the Round Robin merely hastened the governor's victory. In any case, Huey so treasured the Round Robin that it was kept, until the senate adjourned, in a special place. When one of his parish leaders visited the Heidelberg suite and asked to see it, Huey looked at Miss Grosjean, who unbuttoned the top of her dress to reveal the document pinned on the inside of her brassiere.[73]

· 11 ·

FEATHER DUSTING

"It was a fight to the death between gorillas and baboons," the notorious South-baiter H. L. Mencken wrote of Louisiana's 1929 impeachment struggle. "The whole combat was typical of political science in the Hookworm Belt." As for Huey Long, Mencken dismissed him as just another redneck demagogue "with a tough set of vocal cords," who stood out only because of his utter shamelessness. As usual, the Sage of Baltimore proved more a humorist than prophet. Closer to the truth was the novelist Sherwood Anderson, who believed Huey drew his strength from "the terrible South"—a beaten, poverty-stricken land hungering to exact a price for its decades of economic suffering.[1]

Huey became a genius at turning enemies' thrusts to his own advantage. The charges for which he was impeached were, for the most part, valid. Yet to a majority of Louisianians he was able to transfigure his struggle into that of young David versus the Standard Oil Goliath. There was usually enough truth in his accusations to taint his foes with selfishness and lack of vision. On the other hand, there was even more truth in his opponents' complaint that Huey Long believed in nothing but himself— that, in Cecil Morgan's words, "whatever good there was [in one of his proposals], it was inextricably associated with something that added to his power."[2] Most voters, however, apparently believed the Kingfish, and not his critics.

Some of Huey's defenders later claimed the impeachment fight hardened him, and they excused his subsequent ruthlessness as a response to the tactics of those who had attempted to remove him from office. Huey agreed with this assessment. As he told one biographer, "I used to try to get things done by saying 'please.' That didn't work and now. . . . I dynamite 'em out of my path."[3] Yet almost all the evidence points in another direction: being impeached may have made Huey more alert to danger and strengthened his resolve to achieve absolute control of the legislature and the state judiciary, but examples of his trying "to get things done by saying 'please'" were as rare before the impeachment fight as afterward.

Holding on to the governorship after almost losing it was a personal victory, but severe problems remained for Huey Long. A majority in both House and senate still opposed him. Lieutenant Governor Cyr, Chief Justice O'Niell of the state supreme court, and Attorney General Percy Saint were among his bitterest enemies. All daily newspapers and most weeklies had urged his removal from office. Also, the Round Robin that had aborted his senate trial had one disadvantage: seven of the eight impeachment charges voted by the House could be brought up again. If Huey then lost only two or three supporters in the senate, the opposition would have its necessary two-thirds majority to convict. Reminded of this, he said: "I'll just have to grow me a new crop of legislators."[4]

He tried to start a new crop immediately: nine opposition legislators who he believed were vulnerable became the targets of recall petitions. In eight of the nine cases, however, the incumbents retained their seats, at least until the next regular election in 1932. On patronage, Huey was more successful. Since Reconstruction, Louisiana's chief executives had enjoyed great appointive powers; the planter-business oligarchy that ruled the state had assumed that their class, personified by the governor, would always control patronage. Now this power had fallen into the hands of Huey Long. During his first year as governor, he wielded patronage more thoroughly than any of his predecessors, and as soon as the impeachment crisis ended, his attention shifted from managerial positions to the lower-paying state jobs. Even a lowly drawbridge tender at the town of Plaquemine was fired because he had ties to an anti-Long senator.[5]

Harley Bozeman, who since childhood had been Huey's most helpful friend, became a casualty of the impeachment fight and its patronage aftermath. Bozeman, Winn Parish's representative and Long's floor leader in the House, predictably voted against impeachment, but he angered Huey by urging him, during the crisis, to resign the governorship so that he might run for office again, rather than face what Bozeman thought was almost certain conviction by the senate. Presently Huey made Bozeman resign his lucrative position as chairman of Louisiana's Tax Commission. The next year, 1930, Bozeman ran for Huey's old seat on the Public Service Commission and sought the Kingfish's blessing; instead, Huey endorsed a junior partner in his Shreveport law firm, Harvey G. Fields. Bozeman lost, later testified against Long at a United States Senate investigation of Louisiana affairs, and wrote letters to anti-Long newspapers declaring he was "bowed down in shame" for his role in helping Huey's career.[6] The two were never reconciled.

Exasperated by their failure to oust Huey at his senate trial, and reacting to his recall petitions aimed at anti-Long legislators, his enemies next tried a recall drive against him. It died aborning. In the rural parishes, where most voters lived, Huey was accurately described as "stronger . . . today than ever before." The Leesville *Leader*, in poverty-stricken Vernon Parish, reflected this sentiment by exclaiming: "Go to it, Huey P! Give them hell without intermission. Down that satanic crowd which has so long had a strangle hold on the State of Louisiana."[7] A well-to-do, mostly urban minority of voters yearned more than ever to get Huey out of office. When impeachment failed and the recall effort showed no promise, their next move, in June of 1929, was to organize something called the Constitutional League.

Former governor John M. Parker agreed to become president of the Constitutional League. Parker had hoped to spend his twilight years away from politics and telephones at his beloved Bayou Sara farm, where he found some relief from lifelong respiratory problems. But his detestation of Huey Long now overrode other considerations. Parker was not so much opposed to Long's programs as he was to his methods and behavior, which Parker considered "immoral." The elderly patrician-progressive had fought venality in government since the 1880s, and in his view Huey Long was a nightmarish amalgam of the worst in Reconstruction, the Mafia, and the old New Orleans Ring. The Constitutional League, Parker explained, was formed "for the purpose of restoring constitutional government in Louisiana." Its three hundred members, made up primarily of out-of-office politicians, corporation lawyers, and bankers, pledged $100,000 to fight Long's "dictatorship."[8] The League set to work delving into state records and soon came up with evidence of waste and probable graft in the Highway Commission, along with proof that sixteen Longite legislators were "double-dipping," that is, holding salaried positions on various state commissions, boards, and departments. The League scored a success against the latter abuse when Attorney General Saint and the state supreme court agreed that such patronage violated Louisiana's constitution. All sixteen solons were forced to resign their state jobs.[9]

This small victory was the Constitutional League's only success. The wider practice of nepotism, pervasive in Louisiana decades before Huey Long, was not illegal; most pro-Long legislators had relatives, including wives and children, with state jobs. As for his own family, Huey had placed at least twenty-three relatives on the state pay roll by mid-1929. When the League published their names, the governor laughed and said the list was incomplete; he also suggested that the state penitentiary was housing and feeding some of his other relatives at the taxpayers' expense. As he did against most foes, Huey counterattacked by branding the League as just another front for Standard Oil and other greedy interests. By this time, his talent for ridicule was coming forward in virtually every attack; he had a special gift for thinking up vivid, hurtful nicknames to use on organizations or people who opposed him. These tags usually had sufficient appropriateness to stick. Thus the Constitutional League became, in Huey's vocabulary, the "League of Notions." When he tired of that, he called it the "Constipated League."[10]

For all his love of a political fight, Huey's innate shrewdness told him that mid-1929 was a time to hold his combativeness in check. He needed a truce with those of his enemies who were not intractable; the legislature's regular session of 1930 was now on his mind, and without some compromises he would lack a majority behind the new measures he envisioned. In July of 1929, Huey publicly replied to a letter from Harvey Couch, a powerful businessman and organizer of a "citizen's committee." Urging the governor's agreement to proposals aimed at ending "disturbing political conditions," Couch and his associates had pointed out Louisiana's need for new capital investment, which was not likely to come unless a more placid situation prevailed. Huey readily agreed. He dropped his recall efforts against legislators, and Couch and his committee of leading businessmen promised to use their influence to stop a renewal of impeachment proceedings and to promote Huey's program in the 1930 legislature. In return, Huey further promised not to raise taxes on business and explicitly withdrew his demand for a tax on oil refinery products.[11]

Actually, the terms had been worked out before the exchange of letters. Huey and Harvey Couch were old acquaintances—Couch had begun his business career in Winnfield in 1907. By 1929, he was president of the Louisiana and Arkansas Rail Company and Louisiana Power and Light, as well as founder-president of the largest utility companies in Mississippi and Arkansas. Couch was probably the only person friendly with both Huey Long and Standard Oil's management. Huey, for all his rhetoric, was not really anticapitalist; he might seem so to particular concerns—notably Standard Oil—that had crossed him in some fashion, but as *Business Week* observed in 1935, his high-handedness almost always involved political control, not economic domination.[12] Businessmen who respectfully accepted Huey Long as the *political* boss of Louisiana discovered an ally instead of a foe.

Between the truce agreement in July, 1929, and the legislative session of May–July, 1930, Huey and Louisiana experienced a period of relative quiet. The hard-liners of the Constitutional League kept up their fading crusade against Huey, and the Ewing papers fitfully attacked him, but with the major business interests, including Standard Oil, seemingly reconciled to his governorship, the anti-Long forces—who as in times past referred to themselves as the "better element," the "best people," or the "real people"—were in disarray. They had been outmaneuvered by their enemy and deserted by the state's most powerful capitalists, who put profits above all else. Their best chance to remove Huey Long by legal means was past.

At first, the Great Depression hit the industrialized North much harder than it did Louisiana or other southern states. Louisiana's economy, low already, had less distance to fall. But by early 1930, the effects of the previous October's Wall Street crash began to be felt in New Orleans, then elsewhere in the state. Workers were laid off, more people looked for fewer jobs, and prices for the state's chief agricultural products—cotton and sugar—

started dropping. Drought worsened the economic situation. In 1930 the northern and central parishes suffered their worst summer dry spell since 1893; cotton yields were reduced and home gardens ruined.[13] The 1930s began like a grim encore of the 1890s.

The Great Depression and accompanying drought enhanced Huey Long's appeal and power. Obtaining or keeping a state job, however meager the pay, became essential for thousands of Louisianians. Moreover, Huey's highway- and bridge-building program now had the added attractiveness of providing construction work for the growing number of unemployed. At a more prosperous time, believed Harry Gamble (one of the smarter anti-Long leaders), Huey with "all of his talents could not have dominated the people of this state like he did. The time was exactly right for him."[14]

New Orleans' Mardi Gras season of 1930 had to compete with Governor Long for public attention. Huey stayed at his Roosevelt Hotel suite through February and early March, and his behavior while greeting distinguished guests who visited the city during that time aroused suspicions that he was endeavoring to upstage Carnival. Huey had reason to be angry at local patricians for not asking him to any of their exclusive masked balls, for he was the first governor since the Reconstruction Republicans not to receive an invitation. Feeling rejected, he publicly blamed Mardi Gras and other local frivolities for allowing Houston to outhustle New Orleans.[15] Inside him was still the jealous twelve-year-old who threw a rock at the circus elephants parading in Winnfield.

In February, former president Calvin Coolidge and wife Grace vacationed in New Orleans, staying at the Roosevelt Hotel. Unavoidably, the Coolidges met and dined with Huey Long, who delighted reporters by informing the astonished Vermonter, "I'm a hillbilly, more or less, like yourself." When photographers took their picture, Huey suggested a caption: "The ex-President of the United States, and the future one." After the Coolidges left, Long told the press he had inquired about living conditions in the White House and was grieved to learn that, like the old governor's mansion, "it was not in very good shape." So, Huey concluded, "I will have to go up there and tear it down and build another one."[16]

During the final days of Carnival, Huey was visited in his hotel suite by Commander Lothar von Arnauld de la Perière of the German navy, whose cruiser *Emden* had docked in New Orleans as part of a good-will tour of the United States. Accompanying the commander was the German consul in New Orleans. Huey received the formally dressed aristocrats in his favorite bedroom attire, silk pajamas (the bright green pair he wore that day being a Christmas gift from the state bank examiner). The episode caused a minor diplomatic incident, as the German consul believed his nation had been insulted. Huey pretended to make amends the next day with a visit to the *Emden*, this time wearing correct attire furnished by Seymour Weiss. Commander von Arnauld later told reporters he thought the governor "was a very intelligent, interesting and unusual person." Three months later, in Baton Rouge for the legislative session, Huey was visited at the new governor's mansion by Major General Frank McCoy, commander of the United States Fourth Army. Huey received McCoy clad only in underwear. According to the *State-Times*, the general should have congratulated himself on "a narrow escape," as the governor earlier had greeted a Baton Rouge delegation "in the nude." [17]

Such headline-grabbing episodes helped appease Huey's perpetual thirst for attention, but his focus never strayed from his primary objective—to become the master of Louisiana. He had lost majority control of the legislature, but he hoped that his agenda for the 1930 session, endorsed in advance by the state's leading capitalists because he pledged no new taxes on business, would prove too popular to be rejected, and that with its passage he would achieve more power.

When the legislature assembled in May, the governor revealed the top of his agenda: a $68-million bond issue to build 3,000 miles of paved roads, the bonds to be backed by the already-imposed tax on gasoline at the pump. Funds from Huey's 1928 bond issue of $30 million were currently being spent, but only on a "scattering," as he called it, of disconnected highways; a typical parish now had five or ten miles of pavement leading out of the main town. Highway engineers probably thought Huey was crazy to make them build that way, but it proved brilliant political strategy. As Huey later explained, "When the people once knew the pleasure of travelling over paved highways their support of a program to connect up the links was certain." [18]

Later in the session, Huey's floor leaders introduced another bond-issue proposal, this one for $5,000,000 to build a new state capitol. The governor already had commissioned Leon C. Weiss, of the architectural firm of Weiss, Dreyfous, and Seiferth, to design a "skyscraper" capitol to symbolize Louisiana's thrust into modernity. Huey selected not only the basic design, but also the location: a tract just north of downtown Baton Rouge that had been part of LSU before the university moved to its new campus in the mid-1920s. When asked what should be done to the old Gothic-style capitol, Huey suggested, "Turn it over to some collector of antiques." [19]

Huey assumed that his support from the business community, most of all from Harvey Couch and Rudolph Hecht, the New Orleans banker, would induce the legislature to give his bond issues the two-thirds majority required to submit such proposals to the voters. In particular, Huey expected the New Orleans Old Regular organization, with its nineteen representatives and eight senators, to go along. Despite his fulminations against the city machine in past years, Huey had signaled his desire for cooperation by keeping out of the recent (January, 1930) mayoralty election. Even so, the Old Regular ward bosses and their victorious candidate, T. Semmes Walmsley, concluded their interests would not be served by providing Huey Long with more state money to spend. Consequently, the bond-issue amendments failed to obtain the needed two-thirds majority in either house.[20]

Fuming at this unexpected setback, Huey counterattacked on two fronts. He persuaded New Orleans bankers to withhold loans to the city government, and he directed the state Tax Commission to review assessments in Orleans Parish—thereby delaying the collection of municipal taxes. For a time, the city faced bankruptcy. Then, on June 11, the last day new bills could be introduced at the 1930 regular session, Huey shocked his opponents by proposing a constitutional convention. Such a convention to rewrite the state's organic law required approval by public vote, but only a simple majority in the legislature was needed to place the proposal on the ballot. Huey had a majority. The prospect of Huey Long's replacing the Constitution of 1921 with one written under his guidance bestirred ex-governors Sanders, Pleasant, and Parker to lobby against the proposed convention, just as they had worked in opposition to Huey's bond issues. (Under the 1921 constitution, Louisiana governors were limited to one term; Long's foes assumed he was planning to change that.) Despite the high-powered opposition, the House voted for Huey's constitutional convention fifty-six to forty-two, and the proposal would have narrowly passed the senate—but Lieutenant Governor Cyr, as presiding officer, was able to keep it from coming to a floor vote. So Huey lost this round. He took some immediate revenge: he line-item vetoed all office expenses for Attorney General Saint and Lieutenant Governor Cyr; appropriations for them were "unnecessary," he said, because Saint "had become counsel to the Constitutional League and not the Governor," while Cyr's budget listed travel funds that would never be used, since "he ain't going nowhere."[21]

Six days after the legislature adjourned sine die, Huey announced, on July 16, 1930, his candidacy for the United States Senate. Earlier, he had said, "Maybe I will and maybe I won't," when questioned about his plans for the September Democratic senatorial primary. Being a senator, however, provided a better springboard to the White House than did Louisiana's governorship, and Huey had always intended to go to Washington; the only real question was when. His setbacks in the recent legislative session convinced him to try now, even though his gubernatorial term was only half over, against Senator Ransdell, instead of waiting to take on Senator Broussard in 1932.[22] A smashing victory at this time, Huey believed, would cow the legislature into approving his bond-issue proposals at a special session he planned to call; it also should clear up any question about who was the boss of Louisiana. As usual, his instincts were correct.

A few of Huey's enemies were so shortsighted as to welcome his candidacy against Ransdell, even to the point of saying they would vote "to send Huey P. Long to the United States Senate, thus getting rid of him as a factor in state affairs." That silly notion was not typical, for most of Louisiana's old ruling class had finally come to realize that "this shifty youngster," as the Shreveport *Journal* called him, was the most formidable enemy they had faced since Reconstruction, or perhaps ever. "A great menace threatens a free people," State Senator Charles Holcombe warned an anti-Long rally in Hammond. "A great curse has fallen upon us."[23]

Old Colonel Ewing of the *States* summoned up the imagery of his mentor, Major Hearsey, in denouncing the "infamies" of "the little chinkapin-headed misfit now in the Governor's chair." Recalling the New Orleans uprising that led to the dissolution of carpetbag rule, Ewing predicted that sooner or later "the descendants of the valiant heroes of the Fourteenth of September" would find the means to stop "this counterfeit Mussolini."[24]

Huey was one month shy of his thirty-seventh birthday when he announced against Ransdell. The senator, born before the Civil War, was seventy-one. Ransdell first held public office as a district attorney in 1884; he had been in Congress since 1899. In 1912, after thirteen years in the House, Ransdell defeated incumbent senator (and former governor) Murphy J. Foster. From then until he faced Huey Long in 1930, Ransdell was a traditional Louisiana senator—which is to say, a dignified probusiness conservative of mediocre ability who supported a protective tariff on sugar. Ironically, Ransdell had obtained his senate seat by portraying the elderly Foster as lethargic and out-of-date; now, eighteen years later, Ransdell faced a youthful opponent who was more blunt in using the age issue. One of Huey's supporters described Ransdell as "old and childish, liable to kick the bucket at any time," and Huey on the campaign trail was almost as indelicate. Long explained that he had endorsed Ransdell in the 1924 senatorial race against Mayor Thomas of Shreveport only because he "was the lesser of two evils." With feigned sadness he observed, "Even then [Ransdell was] in the twilight of his life." Huey also referred to the senator, who wore a heavy moustache and goatee, as "Trashy-Mouth" and "Old Feather Duster."[25]

The 1928 race for the governorship had been Louisiana's most vituperative political contest of the twentieth century, but in epithet hurling it was eclipsed by the Long-Ransdell senatorial struggle of 1930. The contest, wrote an astute observer, plumbed "the nadir of indecency and frantic desperation." Ransdell tried to uphold a serene, statesmanlike image and refused to call his opponent vile names, yet he unhesitatingly played the old racial card that patrician officeholders had used since Reconstruction. "The negroes," Ransdell claimed, "are praying for Huey Long's election and my defeat." On a more plaintive note, the senator asked audiences: "Do I look to you like a worn out old man or a feather duster?"[26] Apparently most voters thought he did.

With all dailies and most weeklies in the state castigating Huey, sometimes in language that the New York *Times* primly told its readers "cannot be printed here," the Kingfish decided to begin publishing his own journal as an antidote to what he called "the lying newspapers." Huey's paper was an insult processor named the *Louisiana Progress*. It appeared weekly, beginning March 27, 1930. Long's organization continued to issue circulars, but these usually were little more than supplements to material in the *Progress*, which Harnett Kane described as "probably the most cheerfully venomous regular publication in the nation." John D. Klorer, formerly of the *Times-Picayune* staff, was hired as editor. The same method of rapid distribution that worked so well for the circulars—transportation in state vehicles to Long's parish leaders—was utilized for the *Progress*. To make libel suits more difficult, the paper was printed out-of-state, in Meridian, Mississippi.[27]

Cartoons by Trist Wood, a freelance artist, festooned the pages of Huey's *Louisiana Progress*. Governor Long realized that many of his supporters were semiliterate at best, but he knew they were able to appreciate caricatures of those politicians who in the past had failed to support adequate funding for public education. Huey took a special interest in Wood's cartoons, often suggesting themes and captions. Wood also borrowed from Long's stockpile of insulting nicknames, and Ransdell, as depicted in *Progress* cartoons, resembled a confused, desiccated old goat on its last legs, wearing a tag saying "Feather Duster." Colonel "Bow Wow" Ewing also figured in many of Wood's illustrations; since Ewing was sensitive about his age (he had "already passed his allotted three score and ten," Huey pointed out), the *States* publisher looked nearer death every time Wood drew him. Cartoons of J. Y. Sanders, Sr., showed him bent with age, and ex-governor Parker's face appeared as a mass of wrinkles. Huey's *Progress* began by calling him "John M(istake) Parker" and "White Wings," but because Parker was thin to the point of fragility, his nickname soon became "Old Sack of Bones."[28]

The tone of Louisiana politics was never high, despite the old elite's pretensions of gentility. Now the patricians tried to do battle with Huey at his level, ignoring warnings from the Mansfield *Enterprise* that whoever undertakes the "skinning of a skunk . . . cannot fail to be smeared." Parker, speaking at a Ransdell rally, referred to Huey as "a creature devoid of every element of honor and decency," and ex-governor Pleasant compared him to "Marx, Lenin and Trotsky." Mrs. Pleasant was more abusive than her husband. Speaking over KTBS radio in Shreveport, she described Huey as "common beyond words. . . . He has not only common ways, but a common, sordid, dirty soul [with] the greed and coarseness of the swine . . . the venom of the snake, the cruel cowardice of the skulking hyena." Mrs. Pleasant would have been well advised not to have uttered those words, for Huey discovered she had once been hospitalized for mental illness, and he was not loath to make public that fact.[29]

Mayor Walmsley of New Orleans described Huey as a "cur" and a "madman," but that was no match in imagination for what Huey called him. The mayor had a long neck, a balding head, and a reddish face, so Huey pinned on him the nickname "Turkey Head" Walmsley. John P. Sullivan, the New Orleans politician-gambler whose hatred of Huey impelled him back into the camp of the Old Regulars, joined Walmsley in urging Senator Ransdell's reelection, and said the outlaw Jesse James "was a gentleman compared with Long." Huey's simple, effective response was to call him "Bang Tail" Sullivan, in reference to his being legal counsel and manager of the Fair Grounds race track. Sullivan, a burly six feet four, had a history of violent reaction to indignities: thirty years earlier he had briefly been a cadet at West Point, where his defiance of hazing had involved him in twenty-seven fights in one month. Now Sullivan yearned to use his huge fists on Huey Long.[30]

New Orleans' three leading newspapers heaped fierce abuse on Long during the summer of 1930. Huey responded in his *Progress* by having Trist Wood picture the urban dailies as a hideous three-headed snake, hissing "lies, lies," with an occasional "bow wow" from the *States*'s fat head. Huey and the *Progress* targeted Z. Marshall Ballard, editor and part-owner of the *Item* (and its morning edition, the *Tribune*), for the most scandalous portrayal. Ballard had angered the Kingfish by questioning his sanity and sometimes printing his name as "hueyplong." Years earlier, Ewing's *States* had accused Ballard of being a drug addict; in 1930 Huey and the *Progress* revived this charge, with embellishments. Ballard's face on the three-headed snake had hypodermics sticking out of it. Other Wood cartoons of the *Item*'s editor showed hypodermics projecting from his arms and legs, spittle flying from his mouth, and a circle of bats above his head. Huey also verbally assaulted Ballard as "Hop-Needle Marshall, king of the dope fiends."[31]

The Long organization was more efficient and better financed than it had been three years earlier. Then, Huey had been an outsider, complaining about "pie-eaters" on the state payroll. Now, as the chef who baked a bigger pie, he demanded a piece of each slice. The number of persons directly employed by the state had doubled, to approximately ten thousand, and would presently increase.[32] Schoolteachers and others employed by local governments were not yet under the control of Long's machine and thus not required to make political contributions, but that day would come.

Huey's system of "deducts" began with publication of the *Louisiana Progress:* state employees at the managerial level were told to hand over 20 percent of one month's salary to pay for the paper's production costs. Soon the *Progress* financed itself through advertisements, mostly from highway contractors and other businessmen desiring friendship with the governor. Contributions from state employees, however, became standardized—first to help pay for Huey's campaign against Senator Ransdell, and later for other purposes, such as making sure the poll taxes of Long's poorest supporters were paid. The usual "deduct," beginning in August of 1930 for all workers above the manual-labor level, was 10 percent each month, except for the paychecks prior to Christmas and Easter. Dr. Joseph A. O'Hara, president of the state Board of Health and chairman of the Louisiana Democratic Association (Huey's organization in New Orleans), when asked by a United States Senate committee if these contributions were "voluntary," innocently explained: "All the people employed have to pay or had to pay that ten per cent voluntarily."[33]

A secure state job, even a menial one, was highly prized during the Great Depression. Pick-and-shovel workers were assessed only 2 to 5 percent, so they, along with the higher-paid employees who had to pay more, seldom complained about Huey's deducts system. No objections were heard from contractors who built the highways and other public works, and who regularly kicked back 20 percent of their bid agreements to the Long machine. Since the contractors padded their costs to compensate for kickbacks, no one suffered except the taxpayers. When major contracts were awarded, *Progress* editor John Klorer usually functioned as the machine's collector. "You have a $100,000 contract and you owe us $20,000," Klorer would say. Immediate payment in cash was expected.[34] In other states, businessmen frequently obtained favors through bribery. But as Huey once observed: "Only stupid politicians take bribes. I'm my own boss." [35] Huey's method—setting the terms and naming the price—was not bribery, but extortion.

The Long machine had become financially self-supporting. Whatever funds Huey needed for campaigning were generated by his power as governor. But in 1930 he had not yet obtained a clear majority of the state's vote, and in nearly all parishes at the time, the reported returns approximated the votes actually cast. The Long organization was still not in a position to count (or miscount) many ballots. Huey's power still depended upon personal appeal. No matter how overbearing he might be to henchmen or contractors, he dared not alienate the mass of voting citizens. Average folk were exempted from his abusive or rude behavior. "He was . . . abrupt even to friends and high officials but never to ordinary people," recalled one of his bodyguards. "Goddam it," Huey once shouted to reporters, "there ain't but one thing that I'm afraid of—and that's the people." [36]

Whatever his inner feelings may have been toward the crowds hearing him campaign against Senator Ransdell, Huey had a mesmerizing effect on most listeners. His stage presence in 1930 differed from that in 1924 or 1928 only in being more practiced, more skillful. Whether he believed what he said or not, Huey Long was a splendid actor. Supporters and opponents alike agreed that he possessed an electric quality; it was exciting to be near him and to hear his persuasive voice—now amplified by loudspeakers atop a five-thousand-dollar sound truck he recently had purchased. Thomas O. Harris, a Louisiana journalist since the 1890s, searched in vain for words to describe the power that radiated from Huey and drew the masses to him. Harris had never witnessed anything remotely comparable. The old newsman could only deduce that Huey had a secret gift, "an indefinable something." [37]

Physically, the Kingfish hardly cast a godlike image. A few years earlier he had appeared slim and almost handsome, but during two years as governor he had added thirty pounds, mostly to his midsection. The effects of rich food and liquor also showed in his face, which had grown reddish and jowly. Huey's nose, always oversized, was becoming bulbous. Exaggerated *Item* and *Tribune* cartoons showed Long with a grotesque paunch above spindly legs, and a huge, glowing nose. The New York reporter A. J. Liebling described Huey's face as "impudent, porcine and juvenile." That face "gave him the deceptive appearance of a clown," wrote Arthur M. Schlesinger, Jr., "but the darting pop eyes could easily turn from soft to hard, and the cleft chin was strong and forceful." The novelist John Dos Passos, who later saw Huey dozing at his seat in the Senate, described him as looking "like an overgrown small boy with very bad habits indeed."[38]

Chronic lack of sleep harmed Huey's appearance and worsened his innate cantankerousness. Seldom did he sleep more than four hours a night, and even that was fitful. Political ideas occurred to him in dreams, and he would snap awake to make notes on a yellow pad kept on a night table. He seemed to relish making phone calls at two or three in the morning. Even while trying to catch up on rest at "Cousin Jess" Nugent's hunting camp in the swampy woodlands west of Baton Rouge, away from electricity and telephones, the restless Kingfish was apt to rise from his cot and scribble on the yellow pad, while a body-guard held a flashlight. But once each week or ten days, wherever he was staying, fatigue finally overrode his adrenaline and Huey would sleep soundly all night and into the morning.[39]

Whether weary or rested, Huey on the campaign trail typically presented a cheerful, folksy image. During the 1930 race, he promised that as a senator he would be "even less dignified than in the past," and asked "all you people to keep on calling me 'Huey.' " To a mostly French gathering in Abbeville he confided, "I have too much Cajun blood in me to be dignified."[40] His phenomenal memory for names and faces continued to pay political dividends. Ordinary people he had met years before were immensely flattered that this masterful, almost superhuman being called them by their first names and seemed like a friend who was genuinely concerned about their problems. Joe Fisher, a Long leader in Jefferson Parish, heard trappers and fishermen of that district brag that "Huey knows me, he remembers me." To them, he could do no wrong. The best concise explanation of Huey's popularity is that offered by the southern historian Dewey Grantham: "He made the masses feel important."[41]

Whenever the stakes were high in Pelican State politics, as in the Long-Ransdell senatorial contest, racial issues—"the black ace from the bottom of the deck"—inevitably appeared. Old Ransdell, certifiably a patrician, was the last prominent Louisiana officeholder who could recall having an antebellum slave "mammy." He referred to her as "Mother Molly," and during the Civil War she had carried him to safety when Yankee gunboats shelled the Ransdell family's riverside plantation. "When I was a little boy," Ransdell said, "I loved that black mammy almost as much as my own mother." He added that he also "loved my negro playmates." But fond recollections of vanished slaves did not prevent Senator Ransdell from insisting that he should be re-elected because Louisiana's blacks were praying for Huey Long's victory, or from implying Huey was working with the NAACP, an organization the senator indignantly explained was "plotting to make colored people equal to whites."[42]

The Kingfish was more comfortable making class appeals, but because he understood the deadly potency of race in Louisiana politics, he would, whenever attacked along that line, respond in like fashion. Senator Ransdell, Huey discovered, once addressed a prominent black Republican, in a letter salutation, as "Mr." Soon a photographed copy of Ransdell's breach of racial etiquette appeared on the front page of the *Louisiana Progress*. The innocuous letter concerned a minor federal job, but the *Progress* headlined it as "RANSDELL'S POLITICAL LOVE LETTER TO THE NEGRO WALTER COHEN."[43]

As the September 9, 1930, Democratic primary approached, many major American newspapers took alarm because Louisiana's "gauche and grotesque governor," as the Atlanta *Constitution* called Huey, looked like a winner over Senator Ransdell. The San Francisco *Chronicle* hoped a Long victory would not happen, declaring there was "enough Hooey in the Senate now." Long's election would be bad news for the nation and most of all for Louisiana, opined the New York *Times*, for "victory would make him master of the fate of every one in Louisiana." The Washington *Post*, remembering Huey's undressed reception of the German dignitaries and other visitors, wondered if he might decide to bathe nude in Washington's public fountains "or wear a green toga in the Senate."[44]

Meanwhile, Huey was informing Louisiana's voters that if elected, he would not take his Senate seat until 1932. Probably no other American politician ever made so curious a pledge, but Huey had good reason to make it and keep it. Ransdell's current term would expire in March of 1931. If Governor Long then stepped forward to be sworn in as senator, Lieutenant Governor Cyr would become governor, because the terms of the state offices to which Long and Cyr were elected would not end until May of 1932. Huey could not afford to leave the governorship, with all its patronage power, to the Jeanerette dentist. That a Governor Cyr would fire Long's people and hire his own was certain. Cyr and Long had become irreconcilable enemies. "I will not permit Paul Cyr to serve as governor of Louisiana for one holy minute," Huey declared. As to leaving a Senate seat vacant for over a year, Huey gleefully pointed out that with "Old Feather Duster" in it, the seat was vacant anyway.[45]

As Huey's running mate in 1928, Dr. Cyr, described as "an ox of a man who loved to fight," had physically protected the Kingfish from would-be assailants. Now he expressed a desire to get his hands on Huey Long. "I wish," Cyr told another anti-Longite, "I could get that son of a bitch in the woods with me. Only one of us would come out." But the lieutenant governor had to content himself with severely beating a young Long supporter who, shortly before election day, taunted him about Huey's impending victory over Senator Ransdell. The fight occurred in the lobby of New Orleans' Monteleone Hotel. Dr. Cyr came away victorious but bloody, having cut his fist "on his antagonist's teeth."[46]

Huey's extramarital life became an issue during the last week of his campaign against Ransdell. Alice Lee Grosjean, the governor's confidential secretary, had an aunt in Shreveport married to a man named Sam Irby, whose favorite drinking companion happened to be James Terrell, Alice's ex-husband. On September 3, Irby walked into Ransdell's New Orleans headquarters to say he had some interesting information. Huey had given Irby a position with the Highway Commission (many of Alice's relatives and in-laws obtained state jobs). But having recently been discharged, Irby now offered the Ransdell organization "proof" of widespread graft in state government, and possibly other damaging material. Ransdell's staff quickly took Irby to Baton Rouge to speak with an anti-Long district judge, George K. Favrot. Later, Irby met Terrell, who had come down from Arkansas to file suit "against the person responsible for breaking up my home."[47] After talking with Terrell, Irby decided to file a slander suit against Long and O. K. Allen (chairman of the Highway Commission) for saying Irby was a drunkard and a wife beater. On the advice of attorneys, doubtless provided by the Ransdell campaign, Terrell and Irby boarded an airplane for Shreveport, Huey's legal domicile, to file their suits there. They arrived at nightfall and took a room at the Gardner Hotel. Apparently, later in the evening, one of them foolishly telephoned Alice.[48]

Alice promptly sent word to Huey that her ex-husband and

uncle-in-law were "drunk in their room" at the Gardner. Huey and his lieutenants conferred over what should be done. Earl, at this time still loyal to his brother, suggested—according to one conferee—murder, but Huey vehemently rejected bloodshed and reportedly "kicked [Earl] in the ass" for suggesting it. Huey's solution to the Irby-Terrell problem was a quasi-legal kidnapping.[49]

Agents of his Bureau of Criminal Identification, then head-quartered in Shreveport, rushed to the hotel and began pounding on Irby and Terrell's door. Irby telephoned the city police, then leaned out a window to yell, "Help! Help!" But the BCI agents, including Huey's brother-in-law Dave McConnell, his cousin Wade Long, and his bodyguard George McQuiston, entered the room and took the two men away. Irby and Terrell were transported to coastal Jefferson Parish, where Sheriff Frank Clancy was an ally of Huey's. Both were held incommunicado—Irby on Grand Isle, Terrell at Barataria Bay. Irby later claimed he was tied to a tree, tormented by mosquitoes, and injected with morphine.[50] More likely, he and Terrell were merely kept under guard and provided with liquor and fishing tackle.

As soon as word of the abduction got out, Louisiana Attorney General Saint's office filed kidnapping charges against Governor Long in United States District Court. Huey claimed Irby and Terrell were in legal custody for questioning about "missing state documents" and said Ransdell's desperate managers reminded him of "a nigger in a graveyard whistling to keep his courage up."[51] William Wiegand, a New Orleans *Item* reporter, slipped into Huey's Roosevelt Hotel suite, just as a United States marshal served the governor his federal court summons. Huey was in an ill mood, and when he learned who Wiegand was, he said, "You're a son of a bitch." The *Item* reporter responded by striking Huey a glancing blow on the mouth. Huey's bodyguards immediately grabbed Wiegand. "Search him for weapons," the governor ordered. They found none, but continued to hold Wiegand's arms. "Young man," Huey intoned, "you have done a terrible thing. You have struck the governor of Louisiana." The *Item* reporter replied to the effect that he disliked having his mother referred to as a female dog, whereupon Huey slapped Wiegand's face, then apologized for the epithet and said, "Now we're even." Wiegand was escorted out, but the confrontation so upset Huey that he ordered a unit of national guardsmen to assist the bodyguards in protecting him during the last days of the campaign.[52]

A bizarre radio broadcast from the Roosevelt Hotel on Sunday evening, September 7, provided an exciting finale for the Long-Ransdell campaign. Huey's voice informed Louisiana that "Mr. Sam Irby" was present with a message for the good people of the great state. Irby was indeed in Huey's suite, having been brought by plane and auto from Grand Isle. He stepped to the microphone and read a short, prepared statement. "Governor Long," Irby told radio listeners, "is the best friend [I have] in the world." Irby explained that his "kidnapping" was a ploy to expose Long's enemies, and that Ransdell's managers had placed $2,500 under his pillow in the Shreveport hotel. He was now handing this money over to Huey's campaign. Nothing was said during the broadcast about James Terrell (Alice's ex-husband was held at Barataria Bay until the polls closed on Tuesday). Two days after the election, Terrell and Irby appeared in federal court to request that the kidnapping charges be dropped. Irby later was given a job with Harvey Couch's Louisiana Power and Light Company. Terrell, who probably received both money and warnings, went back to live with his mother in Arkansas and kept silent, except to tell reporters he "went fishing with Irby" while visiting Louisiana.[53]

Huey Long, for the first and only time in his meteoric career, personally won a majority of Louisiana's Democratic vote in the September 9 primary. He beat Ransdell 149,640 to 111,451, despite losing New Orleans, Shreveport, and Baton Rouge. The governor carried all but eleven of the state's sixty-four parishes. He even came close to winning New Orleans (38,682 to Ransdell's 43,373) despite Mayor Walmsley and the Old Regulars' opposition. Huey's 57.3 percent of the state-wide vote placed him, as the New York *Times* pointed out, in a position to become the state's "dictator."[54]

Joseph Ransdell, ridiculed by Huey as "senile" and "in the twilight of his life," no doubt took future consolation in living almost twenty years longer than his youthful opponent. The ex-senator retired to Lake Providence, attended Mass daily, and in 1950 was honored by Pope Pius XII with the title Knight Commander of the Order of St. Gregory the Great. Ransdell continued in good health until shortly before he died at ninety-five in 1954. Yet loneliness gradually enveloped him. Outliving old friends as well as enemies, he did not miss being sneered at as "Feather Duster," but lamented that "no one is left to call [me] Joe."[55]

· 12 ·

CORNPONE AND COTTON

Huey's clear victory in the 1930 senatorial primary daunted all but his most adamant foes, and it impelled his powerful business allies again to try mediation between him and the Old Regular New Orleans machine. Now, too, the chastened city politicians were ready for peace. Foremost among those bringing Governor Long and Mayor Walmsley together was Rudolph Hecht, president of New Orleans' largest bank (Hibernia) and chairman of NOPSI, the city's public utility monopoly. At a postelection banquet in the Roosevelt Hotel, Huey seemed almost taken aback by the fulsome praise heaped upon him by Walmsley—the once and future "Turkey Head"—and other former enemies. The governor responded to flattering testimonials from friends and ex-foes by saying he scarcely recognized himself. "I am still hoping it's me here tonight."[1]

Peace banquets aside, Louisiana politics remained habituated to violence. It had been thus since Reconstruction. Revealingly, the same *Progress* issue (September 18) that reported the Roosevelt Hotel banquet, with an accompanying cartoon showing Huey's former enemies bowing before him, also headlined another postelection story: "EARL LONG BEATS SOME TRUTH INTO CAMPAIGN LIAR."[2] The fight happened six days after the election, at one of New Orleans' busiest intersections, Canal and Royal. During the campaign, Huey's younger brother had been accused by an Old Regular subordinate, Frank P. Krieger, of sexually assaulting a young woman. Earl admitted he had some bad habits but said that rape was not one of them, and he swore that Krieger would pay in blood if they ever met. On Monday following

206

the election, Earl saw Krieger on the sidewalk at the intersection, and—in Earl's words—"I beat the living hell out of him." Predictably, he used his teeth as well as his fists on Krieger. The corner of Canal and Royal deserves a historical marker for political violence: Sheriff Ike Broussard of Lafayette Parish had attempted to thrash New Orleans *Item* publisher Dominick O'Malley at the intersection in 1897, and in 1874 ex-governor Henry Clay Warmoth had stabbed a newspaperman to death there with a pocket knife.[3]

Earl's brawling aside, Huey's triumph over Ransdell made him the virtually unquestioned boss of Louisiana, and for the moment the turbid atmosphere of strife and violence surrounding him moderated. The Constitutional League disbanded immediately. On September 16, a week after his election to the Senate, Long called the legislature into special session. Everything on his agenda easily passed, including a motion to expunge all remaining impeachment charges. The legislators approved for submission to the voters constitutional amendments that would authorize $75 million for additional highway and bridge construction, $5 million for the new capitol building, and increased funding for public schools. As part of Huey's bargain with Walmsley's Old Regulars, New Orleans would have its first bridge across the Mississippi—to be called the "Huey P. Long Bridge"—a modern airport, and an annual state appropriation of $700,000 to improve the city's streets. An increased gasoline tax on consumers was to pay for most of the program. Huey was unschooled in economics, but his argument that spending for public works should increase during a time of depression—because construction costs were cheaper and jobs needed more than ever—made good common sense.[4]

Of the hundred legislators in the House, only twenty-one opposed any part of Long's program in the September special session; only six of the thirty-nine senators were still anti-Long. Elderly and deaf Representative Gilbert Dupre of Opelousas was the most outspoken die-hard. Because Long had "won the senatorship," Dupre exclaimed, "I am requested to recant, to surrender, apologize, and eat up what I have spoken. . . . Others may do this. I will not . . . I am going to vote NO." The Kingfish played a practical joke by having a hole drilled in the old capitol's roof, directly above Dupre's desk. It rains often in Baton Rouge, and water pouring in on him was Dupre's punishment for voting against the new capitol. Yet in December of 1931 the old patrician, who earlier had said Huey was a "slimy person" who belonged "in the asylum or the penitentiary," became a paid columnist for Huey's *Progress*, admitting in print that he was doing it because he had fallen into dire poverty (he was also out on bond for having recently shot and killed a man during an argument). Dupre's column in the *Progress* dealt with white supremacy in Louisiana, and claimed that Huey's foe Dudley LeBlanc "associated with negroes."[5]

The lull in Long's stormy career, the drooping spirits among his enemies, emboldened Huey to do something even he might not have dared at another time. He appointed Alice Lee Grosjean secretary of state. On October 8, 1930, James Bailey, who had held the position for fourteen years, suddenly died. Huey explained his appointment of Miss Grosjean to fill Bailey's unexpired term by saying it was imperative to have someone experienced in Louisiana affairs working as secretary of state without delay, since that office had to prepare ballots for elections, and the constitutional amendments for Huey's public-works program were due to be voted on in November. Even Colonel "Bow Wow" Ewing of the *States* defended Huey's choice. Of course, Alice's appointment at age twenty-four to the highest office any woman ever held in Louisiana did, as *Time* magazine noted, "set many a gossipy tongue to wagging."[6]

Interviewed by the press, Secretary of State Grosjean proudly mentioned her family's patrician credentials. Sensitive about being a tenth-grade dropout and about her failed marriage to James Terrell, Alice pointed out that she was a member of the Daughters of the American Revolution and the United Daughters of the Confederacy, and that her paternal grandfather was Major Victor Grosjean, editor-publisher of the by-then-defunct Shreveport *Caucasian*. She also told reporters she did not intend to run for a full term in 1932 because "I prefer to take my politics from the sidelines." She spoke of plans to go with the Kingfish to Washington as his confidential secretary when he took his oath as senator.[7]

Alice phoned her parents to say she was "just thrilled to death" at being secretary of state, and confided to the press that "I'll probably have a little time now to go to dances . . . I love to dance." But her new post required attention first; she quickly ferreted out a twenty-thousand-dollar shortage in Secretary

Bailey's accounts (he had been a foe of Governor Long) and dismissed all of Bailey's relatives, including his widow, from the state pay roll.[8] The usually anti-Long press circumspectly described Alice in such terms as *pretty, charming,* and *well proportioned,* without mentioning reports of her private relationship with the Kingfish. But with tongue in cheek, Long's own *Progress* observed that next to Huey himself, Alice was "probably the best posted individual on affairs of state," and "was in a position to know just what made the wheels go round in Baton Rouge."[9]

The constitutional amendments Huey wanted all easily passed in the November, 1930, general election. The state's Republicans saw no point in running a senatorial candidate, so Long's name was alone on the ballot, and his election became official. Huey's most ardent followers now referred to him not merely as "the Kingfish," but also as "God's great gift to Louisiana . . . and possibly the entire nation." Letters in the *Progress* referred to him as "our next President."[10]

Huey was preparing himself for entry on the national stage, although he would not actually be sworn in as a United States senator until early 1932. Beginning in December of 1930, he elaborated on his theme that redistribution of wealth was a biblical command. Increasingly, he referred to America's, not just Louisiana's, economic distress.[11] The South's chronic poverty, abundantly evident in the Pelican State even during the "prosperity decade" of the 1920s, had elevated Long to the governorship and allowed him to become the state's almost-dictator by 1930. Now, with the Great Depression deepening over the land, America's economy began to resemble poor Louisiana's. Huey saw the similarity and understood the opportunity. "His appeal," a perceptive observer would write the day Long died, "was to the hopeless and despairing. His light burned brightest under a black sky."[12]

Mass suffering did produce a spark of genuine concern in the Kingfish. He really would have liked to improve the conditions of life for ordinary people. Yet since he never specifically helped any of the underclass who were unable to help him—that is, nonvoters such as blacks or state prisoners—the conclusion is inescapable that everything he did in politics was for the purpose of augmenting his own power. He accepted this terrible fact about himself, just as he understood that his compulsion to dominate everyone and to humiliate all who crossed him put his life in extreme peril. Probably no American politician ever feared assassination as much as did Huey Long. But his craving for the spotlight and for mastery over everything around him were addictions that, from boyhood on, he would not or could not control.

In December of 1930, Huey transferred his living quarters, and thus the state's operational center, from his suite in New Orleans' Roosevelt Hotel to the new governor's mansion in Baton Rouge. As senator-elect in addition to being the state's chief executive, Huey became less accessible. Earlier he had said, "Anyone can see the governor of Louisiana at any time," but now he announced limited office hours in the capitol building and a by-appointment-only policy at the mansion.[13] He ordered an oversized bed installed in the mansion, and spent much of his time reclining or sitting up in it, although he slept but little. Marquis Childs, then with the St. Louis *Post-Dispatch*, observed him there in 1931: "He lies on a great bed with an orange cover to receive the interviewer. . . . On a table beside the governor is a bottle of whiskey." Childs watched as a procession of supplicants were admitted to the Kingfish's bedchamber, then ushered out. "It is a levee of state in the ancient manner," Childs realized, recalling the Sun King of France, Louis XIV, for whom Louisiana was named.[14]

Huey's "natural cussedness," to quote a pro-Long but candid legislator during the impeachment fight, intensified as his power grew. Rank-and-file voters still looked upon him as a charismatic, entertaining friend who told them their enemies were his enemies; yet most members of his organization saw an increasingly harsh overlord who required submission to verbal abuse as the price for obtaining favors. His ablest or wealthiest lieutenants—notably Seymour Weiss, Robert Maestri, and John Overton—were exempted from Huey's tongue-lashings, but toward the majority of his entourage he never bothered to hide his contempt.[15] He considered them stupid or greedy or both, and his tirades probably stemmed in part from resentment that he had not attracted better satellites.

Huey had to let these henchmen know what he thought of them, although after he did so their requests were usually granted, and minutes later he was apt to fling a comradely arm around them. Few among his entourage ever loved him, but it was not their love he needed, as he had a sufficiency of that for

210

himself. What he wanted, and obtained, was both domination and companionship. One of the few who did adore him was Jess Nugent, although this cousin of Huey's took some of the worst abuse. Nugent, a well-paid member of the Highway Commission, once attempted to add something to Huey's instructions during a conference of Longites. "I think—" Jess interjected. Huey snapped: "Goddamn you, shut up! If you could *think* I wouldn't have put you on that commission." Two of Huey's Jefferson Parish leaders recalled what he said to Archie Higgins upon appointing him to one of the state courts of appeal: "Archie, I performed a miracle today. I took a broken-down lawyer and made a judge out of him." [16]

A story goes that when Huey appointed James Monroe Smith president of LSU, late in 1930, he glared at Dr. Smith's rumpled attire and handed him a large bill, saying, "God damn you, go out and buy a new suit. At least try to look like a president." [17] That something insulting was said is likely, but what makes this version ring false is its depiction of the Kingfish donating money out of his own pocket. He did not do that. After entering politics, Huey seldom carried anything above small change, relying upon associates to pay for his meals, tips, and gifts to strangers in need. James A. Noe, a future governor, recalled Huey's ordering him to give a poor woman, whose husband was in the penitentiary, fifty dollars. "She thanked Huey over and over again. I said, 'I gave you the money, you should thank me.'" The woman replied, "Yes, but you wouldn't have given it unless he made you." [18] Once when Huey was vacationing in New York, a hotel attendant sold him four tickets to a musical comedy. He was alone at the moment. Slapping a tip on the counter, he said, "Here, sister, this is for you." It was three pennies. [19]

In callousness toward individuals, Huey sometimes resembled a moral idiot. But as to publicity he was clearly a genius. He instinctively knew how to make things he did and said, whether meaningful or not, catch media attention—as the silly cornpone-potlikker controversy of February, 1931, exemplified. A less significant issue would be difficult to imagine. Yet it brought him national, even international, attention.

The sham battle began when the Atlanta *Constitution* commented on an Associated Press dispatch from Louisiana relating Governor Long's fondness for "potlikker" (the juice of vegetable greens, preferably turnip greens, boiled with pieces of salted fat pork). Potlikker was familiar at dinner tables throughout the rural South, usually accompanied by "cornpone"—bread made from corn meal. The Kingfish mentioned that cornpone tasted best when dunked in the greenish liquid. Huey had recently served this Winn Parish stand-by at a banquet for New Orleans bankers, probably to emphasize who was now on top in Louisiana. The *Constitution*, in an editorial footnote to the AP story, questioned Governor Long's etiquette, opining that true southerners crumbled, not dunked, their cornpone in potlikker. Huey now sensed a grand opportunity for publicity.

He sent a humorous telegram defending his dunking position to Julian Harris, editor of the *Constitution*. He signed it "Huey P. Long, LL.D., Governor and U.S. Senator-elect"—the degree being an honorary doctorate of laws recently conferred upon him by Loyola University of the South. Hungry for light news during the worsening Great Depression, America's press and politicians expressed opinions on the issue. The top-ranked radio show, NBC's "Amos 'n' Andy," revealed that Andy crumbled his cornpone, whereas Amos liked it "either way." New York's elegant St. Regis Hotel temporarily added the dish to its menu. Overseas, newspapers in Paris commented on "la controverse cornpone." While the affair lasted, which was about three weeks, Huey relished the attention. He said it was the most fun he had had since becoming governor.[20]

Huey actually liked "potlikker a le dictator," as he jokingly called his special recipe. But he usually consumed richer foods, as indicated by an expanding waistline. He was more gourmand than gourmet. Eating, like sex, was to him a triviality compared with politics. At critical times he seemed to subsist on a particular dish: during the 1929 impeachment fight, he kept ordering strawberries and cream. When on a campaign tour, what Huey put into his stomach was, as Hermann Deutsch wrote, "a matter of complete indifference to him." Deutsch watched Huey consume a noonday meal at the village of Dry Prong in Grant Parish: "Here Mr. Long lunched on crackers, canned Vienna sausages, sliced raw onion and peanut-brittle candy, munching them together quite indiscriminately with every outward evidence of relish and enjoyment."[21]

His underlings dreaded eating out with Huey because of his offensive habit of taking morsels he fancied off their plates. This usually happened in restaurants, less frequently at meals served in the mansion or hotel suites. Some henchmen claimed he did it to draw the attention of diners at nearby tables. The excuse of absent-mindedness also has been offered, with the explanation that Huey was talking politics at the time. Neither explanation suffices: everybody in the restaurant was already watching him, and he always talked politics. The real purpose was to exhibit domination. Taking someone else's food in a public place could hardly be surpassed as a demonstration of who was—as one of Huey's aides described him—"the top dog."[22]

Only while drunk would Huey dare take food from the plates of people he did not know. His drinking, however, had increased since his becoming governor. Huey's inhibitions were fragile in the soberest of times, and because of his nervous disposition and lack of sleep, it did not take much alcohol to produce symptoms of intoxication. "A half pint would put him out," one of his legislative leaders recalled. As with everything else he did, the Kingfish wasted little time in getting high. His favorite tipples were bourbon whiskey and Burgundy wine, sometimes in the same glass. After becoming a senator, he claimed the Ramos gin fizz, a New Orleans specialty, as his preferred drink, even asserting that "my grandpappy introduced it back in 1852"; once he flew the Roosevelt Hotel's head bartender to New York to demonstrate, in front of newsreel cameras, the proper method of concocting gin fizzes.[23] Much to the surprise of almost everybody, Huey in 1934 abruptly stopped drinking. At the same time he quit smoking (because of sinus trouble), went on a diet, and—hardest of all—tried to cease using profanity. He had decided it was time to improve his image before the American people. Huey was never addicted to liquor, smoking, or food. Cursing, however, proved too ingrained a habit to break, although during public appearances he curbed it to the point that only an occasional "hell" or "damn" slipped out.[24]

August, hot and humid, is not one of Louisiana's better months, and August of 1931 was worse than usual, both for heat and for economic misery. With its petroleum and commercial interests, and as a producer of sugar and rice as well as cotton, the state had a more diversified economy than other parts of Dixie. Still, cotton was the principal cash crop. By the late summer of 1931, the depression had buffeted nearly everyone's means of livelihood, and cotton growers suffered even more than most. The price of middling-grade lint cotton fell to 6.3 cents per pound (it had reached almost 20 cents per pound only two years earlier). Six cents was below the cost of growing a pound of cotton, given the price of the insecticides needed to fight the boll weevil. Then, on August 8, just as cotton harvesting was beginning, terrible news came: the United States Department of Agriculture forecast a yield of 15.5 million bales for 1931, which would be the third-largest output in history; the prediction alone was certain to drive prices even lower. Old-style southern politicians—of whom United States senators Ellison "Cotton Ed" Smith of South Carolina and Thomas Heflin of Alabama were salient examples—reacted by condemning the Department of Agriculture's forecast. (As it turned out, the USDA had underestimated a 17-million-bale crop.) But Huey Long responded with a revolutionary proposal: to outlaw the planting of cotton for the next year, 1932.[25]

Governor Long called the idea "drop-a-crop." It would later be referred to as Long's "cotton holiday plan." Huey himself credited Congressman John Sandlin of northwestern Louisiana, who in turn said, "This plan was suggested to me by the farmers in my district."[26] It had plausibility. If the cotton-producing states would act now to pass laws forbidding the growing of cotton next year, Huey prophesied that textile mills and other users of the fiber would have to stockpile the 1931 crop, paying more for it than they otherwise would for the 1931 and 1932 crops combined. Farmers in 1932 could grow other things for sale, such as potatoes, as well as have larger gardens for home use. Huey referred to the Bible (Leviticus, chapter 25) as his authority: "The Lord told us to lay off raising these crops one year out of seven, to let the people have time to consume them." One supporter wrote Huey, "You are the Moses of the cotton farmer."[27]

Even prominent Louisianans who previously had viewed Huey more as Mephistopheles than Moses were drawn to his cotton holiday plan. The New Orleans *Item*, hitherto Long's severest newspaper enemy, praised both the plan and Huey "for placing the interests of the region above his own welfare." In river parishes Huey had never carried, the planter oligarchy rallied behind him. Mayor Walmsley of New Orleans called upon the Kingfish's opponents "to set aside our political differences for the relief of the suffering cotton growers." Not everyone agreed. George Seth Guion, an anti-Long candidate for governor in the upcoming election, insisted that prohibiting the raising of cotton in Louisiana would be unconstitutional and smacked of dictatorship. Cotton brokers, shippers, and industries that used cotton all protested. No one bothered to ask black or white sharecroppers their opinion, and Huey apparently gave no thought to how they were going to survive 1932 without income or credit.[28]

A "New Orleans Cotton Conference," called by Governor Long and attended by representatives from all major cotton-growing states, met late in August and endorsed Huey's proposal that the producing states enact drop-a-crop laws. Promptly, the Louisiana legislature in special session passed a bill making it a crime to plant, gather, or gin cotton within the state during 1932, with a proviso that the governor could suspend the act "if states producing seventy-five percent of the [previous] crop failed to enact similar legislation."[29] It was 1:40 A.M. on Saturday, August 29, when Huey, awakened at the mansion, signed the bill into law. For the benefit of photographers he wore a cotton nightshirt. "Now!" he exclaimed, after the cameras stopped clicking. "I can take this damn thing off!" He then re-donned his silk pajamas.[30]

Only one other state, South Carolina, followed suit by passing drop-a-crop legislation. Others might have done so had not Texas refused. Texas grew more cotton than any other state; the drop-a-crop strategy could not succeed without it. Long's plan enjoyed support from ordinary farmers in the Lone Star State, but was opposed by Governor Ross Sterling, a conservative oil millionaire. Sterling reluctantly called the legislature into special session, but warned he would veto anything "radical or dangerous like the Long plan." Huey wanted to go to Austin and personally argue his case at the Texas capitol, but he dared not depart Louisiana, because Paul Cyr would then become acting governor. Flying to Austin as his representatives were O. K. Allen, Seymour Weiss, and his twelve-year-old son, Russell B. Long. Young Russell explained that "Papa couldn't leave because he was afraid Lieutenant Governor Cyr might make a mess."[31]

But twelve thousand Texas farmers gathered in an Austin park on a warm September night to hear Huey's booming voice address them from the studios of KWKH in Shreveport, 290 miles away. Amplifiers had been hooked to a big radio on the platform. The Kingfish talked into the KWKH microphone while he held a telephone to his ear; at the other end of the line was Seymour Weiss in Austin, keeping him informed of the crowd's reaction. "We'll dry every tear in Texas," Long promised, "if Texas passes this cotton law." As soon as Huey finished, Governor Sterling climbed the platform to speak. Even in person he was no match for Huey's radio oratory. His constituents began booing him. Desperately appealing to Lone Star patriotism, Sterling asked: "What would Sam Houston think if he would suddenly return to life and see the Governor of Louisiana telling the people of his beloved Texas what to do?" The crowd responded with shouts of "Hurray for Huey Long!"[32]

Texas' legislature, however, heeded Governor Sterling and the lobbyists who opposed Long's plan. Drop-a-crop failed; approved instead was a modest acreage-control bill, which a state district judge later declared unconstitutional. Restriction of cotton production would have to wait until 1933, when Congress passed the Agricultural Adjustment Act—which Senator Long, ironically, fought.[33]

Huey conceded that his cotton holiday plan had died in Austin, even as he hurled insults at Sterling and the Texas legislature. Sterling, he said, wallowed in a 35-million-dollar fortune "while the people of the South were starving." Moreover, Texas' legislators were "bought"; they had been "blandished with wine, women and money, bought like a sack of corn, and paid off like a slot machine." The Texas solons responded with billingsgate of their own: Long was a "liar," a "coward," and "poor white trash," besides being the "arrogant jackass who brays from Louisiana." The New York *Times* called this "WAR ACROSS THE SABINE," but it was only a war of words.[34]

Among all the sentiments Huey expressed during the cotton crisis of 1931, none was more revealing than the self-pity he feigned when drop-a-crop was rejected by Texas. "In my lifetime," he declared, "I have met defeat in many fights, in things that meant a great deal to me personally, politically, or financially. It is pretty well known that I have suffered almost every reverse that a living human could endure and survive. But in all the misfortunes of my lifetime, I have never been struck to the heart as I have been in the last twenty-four hours." His defeat, he added, was also a defeat for millions of suffering farmers across the South, farmers now doomed to continue in misery because greedy plutocrats had conspired to kill a fair, reasonable, and Scripture-inspired proposal.[35]

"Well, Wall Street and the money power won, as usual," an Alabamian commiserated with Huey shortly after the cotton fight ended. Another Alabamian, owner of a 5,500-acre plantation, wrote that "a man like Huey P. Long should be President of the United States." The Kingfish, however, said he did not think his presidential ambitions had been helped by the publicity over his fight with Texas politicians and cotton-goods manufacturers: "I have offended too many powerful interests to be nominated by the Democrats or Republicans." [36]

More likely, Huey Long believed that his only possible route to the White House was by having the disadvantaged, across the South and then across the nation, recognize him as their champion—for the masses to see in him both greatness and commonality with them. His defeats would be their defeats, but he would keep on fighting until the money power was toppled and a better society built. With the cotton crisis of 1931, he had taken another step along that road.

· 13 ·

COMPLETE THE WORK

Before Huey could go to Washington without jeopardizing his Louisiana power base, he had to install an obedient successor as governor. The Democratic primary, which meant election, was set for January of 1932. By late summer of 1931 the campaign was already underway. Huey named a slate of candidates for all nine state-wide offices, the first time this had been done in a Louisiana primary election. The "Complete the Work" ticket, as Huey called it, was headed by gubernatorial candidate Oscar K. "O. K." Allen of Winn Parish.[1] O. K.'s history of unswerving loyalty to the Kingfish went back to the day in 1918 when he had loaned Huey five hundred dollars.

This election presented a new difficulty for Huey's enemies. They had been unable to defeat him for governor or for senator even with the Old Regulars of New Orleans delivering majorities against him. Now the city machine, having come to terms with the Kingfish after his 1930 senatorial primary victory, was supporting the Complete the Work ticket.[2] With both Long and the Old Regulars behind him, Allen was certain to come out of New Orleans with a whopping majority—and since Huey had even greater strength in the rural parishes, chances that his hand-picked successor could be beaten were slim at best.

Nevertheless, five opposition candidates announced for governor, of whom two, Dudley J. LeBlanc and George Seth Guion, waged active campaigns. Public Service Commissioner LeBlanc had a sizable bloc of followers among his fellow Cajuns; some viewed him as a French-style Kingfish. As a youth LeBlanc, like Long, had been a traveling salesman, first for Bull Durham tobacco, then peddling Wine of Cardui—the same panacea for gynecological troubles that the teenage Huey sold. In the early 1920s, LeBlanc had recognized Huey Long as a rising star and tried to emulate him, even calling himself "the Poor Man's Friend" and "the Huey P. Long of the Southwest," much to Huey's indignation.[3] By 1926, when LeBlanc was elected to the Public Service Commission, the two were enemies. LeBlanc and his ally on the commission, Francis Williams, controlled the three-man body, but Long, after becoming governor, rendered the PSC nearly impotent by vetoing its legislative appropriations. The other serious anti-Long candidate to announce for the 1932 gubernatorial election, Guion, was a New Orleans lawyer of upper-class background; *Progress* cartoons portrayed him as a vapid aristocrat mouthing such things as, "Shades of my ancestors!"[4]

O. K. Allen, silver-haired and soft-spoken, possessed a dignified appearance but a weak will. Anti-Longites sneered at him as a dimwit, which he was not, and as putty in the hands of the Kingfish, which he was. Growing up in awful poverty on Dugdemona Bayou's "yan side"—a region that even in Winn Parish was looked upon as backward—Allen became a schoolteacher at fifteen (although at the time he had not gone beyond the fourth grade), and later managed a sawmill. He worked hard, eventually owning a small store, and was elected parish assessor in 1916. When Huey won the governorship in 1928, Allen went to the state senate, then became chairman of the Highway Commission—the job he held when Huey picked him to run for governor. O. K. suffered from heart trouble, a condition probably worsened by Huey's abusive domination and the nagging he took at home from his fat and formidable wife, Florence. "Between Huey and his wife," Allen's secretary recalled, "old Oscar really used to catch it."[5]

Huey's decision to run Allen for governor and House Speaker John B. Fournet for lieutenant governor led to serious trouble within the Long family. Earl, Huey's younger brother, had asked Huey to back him for governor; when Huey refused, Earl insisted that he at least be endorsed for lieutenant governor on Allen's ticket. Again the Kingfish said no. Earl was furious, and so were all his and Huey's siblings still residing in Louisiana (brother Shan and sister Callie lived out-of-state and took no part in the controversy). In his autobiography, Huey disingenuously explained that since "it was already being charged I was a dictator" and had too many relatives on the state pay roll, to have backed Earl for either of the top offices "would have been disastrous to the whole ticket."[6] The real reason was that Earl could not be depended upon to obey Huey's commands.

Earl announced for lieutenant governor anyway, and joined the Guion ticket. In the past, Huey and Earl had often argued, but Earl had supported Huey in all his campaigns, and he had been rewarded with one of the most lucrative state jobs, attorney for the inheritance tax collector in Orleans Parish—a position Huey had promised to abolish, saying he would use the saved fee money to help build a tuberculosis hospital along the shore of Lake Pontchartrain (a New Orleans paper soon printed a photograph of Earl Long with the caption, "New Lakefront TB Hospital"). The position paid up to fifteen thousand dollars a year. Earl, as his part of the bargain, had accepted financial responsibility for their aged father and for sister Callie, who still suffered from tuberculosis. But now, in 1931, Huey and Earl became enemies, and joining Earl in his campaign appearances was Julius Long, accompanied by sisters Lottie, Olive, Clara, and Lucille. Their verbal attacks on Huey made no difference in the election's outcome but delighted Huey's enemies, who otherwise had little to cheer about. Old Hugh, the father, made no public statements, but at a rally in Winnfield he appeared on the speaker's stand with Earl and Julius, and reportedly "stamped his feet in approval" when Julius talked about Huey's lack of feeling for the family.[7]

While running for lieutenant governor, Earl aired the Long family's—or at least Huey's—dirty linen. He recalled how as a child Huey insulted other youngsters but would not fight, and how he, Earl, had to do the older brother's battling for him. Julius corroborated these stories. Speaking in the town of Gretna, Earl referred to Huey as "the yellowest physical coward that God ever let live," and dared "big-bellied Huey" to "meet me face to face" in front of the Roosevelt Hotel. Earl also claimed that Huey's wife, Rose, who had endured "a lot of things," was going to vote the Guion ticket. Sister Lucille, in an astonishing analogy, compared Huey's treatment of Earl to Judas Iscariot's betrayal of Christ.[8]

Huey parried these attacks from family members by taking on the role of wounded innocence. He spoke of their "ingratitude" but promised he would nevertheless "be a better brother to Earl and Julius than they are to me." Yet the Kingfish could not resist a few digs at Earl; he called him "the Sorcerer's Apprentice" (without thinking that imagery through) and in several speeches jokingly claimed that Earl was not a blood member of the Long family, but had been an ugly, squawling, abandoned infant that Huey's mother took pity on and brought home.[9] Actually, as both Earl and Huey surely realized in calmer moments, they were the most alike of the Long brothers. Earl did not have Huey's brilliance nor was he as egocentric, but he shared some of the Kingfish's ambition, mannerisms, and political instincts. Earl admired and envied Huey, and obsessively yearned to duplicate his accomplishments. When Earl finally was elected governor in 1948, *Time* magazine unkindly remarked that he "has aped his brother with the beetle-browed assiduousness of a vaudeville baboon learning to roller-skate."[10]

Dr. Paul Cyr, the incumbent lieutenant governor, entered the gubernatorial race with Allen, LeBlanc, Guion, and the also-rans, but he eventually withdrew and threw his support to Guion. Meanwhile, in October of 1931, Cyr had rashly declared himself to be governor of Louisiana, insisting that Huey had vacated that office when he was elected senator in 1930. Cyr—the "Wild Bull of Jeanerette," as he was nicknamed—took an oath as governor before a friendly clerk of court in Shreveport.[11] Momentarily alarmed, Huey (who was in New Orleans at the time) ordered a National Guard unit in Baton Rouge to guard the governor's mansion and the capitol "to prevent Cyr from seizing them," then stuck a pistol in his pocket and drove toward Baton Rouge at ninety-plus miles an hour to take personal command of his armed forces. In the sort of headline usually found over dispatches about banana-republic revolutions, the New York *Times* announced:

HUEY LONG DEFEATS
COUP D'ETAT BY CYR
HOLDS CAPITOL WITH TROOPS[12]

Adept at making his enemies bleed on their own swords, Huey declared that in taking an illegal oath as governor, Dr. Cyr had abandoned the office of lieutenant governor, so "he is now nothing." Huey had Alvin O. King, president *pro tem* of the state senate, sworn in as the new lieutenant governor. Then orders were issued to have Cyr arrested if he showed up at the capitol building. What resembled comic opera presently turned into burlesque, as various persons—some probably encouraged by Long's organization—mocked Cyr's action by coming before notary publics to take an oath as governor of Louisiana. A notary in Baton Rouge halved his usual fifty-cent fee for oath taking, "to aid jobless aspirants." For a few days, Louisianians merrily greeted each other on the street with "Hello, Governor!"[13]

Dr. Cyr, after futilely ordering Adjutant General Ray Fleming to disband his national guardsmen at the state buildings, took his case to court. Huey filed a countersuit. The matter promptly landed in the Louisiana Supreme Court's lap, but the court prudently delayed its decision until after the January, 1932, primary election. During the interval, Cyr never dared enter the capitol building.[14] For the voters, Huey had a simple explanation: Paul Cyr needed to "go back to his tooth chiseling in his smokehouse office in Jeanerette."[15]

O. K. Allen may be the most inept and overshadowed candidate ever to win a landslide victory in any American gubernatorial election. He was an uninspiring speaker who tended to ramble. Having Governor and Senator-elect Long on the platform with him did not help Allen's performance, for Huey always had difficulty keeping silent when someone else was talking, especially when the speaker was one of his underlings. Reporters on the Complete the Work campaign trail grew accustomed to seeing Huey fidget for several minutes, then deliver his unmistakable stage whisper, "Oscar, your time is up!" Even in the short span he was allowed, Allen did not always remember every promise he was supposed to make. Consequently, he received prompting. At New Iberia, O. K. rattled off a prepared list of things he would do for the district, but forgot one important matter. Huey leaned forward, pulled Allen's coattail, and loudly whispered: "Oscar, you are also going to help the hot pepper industry." The unfortunate man, who would be Louisiana's next governor in title only, parroted: "I am also going to help the hot pepper industry."[16]

The crowds at Complete the Work rallies mostly came to see and hear Huey, and his speech was always the highlight. What he actually said seemed to matter little. "I couldn't believe people could be so spellbound by a man," one of his bodyguards recalled. "Old women were crying. People would wait thirty minutes to touch him, to touch his coat sleeves." As the campaign wore on and it became clear that LeBlanc was the strongest anti-Long candidate, Huey concentrated his fire upon the loquacious Cajun.[17] As was his custom when he decided an enemy should be hit a knockout blow, the Kingfish verbally associated LeBlanc with "niggers."

LeBlanc was secretary-treasurer (actually, founder and principal owner) of a burial insurance company named the People's Benevolent Association, located in the town of Thibodaux. The company had both a white and a black division—the latter with a black vice-president—but in Huey's oratorical description, the PBA was a "nigger coffin club" and LeBlanc a thief who fraternized with Negroes in order to cheat them. After a fancy funeral service, said Huey, "I am informed . . . LeBlanc takes the body into a backroom, takes off the shroud, nails them up in a pine box."[18] In another version, Huey claimed that after nightfall LeBlanc and his black partners would "go and dig that coffin up and . . . use that same coffin and shroud to bury everybody with." Huey's *Progress* joined the attack with blatantly racist cartoons and an assertion that LeBlanc "DIVIDED . . . PROFIT ON DEAD COONS WITH NEGRO PARTNER." The Kingfish's favorite punch line during the 1931–1932 campaign was, "LeBlanc ain't got time to be governor because he's got to go back and be secretary-treasurer of that nigger lodge."[19]

LeBlanc responded by endeavoring to "outnigger" Huey. He could not do it, but he tried. A LeBlanc circular described Long and Allen as "nigger lovers" who hired blacks in preference to white people, with a cartoon showing Huey "giving his chulluns free school books" so they might learn how to overthrow white supremacy. LeBlanc also attempted to outpromise Long, an even more difficult feat. He pledged that a LeBlanc administration would provide $30-per-month pensions for elderly Louisianians—to which Huey responded there were at least forty thousand blacks in the state over the age of sixty, so that under LeBlanc's scheme, white taxpayers would be paying $14,400,000 or more per year to support idle old blacks. On the defensive, LeBlanc replied that he "would exclude negroes from the pensions." Only in the use of scatology was LeBlanc even remotely in the Kingfish's league. He frequently referred to Long and Allen as "Huey Piss Long" and "Old Krap Allen."[20]

It was a low campaign, sinking beneath the depths of the

Ransdell-Long senatorial contest. Real issues were almost ignored by LeBlanc, Guion, and Allen (Long). The Complete the Work ticket relied on promises and racism instead of pointing out the real inadequacies of LeBlanc and Guion, and the anti-Long candidates, particularly LeBlanc, offered little except alternative promises and similar racism. Guion did try to make an issue out of probable fraud in the Highway Commission, and both he and LeBlanc attacked Huey's dictatorial style and his hypocritical alliance with the Old Regulars. These legitimate points, however, were seldom mentioned during the last weeks of the campaign. Guion allowed himself to be overshadowed by his running mate, Earl Long, while LeBlanc's mendacity became transparent when he contrasted his war record with that of the "cowardly slacker" Huey Long and called "upon those buddies who fought with me in the trenches for fourteen long months to go to the polls and vote for me next Tuesday." In fact, LeBlanc had been drafted late in World War I and never got nearer the battlefields of France than Camp Hancock in Georgia. "He wasn't even kicked by a mule or bit by a horsefly," Huey chortled.[21]

Ex-governor Parker offered the nearest approach to dignity and sensibility during the campaign. Once again he left his Bayou Sara farm to warn Louisianians against what he perceived as the gravest threat to liberty in the state's history. Parker endorsed neither Guion nor LeBlanc; he was simply against the "unholy alliance" of Huey Long and the New Orleans Ring. Parker had fought the urban machine since the 1880s; his hatred of Huey dated only from 1921 but was becoming more intense each year. In two state-wide radio addresses early in January, 1932, Parker, his voice quavering with emotion and age, pleaded with "the real people" to see to it their children did not have to grow up in a state dominated and degraded by Huey Long.[22] Huey's *Progress* critiqued Parker's remarks under the headline "OLD SACK OF BONES JOHN M. PARKER IN RADIO CROAK HOUR." Huey, speaking in Monroe, made sarcastic references to Parker's "snake farm," and the *Progress* followed with a cartoon showing serpents twining around the old man's legs (Parker's favorite retirement pastime at Bayou Sara was hunting and killing water moccasins and rattlesnakes).[23]

Even though this campaign was the most abusive since 1896, election day of January 19, 1932, lacked some of the excitement surrounding the two previous gubernatorial contests, when Huey Long's name had been on the ballot. This time, as the anti-Long *Madison Journal* admitted a week before votes were cast, "most people have taken it for granted that O. K. Allen and the whole administrative ticket [will] be nominated." No run-off was required. State-wide, Allen won 214,699 votes to LeBlanc's 110,048 and Guion's 53,756, with 1,446 for two minor candidates. Earl Long, as a candidate for lieutenant governor, did slightly better than his running mate, Guion, but still came in a poor third. In contrast to the past, Huey's slate ran better in New Orleans (70.6 percent of the total) than in the rest of the state (51.5 percent).[24] Indeed, it was the city vote, plus highly questionable returns from three suburban parishes—Jefferson, Plaquemines, and St. Bernard—that gave Allen a first-primary majority.

St. Bernard, where 2,194 whites and no blacks were registered as voters, turned in the most stunning totals: 3,152 for Allen and each of the eight other members of the Complete the Work ticket; 0 for LeBlanc; 0 for Guion; 0 for all other candidates on the ballot who were running for state-wide office. St. Bernard Sheriff L. A. Meraux and Judge Leander Perez, whose district included St. Bernard and Plaquemines, evidently wanted to impress the Kingfish with their iron control of local returns; in 1930 Huey had beaten Ransdell 3,979 to 9 in St. Bernard, and now the tiny stain of opposition was wiped off.[25] "We are one large political family," the *St. Bernard Voice* explained, later adding, "with the exception of several ballots which were spoiled." Dudley LeBlanc, studying the St. Bernard totals, wailed: "This would mean that not *one* person voted for me, not my brother Raoul, nor his wife, nor my wife's relatives. Not *one* Cajun vote! Could you believe that?"[26]

More surprising than the manipulated St. Bernard vote was the honest total from Grant Parish, adjoining Winn. Grant, an old Populist and previously Long stronghold, overwhelmingly fundamentalist Protestant and poor, was the only rural north Louisiana parish to vote for LeBlanc (1,458 to 1,370 for Allen and 313 for Guion). An event during the spring of 1931 in the village of Montgomery caused this turnabout. LeBlanc's brother Preston and a campaign aide, Joe Boudreaux, were attacked and beaten for distributing LeBlanc leaflets during a Complete the Work rally; their assailants were Robert and O. R. Brothers, two of Huey's aides. Grant Parish's judge and sheriff were Longites, so Preston LeBlanc and Boudreaux were jailed on a charge of "intent to kill"; the Brothers brothers were not arrested. But a grand jury, hearing the evidence, realized LeBlanc and Boudreaux were in fact victims, and refused to indict them. An elemental sense of fairness, a resentment against thuggery and legal highhandedness, asserted itself in Grant Parish, causing the Long machine to lose one of its hitherto most reliable districts. (In the Montgomery precinct, where most voters had seen the beatings, Dudley LeBlanc got an absolute majority, 138 to 70 for Allen and 19 for Guion.)[27] Everyone in the parish realized that O. K. Allen would almost certainly win a first-primary victory with or without Grant's votes, and must also have known the parish was likely to suffer for its apostasy. The anti-Long ballots were acts of courage.

The Grant Parish vote was also a warning to Huey Long and his organization that overbearing tactics could erode support even among his core constituency. Yet the St. Bernard returns demonstrated something else: a leader who absolutely controlled the election machinery need not depend upon fluctuating popular support. To Huey, only one thing truly mattered: power and more power for himself, by the most expeditious means. Thus the lesson the Kingfish seemed to learn from Grant Parish in 1932 was that if his authority were ever seriously challenged, the St. Bernard way would be the road to follow.

Dr. Cyr's claim to be the rightful governor still hung tenuously in the air. On January 22, three days after Allen's victory in the Democratic primary, the Louisiana Supreme Court, by four to three, dismissed Cyr's suit and opined that "the sole judge" of when Governor Long did, or would, become Senator Long, was the United States Senate itself. Huey decided it was now safe to take his new office, although his term as governor was not scheduled to end, and Allen's begin, until May. On January 25, the Kingfish arrived in Washington on his "Huey P. Long Special" Pullman coach, checked into the Mayflower Hotel, where he received reporters while clad in lavender silk pajamas, then went to the Capitol to take his oath. The moment Huey became a senator, the news was telephoned to Baton Rouge, where Alvin O. King—who had been sworn in as lieutenant governor the previous October when Dr. Cyr "abandoned" that office—immediately took an oath as Louisiana's interim chief executive.[28]

In vain, Cyr drove from Jeanerette to Baton Rouge and set up a rival "seat of government" in a Heidelberg Hotel room. There he issued a pronouncement that "Alvin O. King, at the head of insurrectionary forces has seized the governor's office," and he warned all persons not to deal with the "pretended government." Yet Dr. Cyr was not especially popular even among staunch anti-Long elements, and his manifestos from the Heidelberg were ignored. Three days after moving in, he was evicted from his room, after a to-the-point phone call from Huey to the hotel's owner; Cyr then transferred his "seat of government" to the cheaper Louisian Hotel across the street. Shortly thereafter, "Governor" Cyr returned to Jeanerette and faded from the news, but not before ominously remarking that "a few funerals in this State would help out a lot."[29]

Huey was fond of boasting, then and later, of how much he had done for Louisiana during his almost four years (May, 1928–January, 1932) as governor. Indeed, positive things had been accomplished. Concrete and asphalt had replaced gravel and shell on the main highways; gravel and shell had replaced mud on the secondary roads. From a pathetic 331 miles of paved highways, the state now had 2,301. One hundred new and toll-free bridges across Louisiana's numerous streams were open or under construction, including four major spans across the Red, two each over the Atchafalaya and the Ouachita, and one across the narrows of Lake Pontchartrain. The great Mississippi was still unbridged in Louisiana except for an interstate span on U.S. Route 80 at Vicksburg, but contracts had been let for the Huey P. Long Bridge at New Orleans, destined to open in 1936. All these projects helped to make the Great Depression less stressful in Louisiana by employing thousands who otherwise would have swelled the ranks of those desperately seeking any kind of work. Roads and bridges were Governor Long's most obvious achievements; as Harnett Kane, one of Huey's severest critics, conceded, "He took Louisiana out of the mud."[30]

Next to road and bridge building, Long ranked advances in public education as the greatest legacy of his administration. There were considerable improvements, mainly for white schools, but Huey's claim that he had taken the state's school system from bottom rank to being "the best anywhere in America" was wildly off the mark. Along with providing free schoolbooks for public and parochial schools, his best educational achievement was setting up night schools to combat adult illiteracy. At least 100,000 adult Louisianians who could not read and write in 1928 had been taught to do so by 1932, and most of the beneficiaries were black. The program, however, would not have been as successful without a large contribution from the Chicago-based Julius Rosenwald Fund, and even with the improvement, Louisiana merely climbed from last to next-to-last in literacy, creeping ahead of South Carolina.[31]

Differences in funding for white and black education actually widened during Long's (and later Allen's) administration, and the disparity was more the fault of the state government than of local boards, since the Long-Allen regimes gradually took control of, and provided most of the funding for, school districts throughout the state. The poorer white parishes were helped by an "Equalization Fund" to bring their schools nearer the standards of those for whites in the plantation parishes and in the cities. During the same time, average salaries for black teachers went down while those of white teachers went up. State-wide, more black children were enrolled than ever before, but their dilapidated, ill-equipped classrooms seldom saw improvements. Many "colored schools" had no blackboards or desks, and their free textbooks were usually tattered ones previously used in white schools. Although the state constitution set "a minimum of $12 for each child of school age," actual expenditures in Louisiana by 1933 averaged $44.98 per white child, but only $7.88 per black child. That gap was slightly wider than in 1916, when the figures were, respectively, $20.69 and $4.00.[32]

Louisiana State University benefited from becoming a special pride of the Kingfish. Huey came to identify himself with LSU so closely he customarily referred to it as "my university." His increasing fondness for LSU proved an exception to his rule of never forgiving a slight—he still remembered the "ignorant or bought" professors who in 1910 had awarded him, at age sixteen, a disappointing third place in debate at the annual state rally in Baton Rouge.[33] When Huey first ran for governor, his resentment toward higher education, specifically aimed at Governor Parker's appropriations for LSU, was bluntly expressed. But during his governorship, Long developed a paternalistic feeling toward LSU, and his fondness was buttressed by a realization that favorable publicity for "my university" also enhanced his image.

Huey understood that academic improvements—better teachers, more classrooms, and increased enrollment—were of first importance, and most of the money he spent on LSU went for those purposes. But Huey's personal involvement centered upon the band and the football team. Leading the Fighting Tiger band in parades and cavorting along the sidelines during games might seem juvenile antics for a governor or senator, but it meant increased national publicity. More people read newspaper sports sections than editorial pages.[34] Besides, Huey purely enjoyed performing in front of crowds.

Enrollment and academic standards both rose at LSU during the years of Huey's overlordship. From 1,600 students in 1928, enrollment climbed to approximately 4,000 by 1933. Largely because of Long's largess, improvements in facilities and faculty took LSU from mediocrity to the status of a major southern university. Typically, Huey exaggerated when he boasted, "Today . . . you will find it no. 1, along with Harvard and Yale," but academics at LSU had much improved in the ten years since 1923, when a New York visitor to LSU's library was dismayed to see that Thorstein Veblen's classic *Theory of the Leisure Class*, published in 1899, had never been checked out.[35] By 1933, excellent young scholars, including Cleanth Brooks and Robert Penn Warren, graced LSU's faculty, and within two years the LSU Press and the *Southern Review* would be established.

Less creditably, the Kingfish selected James M. "Jingle Money" Smith as the university's president. Born at Sikes in Winn Parish, Smith had a Ph.D. from Columbia University and was a good administrator, except for being a thief. "There's not a straight bone in Jim's body," Huey was quoted as saying, "but he does what I tell him." Smith also possessed the dignified appearance befitting a college president. He even showed a semblance of dignity several years later when, following conviction for embezzling $500,000 in university funds, *Life* magazine photographed him wearing a striped convict suit at Angola State Prison.[36]

Angola, an eighteen-thousand-acre penal farm in West Feliciana Parish, had been Louisiana's largest penitentiary since 1901, and in its early years was considered a relatively merciful correctional facility. Life there for black convicts seemed, according to investigators, as good as or better than most blacks might expect on the outside as sharecroppers or wage earners.

Although lacking a rehabilitation or even a literacy program, Angola became one of the most humane southern prisons during the years (1916–1923) of General Manager Henry L. "Marse Henry" Fuqua's administration. Fuqua, who later became governor, insisted upon kinder treatment of the convicts, and fired those guards he viewed as "brutal bullies with large whips." He also virtually abandoned use of the humiliating striped uniforms.[37] But Angola and the smaller prison camps operated with a financial deficit. Governor Long decided the prison system could be made self-supporting, and for a time he almost made it so, but at the cost of brutalization.

The Long administration cut expenses by concentrating all state prisoners in Angola and putting the institution under the financial control of R. L. "Tighty" Himes, previously LSU's business manager. (President Smith voiced no objection to Himes's leaving LSU, since Smith preferred a less meticulous bookkeeper.) Under Himes's supervision, Angola was probably the most graft-free segment of state government, but also the cruelest. Floggings increased in number and severity, and striped uniforms again became the standard attire. Huey understood that voter sentiment opposed "coddling" convicts, especially since a majority of the prisoners were black. (Moreover, the relatives of black convicts did not vote.) The New Orleans *Times-Picayune* and ex-governor Pleasant were highly critical of the new harshness at Angola, but Long responded by saying they were simply frustrated because under his regime the penitentiary was "making money."[38]

Huey's claim that state hospitals were vastly improved during his regime was untrue. The "insane asylums" at Pineville and Jackson, he insisted, were snake pits before he became governor; in fact, they were deficient before, during, and after the Long administration. A scholarly study of Louisiana's mental institutions concluded that more improvement took place during the Parker, Fuqua, and Simpson administrations (1920–1928) than during the Long-Allen years (1928–1936). Long's increased funding for Pineville and Jackson, it turned out, went largely toward hiring politically correct staff members and attendants, many of whom were "deadheads" who did little or no work, but whose salaries were subjected to deducts of 5 to 10 percent for the Long organization.[39] The huge Charity Hospital in New Orleans, already the largest facility of its kind in the South, was expanded and improved to the point that white patients no longer slept two to a bed, but the ramshackle main building, a firetrap, was not replaced until after Huey died, and then with federal money. Charity's "colored ward," during the Long years, remained as overcrowded and filthy as ever; its obstetrics section, wrote Carleton Beals, "would disgrace a Quecha Indian village." [40]

As to public aid for the indigent ("relief," the "dole," or "welfare"), Huey Long reflected the conservatism of old Louisiana. French and Spanish tradition in the southern parishes turned to the Catholic church as "the almoner of the poor," and in Protestant north Louisiana neighborhood charity was supposed to look after those among the destitute who deserved help. Even during Reconstruction, the relatively liberal Republican legislature rejected state aid for the indigent because it would "encourage laziness and make . . . Louisiana a receptacle for the poor of other states." [41] In 1880 a state law was finally passed obliging each parish "to make a provision" only for "infirm, sick, and disabled paupers." When Huey Long became governor, six parishes, including Orleans, had poor farms or almshouses, while most rural parishes allotted minuscule sums (usually three or four dollars per family per month) for those, white or black, who qualified for inclusion on what was generally called the "Pauper List." The state's warm climate and reputedly abundant wild foods such as berries, nuts, and fish—its "easy means of securing subsistence," as an LSU sociologist phrased it in 1913—were pointed to as reasons why "the care of paupers is not so serious a problem." [42]

Long, as governor and as senator, agreed on this point with the patrician regime he toppled. Despite increased poverty during the Great Depression, Louisiana did not set up a Department of Public Welfare until 1936 (after Huey was dead), and 97.9 percent of the $33,764,996 spent to provide work for the state's unemployed during the worst years (1933–1934) of the depression came from the federal treasury. Only three other states contributed so small a percentage for unemployment relief. [43] In one of his 1935 Senate speeches, the Kingfish even claimed that in Louisiana, "we never felt the depression . . . until the [federal] dole money began to be put out." According to him, the federal aid discouraged "lazy" people from seeking work or even planting a garden. "In my section," Huey claimed, "a man can go into the country and raise a garden in six weeks time. He can . . . have turnips and corn meal and catch fish and live easier than anywhere on God's green earth. . . . I would say, 'God helps those who help themselves.' "[44]

Huey's opposition to the New Deal's work relief programs (he continued to use the expression "dole money") from 1933 to 1935 chiefly stemmed from the fact that he did not control or disburse those expenditures. In Louisiana, anything of political importance that Huey did not dominate, he fought unreservedly. Meanwhile, he could pretend to be far more liberal or progressive than Franklin D. Roosevelt by proposing the spectacular but simplistic national program of income redistribution he called "Share Our Wealth."

More revealing than Huey's antagonism toward New Deal programs, or his pseudoradical Share Our Wealth alternative, was the Long-controlled legislature's refusal to appropriate state funds for mothers' pensions (as aid for dependent children was then called) or for old age pensions, along with its opposition to extending limitations on the hours of female and child labor to those employed in agriculture. "Picking cotton is fun for kids anyway," Huey pointed out.[45]

The Washington-bound "Huey P. Long Special," which with much fanfare pulled out of New Orleans' train terminal on a January evening in 1932, had on board Huey's wife, Governor-elect Allen, Mayor Walmsley, Seymour Weiss, and various other followers, including Huey's new personal secretary, Earle J. Christenberry. Alice Lee Grosjean, contrary to her expectations, did not accompany her boss to Washington. "I tried to get someone who could handle the job," Huey remarked. Christenberry claimed a world's speed record in stenography.[46] Also, Huey as senator planned to become a national center of attention and eventually a presidential candidate, and he realized the Washington press corps would scrutinize his private life. The nation was not as tolerant as Louisiana. He could not afford to run for president with Rose and the children at home and the vivacious Miss Grosjean at his side. So Alice stayed behind.

Alice also stepped a bit further out of the spotlight. After her interim appointment as Louisiana's secretary of state ended in May of 1932, she was appointed supervisor of public accounts by the Allen administration. She and the Kingfish still met, but less frequently. Late in 1934, Raymond Daniell of the New York

Times was introduced to her by Huey at 6 A.M. in Huey's New Orleans hotel suite; but with her "was a stoutish, gray-haired woman, who turned out to be her mother."[47] Alice would continue to keep the Kingfish's enormous scrapbook collection up to date, even when that meant clipping stories about his assassination. Shortly before that event, in the summer of 1935, she married a man named William A. Tharpe. As soon as he married Alice, Tharpe received a well-paying state job, being appointed secretary of the Louisiana Tax Commission.[48]

· 14 ·

TERROR OF THE BAYOUS

Anticipating a good story, capital correspondents closely watched Huey Long's first day, January 25, 1932, as a United States senator. They were not disappointed. As he strode down the aisle to take his oath, Huey puffed on a cigar, pausing to leave it on the desk of the Democratic minority leader, Joseph T. Robinson of Arkansas. After the swearing in, Huey took his seat on the back row reserved for new senators. He fidgeted at his desk for about ten minutes, apparently expecting other members to come and greet him. When they did not, he darted toward the front to introduce himself—with hugs, back slaps, and chest jabs—to those Republican and Democratic senators who most often stood in the limelight. "Within an hour," observed the New York *Times*, "the Terror of the Bayous . . . was violating every rule of decorum in that august chamber."[1]

For the next few weeks, however, Huey was more often in Louisiana than in Washington. From the time he took his oath until the Seventy-second Congress adjourned on July 16, Huey was absent 81 out of 137 legislative days. Senator David Reed of Pennsylvania remarked in June that it was "indefensible" for Louisiana's junior senator to be away, without good reason, "for weeks at a time." Upon his return, Long explained that "very important business of . . . Louisiana and I think business of the United States" accounted for his absences. In reality, his poor attendance was caused partly by the painful recognition that although he remained, in his words, "a kingfish in Louisiana," he was as yet "but a minnow in the Washington pool."[2]

The role of minnow—of being the most junior of ninety-six

senators—was of course intolerable. Once, he had been a youthful nobody in Louisiana politics; he had transformed himself into a kingfish by first becoming a barracuda. Now, at age thirty-eight, he commenced the same metamorphosis, for the same purpose, in Washington. It was the only way he knew.

Most senators soon began to prefer Long's absence to his presence, and this was notably true of Joe Robinson of Arkansas. As the Senate's minority leader (and after 1932, majority leader), Robinson expected Democratic members, most of all those from the South, to treat him with respect and obedience. He got neither from the Kingfish. Huey had his own agenda, one designed to gain maximum national attention. "He viewed the Senate," to quote T. Harry Williams, "primarily as a forum from which he could advertise Huey Long to the country."[3]

While still a senator-elect, Huey solemnly told reporters the first bill he introduced would be one requiring jew's-harps—simple musical instruments he enjoyed playing—to be manufactured according to his specifications. In fact, his initial proposal was of considerably larger magnitude: a resolution, offered April 21, 1932, that "no person shall have an annual income in excess of $1,000,000," or receive "during his or her lifetime" gifts or inheritances of "more than $5,000,000." The Senate promptly rejected it by voice vote. Huey responded with a fiery speech, "Our Bloated Plutocracy," in which he labeled Senator Robinson, who had opposed the resolution, as "the outer guard of Wall Street." If the Democratic party nominated a candidate in the upcoming presidential election who echoed Robinson's ideas, Huey warned, he would bolt the party and support the Farmer-Laborites (a leftist Minnesota party) or the Republicans—provided either nominated someone who advocated "a reduction of these swollen fortunes." Whirling about as he spoke, mopping his flushed face with a bright pink handkerchief, Huey histrionically resigned from the four Senate committees to which Robinson had appointed him.[4]

Stunned and angry, Senator Robinson accused Long not only of "a comic opera performance that does not do justice to the dramatic talents . . . of the great actor from Louisiana," but also of demagoguery "calculated to arouse class hatreds." Huey replied that actually, he was trying to avert class warfare, and was therefore the "greatest friend" wealthy Americans had, since his plan would allow families such as the Rockefellers and Morgans to keep all they could reasonably spend in one lifetime. After all, Huey continued, he was "advocating what Christ said on earth." For additional sanction, he referred to Buddhism, Confucianism, and "every religion," plus the Declaration of Independence.[5]

From this point, Huey intensified his offensive, making a personal attack on Robinson. On May 3, the Kingfish read into the *Congressional Record* a legal directory's list of the major business clients of Senator Robinson's law firm in Little Rock. (Topping the list, ironically, were the Arkansas Power and Light Company, the Louisiana Power and Light Company, and the Mississippi Power and Light Company—all three founded and presided over by Huey's millionaire supporter Harvey Couch.) When Robinson failed to rise to the bait, Huey on May 23 again read the list into the *Record*, and this time he insinuated that the Arkansas senator was controlled by the New York investment banker Bernard Baruch, whose business Huey described as a "stock marketing racketeering enterprise." Huey called Robinson's law practice "monstrous," adding that "he represents every nefarious corporate interest on the face of the globe. You do not have to eat a whole beef to tell that it is tainted." At this point the vice-president ordered Huey to his seat because he had violated Senate Rule 19: "No senator in debate shall . . . impute to another senator . . . any conduct or motive unworthy or unbecoming a senator." The Kingfish, his voice dripping with sarcasm, denied he meant to imply that "such a man" as Senator Robinson "could to the slightest degree be influenced by the fact that [his vote] might mean hundreds of thousands and millions of dollars to him in the way of lucrative fees."[6]

A few senators wished Huey well and usually voted with him, but none entirely approved of his methods. Essentially a loner, the Kingfish nevertheless became identified with the Senate's so-called Progressive Bloc, made up of George W. Norris of Nebraska, Robert La Follette, Jr., of Wisconsin, William E. Borah of Idaho, Gerald P. Nye of North Dakota, Burton K. Wheeler of Montana, Bronson Cutting of New Mexico, and Henrik Shipstead of Minnesota. Norris, La Follette, Borah, and Nye were nominal Republicans, Wheeler and Cutting liberal Democrats, and Shipstead the sole Farmer-Laborite in the Senate. The Progressive Bloc's unity derived from a belief that President Hoover, along with most Republicans and Democrats in Congress, were wrongly trying to fight the Great Depression by shoring up big business instead of helping ordinary Americans.[7] Huey stood out among the Senate progressives in several ways: he was the most flamboyant, he was the only southerner, and he alone habitually ascribed base motives to conservative opponents.

Although "Young Bob" La Follette at thirty-six was the only Progressive Bloc senator in Huey's age group, it was Burton Wheeler, fifty, who came closest to being an intimate of the Kingfish. "Bolshevik Burt," as his Montana enemies called him, saw a bit of himself in Huey; he too had fought his state's most powerful corporation (Anaconda Copper), and like Huey he believed America's entry into World War I was a terrible mistake. Wheeler worried about stories coming out of Louisiana about Huey's crookedness and dictatorial ways, but "after the way I had been maligned in Montana," he wrote, "I knew enough not to believe the worst about a politician just because it was being passed around." Wheeler was the only senator ever to accompany Huey to Washington nightspots.[8]

Wheeler and George Norris, Huey declared in 1933, "were the boldest, most courageous men I had ever met." Norris, at seventy-one the eldest among the Progressive Bloc, and a man of firm integrity, was the only senator to whom Huey actually deferred. Huey even sought Norris' advice—the highest compliment he could bestow. Yet it would be hard to imagine anyone less resembling the Kingfish in personality or style. Norris did not even have a political organization in his home state, relying only upon his reputation for sincerity of purpose. Although he treated Huey in courteous fashion and thought that, overall, the Kingfish "served a useful purpose," Norris had, according to his best biographer, "in some ways contempt for Huey Long."[9] Very likely the Kingfish saw in the dignified old Nebraskan someone he would have preferred as a father, and possibly—in rare pensive moods—the sort of man and leader he wished he himself might have been.

On the whole, Huey was unimpressed by the Senate. He thought most of its members were pompous, a shortcoming to which he could truly plead innocent. A New Orleans reporter, one of the few on friendly terms with him, asked the Kingfish his opinion of "the greatest deliberative assembly on earth," as the Senate was sometimes called. Huey evidently did not think of it that way, for he replied that "it was just like the Louisiana legislature except it is . . . maybe a little better." As an afterthought, he said: "In the Senate you get some smarter men."[10]

Louisiana and its legislature continued to absorb most of Huey's time. He also had personal affairs in his home state to attend to: early in 1932 he moved both his law practice and legal residence from Shreveport to New Orleans. The new home, a two-story, Mediterranean-style mansion on Audubon Boulevard near Tulane University, previously belonged to an unfortunate gambler named Schwartz; the property had been acquired by Robert Maestri, and Maestri—whom Huey had appointed Louisiana's commissioner of conservation—sold the residence to the Kingfish, presumably on generous terms.[11]

Rose and the three children lived in the Audubon Boulevard mansion, but Huey was seldom home, and they rarely visited Washington. Most of Huey's time in Louisiana was spent either in his twelfth-floor suite at New Orleans' Roosevelt Hotel or in his seventh-floor Heidelberg Hotel suite in Baton Rouge or—by 1935—in an apartment fixed up for him on the twenty-fourth floor of the new state capitol building. Referring to the skyscraper capitol and Huey's presence there, the anti-Long Hammond *Vindicator* remarked, "Birds of prey prefer to nest in high places."[12]

The legislative session of 1932 was the last to assemble in the cramped old capitol and the first to meet in the thirty-four-story new one, dedicated on the day of Governor O. K. Allen's inauguration, May 17. Inevitably, Senator Long arrived from Washington shortly thereafter and remained during most of the session to make sure both Allen and the legislature did as they were told. Higher taxes were to be imposed upon cigarettes, gasoline, and other consumer items to raise money for payment on the road and bridge bonds and for other purposes, including salaries for additional state employees. Another administration bill, clearly aimed at Dudley LeBlanc, provided for strict regulation of burial insurance companies. (During the session, LeBlanc's bodyguard Joe Boudreaux was pistol-whipped inside the capitol building by Huey's bodyguard Louie Jones; Jones, sentenced to prison, got a pardon from Governor Allen.) At the behest of State Senator Jules Fisher of Jefferson Parish, a Long ally who owned a large shrimp-packing plant, a bill limiting the labor of women to eight hours a day was killed.[13]

Huey's popularity in Louisiana would never be greater than during 1932. The anti-Long minority, approximately 40 percent of the voters, detested or mistrusted him as much as ever, but a clear majority of whites were on his side—and if blacks could have voted, surely most would have chosen him over his more conservative opponents. Huey's road construction and other building programs provided desperately needed jobs for blacks as well as whites, and the state pay roll of institutional and office personnel continued to expand at a time when the worsening depression made steady public employment, despite Huey's deduct system, look better than ever. With New Orleans' Old Regular bloc in the legislature still allied with Huey, all bills he wanted zoomed through the legislature by majorities of two thirds or more.[14] As yet the Long organization had no competition to speak of from the federal government in dispensing patronage or funds for work projects. President Hoover, unlike the next occupant of the White House, did not believe in direct government aid to the unemployed, nor was he much interested in Louisiana's political affairs. Thus, the Hoover administration posed no threat to Huey Long's popularity or power.

By 1932, the Kingfish saw even his previously most ferocious newspaper foe, the New Orleans *Item* (and its morning edition, the *Tribune*), on his side. The *Item*'s publisher and major stockholder, James M. Thompson, decided an alliance with Huey might help him win a circulation war with Louisiana's largest newspaper, the unwaveringly anti-Long *Times-Picayune*. The *Item*'s editor and part owner, Z. Marshall Ballard, still hated Huey for calling him "king of the dope fiends," but Ballard knew he had to go along with Thompson or lose his job. The *Item*'s cynical move did bring it more subscribers: Huey concluded that with a real newspaper singing his praises every day, the Long organization's sometimes-weekly, sometimes-monthly house organ, *Louisiana Progress*, was superfluous; its last issue came out on January 12, 1932 (in 1933 it would be revived as the *American Progress*, to promote Huey Long across the nation). State workers who previously had had the cost of subscriptions to the *Louisiana Progress* deducted from their paychecks now found themselves compulsory purchasers of the *Item*. Huey was frank to admit this. "We help those who are with us," he said.[15]

His string of successes did nothing to improve Huey's disposition toward subordinates. Indeed, his browbeating of O. K. Allen grew worse. The mere fact that O. K. held the title of governor bothered Huey, even though Allen was always eager to please the Kingfish and, according to probably reliable accounts, had given Huey a signed, undated letter of resignation. Huey evidently decided "Governor" Allen needed frequent reminding of his underling status. It also must have dawned on the Kingfish that during his absences in Washington, Allen's weak-willed amiability might be manipulated by others for purposes detrimental to the Long machine. Huey decided he needed someone in Baton Rouge to keep watch on Allen. He selected for that task a bright, beefy young New Orleans attorney, Richard W. Leche. Allen was told Leche would be his office manager and personal secretary. Leche understood he was to call Huey in Washington any time problems arose.[16]

Huey was actually "very fond of Oscar," Leche in later years recalled, despite the fact he "used to cuss him unmercifully. Huey felt that was necessary to keep Oscar in line." One story about Governor Allen's role in Huey's machine became a Louisiana legend: "A leaf," Earl Long enjoyed saying, "blew in the window of Allen's office and fell on his desk. He signed it." The leaf story was apocryphal, but various witnesses to Long-Allen meetings told of actual scenes that were painful to watch. One happened during Governor Allen's first legislative session. Huey called out, "Oscar, go get me those goddam bills we was talking about." Allen, embarrassed because others were present, pretended not to hear. "Goddam you Oscar, don't you stall around with me!" Huey yelled. "I can break you as easy as I made you! Get those goddam bills and get 'em on the jump." Allen hastily got the bills.[17]

"Oscar, you sonofabitch, shut up!" Huey roared when Allen tried to interject his thoughts at Long organization caucuses. Pathetically, the governor once pleaded with Huey to stop cursing him in front of others. "Oscar asked me not to call him a grayheaded old sonofabitch in public again," the Kingfish told Mason Spencer, a jovial anti-Long legislator whom Huey personally liked. "Oscar," Huey claimed to have replied, "I don't consider eighteen or twenty people gathered in an informal group to be the public."[18]

Louie Jones, Huey's top bodyguard and assistant superintendent of the state police, witnessed an even more brutal scene. Jones was sitting in the front of Governor Allen's official limousine alongside "Nigger George," a skilled driver who chauffeured for several governors. Huey and Allen were in back. The Kingfish was dozing; as usual, he had slept little the night before. The driver, Jones recalled, "hit a rough spot and threw Huey against the seat." The Kingfish ordered the car stopped and put George out by the side of the road. Governor Allen, summoning up a wisp of courage, protested, "Don't put my driver out!" Huey responded to Louisiana's chief executive, "Shut your goddamn mouth or I will put you out." Allen shut his mouth, Jones moved behind the wheel, and the chauffeur was left to make his way back to Baton Rouge as best he could.[19]

Allen as governor usually endeavored to retain a shred of dignity by remaining silent. He avoided talking to reporters because they were apt to inquire about his puppet status. But to Forrest Davis, a noted journalist adept at interviewing, O. K. confided: "I'm mighty proud to be Long's lieutenant. All the brains and energy that go into running this state come from him. He is the greatest man of his state and generation." In mock dismay when told of Allen's saccharine praise, Huey exclaimed: "Did he say all that? I wish the son of a bitch would mind what he says. He causes me a hell of a lot of grief down there when he goes astray."[20]

Why did Allen think the empty title of governor was worth retaining, when it meant submission to such abuse by Huey and ridicule by observers? No other position, in or out of state government, could have been as humiliating. Allen accepted his lot partly because he was convinced that he was serving a superman; despite everything, he obviously loved Huey, and he shed real tears when making the official announcement, in 1935, of the Kingfish's death.[21] Also, his association with Huey made him rich.

As a child in Winn Parish, O. K. Allen suffered the kind of poverty Huey Long sometimes claimed to have experienced, but never did. Now Allen was on his way to becoming one of Louisiana's wealthiest men because of joint business ventures with the Kingfish. Allen, Huey, Harvey Couch, and Seymour Weiss were the chief owners of a limestone quarry in Winn Parish. Previously, the quarry's crumbly, low-grade rock had been deemed useful only as filler for river embankments, yet during the Long-Allen administrations, any highway contractor doing business with the state was required to purchase it for foundation material. ("The concrete roads being built with Winnfield crushed stone are so strong that even the most powerful testing machines will not break the corings," Huey's *Progress* lied.)[22] Later, in 1934, Allen would become a partner, along with State Senator James A. Noe, Huey Long, and Seymour Weiss, in the Win or Lose Corporation, which dealt in transfers of oil and gas leases on state-owned lands. Since the very politicians who decided how state property was to be utilized owned this corporation, Win or Lose never lost.[23]

In late June of 1932, the Democratic national convention gathered in Chicago to select its presidential candidate. Franklin D. Roosevelt, governor of New York, had a majority of delegates but was short of the two-thirds margin then necessary for nomination. Huey Long took his hand-picked delegation to Chicago, and also brought with him a big trunk packed with new summer clothes, including four suits (one of pongee silk) made by his New Orleans tailor. The Kingfish arrived not only as a United States senator, but also as the Democratic national committeeman from Louisiana, a position previously held by aged Colonel Robert ("Bow Wow") Ewing, who died in 1931. Huey came to Chicago as an avowed supporter of FDR.[24]

Earlier, Long had voiced misgivings about Roosevelt and suggested that the Democratic nomination go to maverick Republican George Norris. But Norris and Senator Wheeler were backing the New York governor, and they helped convince Huey to do the same. Some of Huey's Louisiana followers wanted him to seek the nomination, but the Kingfish realized that as yet he had no national strength and thus no chance. Curiously, the leftist Farmer-Labor party's executive committee offered its presidential nomination to Senator Long, and asked old Jacob Coxey of Ohio, who had led a march of unemployed men—"Coxey's Army"—on Washington during the depression of the 1890s, to be Huey's running mate. Coxey was willing, but not Huey. The Farmer-Laborites had virtually no support outside Minnesota. Huey's comment was revealing: "What is the use being the head of a party if you don't have anybody to rule?"[25]

Huey's overriding reason for siding with Roosevelt at the 1932 convention was one of sheer necessity: the Kingfish's enemies were sending a rival delegation to Chicago, and in the pending floor fight over which Louisiana group to seat, Huey had to have the support of the Roosevelt majority from other states. The anti-Long delegate group, chosen in Shreveport two weeks prior to the national convention, was headed by three ex-governors: J. Y. Sanders, Sr., Ruffin G. Pleasant, and John M. Parker. Huey sneered at them as "just a bunch of exes" and said their false optimism about being seated reminded him of the drunken Irishman who woke up in a graveyard, looked around at all the tombstones, and said: "It's Resurrection morning and I'm the first to rise!"[26]

The anti-Long delegation included a candidate to replace Huey as Louisiana's Democratic national committeeman—John D. ("Squirt") Ewing, a son of the deceased Robert Ewing and publisher of the Shreveport *Times*. The wives of Louisiana's ex-governors also came to Chicago. Predictably, Mrs. Pleasant drew press attention because of her outspokenness. Issuing a statement designed to appeal to female delegates from other states, she said Senator Long was "as far removed from being a representative of the courteous and chivalrous manhood of the South as midnight is from noon." Huey, who had confronted Mrs. Pleasant several times, believed she might be carrying a pistol in her purse, with the intent of taking a shot at him. Of the four armed members of Louisiana's state police who came to Chicago to protect Huey, one was detailed to watch Mrs. Pleasant's movements.[27]

At this point, yet a third Louisiana delegation arrived. The tactic that had worked against Dr. Cyr would be tried again: a serious challenge would be met with other, burlesque challenges. Huey arranged the birth of a mock group calling themselves the "Unterrified Democracy," to present their claims at the Chicago convention. A rowdy meeting in the chamber of the Louisiana House of Representatives elected the "delegation," which pledged itself to State Senator Jules Fisher for president of the United States, and to State Representative George Delesdernier—he whose speech during the impeachment fight had likened Huey to Jesus Christ—for vice-president. (A banner carried by state employees through downtown Baton Rouge read, "Delesdernier, Democracy's Darling.") Of course the burlesque delegates had no likelihood of being seated at Chicago, but they enjoyed a free trip to the Windy City and, in Frank Freidel's words, "indulged in considerable horseplay" while the convention went about its business.[28]

Huey seemed to be everywhere at once during the convention.

"He stormed through hotel corridors, held forth in bars, and invaded [Louis Howe's] quarters with noisy demands," remembered the economist Rexford Tugwell, a member of FDR's "Brain Trust." Howe, Roosevelt's top aide, tried to pacify the Kingfish because he was making "such a disturbance in the halls." Tugwell observed that "this perpetually erupting volcano ... glanced at us [the Brain Trust professors] several times, but having a shrewd instinct for power, he passed us by without notice." Professor Tugwell and his colleagues decided that Long was simply "a pudgy, overdressed loudmouth ... a curiosity, nothing more." They would soon discover otherwise. Meanwhile, Governor William "Alfalfa Bill" Murray of Oklahoma learned about the Kingfish's confiscatory table manners; dropping by Alfalfa Bill's hotel room early one morning, Long ate part of the breakfast Murray had ordered for himself.[29]

The party's credentials committee heard J. Y. Sanders, Sr., then Huey, plead the cases of their rival delegations. Sanders gave what Senator Wheeler described as a "Magnolia and Molasses speech," whereupon Huey, as his embarrassed friend Wheeler admitted, "launched into as coarse a speech as he could make—which was very coarse indeed." Huey's tirade was punctuated by hisses and boos from the ex-governors, their wives, and other anti-Longites in the audience. A majority of the credentials committee voted in favor of Long's delegation, but next afternoon the entire convention had to decide the issue. Huey relished this opportunity to present his case, since CBS and NBC would be broadcasting his words to the nation. Unlike the previous day's performance in front of the credentials committee, the Kingfish's presentation to the convention avoided billingsgate and made a clear, logical case. Boos from the audience gave way to respectful attention, and finally applause. The convention by 638¾ to 514¼ voted to seat Long's delegation. When it became obvious he had won, Huey cast aside his unaccustomed dignity and, noted the New York *Times*, "jumped upon a chair and gesticulated wildly."[30]

Rose Long, making one of her rare public appearances, sat with the Louisiana delegation as "an acting alternate." She had flown to Chicago after the convention began, and now conspicuously walked up and down the aisles on the arm of the Kingfish, who was concerned about stories Mrs. Pleasant and others were spreading about his ungentlemanly behavior—probably with allusions to extramarital sex. He thought the presence of Mrs. Long would repair any damage done. *Time* quoted him as saying he would "show these damned skirts I know how to treat a lady." Reporters trying to interview Mrs. Long at the convention found her reluctant to say anything. Her only quotable remark came when they asked her how long she had been married. Rose replied, "I don't even remember."[31]

The Kingfish played a major role in winning the nomination for Roosevelt. On the third ballot, FDR was still about ninety votes short of the needed two-thirds majority; his support in Mississippi's and Arkansas' delegations seemed on the verge of cracking, and any erosion at that moment might have denied him the nomination and deadlocked the convention. Roosevelt's floor managers turned to Huey for help, and the Kingfish— sweating, rumpled, and wild-eyed—worked over the two neighboring delegations with what Wheeler described as "red-necked eloquence." United States Senator Pat Harrison of Mississippi caught a full load of Huey's style of persuasiveness: "If you break the unit rule, you sonofabitch, I'll go into Mississippi and break you." Reminded of that threat later, Huey admitted: "It is possible that I did make some such statement in the Chicago convention."[32] Both the Mississippi and Arkansas delegations held firm, and on the fourth ballot FDR won the nomination. "Without Long's work," the Bronx's Democratic boss Edward J. Flynn wrote, "Roosevelt might not have been nominated."[33]

Whether Huey's action at the convention was crucial to FDR's victory is debatable, but there is no doubt Roosevelt already mistrusted and even feared the Kingfish. Huey had not yet been admitted into Roosevelt's presence, having spoken to him only by telephone. In the days following Chicago, various party bigwigs, including some from big business, were invited to New York for meetings with the nominee—but Huey was not. The Kingfish was understandably displeased. One day in mid-July he decided to phone the executive mansion in Albany. Roosevelt accepted the call while finishing lunch with Rex Tugwell; FDR beckoned Tugwell and others present to listen, saying, "This would be good."[34]

"God damn it Frank!" crackled the voice from Louisiana. "Don't you know who nominated you? Why do you have Baruch and Young and all those Wall Street sons of bitches up there to see you? How do you think it looks to the country? How can I

explain it to my people?" Tugwell then heard Roosevelt's mellifluous reply, which took "a considerable expenditure of charm
before Huey was pacified." Afterward, FDR stared at the phone
a moment, replaced it on its cradle, and observed: "It's all very
well for us to laugh at Huey. But actually we have to remember
that he really is one of the two most dangerous men in the country." The other, he said, "is Douglas MacArthur."[35]

The Kingfish was determined to be a player in the autumn
campaign against President Hoover, whether Roosevelt liked it
or not. Huey also had political business to attend to in Louisiana, having decided that Senator Edwin S. "Coozan Ed" Broussard, whom he had helped reelect in 1926, should be denied a
third term in 1932. (The Cajun senator had endorsed Paul Cyr's
claim to the governorship the year before and in other ways
manifested an anti-Long attitude.) First, however, the August 9
senatorial primary in neighboring Arkansas drew the Kingfish
into that state.[36]

Hattie Caraway of Arkansas had come to the United States
Senate late in 1931 to complete the term of her recently deceased husband, Senator Thaddeus Caraway. She sat quietly on
the back row of the chamber alongside an unquiet newcomer,
Huey Long. Arkansas politicians were surprised and perhaps
amused when she declared her candidacy for a full term in the
1932 Democratic primary. Mrs. Caraway seemed the prototypi-
cal southern grandmother who, in one journalist's patronizing
words, "ought to be sitting on a porch in a rocking-chair, mend-
ing somebody's socks." She had no organization and almost no
money. Six men were already in the race. The widow Caraway
was expected to run seventh.[37]

At dawn on August 1, a caravan of Louisiana sound trucks and
automobiles, led by a big blue Cadillac, sped across the state
line into Arkansas. Huey sat in the Cadillac's front seat, next to
the driver. In the glove compartment were three items—a Bible,
a throat atomizer, and a pistol. The Kingfish seemed an improbable Sir Galahad, but he was coming to Hattie's rescue for several reasons. She was one of the few senators who had supported
Huey's resolution to place an absolute limit on personal income
and family fortunes, and she usually voted opposite Joe Robinson, Arkansas' senior senator. Most of all, if Huey could pull off
a political miracle outside his home state, America would have
to take notice.[38]

"I'm here," Huey announced in Arkansas, "to get a bunch of potbellied politicians off this little woman's neck." For eight days Huey crisscrossed the state, his advance men racing ahead in a sound truck blaring country music and announcing the Kingfish's imminent arrival. Many thousands of Arkansans already knew his voice from listening to KWKH out of nearby Shreveport; now they could experience him in person. Mrs. Caraway spoke briefly at each stop, but it was Huey's presence that attracted the crowds—the biggest in the history of Arkansas.[39] He was William Jennings Bryan, Barnum's circus, and Billy Sunday rolled into one, and his show was free.

After the caravan's rousing first stop at the town of Magnolia, where a crowd of rural folk had waited since daybreak, a local politician wired a warning to the Little Rock headquarters of one of Caraway's opponents: "A CYCLONE JUST WENT THROUGH HERE AND IS HEADED YOUR WAY. VERY FEW TREES LEFT STANDING."[40] Mrs. Caraway's six rivals tried to engender resentment against this intrusion by a "foreigner," but to no avail. In lonely places between the towns, people stood by the roadside and cheered as the Kingfish's car passed. By the end of the week, Huey's entourage, including Mrs. Caraway, were worn out by the hectic pace, but the Kingfish seemed to gain strength each day. Hermann Deutsch, the perceptive New Orleans reporter who had covered Huey's doings since 1919, noted that even neatly dressed farmers who drove up in new cars and who "came to scoff . . . remained as prey," as Huey spun his web of words. "Fifteen minutes after he began to talk," Deutsch wrote in a *Saturday Evening Post* article, "he would have these same [middle-class] farmers convinced that they were starving and would have to boil their old boots . . . to have something to feed the babies till the Red Cross brought around a sack of meal and a bushel of sweet potatoes [and] the only road to salvation lay in the reelection of Hattie W. Caraway to the Senate."[41]

By the time of his Arkansas campaign, Huey had learned how to deal with an annoyance often experienced at his Louisiana rallies: babies in the crowds tended to start wailing at the sound of the Kingfish's voice. For the Caraway tour Huey designated certain aides to pacify crying babies with water and lollipops; they would hold and rock the stubborn cases, and sometimes even change diapers. The same aides, usually muscular young men, had the additional duty of handling obstreperous drunks.[42]

Huey naturally attacked Wall Street and its "corrupt alliance" with Democratic and Republican leaders, but he did so without maligning Joe Robinson by name. (Senator Robinson had decided to remain neutral in the contest for Caraway's seat.) Those Arkansans who thought they were coming to be entertained by a radical clown were surprised and charmed to hear a man who could also speak glowingly of a better future, then envelop his wrath and humor and promises in an aura of fundamentalist Christian evangelism. "EXPECTED CIRCUS PROVED MORE LIKE OLD-FASHIONED REVIVAL," read the headline over a newspaper summary of his appearance in the mountain town of Mena. Sunday, August 7, found Huey in Little Rock but unable to campaign because all of Arkansas' counties—unlike Louisiana's parishes—observed a strict Protestant Sabbath. Deutsch mischievously asked the Kingfish which church he planned to attend. Huey's old resentment over compulsory attendance during boyhood surfaced, and he replied: "Me go to church? Why I haven't been to a church in so many years I don't know when." Wanting to hear more, the reporter prompted: "But you're always quoting the Bible, and so—" Huey cut him off: "Bible's the greatest book ever written. But I sure don't need anybody I can buy for six bits and a chew of tobacco to explain it to me. When I need preachers I buy 'em cheap."[43]

That Mrs. Caraway, because of Long's help, would do better than earlier predicted was understood by election day. But the returns must have surprised everybody, possibly even the Kingfish. She took 47 percent of the total vote, beating the closest of her six male rivals by more than two to one. No run-off was held. Hattie Caraway thus became the first woman in American history to be elected to a full term in the Senate, and she gave Huey Long his due credit. What he did may not have been "the greatest political miracle of all times," as a Centenary College professor claimed, but it was a stunning achievement that must have sent chills over old-line politicians throughout the South.[44] Where might he go next?

Huey gave the answer while still in Arkansas. "Broussard's been one of Wall Street's own," Huey declared before returning to his home state. "Watch us clean his plow for him next month." To oppose Louisiana's senior senator, Huey selected an underling whom he treated with a measure of respect, John H. Overton. Having the advantage of both Anglo and French ancestry

248

—he could speak Cajun patois—Overton was a well-educated Alexandria lawyer who had supported Huey since the railroad commissioner's race of 1918. He also had served as one of the Kingfish's lawyers in the impeachment fight. But Overton's own political ambitions had never been realized. Eighteen years older than Huey, he had run third in a United States senate race in 1918; for a time, too, he dreamed of becoming governor. But his first significant political office did not come until 1931, when Eighth District Congressman James "Chicken Jim" Aswell died, and (with Huey's endorsement) Overton won the special election.[45]

Overton also gained Huey's blessing for the senatorial contest against Edwin Broussard in the September 13, 1932, Democratic primary. His miracle in Arkansas accomplished, Huey, with Overton in tow, commenced a whirlwind tour of Louisiana on August 20. The handbills and posters read, "HUEY P. LONG," with smaller type underneath: "Speaking on Behalf of John H. Overton." According to one unkind observer, "Many hicks got the idea Huey was running for still another office."[46] Certainly the Kingfish did most of the talking. "Edwin," he shouted, "dassn't blow his nose without orders from Wall Street." Huey also claimed Senator Broussard and President Hoover were so close that "anytime Hoover takes a dose of laudanum, Broussard gets sleepy." For his part, Overton spoke approvingly of Long's plan to redistribute the nation's wealth, but otherwise uttered generalities. Unlike Allen, Overton played his role smoothly, and Huey seldom contradicted him. At one rally, however, Overton was hoarse and made the mistake of explaining that he had laryngitis. Huey kicked the speaker's leg and bellowed: "Laryngitis, hell! You got a sore throat!"[47]

Senator Broussard waged a forlorn campaign, knowing not only that he would probably lose even with an honest count, but also that several parishes were certain to report rigged, lopsided majorities against him. Yet "Coozan Ed" kept up a brave front, telling an Alexandria audience: "I am going to be elected again. They are not going to steal it from me." At another rally, he added, "They are not fooling with a Ransdell," an observation probably annoying to the old ex-senator Huey had defeated two years earlier. Broussard refrained from personal abuse of Overton—the two had been schoolmates—and concentrated his fire on "the dictatorship of Huey P. Long." Senators Broussard and

Long had not spoken since the day Huey went to Washington to be sworn in. Both took pride in that fact.[48]

"Dummy candidates" helped guarantee Broussard's defeat. The use of nonserious candidates in Louisiana Democratic primaries predated Huey Long, but he nourished it into full bloom. Obscure persons would have filing fees paid in their names, and so could select precinct commissioners. Before ballots were printed, these dummy candidates would withdraw. Their designated commissioners, however, were at the polls on election day to "help" illiterate and handicapped voters, to intimidate others, and to assist in the vote count. Huey's organization—the Louisiana Democratic Association, as it was officially called—put up so many Orleans Parish dummies that on election day, 1,119 precinct commissioners in New Orleans worked for Overton; Broussard had 61. (Mayor Walmsley and the Old Regulars, still allied with Huey, also supported Overton, but they were beginning to feel eclipsed within their home territory.) Overton beat Broussard both in New Orleans and state-wide. The tally was 181,464 to 124,935, with the winner carrying forty-eight of sixty-four parishes.[49] Broussard immediately called for a United States Senate investigation. He made no claim to having won the primary, but filed a protest that Overton "was nominated by fraud, trickery, corruption, intimidation," and thus should not be seated. The ensuing investigation by the Senate, lasting into 1933, displayed much of Louisiana's political dirty linen before the nation.[50]

Among other curious discoveries about the state, the Senate investigators learned that even the overt miscounting of votes was not legally punishable. It was a crime under state law to falsify election returns, but the 1932 session of the legislature had killed a bill to specify criminal penalties for those convicted; therefore, in the historian Glen Jeansonne's words, "fixing elections became a crime for which there was no punishment."[51] Almost certainly, Broussard would have lost in an honest count, but the heavy use of dummy candidates' poll workers in south Louisiana probably did cause the defeat of Public Service Commissioner Dudley LeBlanc, who lost a tight contest to Long's candidate, Wade O. Martin. The election of Martin gave Long control of the PSC, since Francis Williams ("France-ass," Huey called him) was now the only anti-Long member of the three-man body.[52]

A seemingly minor episode involving the use of dummy candidates during the Overton-Broussard race occurred in St. Landry Parish. St. Landry was one of the few consistently anti-Long
parishes in south Louisiana, and its state district judge, B.
Henry Pavy, issued an injunction against the use of precinct
commissioners by withdrawn dummy candidates. When the
Democratic executive committee of neighboring Evangeline
Parish, a Long stronghold that was also in Pavy's district, dis-
obeyed the judge's injunction, he ordered five committeemen to
jail. They served no time: Governor Allen telegraphed reprieves,
and the case was later dropped. But for attempting to thwart the
Long machine, Pavy was, three years later, gerrymandered out
of his judgeship. By that time, Pavy's daughter Yvonne had married a youthful Baton Rouge physician, Dr. Carl Austin Weiss.[53]

Overton's victory in the Democratic senatorial primary temporarily freed Huey's time for national politics, as the November, 1932, general election in Louisiana would be only a formality. Early in October, Huey visited New York City in an effort to
persuade Roosevelt's campaign manager, James A. Farley, to
send him across the nation—into all forty-eight states—on a
special train outfitted with loudspeakers to tell people why they
should vote the Democratic ticket. Huey implied that an FDR
victory over Hoover might hinge upon this being done. Farley,
who still viewed the Kingfish as "somewhat of a freak," was appalled at the idea of turning him loose upon the country, but he
did arrange Huey's first face-to-face meeting with FDR. On Sunday, October 9, Huey came to lunch at Roosevelt's Hyde Park
estate. Huey's lifelong urge to annoy people of higher status
showed itself. He was dressed, and talked, even louder than
usual; his bright suit clashed with an orchid-colored shirt and
watermelon-pink tie. At the table, FDR's patrician mother, Sara,
wanted to know, in a voice everyone heard, "Who is that AWFUL
man sitting on my son's right?" Huey said nothing at the moment, but later, to a friend, he remarked of FDR: "By God, I feel
sorry for him. He's got even more sons of bitches in his family
than I've got in mine."[54]

Interviewed in New York after his Hyde Park encounter, Huey
remained silent about the Roosevelts, but opened up concerning
his view of himself. "Politicians are the riffraff of a party," he told
the New York *Times*. "I'm different. I'm a kingfish." He also
opined, "The great trouble with the Democrats is that we have

251

all the votes and no money." Since Republicans possessed lots of money but little public support, Huey proposed "the best thing we could do is to sell President Hoover a million votes for half what he is going to pay to try to get them. We can spare the votes and we could use the money."[55] The reporter seemed unsure whether he was getting a sample of the Kingfish's humor or of his morality.

Farley and the Democratic National Committee arranged a speaking tour for Huey, but it consisted of only four states—the Dakotas, Nebraska, and Kansas. The Kingfish would have to bear all costs. His first stop was to be Bismarck, North Dakota. It was hardly a tour Huey deemed worthy of his talents, but he agreed, and the crowds he drew were as large and enthusiastic as the recent ones in Arkansas. Farley received such glowing reports from Democratic leaders in the Plains States that he realized, too late, that Huey should have been sent to Pennsylvania, the only large state FDR lost to Hoover. Farley later commented, "We never again underrated him."[56]

Along with grudging respect came increasing fear. Both FDR and Farley, who became postmaster general and chief patronage dispenser in the Roosevelt administration, began to regard Huey not as a socialistic rival from the left, but as a would-be fascist dictator of the United States. Rex Tugwell heard FDR compare Huey "to Hitler and his haranguing method, his unscrupulous use of specious appeals, his arousing of hate, envy, fear, and all the animal passions." Farley in 1933 visited Rome and met the Italian dictator Mussolini, who, he wrote, "reminded me of Huey Long."[57]

· 15 ·

GOD SAID SO!

"I've done all I can for Louisiana, now I want to help the rest of
the country," the Kingfish declared in September of 1932, at a
dinner celebrating Overton's victory over Broussard. Having
achieved a near-dictatorship over the Pelican State, Huey
planned to redirect most of his vast energy toward domination
of American politics. But affairs in Louisiana kept intruding.
The Long machine, being a one-man operation, could not function without supervision by its creator.[1]

None of Huey's Louisiana foes could approach his vitality or
genius; neither could any of his lieutenants. The ablest members
of both camps realized this. He was always "three or four curves
ahead of you," a loyalist recalled. Anti-Long leader Cecil Morgan,
looking back from the distance of 1970, admitted: "Huey was so
. . . intelligent that he continually had his enemies off guard."
George Ginsberg, one of many legislators driven out of politics
by Huey, attributed the Kingfish's success as much to stamina as
to genius, saying that "he worked while we slept."[2] Yet some opponents saw his national ambitions as their state's possible salvation, since even Huey could not be in Washington and Baton
Rouge at the same time. And if he continued to shuttle back and
forth—as he in fact did—they reasoned that his abnormal vitality and resourcefulness must eventually be drained.[3]

Franklin D. Roosevelt was scarcely inaugurated, in March of
1933, before Louisiana's Kingfish began causing trouble. "I have
come here," Huey informed the Senate, "to help him [FDR] carry
out his promises to the people." The only promise that mattered,
in Huey's estimation, was a vague statement Roosevelt had

made, in his Chicago speech accepting the Democratic nomination, suggesting "a more equitable opportunity to share in the
distribution of national wealth." As interpreted by the Kingfish,
this was a pledge to support the resolution Long earlier had introduced in the Senate, to impose an absolute limit on incomes
and family fortunes. In the opening days of the Seventy-third
Congress (March, 1933), a similar resolution was submitted, at
Huey's behest, by a Louisiana member of the House of Representatives. It died in committee.[4] The Roosevelt administration
was not about to let Huey Long set the agenda for coping with
the Great Depression.

Grudgingly, Senator Long voted for about half the emergency
New Deal "relief and recovery" legislation that Congress, at
FDR's urging, passed during the spring of 1933. What support he
gave was mixed with criticism. Only by confiscating and redistributing the possessions of millionaires, Huey kept insisting,
could the Great Depression be ended. Just four days after Roosevelt's inauguration, the Kingfish expressed concern that although FDR "is yet a great President . . . I should like to see him
have more advice than he is getting."[5] Huey did not need to specify whose advice he had in mind.

What had happened to Governor Parker of Louisiana in 1920
was, to some degree, happening thirteen years later to President
Roosevelt. Huey had claimed credit for Parker's election and
feigned outrage when the governor did not fulfill his campaign
pledges—as Long defined them. Now the same scenario was
being played out in Washington, with FDR cast in the role of
Parker. Both times, Long's motive was the same: to pose as the
people's young champion, betrayed by old men who, after election, revealed themselves as tools of Wall Street. It logically followed that the people should turn to their true champion: *he*
should be the next governor; *he* should be the next president.

Huey soon discovered Roosevelt to be a vastly more adroit
politician than Parker. For a time FDR attempted to placate
Huey, fearing an open conflict might antagonize the Kingfish's
handful of sympathizers in the Senate—especially Wheeler,
Norris, and Caraway—thus imperiling passage of the New
Deal's emergency legislation. Rex Tugwell, because he was the
smoothest and most liberal of FDR's Brain Trust, was assigned
the unenviable task of "keeping him [Huey] happy," but Tugwell
soon realized "it was impossible. He wanted power, and could

only get it at Franklin's expense." Control of federal patronage in Louisiana was just the beginning of Long's peremptory claims. When his demands were not met, Huey's reaction was to say he "could not be bought." He added, "I was never more disgusted with political life than I am now."[6]

In June, Huey was invited to the White House for what Roosevelt called a "showdown." Jim Farley, who was present, observed that during his conversation with FDR, Long did not take off his straw hat except to occasionally tap it, when emphasizing a point, on the president's elbow or one of his paralyzed knees. Roosevelt showed no anger at Huey's rudeness, but gently let him know that he would not be consulted on federal patronage. Either Huey did not yet realize how important this patronage was going to be or he thought FDR was bluffing, for he came away from the meeting in an upbeat mood. In the coming months, however, as Huey saw his worst Louisiana enemies dispensing federal jobs, and as relief grants and loans from Washington began to compete in size with his total state budget, Huey's frustration and rage steadily mounted. Finally, he told an official with the Federal Emergency Relief Administration: "It's your sucking bastard, and hereafter I'll be giving you . . . and that fucker in the White House unshirted hell every day from now on."[7]

The off-and-on Senate investigation of John Overton's election continued to aggravate Huey. A preliminary inquiry took place in October of 1932, only a month after Senator Broussard's defeat, and in February of 1933, a Senate subcommittee held two weeks of hearings in New Orleans, at the old federal Custom House on Canal Street. Huey was present as Overton's lawyer—a reversal of their roles in the 1929 impeachment fight; the Senate hired as its general counsel Samuel Tilden Ansell, a pugnacious courtroom performer who once was judge advocate general of the United States army. Ansell and Huey locked horns immediately, and the investigation became more a probe of Long than of Overton.[8]

Ansell pried into numerous aspects of Huey's career. "Deducts" and kickbacks were looked into. Dummy candidates were called to the stand and subjected to Ansell's scornful questioning; many appeared to be ignorant of the duties of the offices for which they had filed. Ansell also pulled confused testimony from Huey's most faithful and dull-witted bodyguard, Joe Messina.

More explicit and irksome to Huey were statements under oath by his two brothers Julius and Earl, who willingly testified about Huey's questionable conduct, including his acceptance of cash from utility companies while he was a public service commissioner. "That's a goddamn lie," Huey yelled in reply. Seymour Weiss, keeper of campaign funds for the Long organization, refused to answer several of Ansell's questions "because I do not want to. . . . that is none of your business." (Why Weiss was not cited for contempt remained a mystery.) But of all the testimony found in the 2,755 pages of the Senate committee's final report, the words of Earl Long on page 862 shine as a classic of understatement. Earl looked at Huey and said, "You are not an average human being."[9]

Apparently neither Ansell nor Huey Long had previously encountered anyone as verbally aggressive as the other, and the experience upset them both. At one point, the Senate's counsel invited Huey to step outside the hearing room for a fistfight. Huey accepted, saying, "I will whip hell out of you," but neither walked out the door and no violence occurred. The subcommittee's chairman, Robert Howell (R.-Neb.), gave a progress report to the full Senate on February 22. After wearily observing that "the investigation was conducted under great difficulties," Howell added: "Frankly . . . I do not care to return to Louisiana."[10] He died a month later, and the hearing was not resumed until November of 1933. By then, Overton had taken his seat in the Senate. The November session was chaired by Senator Tom Connally (D.-Tex.), and as before it met in New Orleans. Public interest ran so high that the meeting place was shifted from the Custom House to a building with a large auditorium, and radio microphones were allowed.[11]

Instead of Ansell, who had resigned as Senate counsel, Long and Overton now faced John G. Holland, a Louisianian who had been an investigator for the United States Justice Department. (Ansell was currently suing Long for libel.)[12] Holland also took a strong dislike to Huey, referring to him during the hearing as "the rat from Louisiana who sent Senator Howell to his grave." But Holland also lashed out in another direction: he called Senator Connally "yellow," to which the Texan replied, "I didn't know he was going crazy."[13]

Senator Connally, while in New Orleans, began feeling as if he were outside the United States; he thought the scenes resembled trials in some unstable foreign country. One morning he was unable to enter the hearing room's front door because mobs of both anti- and pro-Long enthusiasts were blocking the corridor. Connally and another senator, along with Hilda Phelps Hammond—leader of the anti-Long Women's Committee of Louisiana—had to climb a fire escape and enter the hearing room by crawling through a side window. Senator Connally's report to the Senate in January of 1934 cited "distressing and deplorable conditions in the politics of the state of Louisiana," but pointed out there was no evidence that Overton participated in, or had guilty knowledge of, the frauds that helped elect him. So Overton would keep his Senate seat. On a personal note, Connally added: "I advise anyone who thinks he knows something about politics to go down to Louisiana and take a postgraduate course."[14]

Huey's enemies were disgusted at the Senate's failure to remove Overton. Yet what most of them had really wanted was an investigation—and a final report—evidencing so much fraud and corruption that Huey himself would be ousted from the Senate and sent to the penitentiary. They did not get that either. But ex-governor Parker, who hated Huey as much as anyone did, proposed a different fate in a letter of April 12, 1933, to Vice-President John Nance Garner: "Senator Huey P. Long knows neither truth, honesty, or decency. His black record in our state is nationally known. Psychiatrists in my presence have stated that he is a dangerous paranoiac. The Senate should have him examined by experts and to save certain trouble *and probable future killing* have him permanently incarcerated in the criminal insane hospital [St. Elizabeth's] in Washington. . . . would appreciate your having this read to the members of the Senate as prompt action should be taken as today he is the greatest menace to American decency and freedom."[15]

Neither the Senate nor Roosevelt's administration took up Parker's suggestion, although the prospect of Huey in a strait jacket at St. Elizabeth's would have appealed to many. But during the early hours of Sunday, August 27, 1933, three days before his fortieth birthday, the Kingfish inflicted upon himself a potentially fatal political wound. Congress had recently adjourned, and Huey was in New York, staying at his customary habitat there, the Hotel New Yorker—which gave him free board because he drew publicity and tourists. As usual, Rose and the children were not with him. The songwriter Gene Buck ("Tulip

Time"), who knew Huey, invited him to a Saturday evening dinner and ball at the exclusive Sands Point Club on Long Island. Huey—always obsessed with time and probably unhappy over his impending birthday—mixed himself several Sazerac cocktails before arriving at the club and, once there, drank far more than he could handle.[16] By midnight he was quite drunk.

Not since his "singing fool" days of 1929 in New Orleans had Huey made such an ass of himself in public. Certainly among his regrets this evening would be that none of his bodyguards was with him. According to eyewitnesses, Huey wandered from table to table, "made himself objectionable with vulgar greetings," and infuriated Dallas Turner, a black musician at the club, by calling him "coon" and "shine." When dinner was served, Huey grabbed a plate from a plump young woman, saying: "You're too fat already. I'll eat this." The club's headwaiter exclaimed, "Senator Long is just a pig!"[17]

Sometime after midnight the lights dimmed for a floor show, and Huey went to the men's room. Presently he emerged with a bleeding cut over his left eye. The New York *Times* decided that this event deserved a front-page headline: "HUEY LONG GETS A BLACK EYE IN ROW AT LONG ISLAND PARTY." Papers across the nation picked up the story. *Collier's* magazine commissioned a gold medal—later deposited in the museum of the American Numismatic Society—"to the unknown hero who hit Huey Long." Neither the assailant nor his motive was positively identified, but most likely Huey had urinated on someone who was either standing at a receptacle next to him or was using one the Kingfish needed for himself. Huey's offense could have been accidental or deliberate; his bodyguard Murphy Roden recalled that even when sober, Huey was "kind of sloppy" when using a bathroom. A congressional doorkeeper claimed that once, in the Senate men's room, the Kingfish "pretended to miss his mark in the urinal and hit another Senator."[18]

"Huey Pee Long," his Louisiana enemies gleefully began calling him. Other names coming into use, in lieu of Kingfish, included Crawfish, Scuttlefish, Phewey Long, and The Hero of Long Island. Earlier in his career, Huey had been involved in more serious trouble, and he never pretended to have dignity, but the Sands Point episode, because of the way it was publicized and perceived not only in Louisiana but across America, hurt his image more than anything ever had. It was almost his

Chappaquiddick. For several days the press, smelling blood, harassed him at every opportunity. Huey most resented news photographers who tried to get shots of his swollen face: "Hit 'em," Huey told his bodyguards when cameramen came near. "Don't let them take my picture."[19] Huey meanwhile declined to answer questions about telegrammed offers he was receiving—for example, to have a ten-round rematch with his unidentified assailant in Chicago's Soldier Field, or to be paid ten thousand dollars per night if he would appear in a freak show at Coney Island.[20]

As most politicians in a similar predicament would have done, Huey at first tried to ignore the Sands Point episode, hoping the hullabaloo would die down. When it did not, he responded in a manner few might have had the gall to do: he told a thumping lie and stuck to it. Huey solemnly informed America that while attending "a charity event" on Long Island, he had been waylaid in the washroom by "thugs" or "gangsters" hired by the Wall Street firm of J. P. Morgan and Company. Only by escaping had his life been saved.[21] (The reason Huey picked Morgan instead of Rockefeller or Baruch was probably his discovery that *Collier's* magazine was tied to the Morgan firm.) Whether his supporters, much less others, believed Huey's fabrication is questionable. But he had to say something, and he assumed the truth would serve him worse.

Ironically, the fallout from Sands Point began just as Huey launched two new efforts at favorable national publicity: his newspaper, revived in August of 1933 as the *American Progress,* and his autobiography, issued in October with a title borrowed from a phrase in one of William Jennings Bryan's speeches— *Every Man a King.* Like virtually all autobiographies by politicians, it was a self-serving recital of his rise from obscurity to prominence and of his triumphs over villains and misguided persons who tried to thwart his plans for a better society. Huey revealed little about his inner self in the book. But at least it was not ghostwritten. Over a period of several months, whenever he found time, he had dictated its chapters to various secretaries. One of them recalled: "He did it without notes. He would stand up and perform each incident."[22]

Huey's organization paid the cost of producing *Every Man a King,* and about 100,000 copies were printed. Slightly more than 20,000 were sold (price: one dollar) in bookstores; most were given away during 1934 and 1935 to those who joined Huey's

Share Our Wealth Society. Reviews of *Every Man a King* ranged from predictable acclaim in the *American Progress* ("one of the most vivid stories ever told") to predictable scorn in the fiercely anti-Long Hammond *Vindicator,* which found it "not even fit to hang with the corn cobs and mail order house catalogs [in outdoor privies]." The few national journals assessing *Every Man a King* were generally censorious. Allan Nevins, a renowned scholar writing in the *Saturday Review of Literature,* found Huey's book disquieting. "It is clear," opined Nevins, "that he is a man of very remarkable gifts . . . but it is also clear that he is unbalanced, vulgar, in many ways ignorant, and quite reckless . . . the most dangerous type of leader in a democracy." [23]

For a time, late in 1933 and into 1934, the fracas on Long Island seemingly had pushed Huey onto an irreversible downhill slide. "It seemed he might be through—even in Louisiana," wrote Hamilton Basso, one of the more detached observers of the Kingfish's career. "I for one did not think he would survive the incident." [24] During October and November, Huey toured the state in an effort to bolster his sagging image and, simultaneously, to build support for a new tax program. He met unaccustomed hostility. Most of those who came to heckle him were probably anti-Long before Sands Point. A deeper indication of trouble, as he looked at audiences smaller than he usually drew, was the absence—or at least silence—of his traditional followers.

The tour began badly and got worse. Huey probably would have encountered antagonism even without Sands Point because of his brash attacks on President Roosevelt. FDR would never be more popular than in 1933; here, just as the Great Depression hit its lowest point, was a president who seemed to be in charge and to care about the suffering of ordinary Americans. For the moment at least, Roosevelt's standing in Louisiana was higher than Huey's, even among much of Long's core clientele. Desperately needed federal relief money had much to do with FDR's popularity. The month Huey began his hapless tour, 325,611 Louisianians—15.5 percent of the state's population—were on unemployment relief, with all the money coming from Washington. By comparison, Long had control of 24,000 jobs at that time, "from college presidencies to seats on a road-grading tractor." These state jobs paid more in total wages than federal relief expenditures, but they affected fewer lives.[25] Hungry people, or those in danger of becoming hungry, are not likely to cheer when someone they perceive as being their benefactor is abused.

Donaldsonville and its South Louisiana Fair, October 15, was Huey's first stop. He almost canceled his tour after this encounter. Expecting twenty thousand enthusiasts to greet him, he found instead only eight hundred unsmiling listeners gathered around the pavilion where he spoke, and immediately a man named Sammy Klotz yelled, "What about that Long Island affair?" Other hecklers took up the cry. Huey, fronted by twenty or more state police and bodyguards, began yelling back, "Come down here . . . and I'll man-to-man it with you. And I won't have five or six men jump on you like they did to me at Sands Point!" That this was happening in Louisiana infuriated Huey, so he added: "I'll Long Island anything that gets in my way around these diggings!" Later, he regained some of his composure and the crowd quieted, but then he began to criticize President Roosevelt and to claim: "He couldn't have been elected without the help of Huey P. Long." When boos and derisive laughter greeted that statement, the senator responded: "Come on down here, and I'll make you giggle! I'll give you a dose of castor oil and laudanum if necessary." Governor Allen, seated next to Huey on the platform, pulled at the Kingfish's arm and pleaded, "Now don't lose your temper."[26] Huey left Donaldsonville angry, confused, and depressed.

Two days later he spoke at Franklinton, in the piney woods of southeastern Louisiana's Washington Parish—a place he always carried. There, on the advice of his local leaders, he did not attack Roosevelt, but he made another mistake. When a heckler said something about Long's failure to serve in the war, Huey gave his usual retort about having a family to support and not being "mad at anybody over there," but this time he added: "Most [who fought in the war] were dragged in by the hair of their head." Veterans' groups were usually friendly toward Huey because of his support of generous benefits, but that statement produced outrage. The American Legion post in the city of Lafayette invited him to repeat what he said in their community, and guaranteed him "the biggest meeting Lafayette ever saw." Huey did not reply to the challenge.[27]

Elsewhere, Huey's audiences were at best apathetic, and more often antagonistic. Part of his tour was taken on the luxurious private rail coach of his friend Harvey Couch, the utilities and railroad millionaire; it seemed odd he would assail "the rich" from such surroundings. On October 20, Huey arrived in Shreveport to dedicate the new Long-Allen Bridge over the Red River and to watch LSU's football team play Arkansas in the city's stadium. As was becoming his custom, he paced the sidelines during the game and exhorted the Fighting Tigers to victory, but on this occasion boos and cries of "Long Island!" and "Hooey!" reverberated in the stands. Some spectators began to throw things, and one bottle narrowly missed Huey's head.[28]

Thirty miles east of Shreveport, at Minden, an anti-Long judge named Harmon C. Drew heard that Huey had accused him of bilking a bank out of three thousand dollars. If the Kingfish repeated the charge in Drew's hometown, the judge planned to assassinate him. Informed of the plot, Huey's bodyguards told Drew he would be killed if he "put a foot on the platform," and Huey defused the situation by not saying anything, during his brief speech, about the judge. "Goddamn I was scared," Huey later admitted to E. P. Roy, head of the state police.[29]

Minden was only one indication that some Louisianians, mostly among the upper class, were ready for bloodshed if that was what it took to rid the state of the Kingfish. Ex-governor Parker had already expressed himself about "probable future killing," and while Huey continued his tour of the state, ex-governor Sanders declared in a Donaldsonville speech: "We need a revolution in Louisiana. . . . we do not have to wait for any election." More explicitly, a new anti-Long journal in Baton Rouge, *Freedom*, proclaimed its battle cry: "Huey P. Long, Jr., must go, regardless of the steps that must be taken to insure his departure."[30]

The last stop on Huey's ill-fated swing around Louisiana was Alexandria, on November 10. Here, in front of the city hall, the largest crowd of his tour—fifteen thousand—greeted him with a mixture of applause and boos. Thousands held up their hands when asked to show support for his program, but at least half the crowd seemed either neutral or negative. As he spoke, rotten eggs and oranges began to splatter on and around the platform; most were hurled from the crowd, although some came from the upper floors of a bank building across the street. Huey was not hit, but several persons near him were, including (according to the *American Progress*) a baby and a Confederate veteran. Then a stink bomb, aimed from the bank, landed close by. State policemen tried to enter the building but were kept out by Alexandria Police Chief Clint O'Malley and his men. Huey called the egg-throwers and hecklers "polecats," and said it made him proud to have such enemies. Yet by now he realized that things must change, and that in some ways he must change, if he was to remain in power in Louisiana and to have any hope of winning the White House. He ruefully commented, "I am like a rooster with a broken wing."[31]

Of Louisiana's eight congressional districts, the Sixth—which included Baton Rouge—had become the most hostile to Long by 1933. The incumbent representative, Bolivar Kemp, maintained a precarious neutrality between the pro- and anti-Long forces, but when Kemp died in June, the Long machine faced a problem: state law required any unexpired congressional term to be filled by prompt election, and in such a contest a Long foe, probably J. Y. Sanders, Jr., would be an almost certain winner. Governor Allen, at Huey's bidding, kept delaying the call for a Democratic primary, using the excuse that during these economic hard times the state's taxpayers should be spared the expense of a special primary and the formal general election required after any primary. It was clearly a stalling tactic. In late November, Allen called a meeting of the Long-controlled Sixth District Democratic Committee, which declared Congressman Kemp's widow, Lallie, "the unopposed Democratic nominee because there will not be time to hold a primary." A general election, with Mrs. Kemp's name the only one on the ballot, was set for eight days later.[32]

This palpable subversion of the democratic process outraged most voters in the district. Long's minority of support in the twelve-parish Sixth evidently grew smaller. Judge Nat Tycer of Hammond deputized a thousand armed men to prevent the December 5 "general election" in the three parishes of his district (one deputy was Hodding Carter, editor of the Hammond *Daily Courier*). The nine parishes where an election *was* held returned a total of 4,801 votes for Lallie Kemp. Later in December, a "citizen's election" took place in the district, and State Senator J. Y. Sanders, Jr.—who loathed Huey only slightly less than did his father—was the only candidate on that ballot; Mrs. Kemp was invited to enter, but declined. The younger Sanders received approximately 15,000 votes in the "citizen's election." Both Sanders and Kemp went to Washington in January of 1934 to claim the seat. The House of Representatives decided neither was lawfully elected. Finally, in April of 1934, in a special primary election, Sanders defeated Long's candidate, state commissioner of agriculture Harry D. Wilson, and became a congressman.[33]

This successful defiance of Huey Long revealed a curious fact about him—a personality trait that set him apart from other leaders with dictatorial propensities. Childhood episodes had hinted at it; encounters during young manhood and in earlier political struggles had indicated it; and his reaction to armed opposition in southeastern Louisiana's Sixth District now offered clear evidence of it: Huey recoiled from bloodshed. He threatened to send the National Guard into the rebellious parishes, but he did not. The state police, although mobilized for action, were not ordered to intervene, even when state trucks carrying ballots for Mrs. Kemp were fired upon. Huey had backed away from serious violence. As to verbal bullying, he exhibited a degree of recklessness perhaps unparalleled in American politics. He craved to bend everybody to his will and seemed to view himself as an Olympian deity above human law. But deadly force was not his way. He would threaten bodily harm, and occasionally slap or hit opponents, but that was the extent of it. Death terrified him. Although Huey began carrying a pistol when he was a teenage salesman, nobody remembered him ever firing at anything—not at a person, an animal, or even a target. His bodyguard Louie Jones believed Huey Long "never shot a gun in his life."[34]

New Orleans' mayoralty election in January of 1934 was yet another defeat for the Kingfish. The Old Regular ward bosses and Mayor Walmsley, desiring closer ties to the Roosevelt administration and believing Long was on the ropes, broke with the Kingfish late in 1933. Walmsley and Huey had always personally disliked each other; their three-year marriage of convenience now dissolved.[35] The mayor—Huey's *Progress* again started calling him "Turkey Head"—faced two opponents in the Democratic primary: Public Service Commissioner Francis Williams, backed by the *Times-Picayune* and most anti-Long patricians in the city; and John Klorer, Sr., who was persuaded to become the candidate of Long's Louisiana Democratic Association. Klorer, previously a nonpolitician civil engineer, was the father of the aggressive young editor of the *Progress*.[36]

It was the ugliest mayoralty election New Orleans had witnessed since the Behrman-McShane contest of 1920. The Old Regulars were accused by both Williams and Long's LDA (Klorer had little to say about anything) not only of tolerating vice, but also of shaking down whores and gamblers and of "looting" municipal funds. Huey made these and other charges in daily radio broadcasts from his hotel suite in the city. Mayor Walmsley swore to make Huey "swallow every insult," even if he had to physically "drag him out of his hotel."[37] The New Orleans *Item*, thinking Huey's day was over, switched sides and endorsed Walmsley. The mayor also welcomed back into his fold John P. Sullivan, who in 1931 had been deposed as an Old Regular ward boss as part of the city machine's agreement with Huey Long. Sullivan—"Bang Tail," as Huey still called him—was emerging as a major consultant on federal patronage because Roosevelt's administration considered him, John M. Parker, and J. Y. Sanders, Sr., to be the three most dependably anti-Long political figures in Louisiana.[38]

Shortly before election day, a threat loomed of civil war between city and state. The trouble grew from a squabble over possession of the Orleans Parish voter-registration rolls. General Ray Fleming of Louisiana's National Guard was told by Governor Allen to mobilize his troops for duty in New Orleans; Mayor Walmsley threatened to swear in "ten thousand special police" if the state militia arrived. But as had happened the month before in the Sixth Congressional District, violence was averted because the state government—that is, Huey—did not press the issue. Fleming's militia was not ordered to Orleans Parish. Mayor Walmsley won reelection by a substantial plurality (45 percent of the total). Klorer ran second (29 percent) and could have insisted on a run-off, but since the third-place finisher, Williams, swore he would never help a Long candidate, Klorer withdrew.[39] For the moment, Huey had to content himself with approving a story in the *American Progress* stating that "Turkey Head" Walmsley once sat at the same luncheon table, in Washington, with Oscar DePriest, "the negro congressman from Chicago."[40]

Huey was in a foul mood when he left New Orleans for Washington late in January of 1934. Before he departed, an Old Regular ward boss, Ulic Burke, had challenged him to a duel and left a pistol cartridge at the Roosevelt Hotel "as [a] calling card"; then Mayor Walmsley followed Huey to Washington with the announced intent of catching him away from his bodyguards and thrashing "the yellow coward." For several days Walmsley lurked about the nation's capital, but to no avail. Three of the Kingfish's toughest bodyguards—including George McQuiston, with his sawed-off shotgun concealed in a paper bag—now lived with Huey in his hotel suite (in March of 1934, Huey and his guards would move from the Mayflower Hotel to more spacious quarters in the Broadmoor); his protectors even took turns sitting watchfully in the Senate gallery, although they were not allowed to carry weapons there. Huey had no real worry about Mayor Walmsley, but he did fear that some assassin from Louisiana might shoot at him from the gallery.[41]

The annoying setbacks did not dampen Huey's self-esteem or aggressiveness, although for a time he shied away from criticizing President Roosevelt. Otherwise, his ill temper seemed worse than ever, probably in large part because of the stress of the changes he forced upon himself early in 1934. After reflecting on the damage done by Sands Point, and on his confessed inability to control himself after a few drinks, Huey gave up alcohol entirely. Simultaneously, he stopped eating rich foods and took more exercise; his weight dropped from over 200 to 175. Because sinus congestion was beginning to bother him, he also put aside the cigars and cigarettes he so enjoyed. He curbed another bad habit—using profanity in public—although this reform proved the hardest of all to sustain. The columnist George Sokolsky marveled that this supposed wild man "could alter his ways of living by act of will." Occasionally, Huey still visited Washington and New York nightspots, but he ordered soft drinks only. During 1935, he would begin drinking liquor again, but never to excess.[42]

Shortly before Christmas of 1934, Huey even tried, briefly, to cultivate the image of a family man by taking Rose on a belated honeymoon. "Mrs. Long and I never had a honeymoon," he informed reporters, "and we're going to have one now." He said they were planning a leisurely journey "out west." As it turned out, he took her only as far as Hot Springs, Arkansas, with two bodyguards tagging along. After a few days, Rose returned to New Orleans and Huey went back to Washington. While in Arkansas, Huey jokingly proclaimed himself "King of the Ozarks," since "all this territory around here is Long territory anyway."

The mayor of one Ozark community did not think this was funny, and said it confirmed his suspicion about Huey that "the man has a wheel loose."[43]

As the Senate discovered during 1934, Huey's tongue was even sharper than before. He and Democratic majority leader Robinson had worked out a truce that held through the year's session, but other senators who crossed him learned firsthand what his Louisiana enemies had known for a decade and more: Huey Long did not play by the rules. Some of the abuse he heaped upon various colleagues may have been delivered simply to gratify his ego, but mostly it represented a calculated effort to draw more national attention to himself and his proposal to confiscate fortunes—the plan he now called Share Our Wealth.

Huey believed that everybody in politics had at least one skeleton in his closet. By demonstrating adeptness at locating and opening closet doors, and doing it so flamboyantly as to make trivial misdeeds seem the essence of greed or evil, he endeavored to cow the Senate into submission. When senators ignored his accusations or insinuations, he would claim that their silence proved the correctness of his charges; yet any who challenged him were in peril of having even worse allegations flung at them, accompanied by threats to come into their states and campaign against them. "Huey," recalled Senator Alben Barkley of Kentucky, "was like a horsefly; he would light on one part of you, sting you, and then, when you slapped at him, fly away to land elsewhere and sting again." Another Democratic senator admitted: "Frankly, we are afraid of him. He is unscrupulous beyond belief. He might say anything about me, something entirely untrue, but it would ruin me in my state. . . . It's like challenging a buzz saw. He will go the limit. It is safer for me and the rest of us to leave him alone." Another senator was more concise: "He doesn't play fair. How can you fight a man like that?"[44]

Two senators, provoked beyond endurance, were ready to physically fight him. After a heated debate with Huey, Carter Glass of Virginia (age seventy-five) "jumped forward toward Senator Long" and had to be restrained by Joe Robinson. Huey explained to the press that he backed away because Glass "was an old man." Senator Bennett C. Clark of Missouri, enraged by Long's needling, shouted that Huey "hid under the bed" during the World War, and offered to whip him "in this chamber or outside at any time." Even President Roosevelt privately expressed a wish to lay hands on the Kingfish. Arthur Krock, a Pulitzer Prize–winning correspondent for the New York *Times*, overheard the president remark during dinner: "If I could, the way I'd handle Huey Long would be physically. He's a physical coward."[45]

But in his next breath, FDR conceded that in verbal exchanges most senators "were more afraid of [Long] than he is of them." Few could even hope to match wits with him, and the Kingfish's fearsome ability at jiggling skeletons led to suspicions he had his own private investigators. Senator Hamilton Lewis of Illinois must have suspected precisely this as he listened to Huey make allegations about Lewis' not always paying his bills. Similarly, after Huey's truce with Joe Robinson ended, he embarrassed the majority leader by somehow raking up a 1924 incident at the Chevy Chase Country Club, when Robinson lost a fistfight with a fellow golfer. Pat Harrison of Mississippi suffered Huey's most vicious foray into senatorial history. Harrison had provoked the Kingfish by saying that "in my view the opinion of the Senator from Louisiana is less respected by the Membership of this body . . . and by the country than that of any other Senator." Huey responded with some advice for Harrison: "Never touch a porcupine unless you expect to get some quills in you."[46] Accompanying the advice was a dose of quills. Huey contrasted his own opposition to World War I ("that damnable fraud against the American people"), and his defense of S. J. Harper of Winnfield, with Harrison's victorious 1918 senatorial campaign against the incumbent, James K. Vardaman, who like Huey's friend Harper, had criticized America's entry into the war. Harrison previously had been a political ally of Vardaman's. Huey explained to the Senate the difference between himself and Harrison: "Now that is my way of standing by my friends. The Senator from Mississippi has another way . . . catch your friend in trouble, stab him in the back and drink his blood." Harrison, noncombative by nature, wanly replied, "I suppose I must console myself with reflecting on what [Long] has done in the case of others."[47]

From that moment on, however, Harrison hated Huey Long, and usually left the chamber when the Kingfish was speaking, which was often. Senator Harry Byrd of Virginia, a friend of Harrison's and a fellow conservative Democrat, said late in 1934 that he could no longer endure being seated next to Long and at the next session of Congress would ask for another location, "even if I have to sit on the Republican side." To those senators who dared criticize him, Huey usually replied with vituperation, but to one charge—that of being egotistical—he smilingly pleaded guilty. Huey admitted, "I have a pretty high opinion of myself."[48]

From the time he entered the Senate until his death, Huey Long introduced numerous bills, resolutions, and motions. Not one passed. Ordinarily he could depend on just five or six votes; twenty votes was about the maximum for anything he sponsored, and even some of those yeas came from right-wing Republicans hoping to embarrass the Roosevelt administration. "I do not believe [you] could get the Lord's Prayer endorsed in this body," Senator Kenneth McKellar of Tennessee told him during a spirited debate. Huey conceded, "I am not a very influential man here."[49] Yet he seemed unconcerned. After all, the Senate did not elect presidents.

The Great Depression showed only slight signs of improvement during 1934, with the next presidential election just two years away. Huey decided that the time had come to begin nation-wide publicity for his plan to redistribute wealth. On February 5 he inserted in the *Congressional Record* "An Appeal to the People of America" to organize in every community a Share Our Wealth Society with the motto Every Man a King. Later that month he boosted the Share Our Wealth plan on a thirty-minute broadcast over the NBC network, which gave him free evening time. Soon favorable letters by the tens of thousands poured into Huey's Washington office. More would follow. Every letter was answered, which at one point required forty-eight secretaries and typists, working in shifts. By 1935, Huey had more employees and a larger suite in the Senate Office Building than any other member.[50]

Most of the expenses for promoting Share Our Wealth, including rent for the extra office space, were paid by the Kingfish— which is to say, by his Louisiana political organization. The society itself charged neither national nor local dues. "The thieves of Wall Street and their newspaper and radio liars," he explained, "would say I had a scheme to get money" if it cost anything to join. Any local SOW society would receive "official" recognition merely by writing Senator Huey P. Long, Washington,

D.C., and informing him of its existence, the names of its officers, and the number of its members. (As a United States senator, he used his free postal privileges to reply.) Realizing that SOW might be branded communistic, Huey assured everyone that his plan was mandated by the Holy Bible and was "the word and work of the Lord." Thus SOW was not really Huey Long's idea, but God's plan—"praised be the name of the Lord," he added—and when it was enacted, Huey promised, "Heaven will be coming nearer to earth."[51]

Share Our Wealth was simple in outline. Personal and family fortunes above "three or four million dollars" would be confiscated. Annual income and inheritance taxes would be steeply raised—up to a flat 100 percent on anything above one million dollars. The national government would transfer this wealth to the poor. Since wealth also consists of goods, Huey proposed to redistribute in kind "so the poor devil who needs a house can get one from some rich bird who has too many houses"; stock in corporations might also be divided among the people. As to how such transfers could actually be accomplished, Huey confessed he had not worked out the details: "I am going to have to call in some great minds to help me." Being pressed for specifics annoyed him. Once, he shrugged off questions by saying that "as soon as I run the crooks out of government I'll get down to methods for putting the plan into effect."[52]

Understandably, with close to half the nation's families in 1934 and 1935 earning less than the $1,250 considered minimal for a "maintenance level" of life, Huey's promised cornucopia of benefits from Share Our Wealth enjoyed widespread appeal. "Every family would make not less than $2,000 to $3,000 per year," he insisted. Moreover, the Long Plan (as he often called Share Our Wealth) would shorten the work week to thirty hours or "maybe less," with a month's annual paid vacation or "maybe more." Each family able to work, he said, would have a guaranteed "family wealth" of "around $5,000—enough for a home, an automobile, a radio, and the ordinary conveniences" ($5,000 in 1934 dollars is the equivalent of almost $50,000 in 1990 dollars). The Long Plan also called for "a moratorium on all debts which people owe that they cannot pay"; free education for every child from grade school through college; and "a pension to all [poor] persons above 60 years of age in an amount sufficient to support them in comfortable circumstances." The latter, Huey claimed, could be accomplished without deductions from wages during the working years. Everything he proposed could be furnished by confiscating the surplus wealth of America's superrich and by the boost in consumer spending and labor productivity that would follow. "God ordered this," Huey insisted, referring to certain passages in the Bible. "God said so!"[53]

The Kingfish freely admitted his ignorance of economic theory. "No," he told Forrest Davis, "I never read a line of Marx or Henry George or any of them economists. It's all the law of God." Huey declared his plan would save capitalism, not destroy it. He even predicted Share Our Wealth would increase the number of millionaires "tenfold, because so many more people could make a million dollars" if the multimillionaires were forced to give up their stranglehold on the American economy. The charge of being a Marxist made him boil. "Communism? Hell no!" he shouted. "This plan is the only defense this country's got against communism."[54]

Referring to the concentration of wealth and what to do about it, Huey frequently quoted the *Saturday Evening Post* article that had so impressed him in 1916. (Once, when not at his best, Huey amused the Senate by blurting: "Here is what the Lord said about it, and here is what the *Saturday Evening Post* said about it too.") The figures from that magazine article were twenty years old and dubious even then; the supposedly updated statistics he used were even less reliable, such as his reference to "600 families at the most, either possessing or controlling 90 percent of all that is in America."[55] Modern scholars who have studied Share Our Wealth point out that Long's plan was unworkable, at least in the form he proposed, because there simply were not enough multimillionaires' fortunes to pay for it. Alan Brinkley cites figures indicating that if every American family received the $5,000 minimum "family wealth" Huey spoke of, then no family could have kept more than about $7,000 in wealth.[56] To attempt the benefits Long promised, a leveling experiment of a magnitude never seen outside the Communist world, and seldom there, would have been necessary.

That Huey actually believed in his Share Our Wealth plan is doubtful. When one of his most cynical henchmen, Richard Leche, cautioned him not to be specific "about how the wealth can be shared," Huey replied: "You're right. I didn't think you were that smart." Another Long politician, H. C. "Happy" Sevier, said the Kingfish once admitted to him that SOW "wouldn't work," but that "when they figure that out I'll have something new for them." Huey's loyal conservation commissioner, Robert Maestri, believed Long proposed Share Our Wealth "only . . . to get attention." The plan, Maestri opined years later, was "a lot of bullshit."[57]

Yet the problem the plan addressed—hunger and rags in the midst of plenty—was real enough, as Huey understood. Moreover, a prime cause of the Great Depression was indeed the inadequate distribution of income, which meant American wage earners and farmers were unable to purchase all the food and manufactured goods the nation produced.[58] So much poverty in a land of abundance did not make sense in either economic or moral terms. The poor and marginally middle class knew something had gone terribly wrong in America, and millions of them were attracted to Long's promise to put things right. Exactly how many joined Share Our Wealth is uncertain, but by April of 1935, his Washington office reported 7,682,768 members in 27,431 clubs, and Long's critics did not dispute those figures. There were clubs in all forty-eight states, but the South had a majority of the total membership, with Louisiana leading the list. California, Minnesota, and New York reported the largest numbers outside the South. Although Huey had no interest in organizing beyond the United States, his radio broadcasts could be heard in parts of Canada, where 17 SOW clubs began meeting in Ontario Province.[59]

Of all the Share Our Wealth clubs, one in New York City drew the most press attention, chiefly because of its controversial president, Eugene S. Daniell, Jr. Like Huey, Daniell said he hated Wall Street; in 1933 he went to jail for throwing two teargas bombs into the ventilating system of the New York Stock Exchange. As a SOW club leader, Daniell created another disturbance on Wall Street by haranguing in front of J. P. Morgan and Company's office. Later, a police emergency squad had to be sent to "stop a disorder" involving Daniell and Communists at New York's Union Square; Marxists tended to congregate there, and they resented his coming in to proselytize. Huey, in an analogous confrontation, went to New York in March of 1934 to debate Norman Thomas, the Socialist party leader, on the merits of Share Our Wealth versus those of socialism. The audience of mostly leftist urbanites puzzled Huey by reacting to his Biblelaced appeal with gales of laughter. A majority of those present thought Thomas won the debate, but afterward it was the King-fish who drew the autograph hunters.[60]

The Reverend Gerald L. K. Smith became Huey's "national organizer" for the Share Our Wealth movement. Smith was one of the ablest but strangest members of Long's entourage. Born and raised in rural Wisconsin, he became a minister in the Christian church (Disciples of Christ). He moved to Louisiana in 1929, at age thirty-one, upon accepting a call from the Kings Highway Christian Church in Shreveport. Smith was a powerful preacher; his sermons often were broadcast over KWKH, and because he denounced big business as well as Satan, Huey Long heard about him and met him. The two discovered they had much in common. "Next to me," Huey reportedly once said, "[Smith is] the greatest rabble rouser in the country." Indeed, as a spellbinder he may have surpassed the Kingfish. But Smith was not in Long's class as a politician. Besides, a severe person-ality disorder seemed to bedevil him. He became increasingly hostile toward Jews, thinking they were working through both communism and capitalism to dominate the world and, inci-dentally, to destroy him. Something else about Smith bothered Shreveport's coroner, Dr. Willis P. Butler, who years later re-called that Smith displayed "a morbid curiosity about cadavers" and liked to attend autopsies, particularly when Butler per-formed one on a young woman who had been murdered.[61]

Smith lost his Shreveport church for several reasons, but his association with Huey Long probably hastened his departure, for the Kings Highway congregation included some of the city's leading anti-Long conservatives. Before Share Our Wealth was organized in 1934, Smith cast about for various opportunities: briefly he signed on as a recruiter for the Silver Shirts, a fascist order based in North Carolina and headed by William Dudley Pelley, who dreamed of seizing control of the United States gov-ernment. The FBI file on Smith includes a letter he wrote early in 1933 to a German American believed to have contacts with the Nazi hierarchy in Berlin; Smith said he was "anxious to get in touch with his Honor, Adolf Hitler," and proposed an organi-zation in America "to overcome the terrible anti-German prop-aganda being promoted by the Jews."[62] Smith never got to meet Hitler. He had to settle for Huey Long.

As Share Our Wealth's chief organizer, Smith stumped Louisiana first, then other southern states, and by 1935 he was addressing northern audiences, including the Minnesota legislature. Although he never explicitly said so, Smith seems to have imagined Huey Long as the future führer of America and himself in the role of Dr. Goebbels. Smith's pro-Nazi and anti-Semitic views, however, had to be kept under wraps during the time he worked for Huey; the Kingfish did not appreciate being compared to Hitler, whether in praise or in condemnation. The ex-preacher would never have dared say in the Kingfish's presence, as he did later on, that "there were too many Jews" in Long's organization. When Huey was assassinated, Smith wrongly concluded that Dr. Carl Weiss, the presumed murderer, was a Jew (the Weiss name is common among Germans both Jew and Gentile). In Smith's mode of thinking, Jews killed Huey as they killed Jesus.[63]

Smith, an archetypical authoritarian personality, adored Huey Long and referred to him as "a superman." Obviously, he desired to shine in the Kingfish's reflected glory. In one frenzied speech he proclaimed that Huey could not be killed: "You can shoot at him but you will miss him. No matter how many times you shoot, the star of the gods is upon his head. . . . He can't be destroyed." Some of Smith's Louisiana meetings were disrupted by rowdies, and in West Feliciana Parish the sheriff and "a group of citizens" escorted him to the parish line, where he was warned not to return. Smith was denounced by the anti-Long press as ungentlemanly because he insulted two of Huey's female enemies—he called Hilda Phelps Hammond "funny face" and referred to "hysterical Mrs. Pleasant who's just twenty jumps out of the insane asylum." An advocate of muscular Christianity, Smith boasted of his ability to overpower assailants and denied he had been "run out" of West Feliciana. "The only thing about me that will run," he said, "is my nose."[64]

Since blacks were the poorest of the poor, they found the Share Our Wealth idea highly appealing. This constituency created something of a dilemma. Admitting black people to SOW would, Huey knew, leave him vulnerable to racist attacks. On the other hand, enrolling blacks would boost his membership figures, and since this was a nation-wide movement designed to launch his presidential candidacy, it would have been both difficult and unwise to ban nonwhite citizens from SOW. Therefore they were admitted. Separate black clubs were organized in

Louisiana and in several northern states, one of the largest being in New York City's Harlem district. Interviewed by the NAACP's *Crisis* magazine early in 1935, Huey forthrightly said Share Our Wealth was meant for blacks as well as whites. "I'm for the poor man—all poor men, black and white, they all gotta have a chance." But the Kingfish inserted an afterthought he hoped would minimize any damage that reports of this interview might do in the South: "In your article, don't say I'm working for niggers. I'm not. . . . 'Every Man a King' . . . means every man, niggers long with the rest, but not specially for niggers."[65]

Louisiana blacks who came to SOW organizing rallies were given a cautionary welcome. "Now you niggers get back to the rear," one of Smith's aides would inform them as the meeting began. "Don't crowd up front where the white folks belong." Blacks were told that although they were "welcome," they must not sign up at this gathering, which was strictly for a "white folks" club. Nevertheless, some of the Kingfish's foes predictably reacted by depicting Share Our Wealth as a vicious plan to transfer white property to blacks. The Bunkie *Record*, fast becoming the most extreme anti-Long weekly in the state, published crude cartoons showing Long hugging fierce-looking Africans. "Many negroes in North Louisiana," according to another questionable source, "have quit work and are expecting a check for $5,000." The Hammond *Vindicator* printed a letter to Senator Long "congratulating" him because "no one has stirred the negroes up like you have since carpetbag and scalawag days." Blacks were reported as believing Huey was also planning to grant them the right to vote.[66]

Whatever his real intentions might have been about sharing wealth among whites or blacks, Huey Long apparently never considered—certainly he never proposed—giving Louisiana's black population the ballot. Instead, his setbacks during 1933 and early 1934 led him to quite another decision: that white voters, having shown fickleness, must effectively be reduced to the political status of blacks. In the past, Louisiana's government had been a dictatorship over blacks. Now it was about to become a dictatorship over all.

· 16 ·

PLAIN DICTATOR

Huey Long's presidential ambitions and his domination of state politics were necessarily intertwined. The money for national promotion of Share Our Wealth came from Louisiana, as did most of the campaign funds he was laying aside for 1936. By 1935, at least one million dollars, mostly deductions from state employees' salaries and kickbacks from contractors, had been squirreled away in what was known as Huey's "deducts box." Huey understood that attaining the White House could take years. If 1936 proved impossible, 1940 might be a better opportunity.[1] His plans required a secure money-and-power base.

Besides, Louisiana must be held for its own sake. Never to be president would be bad enough; not to dominate at least his home state, not to have somewhere to be catered to and feared— to become a nobody whose words and deeds did not crash the headlines—would to him have been akin to death. Once, when the state's major dailies temporarily conspired to ignore him, Huey was heard to say that "it was like being buried alive." Yet his need for attention ranked second to his lust for authority. A 1935 article in *Forum* magazine was roughly accurate in describing him as "wanting power as a normal man wants bread or sex." Raymond Gram Swing, a respected journalist who had interviewed Hitler and Mussolini before he met Huey Long, described Huey as "the embodiment of the appetite for power."[2]

During early 1934, most anti-Long Louisianians optimistically believed they were about to topple the Kingfish. His string of difficulties, beginning with Sands Point the previous August and proceeding through his candidate's defeat in the January mayor's race in New Orleans, convinced them that Huey was, as some gleefully said, "a gone goose." One astute foe was doubtful. Hodding Carter realized that Huey still had his financial and personal resources intact, so "he isn't down yet." Later that year, after Long had confirmed Carter's worst fears, a *Current History* article speculated that if the Kingfish were ever tossed into the Mississippi River by an enraged citizenry, "he probably would bob up on election day with ballots sticking to his coat-tails."[3]

The conversion of Louisiana from a quasi-authoritarian state into a full-fledged dictatorship began at the legislature's biennial regular session in May and June. Anti-Long forces believed that enough representatives had drifted away from Huey to reorganize the House if not the senate; they planned to replace Longite Allen J. Ellender as Speaker with one of their own, George K. Perrault. In case Governor Allen (at Huey's command) tried to prevent this change by calling in the militia, several hundred anti-Long men from across the state were gathering in the capital city to place "armed support behind the reorganization forces." Their leaders met secretly "on the sixth floor of a Baton Rouge business building"—probably the Reymond, an anti-Long enclave.[4]

Without Huey's high-energy presence, the Long machine almost certainly would have lost control of the 1934 legislature, for the Old Regular bloc from New Orleans presumably had shifted to the anti-Long column, and Governor Allen's bumbling address to the solons typified his limits as a leader. "Fundamentally," Allen informed them, "there are two sides of the business affairs of the state, namely: income and expenditures." It was the Kingfish's indefatigable work behind the scenes—promising, flattering, or threatening certain opposition legislators whom he believed, correctly in most cases, to be vulnerable to one or another kind of pressure. "I can frighten or buy ninety-nine out of every one hundred men," Huey once said to a Tulane professor.[5] At this critical time it took only about twenty frightened or bought men to turn things around.

Huey returned to Washington shortly after the session began, thinking the agenda he presented to Allen to present to the legislature would now have easy passage. It did not. Some of the bills were too controversial, and Governor Allen too irresolute, to force them through. Huey had to hasten back to Baton Rouge and again take charge. The Long machine was simultaneously showing its greatest weakness and strength. As the New York *Times* disparagingly noted, "It is a one-man organization." Yet that one man was Huey Long. In a bravado performance rivaling any of his career, the Kingfish stormed in and out of legislative committee meetings and chambers, pushing bills through to final passage. Although having no right to be on the floor (since he held no state or legislative office), he entered either chamber as he pleased and acted as if he were the floor leader. He shouted orders, muttered threats, tolerated no delays. Several bills Huey proposed had been beaten during his absence in Washington; they were now resurrected by being tacked on as amendments to unrelated bills still pending. Every measure Huey wanted— except one he withdrew and later resubmitted at a special session—became law. The opposition steadily eroded; by session's end, two thirds of the House and senate members were voting for anything he wanted. Thomas O. Harris, who had observed state politics since before Huey was born, had never seen anything like this session; after the Kingfish's death, Harris wrote: "For the balance of his days, Huey Long held the Louisiana legislature in the hollow of his hand."[6]

One bill coming out of the 1934 regular session appeared to be a democratic reform. It submitted to the voters a constitutional amendment abolishing the one-dollar-per-year poll-tax requirement for voter registration. The amendment passed overwhelmingly in November. Two other tax measures, simultaneously approved by the voters as constitutional amendments, could also be touted as progressive actions. One provided for homestead exemptions on up to two thousand dollars' valuation; the other levied Louisiana's first income tax, which exempted the poor and reached a modest maximum of 6 percent on incomes over fifty thousand dollars. But all three measures sounded better than they actually were. Blacks were not helped by lifting the poll tax since—as Huey carefully pointed out—the white primary would still keep them away from the ballot box; also, getting rid of the poll tax crippled the New Orleans Old Regulars and certain anti-Long courthouse rings, who customarily had paid it for their client voters. The homestead exemption, it turned out, would not completely go into effect until 1939, and the income tax raised little revenue because it was pegged so low, even at the upper levels.[7]

The drift toward dictatorship was clearly visible in several other laws. One bill, allegedly a reform to stop the "dummy candidate" practice in elections, allowed a state-appointed board the right to select additional commissioners at all precincts. Another act forbade local courts from interfering with the removal of voter lists from registrars' offices. A liquor-control bill took from local government the right to issue alcoholic beverage permits (all such licensing would henceforth be done by the supervisor of public accounts, Alice Lee Grosjean). Also, control of the New Orleans Police Department was transferred from the city to a state-appointed board of police commissioners. When a group of parish and municipal officials came to Baton Rouge to protest their impending loss of authority, Huey candidly told them: "Yes, we may have one big machine, but we'll bust up the little machines throughout the state."[8]

Most ominous of all was Huey's first law to undermine a free press. Ostensibly as a revenue bill, it levied a 2 percent tax on the advertising income of newspapers in Louisiana with circulations of more than twenty thousand. But the Kingfish was not ashamed of its real purpose. "This tax," one of his circulars explained, "should be called a tax on lying, 2 cents per lie." It affected only the dailies in New Orleans and other urban centers, and only one of these papers—the Lake Charles *American Press*—was then on good terms with Long. (In a speech at Lake Charles, Huey said he would like to exempt the *American Press* but could not find a legal way to do so.) The newspapers appealed through the courts, and eventually the United States Supreme Court ruled, in the case of *Grosjean* v. *American Press Co.*, that the law was unconstitutional.[9] But that decision did not come until after Huey was dead, and meanwhile he would devise a more effective method of intimidating the press.

Huey's foes were thunderstruck by his audacity. They had often called him a dictator. Now he really was becoming one. They had sometimes spoken of taking up arms against his regime, and over the years numerous individuals tried—and in some cases had succeeded in—laying hands on him. But beginning with the pivotal summer legislative session of 1934, talk of violence took on a stridency, a seriousness, it had lacked before. Soon there came to be, as J. Y. Sanders, Jr., said, a "wildness in the air."[10]

Phrases out of the nineteenth century seemed to come, as if by ancestral memory, from the mouths of those Louisianians whose

279

parents and grandparents had led the fight against Radical Reconstruction. An anti-Long rally in Baton Rouge, while the legislature was in session, listened to Shreveport's mayor George W. Hardy describe his willingness to use "a hempen rope." Huey was referred to not only with contemporary vulgarity, but also in archaic terms of opprobrium: *blackguard, poltroon, ruffian, mountebank,* and *despot.* The Hammond *Vindicator* believed that "the time has arrived to take down the old musket from over the door, give it a good greasing and be prepared to march on Baton Rouge." [11]

Looking to the past for guidance, Huey Long's enemies came to focus upon the White League uprising of September 14, 1874. Hilda Phelps Hammond was one of several who could recall being taken as children to the marble shaft at the foot of New Orleans' Canal Street and hearing their fathers tell of the Reconstruction-era battle, "where citizens fell fighting for free government." The Bunkie *Record* called upon the "shades of our ancestors" for spiritual help in combatting Longism, and later noted, less elegantly, that conditions in Louisiana had not been this bad since "the time the burr-heads were in power." [12]

A few White League veterans were still living, and one of them volunteered "to get his ancient musket and fight once more." The uprising's sixtieth anniversary came in 1934, and twenty-six survivors showed up for the ceremonies on September 14. The "orator of the day," a distinguished old New Orleanian, described at length the carpetbagger regime in such a way as to parallel it to Huey Long's. He reminded the crowd, "There were red-blooded men in the Louisiana of 1874, however, and they dealt a death blow to the tyranny." [13]

By the time of the White League commemoration in 1934, Louisiana's legislature, on Huey's orders to Allen, had met again. The slide into dictatorship accelerated at this special five-day session in mid-August. New Orleans was Huey's primary target, but several of the new laws, which were rammed through with stunning rapidity, affected the entire state. The governor obtained power to call into active service the Louisiana National Guard for any reason ("when he may deem it necessary"). His authority to grant reprieves from local or district court rulings was made virtually unlimited. The state attorney general—currently Gaston Porterie, whose obedience to the Kingfish rivaled Governor Allen's—gained the power to "relieve, supplant or supersede" district attorneys in all parishes "when [he] may deem it necessary for the protection of the rights and interests of the state." In a measure aimed solely at New Orleans, the city's charter was amended so that any deputized "special police" could not carry arms without permission of the governor.[14]

The August special session also strengthened and made more mysterious the Bureau of Criminal Identification, presently to be referred to as "Huey's Cossacks." Already these plainclothes state detectives had considerable powers of investigation and arrest; now they became the paramount police force of Louisiana, answerable only to the governor. The BCI headquarters were moved from Shreveport to the state capitol building. The number and names of its rank-and-file members were known only to Long's inner circle, but the new superintendent was announced: National Guard brigadier general Louis F. Guerre.[15]

Sin in New Orleans was one of Huey's favorite targets. It had been so since he campaigned for John M. Parker in the gubernatorial race of 1920. Gambling, prostitution, and most other vices known to humankind were always present in Louisiana's easygoing metropolis, and the Kingfish never expressed concern about it except when undertaking a political offensive against the city's Old Regular organization. In the late summer of 1934 he launched a blitzkrieg. Act 27 of the August special session created a special legislative committee, appointed by Governor Allen, to investigate allegations that Mayor Walmsley's administration was connected to immoral activities in New Orleans. The committee's first action was to appoint its counsel—United States Senator Huey P. Long.[16]

"The greatest cesspool of hell that has ever been known to the modern world" was Huey's description of what he and the legislative committee found in New Orleans. The investigation took place during the first week of September, 1934, and its proceedings—in which Long interrogated witnesses whose counsels were not allowed inside the room—were broadcast over WDSU. Pay-offs and votes from vice elements were indeed important to the Old Regular regime, but the primary intent of Huey's crusade seems to have been to frighten the owners and denizens of casinos, bookie joints, and whorehouses into shifting financial and voting support from the Old Regulars to Long's machine. Julius Long denounced Huey's investigation as "a smoke screen," but it was more than that. A Democratic primary election was set for September 11, with several anti-Long congressmen and the sole public service commissioner who still opposed Huey ("France-ass" Williams) up for reelection. Additionally, two Louisiana Supreme Court seats were to be decided, and Long's four-to-three majority hung in the balance.[17]

General Fleming's national guardsmen moved into New Orleans four days prior to the election, after Huey learned the Old Regulars had hired Guy Moloney, a former New Orleans police chief who had become a soldier of fortune in Latin America, to take charge of the now-illegal "special police" on election day. Neither Long nor Mayor Walmsley wanted bloodshed; a patched-together truce specified that the forces of each side would stay away from the polls on election day. Long's candidates won both congressional seats in the New Orleans area, along with the Public Service Commission post and one of the crucial seats on the state supreme court (the other, in southwestern Louisiana, was to be decided in a special October election, made necessary by the fact that Long's incumbent candidate, a brother of Senator John Overton, had died two days before the September 11 primary). But the Kingfish's triumph was not absolute. Five of the state's eight congressmen, led by J. Y. Sanders, Jr., of the Sixth District, declared their allegiance to President Roosevelt instead of Huey Long.[18]

Anti-Longites of various factions understood that FDR represented their best hope of toppling the Kingfish. Even the most conservative of them, who privately must have deplored the New Deal's trend toward a welfare state, embraced Roosevelt if only because he was Huey Long's most powerful foe. "President Roosevelt . . . alone is responsible for the great work being done in behalf of suffering humanity over this land," declared a right-wing and former Ku Klux leader in Tangipahoa Parish. Congressman Cleveland Dear of Louisiana's Eighth District (Huey called him "Dodo" Dear as a prophecy of the congressman's political extinction) made a point of lavishly praising FDR at every opportunity. Ex-governors Sanders, Pleasant, and Parker, pillars of Louisiana patrician society who, ironically, had opposed FDR's nomination in 1932, were now listed among Roosevelt's leaders in the state.[19]

Huey struck back with special wrath at prominent Louisianians who fought him under the aegis of the New Deal. As to Parker's charge that Long's machine had raked in "at least $10 million" in graft, Huey said the former governor was promoting "the same old claptrap and rottenness that he has undertaken to parade [against me] for . . . years." Edward Rightor, an anti-Long New Orleans lawyer who served on the Public Works Administration's Louisiana advisory board, received one of Huey's most insulting nicknames: Long called him "Whistle-britches," presumably because Rightor suffered from flatulence. When Long's old foe John P. "Bang Tail" Sullivan came to Washington in April of 1934 to testify before a Senate committee hearing, Huey characterized him as "this racketeer," adding that "he is a great deal worse than the man who will go into a grave and take a nickel off a dead man's eye." (Sullivan, at the hearing, cursed Huey and threatened him "with a worse beating than he had ever received at Sands Point.") When Huey learned that his boyhood friend Harley Bozeman had gained a position with a federal agency, he referred to Bozeman as a "little pot-bellied character" who "reminds me very much of a chicken snake."[20]

Some of Huey's most indefatigable enemies were women of upper-class background. In 1933, Hilda Phelps Hammond, able and articulate, organized the Women's Committee of Louisiana to promote anti-Long activity in state and nation. Part of the committee's funding came from the sale of heirlooms at its headquarters on New Orleans' St. Peter Street. (One supporter from Alexandria, having no heirloom to contribute, sent a mass of her red-gold hair, with a note saying she had gotten the idea from the character Jo in *Little Women*.) To Mrs. Hammond, whose brother was a *Times-Picayune* executive and whose lawyer husband had been fired by Huey as counsel for two state boards, the Kingfish "represented pure evil." She spent much of the next two years in Washington, lobbying senators and delivering petitions questioning Long's (and Overton's) fitness to be senators. Among other prominent names on the WCL's roster, one of the most recognizable was that of Mrs. John M. Parker.[21]

Huey usually pulled his punches when confronting female opponents, thinking it wiser to meet such attacks by castigating their husbands, brothers, and fathers for "hiding their own slimy faces behind the skirts of their womenfolk. . . . the cowardly wretches!" But he was provoked beyond endurance by Hilda Hammond. Ugly cartoons of her appeared in the *American Progress*, along with references to her as "the antique queen." In one radio broadcast, the Kingfish insinuated Mrs. Hammond's family had African ancestry. Nor did he ignore ex-governor Pleasant's wife, Anne. Mrs. Pleasant, not a member of the WCL and mistrusted by Mrs. Hammond, conducted a private vendetta against the Kingfish. Once, when she made a scene in the office of Supervisor of Public Accounts Alice Lee Grosjean, Huey ordered Mrs. Pleasant out of the state capitol because she was, as he told it, "a drunken cursing woman." In May of 1934, she made the mistake of testifying, without legal counsel, before a United States Senate subcommittee investigating complaints against Huey Long. As Hilda Hammond recalled the episode, Long was allowed to cross-examine Mrs. Pleasant and "humiliated her" by bringing up the fact that she had undergone treatment "for a mental disease." [22]

Huey's war against the Roosevelt administration intensified during late 1934 and into 1935. The hostility was reciprocal. Roosevelt had become alarmed at reports of the Kingfish's growing strength; a secret poll authorized by the Democratic National Committee indicated that Long, as a third-party "Share Our Wealth" presidential candidate, might siphon off enough votes from FDR to throw the race to the Republicans. Reports that the GOP was offering under-the-table financial backing to Long's campaign—"Satan is tempting some Republicans," wrote Arthur Krock—added to the Democrats' worry. Krock also heard the Kingfish boast: "I can take him. He's a phony. I can take this Roosevelt. He's scared of me. I can out-promise him, and he knows it." [23]

Long was the foremost, but not the only, contemporary apostle of discontent. Also fretting the New Dealers was Father Charles E. Coughlin, a mellifluous Catholic priest from Michigan whose popular Sunday broadcasts over CBS echoed some of Huey Long's themes. His and Huey's lists of villains included many of the same names: J. P. Morgan, Bernard Baruch, John D. Rockefeller. But Coughlin and Long also had differences, the most important being one of rival egos. Long once denigrated the priest as "just a political Kate Smith on the air," but publicly he claimed friendship with Coughlin. James Farley, chairman of the DNC, was most concerned that the Kingfish and the radio priest might combine their followings in 1936, and draw in lesser protest groups, such as the pension planners led by Dr. Francis E. Townsend of California and the Farm Holiday Association headed by Iowa's Milo Reno. Yet without the Kingfish to lead them, no meaningful coalition was likely. "Father Coughlin, Reno, Townsend, *et al.*," Rex Tugwell later wrote, "were all pygmies compared with Huey."[24]

Not only was Huey Long considered by Roosevelt's administration to be the only serious threat among the dissidents, but he was also alone among them in having a political power base that could be attacked. And only he was hated by FDR. When Senator Long and the president first fell out, early in 1933, the White House merely denied him patronage. In fact, the New Deal agency spending the most in Louisiana, the Federal Emergency Relief Administration, remained singularly free of either pro- or anti-Long politics until the spring of 1935; Harry J. Early, the state FERA head, refused to submit to partisan pressures. But other federal agencies, particularly the Public Works Administration and the National Recovery Administration, from their beginnings played anti-Long politics in Louisiana. Then, in April of 1935, Early—his neutrality no longer considered tolerable in Washington—was replaced by Frank Peterman, an anti-Long state senator of small ability who immediately politicized the FERA in Louisiana. Not coincidentally, shortly before Peterman replaced Early, the president, at a meeting of the National Emergency Council, ordered: "Don't keep anybody that is working for Huey Long and his crowd! That is a hundred percent!"[25]

Federal money and patronage used against him exasperated Huey Long, but could not destroy him. The Long machine was self-supporting; its survival did not depend upon whether Washington smiled or frowned. Also, recipients of federal relief were not subjected to the intense pressure state jobholders knew. Yet the White House, as Huey discovered, could play another kind of hardball. Since the Long machine's money was believed to come mainly from salary deducts and contractors' kickbacks, and since there was little likelihood Huey or his lieutenants paid much if any income taxes on it, a decision was made in Washington to unleash the Internal Revenue Service upon the Kingfish.[26] The assumption was that Huey would find it difficult to mount a presidential campaign from the penitentiary.

As early as 1930, midway in the Hoover administration, John M. Parker made regular visits to the Washington office of Elmer Irey, chief of intelligence for the Treasury Department and a formidable evidence-gatherer for the department's Internal Revenue Service. The ex-governor's conversations always came to the same point: "When are you going to do something about Long?" But Parker had only accusations, not hard evidence, and the same was true of a flood of anonymous letters Irey began receiving from Louisiana. In the summer of 1932, Irey sent investigators to the Pelican State, and the agent in charge returned to report: "Chief, Louisiana is crawling. Long and his gang are stealing everything in the state . . . and they're not paying taxes on the loot." But soon Irey was ordered to suspend the investigation; Huey's friend Harvey Couch, the utilities magnate who was also a director of Hoover's Reconstruction Finance Corporation, had used his considerable influence with the Treasury Department to have the matter shelved. Huey had no more trouble about taxes until early 1934, when Roosevelt's secretary of the treasury, Henry Morgenthau, Jr., called Irey into his office and told him to resume the probe.[27]

"We decided," Irey later wrote, "that the technique that had put Al Capone and his gang to jail would be reasonably applicable to Huey Long and his gang." The method used against Capone had been to go after his underlings first, discover from paper trails who got pay-offs not reported as income, then trace some of the money up to, as Irey said, "the big man himself." But in Louisiana, as it turned out, this technique did not work quite so well. Late in 1934 a federal grand jury indicted several Long henchmen for income tax evasion. The highest-up among them were Abe Shushan, president of the Orleans Parish Levee Board; State Senator Jules Fisher and his nephew, State Representative Joseph Fisher; and most important, Seymour Weiss, treasurer of the Long machine and Huey's closest confidant.[28]

In April of 1935 a federal jury found Joe Fisher guilty. He drew an eighteen-month sentence. But Fisher was the only Long underling to go on trial prior to Huey's death. (Several years later, Weiss, Shushan, and numerous other Long lieutenants went to prison for various felonies, including tax evasion.) According to Irey in his 1949 memoirs, "The bullet that killed Huey did not save us from a dictator. It merely saved Huey from going to jail." Irey's supposition lacks reality. Huey knew how to sidestep paper trails. He scrupulously paid taxes on all income that came to him by checks (about $25,000 in 1934). Probably little or none of the deducts and kickback money went into Huey's own pockets; his underlings were allowed to take a commission—Huey was outraged to learn how much Shushan had raked off—but the bulk of all the unreported money from graft and extortion seems to have gone into the organization's treasury (which included the deducts box of reserve funds), and the treasury's secrets were known only to Huey and Seymour Weiss. That Huey owned shares in such dubious enterprises as the Louisiana Quarry Company and the Win or Lose Corporation was well known, but in what way he received money from them remained a mystery; however he was paid, it was not by checks of significant amounts. One of the federal prosecutors in the 1934–1935 tax evasion cases privately admitted: "We have no income tax case against Huey Long. We've traced the money coming in, but it all stops at one of his lieutenants."[29]

When Senator Wheeler complained to the president about the administration's vendetta against Huey, Roosevelt answered that Long was "a crook." Retorted Wheeler, "Well, I don't think so, but if he is a crook, he's too smart for you to catch him." Even if direct evidence against the Kingfish had turned up, the difficulty would have remained of persuading juries in his home state to indict and convict him. Dan Moody, the former Texas governor whom Roosevelt cajoled into becoming chief prosecutor of the tax cases, doubted the president's goal could be accomplished. Moody told Irey: "We are not going to convict Huey Long before a Louisiana jury by proving he cheated on his income tax. We may not be able to convict him if we can prove he murdered his mother, but we'll never do it on an income-tax charge. . . . We might embarrass him, but he embarrasses hard."[30]

That Roosevelt used questionable tactics against Huey is manifest. The president in this instance seems to have followed two of the shopworn aphorisms Huey himself often quoted: "You've got to fight fire with fire" and "The end justifies the means."[31] These sentiments, of course, stand among the world's oldest excuses for abusing power. There is no doubt that the 1934–1935 Internal Revenue Service investigation of Long and his cohorts was ordered by the White House for political reasons. Moreover, federal patronage and relief programs in Louisiana became highly politicized; even the previously nonpartisan FERA was turned into an anti-Long instrument in 1935.[32]

Roosevelt was no dictator, but he was also no stranger to devious, underhanded tactics, and his fight with Huey Long provides a view of the dark side of his presidency.

Never one to endure blows in silence, Huey by early 1935 was battling the Roosevelt administration with the same brand of invective he customarily used against his Louisiana enemies. In the Senate and on the radio—he made six broadcasts over NBC during the first three months of 1935—Huey sneered at "Franklin De-lah-no Rosy-felt," whom he nicknamed "Prince Franklin" and "Knight of the Nourmahal," the *Nourmahal* being a yacht, owned by the millionaire Vincent Astor, on which the president sometimes vacationed. Mayor Walmsley told of Huey saying to his cronies: "I have something on that son-of-a-bitch cripple in the White House that will keep him from doing anything against me. I know that he tours around in a boat with a degenerate."[33] But in public Huey sank no lower than castigating the president as a Wall Street tool who compared unfavorably with Hoover. "To get rid of the devil, did we get a witch?" he asked, adding: "With Hoover it was stupidity. With Roosevelt it is betrayal."[34]

Bestowing derisive nicknames was one of Huey's specialties, and several members of Roosevelt's cabinet joined his list of victims. Secretary of the Interior Harold Ickes became the "chinch bug of Chicago"; Secretary of Agriculture Henry Wallace was "Lord Cornwallace, the ignoramus of Iowa"; and Postmaster General Jim Farley became the "Nabob of New York." Also, Huey referred to General Hugh Johnson, former director of the National Recovery Administration, as "Sitting Bull Johnson, the oo-la-la of Oklahoma." Both Johnson and Ickes were acerbic personalities, willing to swap insults with the Kingfish. "Hitler couldn't hold a candle to Huey in the art of the old Barnum ballyhoo," Johnson exclaimed in a nation-wide radio broadcast. Ickes remarked at a press conference that Huey "has halitosis of the intellect." At a cabinet meeting later that day, Roosevelt told Ickes it was "the best thing that has been said about Huey Long."[35]

Of all the people close to the president, Huey most disliked Jim Farley, and considered him the most vulnerable. Besides being postmaster general, Farley still chaired the Democratic National Committee and was chief patronage broker in the Roosevelt administration. Nor did it escape Huey's notice that Farley was a longtime friend of one of the Kingfish's worst foes, John

P. "Bang Tail" Sullivan. Beginning in March of 1934, Long made public attacks on Farley, linking him to Sullivan the "dive keeper" and claiming that since Farley had recently accepted a twenty-dollar Stetson hat as a gift from someone involved in mail contracts, he was guilty of taking a bribe. Most men, Huey opined, can be bought "for $20, or they will not come at all. I think $20 is about Farley's size." [36]

More serious was his assault on Farley beginning February 11, 1935. In the Senate that day, Huey introduced a resolution calling for an investigation of the postmaster general–DNC chairman for various alleged misdeeds, including graft in the awarding of construction contracts, giving away sheets of commemorative postage stamps to friends (including the president, a stamp collector), and being involved in a race-track wire service. Farley, the Kingfish observed, has "slimy, roaming tentacles." Huey denied his attack on Farley was in retaliation for the Internal Revenue campaign against him. Of course it partly was, but his charge of graft had substance and deserved an investigation. When the Senate rejected his resolution by sixty-two to twenty, Huey commented on the contrast between allowing Farley "flagrantly to violate the law," while down in Richland Parish, Louisiana, "10 niggers were sent to the penitentiary for [stealing] one $2 yearling." [37]

From November of 1934 through July of 1935, Huey consolidated his dictatorship over Louisiana with four additional special sessions of the legislature. The November session lasted only five days but passed forty-four bills. Among these were measures creating what was facetiously called a "State Civil Service Commission" with authority over all police and fire departments in Louisiana; this commission, chaired by the governor and made up entirely of Long loyalists, including General Guerre of the Bureau of Criminal Identification, could arbitrarily hire and fire personnel "for the good of the community." (First to be fired was Alexandria's police chief, O'Malley, who had stood by while rotten eggs were thrown at a United States senator.) The national press paid more attention to the November session's Debt Moratorium Act, which provided for a two-year suspension on the payment of all previous debts—subject to approval by the state banking commissioner—except debts owed to governmental agencies. Another law emasculated parish and city tax assessors by empowering the state-appointed Louisiana

Tax Commission "to correct or change any and all assessments on property." While these and other power bills were jammed through without being read in full or debated at all, Huey sat on the dais of the Speaker of the House, then strode over to the senate chamber. The anti-Long minority of legislators watched it all in silence. "What's the use of arguing?" one was heard to say. Their opposition was confined to pushing nay buttons when votes were taken.[38]

For diversion during the hectic autumn of 1934, Huey again turned to LSU football. He understood little about the game, but the excitement and roar of the crowds drew him like a magnet. Also, leading the Tiger band was great fun. This year he involved himself more than previously in the football team's fortunes, for LSU enjoyed its best team in years, and Huey wanted identification with their string of victories. To the dismay of Coach Lawrence F. "Biff" Jones, the Kingfish informed sportswriters that LSU "has the best team in the country" and offered to prove it by having the Fighting Tigers play two other contenders for the national championship, Alabama and Minnesota, "both the same day." Was Huey joking? Perhaps so, but he did not smile when telling an assistant coach that "LSU can't have a losing team because that'll mean I'm associated with a loser."[39]

LSU was twice-tied but unbeaten going into the Vanderbilt game at Nashville on October 27. Huey, as he sometimes did, planned to travel with the team and band. This time he also announced: "No student should miss this trip because of lack of funds." By threatening the Illinois Central Railroad with raising tax assessments on their bridges in Louisiana, he persuaded the company to lower their round-trip fare from nineteen to six dollars. (Earlier in the season Huey had coerced the Ringling Brothers and Barnum and Bailey Circus into canceling a Saturday night performance in Baton Rouge that would have cut into attendance at LSU's home game against Southern Methodist. He had warned of a statute requiring "all animals" brought into Louisiana to be dipped for ticks, and pointed out the difficulty of dipping tigers and elephants.)[40]

Five special trains carried most of LSU's student body to Nashville, and all who needed money for the trip received a small loan from the Kingfish. Over four thousand made the journey. To discourage rowdiness along the way, Huey posted twenty-five state policemen on the trains. (Tennessee's Fish and

Game Commission notified Huey that his police would be considered deputy game wardens, responsible for guarding "whatever wild life you may see fit to import into our State.") Huey had a grand time leading the LSU band in a pregame downtown parade, then watching the Tigers beat Vanderbilt 29 to 0. Three weeks later he took another "Football Special" train, this time without many students, to Jackson, Mississippi, where LSU defeated Ole Miss. Prior to the game, Huey led a downtown parade to the state capitol, where an enthusiastic crowd of Mississippians joined him in a songfest. Governor Bennett Conner had been reluctant to join Huey's parade but finally did so, reported the New York *Times*, after "being pulled off the front porch of the mansion by a Long aide."[41]

Early in December, LSU dropped two close games in a row, to archrival Tulane and to Tennessee. The Kingfish's mood darkened. "Biff Jones may not be the worst coach around," Huey privately grumbled, "but he sure ain't the best." In mid-December, LSU played the season's last game, against Oregon in Tiger Stadium. At halftime, with LSU trailing 0 to 13, Huey strode to the Tiger dressing room ready to give a pep talk; Coach Jones ordered him out, and when Huey said something about being "sick and tired of losing and tying games," Jones announced his intention of resigning as soon as this game was over, regardless of the outcome. LSU came back in the second half to win 14 to 13, but now Huey had to find someone to prepare the Tigers for the 1935 season.[42]

The Kingfish promptly hired Bernie Moore, an assistant on Jones's staff, as the new head coach. Huey also named a new band director, Castro Carazo, and promised him all the money he needed to give LSU the biggest and best university band in the nation. Carazo, hitherto employed by Seymour Weiss as the Roosevelt Hotel's orchestra leader, had recently been summoned to Baton Rouge to compose a tune for the words to a song written by Huey and bearing the same title as his book—"Every Man a King." Huey looked forward to the next football season for stirring music as well as victories. In the summer of 1935, Carazo would be summoned to Huey's apartment high in the state capitol, to help the Kingfish compose a new song: "Touchdown for LSU." Huey anticipated hearing it played at the September 28 opening against Rice.[43]

Long's mixture of benevolence and heavy-handedness in dealing with LSU extended beyond the football stadium. During the November special legislative session, an angry student wrote a letter to the campus newspaper, the *Reveille*, complaining about the Kingfish's "joke" appointment of the football team's star running back, Abe Mickal, to the state senate. Huey had intended the appointment only as a burlesque, and Mickal—who in any case was underage and a resident of McComb, Mississippi—had politely declined the honor. The Kingfish was furious when he saw the letter, especially since the student editor who decided to print it, Jesse Cutrer, was a nephew of one of the legislators who had voted to impeach him as governor in 1929. "That lying uncle of his sold me out for forty dollars," Huey exclaimed. "That's *my* university and I'm not going to stand for any criticism from anybody out there." LSU's president, James M. Smith, summoned the *Reveille*'s staff and told them a faculty censor would be appointed to make sure no negative comments about Senator Long appeared in future issues. Smith claimed "a matter of principle" was involved. On that point twenty-six journalism students agreed: they signed a petition protesting censorship, and consequently were suspended from the university. Most later recanted and came back to LSU, but the seven who held out received anonymous funds for their enrollment in the School of Journalism at the University of Missouri.[44]

A final special session for 1934 was called "by Governor Allen" to meet from December 16 to Christmas Eve. Huey's addiction to power was growing worse. Already, no American politician had ever exercised so much authority over any part of the nation, but Huey did not consider his domination of Louisiana as yet complete. Therefore, this last legislative assemblage of the year transferred most of the remaining power (and with it, patronage) from local governments to the state—which meant to the Long organization. As a result, parish school boards could no longer hire, fire, or fix the salaries of schoolteachers without prior approval of a new State Budget Committee, headed by Governor Allen. All deputy sheriffs must now be approved by the Bureau of Criminal Identification. Most of the session's other thirty-three bills also eroded local self-government, including spite measures aimed specifically at the anti-Long strongholds of Baton Rouge and Alexandria. Act 23 provided "that in the parish in which the state capitol is situated," half the members of its police jury (the name for elected parish governments in Louisiana) would henceforth be appointed by the governor. As for the central Louisiana city where Huey had been so disrespectfully rotten-egged and stink-bombed the year before, a last-minute amendment to an otherwise benign bill declared vacant several municipal offices, including that of Alexandria's mayor. The governor was authorized to fill these "vacancies."[45]

As always, Huey was the directing force behind every bill at the December special session. But one of his least-known lieutenants, George M. Wallace, drafted most of the bills and thought up procedures for speeding them through. Huey had brought Wallace with him to Baton Rouge in 1928 as his chief legal assistant; Wallace continued in that role through the Allen administration, and in 1934 was given the title of assistant attorney general. Like many men near the Kingfish, Wallace came from Winn Parish. In fact he was one of "the wild Wallace boys," as old Hugh Long called them, who had caused little Huey to get the only spanking he ever received from his father. George Wallace, five years older than Huey, was one of Louisiana's best lawyers but periodically became incapacitated by liquor. Harley Bozeman gave a picturesque summary of an episode in Wallace's early career: "He'd just won $75,000 in a case at Shreveport, got drunk, fell out of the Brewster Building, his wife quit him, he was in the calaboose."[46]

Wallace's talents at designing legislation were put to use in the December session. In a last-minute amendment to an otherwise innocuous bill, he hid away a five-cents-per-barrel manufacturer's license tax on all petroleum refined in the state. Distinct from the severance tax, this was the same measure Huey had introduced in the 1929 legislature that impeached and almost removed him as governor. Now, however, the Kingfish was more powerful and adroit; Standard Oil's lobbyists in the capitol building did not realize that their huge refinery in Baton Rouge was about to be hit with this tax until the moment it passed. Long was twice pleased: the refinery tax would both provide a new source of revenue and satisfy his desire to get even with an old enemy.[47] Yet he had another motive, more important than revenue or revenge, in passing this tax. Within two weeks, by early January of 1935, Huey and Standard reached an accord by which Huey would arrange for the legislature, in a February special session, to rebate four fifths of the tax so long as Standard and the smaller refiners kept a pledge to use "at least eighty percent Louisiana oil" in their state refineries (previously, as little as 10 percent of the petroleum processed in Standard's Baton Rouge plant came from in-state wells). Huey now had some leverage, some control, over Standard Oil.[48] Control was always more important to him than money or revenge.

The special legislative sessions of 1934 and 1935 were events alien to the American political experience, and for that reason, as well as because of the presence of the colorful Kingfish, the nation's press took notice. Correspondents for major newspapers and magazines descended on Baton Rouge to gape at the "Longislature." They wrote of what they saw with varying admixtures of awe, levity, disgust, and apprehension. How could this be happening in America? Some tended to blame the Pelican State's troubled past for causing this dictatorship; according to one harsh opinion, "Louisiana is the rotten dog that bred the maggot."[49] But most visiting journalists were now raising another question: was there a real possibility that Huey Long would someday be president of the United States? On one point of speculation virtually all agreed: if the Kingfish ever did occupy the White House, he would try to run America as he was running Louisiana.

Huey endorsed that conclusion. What he was accomplishing in Louisiana would be "a pattern" for his presidency, he frankly said. Yet the charge of dictatorship irritated him, and he always denied he was one. Why should someone who merely carried out the wishes of the people be called a tyrant? Huey cited the re-election of most of his obedient legislators, and the popular majorities of up to seven to one for his constitutional amendments, as proof that his actions reflected popular demands—as well as the word of God. "There is no dictatorship in Louisiana," he explained. "There is a perfect democracy there, and when you have a perfect democracy it is pretty hard to tell it from a dictatorship." The nation's system did not yet measure up to Louisiana's, Huey added. "I believe in old-fashioned American democracy," he told Forrest Davis. "Only we've got to change it around some."[50]

As to how American democracy might be improved, Huey offered various suggestions. Wealth sharing was, of course, one way. But the political system itself could be brought closer to the people, he maintained, not by rewording the United States Constitution, but rather by a broader interpretation of some of that document's clauses. Huey was intrigued by the fact that although the Constitution says Supreme Court justices are to be appointed by the president with the consent of the Senate, it is silent on how many justices there shall be. If the Court, Huey reasoned, becomes "out of touch with what [is] necessary for the public at the time," then Congress itself might "make itself part of the Court," and in effect merge the legislative and judicial branches of government. The principle of separation of powers was foreign to Long's nature. As he had demonstrated in Louisiana, he was willing to preserve it in theory, but not in fact. Centralization of authority in the hands of a powerful executive who accomplished the general will was, to him, the only sensible way to conduct a government. This was, he said, "the principle of leadership."[51]

Leadership to the Kingfish meant setting the terms for everyone he dealt with—including an organized crime boss. In the spring of 1935, Huey met with Frank Costello (destined to become, in *Time's* words, "the most prominent gangster of the 1940s"). He invited Costello, whose New York City gambling enterprises were being shut down by the reform mayor Fiorello LaGuardia, to move his slot machine and handbook activities to New Orleans and its environs. Huey could guarantee police protection. In return, Costello later testified to a federal grand jury, the Long organization would get a substantial yearly fee. Costello readily accepted Long's terms and told his chief associate, Philip "Dandy Phil" Kastel, "to go down there and work the thing out."[52] In Louisiana it was the Kingfish, not the mob, who made an offer that could not be refused.

Inevitably, as Huey Long's Louisiana dictatorship and his seriousness about running for president both became clearer, he was compared with and to the notorious totalitarian rulers of that day: Stalin, Mussolini, and Hitler. Huey most resented being categorized with Hitler—"that son of a bitch"—whose anti-Semitism repelled him. He also dismissed, although not so contemptuously, comparisons with Stalin and Mussolini. With heavy humor, the Kingfish said he would never dose opponents with castor oil, as Mussolini's regime did. Instead, Huey chuckled, "I'll give them Tabasco, and then they'll like Louisiana."[53]

Huey's Share Our Wealth proposals convinced some of his critics that he was a Marxist-Leninist. But Huey did not think so, nor did the wealthy businessmen among his supporters. Early in 1935, *Business Week* magazine assured its readers that capitalism was alive and thriving in Long's Louisiana. Some of Huey's old enemies, such as Ruffin and Anne Pleasant, were convinced he was a Communist, and William Randolph Hearst's New York *American* insisted that Huey, along with Franklin D. Roosevelt, drew his inspiration from "the brain of an oriental fanatic, Nicolai Lenin."[54] Yet Huey always insisted he was actually trying to humanize capitalism so as to save the nation from communism.

In style, Huey was closer to fascism than communism. His Marxist critics and those fascists who admired him agreed on that. "HUEY LONG IS LOUISIANA'S HITLER" headlined the *Daily Worker*. V. F. Calverton and Benjamin Stolberg, two American Marxist writers, pointed out that Long, Hitler, and Mussolini made demagogic appeals to the same groups of people, including businessmen who viewed them as buffers against communism. Stolberg described Long as "an instinctive Machiavellian" who knew how "to exploit the misery and the confusion of the American people" without offering them a genuine (*i.e.*, Marxist) economic program.[55] On the other side of the political spectrum, ultrarightist Lawrence Dennis, an admirer of Hitler and author of *The Coming American Fascism*, saw in Huey "the nearest approach to a national fascist leader" the United States had so far produced. "It takes a man like Long to lead the masses," Dennis wrote. "I think Long's smarter than Hitler, but he needs a good brain trust. . . . He needs a Goebbels."[56] Gerald L. K. Smith had the same idea.

Yet the fascist label does not stick to Huey Long. No European political designation is appropriate. Share Our Wealth was the nearest thing to an ideology he propounded, but it was more a slogan than a system. Fascism connotes military expansionism, whereas Long's foreign policy—such as it was—consisted in letting the rest of the world alone. Even Norman Thomas, who called Huey a fascist, admitted that Louisiana's subservient government looked more like "circus-dogs jumping through hoops than [an] army . . . marching in goose step."[57]

Raw craving for power, for domination of all around him, was the one thing the Kingfish possessed that is essential for a dictator. Of that he had an abundance. But his egotism was freefloating, not anchored to any ideology. Raymond Gram Swing thought Huey might be a "forerunner of fascism" in America, although Swing understood that the fascist label itself did not belong on someone who had no fixed ideas other than belief in himself. Huey Long, wrote Swing, was "plain dictator." [58]

· 17 ·

RIDING THE PALE HORSE

The Great Depression, more traumatic than the one Huey Long was born in, still gripped the nation in 1935. As a true demagogue—and admitting he was one, by his definition—Huey envisioned millions of unhappy voters turning to him and his Share Our Wealth panacea in 1936, with more millions to follow in 1940. No American politician since Aaron Burr was so bold or crafty. Even Burr did not compare in ruthlessness and ambition. The Kingfish planned to rule the United States as president for sixteen years, and in the process destroy both the Democratic and Republican parties.[1]

During early 1935, however, Huey could not devote full attention to pursuit of the presidency because of happenings in Louisiana. His dictatorship was not complete enough for the state machine to function properly without him. Particularly troublesome was anti-Long activity in the capital city's East Baton Rouge Parish. His opposition there included hundreds of mostly upper-middle-class men and women who talked, sometimes openly, of armed revolt and assassination.

In late January a brief revolution did occur in Baton Rouge. A paramilitary organization of anti-Longites, the Square Deal Association, had been formed in more than a dozen parishes; among its members were ex-governors Parker and Pleasant, Mayor Walmsley of New Orleans, and Hilda Phelps Hammond, who joined the association's Woman's Division. Baton Rouge contained the largest Square Deal unit within the state. Huey was kept informed of its plans by Sidney Songy, a member who spied for the Bureau of Criminal Identification. Late on the afternoon of January 25, a mob of Square Dealers, three hundred of them armed, took possession of the East Baton Rouge Parish courthouse in reaction to the Long machine's firing of all parish employees. Members of the Woman's Division brought coffee and sandwiches, but some of them also carried guns.[2]

At Huey's direction, Governor Allen called out the Louisiana National Guard, imposed martial law throughout the parish, and placed Brigadier General Guerre, who also headed the BCI, in command. The parish and its city, by Guerre's proclamation, became the "First Military District." Typical of martial law decrees, crowds were forbidden to gather and civilians could not carry, transport, buy, or sell firearms within the district. But other restrictions were singularly harsh: a crowd was defined as "two or more people," and nothing could be published criticizing state officials. The ban applied to Baton Rouge's two daily newspapers, owned by the Manship family.[3]

The Square Dealers at the courthouse had dispersed by daybreak of January 26, as truckloads of militiamen began entering the city. About eight hundred troops were in Baton Rouge by noon, reinforced with units from the state police. By that time, in the capitol building, around which most of the guardsmen were assembled, Attorney General Porterie was conducting a hearing on Square Deal activities. Songy was the chief witness, and Senator Long did all the questioning. The informer swore he had direct knowledge of a Square Deal plot to murder the Kingfish and that the conspirators included East Baton Rouge Parish District Attorney John Fred Odom and other leading citizens. On the afternoon of the first day of Baton Rouge's military occupation, shortly after Porterie's (Huey's) hearing in the capitol adjourned, about one hundred armed Square Dealers gathered at the Baton Rouge airport. Yet they were not sure for what purpose they had come. Even the leaders only knew they had received short, urgent telephone messages from unidentified voices telling them to "get out to the airport."[4]

The "battle of the airport," shortly before sunset on January 26, was brief and almost bloodless. Within minutes after the Square Dealers drove up, five hundred guardsmen and state police were on the scene; their weapons included machine guns. Huey had finally overcome his reluctance to shed blood. Obviously, the BCI had obtained from Songy or someone else a Square Deal membership list, and the telephone calls had lured those who responded into a trap. Outnumbered five to one, all but a few Square Dealers surrendered after being barraged with tear gas. The rest, including the SD president, Ernest Bourgeois, escaped into nearby woods; Bourgeois later fled to Mississippi. The only casualty was a Square Dealer named George Alessi, who was shot but recovered. Shortly after the "battle" ended, two or three hundred angry spectators, including women and children, came to the airport and began shouting insults at the guardsmen and police. The protestors were dispersed by another volley of tear gas. General Fleming of the Louisiana National Guard summarized the Square Deal's inept revolt as "the kind of insurrection you found in the Latin American countries in the old days."[5]

Baton Rouge became sullenly quiet. Martial law lasted until July, although most troop units were removed in early February. Huey interrogated other witnesses when the hearing on Square Deal activities resumed on February 1. A former deputy sheriff named George "Red" Davis swore he had been offered ten thousand dollars to assassinate the Kingfish, and he implied that East Baton Rouge Parish Sheriff Robert L. Pettit was in on the plot. Davis, a marksman, said he once tried to shoot Huey Long from a great distance by using a rifle with telescopic sights, but became too nervous when the opportunity arrived. Songy previously testified that Square Deal conspirators had prepared to ambush Huey on the highway to New Orleans, at a place called "dead man's curve." Although Davis and Songy may not have been entirely truthful, and no indictments followed the hearing, Long's life undeniably was under increasing peril. Hodding Carter of Hammond wrote in March of 1935: "There are many sane, thoughtful citizens who believe that only through a .45 can the state regain its political and economic sanity."[6]

Two days after the rout of the Square Dealers, America's beloved humorist Will Rogers flew into Baton Rouge airport for an overnight stay in Louisiana's capital city. Rogers' most quoted saying was, "I never met a man I didn't like," but evidently he made an exception in Huey Long's case. The mail carrier who gave Rogers a ride from the airport to the Heidelberg Hotel told reporters that he asked Will what he thought of the Kingfish, but "I can't tell you what he said about Huey!" Rogers, interviewed in the Heidelberg's lobby, refused to answer the same question and instead signed autographs; when a small boy tried to get the humorist's attention by kicking his shins, Rogers took a piece of paper and wrote "Huey Long," with the comment: "Keep that, son, some day it may be valuable." Brigadier General Guerre, Baton Rouge's martial law commander, officially welcomed the famous visitor and invited him to inspect the troops next morning, but Rogers declined, saying he "did not want any plans made for him."[7]

With soldiers still guarding the capitol building, the legislature met briefly in February of 1935 and by concurrent resolution approved the tax reduction agreement Huey had signed with J. C. Hilton, president of Standard Oil of Louisiana.[8] More important was the special session Huey told Allen to call in April. At that session, thirty-four bills were introduced and passed with the usual whirlwind rapidity—thirty-two of them passed in thirty minutes, with only their titles being read. (It was Huey's custom to hold a "caucus" just before each special session to let pro-Long legislators at least know what the bills for which they were going to vote were about.) Among the more controversial measures introduced, one created a new state agency, the Bond and Tax Board, having the authority to approve or disapprove any loan, grant, or bond issue that any parish or municipal government wished to incur or receive; this bill obviously was designed to prevent anti-Long enclaves such as New Orleans or Baton Rouge from receiving additional federal help.[9]

Huey's first state-wide assault on freedom of the press came in another measure passed without debate during the April session—an act "creating a State Printing Board and defining its power and duties." This agency, its members all appointed by the governor, would solely determine which newspapers were eligible to be "the official printer" for governmental subdivisions in Louisiana, including parishes, municipalities, and school boards. As Hodding Carter observed, "For many small newspapers this legal printing meant the difference between survival and failure." Several of the most vehemently anti-Long weeklies in the state suddenly ceased discussing politics. One, the Hammond *Vindicator*, previously an advocate of armed revolution against the Kingfish, decided to "merge with the state administration" and received its anticipated reward from the State Printing Board.[10]

Two other bills, dealing with the conduct of elections, were so authoritarian that even Huey's obedient legislators seemed a bit uneasy. One of the acts set up in each parish a Board of Supervisors of Elections, with two of its three members to be appointed, and subject to removal, by the governor. That act was a preliminary to Act 28, which provided that each parish board of supervisors would, by majority vote, select all commissioners and poll watchers at every precinct. These acts applied only to primary elections; of course, since the early years of the twentieth century, Democratic primaries nearly always had decided who held public offices in Louisiana. Thus, the Long machine would now count all votes in the only elections that mattered. Huey had come to mistrust the voters. According to State Senator Harry Gilbert, an ally, Long said: "I'm always afraid of an election. You can't tell what will happen." Act 28 was designed to prevent any uncertainty. What had transpired in St. Bernard and Plaquemines parishes for years could now be done statewide. The act passed the House sixty-one to twenty-seven, the senate by twenty-nine to ten, and was dutifully signed by Governor Allen.[11]

Just before the House voted, something happened that had not occurred in recent sessions. An opposition member arose to speak. He was Mason Spencer of Madison Parish, the same bulky legislator who had helped restore order at the "Bloody Monday" meeting in 1929. Spencer knew he would be allowed little time, so he looked at Huey Long and said only a few words: "When this ugly thing is boiled down in its own juices, it disfranchises the white people of Louisiana. I am not gifted with second sight, nor did I see a spot of blood on the moon last night, but I can see blood on the polished marble of this capitol, for if you ride this thing through, you will travel with the white horse of death."[12]

"White men," Spencer thought it necessary to add, "have ever made poor slaves." Scattered applause from the galleries accompanied Spencer's last statement. The big representative was more perceptive than most of his anti-Long associates, and he was first among them to grasp an awful truth: Louisiana whites were now as politically helpless as blacks. Westbrook Pegler, a syndicated columnist observing the April session, also realized that these laws were "reducing to the political status of the Negro all of the white people . . . who oppose Der Kingfish."[13]

Actually, Huey Long was reducing *all* white Louisianians (because as voters all were at least potential foes) to the political equivalent of black people. An ironist might say Long was committed to racial equality, after a sort. Indeed, his urge to dominate everybody kept him from being a racist in the usual sense; viewed from his Jovian perspective, all humanity was inferior to the Kingfish. Lesser politicians might worry about public opinion, and about maintaining facades of honor, of truth, of dignity. He was above such trivialities. Huey was, as the essayist Ralph Waldo Emerson said of Napoleon, a *"Jupiter Scapin . . . a sort of scamp Jupiter."* [14]

It was Huey's custom to demean enemies by associating them with blacks. Examples of it abounded: Senator Ransdell was a "buddy" of the black Republican Walter Cohen; Dudley LeBlanc operated a crooked "nigger lodge" to make money off "dead coons"; Shreveport businessman Andrew Querbes once operated a "nigger" saloon and dive; John M. Parker's bodyguard, unlike the white gunmen who protected Huey, was "a little nigger" with a .22 rifle; Mayor Walmsley was involved in burying a Negro cadaver from Charity Hospital so that valuable property could be rezoned as a cemetery, and Walmsley also ate at the same table with a black congressman; Daniel D. Moore, a former *Times-Picayune* managing editor who was briefly internal revenue collector for Louisiana, had presided over a New Orleans clinic "to treat the colored for venereal diseases . . . and established many colored supporters and customers throughout the city." Huey also unfavorably compared the New Orleans Cotton Exchange with "any nigger crap game." [15]

The Kingfish's ultimate way of identifying white enemies with blacks was to say, or at least insinuate, that they had African blood. From 1910 until 1970, Louisiana's legal distinction of race relied upon the *State* v. *Treadaway* decision, which said a person was "colored" who had *any* "negro blood pure or mixed . . . no matter what may be the proportions of the admixture, so long as the negro blood is *traceable.*" [16] The knowledge that interracial sex had been flagrant in Louisiana's early history, and the probability that thousands of light-skinned Creoles of color had passed into the "white" population during the late nineteenth and early twentieth centuries, made questions about ancestry even more explosive than in other southern states. A Louisiana family of the 1930s would not face the prospect of falling into the pariah caste if one of its members, living or dead, were accused of the vilest crimes. But because this was a time of intense racism—of segregation and disfranchisement at its apogee—the charge of even a tinge of black ancestry could prove devastating to the most patrician of white families. Pollution of blood was not to be washed away.

Reckless as he was, Huey did not often resort to asserting or even hinting that a foe had "colored" blood, but he did so in the case of a principal owner of the *Times-Picayune*, Alvin Howard, whom Huey nicknamed "Kinky" Howard because of his nappy black hair. Huey also referred to Leonard Nicholson, another stockholder and executive at the newspaper, as "Liverwurst" Nicholson, presumably because his face was darkly tinged. (Once, in the Senate, Huey sneered that "the *Times-Picayune* . . . claims to be a paper for white supremacy, but one of the leading executives . . . is part negro." He did not specify whether he meant Howard or Nicholson.) According to Carleton Beals, Huey in a New Orleans radio address also made racial insinuations about the family of Hilda Phelps Hammond. At least one of Huey's aides cautioned him to stop saying such things because "he would be killed." [17]

In July of 1935, Huey decided another special legislative session was needed to nail down his Louisiana power base. It turned out to be the last session he would live through. Instead of taking the Washington–New Orleans train, he went by airplane. Flying made Huey uneasy, but he was trying to grow accustomed to it, for he had decided that in 1936 he would become the first campaigner in American history to tour the nation by air. Already he had ordered a private plane built for that purpose, one especially equipped with loudspeakers, so that as he descended from the clouds a city could be told Huey P. Long was about to land and speak. He planned to visit all forty-eight states. [18]

The July session lasted only five days. Twenty-five bills were passed, none being debated. The minority opposition, shrunken by desertion to no more than one fourth of either chamber, did not bother to vote on most roll calls. Most of Huey's former foes who now drifted into his camp were doing so not because they had been "bought," to use one of the Kingfish's favorite words, but because they knew their parishes or districts would get nothing unless peace was made with the Kingfish. As the Abbeville *Meridional* pointed out, this session witnessed a "completing" and a "tightening" of Long's dictatorship. Ironically, it assembled shortly after night had fallen on July 4, Independence Day.[19]

By Act 25, the state Civil Service Commission's authority over hiring and firing was extended to all parish and municipal employees so that these jobs could be removed—in the bill's mocking words—"from political considerations." (Schoolteachers were exempted from this act, but their jobs and salaries were determined by the State Budget Committee, whose power was increased by another act.) Yet another act set up a State Board of Censors, appointed by the governor, with power to prevent any motion picture—including newsreels—from being shown in Louisiana; local governments were specifically forbidden to approve or disapprove of films (twenty-eight representatives and four senators voted against this bill, the highest nay vote recorded at the session). Other measures passed during the July session were designed to bankrupt Mayor Walmsley's administration by forbidding New Orleans to collect real estate, license, or other taxes.[20]

Within days, New Orleans' Old Regular ward bosses capitulated to Huey. By then the city was against the wall, unable to pay its bills, levy taxes, or borrow money. On July 12, thirteen of the seventeen bosses caucused after secret negotiations with Long, and announced they had joined his organization; they also asked Mayor Walmsley to resign. "Turkey Head" refused, saying, "I will never let a draft dodger like Long run me out of office." On July 29, the four remaining ward bosses surrendered to the Kingfish, and two days later the city's council, by a three-to-two vote, passed ordinances stripping the mayor of all authority. Walmsley, wrote a commentator, kept only "his title and office furniture."[21]

In return, the Kingfish promised to see that the state bailed the city out of its financial distress, and he told the ward bosses they would be permitted a role, with some jobs to distribute, in his organization. But when they gathered in his Roosevelt Hotel suite, Huey let them know their place by addressing them as "you birds."[22] By July's end, Huey Long held New Orleans in the same iron grip he had over the rest of the state. Now he could concentrate on Washington affairs and his pursuit of the presidency.

That pursuit had been intensifying since the beginning of

1935. Huey's plans for the next year's presidential race were not yet complete, and rightly so; he understood that some options had to be kept open and that unforeseen developments might require changes in tactics. But his strategy's broad design was clear.

He would offer himself as a candidate at the 1936 Democratic convention. Roosevelt could not be denied renomination, Huey knew that, but he expected to have a substantial number of delegates from the Deep South, and perhaps from some of the Plains States as well. And whatever his delegate strength might be, he was certain to make it a tumultuous convention with acrimony aplenty and massive press and radio coverage of himself and Share Our Wealth. What then? After Roosevelt's nomination for a second term, Huey would announce the formation of a third party, free of domination by Wall Street and dedicated to ending the Great Depression ("Roosevelt's Depression," he enjoyed calling it) by redistributing the wealth of America—a principle supported by the Bible, by every philosopher whose name Huey could think of, and by common sense. The Republicans, he anticipated, would run Hoover or some other "old mossback." But with the nation's liberal majority divided between the Democratic and Share Our Wealth parties, Huey expected a Republican victory in the electoral college.[23]

The Kingfish was uncertain about who would become the third party's candidate in 1936. It might not be he himself, for he was under no delusion that a Share Our Wealth ticket had a realistic chance of taking the White House. But if not Huey Long, the candidate would have to be a maverick liberal of national reputation: Senator Wheeler perhaps, or Borah, or Norris. And Huey expected other dissident leaders—Coughlin, Townsend, Reno—to join the crusade. He was not ruling out his own candidacy; on that point it was too early to decide. In any case he expected to be the headline campaigner, touring the nation in his airplane, and it was his fondest hope that the Share Our Wealth ticket would draw off enough Democratic votes to hand the election to the Republicans. Assuming that happened (and it was a large assumption), then in 1940, after four more years of depression, Huey Long, at age forty-six, would—according to his scenario—win the Democratic nomination and the White House. As his mostly favorable biographer T. Harry Williams conceded, Long "was willing to let the country suffer for four years so that he could then save it."[24]

Leaders of the Democratic party grew increasingly fearful that Huey's strategy might work. (A secret public-opinion poll authorized by the Democratic National Committee in the spring of 1935, conducted for the purpose of determining how much of a threat Huey Long posed, found that approximately 11 percent of America's voters preferred the Kingfish over FDR or a Republican candidate; DNC chairman Farley believed that Huey, on a third-party ticket, might garner as many as six million votes and thereby "have the balance of power in the 1936 election.") "This country was never under a greater menace," exclaimed New Dealer Hugh Johnson in a CBS address on March 4, 1935, referring to the likely political alliance of Long and Father Coughlin. Roosevelt himself kept publicly silent about the Kingfish, although his private views were well known. The president, having unleashed Internal Revenue investigators on Huey, even considered placing Louisiana under federal military occupation. He shelved the idea because such action would surely have revived bitter memories of Reconstruction across the South.[25] But under certain circumstances—if, for example, Congress voted approval—Long, had he lived, might have been deposed from power in Louisiana by federal force.

Roosevelt's most adroit response to the Kingfish was his sponsorship of the Wealth Tax Act of 1935, which sharply raised federal income taxes at the top levels. The increase brought little additional revenue but did soak the very rich with a high surtax, and this approach could be portrayed as, in the president's words, an effort "to equalize the distribution of wealth." More candidly, FDR used the phrase "steal Long's thunder" in a conversation with Raymond Moley of the New Deal's Brain Trust.[26] Huey at first expressed delight at the president's tax message— "I just wish to say, 'Amen!'"—but soon had second thoughts. Three days later the Kingfish read into the *Congressional Record* his letter to the president challenging FDR to endorse (as he knew Roosevelt would not) the entire Share Our Wealth plan. "My elimination from politics would be the immediate and sure result," Huey informed the president; moreover, "loud will be my praise" even if "you . . . continue to oppose me in the Louisiana political arena with all the weapons and sinews which your Public Treasury now affords my enemies."[27]

With the next year's presidential race in mind, Huey began making personal appearances in various American cities. Nearly always he spoke to large and enthusiastic crowds. Doubtless some came merely for entertainment or to see a "dictator" in the flesh. Yet the Kingfish was more confident than ever of his ability to mesmerize. When Senator Wheeler, who tried to stay on good terms with both FDR and Long, heard Huey say about Roosevelt, "I'm going to beat that son of a bitch," the Montanan expressed doubt. "You've never seen the crowds I get," Huey assured him. "But Huey, they come out to see you as a curiosity," Wheeler pointed out. "Yes," Huey agreed. "But when they get there—I get 'em!"[28]

Ten thousand crowded in and around the Georgia capitol building to hear or just catch a glimpse of the Kingfish when he visited Atlanta in February of 1935. He was "in all his glory," marveled the *Constitution*. A reporter from St. Louis, watching his performance, wrote: "He made them laugh, made them cry, and he made them cheer. Time after time his demands for a redistribution of wealth were greeted with wild rebel yells." No rebel yells sounded a month later when Huey spoke in Philadelphia, but the sixteen thousand who packed the city's Convention Hall loudly applauded and cheered his remarks. Next on Huey's speaking schedule was Columbia, South Carolina, where he had a mixed reception; pro-Roosevelt students from the state university annoyed him by unfurling banners that read "We Love Our President" and "Too Much Hooey." The Kingfish shouted, "Don't hold that up back there so people can't see me!"[29]

In April the Iowa State Fair grounds at Des Moines became the test site for Huey's Share Our Wealth rhetoric in the Midwest. He seemed more than satisfied with the result. The enthusiastic crowd heard Milo Reno introduce him as "the hero whom God in his goodness has vouchsafed to his children." At one point in Huey's speech, amidst Biblical quotations and thimble-rigged statistics, he became so worked up that he lapsed from his resolve not to curse in public. "If you can't understand this," he exclaimed, "just shut your damned eyes and believe it." The audience did not seem to mind, and as he left the platform the Kingfish told reporters, "I could take this state like a whirlwind."[30]

Reports of his large crowds and growing radio audience—he was becoming almost a regular on NBC—gave jitters not only to the Roosevelt administration, but to many other observers, of varied political persuasions, who knew what Huey Long had done in Louisiana. The dictator of an American state was running for president, and although his chances still appeared remote, his boundless drive and eerie magnetism were becoming more evident as his national support grew.

"One simply turns away in disgust," editorialized the Charlotte *Observer* "at the thought of [Huey Long in the White House] and yet . . . if the wave of this man's popularity continues, there is no way to estimate the strength and hold and pull upon the people of this country he might eventually develop." Senator Kenneth McKellar of Tennessee told Huey to his face that "many things have happened to the United States since our government was established, but nothing that would be so unspeakable as to have at the head of this nation a man who has the venom and the hatred and the malice toward everyone who disagrees with him that the Senator from Louisiana has." A prominent Texan wrote the President: "I have seen his machine develop into what it is today—from nothing—and I venture to predict that unless he is dealt with summarily, the United States is going to have the first real trouble since 1865." [31]

The real trouble about the Kingfish was one of misdirected talent, of dire character flaws. "No one can tell," wrote Raymond Moley, "what services he could have rendered his state and nation had he chosen to use that mind well." Admirers and detractors agreed that he was a natural leader. H. G. Wells called him "a Winston Churchill who has never been to Harrow." A closer analogy would be to call Huey Long a Theodore Roosevelt without a moral compass.

"I have never known a mind," Moley said of the Kingfish, "that moved with more clarity, decisiveness, and force." Moley was fascinated by him, and Huey, flattered by an Ivy League professor's attention, spent some hours conversing with Moley. "I implored Huey to rise above demagoguery and use his great capacities to act like a statesman." The plea had no effect; Huey demurred, claiming that he "sought no personal gain" in his actions. The tragedy of Huey Long, Moley concluded, was "the deliberate squandering of his talents for tawdry ends . . . the enrichment of his shoddy friends and . . . petty revenge upon his enemies." [32]

Another of Huey's uneasy admirers who tried to change him was Senator Wheeler. It was Huey's habitual self-puffery that distressed Wheeler the most. The Montana Democrat decided to be blunt with the Kingfish, saying (in private), "You disgust your own friends with your boasting." Huey paused before replying, then confessed a sad truth about himself. "The only pleasure I get out of life is boasting," he told Wheeler. "And now you want to take that away from me! When you stop to think of where I've come from and what I've got to do—don't you think I have a right to boast?" Huey's old adversary Thomas O. Harris suspected, as did Senator Wheeler, that the Kingfish was a driven, unhappy man.[33]

The congressional session of 1935, lasting from early January until late August, was more protracted and wordy than any previous Congress in American history. This was the time of the "Second New Deal": Social Security, the Wealth Tax Act, the National Labor Relations Board (Wagner Act), and the biggest jobs-for-the-unemployed relief program ever enacted, the Works Progress Administration. In part, the leftward shift of Roosevelt's administration was a political maneuver to blunt the attacks of Huey Long and others who said the New Deal was not doing enough to help the poor.[34]

Huey opposed most of the Second New Deal legislation. Some of his criticisms, especially of Social Security, were valid. It imposed a regressive tax on laborers' salaries and excluded from coverage workers who would need old-age pensions the most, such as farm laborers. But the Kingfish also resorted to contradiction and hypocrisy: at the same time that he adjured the federal government to assume more of Social Security's cost, he denounced this and other Second New Deal measures as undermining states' rights by investing too much power in the central government. Louisiana would not submit to federal dictatorship, the state's dictator warned. "Our people will remain free."[35]

Huey's avalanche of words takes up more pages in the 1935 *Congressional Record* than the combined remarks of any three other members of either house. In previous sessions he had used the filibustering tactic, but now it became almost his trademark. His tendency to interrupt other senators with questions and comments, sometimes off the subject, grew chronic. His obstructionist, delaying tactics against New Deal legislation may have been promoted in part by spitefulness, but publicity over radio and in the press was surely his chief motive. Some senators' orations could empty the visitors' galleries, but when word spread in the Capitol that the Kingfish had begun to speak or was about to do so, the Senate galleries promptly filled and people lined up outside, waiting their turn for what was considered the best free show in Washington.[36]

Even at that, the galleries thinned toward the latter part of Huey's June 12 filibuster. It lasted fifteen and a half hours, not ending until almost four the next morning. (Robert La Follette, Sr., had set the Senate record with an eighteen-hour filibuster in 1908, but thirty quorum calls had given "Fighting Bob" respite. Huey was allowed only two ten-minute quorum calls during his ordeal; he made a beeline for the men's room when it was over.) During this filibuster, Huey frequently got harassing questions from other senators. Nipping at Huey was now customary; ever since March, at Majority Leader Robinson's instigation, the Kingfish had been receiving payment in kind for his assaults on the administration and on fellow senators. His colleagues' counterattacks continued until adjournment in late August. "Long was nagged and worried," Raymond Moley observed, "like a wild boar among dogs."[37]

Huey was almost never equaled in sarcasm or ridicule, but by session's end he had sustained some hard bites. When he predicted Senator Robinson's defeat in the following year's Arkansas election, the majority leader said it would be "a godsend" to leave the Senate, if being reelected meant he had to continue listening to and looking at Huey Long. Senator Josiah Bailey of North Carolina called Huey's recently composed song, "Every Man a King," a "national hymn for himself" and compared the Kingfish to a "worthless fice [dog]" that "manages to extoll himself in his own esteem by . . . barking! barking!" The galleries were warned frequently for laughing at Senator Long's witticisms, but one day Senator Barkley remarked, "When people go to the circus they ought to be allowed to laugh at the monkey." Senator Lewis Schwellenbach of Washington organized a band of freshman senators who resolved to badger the Kingfish at every opportunity. "We are not going to let him continue to use the Senate," announced Schwellenbach, "as a medium for making himself the fascist dictator of America." Mild-mannered Senator Henry Ashurst of Arizona called Huey "an apostle of despair" and warned him of what happened to the Greek poet Aeschylus, who was killed by a turtle dropped from the sky by an eagle. Let us hope, said Ashurst, "that the American eagle will not be required to drop something upon the head of the Senator from Louisiana."[38]

Only in the Senate did Huey Long discuss foreign policy. In speeches elsewhere he never mentioned the subject, for the rest of the world held no interest for him. He actually boasted of having "never stepped outside the confines of the United States," and said he "probably never will go abroad." In Senate speeches and votes, Huey was unreservedly isolationist and protectionist. If there was any public issue in which Long's stance reflected genuine conviction, it was this one. He said that both the Spanish-American War and America's involvement in World War I had been murderous frauds perpetrated in the interests of Wall Street, and he castigated American imperialism in Latin America for the same reason. He feared another world war was coming and that the United States "by design" would be brought into it. "Get out of Europe! Get out of Asia!" Huey implored. He opposed a naval appropriations bill because "I would prefer to vote this billion dollars to feed the starving rather than for more battleships to kill somebody."[39]

Nor did he want other nations to have influence in American affairs, or to sell their products here. Early in 1935 he opposed United States membership in the World Court, an international tribunal of little authority. "I do not intend to vote for this infernal thing," he told the Senate, "so that Señor Ab Jap or some other something . . . can pass upon our controversies." In one foreign country, however, the Kingfish became something of a hero. He had praised Paraguay for standing up to Rockefeller's Standard Oil Company, which he claimed was backing Bolivia in the current war between the two South American nations. In gratitude, the Paraguayans named a captured jungle stronghold "Fort Senator Long."[40]

Huey's last appearance in the Senate came on August 26, the day the 1935 congressional session adjourned. The day began with routine business, including laying aside a petition from the Women's Committee of Louisiana "praying for an investigation" of Senators Long and Overton (Mrs. Hammond's group had submitted that petition on every Monday Congress met during the past year). Presently, the matter of a deficiency appropriations bill that included the starting costs of Social Security came up, and Huey Long commenced what would be his last filibuster, his

last Senate speech. Pacing up and down, discoursing on whatever came to mind (including Louisiana's "warm, nice, enticing
climate"), refusing to yield except for questions, he talked until
midnight—the time set for adjournment sine die. He thereby
prevented passage of the bill. Because of Long's obstructionism,
President Roosevelt had to divert WPA and NRA funds in order
to begin Social Security.[41]

"I am . . . just having a high-heeled good time," Huey informed
his colleagues, who clearly were not, during his final Senate appearance. He warned senators that some of *them* would be
turned out by the voters, but "there is not enough power under
the canopy of heaven to beat me in an election to come back to
this body. . . . I challenge the whole dad-gummed kit and barrel
of the Democratic party to come down and beat me." In passing,
he referred to the House of Representatives as "435 dumbbells."
Huey went on to make his habitual disclaimer about personal
ambitions, saying, in nearly the same words he had used at Hot
Wells in 1919, that he did not care about a political future: "It
does not mean a thing under the living sun to me. Public office
means nothing." But at one point the Kingfish said something
oddly clashing with his expressed confidence about returning
for next year's session of Congress: "I may not be back here. This
may be my swan song, for all I know."[42]

313

· 18 ·

ORCHIDS AND WILDFLOWERS

Two days after Congress adjourned in 1935, Huey and two body-guards left Washington for New York, where on August 30 he made a radio speech over WOR and marked his forty-second birthday in his free hotel suite at the Hotel New Yorker. The hotel sent up a big cake, along with the vocalist Lila Lee, who sang "Happy Birthday, Dear Huey." Later in the evening the Kingfish went to an uptown supper club, where the radio star Phil Baker came to his table. Baker introduced his pretty eighteen-year-old niece, Cleanthe Carr, to the senator. Miss Carr, an aspiring artist, took a napkin and drew a good likeness of Huey. Admiring the sketch and the girl, Huey asked her to do the illustrations for a new book he had authored, and she agreed.[1]

Early the next morning, August 31, Huey and his bodyguards boarded a train at Grand Central Station for Pennsylvania. During the day he spoke at a Long family reunion near the town of Lebanon and claimed kinship with everybody there, declaring he was "a Pennsylvania Dutchman who, by accident of parental migration, had been born in the South." He added they were all related to "a famous Revolutionary soldier named Huey Long." Then it was on to Harrisburg, where he signed an agreement with the Telegraph Press concerning publication of *My First Days in the White House*, the book he had recently dictated to a secretary.[2]

A utopian novel set in the near future (1937), *My First Days* revealed even less about the real Huey Long than did *Every Man a King*, and in its bland portrayal of the "revived America" a Long presidency would usher in, the work was hardly prophetic.

314

Not even Huey's sardonic wit came through, except for one of his cabinet appointments: he offered ex-president Franklin D. Roosevelt a position FDR was "qualified to fill"—that of secretary of the navy. The book ended with President Long, his program enacted, listening to the cheers of a grateful nation.[3]

From Pennsylvania, Huey's train sped west toward St. Louis, with two stenographers and an editor from the Telegraph Press riding along, working intensely to ready the manuscript for publication. Sunday morning, September 1, the Kingfish changed trains in St. Louis for Oklahoma City, where he was scheduled to make a Labor Day address the following day. Huey almost missed his connection; the station was packed with St. Louisans who had heard that Huey Long was passing through. Arriving in Oklahoma City late Sunday, suffering from hay fever and lack of sleep, Huey managed to revive with a good night's rest. The next day he visited briefly with K. W. Dawson, the now-retired produce wholesaler who had given him a salesman's job back in 1912; he also rode in a Labor Day parade and spoke to a large, applauding crowd at the Oklahoma State Fair grounds. As at Des Moines and elsewhere, Huey once again compared the Democratic and Republican parties to "High Popalorum" and "Low Popahirum"—a mythical patent medicine sold under two labels, although the ingredients of both versions were identical. He also predicted that if Roosevelt and Hoover "or anybody like them" were nominated, "you're going to have another candidate." Many in the crowd responded with a shout often heard in Louisiana: "Pour it on 'em, Huey!"[4]

Leaving Oklahoma City on Labor Day afternoon, Huey and his bodyguards took a southbound train for Dallas, then drove to Shreveport, where he spent the night. Next morning, September 3, Huey rode to Baton Rouge in a state police car. He briefly visited LSU to watch the football team practice, then went to his apartment high in the capitol building and talked far into the night with Governor Allen and George Wallace, Huey's legal adviser.[5] Obviously, another legislative session was in the offing.

Huey remained in the capital until Thursday, September 5, preparing his bills for the session he had decided would begin that weekend. When questioned by reporters he remained noncommittal, saying (with as straight a face as he could manage) that "Oscar hasn't made up his mind" whether a session would be called. Thursday afternoon the Kingfish ate a late lunch in

315

the Heidelberg Hotel's coffee shop, then read an article about his career, written by Hermann Deutsch, in the current *Saturday Evening Post*. Later, Huey's bodyguard Murphy Roden arrived in a big Cadillac to chauffeur him to New Orleans. From his Roosevelt Hotel suite that evening, Huey made a three-hour broadcast over WDSU, blasting his Louisiana foes—particularly the five congressmen who had been "bought" by Roosevelt—and calling the president "a faker" whom he would not believe under oath. Then, for the first time in weeks, Huey spent the night with his family at their Audubon Boulevard residence.[6]

The following morning the Kingfish went to the Roosevelt Hotel and remained there for the next twenty-four hours, meeting with Long machine leaders from various parishes. Most of their talk concerned local matters, but the question of whom the organization would run for governor in 1936 also was discussed (the state constitution limited Allen to one term). Apparently, Huey had not yet decided on Allen's successor. At ten o'clock in the morning of Saturday, September 7, the announcement came that a special legislative session—the seventh in thirteen months—would commence that evening. Huey stayed in New Orleans until midafternoon, playing golf and discussing presidential campaign finances with Seymour Weiss. Then he left for Baton Rouge and the opening of the session.[7]

Governor Allen's call was couched in broad terms, so that bills or amendments Huey might think of at the last minute could be added. But of the twenty-one objectives listed, three were of special interest: the first item on the agenda proposed "to rearrange any of the judicial districts," the eleventh "to provide for the registration of arms and weapons," and the seventeenth "to legislate for the preservation and protection of the powers reserved to the State of Louisiana . . . by the Tenth Amendment to the Constitution of the United States." Number one was, in Huey's thinking, the least important—his leaders in St. Landry and Evangeline parishes had asked for this bill in order to gerrymander Judge B. Henry Pavy out of his seat. (Pavy was almost the only district judge in Louisiana who remained openly hostile to Long's machine.) The weapons registration bill was prompted by Huey's increasing concern about armed revolt and assassination attempts. It would require the owners of automatic weapons, gas grenades, and sawed-off shotguns or rifles to register such possessions with General Guerre's Bureau of

Criminal Identification. The BCI would have the power to dis-approve ownership. Huey denied he planned to amend the bill and make Louisianans register all firearms, but many believed this was his goal.[8]

Had it not been for Huey's perceived need to assert Louisi-ana's "powers" under the Tenth Amendment to the United States Constitution, this session probably would not have been called. Having solidified his dictatorship over the state, the only legal and political threats Huey faced were from the federal govern-ment, not the least of which was the wooing away of his support-ers with jobs. The vaguely worded Tenth Amendment provides that "powers not delegated to the United States by the Consti-tution . . . are reserved to the States," and on this provision the Kingfish decided to pin his efforts to block New Deal spending in Louisiana.

At Huey's behest, Wallace drafted a bill forbidding, within the state, any federal official or employee from disbursing "any pub-lic funds appropriated or made available by the Congress" if, in the opinion of Louisiana's government, such spending en-croached upon states' rights. Violators could be sentenced to twelve months in jail. Wallace later said he told the Kingfish the bill was unconstitutional, but Huey replied: "I don't give a damn. I want you to draw it up anyway." The Washington *Post* considered the bill to be "the broadest and boldest defiance of federal authority since the Civil War."[9] Huey apparently viewed it simply as a delaying tactic. He had arranged to have the 1936 state Democratic primaries, including his senatorial race, moved up to January, only four months away. He expected by litigation to tie up federal funds in Louisiana until after that election.

After the Old Regular's capitulation in July, Huey's Louisiana enemies had no organization worthy of the name. The militants among them were now convinced it would take either federal intervention or assassination to topple the Kingfish. Even armed revolt seemed an unlikely solution—the Square Deal's patheti-cally failed uprising in Baton Rouge discouraged further activ-ity along those lines. Also, as one of Long's veteran foes ad-mitted, the majority of voters probably still approved of the Kingfish, even though their right to remove him by the ballot box had been taken away.[10]

The minority of Louisianans who still defied Huey in 1935

were mostly middle-to-upper class, yet they seemed to have little else in common, and no program at all besides opposition to Long. More than anything else, the anti-Longites were united by fear. The Kingfish's power and control over their lives was steadily growing. Sometimes it seemed that he knew every person in the state, foe as well as friend. His face and his name were ubiquitous—on bridges, highway markers, dedication tablets, in the newspapers, and most of all on posters affixed to buildings, trees, and utility poles. Many nights his voice blared out of the radio for hours on end. In becoming the master of Louisiana, wrote Robert M. Shaw, Huey "had not only beaten down all who had opposed him but had made them afraid." [11]

Late in July of 1935, while Huey was still in Washington, hundreds of anti-Longites gathered for a two-day meeting at the De Soto Hotel in New Orleans. Four of the five pro-Roosevelt Louisiana congressmen were present, along with Mayor Walmsley, ex-governors Sanders and Parker, and the old newsman Thomas O. Harris. Some of Huey's henchmen were also in the hotel with a hidden microphone, and they made what purported to be a recording of his enemies' conversations. On August 9, Senator Long read into the *Congressional Record* an alleged transcript of that recording, mailed to him by Seymour Weiss. Assassinating Huey Long was part of the conference's agenda, according to the transcript. "I would draw a lottery to go out and kill Long," said one unidentified participant. "It would take only 1 man, 1 gun, and 1 bullet." Another voice (according to Huey's reading of the transcript) declared: "I haven't the slightest doubt but that Roosevelt would pardon anyone who killed Long." [12]

The De Soto Hotel conference indeed had participants who mentioned assassination. But as Hodding Carter, who was there, later wrote: "The 'plotting' was limited to such hopefully expressed comments as 'Good God, I wish somebody would kill the son of a bitch.' " The actual business of the conference, as Huey must have known, involved nonlethal matters: deciding whom to put up as candidates in the next January's hopeless election and, more optimistically, presenting a show of anti-Long unity to the Roosevelt administration, so as to encourage the president and the Democratic Congress to do more toward combatting Longism in Louisiana. [13]

By the time Huey's legislature gathered on the evening of September 7, his enemies had reason to believe the federal government, in the not-too-distant future, might decisively intervene in their state. That such an event would uncomfortably resemble Reconstruction seemed to matter little; most anti-Longites in Louisiana looked forward to federal intervention, including military occupation, if that was what it took to get rid of Huey Long. Their attitude resembled that of the White League during Reconstruction itself, when the state's white minority had made it clear they preferred rule by United States troops to government by a hated carpetbagger-black regime. The De Soto Hotel conferees apparently were ready to echo a phrase from one of Major Hearsey's editorials in the Shreveport *Times* of 1874, that "Louisiana must be a *free state* or a military camp."[14]

At the recent session of Congress, in a last-minute action, the Speaker of the House had appointed a seven-member committee "to investigate expenditures of candidates for the House of Representatives, and for other purposes." Not until the next day was it revealed that "other purposes" meant a congressional probe of Huey Long's regime to determine whether Louisiana had a representative form of government as guaranteed by Article IV of the United States Constitution. This investigation, moreover, was not to be some feeble, Overton-style hearing in New Orleans—it would be a formidable inquiry conducted in Washington. When Huey learned what was up, he exclaimed, "I don't care."[15] But he had to be worried, because if as a result of the hearing Congress decided to ask the president to intervene in Louisiana by whatever means necessary, FDR probably would do so, and with relish. At the least, much of Huey's time and energy would be diverted from the 1936 presidential race.

More than federal intervention, the Kingfish feared assassination. Yet to him a potential fate as bad as or worse than being killed was the loss of center stage, and with it control of all around him. That would be a living death. A *Christian Science Monitor* editor, after interviewing him during the summer of 1935, understood that Huey Long had become a victim of himself, and suggested that "pity was more in order than condemnation, pity for his fears and for his tense unhappiness in the grip of the forces which controlled him."[16]

Huey's worry over the odds he faced in his struggle with President Roosevelt had begun to pierce what Russell Owen called "the armor of his self-esteem." Also, apprehension of violent death, as he came to Baton Rouge for what would be the last time, weighed more heavily upon him than before. Prior to leaving Washington, Huey told Senator Vic Donahey: "They'll get me yet." Senator Harry Byrd recalled Huey saying of his Louisiana enemies, "Those people are determined to kill me, and I'm not going to live through it." On the last night he spent with his family, Huey spoke to his wife of a premonition that he would soon be murdered. Yet in public places his bodyguards were seldom able to keep up with his nervous, darting pace: "Nobody could walk in front of him," an aide recalled. Nor would he wear the bulletproof vest that was given him. Earle Christenberry, his secretary, heard Huey say, "I don't need no goddam bulletproof vest." [17]

On Saturday evening, September 7—the session's first night—Huey became enraged at the sight of elderly Thomas O. Harris, who was sitting with friends at the press table in the House of Representatives. Long cursed Harris, Harris cursed back, and the Kingfish's bodyguard George McQuiston slapped the old man, who was then taken to jail and booked as drunk and disorderly. Otherwise, the evening was quiet. All the bills Huey wanted were introduced by number and title, and after the customary suspension of rules, all were immediately referred to the House Ways and Means Committee. Among them was the bill that became Act 3, shifting St. Landry into a judicial district with three pro-Long parishes (Acadia, Lafayette, and Vermilion) in order to prevent Judge Pavy's reelection. [18]

Judge Pavy had held his seat for twenty-five years. The Pavy family was one of the oldest and most influential in St. Landry Parish, but during the judge's first campaign, in 1910, the opposition had spread rumors of "pollution of blood": that in Henry Pavy's wife's family line there was a taint of black ancestry. The accusation must not have been widely believed, since Pavy was elected and had kept his judgeship ever after. According to Judge Isom Guillory, who lived in St. Landry and knew the Pavys well, there was no black ancestry in the Pavy family or in the legitimate family of Mrs. Pavy—but "it was common knowledge that Judge Pavy's wife's father had a Negro family [begat children by a black mistress]." [19] That was the origin of the rumor. When in 1933 Dr. Carl Austin Weiss married Judge Pavy's daughter Yvonne, it is unlikely the young physician knew anything about the old canard of "nigger blood" in his bride's family. But shortly before the end of his and Huey Long's life, he would hear of it.

Dr. Weiss, age twenty-nine in 1935, probably was the best-trained ear, nose, and throat surgeon in Louisiana. Growing up in Baton Rouge, he first attended college at LSU, then transferred to the Tulane University medical school, where he graduated at twenty-one. He interned at New Orleans' Touro Infirmary, at the American Hospital in Paris, and at Bellevue Hospital in New York. He also went to Vienna for postgraduate study. Returning to Baton Rouge in 1932, the thin, bespectacled physician began collateral practice with his father, Dr. Carl Adam Weiss, on the seventh floor of the Reymond Building. The practice was a prominent one. Ex-governor John M. Parker was both a patient and a friend of the elder Dr. Weiss and occasionally had dinner at the physician's home. Once Huey Long himself strode into the Weiss office suite demanding immediate attention for an irritated eye; Dr. Weiss the elder treated him, but was upset by the Kingfish's cursing. A more agreeable patient came in one November day in 1932—Yvonne Pavy, a pretty brunette graduate student and instructor in French at LSU. Dr. Weiss senior introduced her to his son. The two were immediately attracted to each other, and on December 27, 1933, they married in the Catholic church at the Pavy family's hometown of Opelousas. In June of 1935 the couple's first and only baby was born—a son, Carl Austin Weiss, Jr.[20]

Although Huey Long suffered from sinus trouble and young Dr. Weiss was considered the best physician in Baton Rouge for treating it, the two never met until their mutually fatal encounter on the evening of September 8, 1935. Weiss the younger kept away from politics, although he often expressed disgust at Huey Long and "his puppet show in the capitol." His overriding concerns were his family and his profession. Occasionally, people close to the Kingfish did come to the young practitioner's office for treatment. Richard W. Leche and Mrs. Leche considered him "our doctor" and liked him personally. After the assassination, Seymour Weiss and other Long lieutenants claimed the De Soto Hotel transcript indicated that a "Dr. Weiss" was present on the second day of the meeting, July 22. If so, it must have been the elder Weiss, who had accepted a federal appointment (along with other prominent anti-Longites) to the state review committee of the National Recovery Administration. At the day and approximate time when "Dr. Weiss" was alleged to be plotting murder in New Orleans, Dr. Weiss the younger's office records showed that he was attending patients, including Charlotte Davis, the daughter of Huey's sister Lottie.[21]

Questioned years later, some of Long's associates claimed they never heard that the Kingfish was planning to resurrect the rumor about African ancestry in the Pavy family. Others, however, said they knew of it. Most specific was Joe Fisher, who was close to Long, and who recalled: "Huey . . . had warned Pavy for six months to lay off him [or] he would say the Pavys have 'coffee blood.' In some way this got out and Weiss heard about it." Huey, Fisher noted in a tone of admiration, "was like a rattlesnake, he always warned first." It was characteristic of Long, when striking his lowest blows, to resurrect charges someone else had made years earlier; probably the Long organization was not preparing to cite the Kingfish as saying the Pavy family had Negro blood, but rather that Sheriff Marion Swords of St. Landry Parish had said so back in 1910. A few hours before the assassination, Joe David, the New Orleans printer who did all Long's circulars, got a phone call from Huey telling him material for "an important circular" about Judge Pavy would soon be sent. David never learned its contents.[22]

Until after sunset, September 8 was a normal late-summer Sunday at the Weiss household. The family, including the elder Dr. Weiss and his wife, attended early mass at St. Joseph's Catholic Church. The service was conducted by Monsignor Leon Gassler, who was often called upon to give invocations at the legislature—he had done so at the special session's opening gathering the night before, and also on the night of "Bloody Monday" in 1929. At one o'clock the Weiss couples ate a big noonday meal together, then during the hot afternoon drove to the family's cabin on the Amite River. They returned by nightfall, with young Carl and Yvonne going to their unpretentious bungalow on Lakeland Drive, only two blocks from the tall capitol. Nothing Carl had said or done during the day indicated that he was upset or was planning anything rash. The Sunday *Morning Advocate*, which the family had read and discussed, did have a story about the bill to gerrymander Yvonne's father out of his judgeship, but that in itself was not considered a catastrophe;

within the Weiss household, only the older doctor expressed anger about it. But between eight and nine o'clock that evening, young Carl helped tuck the baby into bed, showered, dressed in the white linen suit he had worn to mass that morning, and told Yvonne he "had to go out on a sick call." He drove off in their four-year-old Buick. He carried with him, as he usually did at night, a cheap .32 automatic pistol he had purchased several years earlier in Europe, while visiting Belgium.[23]

Exactly when and from whom Dr. Weiss learned that Huey Long was preparing to revive the African blood allegation against his wife's family is a mystery. Possibly he never heard it, although judging by his action he almost certainly did, probably earlier that day or evening. Whoever phoned him or otherwise informed him would not have been likely to admit it later. No one ever did. Carl Weiss had no history of violence or instability; he was a professional dedicated to saving lives, and by all accounts was happy with his work and his family. Only one thing might have driven him to murder and what amounted to suicide—a threat to the honor and well-being of his wife and infant son. He decided to silence Huey Long before those he most loved were stained by a racial slur.[24] In the Louisiana of 1935, few calamities could be worse than being stigmatized as "colored."

Dr. Weiss parked his Buick along the driveway in front of the brightly lit capitol. Placing the Belgian pistol in a trouser pocket, he climbed the forty-eight terraced granite steps, entered the building, and crossed the lobby to the corridor connecting the governor's office to both the House and senate chambers. There, practically hidden by a marble pillar, he waited. Huey was inside the House chamber, sometimes sitting next to Speaker Allen J. Ellender, sometimes restlessly walking about the floor to check on various members. He stopped a minute at the back row to banter with Representative Mason Spencer— the one who had warned of the "white horse of death." Huey jokingly told Spencer, "You remind me of [an] old nigger woman."[25]

Around nine fifteen, just as the House was about to adjourn, the Kingfish left the chamber and came fast-stepping down the corridor and into the governor's office, then reentered the corridor a minute later. His bodyguards could not anticipate where he might dash next. Dr. Weiss, only a few feet away, his pistol concealed beneath a straw hat, now advanced toward Huey. Precisely what happened next is still a subject of controversy. Three books of differing opinions have been published dealing specifically with the assassination of Huey Long.[26]

Dr. Weiss probably fired first, but his aim was deflected by a blow to his arm by John Fournet, and Long was hit in the abdomen instead of the heart. Huey gave a yelp of pain—"Ohhhh!"—and ran down the corridor. Instantaneously the bodyguards, Murphy Roden first, commenced firing at Weiss with their .38s and .45s.[27] One of the bodyguards' bullets—a ricochet or a misdirected shot—apparently struck the Kingfish along his lower spine. (Merle Welsh, the mortician who prepared Huey for burial, vividly recalled in 1990 that Long's corpse showed two entry wounds: one in the abdomen, the other in the back. Welsh also observed a local Long leader and physician, Clarence Lorio, come into the mortuary after a pretended inquest was completed, and remove a sizable piece of lead from the Kingfish's body. To Welsh, the extracted slug looked bigger than the caliber Dr. Weiss's pistol would have fired.)[28] Maybe the fatal bullet for Huey Long was the accidental one from a bodyguard's pistol. Yet that question shifts attention from the essential point. The Kingfish died as a result of Dr. Weiss pointing a pistol at him.

The physician shuddered momentarily as the bodyguards' bullets tore into his body. He died within seconds. Roden and the others kept firing into him, more than thirty shots, after Weiss lay still.[29] Knowing that they had failed in their primary responsibility added to the bodyguards' rage at the thin young man who had done so audacious and—to them—so monstrous a deed. Yet to thousands of people Weiss was not a murderer, but a hero, and his funeral the next day—conducted by Monsignor Gassler—was, in James Clarke's words, "the largest of any assassin in American history." Among the mourners were the dean emeritus of LSU's law school, the district attorney for East Baton Rouge Parish, Congressman J. Y. Sanders, Jr., and all the members of the Baton Rouge Kiwanis Club. Also standing bareheaded in the pouring rain at the grave site in Roselawn Cemetery was a frail, elderly man who had sent an expensive wreath—ex-governor John M. Parker.[30]

Huey Long still lived, but in agony, as Dr. Weiss's corpse was lowered into the earth. The Kingfish's family and lieutenants who crowded into his sickroom at Our Lady of the Lake Hospital were told the operation performed on him after the shooting had failed to stop his internal hemorrhaging, and that he could not survive additional surgery. The Kingfish responded to Rose and his three children when they were brought to his bedside. "Here is my sweetheart," he said to Rose. He may or may not have recognized his brothers and sisters, who came hoping for a last-minute reconciliation. At times he mumbled something about *My First Days in the White House,* and what a best-seller the book would be. Seymour Weiss bent over to ask him about the location of the deducts box—something Weiss probably already knew—but received no meaningful reply. Alice Lee Grosjean (now married to William Tharpe) did not venture into the dying man's room, but she was observed crying in the hallway outside. At 4:06 A.M. on Tuesday, September 10, thirty hours after the shooting, death came to Huey Long.[31]

Dr. Weiss's funeral had been impressively large, but that of the Kingfish on September 12 was the most lavish and best attended Louisiana ever knew. Not even Jefferson Davis' funeral in 1889 or that of P. G. T. Beauregard in 1893 was comparable. An estimated 175,000 people—most of them crowded into the capitol grounds, with others perched on the limbs of live oak trees or standing on rooftops as far as a quarter-mile away—watched as Huey Long's hermetically sealed bronze casket-within-a-casket was carried down the forty-eight steps toward a central place in the sunken garden facing the great building.[32]

There, in the earth, a copper vault inside a concrete crypt waited. The LSU band marched in slow-step, playing Huey's song, "Every Man a King," at dirge tempo. At the grave site, Gerald L. K. Smith delivered an emotional funeral oration. Hodding Carter, who was present, but not as a mourner, observed: "Close beside the bier crowded the thieves and sycophants of the inner circle. Beyond wept the poor." Personages nearest the grave shared space with flowers of all descriptions. Wreaths and sprays of orchids and lilies of the valley, contributed by Huey's wealthier supporters, were propped next to bunches of wilted offerings from humble folk who on their way to the funeral had halted their old flivvers by the roadside to pick daisies and other wildflowers.[33]

Four years earlier, when construction had begun on the new capitol, Governor Huey Long had watched with great interest as caskets from an abandoned cemetery dating from the 1800s were being disinterred at a site near that chosen for the sunken garden. Huey marveled at how well preserved were the bodies inside those twenty-three unearthed caskets. Harvey Fields, one of his law partners, remembered the Kingfish had said that "when he died he wanted to be buried there also, and his body preserved the same way." His wish was respected.[34] It seemed a pathetic form of immortality, but at least the pale horse would be slowed in carrying Huey Long into dust, into nothingness.

NOTES

CHAPTER 1: Louisiana, 1893

1. New Orleans *Picayune*, January 1, 1894.

2. Charles Hoffman, *The Depression of the Nineties: An Economic History* (Westport, Conn., 1970), 9, 57–58, 285; Baton Rouge *Advocate*, June 2, 30, 1893; Shreveport *Times*, June 9, July 2, August 27, September 20, 1893.

3. *Appleton's Annual Cyclopaedia for 1893* (New York, 1894), 464; New York *Times*, October 5, 8–9, 1893; San Antonio *Express*, quoted in New Orleans *Daily States*, October 13, 17, 1893.

4. Thomas Cary Johnson, *The Life and Letters of Benjamin Morgan Palmer* (Richmond, 1906), 524, 531–32, 659; B. M. Palmer, "Thanksgiving Sermon, Delivered in the First Presbyterian Church, New Orleans, on Thursday, November 29, 1860" (Copy of typescript in Special Collections, Howard-Tilton Memorial Library, Tulane University); Timothy F. Reilly, "Benjamin M. Palmer: Secessionist Become Nationalist," *Louisiana History*, XVIII (Summer, 1977), 291–93.

5. Grace King, *Memories of a Southern Woman of Letters* (New York, 1932), 23, 29; John M. Parker, Letter in Monroe *News-Star*, December 28, 1922; Matthew James Schott, "John M. Parker of Louisiana and the Varieties of American Progressivism" (Ph.D. dissertation, Vanderbilt University, 1969), 21–22.

6. Johnson, *Benjamin Morgan Palmer*, 1–13, 431, 533.

7. Richard Hofstadter, *The American Political Tradition and the Men Who Made It* (New York, 1958), 90–91; Clement Eaton, *The Growth of Southern Civilization* (New York, 1961), 307–308. The mudsill comparison was popularized by another South Carolinian, James H. Hammond.

8. Quoted in Johnson, *Benjamin Morgan Palmer*, 210.

9. Palmer, "Thanksgiving Sermon," 5–6. After the Civil War, Palmer was elected to be the first president of the Southern Historical Society, an organization dedicated to preserving the "true history" of the struggle for southern independence. See Gaines Foster, *Ghosts of the Confederacy: Defeat, the Lost Cause, and the Emergence of the New South* (New York, 1987), 50–51.

10. Charles Reagan Wilson, *Baptized in Blood: The Religion of the Lost Cause, 1865 to 1920* (Athens, Ga., 1980), 73–74.

11. "The Oration of Dr. Palmer," New Orleans *Picayune*, May 31, 1900; Reilly, "Benjamin M. Palmer," 297–300. See also Foster Rhea Dulles, *America's Rise to World Power, 1898–1954* (New York, 1955), 30–32, 59–61.

12. Editorial, New Orleans *Daily States*, September 26, 1893.

13. H. V. and H. W. Poor, *Poor's Manual of the Railroads of the United States, 1895*, XXVII (New York, 1895), 823: Shreveport *Times*, May 17, 1893; Colfax (La.) *Chronicle*, September 1, 1900; New Orleans *Semi-Weekly States*, March 21, 1893; Shreveport *Evening Journal*, February 6, 1900.

14. William I. Hair, "Henry J. Hearsey and the Politics of Race," *Louisiana History*, XVII (Fall, 1976), 393–400; Walter Parker, "New Orleans Reminiscences, 1894–1940" (Bound clippings from New Orleans *Official Daily Court Reporter*, January 22–May 19, 1941), 28, in Special Collections, Howard-Tilton Memorial Library, Tulane University.

15. Walter Parker, "New Orleans Reminiscences," 6; John Wilds, *Afternoon Story: A Century of the New Orleans "States-Item"* (Baton Rouge, 1976), 188–89; New Orleans *Daily States*, February 2, March 27, May 23, June 15, 1893; Margaret Ann Martin, "Colonel Robert Ewing, Louisiana Journalist and Politician" (M. A. thesis, Louisiana State University, 1964), 56, 62.

16. New Orleans *Picayune*, September 18, 1893; New Orleans *Daily States*, September 18–19, 1893; Shreveport *Times*, September 22, 1893. A daily search of the latter two papers described, by name and location, fourteen lynchings in Louisiana for the year 1893. There probably were more.

17. Letter from "A. P. D." in New Orleans *Daily States*, September 20, 1893; Editorial, *ibid.*, September 18, 1893.

18. "Long Talks," *ibid.*, September 20, 1893.

19. Editorial, *ibid.*, October 3, 1893.

20. New York *Herald Tribune*, September 9, 1935. If Huey Long and Henry Long were kin, their relationship is not known.

21. Stuart Omer Landry, *The Battle of Liberty Place* (New Orleans, 1955), *passim;* New Orleans *Daily States*, September 14, 1893; New Orleans *Picayune*, September 15, 1893.

22. Walter G. Cowan *et al.*, *New Orleans Yesterday and Today: A Guide to the City* (Baton Rouge, 1983), 142.

23. The standard and most balanced general study of the state during Reconstruction is Joe Gray Taylor, *Louisiana Reconstructed, 1863–1877* (Baton Rouge, 1974). This should be supplemented with a briefer but more interpretative work, Ted Tunnell's *Crucible of Reconstruction: War, Radicalism, and Race in Louisiana, 1873–1877* (Baton Rouge, 1984).

24. King, *Southern Woman of Letters*, 78.

25. Tunnell, *Crucible of Reconstruction*, 5–6; Roger W. Shugg, *Origins of Class Struggle in Louisiana: A Social History of White Farmers and Laborers During Slavery and After, 1840–1875* (Baton Rouge, 1939), 160–80, 218–29; John C. Wickliffe, "Negro Suffrage a Failure: Should We Abolish It?" *Forum*, XIV (February, 1893), 800.

26. See comments about "the issue white vs. black," in Vermilionville (La.) *Cotton Boll*, July 8, 1874.

27. Charles Nordhoff, *The Cotton States in the Spring and Summer of 1875* (New York, 1876), 4–49; Taylor, *Louisiana Reconstructed*, 202–208, 260–65; J. Mills Thornton, "Fiscal Policy and the Failure of Radical Reconstruction in the

Lower South," in *Religion, Race, and Reconstruction: Essays in Honor of C. Vann Woodward*, ed. J. Morgan Kousser and James M. McPherson (New York, 1982), 349–51, 382–84.

28. George C. Rable, *But There Was No Peace: The Role of Violence in the Politics of Reconstruction* (Athens, Ga., 1984), 132–38; H. Oscar Lestage, Jr., "The White League in Louisiana and Its Participation in Reconstruction Riots," *Louisiana Historical Quarterly*, XVIII (July, 1935), 632–94.

29. Frank L. Richardson, "My Recollections of the Battle of the Fourteenth of September, 1874, in New Orleans, La.," *Louisiana Historical Quarterly*, XVIII (July, 1935), 498–501; Ella Lonn, *Reconstruction in Louisiana: After 1868* (New York, 1918), 271–73; Taylor, *Louisiana Reconstructed*, 293–94; New York *Times*, September 15–17, 1874.

30. *House Reports*, 43d Cong., 2d Sess., No. 261, Pt. 3, pp. 394–401; New Orleans *Picayune*, September 15–17, 1874; Tunnell, *Crucible of Reconstruction*, 212–13; New York *Times*, September 15, 1874.

31. "Official Report of Gen. Fred N. Ogden, Provisional General of the Louisiana State Militia," in New Orleans *Picayune*, October 2, 1874, and in Alcee Fortier, ed., *Louisiana: Comprising Sketches of Counties [sic], Towns, Events, Institutions, and Persons, Arranged in Cyclopedic Form* (2 vols.; Chicago, 1909), II, 643–46; Editorial in New Orleans *Daily States*, May 15, 1893.

32. New York *Times*, September 17, 1874; William Gillette, *Retreat from Reconstruction: 1869–1879* (Baton Rouge, 1979), 118–20; Grace King, *New Orleans: The Place and the People* (New York, 1895), 330.

33. "Parker Tells of Battle to End Carpetbag Rule," New Orleans *Times-Picayune*, September 15, 1924; Landry, *Battle of Liberty Place*, 240; Hernando D. Money, "Chief Justice White," *Independent*, LXX (March 2, 1911), 455–56; New Orleans *Times-Picayune*, May 30, 1921, September 15, 1924.

34. Schott, "John M. Parker," 2–8, 15–21, 24–25.

35. *Ibid.*, 18, 26.

36. Joy J. Jackson, *New Orleans in the Gilded Age: Politics and Urban Progress, 1880–1896* (Baton Rouge, 1969), 31–38, 82–86; John Smith Kendall, *History of New Orleans* (2 vols.; Chicago, 1922), I, 451–54.

37. Kendall, *History of New Orleans*, I, 451; Jackson, *New Orleans in the Gilded Age*, 83, 88–89; Brian Gary Ettinger, "John Fitzpatrick and the Limits of Working-Class Politics in New Orleans, 1892–1896," *Louisiana History*, XXVI (Fall, 1985), 145–46.

38. Schott, "John M. Parker," 23–24; Jackson, *New Orleans in the Gilded Age*, 33, 37, 109.

39. Humbert S. Nelli, *The Business of Crime: Italians and Syndicate Crime in the United States* (New York, 1976), 3–6, 21, 25–26.

40. New Orleans *Times-Democrat*, October 21, 1890; New Orleans *Picayune*, May 16, 1891.

41. Jackson, *New Orleans in the Gilded Age*, 248–49; Nelli, *Business of Crime*, 32; Atlanta *Constitution*, March 16–18, 1891; Robert H. Marr, Jr., "The New Orleans Mafia Case," *American Law Review*, XXV (May–June, 1891), 416. The author of this article about the Hennessy murder was the son of Judge R. H. Marr, who presided at an 1891 trial of Provenzano family members accused of attempting to kill the Matrangas. The Provenzanos were found not guilty. Judge Marr also received the grand jury report of May, 1891, that refused to indict members of

the lynch mob that killed the eleven Sicilians suspected of Chief Hennessy's murder. Something mysterious happened to Judge Marr the next year. In April of 1892, he vanished (see New York *Times*, April 21, 1892). His body was never found.

42. John E. Coxe, "The New Orleans Mafia Incident," *Louisiana Historical Quarterly*, XX (October, 1937), 1085.

43. John C. Wickliffe, "A Jury of 20,000," *Frank Leslie's Illustrated Newspaper*, April 4, 1891; "The Mafia, and What Led to the Lynching," *Harper's Weekly*, XXV (March 28, 1891), 226; John Smith Kendall, "Who Killed de Chief?" *Louisiana Historical Quarterly*, XXII (April, 1939), 517.

44. Schott, "John M. Parker," 34–35; *St. Mary Banner* (Franklin, La.), March 23, 1891; Johnson, *Benjamin Morgan Palmer*, 555.

45. "Report of Grand Jury to the Hon. Robert H. Marr," May 5, 1891, in *Foreign Relations of the United States, House Executive Documents*, 53d Cong., 1st Sess., I, 714–22; Marr, "New Orleans Mafia Case," 430; Editorial, New Orleans *Daily States*, May 13, 1893; Editorial, New Orleans *Picayune*, May 16, 1893.

46. Nelli, *Business of Crime*, 65; John V. Baiamonte, Jr., *Spirit of Vengeance: Nativism and Louisiana Justice, 1921–1924* (Baton Rouge, 1986), 63–65, 191, 236.

47. Jackson, *New Orleans in the Gilded Age*, 252; *Soards' New Orleans City Directory for 1893*, p. 933.

48. For D. C. O'Malley's colorful life, this study relies heavily on John Wilds's *Afternoon Story*, 118–76. See also New Orleans *Item*, November 27, 1920.

49. Baton Rouge *Advocate*, January 19, 1893; Lawrence Goodwyn, *Democratic Promise: The Populist Moment in America* (New York, 1976), 99, 219, 169, 334; William Ivy Hair, *Bourbonism and Agrarian Protest: Louisiana Politics, 1877–1900* (Baton Rouge, 1969), 204–205, 214.

50. Election returns for 1892 are in *Report of Louisiana Secretary of State, 1902*, p. 562; Hair, *Bourbonism and Agrarian Protest*, 209–10. The People's party candidate for governor in 1892, a native of Winn, received a higher percentage of the parish's vote than Huey Long would do in his two races for governor. In 1924 Long obtained 69.9 percent of his home parish's vote; in 1928 he got 69.6 percent. See *Report of Louisiana Secretary of State*, 1925, p. 435; *ibid.*, 1929, foldout sheet at end of volume.

51. "People's Party Platform," New Orleans *Times-Democrat*, February 19, 1892; Colfax (La.) *Chronicle*, October 17, 1891, August 4, 19, 1893; Winnfield (La.) *Comrade*, December 2, 30, 1910.

52. A personal observation. This writer has not seen the "black ace" expression in print, but while growing up in Louisiana during the 1940s and 1950s heard it used many times in reference to inserting racial issues in political campaigns, especially when a white candidate was rumored to have some black ancestry.

53. An estimate based on population, occupation, and home and land tenure figures in *Compendium of the Eleventh Census*, 1890, III, 409–15, 440–51, 710–13, 1081–84.

54. Baton Rouge *Advocate*, October 10, 1893; V. O. Key, Jr., *Southern Politics in State and Nation* (New York, 1949), 160.

55. Memphis *Commercial*, quoted in Baton Rouge *Advocate*, April 6, 1893. For Foster's political life, see Sidney James Romero, "The Public Career of Murphy James Foster, Governor of Louisiana, 1892–1900," *Louisiana Historical Quarterly*,

XXVIII (October, 1945), 1129–1243; and Joy J. Jackson, "Murphy J. Foster," in *The Louisiana Governors: From Iberville to Edwards*, ed. Joseph G. Dawson III (Baton Rouge, 1990), 189–93.

56. Richard Nelson Current, *Those Terrible Carpetbaggers* (New York, 1988), 420.

57. This appointive power under the Constitution of 1879 was given to the governor by allowing him to appoint all officers whose elections were not provided for by this constitution or by subsequent legislative sessions. Also, the governor's power of line-item veto made it difficult for the legislature to assert itself. *Constitution of 1879*, Arts. LXVI–LXXVI; *Projet of a Constitution for the State of Louisiana: With Notes and Studies* (2 vols.; Baton Rouge, 1954), I, 400, 420.

58. *Biographical and Historical Memoirs of Louisiana* (2 vols.; Chicago, 1892), I, 40.

59. For the best study of white Democratic stratagems to reduce black voting, see J. Morgan Kousser, *The Shaping of Southern Politics: Suffrage Restriction and the Establishment of the One-Party South, 1880–1910* (New Haven, 1974). The "dead darkey" comment is to be found in the Natchitoches *Louisiana Populist*, October 22, 1897.

60. New Orleans *Picayune*, February 30, 1898. McEnery's admission is also quoted in Kousser, *Shaping of Southern Politics*, 46.

61. Baton Rouge *Advocate*, September 25, November 13, 1892. This was the official journal for printing state government proceedings. During the late nineteenth century, the *Advocate* was owned and edited by close associates of whoever was governor.

62. Governor Murphy J. Foster interview, New Orleans *Daily States*, January 29, 1893. What was still referred to as "the militia" was actually the National Guard. The guard (militia) was under the authority of the various governors unless called to active duty by the president of the United States.

63. Baton Rouge *Advocate*, May 14, 16, 1893; Chicago *Tribune*, August 22, 1893; Shreveport *Sunday Judge*, April 26, 1896; Natchitoches *Louisiana Populist*, May 1, 1896; Donaldsonville (La.) *Times*, April 22, 24, 1896; Philip D. Uzee, "Republican Politics in Louisiana, 1877–1900" (Ph.D. dissertation, Louisiana State University, 1950), 160.

64. T. Harry Williams, *P. G. T. Beauregard: Napoleon in Gray* (Baton Rouge, 1954), 319–27; New Orleans *Daily States*, February 21, 1893.

65. Hair, *Bourbonism and Agrarian Protest*, 26–30, 109–10, 201–202; John T. White, "The History of the Louisiana Lottery" (M.A. thesis, Tulane University, 1939), 20–27; Frank McGloin, "Shall the Lottery's Charter Be Renewed?" *Forum*, XII (January, 1892), 555–58.

66. Berthold C. Alwes, "The History of the Louisiana State Lottery Company," *Louisiana Historical Quarterly*, XXVII (October, 1944), 1070–71, 1097–1102; Johnson, *Benjamin Morgan Palmer*, 548–64.

67. New Orleans *Picayune*, February 23–24, 1893; Shreveport *Times*, February 24, 1893.

68. "Gen. P. G. T. Beauregard's Will," Shreveport *Times*, March 2, 1893; New Orleans *Semi-Weekly States*, February 24, 1893; Williams, *P. G. T. Beauregard*, 328.

69. New Orleans *Times-Democrat*, February 24, 1893; Williams, *P. G. T. Beauregard*, 328; New Orleans *Daily States*, March 29, 1893.

70. New Orleans *Sunday States*, May 28, 1893; Baton Rouge *Advocate*, May 30,

1893; New York *Times*, May 30, 1893; Hudson Strode, *Jefferson Davis, Tragic Hero: The Last Twenty-five Years, 1864–1889* (New York, 1964), 512–22; New York *Times*, December 12, 1889; Hamilton Basso, *Beauregard: The Great Creole General* (New York, 1933), 304–10. On Beauregard's hatred of Davis, see also Williams, *P. G. T. Beauregard*, 308–11, 318.

71. Varina Jefferson Davis to "The Veterans and People of the Southern States," July 11, 1891 (Copy of typescript in John M. Stone Papers, Mississippi Department of Archives and History, Jackson, Miss.); New Orleans *Picayune*, May 28, 1893; "Beauregard's Will," Shreveport *Times*, March 2, 1893.

72. New York *Times*, December 12, 1889, May 28, 30, 1893; Baton Rouge *Advocate*, May 30, 1893; Davis to Veterans and People, in Stone Papers.

73. "Gen. Fred N. Ogden's Simple Monument," New Orleans *Picayune*, September 15, 1893.

74. F. Raymond Daniell, "Land of the Free," in *We Saw It Happen: The News Behind the News That's Fit to Print,* ed. Hanson W. Baldwin and Shepard Stone (New York, 1938), 95. Daniell does not mention Metairie Cemetery by name but says it was "the cemetery outside New Orleans." At that time the highway from Baton Rouge to New Orleans skirted an edge of Metairie Cemetery.

CHAPTER 2: The Boy Who Would Be Kingfish

1. Huey P. Long, *Every Man a King: The Autobiography of Huey P. Long* (New Orleans, 1933), 2; T. Harry Williams, *Huey Long* (New York, 1969), 19–22; Clara Long Knott interview, in T. Harry Williams Papers, Hill Memorial Library, Louisiana State University; "Earl, Huey Fought," New Orleans *Times-Picayune*, September 7, 1975.

2. Williams, *Huey Long*, 10–11; John Klorer, ed., *The New Louisiana: The Story of the Greatest State in the Nation* (New Orleans, n.d.), 21; Julius Long quoted in New Orleans *Times-Picayune*, September 7, 1975.

3. John Milton Price, "Slavery in Winn Parish," *Louisiana History*, VIII (Spring, 1967), 143–46; *The War of the Rebellion: A Compilation of the Official Records of the Union and Confederate Armies* (130 vols.; Washington, D.C., 1880–1901), Ser. I, Vol. XXVI, Pt. 2, pp. 294, 369; Ella Lonn, *Desertion During the Civil War* (1928; rpr. Gloucester, Mass., 1966), 78–79.

4. James Rorty, "Callie Long's Boy Huey," *Forum*, XCIV (August, 1935), 79, 126–27; Williams, *Huey Long*, 14; Frederick W. Carr, "Huey Long's Father Relates Story of Senator's Boyhood," *Christian Science Monitor*, September 11, 1935.

5. Price, "Slavery in Winn Parish," 137–48; Roger W. Shugg, *Origins of Class Struggle in Louisiana: A Social History of White Farmers and Laborers During Slavery and After, 1840–1875* (Baton Rouge, 1939), 95–102, 327; Williams, *Huey Long*, 16–19.

6. United States Census Returns, 1910: Louisiana Population, Winn Parish, Ward One, Town of Winnfield (Microfilm, University of Georgia Library); Julius Tison Long, "What I Know About My Brother, United States Senator Huey P. Long," *Real America*, II (September, 1933), 35, 37.

7. Rorty, "Callie Long's Boy Huey," 127; Harley B. Bozeman, "Winn Parish as I Have Known It," *Winn Parish Enterprise* (Winnfield, La.), July 11, 18, 1957 (Clippings in Bozeman Scrapbooks, Louisiana State Library, Baton Rouge), Earl K. Long television interview, WBRZ, Channel 2, Baton Rouge, August 28, 1960; Williams, *Huey Long*, 26.

8. Long, *Every Man a King*, 2; "Address by Hon. Ernest S. Clements," *Senate Documents*, 77th Cong., 1st Sess., No. 110, p. 32.

9. Long, *Every Man a King*, 2; Bozeman, "Winn Parish," July 11, 1957, in Bozeman Scrapbooks; Carr, "Huey Long's Father."

10. Bozeman, "Winn Parish," July 11, 1957, in Bozeman Scrapbooks; *Thirteenth Census, 1910: Population*, II, 769; Winnfield (La.) *Comrade*, January 28, 1910.

11. Long, *Every Man a King*, 6; Williams, *Huey Long*, 18–24; Fred Francis interview, in Williams Papers. Francis was the son of a Winnfield banker.

12. *Neues Wiener Tagblatt*, quoted in *Living Age*, CCCLXVIII (April, 1935), 183.

13. Long, *Every Man a King*, 6; Thomas O. Harris, *The Kingfish: Huey P. Long, Dictator* (New Orleans, 1938), 10.

14. United States Census Returns, 1900: Louisiana Population, Winn Parish, Ward One, Town of Winnfield (Microfilm, University of Georgia Library). The statement about white women in rural north Louisiana not working in the fields unless the family was very poor and of low status is a personal observation. This writer was born in Franklin Parish and grew up in that region.

15. Rorty, "Callie Long's Boy Huey," 127.

16. Lottie Long Davis interview, in Williams Papers; "Sapsucker" remark quoted in Williams, *Huey Long*, 314; Huey P. Long's Senate speech of March 5, 1935, reprinted in *American Progress*, April, 1935.

17. Harris, *Kingfish*, 97; Julius T. Long, "What I Know," 37.

18. Colfax (La.) *Chronicle*, December 9, 1899.

19. United States Census Returns, 1900: Louisiana Population, Winn Parish, Ward One; Colfax (La.) *Chronicle*, April 14, 21, 1900.

20. Alan Brinkley, *Voices of Protest: Huey Long, Father Coughlin, and the Great Depression* (New York, 1983), 162–63. One of the Long family's closest neighbors in Winnfield was Robert L. Tannehill, the People's party candidate for governor in 1892. See United States Census Returns, 1900: Louisiana Population, Winn Parish, Ward One.

21. Mildred Adams, "Huey the Great," *Forum*, LXXXIX (February, 1933), 72; Mrs. Robert Parrot interview, in Williams Papers.

22. Lottie Long Davis, Harry Gamble interviews, both in Williams Papers.

23. On Earl doing Huey's fighting for him, see Julius T. Long, "What I Know," 39; Earl K. Long interview, WBRZ, August 28, 1960; Harnett T. Kane, *Louisiana Hayride: The American Rehearsal for Dictatorship, 1928–1940* (New York, 1941), 41. Huey's comment on fighting quoted in his *American Progress*, April, 1935.

24. This and subsequent assessments of Huey Long's reading habits, memory, and knowledge of history vary from those in Williams' *Huey Long*, 31–35, 75–77, 184, because of this author's differing interpretations of interviews and of other sources, particularly Long's numerous statements about himself and his view of history.

25. Lottie Long Davis interview, in Williams Papers.

26. Williams, *Huey Long*, 34; Huey P. Long to Aline McConnell, September 21, 1921, in Huey P. Long Papers, Hill Memorial Library, Louisiana State University; Long, *Every Man a King*, 150; A. J. Liebling, *The Earl of Louisiana* (Baton Rouge, 1970), 102.

27. Kane, *Louisiana Hayride*, 41; Forrest Davis, *Huey Long: A Candid Biography* (New York, 1935), 279.

28. T. H. Harris, *The Story of Public Education in Louisiana* (New Orleans,

1924), 61; Minns Sledge Robertson, *Public Education in Louisiana After 1898* (Baton Rouge, 1952), 9–13; E. F. Gayle, "The Bond Issue," *Louisiana School Review,* XII (September, 1904), 18.

29. Williams, *Huey Long,* 30; Winnfield (La.) *Southern Sentinel,* January 17, 31, March 6, 1908.

30. Long, *Every Man a King,* 6; Harris, *Kingfish,* 11; Williams, *Huey Long,* 41; Huey P. Long to Rev. Alvin Stokes, March 18, 1920, in Huey P. Long Papers.

31. Harris, *Kingfish,* 11; Kane, *Louisiana Hayride,* 40.

32. Julius T. Long, "What I Know," 56; Davis, *Long: A Candid Biography,* 19.

33. Brinkley, *Voices of Protest,* 55; Associated Press interview of members of Senator Long's retinue shortly after his assassination, quoted in Baton Rouge *State-Times,* September 11, 1935.

34. Davis, *Long: A Candid Biography,* 33.

35. Burton L. Hotaling, "Huey Pierce Long as Journalist and Propagandist," *Journalism Quarterly,* XX (March, 1943), 21; John Wilds, *Afternoon Story: A Century of the New Orleans "States-Item"* (Baton Rouge, 1976), 228.

36. Huey P. Long to Dr. George S. Long, July 30, 1919, in Huey P. Long Papers; Rorty, "Callie Long's Boy Huey," 127; Arthur M. Schlesinger, Jr., *The Politics of Upheaval* (Boston, 1960), 68.

37. *American Progress,* January 4, 1934; Williams, *Huey Long,* 43; Julius T. Long, "What I Know," 35; Winnfield (La.) *Southern Sentinel,* October 4, 1907, January 17, 1908.

38. Bozeman, "Winn Parish," August 1, 1957, in Bozeman Scrapbooks; Rorty, "Callie Long's Boy Huey," 127.

39. Grady McWhiney, "Louisiana Socialists in the Early Twentieth Century: A Study of Rustic Radicalism," *Journal of Southern History,* XX (August, 1954), 316–22; *Report of Louisiana Secretary of State,* 1914, foldout opposite p. 226; *ibid.,* 1917, p. 303; James R. Green, *Grass-Roots Socialism: Radical Movements in the Southwest, 1895–1943* (Baton Rouge, 1978), 77, 214–23, 247. Green (214n) quotes the state secretary of Louisiana's Socialist party as saying he believed Huey Long's father was a member of both the Populist and Socialist parties, but available evidence indicates he always voted Democratic. The elder Long did, however, apparently become more radical as he grew poorer in old age. See Rorty, "Callie Long's Boy Huey," 78.

40. Long, *Every Man a King,* 7; Williams, *Huey Long,* 37–38.

41. T. H. Harris, *The Memoirs of T. H. Harris* (Baton Rouge, 1963), 125.

42. *Ibid.*

43. *Ibid.* Harris' account of Huey's words sounds apocryphal, but his *Memoirs* are so candid and factual throughout that the conversations may be accepted as substantially correct.

CHAPTER 3: Selling Anybody Anything

1. Huey P. Long, *Every Man a King: The Autobiography of Huey P. Long* (New Orleans, 1933), 8.

2. Hermann B. Deutsch, "Prelude to a Heterocrat," *Saturday Evening Post,* September 7, 1935, pp. 6–7. For a differing version, see Harley B. Bozeman. "Winn Parish as I Have Known It," *Winn Parish Enterprise* (Winnfield, La.), April 11, May 2, 1957 (Clippings in Bozeman Scrapbooks, Louisiana State Library, Ba-

ton Rouge). For the Winnfield *Comrade* editor's admiration of young Huey, see the issue of November 11, 1910.

3. Lottie Long Davis interview, in T. Harry Williams Papers, Hill Memorial Library, Louisiana State University; T. Harry Williams, *Huey Long* (New York, 1969), 26; Long, *Every Man a King*, 5; Bozeman, "Winn Parish," July 11, 1957, in Bozeman Scrapbooks.

4. Bozeman, "Winn Parish," July 11, 1957, in Bozeman Scrapbooks; Huey P. Long, Sr., "My Boy Huey," in *The New Louisiana: The Story of the Greatest State in the Nation*, ed. John D. Klorer (New Orleans, n.d.), 20.

5. Raymond Gram Swing, "The Menace of Huey Long," *Nation*, January 16, 1935, pp. 69–70.

6. Long, *Every Man a King*, 2. The Huey Long letters concerning his family are in his papers at LSU. Several are cited later in this chapter.

7. Winnfield (La.) *Comrade*, January 28, February 11, 1910.

8. United States Census Returns, 1910: Louisiana Population, Winn Parish, Ward One, Town of Winnfield (Microfilm, University of Georgia Library).

9. Harnett T. Kane, *Louisiana Hayride: The American Rehearsal for Dictatorship, 1928–1940* (New York, 1941), 42; Bozeman, "Winn Parish," July 25, 1957, in Bozeman Scrapbooks; W. Adolphe Roberts, *Lake Pontchartrain* (Indianapolis, 1946), 329; "Incredible Kingfish," *Time*, October 3, 1932, p. 10.

10. Deutsch, "Prelude to a Heterocrat," 7; New York *Times*, September 9, 1935; Kane, *Louisiana Hayride*, 42.

11. Meigs O. Frost, "The Romantic, Fighting Career of Huey Long," New Orleans *States*, August 28, 1927; Williams, *Huey Long*, 51.

12. Bozeman, "Winn Parish," August 15, 1957, in Bozeman Scrapbooks; Rose McConnell Long interview, in Williams Papers; Photograph of the teenage Huey Long in Louisiana State Library, Baton Rouge; Huey and Rose's wedding picture in Julius Tison Long, "What I Know About My Brother, United States Senator Huey P. Long," *Real America*, II (September, 1933), 32.

13. Winnfield (La.) *Comrade*, November 11, 1910. Earlier that year the *Comrade* bought out the rival weekly *Southern Sentinel*, for which Huey had worked as a typesetter and sometime writer.

14. Bozeman, "Winn Parish," August 22, 1957, in Bozeman Scrapbooks; Long, *Every Man a King*, 8; Williams, *Huey Long*, 53–54.

15. Rose McConnell Long interview, in Williams Papers.

16. Long, *Every Man a King*, 8–9; Williams, *Huey Long*, 54–55, 69; C. Vann Woodward, *Origins of the New South, 1877–1913* (Baton Rouge, 1951), 376–77. Huey's account of the salesman period of his life is brief and misleading.

17. Deutsch, "Prelude to a Heterocrat," 7; Williams, *Huey Long*, 55–57.

18. Williams, *Huey Long*, 57.

19. *Ibid.*, 58; Long, *Every Man a King*, 10.

20. New Orleans *Times-Picayune*, September 3, 1935; Hermann B. Deutsch, *The Huey Long Murder Case* (Garden City, N.Y., 1963), 49–50.

21. Long, *Every Man a King*, 11–13; New Orleans *States*, August 28, 1927; Williams, *Huey Long*, 60–61.

22. The author concedes that this is speculation, but it is entirely consistent with Huey Long's behavior patterns. In any case it seems unlikely that any state university law school in 1912 would knowingly admit him without a high school diploma.

23. Huey P. Long to Dr. George S. Long, March 22, 1920, Huey P. Long to Julius T. Long, April 1, 1920, both in Huey P. Long Papers, Hill Memorial Library, Louisiana State University.

24. Long, *Every Man a King*, 13–14; Mildred Adams, "Huey the Great," *Forum*, LXXXIX (February, 1933), 72; Williams, *Huey Long*, 61.

25. Deutsch, "Prelude to a Heterocrat," 7; Williams, *Huey Long*, 62–64; Harvey G. Fields, *A True History of the Life, Works, Assassination, and Death of Huey Pierce Long* (Farmerville, La., 1945), 23.

26. Bozeman, "Winn Parish," September 19, 1957, in Bozeman Scrapbooks; Long, *Every Man a King*, 14–15.

27. William D. Miller, *Mr. Crump of Memphis* (Baton Rouge, 1964), 62; Williams, *Huey Long*, 65.

28. Long, *Every Man a King*, 14–15; *Christian Science Monitor*, September 10, 1935.

29. Shreveport *Times*, December 16–21, 1912.

30. Bozeman, "Winn Parish," September 26, 1957, in Bozeman Scrapbooks.

31. New Orleans *States*, August 28, 1927; Williams, *Huey Long*, 66–67.

32. "Long's Marriage 22 Years Ago Revealed in Musty Ledger Here," Memphis *Commercial Appeal*, September 11, 1935; Rose McConnell Long interview, in Williams Papers. Rose Long filled out her husband's unexpired Senate term (1935–36) but did not seek election to a full term. Their son, Russell B. Long, would be elected to the Senate in 1950 and serve thirty-seven years, retiring voluntarily (having never lost an election) in 1987. The Long family provides the only father-mother-child combination in the U.S. Senate dynasties.

33. Williams, *Huey Long*, 67–68; Memphis *Commercial Appeal*, September 11, 1935; Long, *Every Man a King*, 15.

34. John Kingston Fineran, *The Career of a Tinpot Napoleon: A Political Biography of Huey P. Long* (New Orleans, 1932), 8; Arthur J. Cramp, comp., *Nostrums and Quackery: Articles on the Nostrum Evil, Quackery, and Allied Matters Affecting the Public Health . . . From the Journal of the American Medical Association* (2 vols.; Chicago, 1921), II, 166–72.

35. James Harvey Young, *The Medical Messiahs: A Social History of Health Quackery in Twentieth Century America* (Princeton, 1967), 142. The Chattanooga Medical Company sued the AMA for libel because of its charges against Wine of Cardui and the company's owner. The company won its suit but was awarded damages of only one cent.

36. Williams, *Huey Long*, 68; Adams, "Huey the Great," 75.

37. Bozeman, "Winn Parish," October 3, 1957, in Bozeman Scrapbooks; Williams, *Huey Long*, 72; Thomas O. Harris, *The Kingfish: Huey P. Long, Dictator* (New Orleans, 1938), 13.

38. Julius T. Long, "What I Know," 34–35; Julius T. Long to Huey P. Long, September 7, 1921, Huey P. Long to Julius T. Long, September 8, 1921, both in Huey P. Long Papers; Long, *Every Man a King*, 15.

39. Long, *Every Man a King*, 15; New Orleans *States*, August 28, 1927; Charles J. Rivet interview, in Williams Papers; George E. Sokolsky, "Huey Long," *Atlantic Monthly*, CLVI (November, 1935), 525–26.

40. Long, *Every Man a King*, 16–17.

41. *Ibid.*, 17; Kane, *Louisiana Hayride*, 44.

CHAPTER 4: Ruling the Roost

1. Bastrop (La.) *Clarion-Appeal*, quoted in Opelousas (La.) *Courier*, April 18, 1896.

2. "Address of the Democratic State Central Committee," Shreveport *Evening Judge*, May 6, 1896.

3. *Appleton's Annual Cyclopaedia for 1901* (New York, 1902), 705; New Orleans *Times-Democrat*, August 2, 1901; *Compendium of the Eleventh Census, 1890*, I, 470; Kelly Miller, "The Expansion of the Negro Population," *Forum*, XXIX (February, 1902), 677.

4. Neal R. Peirce, *The Deep South States of America: People, Politics, and Power in the Seven Deep South States* (New York, 1974), 121.

5. Joel Williamson, *A Rage for Order: Black-White Relations in the American South Since Emancipation* (New York, 1986), 78–151. *A Rage for Order* is an abridgement, but with all the themes and most examples intact, of Williamson's monumental *The Crucible of Race* (New York, 1984), a brilliant study of the roots and results of racism in the South. For Major Hearsey's editorial, "The Negro Problem and Its Final Solution," see New Orleans *Daily States*, August 7, 1900, and subsequent editorials on August 16 and 19. Hearsey's "final solution" included genocide if blacks did not submit to being "ruled with an iron hand."

6. Paul L. Haworth, "Negro Disfranchisement in Louisiana," *Outlook*, LXXI (May 17, 1902), 164.

7. St. Francisville (La.) *True Democrat*, August 31, 1901.

8. Quoted in Ray Stannard Baker, *Following the Color Line: American Negro Citizenship in the Progressive Era* (New York, 1964), 241. For a cogent discussion of the *Herrenvolk* democracy concept in the South, see George M. Fredrickson's essay, "Aristocracy and Democracy in the Southern Tradition," in *The Southern Enigma: Essays on Race, Class, and Folk Culture*, ed. Walter J. Fraser, Jr., and Winfred B. Moore, Jr. (Westport, Conn., 1983), 97–103.

9. Michael J. Cassity, *American Race Relations to 1900* (Westport, Conn., 1985), xxv–xxx; Florette Henri, *Black Migration: Movement North, 1900–1920* (Garden City, N.Y., 1976), 1–22; Haworth, "Negro Disfranchisement in Louisiana," 166.

10. W. T. Brashear, "Resources of St. Landry," in *Proceedings of the Eighth Annual Session of the Louisiana State Agricultural Society* (Baton Rouge, 1894), 124.

11. Charles E. Wynes, "The Reverend Quincy Ewing: Southern Racial Heretic in the 'Cajun' Country," *Louisiana History*, VII (Summer, 1966), 222–28; Quincy Ewing, "The Heart of the Race Problem," *Atlantic Monthly*, CIII (March, 1909), 389–97; Morton Sosna, *In Search of the Silent South* (New York, 1977), 18.

12. Frederick W. Williamson and George T. Goodman, eds., *Eastern Louisiana: A History of the Watershed of the Ouachita River and Florida Parishes* (2 vols.; Louisville, Ky., 1939), II, 804; William Ivy Hair, *Bourbonism and Agrarian Protest: Louisiana Politics, 1877–1900* (Baton Rouge, 1969), 250; Shreveport *Evening Journal*, February 16, 1900; Review of A. A. Gunby's *Two Addresses on Negro Education in the South*, in *Nation*, December 10, 1903, p. 473.

13. James R. Green, *Grass-Roots Socialism: Radical Movements in the Southwest, 1895–1943* (Baton Rouge, 1978), 204–23. See also Covington Hall, "Labor

Struggles in the Deep South" (Typescript in Special Collections, Howard-Tilton Memorial Library, Tulane University), 136–39, 189–91.

14. New Orleans *Lumberjack*, June 19, 1913; New Orleans *Voice of the People*, June 17, August 21, 1913, February 5, 1914. The *Lumberjack*, organ of the "Red" BTW-IWW, was first published in Alexandria, then moved to New Orleans and later (July, 1913) changed its name to *Voice of the People*.

15. *Report of Louisiana Bureau of Statistics for Labor*, 1906–1907, pp. 43–44; Philip Foner, *History of the Labor Movement in the United States* (3 vols.; New York, 1964), III, 250–53; Oscar Ameringer, *If You Don't Weaken* (New York, 1940), 201, 214–17.

16. Quoted in Ameringer, *If You Don't Weaken*, 218–19.

17. Foner, *History of the Labor Movement*, III, 250–53; Ameringer, *If You Don't Weaken*, 197, 201, 216–21.

18. Advertisement for Bogalusa in *Country Life*, XXXVI (August, 1919), 2; Charles W. Goodyear, *Bogalusa Story* (Buffalo, N.Y., 1950), 18, 42, 47, 94, 127. My description of the Great Southern Lumber Company's operation is not as rosy as the image presented in *Bogalusa Story*, but it is based largely on the information presented there. In 1937, Great Southern's operation merged into the Gaylord Container Corporation.

19. Goodyear, *Bogalusa Story*, 127; *Report of Louisiana Department of Labor and Industrial Statistics*, 1919–20, p. 76; New York *Times*, November 23, 1919; "Report on Situation at Bogalusa, Louisiana, by President of Louisiana State Federation of Labor [J. T. Greer]," February 4, 1920, in Herbert J. Seligmann, *The Negro Faces America* (New York, 1920), 311–19.

20. Bogalusa (La.) *Enterprise and American*, November 27, December 11, 1919; Paul Ted McCulley, "Black Protest in Louisiana, 1898–1928" (M.A. thesis, Louisiana State University, 1970), 26; Goodyear, *Bogalusa Story*, 114–15, 134.

21. Jack Temple Kirby, *Darkness at the Dawning: Race and Reform in the Progressive South* (Philadelphia, 1972), 5.

22. Virginia R. Dominguez, *White by Definition: Social Classification in Creole Louisiana* (New Brunswick, N.J., 1986), 131, 140–41.

23. For representative samples of the new, coarser style of racial epithets beginning in 1896, see New Orleans *States*, quoted in Lake Providence (La.) *Banner Democrat*, February 1, 1896, and in *Iberville South* (Plaquemine, La.), February 1, 22, April 15, 1896; Baton Rouge *Advocate*, March 4, 17, April 3, 1896; New Orleans *Picayune*, March 3, 1896.

24. *Acts*, 1890, No. 111; *Plessy v. Ferguson*, 163 U.S. 537 (1896); Charles A. Lofgren, *The Plessy Case: A Legal-Historical Interpretation* (New York, 1987), *passim*.

25. Roger A. Fischer, *The Segregation Struggle in Louisiana, 1862–77* (Urbana, Ill., 1974), *passim*; C. Vann Woodward, *The Strange Career of Jim Crow* (3d ed.; New York, 1974), *passim*; Abbeville (La.) *Meridional*, August 16, 1902.

26. George M. Fredrickson, *The Black Image in the White Mind: The Debate on Afro-American Character and Destiny, 1817–1914* (New York, 1971), 282; *St. Landry Clarion* (Opelousas, La.), February 4, 1911.

27. New Orleans *Times-Democrat*, September 3, 1900; *Harlequin*, I (January 3, 1900), 8, (May 5, 1900), 2; Mark Sullivan, *Our Times: The United States, 1900–1925* (6 vols.; New York, 1930), III, 369–73, 385. The type of entertainment de-

scribed used black performers and differed from the more benign "blackface" minstrel shows of earlier times.

28. Quoted in Henri, *Black Migration*, 225. This writer, as a child in rural Louisiana, listened to older residents recall "hit the coon" games at parish fairs.

29. *Report of Louisiana Secretary of State*, 1902, pp. 556–57, 564; *Harlequin*, I (April 4, 1900), 4; John R. Kemp, ed., *Martin Behrman of New Orleans: Memoirs of a City Boss* (Baton Rouge, 1977), 66.

30. New Orleans *Times-Democrat*, November 1, 1900; Franklin (La.) *Vindicator-News*, quoted in New Orleans *Picayune*, July 23, 1901.

31. C. Vann Woodward, *Origins of the New South, 1877–1913* (Baton Rouge, 1951), 373; Paul Lewinson, *Race, Class, and Party: A History of Negro Suffrage and White Politics in the South* (1932; rpr. New York, 1965), 112, 230; Steven F. Lawson, *Black Ballots: Voting Rights in the South, 1944–1969* (New York, 1976), 23–46.

32. *Acts*, 1906, No. 49; *Report of Louisiana Secretary of State*, 1904, p. 52, 1929 [listing 1928 registration figures], 328–29. The discrepancy of 795 between registration and affiliation in the figures for 1928 probably reflects failure to list registrants not considered either "white" or "colored," *i.e.*, Asians and Amerindians. In Louisiana, *colored* by law meant anyone of any degree of black African ancestry.

33. New Orleans *Weekly Louisianian*, March 6, 1880; Harry D. Wilson quoted in New Orleans *Picayune*, October 15, 1900.

34. *Acts*, 1902, No. 64; Germaine A. Reed, "Race Legislation in Louisiana, 1864–1920," *Louisiana History*, VI (Fall, 1965), 186–87; August Meier and Elliott Rudwick, "The Boycott Movement Against Jim Crow Streetcars in the South, 1900–1906," *Journal of American History*, LV (March, 1969), 765–75.

35. "New Troubles Abrew," *Harlequin*, I (January 3, 1900), 3; *Acts*, 1908, No. 176; New Orleans *Weekly Louisianian*, June 19, 1880; Dale A. Somers, "Black and White in New Orleans: A Study in Urban Race Relations, 1865–1900," *Journal of Southern History*, XL (1974), 28–29.

36. *Acts*, 1912, No. 117; Reed, "Race Legislation in Louisiana," 381–82; *Acts*, 1914, No. 235.

37. Dewey W. Grantham, Jr., "Dinner at the White House: Theodore Roosevelt, Booker T. Washington, and the South," *Tennessee Historical Quarterly*, XVII (1958), 112–30; George Sinkler, *The Racial Attitudes of American Presidents, from Abraham Lincoln to Theodore Roosevelt* (Garden City, N.Y., 1971), 371–72; Henri, *Black Migration*, 48.

38. Baton Rouge *Advocate*, February 22, 1898; St. Francisville (La.) *True Democrat*, October 26, 1901; William Benjamin Smith, *The Color Line: A Brief in Behalf of the Unborn* (New York, 1905), 21; Grantham, "Dinner at the White House," 122.

39. Fredrickson, *Black Image*, 272; Bennett H. Wall, ed., *Louisiana: A History* (2d ed.; Arlington Heights, Ill., 1990), 244–45; Williamson, *Rage for Order*, 84–85; W. J. Cash, "The Mind of the South," *American Mercury*, XVIII (October, 1929), 190.

40. Mary Ross, "Where Lynching Is a Habit," *Survey*, LXIX (February 15, 1923), 627; William Ivy Hair, *Carnival of Fury: Robert Charles and the New Orleans Race Riot of 1900* (Baton Rouge, 1976), 184–85; New Orleans *Times-Democrat*,

September 22, 1900; New Orleans *Picayune,* quoted in *Richland Beacon-News* (Rayville, La.), November 2, 1901.

41. *Richland Beacon-News* (Rayville, La.), November 9, 1901, January 4, 1913; New Orleans *Daily States,* June 4, 1898; "Address of Governor Blanchard," *Louisiana Senate Journal,* 1906, p. 23; *St. Landry Clarion* (Opelousas, La.), December 28, 1912. See also Mansfield (La.) *Enterprise,* quoted in Shreveport *Caucasian,* December 2, 1909, for the following comment: "All talk about [stopping lynching] is sentimental nonsense, and the man who talks that way don't mean what he says."

42. Carl A. Brasseaux, "The Moral Climate of French Colonial Louisiana, 1699–1763," *Louisiana History,* XXVII (Winter, 1986), 31–35; David C. Rankin, "The Tannenbaum Thesis Reconsidered: Slavery and Race Relations in Antebellum Louisiana," *Southern Studies,* XVIII (Spring, 1979), 21–22; Pierre L. van den Berghe, *The Ethnic Phenomenon* (New York, 1981), 109; "Negrophobia and Niggerloving," Editorial in New Orleans *Daily States,* February 13, 1900.

43. Joel Williamson, *New People: Miscegenation and Mulattoes in the United States* (New York, 1980), 22–23, 66–67, 76–90, 93; Dominguez, *White by Definition,* 159–60; Baker, *Following the Color Line,* 156–57; *Literary Digest,* March 18, 1922, p. 44. John Blassingame estimates that every year from 1875 to the 1890s, one hundred to five hundred Louisianians with small degrees of black African ancestry "crossed over" and became identified with whites. See John Blassingame, *Black New Orleans, 1860–1880* (Chicago, 1973), 201. The number who "crossed over" may have exceeded five hundred per year during the late 1890s, as racism became more virulent.

44. Shreveport *Caucasian,* July 6, 1909.

45. New Orleans *Southwestern Presbyterian,* November 4, 1901; Smith, *Color Line,* 15–16, 21, 186–89.

46. *Harlequin,* I (January 3, 1900), 3; Oliver La Farge, *Raw Material* (Boston, 1942), 121.

47. Dominguez, *White by Definition,* 24–26; Williamson, *New People,* 23, 93; Blassingame, *Black New Orleans,* 206–207; New Orleans *Mascot,* October 3, 1894, October 21, 1893.

48. *Acts,* 1894, No. 54; New Orleans *Times-Democrat,* February 6, 1906, quoted in Baker, *Following the Color Line,* 166; A. A. Gunby, *Two Addresses on Negro Education in the South* (New Orleans, 1903), 6–7.

49. Albert Phelps, *Louisiana: A Record of Expansion* (Boston, 1905), 299.

50. *Acts,* 1908, No. 87; *Louisiana House Journal,* 1908, p. 516; *Louisiana Senate Journal,* 1908, pp. 363–64; Dominguez, *White by Definition,* 30.

51. *State* v. *Treadaway,* 126 La., 300, 501, 508, 511–12 (1910); Harriet Spiller Daggett, *Legal Essays on Family Law* (Baton Rouge, 1935), 20–22; *Louisiana House Journal,* 1910, p. 12; *Acts,* 1910, No. 206.

52. *State* v. *Treadaway* (1910), quoted in Daggett, *Legal Essays,* 11–12. Italics mine.

53. Charles S. Mangum, Jr., *The Legal Status of the Negro* (Chapel Hill, 1940), *passim;* Williamson, *New People,* 97–98; "When Is a Caucasian Not a Caucasian?" *Independent,* LXX (March 2, 1911), 478–79.

54. "When Is a Caucasian Not a Caucasian?" 478–79.

55. Daggett, *Legal Essays,* 24–25; New Orleans *Picayune,* quoted in *Crisis,* V (January, 1913), 118, and in Chicago *Broad Ax,* December 7, 1912.

56. New Orleans *Picayune*, November 29, 1912, quoted in "How Miscegenation Laws Work," *Independent*, LXXIV (January 2, 1913), 12.

57. Hermann B. Deutsch, *The Huey Long Murder Case* (Garden City, N.Y., 1963), 110–11. Not until 1970 did the Louisiana legislature approve a statute specifying the degree of ancestry that divided white from black identity: anyone of one thirty-second or more "Negro blood" was defined as a black person. The 1970 act was repealed in 1983. Since then Louisiana has not used any fraction or equation to determine racial designation—parents are free to specify the race of their children, regardless of appearances, on birth certificates; but in order to change an identity on birth or other records, the 1983 act requires a "preponderance of evidence," which calls for court interpretation. See "Louisiana Drops Racial Fractions," New York *Times*, June 26, 1983, and Dominguez, *White by Definition*, 2–4, 52–53.

CHAPTER 5: Lawyer Long

1. Julius Tison Long, "What I Know About My Brother, United States Senator Huey P. Long," *Real America*, II (September, 1933), 35; Julius T. Long to Huey P. Long, September 7, 1921, in Huey P. Long Papers, Hill Memorial Library, Louisiana State University; Thomas O. Harris, *The Kingfish: Huey P. Long, Dictator* (New Orleans, 1938), 13.

2. Huey P. Long to Julius T. Long, September 8, 1921, Julius T. Long to Huey P. Long, September 7, 1921, both in Huey P. Long Papers; Huey P. Long, *Every Man a King: The Autobiography of Huey P. Long* (New Orleans, 1933), 18; T. Harry Williams, *Huey Long* (New York, 1969), 80, 86; Meigs O. Frost, "The Romantic, Fighting Career of Huey Long," New Orleans *States*, August 28, 1927.

3. Long, *Every Man a King*, 18, 22–23.

4. Dave McConnell interview, in T. Harry Williams Papers, Hill Memorial Library, Louisiana State University; Harley B. Bozeman, "Winn Parish as I Have Known It," *Winn Parish Enterprise* (Winnfield, La.), October 17, November 7, 1957 (Clippings in Bozeman Scrapbooks, Louisiana State Library, Baton Rouge); Williams, *Huey Long*, 80–87.

5. *Congressional Record*, 74th Cong., 1st Sess., 7049; Long, *Every Man a King*, 37–39; John Tebbel, *George Horace Lorimer and the "Saturday Evening Post"* (Garden City, N.Y., 1948), 42.

6. Harris, *Kingfish*, 14.

7. *Time*, January 30, 1928, p. 10; John H. Overton to Huey P. Long, August 24, 1915, in Huey P. Long Papers.

8. Peter Finney, *The Fighting Tigers: Seventy-five Years of LSU Football* (Baton Rouge, 1968), 7–8; John R. Kemp, ed., *Martin Behrman of New Orleans: Memoirs of a City Boss* (Baton Rouge, 1977), 278–80; *American Progress*, January 4, 1934.

9. New Orleans *Daily States*, May 13, 1893; Matthew James Schott, "John M. Parker of Louisiana and the Varieties of American Progressivism" (Ph.D. dissertation, Vanderbilt University, 1969), 209–10, 231, 249–51; William Henry Harbaugh, *The Life and Times of Theodore Roosevelt* (New York, 1963), 387–423.

10. Schott, "John M. Parker," 210, 217–41; Abbeville (La.) *Meridional*, November 7, 1914; *Report of Louisiana Secretary of State, 1917*, p. 303.

11. New Orleans *Times-Picayune*, September 15, 25, 1915, January 19–20, March 23, 1916; Schott, "John M. Parker," 143–48, 249–55.

12. Schott, "John M. Parker," 91–94; Colfax (La.) *Chronicle*, October 26, 1907; Theodore Roosevelt, *A Book-Lover's Holidays in the Open* (New York, 1926), 140–44, Vol. II of Roosevelt, *Outdoor Pastimes of an American Hunter*, 2 vols.

13. *Report of Louisiana Secretary of State*, 1917, p. 287; *Avoyelles Weekly News* (Marksville, La.), March 11, 1916 (Clipping in James B. Aswell Papers, Hill Memorial Library, Louisiana State University); *Tensas Gazette* (St. Joseph, La.), March 17, 1916; Schott, "John M. Parker," 178, 191, 257–65.

14. *Report of Louisiana Secretary of State*, 1917, pp. 141–42; *Louisiana House Journal*, 1916, pp. 1019–20; *Louisiana Senate Journal*, 1916, p. 79; Colfax (La.) *Chronicle*, April 29, 1916; New York *Times*, June 11, 1916; Harbaugh, *Theodore Roosevelt*, 459–62; Schott, "John M. Parker," 287–88, 300.

15. Long, *Every Man a King*, 22–25; Williams, *Huey Long*, 85–87; Bozeman, "Winn Parish," November 7, 1957, in Bozeman Scrapbooks; Hermann B. Deutsch, "Prelude to a Heterocrat," *Saturday Evening Post*, September 7, 1935, p. 85.

16. Harry Gamble interview, in Williams Papers. In *Every Man a King*, 29, Long boasted: "My practice soon grew to such proportions that it approximated, in the number of cases handled, as much as that of the balance of the bar of Winnfield combined."

17. Long, *Every Man a King*, 25–28; *Acts*, 1914, No. 20; [Huey P. Long] to Governor Ruffin G. Pleasant, May 3, 1916, in Huey P. Long Papers.

18. Long, *Every Man a King*, 28, Huey P. Long press release, *ca.* September 1923, in Huey P. Long Papers; Huey P. Long to J. W. Mansell, May 23, 1916, in Huey P. Long Papers; Louis Cochran, "The Louisiana Kingfish," *American Mercury*, XXVI (July, 1932), 286.

19. Long, *Every Man a King*, 31; Huey P. Long to S. M. Broussard, January 8, 1920, Huey P. Long to Julius T. Long, June 2, 1920, both in Huey P. Long Papers.

20. Leonard P. Ayres, *The War with Germany: A Statistical Summary* (Washington, D.C., 1919), 23, 28; Grace King, *Memories of a Southern Woman of Letters* (New York, 1932), 364. In all, 65,988 Louisiana enlisted men, counting black and white, served in the U.S. army during World War I. Adding army officers, and navy and marine personnel, the total number of servicemen from the state approximated 72,000.

21. For an overview of World War I's economic impact on the South, including Louisiana, see George B. Tindall, *The Emergence of the New South, 1913–1945* (Baton Rouge, 1967), 53–61. See also A. B. Genung, "Agriculture in the World War Period," in *Farmers in a Changing World: Yearbook of Agriculture, 1940* (Washington, D.C., 1940), 285; James E. Boyle, *Cotton and the New Orleans Cotton Exchange* (Garden City, N.Y., 1934), 186.

22. J. Douglas Helms, "The Cotton Boll Weevil in Texas and Louisiana, 1892–1907" (M.A. thesis, Florida State University, 1970), 48–49, 72–73; Shreveport *Times*, September 19, 1907; *Tensas Gazette* (St. Joseph, La.), June 15, 1917.

23. Helen B. Pendleton, "Cotton Pickers in Northern Cities," *Survey*, XXXVII (February 17, 1917), 569–70; Robert Higgs, "The Boll Weevil, the Cotton Economy, and Black Migration, 1910–1930," *Agricultural History*, L (April, 1976), 335–50; Florette Henri, *Black Migration: Movement North, 1900–1920* (Garden City, N.Y., 1976), 51; Paul Ted McCulley, "Black Protest in Louisiana, 1898–1928" (M.A. thesis, Louisiana State University, 1970), 81.

24. *Abstract of the Fourth Census, 1920*, p. 101.

25. Tindall, *Emergence of the New South*, 51; *Acts*, 1918, Nos. 139, 188; Colfax

(La.) *Chronicle*, July 20, 1918; Herbert J. Seligmann, *The Negro Faces America* (New York, 1920), 196–97; Seth Keith, "Over Half a Century of Service," *Watchtower*, XC (August 15, 1969), 509.

26. Colfax (La.) *Chronicle*, April 14, 1917; *Tensas Gazette* (St. Joseph, La.), June 15, 1917; Henri, *Black Migration*, 305.

27. *Congressional Record*, 73d Cong., Special Sess., 275; Deutsch, "Prelude to a Heterocrat," 85; Statement by W. T. Heflin in "Huey Long No Slacker" (Advertisement in Shreveport *Times*, October 5, 1927). A less candid version of Heflin's statement appeared in *Louisiana Progress*, September 4, 1930.

28. Deutsch, "Prelude to a Heterocrat," 85; "Reply to Pleasant" (Typescript press release *ca.* September, 1923, in Huey P. Long Papers).

29. Williams, *Huey Long*, 72–73, 114; "Charges Against S. J. Harper by Assistant U.S. Attorney J. H. Jackson, Before a Federal Grand Jury, Alexandria, La., February 13, 1918," copy in Huey P. Long Papers.

30. New Orleans *Times-Picayune*, February 22, 1918; "Charges Against Harper," in Huey P. Long Papers; Harris, *Kingfish*, 18–19.

31. Huey P. Long to R. O. Jackson, August 14, 1919, in Huey P. Long Papers.

32. William Preston, Jr., *Aliens and Dissenters: Federal Suppression of Radicals, 1903–1933* (New York, 1966), 145, 147, 247–61; Long, *Every Man a King*, 34–36; Harnett T. Kane, *Louisiana Hayride: The American Rehearsal for Dictatorship, 1928–1940* (New York, 1941), 44–45.

33. Huey P. Long to Duncan H. Chamberlain, Jr., March 21, 1918, in Huey P. Long Papers; New Orleans *Times-Picayune*, February 22, 1918; Alexandria *Town Talk*, March 20, 1918 (Clipping in James B. Aswell Papers).

34. Statement of Senator S. J. Harper in Colfax (La.) *Chronicle*, May 18, 1918. See also Delos Johnson to Huey P. Long, May 14, 1918, in Huey P. Long Papers.

CHAPTER 6: Commissioner Long

1. *Constitution of 1898*, Art. CCLXXXIII; *Constitution of 1913*, Art. CCLXXXIII; T. Harry Williams, *Huey Long* (New York, 1969), 120–21.

2. Huey P. Long, *Every Man a King: The Autobiography of Huey P. Long* (New Orleans, 1933), 39–40; Julius Tison Long, "What I Know About My Brother, United States Senator Huey P. Long," *Real America*, II (September, 1933), 35–36; Huey P. Long to R. O. Jackson, August 14, 1919, in Huey P. Long Papers, Hill Memorial Library, Louisiana State University.

3. O. B. Thompson interview, in T. Harry Williams Papers, Hill Memorial Library, Louisiana State University; *Louisiana Progress*, March 27, May 15, July 17, August 7, 1930, January 2, 1932; *American Progress*, January 4, 1935.

4. *Louisiana House Journal*, 5th Extra Session, 1929, pp. 358, 447–48; Thomas O. Harris, *The Kingfish: Huey P. Long, Dictator* (New Orleans, 1938), 255–56; "Long Expected It," Washington *Evening Star*, September 9, 1935.

5. Michael Berger, *The Devil Wagon in God's Country: The Automobile and Social Change in Rural America, 1893–1929* (Hamden, Conn., 1979), 30–31; Winnfield (La.) *Comrade*, November 11, 1910; Hermann B. Deutsch, "Huey Long of Louisiana," *New Republic*, November 11, 1931, p. 349; Huey P. Long to The Biggest Little Store, March 22, 1918, in Huey P. Long Papers.

6. Long, *Every Man a King*, 40–41; Hermann B. Deutsch, "Prelude to a Heterocrat," *Saturday Evening Post*, September 7, 1935, p. 86.

7. Letter from Huey P. Long in New Orleans *Item*, March 1, 1918, quoted in

Long, *Every Man a King*, 37–39. Huey used figures on the maldistribution of wealth and unequal educational opportunities in the United States he had seen in a *Saturday Evening Post* article of September 23, 1916. He continued to cite this article during the 1930s. See *Louisiana Progress*, June, 1931.

8. Long, *Every Man a King*, 39–40; *Louisiana Progress*, September 4, 1930.

9. Harnett T. Kane, *Louisiana Hayride: The American Rehearsal for Dictatorship, 1928–1940* (New York, 1941), 77, 92–94; Long, *Every Man a King*, 19–22, 40.

10. *Report of Louisiana Secretary of State*, 1919, pp. 345, 349; Delos Johnson to Huey P. Long, October 22, 1918, in Huey P. Long Papers.

11. Ben C. Dawkins to Huey P. Long, October 31, 1918, Huey P. Long to the Federal Land Bank of New Orleans, June 10, 1919, Huey P. Long to Julius T. Long, December 16, 1918, all in Huey P. Long Papers; Harris, *Kingfish*, 21–23.

12. Brady M. Banta, "The Pine Island Situation: Petroleum, Politics, and Research Opportunities in Southern History," *Journal of Southern History*, LII (November, 1986), 590–91; Long, *Every Man a King*, 41–42; Harris, *Kingfish*, 22–23.

13. For Thomas O. Harris' first meeting with Huey, see Harley B. Bozeman, "Winn Parish as I have Known It," *Winn Parish Enterprise* (Winnfield, La.), November 7, 1957 (Clipping in Bozeman Scrapbooks, Louisiana State Library, Baton Rouge).

14. *Acts*, 1906, No. 36; George B. Tindall, *The Emergence of the New South, 1913–1945* (Baton Rouge, 1967), 91; Mabel Brasher, *Louisiana: A Study of the State* (Richmond, 1929), 178, 244. See also John L. Loos, *Oil on Stream! A History of the Interstate Oil Pipe Line Company, 1909–1959* (Baton Rouge, 1959).

15. Shreveport *Times*, March 26, 1919; Brady M. Banta, "The Regulation and Conservation of Petroleum Resources in Louisiana, 1901–1940" (Ph.D. dissertation, Louisiana State University, 1981), 123–30; New Orleans *Times-Picayune*, June 27, 1919.

16. New Orleans *Times-Picayune*, June 28, 1919; Banta, "Regulation and Conservation," 130–31.

17. Banta, "Pine Island Situation," 599–600; Long, *Every Man a King*, 46.

18. Alexandria *Town Talk*, July 3–4, 1919; New Orleans *States*, July 5, 1919.

19. Deutsch, "Huey Long of Louisiana," 350; New Orleans *Times-Picayune*, July 5, 1919; New Orleans *States*, July 5, 1919.

20. New Orleans *States*, July 5, 1919.

21. Alexandria *Town Talk*, July 5, 1919; J. Martian Hamley to U.S. Senator Edward J. Gay, July 7, 12, 1919, in Edward J. Gay Papers, Hill Memorial Library, Louisiana State University; Huey P. Long to Dr. George S. Long, July 30, 1919, in Huey P. Long Papers.

22. Matthew James Schott, "John M. Parker of Louisiana and the Varieties of American Progressivism" (Ph.D. dissertation, Vanderbilt University, 1969), 336–42; Huey P. Long to H. A. Ashby, January 10, 1920, in Huey P. Long Papers; Homer (La.) *Guardian-Journal*, September 10, 24, 1919; New Orleans *Times-Picayune*, January 13–14, 1920.

23. Schott, "John M. Parker," 315–24; New Orleans *Times-Picayune*, September 20, 1917; William Henry Harbaugh, *The Life and Times of Theodore Roosevelt* (New York, 1963), 471–74.

24. Parker political advertisement in Homer (La.) *Guardian-Journal*, December 10, 1919; Spencer Phillips, "Administration of Governor Parker" (M.A. thesis, Louisiana State University, 1933), 23–24; Schott, "John M. Parker," 250, 419.

25. Phillips, "Governor Parker," 24–33; Perry H. Howard, *Political Tendencies in Louisiana* (Rev. ed.; Baton Rouge, 1971), 211; John R. Kemp, ed., *Martin Behrman of New Orleans: Memoirs of a City Boss* (Baton Rouge, 1977), 291.

26. Huey P. Long to Harley Bozeman, November 28, 1919, in Huey P. Long Papers; Al Rose, *Storyville, New Orleans: Being an Authentic, Illustrated Account of the Notorious Red-Light District* (University, Ala., 1974), 42–46. For twenty years, Tom Anderson listed his occupation in the *Louisiana House Journal* as "merchant," but did not specify merchant of what.

27. "Thomas C. Anderson," in David H. Brown, comp., *A History of Who's Who in Louisiana Politics in 1916* (N.p., 1916), 82; Typescript and handwritten notes of Huey P. Long's speeches during the Parker-Stubbs campaign of 1919–20, p. 1, in Huey P. Long Papers; "Why Railroad Lawyer Stubbs is Supported by Standard Oil, New Orleans Ring, and the Tom Anderson Red Light Organization," Long advertisement in Homer (La.) *Guardian-Journal*, December 10, 1919.

28. Kemp, ed., *Martin Behrman*, 307–12; New Orleans *Times-Picayune*, January 13–15, 1920.

29. Alexandria *Town Talk*, January 14–15, 1920; Monroe *News-Star*, February 26, 1916 (Clipping in James B. Aswell Papers, Hill Memorial Library, Louisiana State University); Colfax (La.) *Chronicle*, December 20, 1919.

30. Huey P. Long to J. L. Ferguson, January 26, 1920, in Huey P. Long Papers; Homer (La.) *Guardian-Journal*, December 10, 1919; *Report of Louisiana Secretary of State*, 1919, pp. 278–79; Paul Lewinson, *Race, Class, and Party: A History of Negro Suffrage and White Politics in the South* (1932; rpr. New York, 1965), 112, 230–32.

31. Jack Temple Kirby, *Rural Worlds Lost: The American South, 1920–1960* (Baton Rouge, 1987), 5, 315–16; T. Arnold Hill, "Why Southern Negroes Don't Go South," *Survey*, XLIII (November, 1919), 183–85; Neil Fligstein, *Going North: Migration of Blacks and Whites from the South, 1900–1950* (New York, 1981), 91.

32. Homer (La.) *Guardian-Journal*, November 12, 1919; James E. Boyle, *Cotton and the New Orleans Cotton Exchange* (Garden City, N.Y., 1934), 186; Sheriff T. R. Hughes of Caddo Parish to U.S. Senator Edward J. Gay, October 21, 1919, in Gay Papers; Paul Ted McCulley, "Black Protest in Louisiana, 1898–1928" (M.A. thesis, Louisiana State University, 1970), 62–63, 65; Shreveport *Journal*, August 29, 1919.

33. Quoted in Florette Henri, *Black Migration: Movement North, 1900–1920* (Garden City, N.Y., 1976), 308. See also Herbert J. Seligmann, "Democracy and Jim-Crowism," *New Republic*, September 3, 1919, p. 151.

34. "Lynchings in 1919," *Literary Digest*, January 17, 1920, p. 20.

35. McCulley, "Black Protest in Louisiana," 107–108; Shreveport *Times*, January 31, 1919; Shreveport *Journal*, February 1, 1919.

36. "The Monroe Horror," Editorial, New Orleans *Times-Picayune*, May 13, 1919; Shreveport *Journal*, May 16, 1919; Herbert J. Seligmann, "Protecting Southern Womanhood," *Nation*, June 14, 1919, pp. 938–39; "Nurses Tell of Visits by Mob," Monroe *News-Star*, May 1, 1919.

37. Harley Bozeman to Huey P. Long, November 26, 1919, Huey P. Long to Harley Bozeman, November 19, 1919, both in Huey P. Long Papers.

38. Roy Wilkins, "Huey Long Says: An Interview with Louisiana's Kingfish," *Crisis*, XLII (February, 1935), 41, 52; Huey P. Long, "Our National Plight," *Louisiana Progress*, August 18, 1931.

39. Huey P. Long to Samuel A. Montgomery, June 12, 1920, in Huey P. Long Papers.

40. Huey P. Long to W. W. White, December 11, 1919, in Huey P. Long Papers; *Report of Louisiana Secretary of State*, 1921, pp. 424, 433–34.

CHAPTER 7: Disgusted

1. New Orleans *Times-Picayune*, May 18, 1920; Colfax (La.) *Chronicle*, May 22, 1920; Matthew James Schott, "John M. Parker of Louisiana and the Varieties of American Progressivism" (Ph.D. dissertation, Vanderbilt University, 1969), 350.

2. Schott, "John M. Parker," 344–45, 362; Huey P. Long to D. H. Finley, February 14, 1920, in Huey P. Long Papers, Hill Memorial Library, Louisiana State University; Brady M. Banta, "The Pine Island Situation: Petroleum, Politics, and Research Opportunities in Southern History," *Journal of Southern History*, LII (November, 1986), 601–605; *Acts*, 1920, Nos. 73 and 76.

3. Brady M. Banta, "The Regulation and Conservation of Petroleum Resources in Louisiana, 1901–1940" (Ph.D. dissertation, Louisiana State University, 1981), 247–69; T. Harry Williams, *Huey Long* (New York, 1969), 141–42.

4. Baton Rouge *State-Times*, April 28, 1920; Shreveport *Times*, May 2, 1920; Banta, "Regulation and Conservation," 166–69; *Acts*, 1920, No. 31; Schott, "John M. Parker," 359–60, 364–69.

5. Schott, "John M. Parker," 368; Banta, "Pine Island Situation," 600n; Huey P. Long to Leland H. Moss, November 9, 1920, in Huey P. Long Papers.

6. Huey P. Long to R. O. Jackson, August 14, 1919, Huey P. Long to Julius T. Long, February 23, April 8, 1920, all in Huey P. Long Papers.

7. Callie Long to Huey P. Long, *ca.* March 15, August 4, 1919, Huey P. Long to Callie Long, January 19, 1920, Huey P. Long to Julius T. Long, April 8, February 23, 1920, all *ibid.*

8. Huey P. Long to Julius T. Long, January 9, 1920, Charles J. Rivet to Huey P. Long, December 13, 1919, both *ibid.;* Williams, *Huey Long*, 315; "Earl, Huey Fought," New Orleans *Times-Picayune*, September 7, 1975; Huey P. Long to Callie Long, January 19, 1920, in Huey P. Long Papers.

9. Callie Long interview, Memphis *Commercial Appeal*, September 12, 1935.

10. Huey P. Long to Julius T. Long, January 29, 1920, Huey P. Long to Charles L. Orr, November 24, 1920, both in Huey P. Long Papers; Julius Tison Long, "What I Know About My Brother, United States Senator Huey P. Long," *Real America*, II (September, 1933), 35.

11. Huey P. Long to Julius T. Long, August 21, 1921 (Photocopy in Julius T. Long, "What I Know," 37); Julius T. Long to Huey P. Long, September 7, 1921, Huey P. Long to Julius T. Long, September 8, November 12, 1921, all in Huey P. Long Papers.

12. See chaps. 2 and 3.

13. Huey P. Long to Dr. George S. Long, April 12, 1920, December 22, 1921, in Huey P. Long Papers.

14. Huey P. Long to Mrs. R. W. Davis (Charlotte Long Davis), March 18, 1920, *ibid.*

15. Huey P. Long to Aline McConnell, November 17, 1920, *ibid.* Even so, Huey put David and Lee McConnell on the state pay roll, with good salaries, after he became governor. See Webster Smith, *The Kingfish: A Biography of Huey P. Long* (New York, 1933), 183–84.

16. Huey P. Long to Dr. Arthur D. Long, February 19, August 29, 1921, Huey P. Long to Aline McConnell, May 23, September 13, 21, October 25, 1921, all in Huey P. Long Papers. See also numerous letters from Aline to Huey during 1921, *ibid.*

17. Huey P. Long to Aline McConnell, September 21, 1921, *ibid.*

18. *Constitution of 1913*, Art. LXII; Huey P. Long to Dr. George S. Long, July 30, 1919, in Huey P. Long Papers.

19. *Report of Louisiana Secretary of State*, 1921, pp. 603–604; George M. Reynolds, *Machine Politics in New Orleans, 1897–1926* (New York, 1936), 210–12, 215.

20. My summary of the New Orleans Ring and its objectives relies heavily on three books, of which Haas's is the most recent and useful: Reynolds, *Machine Politics in New Orleans;* John R. Kemp, ed., *Martin Behrman of New Orleans: Memoirs of a City Boss* (Baton Rouge, 1977); Edward F. Haas, *Political Leadership in a Southern City: New Orleans in the Progressive Era, 1896–1902* (Ruston, La., 1988).

21. Kemp, ed., *Martin Behrman*, 1–6. Behrman wrote his memoirs for the New Orleans *Item* during 1922 and 1923, and John R. Kemp edited the ex-mayor's recollections for this book.

22. *Ibid.*, 108–10, 34–42; Harnett T. Kane, *Louisiana Hayride: The American Rehearsal for Dictatorship, 1928–1940* (New York, 1941), 32; Reynolds, *Machine Politics in New Orleans*, 160–61, 227–28.

23. Reynolds, *Machine Politics in New Orleans*, 233–37; Haas, *Political Leadership*, 28–29, 91; Frank Putnam, "New Orleans in Transition," *New England Magazine*, XXXVI (April, 1907), 227–39; Matthew J. Schott, "The New Orleans Machine and Progressivism," *Louisiana History*, XXIV (Spring, 1983), 142–49; Alexandria *Town Talk*, August 11–12, 1925; H. L. Mencken, "The Calamity of Appomattox," *American Mercury*, XXI (September, 1930), 30.

24. Adam Fairclough, "The Public Utilities Industry in New Orleans: A Study in Capital, Labor, and Government, 1894–1929," *Louisiana History*, XXII (Winter, 1981), 47–57; Kemp, ed., *Martin Behrman*, xvii–xviii; Reynolds, *Machine Politics in New Orleans*, 136, 155–56, 230–35.

25. Reynolds, *Machine Politics in New Orleans*, 210–16; Allan P. Sindler, *Huey Long's Louisiana: State Politics, 1920–1952* (Baltimore, 1956), 41.

26. Huey P. Long to Charles L. Orr, November 24, 1920, in Huey P. Long Papers; *Report of Louisiana Secretary of State*, 1921, pp. 603–604. Long also opposed the 1921 convention because the constitution it would write was not to be submitted to the voters for ratification. See Matthew J. Schott, "Progressives Against Democracy: Electoral Reform in Louisiana, 1894–1921," *Louisiana History*, XX (Summer, 1979), 257–58.

27. New Orleans *Times-Picayune*, January 31, 1920, quoted in Kemp, ed., *Martin Behrman*, 319.

28. *Constitution of 1921*, Art. X, Sec. 21; Baton Rouge *State-Times*, April 7, May 26, June 14, 1921; Banta, "Regulation and Conservation," 171–89.

29. Bennett H. Wall, ed., *Louisiana: A History* (2d ed.; Arlington Heights, Ill., 1990), 275; Major Richardson [chief of state engineers] interview, New Orleans *Times-Democrat*, October 25, 1900; Sindler, *Huey Long's Louisiana*, 43–44.

30. John M. Parker to Sam C. Butterfield, October 30, 1922, in Governor's Correspondence, Hill Memorial Library, Louisiana State University; *Constitution of 1921*, Art. X, Sec. 1; *Acts*, 1934, No. 21.

31. *Constitution of 1921*, Art. XIV, Sec. 15; Kemp, ed., *Martin Behrman*, 320–

21; Reynolds, *Machine Politics in New Orleans,* 67–68. Parker's capitulation on civil service lost him the approval of the New Orleans *Item,* previously his strongest newspaper supporter.

32. *Constitution of 1921,* Art. XXII, Sec. 1, Pt. 9; Carmen Lindig, *The Path from the Parlor: Louisiana Women, 1879–1920* (Lafayette, La., 1986), 157–64.

33. *Guinn* v. *United States,* 238 U.S. 347 (1915).

34. *Constitution of 1921,* Art. VIII, Sec. 1; *Report of Louisiana Secretary of State,* 1929, pp. 328–29. Of the 1,960 registered "colored" voters in 1928, only 307 were female. Of the state's total black registrants, Orleans Parish had 1,723 (88 percent). Forty-one of the sixty-four parishes, including those with the highest percentage of black population, listed none.

35. *Constitution of 1921,* Arts. IV, VI, VII. The quotation on female labor is from Art. IV, Sec. 6.

36. Mark T. Carleton, "The Louisiana Constitution of 1974," in *Louisiana Politics: Festival in a Labyrinth,* ed. James Bolner (Baton Rouge, 1982), 17–19; Parker quoted in Schott, "John M. Parker," 402.

37. *The History and the Government of Louisiana: Research Study No. 17 of Louisiana Legislative Council* (Baton Rouge, 1964), 78; Carleton, "Louisiana Constitution of 1974," in *Louisiana Politics,* ed. Bolner, 18.

38. Huey P. Long, *Every Man a King: The Autobiography of Huey P. Long* (New Orleans, 1933), 56–58; Williams, *Huey Long,* 146, 162–66; Banta, "Regulation and Conservation," 182–83.

39. Long, *Every Man a King,* 59–60; Colfax (La.) *Chronicle,* November 5, 1921; Mildred Adams, "Huey the Great," *Forum,* LXXXIX (February, 1933), 72–73; Williams, *Huey Long,* 148–49.

40. "Field of Honor," Shreveport *Times,* March 1, 1893. For a summary of dueling's antebellum popularity, see Bertram Wyatt-Brown, *Honor and Violence in the Old South* (New York, 1986), 142–53.

41. Kemp, ed., *Martin Behrman,* 124–25, 129–30; John Wilds, *Afternoon Story: A Century of the New Orleans "States-Item"* (Baton Rouge, 1976), 172–74.

42. Thomas O. Harris, *The Kingfish: Huey P. Long, Dictator* (New Orleans, 1938), 24–25; Julius T. Long, "What I Know," 35–36; Shreveport *Times,* November 3, 9, 1921; Colfax (La.) *Chronicle,* November 11, 1921. There are differing accounts as to who paid the dollar fine. Huey later claimed Judge Brunot paid fifty cents of it. Long, *Every Man a King,* 62–63.

43. Harris, *Kingfish,* 24; Williams, *Huey Long,* 167–68.

44. Lake Charles (La.) *American Press,* September 5, 1921; Williams, *Huey Long,* 234.

45. Carleton Beals, *The Story of Huey P. Long* (Philadelphia, 1935), 50; Shreveport *Journal,* January 16, 1923; Harris, *Kingfish,* 25–26; New Orleans *States,* November 14, 1921 (Clipping in Huey P. Long Scrapbooks, Hill Memorial Library, Louisiana State University).

CHAPTER 8 : *Long Our Next Governor*

1. Edwin W. Edwards, "The Role of the Governor in Louisiana Politics: An Historical Analysis," *Louisiana History,* XV (Spring, 1974), 101.

2. Thomas O. Harris, *The Kingfish: Huey P. Long, Dictator* (New Orleans, 1938), 25; Huey P. Long press release attacking Judge Palmer, *ca.* 1923 (Type-

script in Huey P. Long Papers, Hill Memorial Library, Louisiana State University).

3. Rich P. Parker to Huey P. Long, April 4, 1923, Donelson Caffery to Huey P. Long, January 8, 10, May 23, 26, 30, 1923, all in Huey P. Long Papers. For Rich Parker's Socialist party background, see Winnfield *Comrade*, August 5, 1910.

4. St. Francisville (La.) *True Democrat*, quoted in Kentwood (La.) *Commercial*, May 9, 1913; *Louisiana House Journal*, 1912, pp. 17–18; J. Y. Sanders, "The Senatorial Campaign of 1926," chap. 11, pp. 1–2 (Typescript in Jared Y. Sanders Papers, Hill Memorial Library, Louisiana State University).

5. New Orleans *Picayune*, January 6, 1899; Michael Berger, *The Devil Wagon in God's Country: The Automobile and Social Change in Rural America, 1893–1929* (Hamden, Conn., 1979), 44; Abbeville (La.) *Meridional*, January 4, 18, 1919; New Orleans *Item*, quoted in *Literary Digest*, October 21, 1922, p. 44.

6. Colfax (La.) *Chronicle*, July 5, 26, 1919. See also New Orleans *Times-Picayune*, July 2, 1919.

7. A. W. McClellan to John M. Parker, April 18, 1922, J. H. Halland to Parker, April 21, 1922, Secretary to the Governor [Thomas O. Harris] to Mrs. Lillian W. Chase, June 20, 1922, all in Governor's Correspondence, Hill Memorial Library, Louisiana State University; Allan P. Sindler, *Huey Long's Louisiana: State Politics, 1920–1952* (Baltimore, 1956), 43–45.

8. *Compendium of the Eleventh Census*, 1890, I, 748, III, 314; *Statistical Abstract of the United States*, 1921, pp. 120–21.

9. *Louisiana School Review*, XIII (January, 1906), 78–79; *Louisiana Department of Education Report*, 1924–25, p. 65.

10. *Constitution of 1898*, Art. CCXLVIII; *Constitution of 1921*, Art. XII, Sec. 14; Colfax (La.) *Chronicle*, September 1, 1900.

11. See comparisons of white illiteracy by parishes in *Louisiana School Review*, XIII (January, 1906), 78–79; *Louisiana Superintendent of Education Report*, 1908–1909, pp. 51–52; *Louisiana Superintendent of Education Report*, 1912–13, pp. 26, 215; House Bill No. 87 [to virtually terminate black public education], in *Louisiana House Journal*, 1904, p. 110; *Louisiana Department of Education Report*, 1922–23, Pt. 1, p. 6, 16–17, 53, Pt. 2, pp. 40–45; *Louisiana Department of Education Report*, 1923–24, pp. 9–10, 12, 14, 13, 47; Harris' statement on transportation quoted in Jane Ellen McAllister, *The Training of Negro Teachers in Louisiana* (New York, 1929), 19; *Acts*, 1916, No. 27.

12. New Orleans *Times-Picayune*, September 1, 1923; *Speech and Platform of Huey P. Long* (Pamphlet, ca. 1923, in Huey P. Long Scrapbooks, Hill Memorial Library, Louisiana State University); T. Harry Williams, *Huey Long* (New York, 1969), 198–99.

13. Carleton Beals, *The Story of Huey P. Long* (Philadelphia, 1935), 55–56; Hamilton Basso, "Huey Long and His Background," *Harper's Monthly*, CLXX (May, 1935), 663–65, 670; W. J. Cash, *The Mind of the South* (New York, 1960), 293.

14. Webster Smith, *The Kingfish: A Biography of Huey P. Long* (New York, 1933), 31–32; Rose Lee, "Senator Long at Home," *New Republic*, May 30, 1934, p. 67; Williams, *Huey Long*, 200; Harnett T. Kane, *Louisiana Hayride: The American Rehearsal for Dictatorship, 1928–1940* (New York, 1941), 48; Russell Owen, "Huey Long Keeps Washington Guessing," *New York Times Magazine*, January 29, 1933, p. 14.

15. Sindler, *Huey Long's Louisiana*, 48; Perry H. Howard, *Political Tendencies*

in Louisiana (Rev. ed.; Baton Rouge, 1971), 227–29; Mark T. Carleton, *Politics and Punishment: The History of the Louisiana State Penal System* (Baton Rouge, 1971), 107, 111; George M. Reynolds, *Machine Politics in New Orleans, 1897–1926* (New York, 1936), 217–222.

16. New Orleans *Daily States,* July 4, 1911 (Clipping in James B. Aswell Papers, Hill Memorial Library, Louisiana State University); Edward Rightor to Charles K. Fuqua, December 28, 1911, in Charles K. Fuqua Papers, Hill Memorial Library, Louisiana State University; Howard, *Political Tendencies,* 202–203; *Report of Louisiana Secretary of State, 1912,* Pt. 2, "Recapitulation," p. 129ff.; John R. Kemp, ed., *Martin Behrman of New Orleans: Memoirs of a City Boss* (Baton Rouge, 1977), 270n; Dave H. Brown, comp., *A History of Who's Who in Louisiana Politics in 1916* (N.p., 1916), 39–40.

17. *Lafourche Comet* (Thibodaux, La.), January 3, 1924.

18. Harvey G. Fields, *A True History of the Life, Works, Assassination, and Death of Huey Pierce Long* (Farmerville, La., 1945), 27; Beals, *Story of Long,* 60; Huey P. Long to E. R. Bernstein, December 30, 1924, in Huey P. Long Papers; Williams, *Huey Long,* 104, 201; Julius Tison Long, "Julius T. Long Unmasks His Brother, U.S. Senator Huey P. Long," *Real America,* II (October, 1933), 55; *Senate Hearings on Campaign Expenditures,* 72d Cong., 2d Sess., Pt. 1, p. 953.

19. New Orleans *Times-Picayune,* August 17, September 1, 30, 1923; New Orleans *Item,* December 22, 1923; Sindler, *Huey Long's Louisiana,* 48; Williams, *Huey Long,* 196–97.

20. Dave McConnell interview, in T. Harry Williams Papers, Hill Memorial Library, Louisiana State University; Huey P. Long, *Every Man a King: The Autobiography of Huey P. Long* (New Orleans, 1933), 74–75; Hermann B. Deutsch, "Prelude to a Heterocrat," *Saturday Evening Post,* September 7, 1935, p. 87.

21. Long, *Every Man a King,* 73–74.

22. New Orleans *Morning Tribune,* October 9, 1930 (Clipping in E. A. Conway Scrapbooks, Louisiana State Library, Baton Rouge); Beals, *Story of Long,* 192; Colfax (La.) *Chronicle,* March 12, 1926.

23. For the Long-Grosjean relationship, and differing versions of it, see Williams, *Huey Long,* 254–55, 317–18, 471–73, 488–89; Sam Irby, *Kidnaped by the Kingfish: With Intimate Details of This and Other Crimes of Huey P. Long* (New Orleans, 1932), 21–23; Beals, *Story of Long,* 192–97; H. Lester Hughes, Richard W. Leche interviews, both in Williams Papers; Kane, *Louisiana Hayride,* 83–84; "Long's Latest," *Time,* October 20, 1930.

24. Shreveport *Times,* December 3, 1923; Colfax (La.) *Chronicle,* December 8, 1923; Abbeville (La.) *Meridional,* September 22, 1923; Dudley J. LeBlanc to Huey P. Long, December 4, 1923, in Huey P. Long Papers; Theophile Landry interview, in Williams Papers; Julius Long, quoted in Arthur M. Schlesinger, Jr., *The Politics of Upheaval* (Boston, 1960), 51.

25. Open letter from Huey P. Long to John M. Parker, October 28, 1923, in Huey P. Long Papers; New Orleans *Times-Picayune,* November 12, 1923; Long, *Every Man a King,* 75–76; Sindler, *Huey Long's Louisiana,* 49.

26. Hiram Wesley Evans, "The Klan's Fight for Americanism," *North American Review,* CCXXIII (Spring, 1926), 35–63; John Higham, *Strangers in the Land: Patterns of American Nativism, 1860–1925* (New York, 1963), 286–97; "The Murders of Mer Rouge," *Literary Digest,* January 13, 1923, pp. 10–12; New York *Times,* November 20, 22, 1922, April 17, 20, 1923.

27. Kenneth E. Harrell, "The Ku Klux Klan in Louisiana, 1920–1930" (Ph.D. dissertation, Louisiana State University, 1966), v–vi, 111–17, 132, 321–26; Mabel Brasher, *Louisiana: A Study of the State* (Atlanta, 1929), 17–18; T. Lynn Smith and Homer L. Hitt, *The People of Louisiana* (Baton Rouge, 1952), 128–30; Sindler, *Huey Long's Louisiana*, 31.

28. David M. Chalmers, *Hooded Americanism: The History of the Ku Klux Klan* (New York, 1965), 59; Harrell, "Klan in Louisiana," 113–25.

29. Unidentified clipping from Shreveport newspaper, *ca.* 1922, quoting Rev. M. E. Dodd, in Huey P. Long Scrapbooks; Charles C. Alexander, *The Ku Klux Klan in the Southwest* (Lexington, Ky., 1965), 43, 98–99; Matthew James Schott, "John M. Parker of Louisiana and the Varieties of American Progressivism" (Ph.D. dissertation, Vanderbilt University, 1969), 420–21. Long opposed Thomas for political and personal reasons, not because Thomas was backed by the Klan.

30. Harrell, "Klan in Louisiana," 125–29; Chalmers, *Hooded Americanism*, 32–34, 59; Kenneth T. Jackson, *The Ku Klux Klan in the City, 1915–1930* (New York, 1967), 238–40; Leonard Lanson Cline, "In Darkest Louisiana," *Nation*, March 14, 1923, p. 293.

31. George B. Tindall, *The Emergence of the New South, 1913–1945* (Baton Rouge, 1967), 192; Alexander, *Klan in the Southwest*, 43; Harrell, "Klan in Louisiana," 268–69; Leesville (La.) *Leader*, March 16, 1922.

32. Morehouse and Richland reported slightly fewer lynchings, prior to 1922, than three other parishes (Ouachita, Caddo, and Bossier), but those three were more populous. Mary Ross, "Where Lynching Is a Habit," *Survey*, LXIX (February 15, 1923), 626–27.

33. *Morehouse Clarion* (Bastrop, La.), September 2, 16, 1881. Commenting upon the cattle rustler's fate, the *Richland Beacon* (Rayville, La.), October 1, 1881, also chortled about "cow-PITAL punishment," but ominously added, "We know a great many worse things are continually being done in our vicinity."

34. Alton Earl Ingram, "The Twentieth Century Ku Klux Klan in Morehouse Parish, Louisiana" (M.A. thesis, Louisiana State University, 1961), 27; New Orleans *Times-Picayune*, January 10, 1923; Harrell, "Klan in Louisiana," 189–90.

35. Skipwith quoted in John Rogers, *The Murders of Mer Rouge: The True Story of an Atrocity Unparalleled in the Annals of Crime* (St. Louis, 1923), 20 (Copy in Joseph P. Hornor Collection, Hill Memorial Library, Louisiana State University); Harrell, "Klan in Louisiana," 196–99.

36. *Morehouse Enterprise* (Bastrop, La.), May 26, July 28, 1922; Rogers, *Murders of Mer Rouge*, 21–23; Harrell, "Klan in Louisiana," 196–99.

37. Robert L. Duffus, "How the Ku Klux Klan Sells Hate," *World's Work*, XLVI (July, 1923), 175–76; Harrell, "Klan in Louisiana," 208–11; *Morehouse Enterprise* (Bastrop, La.), September 1, December 22, 1922.

38. Rogers, *Murders of Mer Rouge*, 21–22.

39. Cline, "In Darkest Louisiana," 292–93; Harrell, "Klan in Louisiana," 199–207; *Morehouse Enterprise* (Bastrop, La.), August 4, December 29, 1922; New Orleans *Times-Picayune*, December 30, 1922, January 11, 1923. The reason for the shootout between Drs. McCoin and Thom was said to be "professional jealousy."

40. Rogers, *Murders of Mer Rouge*, 23; Schott, "John M. Parker," 424–26.

41. John M. Parker to M. M. Mallary, June 20, 1922, Secretary to the Governor to Mrs. Lillian W. Chase, June 20, 1922, John M. Parker to George B. Campbell,

September 4, 1922, all in Governor's Correspondence; Schott, "John M. Parker," 409–10.

42. Schott, "John M. Parker," 429–32; New York *Times*, November 20, 1922. See also identical letters from John M. Parker to U.S. Senators Joseph E. Ransdell and Edwin S. Broussard, November 24, 1922, in Governor's Correspondence. The italics in the quotation from the letter to Harding are mine.

43. *Morehouse Enterprise* (Bastrop, La.), November 10, December 22, 1922; New Orleans *Times-Picayune*, November 29, December 24, 1922; Schott, "John M. Parker," 437; Chalmers, *Hooded Americanism*, 62.

44. Cline, "In Darkest Louisiana," 292–93; New York *Times*, November 22, 1922, February 22, April 17, 19–20, 1923; "Mer Rouge Murders Unpunished," *Literary Digest*, March 31, 1923, pp. 10–11; Abbeville (La.) *Meridional*, January 6, 1923; Schott, "John M. Parker," 439; Harrell "Klan in Louisiana," 232–62.

45. Abbeville (La.) *Meridional*, April 7, 1923; St. Martinville (La.) *Messenger*, quoted *ibid.;* New Orleans *Times-Picayune*, April 7, 1923. See also Donaldsonville (La.) *Chief*, January 13, 1923.

46. Harrell, "Klan in Louisiana," 291–92. See also Colfax (La.) *Chronicle*, July 22, September 2, 1922; *Richland Beacon-News* (Rayville, La.), August 5, 1922.

47. New Orleans *Times-Picayune*, August 27, October 6, 1923; Harrell, "Klan in Louisiana," 329–32; Bouanchaud circular, *ca.* 1923, in Huey P. Long Scrapbooks; Baton Rouge *State-Times*, January 12, 1924.

48. Harrell, "Klan in Louisiana," 333–34; Baton Rouge *State-Times*, September 30, 1923; Abbeville (La.) *Meridional*, December 15, 1923; Reynolds, *Machine Politics in New Orleans*, 149, 218–19.

49. Harris, *Kingfish*, 27–28; Kane, *Louisiana Hayride*, 51; Huey P. Long to Dr. George S. Long, December 22, 1921, in Huey P. Long Papers.

50. Smith, *Kingfish*, 35–36; Harrell, "Klan in Louisiana," 335–37, 357. See also Fuqua ad in Alexandria *Town Talk*, January 11, 1924.

51. Huey P. Long press release, *ca.* October, 1923 (Typescript in Huey P. Long Papers); "Why We Are for Huey P. Long!" (Circular, *ca.* September, 1923, in Huey P. Long Scrapbooks); Abbeville (La.) *Meridional*, September 22, 1923.

52. *Morehouse Enterprise* (Bastrop, La.), November 9, 1923; Harrell, "Klan in Louisiana," 258–59; Colfax (La.) *Chronicle*, November 10, 1923. Skipwith's little fine was mentioned, with grim humor, in *New Republic*, November 28, 1923, p. 18, as "the heavy hand of justice in Louisiana."

53. New Orleans *States*, January 11, 13, 1924.

54. Long, *Every Man a King*, 76–77; *Report of Louisiana Secretary of State*, 1925, p. 372 (residents of Clay community in Jackson Parish voted at the Ansley Precinct); Baton Rouge *State-Times*, January 15, 1924; New Orleans *States*, January 15, 1924.

55. *Report of Louisiana Secretary of State*, 1925, pp. 402, 435.

56. *Ibid.*, 480; Colfax (La.) *Chronicle*, February 23, 1924; *Morehouse Enterprise* (Bastrop, La.), January 18, February 22, 1924.

57. *Madison Journal* (Tallulah, La.), February 2, 1924; Schott, "John M. Parker," 456–59; Huey P. Long press release, *ca.* January 20, 1924 (Typescript in Huey P. Long Papers).

58. *Lafourche Comet* (Thibodaux, La.), January 3, 10, 1924; *Richland Beacon-News* (Rayville, La.), January 12, 1924; *Madison Journal* (Tallulah, La.), January 26, 1924; Letter from J. M. Downey in New Orleans *Times-Picayune*, January 26, 1924 (Clipping in Huey P. Long Scrapbooks).

CHAPTER 9: Rising and Shining

1. Huey P. Long, *Every Man a King: The Autobiography of Huey P. Long* (New Orleans, 1933), 77–78.

2. Adras Laborde, *A National Southerner: Ransdell of Louisiana* (New York, 1951), 107–11; Telegram from Dudley J. LeBlanc to Huey P. Long, September 11, 1924, in Huey P. Long Papers, Hill Memorial Library, Louisiana State University; Long, *Every Man a King*, 79.

3. T. Harry Williams, *Huey Long* (New York, 1969), 220; J. Y. Sanders, "The Senatorial Campaign of 1926," chap. 3, p. 8 (Typescript in Jared Y. Sanders Papers, Hill Memorial Library, Louisiana State University). See also Maude Hearn O'Pry, *Chronicles of Shreveport* (Shreveport, 1928), 204.

4. Kenneth E. Harrell, "The Ku Klux Klan in Louisiana, 1920–1930" (Ph.D. dissertation, Louisiana State University, 1966), 295–97, 320–23, 348–53; David M. Chalmers, *Hooded Americanism: The History of the Ku Klux Klan* (New York, 1965), 65. For Sheriff Carpenter's shortage and removal, see John M. Parker to A. V. Coco, January 21, 1924, Parker to J. F. Carpenter, January 22, 1924, both in Governor's Correspondence, Hill Memorial Library, Louisiana State University; and Colfax (La.) *Chronicle*, March 1, 1924.

5. *Acts*, 1924, Nos. 2 and 3; Harrell, "Klan in Louisiana," 132, 343–50; Charles C. Alexander, *The Ku Klux Klan in the Southwest* (Lexington, Ky., 1965), 26.

6. *Compilation of Louisiana Democratic Primary Returns*, September 9, 1924, pp. 49, 51; *Louisiana Progress*, August 7, 1930.

7. *Compilation of Louisiana Democratic Primary Returns*, September 9, 1924, Parish of Winn, 47–48; Huey P. Long to Henry Jastremski, July 7, 1924, in Huey P. Long Papers; Williams, *Huey Long*, 221–22.

8. New Orleans *Times-Picayune*, January 4, 6, 8, February 9, 1925, January 13, 1926; George M. Reynolds, *Machine Politics in New Orleans, 1897–1926* (New York, 1936), 219–23; Walter G. Cowan *et al., New Orleans Yesterday and Today: A Guide to the City* (Baton Rouge, 1983), 164; John R. Kemp, ed., *Martin Behrman of New Orleans: Memoirs of a City Boss* (Baton Rouge, 1977), 329, 335–41.

9. Thomas O. Harris, *The Kingfish: Huey P. Long, Dictator* (New Orleans, 1938), 29–31; Sanders, "Senatorial Campaign of 1926," chap. 8, p. 9; Abbeville (La.) *Meridional*, October 13, 1900.

10. *Report of Louisiana Secretary of State*, 1912, Pt. 2, "Recapitulation," 129ff.; *Ibid.*, 1921, pp. 576–77; Hewitt Bouanchaud to Edward J. Gay, May 26, 1919, in Edward J. Gay Papers, Hill Memorial Library, Louisiana State University.

11. Sanders, "Senatorial Campaign of 1926," chap. 3, pp. 1–3, chap. 5, pp. 6–7, chap. 7, pp. 9–10; Kemp, ed., *Martin Behrman*, 265–72; Colfax (La.) *Chronicle*, August 27, 1926; *Tensas Gazette* (St. Joseph, La.), November 10, 1911, February 2, 1912. For a succinct description of J. Y. Sanders' oratorical themes, see Winnfield (La.) *Southern Sentinel*, January 17, 1908.

12. Long, *Every Man a King*, 82–83; Julius T. Long to Edwin S. Broussard, April 24, 1926, in Huey P. Long Papers; Carleton Beals, *The Story of Huey P. Long* (Philadelphia, 1935), 70–71; *Nouveau Petit Larousse* (Paris, 1972), 1614; Sanders, "Senatorial Campaign of 1926," chap. 6, p. 4; *Governor Sanders Nails Long with Record* (Pamphlet, *ca.* 1926, in Sanders Papers).

13. Sanders, "Senatorial Campaign of 1926," chap. 7, p. 101; Reinhard H. Luthin, *American Demagogues: Twentieth Century* (1954; rpr. Gloucester, Mass., 1959), 244.

14. *Compilation of Louisiana Democratic Primary Returns,* September 14, 1926, pp. 67–68; Long, *Every Man a King,* 82–83; Harris, *Kingfish,* 31.

15. Long, *Every Man a King,* 83–84; Beals, *Story of Long,* 71–72; Williams, *Huey Long,* 241–42.

16. Paul E. Ticks column, "Louisiana Politics and Politicians," Shreveport *Caucasian,* June 14, 1927.

17. Williams, *Huey Long,* 104–105; Long, *Every Man a King,* 87; Harnett T. Kane, *Louisiana Hayride: The American Rehearsal for Dictatorship, 1928–1940* (New York, 1941), 53; Hermann B. Deutsch, "Prelude to a Heterocrat," *Saturday Evening Post,* September 7, 1935, p. 86.

18. Williams, *Huey Long,* 97.

19. John Kingston Fineran, *The Career of a Tinpot Napoleon: A Political Biography of Huey P. Long* (New Orleans, 1932), 14–15; New Orleans *States,* October 10, 1921 (Clipping in Huey P. Long Scrapbooks, Hill Memorial Library, Louisiana State University).

20. Beals, *Story of Long,* 71; Fineran, *Tinpot Napoleon,* 15; Williams, *Huey Long,* 239–40; Colfax (La.) *Chronicle,* October 1, 1926.

21. Shreveport *Caucasian,* November 29, 1927, approvingly quoting *Richland Beacon-News* (Rayville, La.).

22. I. A. Newby, *The South: A History* (New York, 1978), 380–84; John A. Garraty, *The Great Depression* (Garden City, N.Y., 1987), 52–53.

23. Frederick Simpich, "The Great Mississippi Flood of 1927," *National Geographic,* LII (September, 1927), 243–89; Dr. Isaac Monroe Cline, quoted in Pete Daniel, *Deep'n as It Come: The 1927 Mississippi River Flood* (New York, 1977), 77.

24. "America's Yellow Dragon on the Rampage," *Literary Digest,* May 21, 1927, pp. 36–40; Daniel, *Deep'n as It Come,* 7; George W. Healy, Jr., *A Lifetime on Deadline: Self-Portrait of a Southern Journalist* (Gretna, La., 1976), 42; Colfax (La.) *Chronicle,* April 22, 1927.

25. New Orleans *Daily States,* June 2, 1893; New Orleans *States,* November 29, 1927; New York *Times,* April 18, 22, 1927; Colfax (La.) *Chronicle,* May 6, 1927; *Tensas Gazette* (St. Joseph, La.), May 6, 13, 1927; Simpich, "Great Mississippi Flood," 248.

26. New York *Times,* May 1–2, 1927; Healy, *Lifetime on Deadline,* 44–47. A Red Cross map of the total overflow area is reproduced in Daniel, *Deep'n as It Come,* 85.

27. Herbert Treadwell Wade, ed., *The New International Yearbook: A Compendium of the Year's Progress for the Year 1927* (New York, 1928), 480; New York *Times,* April 28, 1927; "Catastrophe," *Time,* May 30, 1927, pp. 8–9; Helen Murphy, "Overflow Notes," *Atlantic Monthly,* XXL (August, 1927), 225, 230.

28. *Nation,* May 25, 1927, p. 571; Daniel, *Deep'n as It Come,* 90; *Time,* June 6, 1927, p. 15; *Tensas Gazette* (St. Joseph, La.), May 6, 13, 1927; Colfax (La.) *Chronicle,* May 6, 1927.

29. Will Irwin quoted in "Personal Glimpse," *Literary Digest,* July 30, 1927, pp. 39–40.

30. Simpich, "Great Mississippi Flood," 285–87; W. M. Black, "The Problem of the Mississippi," *North American Review,* CCXXIV (December, 1927), 639–40; *Time,* June 13, 1927, p. 12; "National Flood Control," *Nation,* November 2, 1927, p. 467; Daniel, *Deep'n as It Come,* 150–51.

31. Beals, *Story of Long,* 78; Williams, *Huey Long,* 246; John H. Overton,

Speech delivered at Huey P. Long rally, August 25, 1927 (Typescript in Huey P. Long Papers).

32. Harris, *Kingfish*, 31–32; Long, *Every Man a King*, 92–93; Healy, *Lifetime on Deadline*, 44.

33. Shreveport *Caucasian*, July 9, 1927; L. A. Meraux to O. H. Simpson, in New Orleans *States*, August 24, 1927; Ruston (La.) *Leader*, September 28, 1927 (Clipping in Huey P. Long Papers).

34. A. W. Newlin to James B. Aswell, March 12, 1927, in James B. Aswell Papers, Hill Memorial Library, Louisiana State University; James B. Aswell to J. Floyd Hodges, March 8, 1927, in James B. Aswell, Jr., and Family Papers, Hill Memorial Library, Louisiana State University. Other letters in the Aswell collections during the early months of 1927 appeal to Congressman Aswell to run against Long.

35. Hammond (La.) *Vindicator*, July 15, 1927 (Clipping in Huey P. Long Scrapbooks); Matthew James Schott, "John M. Parker of Louisiana and the Varieties of American Progressivism" (Ph.D. dissertation, Vanderbilt University, 1969), 466, 476.

36. Robert Ewing to James B. Aswell, June 29, 1927, in James B. Aswell Papers, New Orleans *Times-Picayune*, July 9, 1927; Shreveport *Caucasian*, July 9, September 18, 1927.

37. Harris, *Kingfish*, 32; Shreveport *Caucasian*, July 15, August 22, November 8, 11, 1927; Homer (La.) *Guardian-Journal*, September 7, 1927 (Clipping in Huey P. Long Papers); Roland B. Howell interview, in T. Harry Williams Papers, Hill Memorial Library, Louisiana State University.

38. Baton Rouge *Morning Advocate*, August 4, 1927; Shreveport *Times*, August 4, 1927; Kane, *Louisiana Hayride*, 54. Huey's "Every Man a King" slogan was adopted from a speech by William Jennings Bryan.

39. Shreveport *Times*, August 4, 1927; New Orleans *Times-Picayune*, November 4, 1927; Donaldsonville (La.) *Chief*, August 6, 1927 (Clipping in Huey P. Long Scrapbooks).

40. Beals, *Story of Long*, 78–79; Shreveport *Times*, August 4, 1927. Italics mine.

41. Reynolds, *Machine Politics in New Orleans*, 186–87; *St. Bernard Voice* (Arabi, La.), November 3, December 8, 1923, January 12, 1924; Beals, *Story of Long*, 78–79; Paul Cyr quoted in Shreveport *Times*, March 22, 1929; Colfax (La.) *Chronicle*, August 19, October 7, November 18, 1927.

42. Colfax (La.) *Chronicle*, November 18, 1927.

43. Huey P. Long, "Signed Reply to the Last Attack Made Upon Him by L. E. Thomas," October 22, 1927 (Typescript in Huey P. Long Scrapbooks); New Orleans *States*, October 23, 1927; Shreveport *Times*, November 25, 1927.

44. Long, *Every Man a King*, 98–99; Monroe *News-Star*, September 15, 1927; Overton, Speech at Long rally, August 25, 1927. (The comment about Wilson's "autobiography" was first uttered by Overton, and Long liked it so much he later used it.)

45. Healy, *Lifetime on Deadline*, 63.

46. *Time*, January 30, 1928, p. 10; John Wilds, *Afternoon Story: A Century of the New Orleans "States-Item"* (Baton Rouge, 1976), 230–32; Thomas O. Harris to John M. Parker, July 22, 1922, in Governor's Correspondence, Hill Memorial Library, Louisiana State University.

47. New Orleans *States*, November 29, December 12, 1927; Shreveport *Caucasian*, December 5, 1927; *Time*, January 30, 1928, p. 10; New Orleans *Times-Picayune*, January 16, 1928.
48. Burton L. Hotaling, "Huey Pierce Long as Journalist and Propagandist," *Journalism Quarterly*, XX (March, 1943), 21–24. Huey's *Louisiana Progress* began publication on March 27, 1930.
49. New Orleans *Times-Picayune*, April 7, 12, 14, 1922. WAAB's signal was weak. Even in the city, static sometimes made reception difficult in 1922, and the station management was thrilled to learn that one night it was heard in Hammond, forty-five air miles away.
50. New Orleans *States*, January 11, 13, 1924, August 9, 1925; Francis Chase, Jr., *Sound and Fury: An Informal History of Broadcasting* (New York, 1942), 19–20, 87; C. Joseph Pusateri, "The Stormy Career of a Radio Maverick, W. K. Henderson of KWKH," *Louisiana Studies*, XV (Winter, 1976), 389–90.
51. Williams, *Huey Long*, 255.
52. Harvey G. Fields, *A True History of the Life, Works, Assassination, and Death of Huey Pierce Long* (Farmerville, La., 1945), 27, 68; Williams, *Huey Long*, 252–53; Edward F. Haas, "New Orleans on the Half-Shell: The Maestri Era, 1936–1946," *Louisiana History*, XIII (Summer, 1972), 284.
53. M. Maestri to Acting Mayor William Mehle, June 10, 1902 (complaining about assessments on his Storyville properties), in Mayor's Office Correspondence, City Archives Department, New Orleans Public Library; Al Rose, *Storyville, New Orleans: Being an Authentic, Illustrated Account of the Notorious Red-Light District* (University, Ala., 1974), 39, 133; *Who's Who in America*, XXI (Chicago, 1940), 1668; Kane, *Louisiana Hayride*, 241.
54. Haas, "New Orleans on the Half-Shell," 283–84; Hermann B. Deutsch, "New Orleans Politics: The Greatest Free Show on Earth," in *The Past as Prelude: New Orleans, 1718–1968*, ed. Hodding Carter (New Orleans, 1968), 328.
55. Long, *Every Man a King*, 94–97; Shreveport *Caucasian*, July 9, 1927; Fields, *True History*, 27; Williams, *Huey Long*, 256–57.
56. Williams, *Huey Long*, 268–69; Long, *Every Man a King*, 100; Shreveport *Times*, November 25, 27, 1927.
57. Arthur Marvin Shaw, "The First Time I Saw Huey," *Southwest Review*, XXXV (Winter, 1950), 61.
58. Long, *Every Man a King*, 100–101; New York *Times*, November 27, 1927; Shreveport *Caucasian*, November 27–28, 1927; W. Adolphe Roberts, *Lake Pontchartrain* (Indianapolis, 1946), 331.
59. Sanders, "Senatorial Campaign of 1926," chap. 8, pp. 1–10, chap. 9, pp. 1–9, 27–28, chap. 11, pp. 13–21; Shreveport *Times*, August 4, 1927; New Orleans *States*, July 17, October 20, 26, 1927; New Orleans *Times-Picayune*, November 16, 1927.
60. For varying accounts of the Long-Sanders brawl, see New Orleans *States*, November 15, 1927; New York *Times*, November 16, 1927; New Orleans *Times-Picayune*, November 16, 1927; New Orleans *Morning Tribune*, November 16, 1927 (Clipping in Huey P. Long Scrapbooks); and Beals, *Story of Long*, 81–82.
61. New Iberia (La.) *Enterprise*, July 23, 1927 (Clipping in Huey P. Long Scrapbooks); *Richland Beacon-News* (Rayville, La.), November 26, 1927; Shreveport *Caucasian*, October 22, December 5, 1927; Colfax (La.) *Chronicle*, December 2, 1927; New Orleans *Federationist*, quoted in Shreveport *Caucasian*, November 14, 1927.

62. Sanders, "Senatorial Campaign of 1926," chap. 6, p. 3; Alan Brinkley, *Voices of Protest: Huey Long, Father Coughlin, and the Great Depression* (New York, 1983), 20.

63. Kane, *Louisiana Hayride*, 55; Williams, *Huey Long*, 265; New Orleans *States*, January 5, 1928; Ernest Clements, Oscar Guidry, J. L. Hutchinson interviews, in Williams Papers; Houma (La.) *Courier*, November 3, 1927 (Clipping in Huey P. Long Scrapbooks); Abbeville (La.) *Meridional*, November 5, 1927.

64. Long, *Every Man a King*, 99.

65. *Tensas Gazette* (St. Joseph, La.), December 30, 1927; Shreveport *Journal*, September 5, 1927; *Report of Louisiana Secretary of State*, 1929, foldout sheet of election returns at end of volume; Perry H. Howard, *Political Tendencies in Louisiana* (Rev. ed.; Baton Rouge, 1971), 231–32.

66. New Orleans *Item-Tribune*, January 18, 1928 (Clipping in Huey P. Long Scrapbooks); Williams, *Huey Long*, 279n.

67. New Orleans *Morning Tribune*, January 21, 23, 1928 (Clippings in Huey P. Long Scrapbooks); Long, *Every Man a King*, 104–105; New Orleans *Times-Picayune*, January 20, 23, 1928.

68. *Louisiana House Journal*, Regular Session, 1928, pp. 24–25; Hamilton Basso, "Huey Long and His Background," *Harper's Monthly*, CCLXX (May, 1935), 664.

CHAPTER 10: "I'm the Kingfish"

1. New York *Times*, January 29, 1928.

2. Mark Twain, *Life on the Mississippi* (New York, 1961), 237; Forrest Davis, *Huey Long: A Candid Biography* (New York, 1935), 96; New Orleans *Picayune*, May 22, 1928; Sidney J. Romero, "The Inaugural Addresses of the Governors of the State of Louisiana," *Louisiana History*, XIV (Summer, 1973), 252; Thomas O. Harris, *The Kingfish: Huey P. Long, Dictator* (New Orleans, 1938), 39. Huey at thirty-four was Louisiana's second-youngest governor. Republican Henry Clay Warmoth, inaugurated in 1868 at age twenty-six, was the youngest.

3. Huey P. Long, *Every Man a King: The Autobiography of Huey P. Long* (New Orleans, 1933), 106–107; Harris, *Kingfish*, 36–37; T. Harry Williams, *Huey Long* (New York, 1969), 287–88.

4. Webster Smith, *The Kingfish: A Biography of Huey P. Long* (New York, 1933), 49–51; Allan P. Sindler, *Huey Long's Louisiana: State Politics, 1920–1952* (Baltimore, 1956), 59–60; Bennett H. Wall, ed., *Louisiana: A History* (2nd ed.; Arlington Heights, Ill., 1990), 275–76; Henry Larcade, Jr., interview, in T. Harry Williams Papers, Hill Memorial Library, Louisiana State University; J. Y. Sanders, "The Senatorial Campaign of 1926," chap. 11, pp. 9, 21 (Typescript in Jared Y. Sanders Papers, Hill Memorial Library, Louisiana State University).

5. "State Budget," in *Acts*, Regular Session, 1928, pp. 169–89; Richard Lawrence Gordon, "The Development of Louisiana's Public Mental Institutions, 1735–1940" (Ph.D. dissertation, Louisiana State University, 1978), 338–39.

6. Williams, *Huey Long*, 296–98; Edward A. Haggerty, Sr., interview, in Williams Papers; Smith, *Kingfish: A Biography*, 50; Arthur M. Schlesinger, Jr., *The Politics of Upheaval* (Boston, 1960), 47.

7. Cecil Morgan, Norman Bauer, Mason Spencer, J. Y. Sanders, Jr., interviews, all in Williams Papers; David H. Zinman, *The Day Huey Long Was Shot* (New York, 1963), 52–59; Baton Rouge *Morning Advocate*, ca. 1933, quoted in

James W. Clarke, *American Assassins: The Darker Side of Politics* (Princeton, 1982), 227.

8. Norman Bauer, Cecil Morgan interviews, both in Williams Papers; *Madison Journal* (Tallulah, La.), September 13, 1935; Hodding Carter, "Huey Long: American Dictator," in Isabel Leighton, ed., *The Aspirin Age, 1919–1941* (New York, 1963), 360. The Carter essay is a revised version of his article in *American Mercury* magazine in 1949.

9. Brady M. Banta, "The Regulation and Conservation of Petroleum Resources in Louisiana, 1901–1940" (Ph.D. dissertation, Louisiana State University, 1981), 333–50; *Report of Louisiana Secretary of State*, 1929, foldout of 1928 amendment returns at end of volume; Long, *Every Man a King*, 112–14.

10. *Acts*, Regular Session, 1928, No. 204; Roy Wilkins, "Huey Long Says: An Interview with Louisiana's Kingfish," *Crisis*, XLII (February, 1935), 52.

11. *Acts*, Regular Session, 1928, No. 99; *Acts*, First Extra Session, 1934, No. 9.

12. Williams, *Huey Long*, 321–23; *Louisiana House Journal*, Fifth Extra Session, 1929, pp. 29–31; Jerome Beatty, "You Can't Laugh Him Off!" *American Magazine*, CXV (January, 1933), 115; New York *Herald Tribune*, September 9, 1935; Harnett T. Kane, *Louisiana Hayride: The American Rehearsal for Dictatorship, 1928–1940* (New York, 1941), 399.

13. Humbert S. Nelli, *The Business of Crime: Italians and Syndicate Crime in the United States* (New York, 1976), 188; Kane, *Louisiana Hayride*, 370, 397–401.

14. *Congressional Record*, 74th Cong., 1st Sess., 11,454. Huey's Louisiana history lesson to the Senate was reprinted by his *American Progress*, August, 1935.

15. Alan Brinkley, *Voices of Protest: Huey Long, Father Coughlin, and the Great Depression* (New York, 1983), 26; Carleton Beals, *The Story of Huey P. Long* (Philadelphia, 1935); Kane, *Louisiana Hayride*, 63.

16. New Orleans *Times-Picayune*, June 26, 1928; Harris, *Kingfish*, 42–43; Stella O'Conner, "The Charity Hospital of New Orleans," *Louisiana Historical Quarterly*, XXXI (January, 1948), 87–88; Williams, *Huey Long*, 290–94.

17. Huey P. Long, Speech delivered at New Orleans rally, August 25, 1927 (Typescript in Huey P. Long Scrapbooks, Hill Memorial Library, Louisiana State University); Adam Fairclough, "The Public Utilities Industry in New Orleans: A Study in Capital, Labor, and Government, 1894–1929," *Louisiana History*, XXII (Winter, 1981), 49–50, 55–59; Harris, *Kingfish*, 44.

18. Williams, in *Huey Long*, 299–302, praises Long for his NOPSI negotiations, which after all brought natural gas to New Orleans. For another view, critical both of Long and of Williams' interpretation of the gas controversy, see Fairclough, "Public Utilities Industry," 57–60.

19. Fairclough, "Public Utilities Industry," 60; Kane, *Louisiana Hayride*, 65.

20. Smith, *Kingfish: A Biography*, 53–54; Beals, *Story of Long*, 111; Mildred Adams, "Huey the Great," *Forum*, LXXXIX (February, 1933), 73; Sam Irby, *Kidnaped by the Kingfish: With Intimate Details of This and Other Crimes of Huey P. Long* (New Orleans, 1932), 25; Williams, *Huey Long*, 321.

21. Williams, *Huey Long*, 316–18; Irby, *Kidnaped by the Kingfish*, 12–13; Sam Irby was Ms. Grosjean's uncle-in-law, and for a time had a state job and lived in room 718, next to hers, in the Heidelberg Hotel.

22. David Zinman, "Seymour Weiss Is Man Who Climbed Back from Disaster," Baton Rouge *Morning Advocate*, August 5, 1963; Irby, *Kidnaped by the Kingfish*, 11–12; Carter, "Huey Long," in *Aspirin Age*, ed. Leighton, 340; *Who Was Who in America*, V (1973), 766; Williams, *Huey Long*, 374–75.

23. Kane, *Louisiana Hayride*, 81; "Seymour Weiss," in *Louisiana Today*, ed. James M. Thomson (N.p., 1939), 182; Seymour Weiss interview, in Williams Papers.

24. Long, *Every Man a King*, 223–25; Irby, *Kidnaped by the Kingfish*, 26; New Orleans *States*, March 18, 1929; *Louisiana House Journal*, Fifth Extra Session, 1929, pp. 727–32.

25. Steven D. Zink, "Cultural Conflict and the 1928 Presidential Campaign in Louisiana," *Southern Studies*, XVII (Summer, 1978), 175–97; George B. Tindall, *The Emergence of the New South, 1913–1945* (Baton Rouge, 1967), 246–51; H. L. Mencken column in Baltimore *Evening Sun*, July 30, 1928, reprinted in *H. L. Mencken on Politics: A Carnival of Buncombe*, ed. Malcolm Moos (New York, 1960), 167.

26. W. C. Pegues interview, in Williams Papers.

27. Farmerville (La.) *Gazette*, September 19, 1928, quoted in Zink, "Cultural Conflict and 1928 Presidential Campaign," 191; Alexandria *Town Talk*, October 18, 1928, quoted in Williams, *Huey Long*, 328; Barbara C. Wingo, "The 1928 Presidential Election in Louisiana," *Louisiana History*, XVIII (Fall, 1977), 419.

28. Hermann B. Deutsch, "Kingdom of the Kingfish," New Orleans *Item*, August 13, 1939; Perry H. Howard, *Political Tendencies in Louisiana* (Rev. ed.; Baton Rouge, 1971), 297–99.

29. T. H. Harris, *The Memoirs of T. H. Harris* (Baton Rouge, 1963), 160–61; Beals, *Story of Long*, 95.

30. *Louisiana House Journal*, Fifth Extra Session, 1929, pp. 651–61; Williams, *Huey Long*, 651.

31. Long, *Every Man a King*, 115; *Louisiana House Journal*, Fifth Extra Session, 1929, pp. 661–62.

32. *Louisiana House Journal*, Fifth Extra Session, 1929, pp. 661–62; New Orleans *Times-Picayune*, April 20, 1929.

33. Hamilton Basso, "Huey Long and His Background," *Harper's Monthly*, CLXX (May, 1935), 664; Deutsch, "Kingdom of the Kingfish," New Orleans *Item*, August 23, 1939; Davis, *Long: A Candid Biography*, 28, 32; Williams, *Huey Long*, 312–13.

34. Harris, *Kingfish*, 39–40.

35. See 1929 cartoons of Huey Long, particularly in the New Orleans *Item* and its morning edition, the *Tribune*, in E. A. Conway Scrapbooks, Louisiana State Library, Baton Rouge. New Orleans *Item* quoted in *Literary Digest*, April 6, 1929, p. 8.

36. New Orleans *Times-Picayune*, February 9–10, 14, 1929; Beals, *Story of Long*, 103–105; New York *Times*, August 13, 1928, April 25, 1929; Williams, *Huey Long*, 340–45.

37. Long, *Every Man a King*, 226–28; Beals, *Story of Long*, 107–109; Colfax (La.) *Chronicle*, January 4, 1929; New Orleans *Times-Picayune*, February 2, 1929.

38. Mansfield (La.) *Enterprise*, January 2, 1929; Smith, *Kingfish: A Biography*, 57–58; Long, *Every Man a King*, 130–31.

39. Beals, *Story of Long*, 103, 108–109; "The Handsome Governor—A Studio Party—A Raid," *Denver Post Magazine*, July 14, 1929 (Clipping in Conway Scrapbooks); *Louisiana House Journal*, Fifth Extra Session, 1929, pp. 791–97.

40. Herbert Asbury, "The Noble Experiment of Izzy and Moe," in *Aspirin Age*, ed. Leighton, 47; Smith, *Kingfish: A Biography*, 145; Kane, *Louisiana Hayride*, 82; "Louisiana's 'Stormy Petrel,' " *Literary Digest*, April 6, 1929, p. 8.

41. New York *Times*, April 5, 1929; George W. Healy, Jr., *A Lifetime on Deadline: Self-Portrait of a Southern Journalist* (Gretna, La., 1976), 64–65; Irby, *Kidnaped by the Kingfish*, 24–25.

42. *Louisiana House Journal*, Fifth Extra Session, 1929, pp. 217–23.

43. *Ibid.*, 219, 226, 230.

44. Long, *Every Man a King*, 122–25; Banta, "Regulation and Conservation," 34–47.

45. Tindall, *Emergence of the New South*, 363; Harris, *Kingfish*, 49–52.

46. *Louisiana House Journal*, Fifth Extra Session, 1929, p. 376.

47. *Ibid.*, 129; Baton Rouge *State-Times*, March 21, 1929.

48. *Louisiana House Journal*, Fifth Extra Session, 1929, p. 132; Shreveport *Times*, March 22, 1929.

49. Williams, *Huey Long*, 354–55; Smith, *Kingfish: A Biography*, 90.

50. Warmoth's diary quoted in Richard Nelson Current, *Those Terrible Carpetbaggers* (New York, 1988), 420. Warmoth in 1872 was suspended from office after being impeached by the House, but the Constitution of 1921, under which Huey's impeachment and trial took place, specified that the governor was not to be suspended by impeachment; he could be forced to vacate the office only by a senate trial in which two thirds voted to convict.

51. Beals, *Story of Long*, 116–17; New Orleans *Times-Picayune*, March 26, 1929; *Louisiana House Journal*, Fifth Extra Session, 1929, pp. 26–29.

52. Thomas O. Harris, "Red-Blooded Men Expose Fraud to Vote to Adjourn," New Orleans *States*, March 26, 1929; Williams, *Huey Long*, 356–59.

53. Beals, *Story of Long*, 117–18; New Orleans *Item*, March 26–27, 1929; Harris, *Kingfish*, 55–56; Smith, *Kingfish: A Biography*, 80–81.

54. Williams, *Huey Long*, 358; New Orleans *Item*, March 26, 27, 1929; Smith, *Kingfish: A Biography*, 84–85.

55. New Orleans *Times-Picayune*, March 27, 1929; *Louisiana House Journal*, Fifth Extra Session, 1929, 27–33; Smith, *Kingfish: A Biography*, 86.

56. Harris, *Kingfish*, 58–61; Mason Spencer interview, in Williams Papers.

57. Abbeville (La.) *Meridional*, April 27, 1929.

58. *Louisiana House Calendar*, Fifth Extra Session, 1929, pp. 12–54; *Louisiana Senate Journal*, Fifth Extra Session, 1929, pp. 186–87.

59. *Louisiana House Journal*, Fifth Extra Session, 1929, p. 219; Bailey quoted in John Kingston Fineran, *The Career of a Tinpot Napoleon: A Political Biography of Huey P. Long* (New Orleans, 1932), 78.

60. *Louisiana House Journal*, Fifth Extra Session, 1929, pp. 288, 195; Williams, *Huey Long*, 375; Sindler, *Huey Long's Louisiana*, 64n.

61. Smith, *Kingfish: A Biography*, 131–32; *Louisiana House Journal*, Fifth Extra Session, 1929, p. 798.

62. Beals, *Story of Long*, 161; Williams, *Huey Long*, 385.

63. *Constitution of 1921*, Art. IX, Sec. 2.

64. Williams, *Huey Long*, 365; Harris, *Kingfish*, 61–65; Circular, "The Same Fight Again," quoted in Long, *Every Man a King*, 152–53.

65. Burton L. Hotaling, "Huey Pierce Long as Journalist and Propagandist," *Journalism Quarterly*, XX (March, 1943), 22–23; Beals, *Story of Long*, 140–43, 154; Smith, *Kingfish: A Biography*, 149–55.

66. Williams, *Huey Long*, 353–54; Long, *Every Man a King*, 146–48; Kane, *Louisiana Hayride*, 73–74.

67. Beals, *Story of Long*, 159–60; New York *Times*, April 4–5, 1929.

68. *Louisiana House Journal,* Fifth Extra Session, 1929, pp. 291–92. See also New York *Times,* April 7, 1929; Fineran, *Tinpot Napoleon,* 72–73.

69. Smith, *Kingfish: A Biography,* 116–17.

70. "Copy of Writ of Summons or Citation Served on Huey P. Long, April 27, 1929," *Louisiana Senate Journal,* Fifth Extra Session, 1929, pp. 178–87; O'Niell quoted in Williams, *Huey Long,* 383; Shreveport *Times,* March 22, 1929.

71. New York *Times,* April 28, May 15–17, 1929; *Louisiana Senate Journal,* Fifth Extra Session, 1929, pp. 201–209; Harris, *Kingfish,* 58–61, 69–70; Healy, *Lifetime on Deadline,* 66–67; Glen Jeansonne, *Leander Perez: Boss of the Delta* (Baton Rouge, 1977), 66–67.

72. *Louisiana Senate Journal,* Fifth Extra Session, 1929, pp. 265–70.

73. Long, *Every Man a King,* 160–61; "Louisiana's Impeachment Bomb Ends in Smoke," *Literary Digest,* June 1, 1929, pp. 10–11; Williams, *Huey Long,* 398–400; H. Lester Hughes interview, in Williams Papers.

CHAPTER 11: Feather Dusting

1. H. L. Mencken, "The Glory of Louisiana," *Nation,* May 3, 1933, pp. 507–508; Sherwood Anderson quoted in Arthur M. Schlesinger, Jr., *The Politics of Upheaval* (Boston, 1960), 52.

2. John F. Carter [Unofficial Observer], *American Messiahs* (New York, 1935), 8; Cecil Morgan to Bell I. Wiley, May 9, 1970, copy in Manuscripts Section, Howard-Tilton Memorial Library, Tulane University.

3. T. Harry Williams, *Huey Long* (New York, 1969), 408–10; Forrest Davis, *Huey Long: A Candid Biography* (New York, 1935), 119.

4. George M. Coad, "Move in Louisiana for Long's Recall," New York *Times,* May 26, 1929; Hermann B. Deutsch, "Kingdom of the Kingfish," New Orleans *Item,* August 21, 1939.

5. Abbeville (La.) *Meridional,* May 25, 1929; Colfax (La.) *Chronicle,* July 19, August 2, 1929; Thomas O. Harris, *The Kingfish: Huey P. Long, Dictator* (New Orleans, 1938), 77–78; Carleton Beals, *The Story of Huey P. Long* (Philadelphia, 1935), 168–69.

6. *Senate Hearings on Campaign Expenditures,* 72d Cong., 2d Sess., Pt. 1, pp. 917–18; Williams, *Huey Long,* 370; Julius Tison Long, "What I Know About My Brother, United States Senator Huey P. Long," *Real America,* II (September, 1933), 37–38; Bozeman advertisement in *Louisiana Progress,* September 4, 1930; Shreveport *Journal,* August 30, 1930; Harley B. Bozeman to Editor, Hammond (La.) *Vindicator,* December 4, 1933.

7. New York *Times,* May 26, 1929; Bogalusa (La.) *News,* quoted in *Literary Digest,* June 1, 1929, p. 10; Leesville (La.) *Leader,* quoted in Mansfield (La.) *Enterprise,* April 25, 1929.

8. Matthew James Schott, "John M. Parker of Louisiana and the Varieties of American Progressivism" (Ph.D. dissertation, Vanderbilt University, 1969), 476–82; New Orleans *States,* June 11, 1929; Shreveport *Journal,* June 12, 1929; Williams, *Huey Long,* 422.

9. Webster Smith, *The Kingfish: A Biography of Huey P. Long* (New York, 1933), 182–84; Williams, *Huey Long,* 423; *Saint v. Allen,* 169 La. 1046 (1930), cited in *Constitutions of the State of Louisiana,* ed. Benjamin Wall Dart (Indianapolis, 1932), 46.

10. Smith, *Kingfish: A Biography,* 182–84; Huey P. Long, *Every Man a King:*

NOTES TO PAGES 191-97
NOTES TO PAGES 191-97

The Autobiography of Huey P. Long (New Orleans, 1933), 183–89; Beals, *Story of Long,* 166; Harris, *Kingfish,* 79–80.

11. New Orleans *Times-Picayune,* July 19–21, 1929; Colfax (La.) *Chronicle,* July 26, August 2, 1929; Harris, *Kingfish,* 79.

12. Harley B. Bozeman, "Winn Parish as I Have Known It," *Winn Parish Enterprise* (Winnfield, La.), May 30, 1957 (Clipping in Bozeman Scrapbooks, Louisiana State Library, Baton Rouge); *Who's Who in America,* XVI (Chicago, 1930), 586; "Dictated but Not Dead," *Business Week,* February 9, 1935, pp. 12–13.

13. Roman Heleniak, "Local Reaction to the Great Depression in New Orleans, 1929–1933," *Louisiana History,* X (Fall, 1969), 209–16; George B. Tindall, *The Emergence of the New South, 1913–1945* (Baton Rouge, 1967), 354–55; Colfax (La.) *Chronicle,* August 8, 27, 1930.

14. Harry Gamble interview in T. Harry Williams Papers, Hill Memorial Library, Louisiana State University.

15. Beals, *Story of Long,* 173–74.

16. New Orleans *Times-Picayune,* February 14, 1930; Williams, *Huey Long,* 429–30; Harnett T. Kane, *Louisiana Hayride: The American Rehearsal for Dictatorship, 1928–1940* (New York, 1941), 86–87; Shreveport *Journal,* February 14, 1930.

17. "Undressed Governor, " *Time,* June 16, 1930, p. 19; New Orleans *Times-Picayune,* March 10, 1930; Baton Rouge *State-Times,* quoted in Smith, *Kingfish: A Biography,* 188–89.

18. Harris, *Kingfish,* 81–82; Long, *Every Man a King,* 201.

19. New Orleans *Times-Picayune* (Clipping, *ca.* February, 1930, in E. A. Conway Scrapbooks, Louisiana State Library, Baton Rouge); Shreveport *Journal,* May 19, 1930; Williams, *Huey Long,* 427–28.

20. Allan P. Sindler, *Huey Long's Louisiana: State Politics, 1920–1952* (Baltimore, 1956), 68–69; Harris, *Kingfish,* 84–85; Smith, *Kingfish: A Biography,* 193–94.

21. Beals, *Story of Long,* 180–81; Williams, *Huey Long,* 450–53; Long, *Every Man a King,* 210; Deutsch, "Kingdom of the Kingfish," New Orleans *Item,* August 23, 1939.

22. *Louisiana Progress,* April 24, July 17, 1930; New York *Times,* July 20, 1930.

23. Shreveport *Journal,* quoted in Mansfield (La.) *Enterprise,* August 21, 1930; State Senator Holcombe quoted in Adras Laborde, *A National Southerner: Ransdell of Louisiana* (New York, 1951), 189.

24. New Orleans *States,* quoted in *Time,* June 16, 1930, p. 19.

25. *Biographical Directory of the American Congress, 1774–1927* (Washington, D.C., 1928), 1444; George Q. Flynn, "A Louisiana Senator and the Underwood Tariff," *Louisiana History,* X (Winter, 1969), 6–7; Hammond (La.) *Vindicator,* July 15, 1927; *Louisiana Progress,* July 24, August 7, 1930; Beals, *Story of Long,* 186.

26. Harris, *Kingfish,* 87, quoting Carleton Beals; Laborde, *National Southerner,* 187–88; Baton Rouge *Morning Advocate,* September 7, 1930.

27. New York *Times,* August 31, 1930; Kane, *Louisiana Hayride,* 78; Earle J. Christenberry interview, in Williams Papers.

28. Burton L. Hotaling, "Huey Pierce Long as Journalist and Propagandist," *Journalism Quarterly,* XX (March, 1943), 24; Long, *Every Man a King,* 188; Joseph David interview, in Williams Papers; *Louisiana Progress,* March 27, April 17, May 15, 29, June 12, July 24, 31, 1930, January 12, 1932.

29. Mansfield (La.) *Enterprise*, May 8, 1930; Baton Rouge *State-Times*, September 4, 1930; Beals, *Story of Long*, 188; Shreveport *Journal*, August 26, 1930; John Herrick, "Huey Long Foes Spill It All," Chicago *Tribune*, May 30, 1934.

30. Baton Rouge *State-Times*, June 19, 1930; Chick Frampton interview, in Williams Papers; *American Progress*, April 5, August 7, 1934; Williams, *Huey Long*, 166–67, 470, 690–91; New York *Times*, April 5, 1934.

31. *Louisiana Progress*, May 29, June 5, 12, July 3, 17, 31, August 7, 1930; Beals, *Story of Long*, 188; Harris, *Kingfish*, 87.

32. Williams, *Huey Long*, 755; Sindler, *Huey Long's Louisiana*, 101; Hodding Carter, "Louisiana Limelighter," *Review of Reviews*, XCI (March, 1935), 28.

33. New Orleans *Times-Picayune*, March 27, 1930; Hotaling, "Long as Journalist," 24–25; Harris, *Kingfish*, 98; Kane, *Louisiana Hayride*, 206; *Senate Hearings on Campaign Expenditures*, 72d Cong., 2d Sess., Pt. 1, p. 428.

34. Elmer L. Irey and William J. Slocum, *The Tax Dodgers: The Inside Story of the T-Men's War with America's Political and Underworld Hoodlums* (New York, 1949), 94, 111; Norman Lant interview, in Williams Papers.

35. "Washington Reporter's Glimpse of Huey Long," St. Louis *Post-Dispatch*, September 11, 1935.

36. M. J. Kavanaugh interview, in Williams Papers; Huey Long quoted in Schlesinger, *Politics of Upheaval*, 54.

37. Kavanaugh, Paul Flowers interviews, in Williams Papers; Louis Cochran, "The Louisiana Kingfish," *American Mercury*, XXVI (July, 1932), 283; Harris, *Kingfish*, 113.

38. Cartoon, New Orleans *Morning Tribune*, August 4, 1930, in Conway Scrapbooks; A. J. Liebling, *The Earl of Louisiana* (Baton Rouge, 1970), 9; Schlesinger, *Politics of Upheaval*, 48; John Dos Passos, "Washington: The Big Tent," *New Republic*, March 14, 1934, p. 120.

39. W. M. Hallack, Theophile Landry, Louie Jones interviews, in Williams Papers; Baton Rouge *State-Times*, September 11, 1935.

40. Beals, *Story of Long*, 186; New Orleans *Times-Picayune*, August 31, 1930.

41. Joe Fisher interview, in Williams Papers; Dewey W. Grantham, *The Life and Death of the Solid South* (Lexington, Ky., 1988), 86.

42. Laborde, *National Southerner*, 1–4, 26; Baton Rouge *Morning Advocate*, September 7, 1930; Williams, *Huey Long*, 469.

43. *Louisiana Progress*, September 4, 1930.

44. Atlanta *Constitution*, September 9, 1930; San Francisco *Chronicle*, quoted in Baton Rouge *State-Times*, July 30, 1930; George M. Coad, "Virulent Campaign Waged in Louisiana," New York *Times*, August 31, 1930; Washington *Post* quoted in New Orleans *Times-Picayune*, June 12, 1930.

45. *Louisiana Progress*, August 28, 1930; Hermann B. Deutsch, "Huey Long: The Last Phase," *Saturday Evening Post*, October 12, 1935, p. 84.

46. Williams, *Huey Long*, 270; John Nuckolls interview, in Williams Papers; New Orleans *States*, August 30, 1930 (Clipping in Conway Scrapbooks).

47. For Irby's none-too-trustworthy account of events, see Sam Irby, *Kidnaped by the Kingfish: With Intimate Details of This and Other Crimes of Huey P. Long* (New Orleans, 1932), 21–22, 45–48; New Orleans *Item-Tribune*, September 7, 1930 (Clipping in Conway Scrapbooks); Beals, *Story of Long*, 193.

48. Irby, *Kidnaped by the Kingfish*, 46–49; Deutsch, "Kingdom of the Kingfish," New Orleans *Item*, August 24, 1939.

49. Williams, *Huey Long*, 472–73. Irby, on the other hand, believed Huey suggested killing him, and Earl talked the Kingfish out of it. See Irby, *Kidnaped by the Kingfish*, 48–54.

50. Shreveport *Journal*, September 6, 1930; Atlanta *Constitution*, September 6, 1930; Irby, *Kidnaped by the Kingfish*, 48–54.

51. New Orleans *Times-Picayune*, September 7, 1930; Beals, *Story of Long*, 196.

52. Baton Rouge *Morning Advocate*, September 9, 1930; John Wilds, *Afternoon Story: A Century of the New Orleans "States-Item"* (Baton Rouge, 1976), 234; Williams, *Huey Long*, 474; New York *Times*, September 9, 1930.

53. Harris, *Kingfish*, 88–89; New York *Times*, September 9, 1930; John Kingston Fineran, *The Career of a Tinpot Napoleon: A Political Biography of Huey P. Long* (New Orleans, 1932), 136–37; Baton Rouge *State-Times*, September 10, 1930; Shreveport *Journal*, September 11, 1930. Irby later had the poor judgment to again attempt a lawsuit against Huey Long. This led to his arrest and temporary confinement in a mental hospital. Later he moved to Mississippi and, with the assistance of the anti-Long journalist John K. Fineran, wrote a semitruthful booklet about his misadventures, *Kidnaped by the Kingfish*.

54. *Report of Louisiana Secretary of State*, 1931, p. 69; Sindler, *Huey Long's Louisiana*, 71–73; George M. Coad, "Louisiana Expects Troublous Times," New York *Times*, September 14, 1930.

55. *Time*, August 9, 1954, p. 80; Laborde, *National Southerner*, 215, 236.

CHAPTER 12: Cornpone and Cotton

1. *Louisiana Progress*, September 18, 1930; New Orleans *Item*, September 18, 1930; Huey P. Long, *Every Man a King: The Autobiography of Huey P. Long* (New Orleans, 1933), 235.

2. *Louisiana Progress*, September 18, 1930.

3. New Orleans *Times-Picayune*, September 16, 1930; *Louisiana Progress*, September 18, 1930; John Wilds, *Afternoon Story: A Century of the New Orleans "States-Item"* (Baton Rouge, 1976), 108–109, 129; Henry Clay Warmoth, *War, Politics, and Reconstruction: Stormy Days in Louisiana* (New York, 1930), 242–43.

4. Allan P. Sindler, *Huey Long's Louisiana: State Politics, 1920–1952* (Baltimore, 1956), 74–75; New Orleans *Times-Picayune*, September 17, 1930; Thomas O. Harris, *The Kingfish: Huey P. Long, Dictator* (New Orleans, 1938), 90–91; Bogalusa (La.) *News*, September 19, 1930 (Clipping in E. A. Conway Scrapbooks, Louisiana State Library, Baton Rouge).

5. Baton Rouge *State-Times*, September 17, 1930; Sindler, *Huey Long's Louisiana*, 74; Gilbert L. Dupre, Column in *Louisiana Progress*, November 10, 1931; New Orleans *Times-Picayune*, December 2, 1931. Dupre's earlier castigation of Huey Long is quoted in *Madison Journal* (Tallulah, La.), August 15, 1930. For two accounts of the leak over Dupre's head, see Long, *Every Man a King*, 239, and T. Harry Williams, *Huey Long* (New York, 1969), 484–85. Sindler assumed the story was apocryphal, but according to Huey's contemporaries interviewed by Williams, the Kingfish really did order a hole bored in the capitol roof.

6. New Orleans *States*, October 8–9, 1930 [esp. editorial on Alice Grosjean's appointment, October 9]; Baton Rouge *Morning Advocate*, October 9, 1930; *Time*, October 20, 1930, pp. 18–19.

7. New Orleans *Morning Tribune*, October 9, 1930 (Clipping in Conway Scrapbooks); New Orleans *Times-Picayune*, October 9, 1930.

8. *Time*, October 20, 1930, p. 19; *Avoyelles Times* (Marksville, La.), October 11, 1930 (Clipping in Conway Scrapbooks); John Kingston Fineran, *The Career of a Tinpot Napoleon: A Political Biography of Huey P. Long* (New Orleans, 1932), 140.

9. New Orleans *Morning Tribune*, October 9, 16, 1930 (Clippings in Conway Scrapbooks); New Orleans *States*, October 9, 1930; "Salute!" [editorial on Alice Grosjean], *Louisiana Progress*, October 16, 1930.

10. *Acts*, Sixth Extra Session, 1930, pp. 5–31; *Louisiana Progress*, November 6, December, 1930, January, July 15, 1931. The *Progress* appeared monthly from December, 1930, until July 15, 1931, then resumed weekly publication.

11. Huey Long, article in *Louisiana Progress*, December, 1930, and *ibid.*, January, 1931; Prescott (Ark.) *Evening Courier*, quoted in *Louisiana Progress*, January, 1931.

12. Raymond Clapper, "Between You and Me," Column in Washington *Post*, September 11, 1935.

13. New York *Times*, December 7, 1930.

14. Marquis W. Childs, "Governor, Senator-Elect, and a 'Prisoner' in His Own State," *St. Louis Post-Dispatch Sunday Magazine*, March 22, 1931 (Clipping in Conway Scrapbooks).

15. *Louisiana House Journal*, Fifth Extra Session, 1929, p. 380; Mrs. John H. Overton, Harry Gamble interviews, both in T. Harry Williams Papers, Hill Memorial Library, Louisiana State University; Hermann B. Deutsch, "Paradox in Pajamas," *Saturday Evening Post*, October 5, 1935, pp. 14–15.

16. Webster Smith, *The Kingfish: A Biography of Huey P. Long* (New York, 1933), 183; Jess Nugent, Fred Blanche, John Fleury, Joe Fisher interviews, all in Williams Papers.

17. Williams, *Huey Long*, 502. Williams properly considered this story "dubious." For another version, see Harnett T. Kane, *Louisiana Hayride: The American Rehearsal for Dictatorship, 1928–1940* (New York, 1941), 214–15.

18. James A. Noe interview, in Williams Papers.

19. "Nor Long Remember," *New Yorker*, September 21, 1935, pp. 14–15.

20. William F. Mugleston, "Cornpone and Potlikker: A Moment of Relief in the Great Depression," *Louisiana History*, XVI (Summer, 1975), 279–88. Atlanta *Constitution*, February 13, 17, 18, 1931; New York *Times*, February 27, 28, 1931.

21. Mugleston, "Cornpone and Potlikker," 281; Deutsch, "Paradox in Pajamas," 14.

22. Williams, *Huey Long*, 320–21; Richard Foster, W. A. Cooper, Robert O'Neal, Richard W. Leche interviews, all in Williams Papers.

23. *Time*, September 11, 1933; Otho Long, Henry Larcade, Jr., Richard Foster interviews, all in Williams Papers; New York *Times*, July 26, 1935.

24. Forrest Davis, *Huey Long: A Candid Biography* (New York, 1935), 275; F. Raymond Daniell, "Land of the Free," in *We Saw It Happen: The News Behind the News That's Fit to Print*, ed. Hanson W. Baldwin and Shepard Stone (New York, 1938), 91; Raymond Gram Swing, *Forerunners of American Fascism* (New York, 1935), 82; Des Moines *Sunday Register*, April 28, 1935, and Grinnell (Iowa) *Register*, April 29, 1935 (Clippings in Huey P. Long Scrapbooks, Hill Memorial Library, Louisiana State University).

25. Robert E. Snyder, *Cotton Crisis* (Chapel Hill, 1984), xvi, 1–13, 33–34; New

Orleans *Times-Picayune*, August 9, 1931; James E. Boyle, *Cotton and the New Orleans Cotton Exchange* (Garden City, N.Y., 1934), 139, 187.

26. "Governor Long's Drop-a-Crop Cotton Plan," *Literary Digest*, September 19, 1931, pp. 8–9; Robert E. Snyder, "Huey Long and the Cotton-Holiday Plan of 1931," *Louisiana History*, XVIII (Spring, 1977), 140n; Snyder, *Cotton Crisis*, 41.

27. New York *Times*, August 17, 1931; Telegram from Huey P. Long to selected officials of the cotton-producing states, *ca.* August 16, 1931 (Typescript in Huey P. Long Papers, Hill Memorial Library, Louisiana State University); Snyder, "Huey Long and the Cotton-Holiday," 139–40, 147; Alan Brinkley, *Voices of Protest: Huey Long, Father Coughlin, and the Great Depression* (New York, 1983), 39.

28. New Orleans *Item*, September 18, 1931; Williams, *Huey Long*, 532; Snyder, *Cotton Crisis*, 46–47; New Orleans *Times-Picayune*, August 18, 1931; Anthony J. Badger, "Huey Long and the New Deal," in *Nothing Else to Fear: New Perspectives on America in the Thirties*, ed. Stephen W. Baskerville and Ralph Willett (Manchester, Eng., 1985), 92.

29. "No More Cotton?" *Time*, August 31, 1931, p. 11; *Louisiana Senate Journal*, Seventh Extra Session, 1931, p. 4; *Acts*, Seventh Extra Session, 1931, No. 1; Snyder, "Huey Long and the Cotton-Holiday," 152.

30. New Orleans *Times-Picayune*, August 30, 1931; Carleton Beals, *The Story of Huey P. Long* (Philadelphia, 1935), 211.

31. New York *Times*, September 15, 16, 1931; Snyder, *Cotton Crisis*, 93–103; "Drop-a-Crop," *Time*, September 21, 1931, pp. 11–12.

32. Baton Rouge *State-Times*, September 10, 1931; Snyder, *Cotton Crisis*, 101–102; *Time*, September 21, 1931, p. 12.

33. Snyder, *Cotton Crisis*, 107–14, 126–27; Badger, "Huey Long and the New Deal," in *Nothing Else to Fear*, ed. Baskerville and Willett, 90–92.

34. Harris, *Kingfish*, 96–97; New York *Times*, September 16, 17, 1931; Beals, *Story of Long*, 212; Editorial, New York *Times*, September 18, 1931.

35. Snyder, "Huey Long and the Cotton-Holiday," 158–59.

36. R. W. Brooks to Huey P. Long, September 18, 1931, J. M. Black, Jr., to Huey P. Long, September 2, 1931, both in Huey P. Long Papers; New Orleans *Times-Picayune*, September 4, 1931. See also Snyder, "Huey Long and the Cotton-Holiday," 159–60.

CHAPTER 13: Complete the Work

1. Huey P. Long, *Every Man a King: The Autobiography of Huey P. Long* (New Orleans, 1933), 260; *Louisiana Progress*, November 10, 1931.

2. Baton Rouge *State-Times*, July 3, 1931; New York *Times*, July 12, 1931. The Old Regulars also agreed that Huey could name almost half their candidates for the state legislature in the 1932 election. In return, Huey promised abundant patronage and no interference in the next city election, set for January of 1934. See T. Harry Williams, *Huey Long* (New York, 1969), 526–27.

3. Letters and telegrams from Dudley J. LeBlanc to Huey P. Long, August 16, 1922, August 22, September 9, 16, 1924, Long to LeBlanc, September 29, 1924, all in Huey P. Long Papers, Hill Memorial Library, Louisiana State University. For LeBlanc's background and career, see Floyd Martin Clay, *Coozan Dudley LeBlanc: From Huey Long to Hadacol* (Gretna, La., 1973).

4. Clay, *Coozan Dudley LeBlanc*, 56–58; Abbeville (La.) *Meridional*, December 9, 1930, July 11, 1931; Williams, *Huey Long*, 529–30; *Louisiana Progress*, July 15, 1931, January 12, 1932.

5. Long, *Every Man a King*, 19–22, 40, 118–19; *Louisiana Progress*, January 12, 1932; Harley B. Bozeman, "Winn Parish as I Have Known It," *Winn Parish Enterprise* (Winnfield, La.), January 24, 1959 (Clipping in Bozeman Scrapbooks, Louisiana State Library, Baton Rouge); "Allen, Oscar K.," in *National Cyclopaedia of American Biography*, XXVII (Clifton, N.J., 1940), 435–36; Richard W. Leche interview, in T. Harry Williams Papers, Hill Memorial Library, Louisiana State University.

6. Stan Opotowsky, *The Longs of Louisiana* (New York, 1960), 58–59; Long, *Every Man a King*, 260.

7. Julius Tison Long, "What I Know About My Brother, United States Senator Huey P. Long," *Real America*, II (September, 1933), 36; Stephen Hess, "The Long, Long Trail," *American Heritage*, XVII (August, 1966), 70; Williams, *Huey Long*, 528–29, 536; Carleton Beals, *The Story of Huey P. Long* (Philadelphia, 1935), 217–18.

8. New Orleans *Times-Picayune*, January 19, 1932, September 7, 1975; Beals, *Story of Long*, 218; Williams, *Huey Long*, 536; Shreveport *Journal*, January 8, 1932.

9. New Orleans *Times-Picayune*, September 7, 1935; Morgan D. Peoples, "Earl Kemp Long: The Man from Pea Patch Farm," *Louisiana History*, XVII (Fall, 1976), 385–86; Williams, *Huey Long*, 537–38.

10. *Time* quoted in Hess, "Long, Long Trail."

11. *Bienville Democrat* (Arcadia, La.), November 12, 1931 (Clipping in E. A. Conway Scrapbooks, Louisiana State Library, Baton Rouge); New Orleans *Times-Picayune*, October 14, 15, 1931; John Kingston Fineran, *The Career of a Tinpot Napoleon: A Political Biography of Huey P. Long* (New Orleans, 1932), 151–68.

12. New York *Times*, October 14, 1931.

13. Louis Cochran, "The Louisiana Kingfish," *American Mercury*, XXVI (July, 1932), 286–87; Harnett T. Kane, *Louisiana Hayride: The American Rehearsal for Dictatorship, 1928–1940* (New York, 1941), 85; New York *Times*, October 15–17, November 4, 1931.

14. New Orleans *Times-Picayune*, October 14, 15, 1931; New York *Times*, October 4, November 4, 19, 1931, January 23, 1932; Allan P. Sindler, *Huey Long's Louisiana: State Politics, 1920–1952* (Baltimore, 1956), 76.

15. New Orleans *States*, November 26, 1931 (Clipping in John H. Overton Papers, Archives Division, Northwestern State University, Natchitoches, La.).

16. Fineran, *Tinpot Napoleon*, 168–70; New Orleans *States*, November 26, 1931; Edgar Poe, "Hitting the Campaign Trail with the Longs," New Orleans *Times-Picayune*, September 7, 1975.

17. M. J. Kavanaugh interview, in Williams Papers; *Louisiana Progress*, August 18, November 10, 1931.

18. Clay, *Coozan Dudley LeBlanc*, 85–86; James Harvey Young, *The Medical Messiahs: A Social History of Health Quackery in Twentieth Century America* (Princeton, 1967), 318–19; New Orleans *Times-Picayune*, December 6, 1931; Chick Frampton interview, in Williams Papers.

19. *Louisiana Progress*, August 18, 1931; Williams, *Huey Long*, 538.

20. "Dudley J. LeBlanc Answers the Lies of Huey P. Long" (LeBlanc circular in Conway Scrapbooks); Colfax (La.) *Chronicle*, December 17, 1931; *Louisiana Progress*, August 18, 1931, January 12, 1932; Clay, *Coozan Dudley LeBlanc*, 92.

21. New York *Times*, January 10, 1932; *Louisiana Progress*, November 10, 1931, January 12, 1932; Shreveport *Journal*, October 23, 1931; Clay, *Coozan Dudley LeBlanc*, 21, 83–85; Beals, *Story of Long*, 219–21.

22. New Orleans *Times-Picayune*, January 7, 1932; Beals, *Story of Long*, 222–23.

23. *Louisiana Progress*, January 12, 1932; Beals, *Story of Long*, 221; Matthew James Schott, "John M. Parker of Louisiana and the Varieties of American Progressivism" (Ph.D. dissertation, Vanderbilt University, 1969), 493.

24. *Madison Journal* (Tallulah, La.), January 8, 1932; *Report of Louisiana Secretary of State*, 1933, foldout following p. 352.

25. *Report of Louisiana Secretary of State*, 1931, p. 358; *Ibid.*, 1933, foldout following p. 351; Glen Jeansonne, *Leander Perez: Boss of the Delta* (Baton Rouge, 1977), 16–22, 72–73.

26. *St. Bernard Voice* (Arabi, La.), September 13, 1930, January 23, 1932; Clay, *Coozan Dudley LeBlanc*, 97–98.

27. *Report of Louisiana Secretary of State*, 1933, foldout following p. 351; Colfax (La.) *Chronicle*, April 16, 30, 1931, January 21, 1932.

28. New York *Times*, January 23, 26, 1932; New Orleans *Times-Picayune*, January 24–26, 1932; "A Louisiana Kingfish in Washington," *Literary Digest*, February 6, 1932, p. 7.

29. Thomas O. Harris, *The Kingfish: Huey P. Long, Dictator* (New Orleans, 1938), 100–102; Williams, *Huey Long*, 542–43; New York *Times*, January 25, 1932. For Huey's account of his phone conversation with Roy Heidelberg, owner of the hotel, see Long, *Every Man a King*, 288.

30. Long, *Every Man a King*, 282–84; *Congressional Record*, 72d Cong., 2d Sess., 4673–74; Williams, *Huey Long*, 546–47; Kane, *Louisiana Hayride*, 141.

31. *Congressional Record*, 72d Cong., 2d Sess., 4674; Long, *Every Man a King*, 281; *Louisiana Progress*, September 25, 1930; Minns Sledge Robertson, *Public Education in Louisiana After 1898* (Baton Rouge, 1952), 116–17; *Abstract of the Fifteenth Census, 1930*, p. 28.

32. Robertson, *Public Education in Louisiana*, 157–60, 182–83, 188–92; *Louisiana Schools*, XII (November, 1934), 8; *Constitution of 1921*, Art. XII, Sec. 14; Carleton Beals and Abel Plenn, "Louisiana's Black Utopia," *Nation*, October 30, 1935, p. 504; *Louisiana Department of Education Report*, 1915–16, Pt. 1, p. 9.

33. See chap. 2.

34. Long, *Every Man a King*, 246–49; Williams, *Huey Long*, 492–509; Fred Digby, Lawrence M. "Biff" Jones, Troy H. Middleton interviews, all in Williams Papers; John F. Carter [Unofficial Observer], *American Messiahs* (New York, 1935), 14–15.

35. Don Wharton, "Louisiana State University," *Scribner's Magazine*, CII (September, 1937), 33–34; Fred C. Frey interview, in Williams Papers; *Congressional Record*, 73d Cong., 1st Sess., 5270; Victor G. Gough, "Backward Louisiana," letter in *New Republic*, August 1, 1923, p. 261.

36. Ronda Cabot Tentarelli, "The Life and Times of the *Southern Review*," *Southern Studies*, XVI (Summer, 1977), 139–51; Thomas W. Cutrer, "Conference

on Literature and Reading in the South and Southwest, 1935," *Southern Review,* n.s., XXI (April, 1985), 261–65; Kane, *Louisiana Hayride,* 212–16, 276–88, 385; Middleton interview, in Williams Papers; Beals, *Story of Long,* 391. For the photo of Dr. Smith in prison garb, see *Life,* December 11, 1939, p. 31.

37. Mark T. Carleton, *Politics and Punishment: The History of the Louisiana State Penal System* (Baton Rouge, 1971), 90–109, 138; John R. Pleasant, Jr., "Ruffin G. Pleasant and Huey P. Long on the Prisoner-Stripe Controversy," *Louisiana History,* XV (Fall, 1974), 160–61.

38. Baton Rouge *Morning Advocate,* May 16, 1932; Carleton, *Politics and Punishment,* 126–32; Pleasant, "Prisoner-Stripe Controversy," 363–66;

39. *Congressional Record,* 73d Cong., 2d Sess., 1556; Elizabeth Wisner, *Public Welfare Administration in Louisiana* (Chicago, 1930), 114–31; Richard Lawrence Gordon, "The Development of Louisiana's Public Mental Institutions, 1735–1940" (Ph.D. dissertation, Louisiana State University, 1978), 338–39, 436–37.

40. Wisner, *Public Welfare,* 199; John Robert Moore, "The New Deal in Louisiana," in *The New Deal: The State and Local Levels,* ed. John Braeman *et al.* (Columbus, Ohio, 1975), 157; Beals and Plenn, "Louisiana's Black Utopia," 504.

41. Lillie H. Nairne, "A Study of the Administration of Relief to the Unemployed in Louisiana" (M.S. thesis, Tulane University, 1935), 1–4, 121; Wisner, *Public Welfare,* 29–31.

42. Wisner, *Public Welfare,* 29–31; William O. Scruggs, "Parish Government in Louisiana," *Annals of the American Academy of Political and Social Science,* LXVII (May, 1913), 45.

43. Moore, "New Deal in Louisiana," in *New Deal: State and Local,* ed. Braeman *et al.,* 141. For Louisiana figures on unemployment relief (1933–34), see "Emergency Relief Expenditures by States," *Congressional Record,* 74th Cong., 1st Sess., 3947–48.

44. *Congressional Record,* 74th Cong., 1st Sess., 3444–48.

45. Nairne, "Relief to the Unemployed in Louisiana," 3–4; *Acts,* 1930, No. 71; Anthony J. Badger, "Huey Long and the New Deal," in *Nothing Else to Fear: New Perspectives on America in the Thirties,* ed. Stephen W. Baskerville and Ralph Willett (Manchester, Eng., 1985), 72.

46. New Orleans *Times-Picayune,* January 24–26, 1932; Williams, *Huey Long,* 552; *Congressional Record,* 73d Cong., 2d Sess., 6190; "Share-the-Wealth Wave," *Time,* April 1, 1935, p. 16.

47. *Louisiana Senate Journal,* Sixth Regular Session, 1932, p. 1410; "Alice in Wonderland," Hammond (La.) *Vindicator,* September 22, 1933; F. Raymond Daniell, "Land of the Free," in *We Saw It Happen: The News Behind the News That's Fit to Print,* ed. Hanson W. Baldwin and Shepard Stone (New York, 1938), 93–94.

48. New York *Times,* February 18, 19, 1939.

CHAPTER 14: Terror of the Bayous

1. *Congressional Record,* 72d Cong., 1st Sess., 2596; New Orleans *States,* January 25, 26, 1932; New York *Times,* January 26, 28, 31, 1932.

2. Alan Brinkley, *Voices of Protest: Huey Long, Father Coughlin, and the Great Depression* (New York, 1982), 42; *Congressional Record,* 72d Cong., 1st Sess., 13,443; New York *Times,* January 26, 1932.

3. T. Harry Williams, *Huey Long* (New York, 1969), 560. Overall, Williams' biography treats Long more sympathetically than this book, but in several passages Williams concedes, or almost concedes, that Huey's primal motivation throughout his life was self-aggrandizement. In particular, see pp. 37, 315, 515–16, 750–52.

4. New York *Times*, May 25, 1931, April 30, 1932; *Congressional Record*, 72d Cong., 1st Sess., 8556, 9202, 9212–14.

5. *Congressional Record*, 72d Cong., 1st Sess., 9216–19.

6. Washington *Post*, May 4, 13, 1932; *Congressional Record*, 72d Cong., 1st Sess., 9482–83; 10,062–65.

7. Anthony J. Badger, "Huey Long and the New Deal," in *Nothing Else to Fear: New Perspectives on America in the Thirties*, ed. Stephen W. Baskerville and Ralph Willett (Manchester, Eng., 1985), 81; John D. Hicks, *Republican Ascendancy, 1921–1933* (New York, 1960), 89–90, 129; Brinkley, *Voices of Protest*, 77–78, 302.

8. Burton K. Wheeler, *Yankee from the West* (Garden City, N.Y., 1962), 282–90; "Share-the-Wealth Wave," *Time*, April 1, 1935, p. 16. A cogent summary of Wheeler's career is in Arthur M. Schlesinger, Jr., *The Politics of Upheaval* (Boston, 1960), 136–39.

9. Huey P. Long, *Every Man a King: The Autobiography of Huey P. Long* (New Orleans, 1933), 289; Richard Lowitt, *George W. Norris: The Triumph of a Progressive* (Urbana, Ill., 1978), 136.

10. Chick Frampton interview, in T. Harry Williams Papers, Hill Memorial Library, Louisiana State University.

11. *Congressional Record*, 73d Cong., 1st Sess., 5268; Williams, *Huey Long*, 555.

12. Rose Lee, "Senator Long at Home," *New Republic*, May 30, 1934, p. 66; Hermann B. Deutsch, *The Huey Long Murder Case* (Garden City, N.Y., 1963), 64; Hammond (La.) *Vindicator*, October 6, 1933.

13. *Louisiana House Journal*, Sixth Regular Session, 1932, pp. 7–8, 19–22; New York *Times*, June 3, 15, 1932; "Incredible Kingfish," *Time*, October 3, 1932; Williams, *Huey Long*, 568–71; Carleton Beals, *The Story of Huey P. Long* (Philadelphia, 1935), 233–35, 336.

14. See *Louisiana House Journal* and *Louisiana Senate Journal*, Sixth Regular Session, 1932, *passim*.

15. John Wilds, *Afternoon Story: A Century of the New Orleans "States-Item"* (Baton Rouge, 1976), 234–37. See also *Louisiana Progress*, January 12, 1932, and *American Progress*, August 24, 1933. Wilds points out that although Thompson's *Item* temporarily gained from an alliance with Long, the move hurt his newspaper's credibility and "was ruinous ultimately."

16. Richard W. Leche interview, in Williams Papers; Allan P. Sindler, *Huey Long's Louisiana: State Politics, 1920–1952* (Baltimore, 1956), 119n; John Kingston Fineran, *The Career of a Tinpot Napoleon: A Political Biography of Huey P. Long* (New Orleans, 1932), 165; Williams, *Huey Long*, 566–67.

17. Leche interview, in Williams Papers; Stephen Hess, "The Long, Long Trail," *American Heritage*, XVII (August, 1966), 72; *Time*, October 3, 1932, p. 10.

18. Brinkley, *Voices of Protest*, 27; Mason Spencer interview, in Williams Papers.

19. Louie Jones interview, in Williams Papers. This was not the only time Huey put a chauffeur out on the highway. Two other such episodes are described—one in Wheeler, *Yankee from the West*, 285, another in Hermann B. Deutsch, "Paradox in Pajamas," *Saturday Evening Post*, October 5, 1935, p. 15.

20. Forrest Davis, *Huey Long: A Candid Biography* (New York, 1935), 34–35. Davis primly quoted Huey as referring to Allen as "the so-and-so," but most likely the actual words were his standard ones on such occasions.

21. "Mourners, Heirs, Foes," *Time*, September 23, 1935, p. 15.

22. Julius Tison Long, "Julius T. Long Unmasks His Brother, U.S. Senator Huey P. Long," *Real America*, II (October, 1933), 53–54; Harley B. Bozeman, "Winn Parish as I Have Known It," *Winn Parish Enterprise* (Winnfield, La.), August 7, 1958 (Clipping in Bozeman Scrapbooks, Louisiana State Library, Baton Rouge); Sam Irby, *Kidnaped by the Kingfish: With Intimate Details of This and Other Crimes of Huey P. Long* (New Orleans, 1932), 38–41. Irby's booklet has many distortions, but he had been a "chemist" with the Louisiana Highway Department and was personally involved in a scheme to boost the price contractors had to pay for Winnfield limestone by pouring oil into the quarried material and calling this mixture "amesite." For official praise of "Winnfield crushed stone," see *Louisiana Progress*, May, 1931.

23. Elmer L. Irey and William J. Slocum, *The Tax Dodgers: The Inside Story of the T-Men's War with America's Political and Underworld Hoodlums* (New York, 1949), 96–97; Williams, *Huey Long*, 825–27; Harnett T. Kane, *Louisiana Hayride: The American Rehearsal for Dictatorship, 1928–1940* (New York, 1941), 160, 176, 444n.

24. William E. Leuchtenburg, *Franklin D. Roosevelt and the New Deal, 1932–1940* (New York, 1963), 4–7; New York *Times*, June 22, 27, 1932; Wilds, *Afternoon Story*, 192; Long, *Every Man a King*, 301–303.

25. New York *Times*, May 1, June 18, 1932; Wheeler, *Yankee from the West*, 285; *Louisiana Progress*, January, 1931; Beals, *Story of Long*, 238; *Congressional Record*, 74th Cong., 1st Sess., 9124–25. After Huey declined it, Jacob Coxey accepted the Farmer-Labor party's presidential nomination and received only 7,309 votes out of 44 million cast. Most of Coxey's vote came from Minnesota. See Richard B. Morris, ed., *Encyclopedia of American History* (New York, 1953), 340.

26. Shreveport *Times*, June 15–17, 1932; Frank Freidel, *Franklin D. Roosevelt: The Triumph* (Boston, 1956), 279; Beals, *Story of Long*, 236–39.

27. New York *Times*, June 26, 1932; Williams, *Huey Long*, 576.

28. Webster Smith, *The Kingfish: A Biography of Huey P. Long* (New York, 1933), 263–65; Williams, *Huey Long*, 574–75; Freidel, *Roosevelt: The Triumph*, 301–302.

29. R. G. Tugwell, *The Brains Trust* (New York, 1968), 230–31; Long, *Every Man a King*, 304–305. Huey attributed his eating Governor Murray's breakfast to absent-mindedness.

30. Wheeler, *Yankee from the West*, 286; James A. Farley, *Jim Farley's Story: The Roosevelt Years* (New York, 1948), 15–16; New York *Times*, June 28, 29, 1932.

31. *Time*, October 3, 1932, p. 10; "Lets 'Kingfish' Do Talking," New York *Times*, June 28, 1932.

32. Wheeler, *Yankee from the West*, 286–87; Freidel, *Roosevelt: The Triumph*,

NOTES TO PAGES 245-50

306–11; Thomas L. Stokes, *Chip off My Shoulder* (Princeton, 1940), 321–22; *Congressional Record*, 73d Cong., 2d Sess., 6092.

33. Edward J. Flynn, *You're the Boss* (New York, 1947), 101.

34. Tugwell, *Brains Trust*, 430–31.

35. Edward Robb Ellis, *A Nation in Torment: The Great American Depression, 1929–1939* (New York, 1971), 390–91; Rexford G. Tugwell, *The Democratic Roosevelt* (Garden City, N.Y., 1957), 349.

36. *Louisiana Progress*, August 18, 1931; Long, *Every Man a King*, 252–58; *Time*, September 12, 1932, p. 48.

37. Brinkley, *Voices of Protest*, 47–48; Hermann B. Deutsch, "Hattie and Huey," *Saturday Evening Post*, October 15, 1932, pp. 6–7.

38. Stuart Towns, "A Louisiana Medicine Show: The Kingfish Elects an Arkansas Senator," *Arkansas Historical Quarterly*, XXV (Summer, 1966), 119–22; *Congressional Record*, 72d Cong., 1st Sess., 25, 192–93; Deutsch, *Long Murder Case*, 22–25.

39. *Time*, October 3, 1932; New Orleans *Item*, August 1, 2, 1932; Brinkley, *Voices of Protest*, 49.

40. Deutsch, *Long Murder Case*, 23; Williams, *Huey Long*, 589–90.

41. New York *Times*, July 31, August 2, 1932; Deutsch, "Hattie and Huey," 90.

42. Long, *Every Man a King*, 313; Beals, *Story of Long*, 243.

43. Hermann B. Deutsch, "Huey Long: The Last Phase," *Saturday Evening Post*, October 12, 1935, p. 82; Deutsch, *Long Murder Case*, 24–25. Deutsch covered Huey's Arkansas campaign for the New Orleans *Item*—pro-Long at the time—so Huey assumed his remark about church attendance and preachers would not appear in the press. Indeed, Deutsch waited until 1963 before putting the conversation in print.

44. New York *Times*, August 11, 1932; Brinkley, *Voices of Protest*, 52–53; Arthur Marvin Shaw, "The First Time I Saw Huey," *Southwest Review*, XXXV (Winter, 1950), 63.

45. Mrs. John H. Overton interview, in Williams Papers; New Orleans *States*, September 9, 1932 (Clipping in John H. Overton Papers, Archives Division, Northwestern State University, Natchitoches, La.); *Report of Louisiana Secretary of State*, 1919, p. 344; *Louisiana Progress*, April, 1931.

46. New Orleans *Times-Picayune*, August 21–23, 1932; Beals, *Story of Long*, 248.

47. New Orleans *Item*, August 23, 1932 (Clipping in Overton Papers); Beals, *Story of Long*, 248; Robert Brothers interview, in Williams Papers; Williams, *Huey Long*, 597.

48. Alexandria *Town Talk*, August 22, 1932; New Orleans *Times-Picayune*, August 15, 1932; *Congressional Record*, 72d Cong., 2d Sess., 2817–28, 4994.

49. Sindler, *Huey Long's Louisiana*, 37, 81–82; Williams, *Huey Long*, 596–97; *Report of Louisiana Secretary of State*, 1933, p. 3.

50. Thomas O. Harris, *The Kingfish: Huey P. Long, Dictator* (New Orleans, 1938), 119; *Congressional Record*, 72d Cong., 2d Sess., 4993.

51. *Senate Hearings on Campaign Expenditures*, 72d Cong., 2d Sess., Pt. 1, 654–55, 692–93; *Congressional Record*, 73d Cong., 2d Sess., 1554–56, 1564–65; Glen Jeansonne, *Leander Perez: Boss of the Delta* (Baton Rouge, 1977), 72.

52. New Orleans *Item*, September 14, 1932; *Senate Hearings on Campaign Expenditures*, 72d Cong., 2d Sess., Pt. 1, pp. 174, 179.

53. New York *Times*, September 11, 1932; Sindler, *Huey Long's Louisiana*, 82n; Deutsch, *Long Murder Case*, 43; James W. Clarke, *American Assassins: The Darker Side of Politics* (Princeton, 1982), 228.

54. James A. Farley, *Behind the Ballots* (New York, 1938), 170–71; Grace Tully, *FDR, My Boss* (New York, 1949), 323–24; Williams, *Huey Long*, 601–602.

55. New York *Times*, October 11, 1932.

56. *Ibid.*, October 16, 1932; New Orleans *Times-Picayune*, October 26, 1932; Williams, *Huey Long*, 602–603; Farley, *Behind the Ballots*, 171.

57. Tugwell, *Democratic Roosevelt*, 349; Farley, *Jim Farley's Story*, 45.

CHAPTER 15: God Said So!

1. "Incredible Kingfish," *Time*, October 3, 1932, p. 10; F. Raymond Daniell, "Louisiana Becomes an Authoritarian State," New York *Times*, February 10, 1935.

2. Waldo Dugas, George Ginsberg interviews, both in T. Harry Williams Papers, Hill Memorial Library, Louisiana State University; Cecil Morgan to Bell I. Wiley, May 9, 1970, in Manuscripts Section, Howard-Tilton Memorial Library, Tulane University.

3. New York *Times*, February 10, 1935; Harnett T. Kane, *Louisiana Hayride: The American Rehearsal for Dictatorship, 1928–1940* (New York, 1941), 92.

4. Samuel I. Rosenman, comp., *The Public Papers and Addresses of Franklin D. Roosevelt* (13 vols.; New York, 1938–50), I, 659; *Congressional Record*, 73d Cong., 1st Sess., 124–25, 155, 275–76, 3323.

5. Alan Brinkley, *Voices of Protest: Huey Long, Father Coughlin, and the Great Depression* (New York, 1983), 60–62; *Congressional Record*, 73d Cong., 1st Sess., 55.

6. New York *Times*, April 15, 1933; Rexford G. Tugwell, *The Democratic Roosevelt* (Garden City, N.Y., 1957), 298, 348, 350; *Congressional Record*, 73d Cong., 1st Sess., 4261–62.

7. James A. Farley, *Behind the Ballots* (New York, 1938), 240–43; John Salmond, *A Southern Rebel: The Life and Times of Aubrey Willis Williams, 1890–1965* (Chapel Hill, 1983), 45–46.

8. T. Harry Williams, *Huey Long* (New York, 1969), 604–18; *Senate Hearings on Campaign Expenditures*, 72d Cong., 2d Sess., Pt. 1, *passim.*

9. *Senate Hearings on Campaign Expenditures*, 72d Cong., 2d Sess., Pt. 1, 3, 19–20, 38, 52–57, 85, 282–83, 554–66, 587–98, 817–22, 835–62, 953–54, 1002–18; New Orleans *Times-Picayune*, February 3, 4, 10, 18, 1933; *Congressional Record*, 72d Cong., 2d Sess., 4687–89; Thomas O. Harris, *The Kingfish: Huey P. Long, Dictator* (New Orleans, 1938), 119–25.

10. Williams, *Huey Long*, 613–14; New Orleans *Times-Picayune*, February 12, 1933; *Congressional Record*, 72d Cong., 2d Sess., 4691.

11. Tom Connally and Alfred Steinberg, *My Name Is Tom Connally* (New York, 1954), 167–68; *Senate Hearings on Campaign Expenditures*, 73d Cong., 2d Sess., Pt. 2, pp. 1122, 1136.

12. *Congressional Record*, 72d Cong., 2d Sess., 4658–59, 4713; Harris, *Kingfish*, 125–26; New York *Times*, November 6, 1934. Because of congressional immunity, Huey could not be sued for saying, in the Senate, that S. T. Ansell was "a thief of the . . . lowest order of crookdom," but when he used similar words in a

circular, he was open to a libel suit. The case was still pending at the time of Long's death.

13. "Committed in a Cathedral," *Time*, December 4, 1933, p. 14.

14. Connally and Steinberg, *Tom Connally*, 168; *Congressional Record*, 73d Cong., 2d Sess., 1552–64.

15. John M. Parker to John Nance Garner, April 12, 1933, in John M. Parker Papers, Southern Historical Collection, University of North Carolina, Chapel Hill. Italics mine.

16. New York *Times*, August 29, 1933; Williams, *Huey Long*, 648–49. The Hotel New Yorker confirmed Huey's boast that he stayed there free of charge (see New York *Times*, September 7, 1935).

17. New York *Herald Tribune*, August 30, 1933; "In a Washroom," *Time*, September 11, 1933, pp. 16–17.

18. New York *Times*, August 29, 1933; *Times* (London), September 22, 1933; Owen P. White, *The Autobiography of a Durable Sinner* (New York, 1942), 270–71; Murphy Roden interview, in Williams Papers; William Miller and Frances Spatz Leighton, *Fishbait: The Memoirs of a Congressional Doorkeeper* (Englewood Cliffs, N.J., 1977), 15.

19. Hammond (La.) *Vindicator*, September 8, October 20, November 17, 1933; Hilda Phelps Hammond, *Let Freedom Ring* (New York, 1936), 128; New Orleans *Times-Picayune*, August 31, September 1, 1933; New York *Times*, August 31, 1933. See also Hodding Carter, "Kingfish to Crawfish," *New Republic*, January 24, 1934, pp. 302–303.

20. Brinkley, *Voices of Protest*, 66; New York *Times*, August 31, 1933.

21. *American Progress*, September 7, 1933; *Time*, September 11, 1933, p. 17; Harris, *Kingfish*, 143.

22. Burton L. Hotaling, "Huey Pierce Long as Journalist and Propagandist," *Journalism Quarterly*, XX (March, 1943), 26–27; Mary B. Walle, quoted in Williams, *Huey Long*, 644.

23. Hotaling, "Long as Journalist," 27; *American Progress*, October 19, 1933; Hammond (La.) *Vindicator*, November 2, 1933; Allan Nevins, "One of Our Conquerers," *Saturday Review of Literature*, December 9, 1933, p. 324.

24. Hamilton Basso, "Huey Long and His Background," *Harper's Monthly*, CLXX (May, 1935), 671. In the years after Long's death, Basso reflected upon the Kingfish's career and its threat to democracy in America, and became more critical. See his *Mainstream* (New York, 1943), 179–95.

25. John A. Garraty, *The Great Depression* (Garden City, N.Y., 1987), 182–85; John Robert Moore, "The New Deal in Louisiana," in *The New Deal: The State and Local Levels*, ed. John Braeman *et al.* (Columbus, Ohio, 1975), 145–46; Hodding Carter, "Louisiana Limelighter," *Review of Reviews*, XCI (March, 1935), 28.

26. New Orleans *Times-Picayune*, October 16, 1933; *Time*, October 23, 1933, p. 42; New York *Times*, October 17, 1933.

27. Hammond (La.) *Vindicator*, October 27, 1933; Mason Dixon, "Senator Long Faces Revolt in Louisiana," New York *Times*, November 5, 1933.

28. "Long Assails Rich from Private Car," New York *Times*, October 22, 1933; Forrest Davis, *Huey Long: A Candid Biography* (New York, 1935), 202; Shreveport *Journal*, quoted in Hammond (La.) *Vindicator*, October 27, 1933.

29. New York *Times*, November 11, 1933; Davis, *Long: A Candid Biography*, 202; Murphy Roden, E. P. Roy interviews, both in Williams Papers.

30. Parker to Garner, April 12, 1933, in Parker Papers, University of North

Carolina, Chapel Hill; Hammond (La.) *Vindicator,* November 3, 1933; Baton Rouge *Freedom,* quoted in Colfax (La.) *Chronicle,* November 24, 1933.

31. *American Progress,* November 16, 1933; New York *Times,* November 10–11, 1933.

32. *Congressional Record,* 73d Cong., 2d Sess., 1510–11; Hammond (La.) *Vindicator,* November 24, December 1, 1933; *American Progress,* November 23, 1933; "Revolting Parishes," *Time,* December 18, 1933, p. 11.

33. Hodding Carter, "Huey Long: American Dictator," in *The Aspirin Age, 1919–1941,* ed. Isabel Leighton (New York, 1963), 342–43; *Congressional Record,* 73d Cong., 2d Sess., 1510–21; Hammond (La.) *Vindicator,* April 27, 1934.

34. Carter, "Kingfish to Crawfish," 304; Louie Jones interview, in Williams Papers.

35. New Orleans *Times-Picayune,* December 20, 21, 1933; New York *Times,* October 1, December 21, 1933; Williams, *Huey Long,* 670–71. Prior to their break, Mayor Walmsley and Long met several times in Long's hotel suite but could not agree on a ticket for the lesser municipal offices. The seventeen Old Regular ward bosses made Walmsley's decision for him—they voted 12–5 against continuing the OR-Long alliance.

36. *American Progress,* December 28, 1933, January 4, 18, 1934; New Orleans *Times-Picayune,* January 21–23, 1934.

37. *American Progress,* January 4, 18, 1934; New York *Times,* January 23, 1934; Davis, *Long: A Candid Biography,* 208–209.

38. New Orleans *Item,* January 19, 22, 1934; *American Progress,* January 18, 1934; Allan P. Sindler, *Huey Long's Louisiana: State Politics, 1920–1952* (Baltimore, 1956), 60n, 75n; Matthew James Schott, "John M. Parker of Louisiana and the Varieties of American Progressivism" (Ph.D. dissertation, Vanderbilt University, 1969), 490–91.

39. New Orleans *Times-Picayune,* January 22, 23, 1934; Williams, *Huey Long,* 674–75; Hammond (La.) *Vindicator,* January 26, 1934.

40. *American Progress,* February 1, 1934. Whether he was in Louisiana or in Washington, Huey kept close supervision over everything that went into the *Progress.* See Hotaling, "Long as Journalist," 26.

41. New York *Times,* January 28, 30, 1934; Carter, "Huey Long," in *Aspirin Age,* ed. Leighton, 353; Williams, *Huey Long,* 678–79; *Congressional Record,* 74th Cong., 1st Sess., 12,790.

42. W. C. Pegues, Theophile Landry interviews, both in Williams Papers; Des Moines *Sunday Register,* April 28, 1935 (Clipping in Huey P. Long Scrapbooks, Hill Memorial Library, Louisiana State University); George E. Sokolsky, "Huey Long," *Atlantic Monthly,* CLVI (November, 1935), 525; New York *Times,* February 10, July 25, 1935.

43. John F. Carter [Unofficial Observer], *American Messiahs* (New York, 1935), 5–6; Williams, *Huey Long,* 679–80; New York *Times,* November 26, 28, 1934.

44. Alben W. Barkley, *That Reminds Me* (Garden City, N.Y., 1954), 159; Boston *Post,* March 10, 1935, quoted in Williams, *Huey Long,* 681; Russell Owen, "Huey Long Gives His View of Dictators," *New York Times Magazine,* February 10, 1935, p. 3.

45. New York *Herald Tribune,* March 12, 1933; New York *Times,* March 12, 13, 1933, April 6, 1934; Arthur Krock, *Memoirs: Sixty Years on the Firing Line* (New York, 1968), 170.

46. Krock, *Memoirs,* 170; Rodney Dutcher, "Long Detested, but Still Feared,"

New Orleans *States*, April 14, 1934; "The Pied Pipers," *Time*, March 28, 1935, p. 15; *Congressional Record*, 73d Cong., 2d Sess., 6081, 6093, 6105.

47. *Congressional Record*, 73d Cong., 2d Sess., 6093, 6097.

48. Burton K. Wheeler, *Yankee from the West* (Garden City, N.Y., 1962), 284; Brinkley, *Voices of Protest*, 77; New York *Times*, November 15, 1934; *Congressional Record*, 74th Cong., 1st Sess., 1836.

49. *Congressional Record*, 74th Cong., 1st Sess., 7913, 7916.

50. *Ibid.*, 73d Cong., 2d Sess., 1920–21, 3450–53; "Share-the-Wealth Wave," *Time*, April 1, 1935, p. 16; Hotaling, "Long as Journalist," 26n.

51. *Congressional Record*, 73d Cong., 2d Sess., 1920–21. Dime-size lapel buttons were sold to local Share Our Wealth clubs at cost—six dollars per thousand. *American Progress*, March 1, 1934.

52. "Redistribution of Wealth," Radio address by Huey P. Long, in *Congressional Record*, 74th Cong., 1st Sess., 410–12; New York *Times*, March 9, 10, 1935.

53. Selden C. Menefee, "Standard of Living," *Survey*, LXXIII (September, 1937), 281–82; *Historical Statistics of the United States: Colonial Times to 1970* (Washington, D.C., 1975), Pt. 1, 210–11; *Statistical Abstract of the United States*, 1982–83; Bureau of Labor Statistics, *CPI Detailed Report*, February, 1990 (Washington, D.C., 1990), 1, 3. The synopsis of Long's evolving Share Our Wealth plan is derived from articles in the *American Progress*, February 15, March 22, 1934, April, 1935, and from three NBC radio broadcasts reprinted in the *Congressional Record*, 73d Cong., 2d Sess., 3450–53, 74th Cong., 1st Sess., 410–12, 7048–50. The biblical chapters and verses that Huey usually cited as authority for Share Our Wealth were Lev. 25:10, Deut. 15:1–2, Neh. 5, Eccles. 5:9, and James 5:1–4.

54. Davis, *Long: A Candid Biography*, 42–43; *Congressional Record*, 74th Cong., 1st Sess., 411; New York *Times*, March 9, 1935.

55. *Congressional Record*, 73d Cong., 2d Sess., 5990, 74th Cong., 1st Sess., 3438.

56. Brinkley, *Voices of Protest*, 73; Anthony J. Badger, "Huey Long and the New Deal," in *Nothing Else to Fear: New Perspectives on America in the Thirties*, ed. Stephen W. Baskerville and Ralph Willett (Manchester, Eng., 1985), 93.

57. Richard W. Leche, H. C. Sevier interviews, both in Williams Papers; Michael L. Kurtz and Morgan D. Peoples, *Earl K. Long: The Saga of Uncle Earl and Louisiana Politics* (Baton Rouge, 1990), 82.

58. Garraty, *Great Depression*, 10; David A. Shannon, *Between the Wars: America, 1919–1941* (Boston, 1979), 149–50.

59. *Time*, April 1, 1935, p. 17; Williams, *Huey Long*, 700–701; John F. Carter [Observer], *American Messiahs*, 22–23.

60. New York *Times*, August 5, 13, 1933, March 3, 1934, June 2, 1935; *Time*, April 1, 1935, p. 17; Williams, *Huey Long*, 694.

61. Glen Jeansonne, *Gerald L. K. Smith: Minister of Hate* (New Haven, 1988), 11–27, 101–205. This superb biography is the definitive work on G. L. K. Smith, who in later years (he died in 1976) became America's most anti-Semitic ultra-right evangelist.

62. *Ibid.*, 28–31. Jeansonne obtained Smith's FBI file through the Freedom of Information Act.

63. Alan A. Michie and Frank Ryhlick, *Dixie Demagogues* (New York, 1939), 118; Jeansonne, *G. L. K. Smith*, 102–105. The notion that Huey Long's assassina-

tion was a Jewish plot first appeared in an American Nazi publication, *American Bulletin*, shortly after his death. See *New Republic*, December 18, 1935, p. 158.

64. Gerald L. K. Smith, "Or Superman?" *New Republic*, February 13, 1935, pp. 14–15; *American Progress*, February 22, May 29, 1934; Kane, *Louisiana Hayride*, 152; *Time*, April 1, 1935, p. 17.

65. Williams, *Huey Long*, 702; Roy Wilkins, "Huey Long Says: An Interview with Louisiana's Kingfish," *Crisis*, LXII (February, 1935), 52.

66. Carleton Beals and Abel Plenn, "Louisiana's Black Utopia," *Nation*, October 30, 1935, p. 505; Bunkie (La.) *Record*, July 19, 1935; Hammond (La.) *Vindicator*, May 11, 1934.

CHAPTER 16: Plain Dictator

1. T. Harry Williams, *Huey Long* (New York, 1969), 821–22; Forrest Davis, *Huey Long: A Candid Biography* (New York, 1935), 272–73.

2. "Huey Long," *Christian Century*, LII (September 18, 1935), 1167; Fred Digby interview, in T. Harry Williams Papers, Hill Memorial Library, Louisiana State University; James Rorty, "Callie Long's Boy Huey," *Forum*, XCIV (August, 1935), 127; Raymond Gram Swing, *Forerunners of American Fascism* (New York, 1935), 81.

3. Harnett T. Kane, *Louisiana Hayride: The American Rehearsal for Dictatorship, 1928–1940* (New York, 1941), 105; Hodding Carter, "Kingfish to Crawfish," *New Republic*, January 24, 1934, p. 305; F. Raymond Daniell, "The Gentleman from Louisiana," *Current History*, XLI (November, 1934), 177.

4. Hammond (La.) *Vindicator*, May 11, 1934; Hermann B. Deutsch, "Kingdom of the Kingfish," New Orleans *Item*, September 4, 1939; Thomas O. Harris, *The Kingfish: Huey P. Long, Dictator* (New Orleans, 1938), 160–62.

5. *Louisiana Senate Journal*, Seventh Regular Session, 1934, p. 7; Harris, *Kingfish*, 163–64; Charles E. Dunbar, Jr., interview, in Williams Papers.

6. Baton Rouge *State-Times*, June 21–25, 1934; F. Raymond Daniell, "Louisiana Becomes an Authoritarian State," New York *Times*, February 10, 1935; Williams, *Huey Long*, 717–19; Harris, *Kingfish*, 164.

7. *Acts*, Regular Session, 1934, Nos. 21, 78, 230; V. O. Key, Jr., *Southern Politics in State and Nation* (New York, 1949), 603; Williams, *Huey Long*, 720–21; Carleton Beals, *The Story of Huey P. Long* (Philadelphia, 1935), 270.

8. Allan P. Sindler, *Huey Long's Louisiana: State Politics, 1920–1952* (Baltimore, 1956), 89–91; New Orleans *Times-Picayune*, July 8–12, 1934; Davis, *Long: A Candid Biography*, 213.

9. F. Raymond Daniell, "Once More Huey Long Calls the Dance," *New York Times Magazine*, September 2, 1934, p. 3; Sindler, *Huey Long's Louisiana*, 89–90; Raymond Gram Swing, "The Menace of Huey Long," *Nation*, January 16, 1935, p. 70; Tom Wallace, "Who's Huey in Louisiana," San Francisco *Chronicle*, February 24, 1935 (Clipping in Huey P. Long Scrapbooks, Hill Memorial Library, Louisiana State University); *Grosjean v. American Press Co.*, 297 U.S. 233 (1936).

10. J. Y. Sanders, Jr., interview, in Williams Papers.

11. New Orleans *Times-Picayune*, June 12, 13, 1934; Davis, *Long: A Candid Biography*, 214; W. Adolphe Roberts, *Lake Pontchartrain* (Indianapolis, 1946), 336; Bunkie (La.) *Record*, September 7, 24, 1934, July 19, 1935; Hammond (La.) *Vindicator*, June 15, 1934.

12. Hilda Phelps Hammond, *Let Freedom Ring* (New York, 1936), 20–21; Bunkie (La.) *Record*, August 24, 1934, January 4, 1935.

13. Westbrook Pegler, "Fair Enough," column in Washington *Post*, September 12, 1935; New Orleans *Times-Picayune*, September 15, 1934.

14. *Acts*, First Extra Session, 1934, Nos. 7, 8, 24; Harris, *Kingfish*, 173–75. Huey's *American Progress*, August 7, 1934, claimed Mayor Walmsley was deputizing touts and pimps as "special police."

15. *Acts*, First Extra Session, 1934, No. 9; Davis, *Long: A Candid Biography*, 18; "An American Dictator," *Times* (London), April 25, 1935; Louis F. Guerre interview, in Williams Papers.

16. *Acts*, First Extra Session, 1934, No. 27; Williams, *Huey Long*, 728–29; Harris, *Kingfish*, 175–76.

17. *Congressional Record*, 74th Cong., 1st Sess., 153; New Orleans *Times-Picayune*, September 3–11, 1934; Baton Rouge *State-Times*, September 11, 1934; Carleton Beals, "Sharing Vice and Votes," *Nation*, October 2, 1935, p. 379.

18. New Orleans *Times-Picayune*, September 8–10, 1934; Atlanta *Constitution*, September 10, 1934; Williams, *Huey Long*, 733–36; Harris, *Kingfish*, 175–79, 221–22.

19. George B. Campbell, "Roosevelt—Not Long—Deserves Praise," Hammond (La.) *Vindicator*, December 8, 1933; *Congressional Record*, 74th Cong., 1st Sess., 6937–38; Betty Marie Field, "The Politics of the New Deal in Louisiana, 1933–1939" (Ph.D. dissertation, Tulane University, 1973), 8–11.

20. *Congressional Record*, 73d Cong., 1st Sess., 1712, 2d Sess., 6480–81; 74th Cong., 1st Sess., 9097–98; New York *Times*, April 5, 1934; *American Progress*, January 18, 1934, February 1, 1935.

21. Pamela Tyler, "Silk Stockings and Ballot Boxes: Women of the Upper Class and New Orleans Politics, 1930–1955" (Ph.D. dissertation, Tulane University, 1989), 41, 46–47, 63, 74–75; Hammond, *Let Freedom Ring*, 203–207; *Congressional Record*, 73d Cong., 2d Sess., 1558–59.

22. *Congressional Record*, 73d Cong., 2d Sess., 1559, 1562; Beals, *Story of Long*, 178; *American Progress*, November 16, 23, 1933, January 4, 1935; Shreveport *Journal*, June 16, 1932; New York *Times*, May 31, 1933; Tyler, "Silk Stockings," 81; John Herrick, "Huey Long Foes Spill It All," Chicago *Tribune*, May 30, 1934; Hammond, *Let Freedom Ring*, 209.

23. Alan Brinkley, *Voices of Protest: Huey Long, Father Coughlin, and the Great Depression* (New York, 1983), 207–209; Arthur Krock, "In Washington," column in New York *Times*, March 27, 1935; Robert E. Snyder, "Huey Long and the Presidential Election of 1936," *Louisiana History*, XVI (Spring, 1975), 128.

24. William E. Leuchtenburg, *Franklin D. Roosevelt and the New Deal, 1932–1940* (New York, 1963), 88–103; Brinkley, *Voices of Protest*, 209–15; Rexford G. Tugwell, *The Democratic Roosevelt* (Garden City, N.Y., 1957), 350.

25. Field, "New Deal in Louisiana," 16–21; Arthur M. Schlesinger, Jr., *The Politics of Upheaval* (Boston, 1960), 243–44.

26. Williams, *Huey Long*, 755–58, 795–96; *Congressional Record*, 74th Cong., 1st Sess., 156.

27. Elmer L. Irey and William J. Slocum, *The Tax Dodgers: The Inside Story of the T-Men's War with America's Political and Underworld Hoodlums* (New York, 1949), 89–92; Burton K. Wheeler, *Yankee from the West* (Garden City, N.Y., 1962), 290–91.

28. Irey and Slocum, *Tax Dodgers*, 92; Field, "New Deal in Louisiana," 180–83.

29. New Orleans *Times-Picayune*, April 27, 1935; Kane, *Louisiana Hayride*, 403–404, 424–26; David Zinman, "Seymour Weiss Is Man Who Climbed Back from Disaster," Baton Rouge *Morning Advocate*, August 5, 1963; Irey and Slocum, *Tax Dodgers*, 111; *Congressional Record*, 74th Cong., 1st Sess., 4451; Harris, *Kingfish*, 224–25; Williams, *Huey Long*, 820, 827–28.

30. Wheeler, *Yankee from the West*, 282; Irey and Slocum, *Tax Dodgers*, 95–96.

31. Daniell, "Gentleman from Louisiana," 172; Dunbar and Chick Frampton interviews, both in Williams Papers.

32. Irey and Slocum, *Tax Dodgers*, 94–95; Field, "New Deal in Louisiana," 1–194; Owen P. White, *The Autobiography of a Durable Sinner* (New York, 1942), 273–75.

33. Brinkley, *Voices of Protest*, 169; "The Pied Pipers," *Time*, March 18, 1935, p. 15; *American Progress*, June, 1935; Field, "New Deal in Louisiana," 187.

34. *Congressional Record*, 74th Cong., 1st Sess., 1832, 11,518; Field, "New Deal in Louisiana," 93.

35. New York *Times*, April 23, 1935; "Des Moines Holiday," *Time*, May 6, 1935, p. 19; *Congressional Record*, 74th Cong., 1st Sess., 2943, 6110; Harold L. Ickes, *The Secret Diary of Harold L. Ickes: The First Thousand Days* (New York, 1953), 346.

36. *Congressional Record*, 73d Cong., 2d Sess., 3899–3900.

37. Terry L. Jones, "An Administration Under Fire: The Long-Farley Affair of 1935," *Louisiana History*, XXVIII (Winter, 1987), 5–17; *Congressional Record*, 74th Cong., 1st Sess., 1782, 1794, 1797, 1831, 2398, 7441–42, 9364. Huey predicted (pp. 7441–42) that the next time he struggled with Jim Farley he would "bury him face down, so that every time he scratches he will go nearer home."

38. *Acts*, Second Extra Session, 1934, Nos. 2, 18, 22; Hodding Carter, "Louisiana Limelighter," *Review of Reviews*, XCI (March, 1935), 28, 64; Atlanta *Constitution*, November 16, 1934; New York *Times*, November 14, 17, 1934.

39. Davis, *Long: A Candid Biography*, 225–26; New York *Times*, November 7, 1934; Williams, *Huey Long*, 505.

40. Peter Finney, *The Fighting Tigers: Seventy-five Years of LSU Football* (Baton Rouge, 1968), 117–22.

41. "An Invasion of Tennessee," *Times* (London), October 24, 27, 1934; Atlanta *Constitution*, October 27, 28, 1934; New York *Times*, November 18, 1934.

42. Finney, *Fighting Tigers*, 126–33; New Orleans *Times-Picayune*, December 17–19, 1934.

43. New York *Times*, December 20, 1934; Finney, *Fighting Tigers*, 129–31, 133; *American Progress*, January 4, 1935; *Congressional Record*, 74th Cong., 1st Sess., 14,727.

44. Williams, *Huey Long*, 774–78; Baton Rouge *State-Times*, December 4, 5, 1934; *New Republic*, December 12, 1934, p. 115. As if to justify Huey's censorship of LSU's *Reveille*, the *American Progress* pointed out (January 4, 1935) that the editors of Tulane's student newspaper, *Hullabaloo*, had been "fired" in 1926 for criticizing a faculty member.

45. *Acts*, Third Extra Session, 1934, Nos. 17, 22, 27; New York *Times*, December 16–21, 1934; *Nation*, January 2, 1935, p. 3; Hermann B. Deutsch, "Kingdom of the Kingfish," New Orleans *Item*, September 12, 1939.

46. Washington *Evening Star*, September 10, 1935; New York *Times*, September 11, 1935; Williams, *Huey Long*, 287, 745, 860; Huey P. Long, Sr., "My Boy Huey," in *The New Louisiana: The Story of the Greatest State in the Nation*, ed. John

D. Klorer (New Orleans, n.d.), 20; Harley Bozeman interview, in Williams Papers.

47. George M. Wallace interview, in Williams Papers; *Acts*, Third Extra Session, 1934, No. 15; Brady Michael Banta, "The Regulation and Conservation of Petroleum Resources in Louisiana, 1901–1940" (Ph.D. dissertation, Louisiana State University, 1981), 356.

48. Baton Rouge *State-Times*, January 5, 6, 1935; Banta, "Regulation and Conservation," 357–61.

49. New York *Times*, November 15, 17, 18, 1934, April 17, 1935; San Francisco *Chronicle*, February 17, 18, 1935; Arnold S. Fulton, "First Month of Dictator Long," *Nation*, August 14, 1935, pp. 179–81; Rorty, "Callie Long's Boy Huey," 127.

50. *Congressional Record*, 74th Cong., 1st Sess., 152; Williams, *Huey Long*, 741; Schlesinger, *Politics of Upheaval*, 66–67; Davis, *Long: A Candid Biography*, 34.

51. *Congressional Record*, 73d Cong., 1st Sess., 1125; Swing, "Menace of Huey Long," 36–38; Davis, *Long: A Candid Biography*, 35.

52. Frank Costello's testimony and activities cited in Humbert S. Nelli, *The Business of Crime: Italians and Syndicate Crime in the United States* (New York, 1976), 188–89, 224–25. See also Michael L. Kurtz and Morgan D. Peoples, *Earl K. Long: The Saga of Uncle Earl and Louisiana Politics* (Baton Rouge, 1990), 86; Richard Behar, "The Underworld Is Their Oyster," *Time*, September 3, 1990, p. 56; Kane, *Louisiana Hayride*, 397, 402. In *Huey Long*, 825, T. Harry Williams questions Costello's testimony about being invited into New Orleans by the Kingfish, since "in 1935 Huey could not have provided this protection . . . for the city government was controlled by his bitter enemy Semmes Walmsley." But this assertion ignores the fact that New Orleans had already lost control of its law enforcement (even the mayor's "special police" could not carry arms without the governor's permission), and by July of 1935 Mayor Walmsley was stripped of all remaining power by his own Old Regular organization, when it capitulated to Huey Long.

53. Russell Owen, "Huey Long Gives His View of Dictators," *New York Times Magazine*, February 10, 1935, p. 3; Allan A. Michie and Frank Ryhlick, *Dixie Demagogues* (New York, 1939), 112; George E. Sokolsky, "Huey Long," *Atlantic Monthly*, CLVI (November, 1935), 532.

54. "Dictated but Not Dead," *Business Week*, February 9, 1935, pp. 12–13; New York *American*, quoted in *Congressional Record*, 74th Cong., 1st Sess., 10, 146–48.

55. New York *Daily Worker*, March 21, 1935 (Clipping in Huey P. Long Scrapbooks); V. F. Calverton, "Our Future Dictator," *Scribner's Magazine*, XCVII (May, 1935), 171–75; Benjamin Stolberg, "Dr. Huey and Mr. Long," *Nation*, September 25, 1935, pp. 344–46.

56. John A. Garraty, *The Great Depression* (Garden City, N.Y., 1987), 210–11; Schlesinger, *Politics of Upheaval*, 77.

57. Norman Thomas, *After the New Deal, What?* (New York, 1936), 149.

58. Swing, "Menace of Huey Long," 38.

CHAPTER 17: Riding the Pale Horse

1. To the charge of demagoguery Long pleaded guilty, but claimed "in the old Greek parlance that meant the language which was acceptable to the majority."

Congressional Record, 74th Cong., 1st Sess., 10,148. The Kingfish's plans for America under his presidency are discussed in Hamilton Basso, *Mainstream* (New York, 1943), 193–94, and in Forrest Davis, *Huey Long: A Candid Biography* (New York, 1935), 21–22, 41, 271–85. Davis interviewed Long on the subject.

2. Thomas O. Harris, *The Kingfish: Huey P. Long, Dictator* (New Orleans, 1938), 197–202; New Orleans *Times-Picayune,* January 19, 27, 1935; T. Harry Williams, *Huey Long* (New York, 1969), 784–86; New York *Times,* January 27, 28, February 1, 1935; Ed Reed, *Requiem for a Kingfish: The Strange and Unexplained Death of Huey Long* (Baton Rouge, 1986), 115.

3. New Orleans *Item-Tribune,* January 27, 1935 (Clipping in Huey P. Long Scrapbooks, Hill Memorial Library, Louisiana State University); New York *Times,* January 27, 1927; Williams, *Huey Long,* 787.

4. Davis, *Long: A Candid Biography,* 233–34; New Orleans *Times-Picayune,* January 27, 1935; Williams, *Huey Long,* 789.

5. Harris, *Kingfish,* 205; New York *Times,* January 27, 30, 1935; *Congressional Record,* 74th Cong., 1st Sess., 1370; *New Republic,* February 6, 1935, pp. 344–45; Ray Fleming interview, in T. Harry Williams Papers, Hill Memorial Library, Louisiana State University.

6. New York *Times,* February 3, 1935; Reed, *Requiem for a Kingfish,* 117; Hodding Carter, "Louisiana Limelighter," *Review of Reviews,* XCI (March, 1935), 24.

7. Baton Rouge *State-Times,* January 29, 1935; Hammond (La.) *Vindicator,* February 1, 1935.

8. A photocopy of the formal agreement between Long and Hilton is reproduced in Harris, *Kingfish,* 203; New Orleans *Times-Picayune,* February 26, 27, 1935.

9. The Bond and Tax Board consisted of loyal Longites: the governor, lieutenant governor, attorney general, secretary of state, and the supervisor of public accounts (Alice Lee Grosjean). Betty Marie Field, "The Politics of the New Deal in Louisiana, 1933–1939" (Ph.D. dissertation, Tulane University, 1973), 142–43; New York *Times,* April 17, 19, 1935; *Congressional Record,* 74th Cong., 1st Sess., 6112–13; New Orleans *Item,* April 23, 1935.

10. *Acts,* Second Extra Session, 1935, No. 8; Hodding Carter, "Huey Long, American Dictator," in *The Aspirin Age, 1919–1941,* ed. Isabel Leighton (New York, 1949), 36; Harris, *Kingfish,* 280; Hammond (La.) *Vindicator,* July 19, 1935.

11. *Acts,* Second Extra Session, 1935, Nos. 5, 28; *Louisiana House Calendar,* April 17, 1935, p. 9; *Louisiana Senate Calendar,* April 20, 1935, p. 9; Harry Gilbert quoted in Glen Jeansonne, "The Apotheosis of Huey Long," *Biography,* XII (Fall, 1989), 290; New York *Times,* April 18, 20, 1935.

12. Baton Rouge *Morning Advocate,* April 18, 1935; Hodding Carter, "Huey Long's Louisiana Hayride," *American Mercury,* LXVII (April, 1949), 436.

13. Baton Rouge *Morning Advocate,* April 18, 1935; Pegler's column quoted in Harnett T. Kane, *Louisiana Hayride: The American Rehearsal for Dictatorship, 1928–1940* (New York, 1941), 114.

14. Ralph Waldo Emerson, *Representative Men* (Boston, 1884), 243.

15. *Louisiana Progress,* July 3, 17, September 4, 1930, August 18, 1931, January 12, 1932; *American Progress,* September 28, 1933, February 1, 1934, March, 1935; *Louisiana House Journal,* Fifth Extra Session, 1929, pp. 218–19. *Congressional Record,* 73d Cong., 2d Sess., 1934, 6539.

16. Italics mine. *State* v. *Treadaway* (1910) quoted in Harriet Spiller Daggett, *Legal Essays on Family Law* (Baton Rouge, 1935), 11–12.

17. Edward A. Haggerty, Sr., Russell B. Long, E. J. Oakes interviews with T. Harry Williams, in Williams Papers; *American Progress*, September 21, 1933; *Congressional Record*, 72d Cong., 2d Sess., 2812; Carleton Beals, *The Story of Huey P. Long* (Philadelphia, 1935), 178.

18. New York *Times*, July 4, 1935; Williams, *Huey Long*, 844.

19. Abbeville (La.) *Meridional*, July 13, 1935; Baton Rouge *State-Times*, July 5, 6, 1935.

20. *Acts*, Third Extra Session, 1935, Nos. 6, 16, 25; New Orleans *Times-Picayune*, July 6, 7, 1935; Colfax (La.) *Chronicle*, July 12, 1935; Harris, *Kingfish*, 218–19.

21. New Orleans *Times-Picayune*, July 13, 14, 30, 1935; New York *Times*, July 25, 1935; Harris, *Kingfish*, 219–20; Williams, *Huey Long*, 852–54; Hammond (La.) *Vindicator*, July 19, 1935.

22. Williams, *Huey Long*, 853; Arnold S. Fulton, "First Month of Dictator Long," *Nation*, August 14, 1935, pp. 179–80.

23. New York *Times*, April 6, July 26, 1935; Davis, *Long: A Candid Biography*, 251, 253; *Congressional Record*, 74th Cong., 1st Sess., 5114; Kane, *Louisiana Hayride*, 125–27.

24. Thomas L. Stokes, *Chip off My Shoulder* (Princeton, 1940), 402; Robert E. Snyder, "Huey Long and the Presidential Election of 1936," *Louisiana History*, XVI (Spring, 1975), 124–25; Kane, *Louisiana Hayride*, 125; George E. Sokolsky, "Huey Long," *Atlantic Monthly*, CLVI (November, 1935), 523; Williams, *Huey Long*, 844.

25. Arthur M. Schlesinger, Jr., *The Politics of Upheaval* (Boston, 1960), 250; New York *Times*, March 5, 10, 1935; Alan Brinkley, *Voices of Protest: Huey Long, Father Coughlin, and the Great Depression* (New York, 1983), 79–80, 208–209. Brinkley's *Voices of Protest*, Appendix II, pp. 284–86, summarizes the results of Emil Hurja's poll conducted for the Democratic National Committee in 1935.

26. Schlesinger, *Politics of Upheaval*, 325–34; Raymond Moley, *After Seven Years* (New York, 1939), 305.

27. New York *Times*, June 20, 1935; Huey P. Long to Franklin D. Roosevelt, June 22, 1935, read into *Congressional Record*, 74th Cong., 1st Sess., 9906–9907.

28. Francis Brown, "Pied Pipers of the Economic Depression," *New York Times Magazine*, March 17, 1935, p. 20; Burton K. Wheeler, *Yankee from the West* (Garden City, N.Y., 1962), 284.

29. Atlanta *Constitution*, February 6, 1935; St. Louis *Post-Dispatch*, quoted in Davis, *Long: A Candid Biography*, 259; Philadelphia *Inquirer*, March 15, 1935 (Clipping in Huey P. Long Scrapbooks); New York *Times*, March 24, 1935.

30. Des Moines *Sunday Register*, April 28, 1935 (Clipping in Huey P. Long Scrapbooks); Robert Morss Lovett, "Hue [*sic*] Long Invades the Middle West," *New Republic*, May 15, 1935, pp. 10–12.

31. Charlotte *Observer*, March 26, 1935 (Clipping in Huey P. Long Scrapbooks); *Congressional Record*, 74th Cong., 1st Sess., 7440; Harold L. K. Van Burean to Franklin D. Roosevelt, February 2, 1935, quoted in Snyder, "Huey Long and the Presidential Election of 1936," 123–24.

32. Raymond Moley, *Twenty-seven Masters of Politics* (New York, 1949), 221; Raymond Moley, *The First New Deal* (New York, 1966), 372–73.

33. Wheeler, *Yankee from the West*, 284; Harris, *Kingfish*, 242.

34. Schlesinger, *Politics of Upheaval*, 385–422; Brinkley, *Voices of Protest*, 247.

35. William E. Leuchtenburg, *Franklin D. Roosevelt and the New Deal, 1932–1940* (New York, 1963), 132; *Congressional Record*, 74th Cong., 1st Sess., 9296–97; 11,517–19.

36. Arthur Krock, "In Washington," column in New York *Times*, March 12, 1935; Stephen Hess, "The Long, Long Trail," *American Heritage*, XVII (August, 1966), 70; Wheeler, *Yankee from the West*, 282.

37. "Feet to Fire," *Time*, June 24, 1935, pp. 10–12; Moley, *Twenty-seven Masters*, 228. Huey's filibuster fills eighty-four double-columned pages in the *Congressional Record*, 74th Cong., 1st Sess., 9091–9177.

38. *Congressional Record*, 74th Cong., 1st Sess., 3016, 7363, 7435, 7440, 7416, 9156, 9364–65; Schlesinger, *Politics of Upheaval*, 251; Alben W. Barkley, *That Reminds Me* (Garden City, N.Y., 1954), 161.

39. *Congressional Record*, 73d Cong., 2d Sess., 3375, 3793, 5097–5105, 74th Cong., 1st Sess., 1131–32, 14,250–51, 14,442.

40. *Time*, February 11, 1935, p. 14; *Congressional Record*, 74th Cong., 1st Sess., 1131–32; New York *Times*, May 31, August 19, 1934, September 11, 1935.

41. Washington *Post*, August 27, 1935; New York *Times*, August 27, 28, 1935; *Congressional Record*, 74th Cong., 1st Sess., 14,691, 14,718–52; Arthur M. Schlesinger, Jr., *The Coming of the New Deal* (Boston, 1958), 312.

42. *Congressional Record*, 74th Cong., 1st Sess., 14,722, 14,727–28, 14,731, 14,742–43, 14,747, 14,752; *Time*, September 2, 1935, p. 11.

CHAPTER 18: Orchids and Wildflowers

1. New York *Times*, August 31, September 7, 1935; Hermann B. Deutsch, *The Huey Long Murder Case* (Garden City, N.Y., 1963), 46–48.

2. New York *Times*, September 1, 1935; T. Harry Williams, *Huey Long* (New York, 1969), 846–47.

3. Huey Pierce Long, *My First Days in the White House* (Harrisburg, Pa., 1935), 18–19, 141.

4. Deutsch, *Long Murder Case*, 49–50; St. Louis *Post-Dispatch*, September 2, 1935; New Orleans *Times-Picayune*, September 3, 1935.

5. Baton Rouge *Morning Advocate*, September 4, 1935; New Orleans *Times-Picayune*, September 4, 1935; Deutsch, *Long Murder Case*, 51.

6. Deutsch, *Long Murder Case*, 55–57; New Orleans *Times-Picayune*, September 6, 1935.

7. Baton Rouge *State-Times*, September 7, 1935; New York *Herald Tribune*, September 8, 1935; Seymour Weiss interview, in T. Harry Williams Papers, Hill Memorial Library, Louisiana State University; Deutsch, *Long Murder Case*, 59–64.

8. *Louisiana Senate Journal*, Fifteenth Extra Session, 1935, p. 4; *Acts*, Fourth Extra Session, 1935, No. 17; New York *Times*, September 8, 1935; Ed Reed, *Requiem for a Kingfish: The Strange and Unexplained Death of Huey Long* (Baton Rouge, 1986), 21–22. The use of different numbers for the same session, given above, is due to the *Louisiana Journals'* and *Acts's* using a separate serial identification.

9. New York *Times*, September 8, 9, 1935; Williams, *Huey Long*, 860–61; Washington *Post*, September 9, 1935.

10. Tom Wallace, "Who's Huey in Louisiana," San Francisco *Chronicle*, February 17, 18, 21, 22, 24, 26–28, 1935 (Clippings in Huey P. Long Scrapbooks, Hill Memorial Library, Louisiana State University); Thomas O. Harris, *The Kingfish: Huey P. Long, Dictator* (New Orleans, 1938), 208, 272, 279–80.

11. Cecil Morgan to Bell I. Wiley, May 9, 1970, copy in Manuscripts Section, Howard-Tilton Memorial Library, Tulane University; Robert Angelle, Harry Gilbert, Robert D. Jones, Theophile Landry, Harvey Peltier interviews, in Williams Papers; New York *Times*, November 3, 1933, March 17, 1935; Arthur Marvin Shaw, "The First Time I Saw Huey," *Southwest Review*, XXXV (Winter, 1950), 64.

12. *Louisiana Progress*, August, 1935; Harris, *Kingfish*, 221–22, 260–62; Seymour Weiss interview, in Williams Papers; *Congressional Record*, 74th Cong., 1st Sess., 12,786–91.

13. Hodding Carter, "Huey Long's Louisiana Hayride," *American Mercury*, LXVII (April, 1949), 443; Harris, *Kingfish*, 221–23.

14. Shreveport *Times*, September 16, 1874, quoted in H. Oscar Lestage, Jr., "The White League in Louisiana and Its Participation in Reconstruction Riots," *Louisiana Historical Quarterly*, XVIII (July, 1935), 695. Major Henry J. Hearsey, before founding the New Orleans *States* in 1880, had been the editor of the Shreveport *Times* during Reconstruction.

15. Index to Proceedings and Debates, *Congressional Record*, 74th Cong., 1st Sess., House Res. 347; *Congressional Record*, 74th Cong., 1st Sess., 14,382, 14,820–21; Washington *Post*, August 28, 1935; "Spotlight Again Plays on Long," *Literary Digest*, September 7, 1935, p. 8.

16. *Christian Science Monitor*, September 10, 1935.

17. Russell Owen, "Huey Long Keeps Washington Guessing," *New York Times Magazine*, January 29, 1933, p. 14; Baton Rouge *State-Times*, September 11, 1935; Williams, *Huey Long*, 791; New Orleans *Times-Picayune*, September 7, 1975; Deutsch, *Long Murder Case*, 148.

18. New York *Herald Tribune*, September 9, 1935; Deutsch, *Long Murder Case*, 66–67; *Acts*, Fourth Extra Session, 1935, No. 3.

19. *St. Landry Clarion* (Opelousas, La.), February 29, March 12, 19, 26, April 9, 1910; Isom Guillory interview, in Williams Papers; Baton Rouge *State-Times*, April 29, 1943 (Clipping in Vertical File, Hill Memorial Library, Louisiana State University). Deutsch, in *Huey Long Murder Case* (p. 43), identified Sheriff Marion Swords of St. Landry as the chief disseminator of the rumor about "Negro blood" in the Veazie family (Judge Pavy's wife's family), but Deutsch incorrectly dated the judge's first election as 1908. It was 1910. The *St. Landry Clarion's* coverage of Judge Pavy's first campaign (cited above) did not specifically refer to the racial rumor, but a Pavy advertisement in the March 19 issue mentioned a "slanderous pamphlet" being circulated by the opposition, without specifying its contents.

20. David H. Zinman, *The Day Huey Long Was Shot* (New York, 1963), 58–82; New Orleans *Item*, September 9, 10, 1935 (Clippings in E. A. Conway Scrapbooks, Louisiana State Library, Baton Rouge); William H. Vahey, Jr., "Idealism Is Held Motive of Weiss in Slaying Long," *Washington Post Magazine*, September 29, 1935, p. 12.

21. Vahey, "Idealism Is Held Motive," 12; Richard W. Leche, Seymour Weiss interviews, both in Williams Papers; Betty Marie Field, "The Politics of the New Deal in Louisiana, 1933–1939" (Ph.D. dissertation, Tulane University, 1973), 21; New Orleans *Times-Picayune*, September 14, 1935. Field's dissertation, however, confuses young Dr. Weiss with his father.

22. Joe Fisher interview, in Williams Papers; Deutsch, *Long Murder Case*, 43; James W. Clarke, *American Assassins: The Darker Side of Politics* (Princeton, 1982), 236; Williams, *Huey Long*, 863.

23. New Orleans *Item*, September 9, 1935; Zinman, *Day Long Was Shot*, 85–90; Deutsch, *Long Murder Case*, 69–70, 75–76; New York *Times*, September 10, 1935; "Widow Denies Weiss Party to Death Plot," Memphis *Commercial Appeal*, September 14, 1935.

24. This view of Dr. Weiss's motive is in general agreement with the conclusions of Deutsch, *Long Murder Case*, 163–69, and Clarke, *American Assassins*, 236–37.

25. Charles East, "The Death of Huey Long: A Photographic Essay," *Southern Review*, XXI (April, 1985), 248–49; Zinman, *Day Long Was Shot*, 92, 112–14; Deutsch, *Long Murder Case*, 21–22, 86.

26. The three books, previously cited by full title, are: Deutsch, *Long Murder Case;* Zinman, *Day Long Was Shot;* and Reed, *Requiem for a Kingfish.* See also T. Harry Williams, "Louisiana Mystery: An Essay Review," *Louisiana History*, VI (Summer, 1965), 287–91.

27. John Fournet, Murphy Roden interviews, both in Williams Papers; Zinman, *Day Long Was Shot*, 115–16.

28. Merle Welsh, a young mortician in 1935, was Baton Rouge's only licensed funeral director and embalmer at that time. He prepared both Huey Long and Dr. Weiss for burial. Welsh remembers that the coroner's jury examination of Long's body was "a farce," and that *both* the bullet holes he (Welsh) observed in Huey's body appeared to be entry wounds—not entry and exit, as the coroner's jury report stated. Author's conversation with Merle Welsh, May 15, 1990.

29. New Orleans *Item*, September 9, 1935. Merle Welsh transported Dr. Weiss's body from the capitol and assisted at the subsequent coroner's examination. Coroner Thomas Bird asked Welsh to count the number of bullet holes, and after he enumerated the sixty-first (these including both entry and exit wounds), the coroner said: "That's enough. You can stop counting now." Author's conversation with Merle Welsh, May 15, 1990.

30. Baton Rouge *State-Times*, September 9, 10, 1935; Clarke, *American Assassins*, 238; New York *Times*, September 10, 1935; Bunkie (La.) *Record*, September 13, 1935.

31. E. L. Sanderson, "Final Hours of Long Revealed by Doctor," New York *Times*, September 11, 1935; Memphis *Commercial Appeal*, September 10–12, 1935; Colfax (La.) *Chronicle*, September 13, 1935; Williams, *Huey Long*, 876; "Mourners, Heirs, Foes," *Time*, September 23, 1935, p. 15.

32. *American Progress*, September, 1935; New Orleans *Times-Picayune*, September 13, 1935, September 7, 1975; Atlanta *Constitution*, September 13, 1935.

33. Glen Jeansonne, *Gerald L. K. Smith: Minister of Hate* (New Haven, 1988), 41–42; Hodding Carter, "Huey Long: American Dictator," in *The Aspirin Age*,

1919–1941, ed. Isabel Leighton (New York, 1949), 362–63; New York *Times*, September 13, 1935; St. Louis *Post-Dispatch*, September 13, 1935.

34. "Baton Rouge Post Cemetery" (Historical marker adjacent to the Arsenal Museum, state capitol grounds, Baton Rouge); St. Louis *Post-Dispatch*, September 13, 1935; Harvey G. Fields, *A True History of the Life, Works, Assassination, and Death of Huey Pierce Long* (Farmerville, La., 1945), 65.

BIBLIOGRAPHICAL ESSAY

"More bunkum has been written about Huey Long and his place in history than any man in this region I know of," former Louisiana governor Sam Jones once grumbled. Jones's charge has some foundation. Contemporaneous journalists as well as later writers agree only that the Kingfish was preternaturally intelligent and gifted with oratorical power; on virtually all else they seem to be describing different people when assessing Louisiana's most famous politician.

Practically all the books and articles about Huey Long contribute something to an understanding of this complex, driven man. Yet although several writers have attempted brief forays into explanations of why Louisiana appeared ripe for someone like Long, none has made an extensive effort to describe the economic, political, and racial complexities of the state during the years of Huey Long's lifetime. The Kingfish was much more than a product of his environment—in some ways he was, as he loved to boast, sui generis—but the peculiarities of his native state gave him opportunities (and temptations) that other locales would have denied him. The need this book tries to fulfill is the telling of Long's life story in the broad context of his time and place.

The sources that proved most valuable in illuminating the Kingfish and his realm are discussed below. Elsewhere, the numbered notes cite all primary material and secondary writings used in individual chapters.

GOVERNMENT DOCUMENTS

Two sets of state documents are indispensable for understanding Louisiana during Huey Long's lifetime: the *Official Journals* of the House of Representatives and senate, and the *Acts* of the General Assembly (renamed the "Legislature" by the Constitution of 1921). Every volume of these resources from the 1890s through 1935 was carefully examined, and the *Official Journals* and *Acts* of the years 1928 to 1935 disclose the extent to which Huey Long was able to impose authoritarian rule on Louisiana. Studying the bills he pushed through the legislature, notably those of the 1934 and 1935 special sessions, makes unavoidable the conclusion that he was an actual dictator. The *Reports* of Louisiana's secretary of state, usually issued biennially, provide parish-by-parish election and registration statistics from 1900 through 1935 (individual precinct returns are given for many elections). Since registration figures were broken down by race as well as by political affiliation, the almost total disfranchisement of blacks during this period is starkly revealed. Other useful state documents include the annual or biennial *Reports* of the superintendent of public education, state treasurer, Department of Labor, Conservation Commission, and Board of Charities and Corrections. For Louisiana's constitutions of 1898, 1913, and 1921, see Benjamin Wall Dart, ed., *Constitutions of the State of Louisiana and Selected Federal Laws* (Indianapolis, 1932).

Among federal documents, the *Congressional Record* is paramount for researching Huey Long's national career. During his three and a half years in Washington, Long managed to put vastly more words into the *Congressional Record* than any other senator. Its pages also reveal the extent to which Long was feared or hated by numerous senators. The 1932–1933 Senate subcommittee investigation of Long and Louisiana affairs is recorded in the almost 3,000 pages of the *Senate Hearings on Campaign Expenditures*, 72d Cong., 2d Sess. The subcommittee's findings are in *Senate Campaign Expenditures, 1932, Louisiana*, 73d Cong., 2d Sess., No. 191. Manuscript census returns of the United States *Twelfth Census* (1900) and *Thirteenth Census* (1910) for Winn Parish, Louisiana, provide information about the Long family and their Winnfield neighbors.

MANUSCRIPT COLLECTIONS

The Huey P. Long Papers, the Huey P. Long Scrapbooks, and the Interview Collection in T. Harry Williams' Papers—all in the Louisiana and Lower Mississippi Valley Collections, Hill Memorial Library, Louisiana State University at Baton Rouge—were three vital primary sources for this study. The Long Papers are in three parts: his personal papers, the Public Service Commission file, and a private law cases file. The Williams Papers include typescripts of more than two hundred interviews, mostly conducted by Professor Williams during the 1950s and early 1960s, of persons who knew Huey Long, including many of his surviving relatives. Professor Williams made extensive use of these recollections in his 1969 biography, *Huey Long*—as has this writer. Other collections at LSU that shed additional light on Louisiana's public affairs during Huey Long's lifetime are the Governor's Correspondence (John

M. Parker, 1920–1924); Jared Y. Sanders Papers; James B. Aswell Papers; James B. Aswell, Jr., and Family Papers; Caffery Family Papers; Edward J. Gay Papers; Joseph E. Ransdell Papers; Ladislas Lazaro Papers; Charles K. Fuqua Papers; Walter J. Dietz Papers; Chaplin, Breazeale, and Chaplin Papers; Edward L. Stevens Papers; and the Joseph P. Hornor Collection.

Two collections at the Louisiana State Library, Baton Rouge, were most helpful: the Harley B. Bozeman Scrapbooks and the E. A. Conway Scrapbooks. Bozeman, who was Huey Long's closest childhood friend and his fellow traveling salesman, wrote a series of articles, "Winn Parish as I Have Known It," for a Winnfield newspaper between 1957 and 1969, and these reminiscences, many about Huey and his family, form the content of the scrapbooks. The Conway Collection, seven large scrapbooks, consists of newspaper clippings and political circulars and pamphlets for and against Huey Long, from 1929 to 1935. At the Howard-Tilton Memorial Library, Tulane University, New Orleans, is the William B. Wisdom Collection of publications about Huey Long. The Archives Division of Northwestern State University's library, in Natchitoches, holds the John H. Overton Papers and a Ku Klux Klan Collection of pamphlets from the post–World War I period.

THESES AND DISSERTATIONS

Unpublished monographs provided telling perspectives on Louisiana during Huey Long's life. Of greatest value was Matthew James Schott, "John M. Parker of Louisiana and the Varieties of American Progressivism" (Ph.D. dissertation, Vanderbilt University, 1969). Governor Parker, a patrician, business-oriented Louisiana progressive, was in many ways Long's antithesis—and one of the Kingfish's most determined enemies. Brady Michael Banta, "The Regulation and Conservation of Petroleum Resources in Louisiana, 1901–1940" (Ph.D. dissertation, Louisiana State University, 1981), offers extensive information on the extraction (and misuse) of the state's most important mineral properties during both the pre-Long and Long eras. Richard Lawrence Gordon, "The Development of Louisiana's Public Mental Institutions, 1735–1940" (Ph.D. dissertation, Louisiana State University, 1978), is a story, in Gordon's words, "of failure wrapped in a veneer of success." These institutions were heavily politicized, most of all during Huey Long's regime. Lillie H. Nairne, "A Study of the Administration of Relief to the Unemployed in Louisiana" (M.S. thesis, Tulane University, 1935), points out that Huey Long's regime showed no more concern for the unemployed than did its predecessors, leaving minuscule "poor relief" to be handled by parish governments, as it had been since passage of the Pauper Act of 1890. Paul Ted McCulley, "Black Protest in Louisiana, 1898–1928" (M.A. thesis, Louisiana State University, 1970), describes the futile efforts of blacks to contest disfranchisement and segregation. Kenneth E. Harrell, "The Ku Klux Klan in Louisiana, 1920–1930" (Ph.D. dissertation, Louisiana State University, 1966), is the best single source on that subject, and Harrell describes how the Klan issue clouded Huey Long's first (1923–1924) run for the governorship. Alton Earl Ingram, "The Twentieth Century Ku Klux Klan in Morehouse Parish" (M.A. thesis, Louisiana State University, 1961) focuses on the storm center of Klan activity in the state. Margaret Ann Martin, "Colonel Robert Ewing, Louisiana Journalist and Politician" (M.A. thesis, Louisiana State University, 1964), surveys the career of a press lord who was once an ally, then an enemy, of Huey Long. Edward Francis Renwick, "The Longs' Legislative Lieutenants" (Ph.D. dissertation, University of Arizona, 1967), discusses the roles of subordinates in both Huey and Earl Long's administrations. The best study of the struggle between Long and the Roosevelt administration over New Deal activity in Louisiana is Betty Marie Field, "The Politics of the New Deal in Louisiana, 1933–1939" (Ph.D. dissertation, Tulane University, 1973). The activities of Hilda Phelps Hammond and other patrician women who opposed Huey Long are described in Pamela Tyler, "Silk Stockings and Ballot Boxes: Women of the Upper Class and New Orleans Politics, 1930–1955" (Ph.D. dissertation, Tulane University, 1989).

NEWSPAPERS AND PERIODICALS

Louisiana newspapers are essential sources for anyone writing about social and political issues in Huey Long's time. Most of the newspapers mentioned here are available on microfilm in the libraries of either Louisiana State University or Tulane University, in the New Orleans Public Library, or in the State Library in Baton Rouge. The state's urban dailies and rural weeklies generally possessed more verve than objectivity or accuracy, but the press provides a flavor of the past, and gems of truth can be found amidst the dross. The morning New Orleans *Picayune* and the *Times-Democrat* (merging as the *Times-Picayune* in 1914) finally became the state's leading newspaper, but during most of the period it was locked in a circulation and advertising war with the afternoon *Item* and that paper's morning edition, the *Tribune*. The afternoon *States* was also a hot competitor until it ran into financial difficulties and was purchased by the *Times-Picayune* in 1933. Only the *Times-Picayune* was a consistent foe of Huey Long. The *States* sided with him over the years 1928 to 1930, and the *Item* (and *Tribune*), despite intense previous opposition, in 1931 began supporting the Kingfish—in return for which state employees became compulsory subscribers to the paper.

Several other Louisiana dailies, particularly those in Shreveport and Baton Rouge, provided considerable information. The Shreveport sources included the *Times*, the *Journal*, and—until its demise in 1928—

the *Caucasian*. For Baton Rouge and affairs at the state capitol, the *Morning Advocate* and *State-Times* proved helpful for most of the period. Specific events were researched in other dailies, particularly the Monroe *News-Star*, the Alexandria *Town Talk*, and the Lake Charles *American Press*. Among Louisiana weeklies, the Colfax *Chronicle* proved so attuned to state affairs that it was read for every issue from the 1890s to 1935. Huey Long's own journal, the *Louisiana Progress*, published episodically beginning in 1930 (its name was changed to the *American Progress* in 1933), was an essential source. Many small-town weeklies were valuable for specific periods in their extant files, notably the Abbeville *Meridional*, *St. Bernard Voice* (Arabi), *Morehouse Enterprise* (Bastrop), *Bossier Banner* (Benton), Bogalusa *Enterprise and American*, Bunkie *Record*, Donaldsonville *Chief*, Hammond *Vindicator*, Homer *Guardian-Journal*, Kentwood *Commercial*, Lake Providence *Sentry*, Mansfield *Enterprise*, *Assumption Pioneer* (Napoleonville), Opelousas *Courier*, *St. Landry Clarion* (Opelousas), *Richland Beacon-News* (Rayville), St. Francisville *True Democrat*, *Tensas Gazette* (St. Joseph), *Madison Journal* (Tallulah), *Lafourche Comet* (Thibodaux), Winnfield *Comrade*, and Winnfield *Southern Sentinel*. Unfortunately, only fragmentary holdings exist of the few black newspapers published in Louisiana during the late nineteenth and early twentieth centuries, such as the Baton Rouge *Observer* (1900) and the Shreveport *Afro-American* (1932). Microfilm copies are extant, however, for a Marxist (Industrial Workers of the World) publication, the Alexandria *Lumberjack*, that attempted during 1913 and 1914 to promote biracial solidarity among laborers. During this time the paper changed names and location, surfacing in New Orleans as the *Voice of the People*.

The New York *Times* was the most valuable of all out-of-state newspapers for the entire period, especially for the years of Long's rule in Louisiana. Other out-of-state journals researched for particular events include the New York *Herald Tribune*, Washington *Post*, Chicago *Tribune*, Atlanta *Constitution*, Memphis *Commercial Appeal*, St. Louis *Post-Dispatch*, and the *Christian Science Monitor*.

National periodicals read extensively—some for Long's career and others also for articles about earlier Louisiana affairs—include *American Magazine*, *American Mercury*, *Arena*, *Atlantic Monthly*, *Century*, *Crisis*, *Forum*, *Harper's Monthly*, *Independent*, *Leslie's Illustrated Weekly*, *Liberty*, *Literary Digest*, *McClure's Magazine*, *Nation*, *New Republic*, *North American Review*, *Outlook*, *Saturday Evening Post*, *Survey*, *Time*, and *World's Work*.

JOURNAL ARTICLES

Dozens of scholarly articles on aspects of Louisiana history from the 1890s to the 1930s, or on Huey Long himself, are cited in the notes. All of these articles that were of appreciable help—plus a few that were not cited but did add to my understanding of Louisiana in Long's lifetime—are listed below, in alphabetical order by author.

For articles about Louisiana's social, economic, and political affairs (other than Long's career), see especially: Berthold C. Alwes, "The History of the Louisiana State Lottery Company," *Louisiana Historical Quarterly*, XXVII (October, 1944); Pamela D. Arceneaux, "Guidebooks to Sin: The Blue Books of Storyville," *Louisiana History*, XXVIII (Fall, 1987); Riley E. Baker, "Negro Voter Registration in Louisiana, 1879–1964" *Louisiana Studies*, IV (Winter, 1965); Brady M. Banta, "The Pine Island Situation: Petroleum, Politics, and Research Opportunities in Southern History," *Journal of Southern History*, LII (November, 1986); Damon L. Barbat, "The Illegitimate Birth of the Mafia in New Orleans," *Southern Studies*, XXIV (Fall, 1985); Bernard A. Cook, "Covington Hall and Radical Rural Unionization in Louisiana," *Louisiana History*, XVIII (Spring, 1977); John E. Coxe, "The New Orleans Mafia Incident," *Louisiana Historical Quarterly*, XX (October, 1937); Henry C. Dethloff and Robert R. Jones, "Race Relations in Louisiana, 1877–1898," *Louisiana History*, IX (Fall, 1968); Edwin W. Edwards, "The Role of the Governor in Louisiana Politics: An Historical Analysis," *Louisiana History*, XV (Spring, 1974); Brian Gary Ettinger, "John Fitzpatrick and the Limits of Working-Class Politics in New Orleans, 1892–1896," *Louisiana History*, XXV (Fall, 1985); Wayne M. Everard, "Bourbon City: New Orleans, 1878–1900," *Louisiana Studies*, XI (Fall, 1972); Adam Fairclough, "The Public Utilities Industry in New Orleans: A Study in Capital, Labor, and Government, 1894–1929," *Louisiana History*, XXII (Winter, 1981); George Q. Flynn, "A Louisiana Senator and the Underwood Tariff," *Louisiana History*, X (Winter, 1969); Philip S. Foner, "The IWW and the Black Worker," *Journal of Negro History*, LV (January, 1970); Craig L. Foster, "Tarnished Angels: Prostitution in Storyville, New Orleans, 1900–1910," *Louisiana History*, XXXI (Winter, 1990); Edward F. Haas, "New Orleans on the Half-Shell: The Maestri Era, 1936–1946," *Louisiana History*, XIII (Summer, 1972); William I. Hair, "Henry J. Hearsey and the Politics of Race," *Louisiana History*, XVII (Fall, 1976); Roman Heleniak, "Local Reaction to the Great Depression in New Orleans, 1929–1933," *Louisiana History*, X (Fall, 1969); Joy Jackson, "Prohibition in New Orleans: The Unlikeliest Crusade," *Louisiana History*, XIX (Summer, 1978); Glen Jeansonne, "Partisan Parson: An Oral History Account of the Louisiana Years of Gerald L. K. Smith," *Louisiana History*, XXIII (Spring, 1982); John Smith Kendall, "Who Killed de Chief?" *Louisiana Historical Quarterly*, XXII (April, 1939); H. Oscar Lestage, Jr., "The White League in Louisiana and Its Participation in Reconstruction Riots," *Louisiana Historical Quarterly*, XVIII (July, 1935); Grady McWhiney, "Louisiana Socialists in the Early Twentieth Century: A Study of Rustic Radicalism," *Journal of Southern History*, XX (August, 1954);

Robert H. Marr, Jr., "The New Orleans Mafia Case," *American Law Review,* XXV (May–June, 1891); August Meier and Elliott Rudwick, "The Boycott Movement Against Jim Crow Streetcars in the South, 1900–1906," *Journal of American History,* LV (March, 1969); Jean M. Palmer, "The Impact of World War I on Louisiana's Schools and Community Life," *Louisiana History,* VII (Fall, 1966); John Milton Price, "Slavery in Winn Parish," *Louisiana History,* VIII (Spring, 1967); C. Joseph Pusateri, "The Stormy Career of a Radio Maverick, W. K. Henderson of KWKH," *Louisiana Studies,* XV (Winter, 1976); Germaine A. Reed, "Race Legislation in Louisiana, 1864–1920," *Louisiana History,* VI (Fall, 1965); Timothy F. Reilly, "Benjamin M. Palmer: Secessionist Become Nationalist," *Louisiana History,* XVIII (Summer, 1977); Martin Reuss, "The Army Corps of Engineers and Flood-Control Politics on the Lower Mississippi," *Louisiana History,* XXIII (Spring, 1982); Matthew J. Schott, "Class Conflict in Louisiana Voting Since 1877: Some New Perspectives," *Louisiana History,* XII (Spring, 1971); Schott, "Progressives Against Democracy: Electoral Reform in Louisiana, 1894–1921," *Louisiana History,* XX (Summer, 1979); Schott, "The New Orleans Machine and Progressivism," *Louisiana History,* XXIV (Spring, 1983); William O. Scruggs, "Parish Government in Louisiana," *Annals of the American Academy of Political and Social Science,* LXVII (May, 1913); Barbara C. Wingo, "The 1928 Presidential Election in Louisiana," *Louisiana History,* XVIII (Fall, 1977); Charles F. Wynes, "The Reverend Quincy Ewing: Southern Racial Heretic in the 'Cajun' Country," *Louisiana History,* VII (Summer, 1966); Steven D. Zink, "Cultural Conflict and the 1928 Presidential Campaign in Louisiana," *Southern Studies,* XVII (Summer, 1978).

For articles about Huey Long, see especially: Alan Brinkley, "Huey Long, the Share Our Wealth Movement, and the Limits of Depression Dissidence," *Louisiana History,* XXII (Spring, 1981); F. Raymond Daniell, "The Gentleman from Louisiana," *Current History,* XLI (November, 1934); Henry C. Dethloff, "The Longs: Revolution or Populist Retrenchment?" *Louisiana History,* XIX (Fall, 1978); Charles East, "The Death of Huey Long: A Photographic Essay," *Southern Review,* n.s., XXI (April, 1985); Burton L. Hotaling, "Huey Pierce Long as Journalist and Propagandist," *Journalism Quarterly,* XX (March, 1943); Glen Jeansonne, "Challenge to the New Deal: Huey P. Long and the Redistribution of National Wealth," *Louisiana History,* XXI (Fall, 1980); Jeansonne, "Huey P. Long: A Political Contradiction," *Louisiana History,* XXXI (Winter, 1990); Jeansonne, "The Apotheosis of Huey Long," *Biography,* XII (Fall, 1989); Terry L. Jones, "An Administration Under Fire: The Long-Farley Affair of 1935," *Louisiana History,* XXVIII (Winter, 1987); John Adam Moreau, "Huey Long and His Chroniclers," *Louisiana History,* VI (Spring, 1965); William F. Mugleston, "Cornpone and Potlikker: A Moment of Relief in the Great Depression," *Louisiana History,* XVI

(Summer, 1975); John R. Pleasant, Jr., "Ruffin G. Pleasant and Huey P. Long on the Prisoner-Stripe Controversy," *Louisiana History*, XV (Fall, 1974); Matthew J. Schott, "Huey Long: Progressive Backlash?" *Louisiana History*, XXVII (Spring, 1986); Arthur Marvin Shaw, "The First Time I Saw Huey," *Southwest Review*, XXXV (Winter, 1950); Robert E. Snyder, "Huey Long and the Cotton-Holiday Plan of 1931," *Louisiana History*, XVIII (Spring, 1977); Snyder, "Huey Long and the Presidential Election of 1936," *Louisiana History*, XVI (Spring, 1975); Snyder, "The Concept of Demagoguery: Huey Long and His Literary Critics," *Louisiana Studies*, XV (Spring, 1976); Stuart Towns, "A Louisiana Medicine Show: The Kingfish Elects an Arkansas Senator," *Arkansas Historical Quarterly*, XXV (Summer, 1966); Courtney Vaughn, "The Legacy of Huey Long," *Louisiana History*, XX (Winter, 1979); T. Harry Williams, "Louisiana Mystery: An Essay Review," *Louisiana History*, VI (Summer, 1965); Williams, "The Gentleman from Louisiana: Demagogue or Democrat?" *Journal of Southern History*, XXVI (February, 1960).

BOOKS

The Kingfish casts a wide shadow over twentieth-century Louisiana, and most books about the state since 1900 are perforce concerned either entirely or in part with Huey Long or what is called the "Long dynasty." Several biographies deal with politicians whose names were not Long, but in almost all of these the Kingfish makes a scene-stealing entry. A rare exception is John R. Kemp, ed., *Martin Behrman of New Orleans: Memoirs of a City Boss* (Baton Rouge, 1977), the edited 1920s memoirs of a five-term New Orleans mayor; Behrman's career was over before Long became governor. Adras Laborde, *A National Southerner: Ransdell of Louisiana* (New York, 1951), chronicles the life of Senator Joseph Ransdell, whom Huey unseated in 1930. Floyd Martin Clay, *Coozan Dudley LeBlanc: From Huey Long to Hadacol* (Gretna, La., 1973), depicts the colorful career of a Cajun politician who dared oppose the Kingfish. Glen Jeansonne has written two perceptive biographies of men important in Huey Long's organization: *Leander Perez: Boss of the Delta* (Baton Rouge, 1977); and *Gerald L. K. Smith: Minister of Hate* (New Haven, 1988). Michael L. Kurtz and Morgan D. Peoples, *Earl K. Long: The Saga of Uncle Earl and Louisiana Politics* (Baton Rouge, 1990), clearly describes Huey's influence on his younger, imitative brother. A concise account of Louisiana's twentieth-century history may be found in Parts 3 and 4 of Bennett H. Wall, ed., *Louisiana: A History* (2d ed.; Arlington Heights, Ill., 1990).

Of the many books about the Huey Long, two were written (more precisely, dictated to secretaries) by the Kingfish himself. Shortly before his fortieth birthday, Huey published *Every Man a King: The Autobiography of Huey P. Long* (New Orleans, 1933). It is as self-serving as most politicians' autobiographies, with little disclosure of the author's inner self, but its folksy, humorous style does suggest why Huey enjoyed such popular appeal. At the time of his assassination, Huey was overseeing publication of a book designed to promote his bid for the presidency: *My First Days in the White House* (Harrisburg, Pa., 1935) took the form of a novel, set two years in the future, portraying a happy, post-depression America under President Huey P. Long. Curiously bland, it lacks the sardonic wit of *Every Man a King* and reveals nothing about the author except his enormous ego. Two well-edited books of readings contain portions of Huey's books as well as selections from what contemporaries and historians have written about the Kingfish: Henry C. Dethloff, ed., *Huey P. Long: Southern Demagogue or American Democrat?* (Boston, 1967), and Hugh Davis Graham, ed., *Huey Long* (Englewood Cliffs, N.J., 1970).

Three biographies of Long appeared during the last years of his brief life, and another just two months after his death. The first was an extended diatribe by John Kingston Fineran, its posture revealed in the title: *The Career of a Tinpot Napoleon: A Political Biography of Huey P. Long* (New Orleans, 1932). On the title page, Fineran "cordially invited" Long to sue him for criminal libel. More factual and less choleric, although strongly critical, is Webster Smith, *The Kingfish: A Biography of Huey P. Long* (New York, 1933). Smith's book is most useful for Long's 1929 impeachment. Forrest Davis, *Huey Long: A Candid Biography* (New York, 1935), came out a few weeks before Long's death. A skilled interviewer, Davis was appalled by Long's frankly stated desire to "break up" both major parties and occupy the White House for sixteen years. Davis tried to be fair to his subject, but concluded that the Kingfish "was the most dangerous man in America." Carleton Beals, *The Story of Huey P. Long* (Philadelphia, 1935), published shortly after Long was killed, is severely critical of both Louisiana and the Kingfish, describing Huey as a Latin American–style dictator. Beals attacked from the left, pointing out that blacks were no better off in Long's Louisiana than before. But he also excoriated Huey's Louisiana foes, saying that their "one ambition has been to maintain the old plantation-corporation status quo which has already made the state the most backward entity in the Union."

Three years after the Kingfish died, an elderly Louisiana journalist, Thomas O. Harris, who had followed Huey's political career since its beginning in 1918 and had known him even earlier, published *The Kingfish: Huey P. Long, Dictator* (New Orleans, 1938). Harris, a close friend of ex-governor Parker, detested Huey personally but attempted to be objective; his account is generally factual. Because Harris was an eyewitness to many of the events described, the book constitutes a primary source. Harris also came to understand that the Kingfish, beneath his laughing exterior, was an unhappy man.

In the aftermath of scandals that sent several of the deceased King-fish's henchmen to prison, a New Orleans journalist and popular writer, Harnett T. Kane, published *Louisiana Hayride: The American Rehearsal for Dictatorship, 1928–1940* (New York, 1941). The book has been criti-cized for superficiality and for anti-Long bias, but it is superbly written and is better on the scandals surrounding Huey's successors than on the Kingfish's career.

Partly in response to Kane, Harvey G. Fields—one of Huey's most devoted followers—wrote *A True History of the Life, Works, Assassina-tion, and Death of Huey Pierce Long* (Farmerville, La., 1945). The book is artless and hagiographic, but it is something of a primary source. Fields includes a chilling description of Long selecting his own grave site.

The first academic work to analyze twentieth-century Louisiana pol-itics is Allan P. Sindler, *Huey Long's Louisiana: State Politics, 1920–1952* (Baltimore, 1956). Sindler points out that Louisiana's backwardness gave Long the opportunity to rise to power, but concludes that the King-fish did more harm than good, and that Huey Long's legacy was "mor-ally enervating." Two popular, less analytical books appeared eight years later: Stan Opotowsky, *The Longs of Louisiana* (New York, 1960), and Thomas Martin, *Dynasty: The Longs of Louisiana* (New York, 1960). Both are critical of Huey Long's methods but credit him for materially improving the state.

Although Huey Long is only one of the cast of characters in Arthur M. Schlesinger, Jr., *The Politics of Upheaval* (Boston, 1960)—the third volume of Schlesinger's monumental *Age of Roosevelt*—the author de-votes one striking chapter, "The Messiah of the Rednecks," to Huey. Pithy and unflattering, it is the sharpest cameo study of the Kingfish. The best one-volume study of American politics in the 1930s is William E. Leuchtenburg, *Franklin D. Roosevelt and the New Deal, 1932–1940* (New York, 1963). In the chapter "Waiting for Lefty," Leuchtenburg places Huey Long's challenge to the New Deal in perspective.

For many years Professor T. Harry Williams gathered material—in-cluding conducting more than two hundred interviews of persons who knew Huey Long—in preparation for a massive biography destined to win a Pulitzer Prize: *Huey Long* (New York, 1969). The book is richly detailed and skillfully blends narrative with analysis. Williams con-cedes that the Kingfish loved power and eventually became obsessed with it, yet offers excuses for most of his actions. He credits Long with sincerity of purpose. In the opinion of this writer, Williams was overly sympathetic to Huey Long. But Professor Williams was a great scholar and teacher, and one of the things this writer, as a student at LSU, learned from him was that historians may honestly and respectfully disagree.

Alan Brinkley, *Voices of Protest: Huey Long, Father Coughlin, and the Great Depression* (New York, 1983), is a scholarly analysis of both Long and another charismatic demagogue, the Catholic priest Charles E. Coughlin of Michigan, and of the movements they founded during the depression years of the 1930s. Brinkley is more critical of Long than was Williams, but he gives the Kingfish credit for addressing real economic problems, although Long's Share Our Wealth solution was, as Brinkley points out, simplistic and flawed. C. Vann Woodward described *Voices of Protest* as "a sensitive and subtle work moderated by grace and restraint."

Questions about the death of Huey Long remain. Three books of differing opinions have been published specifically about the assassination: Hermann B. Deutsch, *The Huey Long Murder Case* (Garden City, N.Y., 1963); David H. Zinman, *The Day Huey Long Was Shot* (New York, 1963); and Ed Reed, *Requiem for a Kingfish: The Strange and Unexplained Death of Huey Long* (Baton Rouge, 1986). All three books explore interesting facets of the events leading up to Long's death and speculate about the motives of Long's presumed assassin, Dr. Carl Austin Weiss. This writer (1) agrees with Deutsch that Dr. Weiss's probable motive in confronting the Kingfish was fear that Long was about to revive an old rumor concerning Negro blood in Mrs. Weiss's family, (2) agrees with Reed that the Kingfish was probably accidentally hit by one of his bodyguards' bullets, but (3) disagrees with Reed's conclusion that Dr. Weiss did not also shoot Huey Long. Reed's fascinating interview with Merle Welsh, the mortician who prepared both Dr. Weiss and Huey Long for their funerals, was confirmed by this writer when he talked with Mr. Welsh in May of 1990.

INDEX

McConnell, David, 74, 106, 204, 346*n*15
McConnell, Lee, 106, 346*n*15
McConnell, Rose. *See* Long, Rose McConnell
McEnery, Samuel D., 18–19, 20, 21
McKellar, Kenneth, 269, 309
McQuiston, George, 165, 204, 266, 320
McShane, Andrew, 111, 113, 141, 265
Maestri, Robert S., 155, 166, 182, 184, 210, 238, 272
Mafia, 2, 12–13, 14, 15, 66, 76, 94
Maloney, Paul, 142, 156
Manship, Charles, 178, 181, 185
Martin, Wade O., 250
Martin, Whitmel Pugh, 76
Mencken, H. L., 110, 170, 187
Meraux, L. A., 150, 225
Messina, Joe, 165, 166, 169, 182, 255
Moley, Raymond, 307, 309, 311
Moore, Randall, 144, 177
Moran, Jimmy. *See* Brocato, James
Morgan, Cecil, 163, 164, 179, 187, 253
Mussolini, Benito, 252, 276, 295, 296

New Deal, 216, 232, 254, 282, 284, 285, 287, 307, 310, 312–13, 317
New Regulars, 124, 125–26, 155–56
Newspapers, freedom of, 279, 301
Nicholson, Leonard, 304
Noe, James A., 211, 242
Norris, George W., 236, 237, 242, 254, 306
Nugent, Jess, 201, 211

Odom, John Fred, 299
Ogden, Frederick N., 9, 22–23
Oil and gas industry, 89–92, 94, 101–103, 107, 111, 112, 118, 119, 164, 167, 177–78, 179, 191, 293–94, 301
Old Regulars, 124, 126, 152, 156, 194, 206, 207, 218, 239, 250, 264–65, 277, 281, 282, 305, 317, 366*n*2, 375*n*35, 380*n*52
O'Malley, Clint, 263, 289
O'Malley, Dominick C., 13–14, 15, 117, 207
O'Niell, Charles, 185, 186, 188

Orleans Democratic Association (ODA), 111, 113, 124
Overton, John H., 75, 77, 185, 210, 248–50, 251, 253, 255, 256, 257, 282, 312

Palmer, Benjamin M., 1–4, 10, 11, 14, 20, 21, 56, 57, 171, 327*n*9
Palmer, James, 117, 119
Parker, John M.: and Huey Long, 2, 93, 101–103, 111, 112, 115–17, 127–28, 157, 194, 197, 224, 254, 257, 262, 265, 282–83, 285–86, 318; family and friends of, 2, 11, 164, 321; childhood of, 10; and love of country life, 11, 27; and New Orleans Ring, 11–12, 109, 111, 113, 132, 224; and lynchings of presumed *mafiosi*, 12–15, 76, 132; gubernatorial campaigns of, 34, 75, 76–78, 93–96, 97, 99–100, 281; as governor, 101–103, 107, 111–17, 121, 124, 127–28, 132–34, 136, 140, 141, 157, 161, 162, 168, 228, 230; and Ku Klux Klan, 132–34, 136, 140; and Flood of 1927, pp. 147–48; after governorship, 150; and Constitutional League, 189–90; at 1932 Democratic national convention, 243; and support for Franklin Roosevelt, 282; and Square Deal Association, 298; bodyguard of, 303; and death of Carl Austin Weiss, 324
Parker, John M., Sr., 10, 11
Pavy, B. Henry, 251, 316, 320, 322, 384*n*19
People's party. *See* Populism
Perez, Leander, 185, 186, 225
Perrault, George K., 179, 180, 277
Petroleum industry. *See* Oil and gas industry
Pleasant, Anne, 197–98, 243, 244, 274, 284, 296
Pleasant, Ruffin G., 75, 76, 78, 83, 90–94, 96, 111, 121, 125, 168, 194, 197, 230, 243, 282, 296, 298
Plessy v. *Ferguson*, 61–62, 64, 165
Populism, 15–19, 29–30, 36, 37, 55, 58, 61, 120, 125, 334*n*39

Sterling, Ross, 215, 216
Stolberg, Benjamin, 296
Stubbs, Frank P., 95, 96, 97, 100
Sullivan, John P., 93, 113, 118, 124,
    125–26, 128, 141, 155, 159, 167,
    174, 176, 198, 265, 283, 288–89
Swing, Raymond Gram, 40–41, 276,
    296–97
Swords, Marion, 322, 384*n*19

Tannehill, Robert L., 16, 333*n*20
Taylor, Shelby, 118, 143
Terrell, James, 127, 203–205, 208
Textbooks. *See* Education
Tharpe, William A., 233, 325
Thomas, Lee E., 77–78, 93, 129, 140,
    141, 150, 156, 172, 196
Thomas, Norman, 272, 296
Thompson, James M., 239, 370*n*15
Tison, Caledonia. *See* Long, Caledonia
    Tison "Callie"
Townsend, Francis E., 284, 306
Tugwell, Rexford, 244, 245–46, 252,
    254–55, 285
Tycer, Nat, 263

Unions. *See* Labor unions

Vardaman, James K., 268
Vidrine, Arthur, 166–67
Voitier, Paul, 165
Voting requirements and registration,
    62, 113–14, 278, 301–302

Wallace, George M., 30, 40, 293, 315,
    317
Wallace, Henry, 288
Wallace, J. T., 30, 40
Walmsley, T. Semmes, 194, 198, 205–
    207, 214, 232, 250, 264–66, 281,
    282, 288, 298, 303, 305, 318, 375*n*35,
    380*n*52

Warmoth, Henry Clay, 7, 8, 18, 162,
    179, 207, 357*n*2, 360*n*50
Warren, Robert Penn, 229
Washington, Booker T., 65–66, 67, 78
Weiss, Carl Adam, 163–64, 321, 322–
    23
Weiss, Carl Austin, 7, 72, 164, 251,
    274, 320–25, 385*nn*28–29
Weiss, Leon C., 194
Weiss, Seymour, 168–69, 182, 193,
    210, 215, 216, 232, 241, 242, 256,
    286, 287, 291, 316, 318, 321, 325
Weiss, Yvonne Pavy, 251, 321, 322–23
Weller, Daniel R., 183
Wells, H. G., 309
Welsh, Merle, 324, 385*nn*28–29
Wheeler, Burton K., 236, 237, 242,
    244, 245, 254, 287, 306, 308, 309–10
White, Edward D., 10–11, 21
White League, 7, 8, 9–11, 17, 22, 23,
    94, 280, 319
Wiegand, William, 204
Wilkins, Roy, 165
Wilkinson, John D., 144
Wilkinson, Theodore, 36
Williams, Augustus "Gus," 125–26,
    137, 155, 167
Williams, Francis, 118, 125–26, 137,
    143–44, 155, 167, 219, 250, 264–65,
    282
Williams, T. Harry, 27, 235, 306
Williamson, Joel, 56
Williams v. *Mississippi*, 62
Wilson, Harry D., 64–65, 97, 264
Wilson, Riley J., 149, 150, 152–54,
    156, 157, 160
Wilson, Woodrow, 48, 76, 80, 84, 94
Wood, Trist, 197, 198
Woodward, C. Vann, 63
World War I, 80–84, 94, 95, 237, 261,
    312, 342*n*20